ZAGAT
2016

New York City
Restaurants

EDITORS
Curt Gathje and Emily Rothschild
with Carol Diuguid

PRODUCTION EDITOR
Aynsley Karps

COORDINATOR
Larry Cohn

Published and distributed by
Zagat Survey, LLC
76 Ninth Avenue
New York, NY 10011
feedback@zagat.com
www.zagat.com

ABOUT ZAGAT

In 1979, we asked friends to rate and review restaurants purely for fun. The term "user-generated content" had yet to be coined. That hobby grew into Zagat; 37 years later, we have loyal reviewers around the globe and have covered restaurants, hotels, nightlife and more. Along the way, we evolved from being a print publisher to a digital content provider. You can find us on zagat.com and across the Google products you use every day.

The reviews in this guide are based on feedback from avid diners. The ratings reflect the average scores submitted for each establishment, while the text is based on quotes from, or paraphrasings of, diners' comments. Ratings and reviews have been updated throughout this edition based on our most recent results. Phone numbers, addresses and other factual data were correct to the best of our knowledge when published in this guide.

Nina and Tim

Nina & Tim Zagat

ACKNOWLEDGMENTS

First and foremost, we thank the thousands of people who contributed ratings and reviews – they are the real authors of this guide.

We also thank Brian Albert, Thomas Briechle, Caley Goldblatt, Miranda Levenstein, Soo Jin Oh, Bernard Onken, Catherine Quayle and Anna Zappia, as well as the following members of our staff: Reni Chin, Kelly Dobkin, Brian Farnham, Jeff Freier, Michelle Golden, Justin Hartung, Tiffany Herklots, Alex Horowitz, Anna Hyclak, Ryutaro Ishikane, Michele Laudig, Caitlin Miehl, Polina Paley, Albry Smither, Amanda Spurlock, Art Yagci and Kyle Zolner.

JOIN IN

To improve our guides, we solicit your comments – positive or negative; it's vital that we hear your opinions. Just contact us at **feedback@zagat.com.**

CONTENTS

NEW YORK CITY AT A GLANCE

KEY STATS

- **2,237 restaurants**
- **119 new restaurants**
- **82 new branches of existing places**
- **136 neighborhoods covered**
- **98 cuisines covered**

BIG WINNERS

Top Food: **Le Bernardin**
Top Decor: **Four Seasons**
Top Service: **Le Bernardin**
Top Newcomer: **Shuko**
Most Popular: **Le Bernardin**

OUTER-BOROUGH CHAMPS

Brooklyn: **Peter Luger**
Queens: **Vesta**
Bronx: **Roberto's**
Staten Island: **Denino's**

TOP CUISINES/SPECIALTIES

American: **Gotham Bar & Grill**
BBQ: **Fette Sau**
Burger Joint: **Burger Joint**
Chicken Joint: **Flor de Mayo**
Chinese: **Decoy**
Dim Sum: **RedFarm**
Dumplings: **Prosperity Dumpling**
French: **Le Bernardin**
Greek: **Milos**
Japanese: **Sushi Yasuda**
Italian: **Marea**
Korean: **Jungsik**
Lobster Roll: **Pearl Oyster Bar**
Pizza: **Paulie Gee's**
Ramen: **Chuko**
Steakhouse: **Peter Luger**
Tacos: **Los Tacos**
Thai: **Ayada**

NEW YORK CITY AT A GLANCE

WORD CLOUD

A look at the most commonly used words in this book's reviews. Service remains top-of-mind for diners and Italian and American remain their perennial favorite cuisines.

COMINGS & GOINGS

Many NYC stalwarts were reborn in new digs. *Sex and the City*-era hot spot **Asia de Cuba,** '80s pioneer **Jams** and the iconic **Rainbow Room** reopened after being off the scene for many years. **Amanda Cohen's Dirt Candy, David Chang's Momofuku Ko,** Danny Bowien's **Mission Chinese** and **Danny Meyer's Untitled** also made re-entrances in more spacious surrounds.

At the same time, we bid adieu to longtime staples including **Commerce, Edison Cafe, Five Points, The Grocery, The Harrison, Josie's, Megu, Olives, Ouest** and the original outpost of **The Palm,** while relatively new, high-end places like **Alder, The Elm** and **Marco's** also surprised with their exits.

Zagat.com STATS

Most searched cuisines
1. Italian
2. Sushi
3. Steak
4. Pizza
5. Mexican

Most searched restaurants
1. The NoMad
2. Capital Grille
3. Il Mulino
4. Nobu
5. Perry St.
6. Scarpetta
7. Tao
8. Carmine's
9. Marea
10. Sushi of Gari

NEWS & TRENDS

NEWCOMERS AT A GLANCE

A look at the cuisines of our 119 newcomers

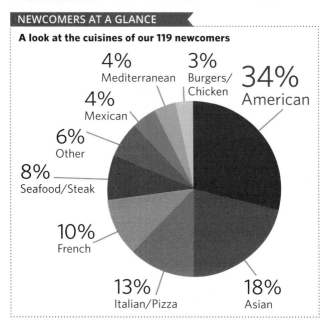

- 4% Mediterranean
- 3% Burgers/Chicken
- 34% American
- 4% Mexican
- 6% Other
- 8% Seafood/Steak
- 10% French
- 13% Italian/Pizza
- 18% Asian

BIG TRENDS

- **Food halls keep coming,** with **City Kitchen, Gansevoort Market** and **Le District** all opening, while others like the **Anthony Bourdain** market at Pier 57 and **UrbanSpace Vanderbilt** near Grand Central are on the way.

- **Prix fixe-only dining is on the upswing,** with a number of established places like **Aldea, Betony, Dovetail** and the **Rainbow Room** switching to set menus, and the debut of set-price newcomers **Delaware & Hudson, Gabriel Kreuther, One Dine, O Ya, Semilla** and **Shuko.**

- **The rise of Battery Park City and the Financial District continues.** Last year brought the hit food hall **Hudson Eats,** recently joined by **Le District.** And with the opening of One World Trade Center, the area is busier than ever. High-profile projects on the horizon include a four-story restaurant/lounge complex from **April Bloomfield** and **Ken Friedman**; outposts of **Jose Garces'** Philly hit, **Amada,** and **Joël Robuchon's** reimagined **L'Atelier,** both in Brookfield Place; and new ventures from **Tom Colicchio, Wylie Dufresne** and **Keith McNally** in neighborhood hotels.

- **Vegetable-centric menus** continue their ascent at hot spots **Cafe Clover, Dirt Candy, Little Park, Semilla** and **Untitled.**

- **Chicken remains a focus,** with **David Chang** and **Marcus Samuelsson** debuting bird-focused joints (**Fuku, Streetbird**) and **Danny Meyer** adding a chicken burger at **Shake Shack.**

- **Though its bar scene never cools off, Brooklyn's restaurants** had a lower-key year – especially compared to the borough's recent history of splashier openings. In addition, high-profile, higher-end entries **The Elm, The Grocery** and **Marco's** all closed their doors.

KEY NEWCOMERS

Our editors' picks among this year's arrivals (see map at the back of this book; full newcomers list on p. 323).

INSTANT HITS

The Clocktower
Fuku
Javelina
Kang Ho Dong Baekjeong
Polo Bar
Seamore's
Superiority Burger
Upland

NAME CHEFS

Cosme (Enrique Olvera)
Fuku (David Chang)
Gabriel Kreuther (Gabriel Kreuther)
Jams (Jonathan Waxman)
Little Park (Andrew Carmellini)
Lupulo (George Mendes)
Santina (Mario Carbone/Rich Torrisi)
Streetbird (Marcus Samuelsson)
Via Carota (Jody Williams/Rita Sodi)

SPLASHY SPACES

Chefs Club
Chevalier
The Clocktower
Gabriel Kreuther
Santina
Zuma

SEASONAL FOCUS

Almanac
Cafe Clover
Delaware & Hudson
Jams
Little Beet Table
Little Park
Semilla

ASIAN SPICE

Mu Ramen
Noreetuh
Oiji
O Ya
Ramen Lab
Shuko

NEIGHBORHOOD STARS

Bowery Meat Co.
Pizza Beach
Rebelle
The Ribbon
Rosie's
Sessanta
Tijuana Picnic
Tuome
Vic's
Wildair

PROJECTS ON TAP

Along with the upcoming Battery Park City/FiDi projects mentioned on p. 8, here are more high-profile projects coming soon.

Carla Hall's Southern Kitchen: *The Chew* star's first restaurant, specializing in Nashville-style hot chicken plus other comfort eats

High Street on Hudson: Outpost of Philly chef **Eli Kulp**'s notable New American cafe in the West Village

La Sirena: Long-awaited Italian trattoria from **Mario Batali** and **Joe Bastianich** in the Maritime Hotel

Momosan Ramen & Sake: Masaharu Morimoto's first-ever ramen place, in Murray Hill

Sadelle's: Mario Carbone and Rich Torrisi's high-end take on a bagel shop/Jewish appetizing joint in SoHo

Salvation Burger: Burger joint from **April Bloomfield** and **Ken Friedman** in East Midtown's Pod 51 Hotel

For more information on hot openings and to rate and review new restaurants, check out zagat.com.

MOST POPULAR

These places are plotted on the map at the back of this book.

① **Le Bernardin** | *French/Seafood*

② **Peter Luger** | *Steak*

③ **Gramercy Tavern** | *American*

④ **Shake Shack** | *Burgers*

⑤ **Gotham Bar & Grill** | *American*

⑥ **Bouley** | *French*

⑦ **Union Square Cafe** | *American*

⑧ **ABC Kitchen** | *American*

⑨ **5 Napkin Burger** | *Burgers*

⑩ **21 Club** | *American*

⑪ **Daniel** | *French*

⑫ **Jean-Georges** | *French*

⑬ **Capital Grille** | *Steak*

⑭ **Atlantic Grill** | *Seafood*

⑮ **Katz's Delicatessen** | *Deli*

⑯ **Carmine's** | *Italian*

⑰ **Marea** | *Italian/Seafood*

⑱ **Rosa Mexicano** | *Mexican*

⑲ **2nd Ave Deli** | *Deli/Kosher*

⑳ **Bareburger** | *Burgers*

㉑ **Del Frisco's** | *Steak*

㉒ **Babbo** | *Italian*

㉓ **Eleven Madison Park** | *Amer.*

㉔ **Balthazar** | *French*

㉕ **Del Posto** | *Italian*

㉖ **Becco** | *Italian*

㉗ **Jean-Georges' Nougatine** | *Fr.*

㉘ **Café Boulud** | *French*

㉙ **The Palm** | *Steak*

㉚ **La Grenouille** | *French*

㉛ **Wolfgang's Steakhse.** | *Steak*

㉜ **Keens Steakhse.** | *Steak*

㉝ **Boulud Sud** | *Mediterranean*

㉞ **Il Mulino** | *Italian*

㉟ **Nobu** | *Japanese*

㊱ **Per Se** | *American/French*

㊲ **Bar Boulud** | *French*

㊳ **Eataly** | *Food Mkt./Italian*

㊴ **Four Seasons** | *American*

㊵ **Fig & Olive** | *Mediterranean*

㊶ **Carnegie Deli** | *Deli*

㊷ **The Smith*** | *American*

㊸ **Blue Water Grill** | *Seafood*

㊹ **The Modern** | *American/Fr.*

㊺ **Ai Fiori** | *Italian*

㊻ **Lincoln** | *Italian*

㊼ **Bobby Van's** | *Steak*

㊽ **Aquagrill** | *Seafood*

㊾ **Meatball Shop** | *Sandwiches*

㊿ **Sarabeth's** | *American*

Lists exclude places with low votes, unless otherwise indicated

* Indicates a tie with restaurant above

WINNERS

TOP FOOD

29 **Le Bernardin** | *French/Seafood*	27 **Union Square Cafe** | *Amer.*
29 **Bouley** | *French*	27 **Sea Fire Grill** | *Seafood*
29 **Daniel** | *French*	27 **Nobu** | *Japanese*
28 **Jean-Georges** | *French*	27 **Benjamin Steak Hse.** | *Steak*
28 **Gotham Bar & Grill** | *American*	27 **Pearl Oyster** | *Seafood*
28 **Peter Luger** | *Steak*	27 **Sushi Nakazawa** | *Japanese*
28 **Eleven Madison Park** | *Amer.*	27 **Aquagrill** | *Seafood*
28 **Blue Hill** | *American*	27 **Estela** | *American/Med.*
28 **Per Se** | *American/French*	27 **15 East** | *Japanese*
28 **Gramercy Tavern** | *American*	27 **Bâtard** | *American/Euro.*
28 **Graffiti** | *Eclectic*	27 **Bohemian** | *Japanese*
27 **La Grenouille** | *French*	26 **Vesta** | *Italian*
27 **Sushi Yasuda** | *Japanese*	26 **Tocqueville** | *Amer./French*
27 **Marea** | *Italian/Seafood*	26 **Brushstroke** | *Japanese*
27 **Jean-Georges' Nougatine** | *Fr.*	26 **Di Fara** | *Pizza*
27 **Milos** | *Greek/Seafood*	26 **Rubirosa** | *Italian/Pizza*
27 **L'Artusi** | *Italian*	26 **River Café** | *American*
27 **Annisa** | *American*	26 **Russ & Daughters** | *Jewish*
27 **Del Posto** | *Italian*	26 **Porter House** | *Steak*
27 **Café Boulud** | *French*	26 **Fette Sau** | *BBQ*

TOP DECOR

28 **Four Seasons**	27 **Per Se**
28 **Daniel**	27 **Del Posto**
28 **Asiate**	27 **Carlyle Restaurant**
28 **Bouley**	27 **Riverpark**
28 **Rainbow Room**	27 **Tao**
28 **Le Bernardin**	27 **Lincoln**
28 **River Café**	27 **Gotham Bar & Grill**
28 **La Grenouille**	26 **Buddakan**
28 **Jean-Georges**	26 **Park Avenue**
28 **Eleven Madison Park**	26 **Morimoto**

TOP SERVICE

29 **Le Bernardin**	27 **Del Posto**
29 **Daniel**	27 **Gotham Bar & Grill**
28 **Bouley**	27 **Graffiti**
28 **Eleven Madison Park**	27 **River Café**
28 **Jean-Georges**	26 **Sushi Nakazawa**
28 **Per Se**	26 **Annisa**
28 **La Grenouille**	26 **Sea Fire Grill**
27 **Gramercy Tavern**	26 **Café Boulud**
27 **Four Seasons**	26 **Union Square Cafe**
27 **Blue Hill**	26 **River Park**

TOP FOOD

AMERICAN

- 28 **Gotham Bar & Grill**
- 28 **Eleven Madison Park**
- 28 **Blue Hill**
- 28 **Per Se**
- 28 **Gramercy Tavern**
- 27 **Annisa**
- 27 **Union Square Cafe**
- 27 **Juni**
- 27 **Estela**
- 27 **Bâtard**
- 26 **Tocqueville**
- 26 **River Café**

ASIAN

- 26 **Pig and Khao**
- 25 **Buddakan**
- 24 **Asiate**
- 24 **Spice Market**
- 24 **Talde**
- 24 **Red Bamboo**
- 24 **Tao**
- 24 **Khe-Yo**

AUSTRIAN/SWISS/GERMAN

- 25 **Wallsé**
- 25 **Cafe Katja**
- 24 **Zum Stammtisch**
- 23 **Mont Blanc**
- 22 **Blaue Gans**
- 22 **Café Sabarsky/Fledermaus**
- 22 **Edi & The Wolf**
- 21 **Zum Schneider**

BAKERIES

- 26 **Bakeri**
- 25 **Dominique Ansel Bakery**
- 25 **Four & Twenty Blackbirds**
- 25 **ChikaLicious Dessert Club**
- 25 **Blue Ribbon Bakery**
- 24 **Ferrara**
- 24 **La Bergamote**
- 24 **Balthazar**

BARBECUE

- 26 **Fette Sau**
- 25 **Hometown BBQ**
- 25 **Mighty Quinn's**
- 24 **BrisketTown**
- 24 **Butcher Bar**
- 23 **Mable's Smokehouse**
- 23 **Morgans BBQ**
- 22 **Daisy May's**

BURGER JOINTS

- 25 **Burger Joint**
- 24 **Amsterdam Burger Co.**
- 23 **Black Iron Burger**
- 23 **DuMont Burger**
- 23 **Corner Bistro**
- 22 **Burger Bistro**
- 22 **Shake Shack**
- 22 **Zaitzeff**

CARIBBEAN

- 24 **Cuba**
- 23 **Ali's Roti**
- 23 **Negril**
- 23 **Victor's Cafe**
- 23 **Havana Alma de Cuba**
- 23 **Miss Lily's**
- 23 **Guantanamera**
- 23 **Sazon**

CHICKEN

- 23 **Flor de Mayo**
- 23 **Pio Pio**
- 23 **BonChon**
- 22 **BarKogi**
- 21 **Coco Roco**
- 21 **Blue Ribbon Fried Chicken**
- 21 **Kyochon Chicken**
- 21 **Hill Country Chicken**

CHINESE

- 26 **Decoy**
- 25 **White Bear**

25 **Biang!**
25 **Fung Tu**
24 **Shanghai Cafe**
24 **Prosperity Dumpling**
24 **Cafe China**
24 **RedFarm**

COFFEE

25 **La Colombe**
25 **Birch Coffee**
24 **Abraço Espresso**
24 **Blue Bottle**
24 **Toby's Estate**
23 **Stumptown**
23 **Sweetleaf**
23 **Ninth Street Espresso**

DELIS

25 **Mill Basin Deli**
25 **David's Brisket House**
25 **Barney Greengrass**
25 **Katz's Delicatessen**
24 **Liebman's Delicatessen**
23 **Sarge's**
23 **Pastrami Queen**
23 **B & H Dairy**

DESSERT
(see also Bakeries, Ice Cream)

25 **ChikaLicious Dessert Bar**
25 **Chocolate Room**
24 **Spot Dessert Bar**
22 **Café Sabarsky/Fledermaus**
19 **Serendipity 3**
19 **Junior's**
19 **Omonia Cafe**
18 **Cafe Lalo**

DIM SUM

24 **RedFarm**
24 **Pacificana**
23 **Oriental Garden**
22 **Buddha Bodai**
22 **Ping's Seafood**

21 **Golden Unicorn**
21 **Jing Fong**
21 **Nom Wah Tea Parlor**

DUMPLINGS

24 **Prosperity Dumpling**
24 **Dumpling Man**
24 **Mimi Cheng's**
23 **The Bao**
22 **Vanessa's Dumpling House**
22 **Mandoo Bar**
22 **Excellent Dumpling House**
22 **Dumpling Galaxy**

FOOD HALLS

26 **Smorgasburg**
25 **City Kitchen** ▽
24 **Eataly**
23 **Berg'n**
22 **New World Mall**
21 **Plaza Food Hall**
20 **Gotham West Market**
19 **Hudson Eats**

FRENCH

29 **Le Bernardin**
29 **Bouley**
29 **Daniel**
28 **Jean-Georges**
27 **La Grenouille**
27 **Café Boulud**
26 **Chef's Table/Brooklyn Fare**
26 **Picholine**

FRENCH BISTRO

25 **Buvette**
25 **Le Gigot**
25 **Minetta Tavern**
24 **Dirty French**
24 **La Sirène**
24 **db Bistro Moderne**
24 **JoJo**
24 **Lucien**

TOP FOOD

TOPS BY CUISINE/SPECIALTY

GLUTEN-FREE OPTIONS

27 Del Posto
26 Rubirosa
26 Caracas Arepa Bar
24 Hu Kitchen
24 Galli
23 Risotteria
22 Friedman's
22 Little Beet Table

GREEK

27 Milos
26 Avra
26 Taverna Kyclades
26 Pylos
25 Agnanti
25 Elias Corner
25 Telly's Taverna
24 Bahari Estiatorio

ICE CREAM

27 Ample Hills Creamery
26 Jacques Torres Ice Cream
26 Lemon Ice King
26 Morgenstern's Finest
25 Grom
25 Il Laboratorio
25 Ralph's Famous
25 Big Gay Ice Cream

INDIAN

26 Tamarind
25 Amma
24 Junoon
24 Awadh
24 Vatan
24 Bukhara Grill
24 Moti Mahal Delux
24 Dawat

ITALIAN

27 Marea
27 L'Artusi

27 Del Posto
26 Vesta
26 Rubirosa
26 San Matteo
26 Supper
26 Don Peppe
26 Ai Fiori
26 Babbo
26 Al Di La
26 Scalini Fedeli

JAPANESE/SUSHI

27 Sushi Yasuda
27 Nobu
27 Sushi Nakazawa
27 15 East
27 Bohemian
26 Brushstroke
26 Masa
26 Kyo Ya
26 Zenkichi
26 Shuko
26 Morimoto
26 Sasabune

KOREAN

26 Jungsik
25 Danji
25 Kristalbelli
24 Hangawi
24 Hanjan
24 New WonJo
24 Franchia
23 Kang Ho Dong Baekjeong

KOSHER

25 Mill Basin Deli
24 Liebman's Delicatessen
24 Reserve Cut
24 Peacefood Café
23 Caravan of Dreams
23 Sacred Chow
23 Pastrami Queen
23 2nd Ave Deli

TOP FOOD

LOBSTER ROLLS

27 **Pearl Oyster Bar**
25 **Ed's Lobster Bar**
24 **Mary's Fish Camp**
24 **Cull & Pistol**
24 **Luke's Lobster**
24 **Red Hook Lobster Pound**
24 **Burger & Lobster**
23 **Mermaid Inn**

MEDITERRANEAN

27 **Olea**
26 **Little Owl**
26 **Convivium Osteria**
26 **Gato**
25 **Amali**
25 **Boulud Sud**
25 **Alta**
25 **Il Buco**

MEXICAN
(see also Taquerias)

26 **Casa Enrique**
25 **Cosme**
25 **Gran Electrica**
24 **Chavela's**
24 **Mesa Coyoacan**
24 **Ofrenda**
24 **Black Ant**
24 **Barrio Chino**

MIDDLE EASTERN

26 **Tanoreen**
26 **Taïm**
25 **Bar Bolonat**
25 **Balaboosta**
24 **Ilili**
24 **Balade**
24 **Mimi's Hummus**
24 **Almayass**

NEWCOMERS

26 **Shuko**
26 **Almanac**
26 **Javelina**
26 **Tuome**
26 **Little Park**
26 **Delaware & Hudson**
25 **Upland**
25 **Cosme**

NOODLE SHOPS
(see also Ramen)

25 **Biang!**
25 **Ootoya**
24 **Great NY Noodle Town**
23 **Soba-ya**
23 **Cocoron**
23 **Tasty Hand-Pulled Noodles**
23 **Soba Totto**
23 **Xi'an Famous Foods**

PIZZA

27 **Paulie Gee's**
27 **Totonno's**
26 **Lucali**
26 **Di Fara**
26 **Denino's**
26 **Emily**
26 **Juliana's**
26 **Roberta's**

RAMEN

26 **Chuko**
25 **Ippudo**
24 **Mu Ramen**
24 **Minca**
24 **Totto Ramen**
23 **Kung Fu Ramen**
23 **Hide-Chan**
23 **Jin Ramen**

TOP FOOD

TOPS BY CUISINE/SPECIALTY

RAW BARS

- 27 Pearl Oyster Bar
- 27 Upstate
- 27 Aquagrill
- 26 Maison Premiere
- 25 Blue Ribbon
- 25 Esca
- 25 Oceana
- 25 Lure Fishbar

SANDWICHES
(see also Delis)

- 27 Alidoro
- 26 Il Bambino
- 25 Untamed Sandwiches
- 25 Press 195
- 24 Defonte's
- 24 Banh Mi Saigon
- 23 Taboonette
- 23 Num Pang

SEAFOOD

- 29 Le Bernardin
- 27 Marea
- 27 Milos
- 27 Sea Fire Grill
- 27 Aquagrill
- 26 Avra
- 26 Taverna Kyclades
- 25 Bocelli

SOUTH AMERICAN

- 26 Caracas Arepa Bar
- 25 Fogo de Chão
- 24 Churrascaria Plataforma
- 24 Chimichurri Grill
- 24 Raymi
- 23 Buenos Aires
- 23 Arepas Café
- 23 Pio Pio

SOUTHERN/SOUL

- 25 Brooklyn Star
- 25 Melba's
- 24 Egg
- 24 Sweet Chick
- 24 Pies-N-Thighs
- 24 Queens Comfort
- 24 Root & Bone
- 24 Peaches

SPANISH/TAPAS

- 27 La Vara
- 25 Huertas
- 25 Casa Mono
- 24 Beso
- 24 Txikito
- 24 Toro
- 24 Bar Jamón
- 24 Alcala

STEAKHOUSES

- 28 Peter Luger
- 27 St. Anselm
- 27 Benjamin Steak House
- 26 Porter House NY
- 26 BLT Prime
- 26 Keens
- 26 Quality Meats
- 26 Club A Steak House
- 26 Wolfgang's
- 25 Ruth's Chris
- 25 Maloney & Porcelli
- 25 Sparks

TAQUERIAS

- 27 Los Tacos
- 24 Tortilleria Nixtamal
- 24 Tacombi
- 24 Pampano Taqueria

More on zagat.com

TOP FOOD

TOPS BY CUISINE/SPECIALTY

23 **Toloache Taqueria**
23 **La Esquina**
23 **Oaxaca**
22 **Empellón Taqueria**

THAI

26 **Ayada**
26 **Sripraphai**
26 **Pok Pok Ny**
26 **Pure Thai Cookhouse**
25 **Uncle Boons**
25 **Kin Shop**
24 **Ngam**
24 **Erawan**

TURKISH

26 **Taci's Beyti**
23 **Sip Sak**
23 **Uskudar**
23 **Akdeniz**
22 **Sahara**
22 **Turkish Kitchen**

22 **Pasha**
21 **Beyoglu**

VEGETARIAN

26 **Taïm**
26 **Candle 79**
25 **Dirt Candy**
25 **Blossom**
24 **Candle Cafe**
24 **Hangawi**
24 **V-Note**
24 **Vatan**

VIETNAMESE

24 **Banh Mi Saigon**
23 **Omai**
23 **Indochine**
23 **Pho Bang**
22 **Nha Trang**
22 **Le Colonial**
22 **Vietnaam**
20 **Hanco's**

TOPS BY NEIGHBORHOOD: MANHATTAN

BATTERY PARK CITY

25 **North End Grill**
25 **Mighty Quinn's**
25 **Blue Ribbon Sushi**
23 **Num Pang**
22 **Blue Smoke**
22 **Shake Shack**
22 **Dos Toros**
21 **Parm**

THE BOWERY

24 **Saxon + Parole**
24 **Bar Primi**
24 **Great NY Noodle Town**
24 **Pearl & Ash**
22 **Bacchanal**
22 **DBGB**

22 **Cherche Midi**
22 **Hecho en Dumbo**

CHELSEA

27 **Los Tacos**
27 **Del Posto**
26 **Morimoto**
26 **Colicchio & Sons**
26 **Sushi Seki**
25 **Scarpetta**
25 **Da Umberto**
25 **Old Homestead**

CHINATOWN

24 **Great NY Noodle Town**
23 **Tasty Hand-Pulled Noodles**
23 **Oriental Garden**

TOP FOOD

TOPS BY NEIGHBORHOOD: MANHATTAN

23 **Peking Duck House**
23 **456 Shanghai Cuisine**
23 **Xi'an Famous Foods**
22 **Hop Kee**
22 **Buddha Bodai**

EAST 40s

27 **Sushi Yasuda**
27 **Sea Fire Grill**
27 **Benjamin Steak House**
26 **Avra**
26 **Wolfgang's Steakhouse**
25 **Sparks**
25 **Sakagura**
25 **Hatsuhana**

EAST 50s

27 **La Grenouille**
26 **Four Seasons**
26 **Aquavit**
26 **Club A Steak House**
26 **Wolfgang's Steakhouse**
25 **Amma**
25 **Maloney & Porcelli**
25 **Felidia**

EAST 60s

29 **Daniel**
26 **Sushi Seki**
25 **Amali**
25 **Tiella**
25 **Il Mulino Uptown**
24 **Scalinatella**
24 **Ravagh**
24 **JoJo**

EAST 70s

27 **Café Boulud**
26 **Sasabune**
26 **Sushi of Gari**
26 **Candle 79**
25 **Tanoshi Sushi**
24 **Caravaggio**

24 **Candle Cafe**
24 **V-Note**

EAST 80s

26 **San Matteo**
25 **Elio's**
25 **Sistina**
25 **The Simone**
25 **Giovanni Venticinque**
24 **Erminia**
24 **Ristorante Morini**
24 **Luke's Lobster**

EAST 90s/EAST HARLEM

24 **Nick's**
24 **Paola's**
23 **Rao's**
23 **Pio Pio**
23 **Sfoglia**
22 **Table d'Hôte**
22 **Pascalou**
22 **El Paso**

EAST VILLAGE

28 **Graffiti**
27 **Upstate**
26 **Kyo Ya**
26 **Momofuku Ko**
26 **Supper**
26 **The Eddy**
26 **Caracas Arepa Bar**
26 **Tuome**

FINANCIAL DISTRICT

25 **Capital Grille**
24 **Delmonico's**
24 **Reserve Cut**
24 **Luke's Lobster**
24 **Adrienne's Pizzabar**
23 **Morton's**
23 **Toloache Taqueria**
23 **Cipriani Club 55**

TOP FOOD

TOPS BY NEIGHBORHOOD: MANHATTAN

FLATIRON/UNION SQUARE

28 **Eleven Madison Park**
28 **Gramercy Tavern**
27 **Union Square Cafe**
27 **15 East**
26 **Tocqueville**
26 **ABC Kitchen**
25 **Craft**
25 **Cosme**

GRAMERCY PARK

26 **BLT Prime**
26 **Javelina**
25 **Novitá**
25 **Casa Mono**
25 **Maialino**
24 **Bar Jamón**
24 **Yama**
23 **Morton's Grille**

GREENWICH VILLAGE

28 **Gotham Bar & Grill**
28 **Blue Hill**
26 **Shuko**
26 **Babbo**
26 **Neta**
26 **Tomoe Sushi**
25 **Ribalta**
25 **Alta**

HARLEM

25 **Melba's**
23 **The Cecil**
23 **Lido**
23 **Amy Ruth's**
22 **Chez Lucienne**
22 **Madiba**
22 **Red Rooster**
22 **Ponty Bistro**

LITTLE ITALY

24 **Shanghai Cafe**
24 **Pellegrino's**
24 **Banh Mi Saigon**
23 **Angelo's of Mulberry St.**
23 **Wild Ginger**
23 **Pepe Rosso Social**
23 **Il Cortile**
23 **Nyonya**

LOWER EAST SIDE

26 **Russ & Daughters Cafe**
26 **Pig and Khao**
25 **Clinton St. Baking Co.**
25 **Dirt Candy**
25 **Contra**
25 **Katz's Delicatessen**
25 **Cafe Katja**
25 **Blue Ribbon Sushi Izakaya**

MEATPACKING

25 **Sushi Dojo Express**
25 **Ed's Lobster Bar**
24 **Valbella**
24 **Spice Market**
24 **Tacombi at Gansevoort Mkt.**
23 **Santina**
23 **Catch**
23 **STK**

MURRAY HILL

27 **Alidoro**
27 **Juni**
26 **Riverpark**
26 **Wolfgang's Steakhouse**
25 **Villa Berulia**
25 **Upland**
24 **Nick's**
24 **Hangawi**

NOHO

27 **Bohemian**
26 **Gato**
25 **Bond St**
25 **Bianca**
25 **Il Buco**
24 **Saxon + Parole**

TOPS BY NEIGHBORHOOD: MANHATTAN

24 **Il Buco Alimentari**
22 **Aroma Kitchen**

NOLITA

27 **Estela**
26 **Rubirosa**
26 **Taïm**
26 **Musket Room**
25 **Uncle Boons**
25 **Balaboosta**
24 **Lombardi's**
24 **Public**

NOMAD

26 **NoMad**
25 **NoMad Bar**
24 **Ilili**
24 **Marta**
24 **Ben & Jack's Steak House**
22 **The Breslin**
22 **Maysville**
22 **Hillstone**

PARK AVENUE SOUTH

25 **Upland**
25 **Park Avenue**
23 **Morton's Grille**
23 **Forcella**
22 **Hillstone**
22 **Florian**
22 **Little Beet Table**
22 **Dos Toros**

SOHO

27 **Alidoro**
27 **Aquagrill**
26 **Osteria Morini**
25 **Rouge et Blanc**
25 **Il Mulino Prime**
25 **Blue Ribbon**
25 **Blue Ribbon Sushi**
25 **David Burke Kitchen**

TRIBECA

29 **Bouley**
28 **Mehtaphor**
27 **Nobu**
27 **Bâtard**
26 **Brushstroke**
26 **Sushi of Gari**
26 **Tamarind**
26 **Scalini Fedeli**

WEST 30s

26 **Keens**
26 **Ai Fiori**
25 **Untamed Sandwiches**
25 **Kristalbelli**
24 **Delmonico's Kitchen**
24 **Spot Dessert Bar**
24 **New WonJo**
24 **David Burke Fabrick**

WEST 40s

26 **Sushi of Gari**
26 **Wolfgang's Steakhouse**
25 **Aureole**
25 **Del Frisco's**
25 **Esca**
25 **Strip House**
25 **Oceana**
25 **Ootoya**

WEST 50s

29 **Le Bernardin**
28 **Per Se**
27 **Marea**
27 **Milos**
27 **Nobu 57**
26 **Porter House**
26 **Masa**
26 **The Modern**

WEST 60s

28 **Jean-Georges**
26 **Picholine**

TOP FOOD

TOPS BY NEIGHBORHOOD: MANHATTAN

26 **Telepan**
25 **Boulud Sud**
25 **Lincoln**
25 **Blossom du Jour**
24 **Bar Boulud**
23 **Atlantic Grill**

WEST 70s

26 **Gari**
25 **Dovetail**
24 **RedFarm**
23 **Ocean Grill**
23 **Tessa**
23 **Saravanaa Bhavan**
23 **Risotteria**
23 **Burke & Wills**

WEST 80s

25 **Barney Greengrass**
25 **Blossom**
24 **Candle Cafe West**
24 **Milling Room**
24 **Luke's Lobster**

24 **Peacefood Café**
23 **Bustan**
23 **Spiga**

WEST 90s & UP

24 **Gennaro**
24 **Awadh**
24 **Pisticci**
24 **Amsterdam Burger Co.**
23 **Thai Market**
23 **Covo**
23 **Flor de Mayo**
23 **Jin Ramen**

WEST VILLAGE

27 **L'Artusi**
27 **Annisa**
27 **Pearl Oyster Bar**
27 **Sushi Nakazawa**
26 **Perry St.**
26 **Almanac**
26 **Mas (Farmhouse)**
26 **Decoy**

TOPS BY NEIGHBORHOOD: BROOKLYN

BAY RIDGE

26 **Tanoreen**
25 **David's Brisket House**
24 **Fushimi**
24 **Gino's**
24 **Chadwick's**
24 **Areo**
23 **Arirang Hibachi Steakhouse**
23 **Tuscany Grill**

BOERUM HILL/COBBLE HILL

27 **La Vara**
26 **Battersby**
26 **Hibino**
26 **Rucola**
25 **French Louie**

25 **Chocolate Room**
24 **Ki Sushi**
23 **Wild Ginger**

BKLYN. HEIGHTS/DUMBO

26 **River Café**
26 **Juliana's**
25 **Colonie**
25 **Noodle Pudding**
25 **Gran Electrica**
25 **Henry's End**
24 **Jack the Horse Tavern**
24 **Queen**

CARROLL GARDENS

26 **Lucali**
26 **Dover**

TOP FOOD

TOPS BY NEIGHBORHOOD: BROOKLYN

26 **Buttermilk Channel**
25 **Frankies Spuntino**
24 **Prime Meats**
24 **Fragole**
24 **Wilma Jean**
24 **Brooklyn Farmacy**

CROWN HEIGHTS/BED-STUY

25 **David's Brisket House**
25 **Do or Dine**
25 **Mayfield**
24 **Chavela's**
24 **Peaches**
24 **Aita**
24 **Ali's Roti**
23 **Berg'n**

FT. GREENE/CLINTON HILL

27 **Olea**
26 **Emily**
26 **Locanda Vini & Olii**
25 **Speedy Romeo**
24 **Aita**
23 **Habana Outpost**
23 **Walter's**
23 **Oaxaca**

GREENPOINT

27 **Paulie Gee's**
25 **Five Leaves**
24 **Lobster Joint**
24 **Fornino**
23 **Littleneck Outpost**
23 **Scalino**
23 **Xi'an Famous Foods**
21 **Calexico**

PARK SLOPE

26 **Rose Water**
26 **Al Di La**
26 **Convivium Osteria**
25 **Chocolate Room**
25 **Stone Park Café**
25 **Blue Ribbon Brooklyn**
24 **Talde**
24 **Bogota Latin Bistro**

PROSPECT HEIGHTS

26 **Chuko**
26 **Bar Chuko**
25 **Bar Corvo**
24 **James**
24 **Saul**
23 **Morgans BBQ**
22 **The Vanderbilt**
21 **Tom's**

RED HOOK/COLUMBIA ST.

26 **Pok Pok NY**
25 **Hometown BBQ**
25 **Pok Pok Phat Thai** ▽
25 **Good Fork**
24 **Defonte's**
24 **Red Hook Lobster Pound**
23 **Fort Defiance**
21 **Calexico**

WILLIAMSBURG

28 **Peter Luger**
27 **St. Anselm**
26 **Fette Sau**
26 **Zenkichi**
26 **Maison Premiere**
26 **Caracas Brooklyn**
26 **Delaware & Hudson**
25 **Diner**

BROOKLYN: OTHER AREAS

26 **Totonno's** (Coney Island)
25 **Chef's Table/Bklyn. Fare** (Dtwn.)
25 **Di Fara** (Midwood)
25 **Roberta's** (Bushwick)
25 **Taci's Beyti** (Sheepshead Bay)
24 **Mill Basin Deli** (Flatlands)
24 **Northeast Kingdom** (Bushwick)
23 **Momo Sushi Shack** (Bushwick)

TOP FOOD

TOPS BY NEIGHBORHOOD: OTHER BOROUGHS

BRONX

- 25 | **Roberto's**
- 25 | **Enzo's**
- 25 | **Original Crab Shanty**
- 24 | **Liebman's Delicatessen**
- 24 | **NYY Steak**
- 24 | **Beccofino**
- 24 | **Emilia's**
- 24 | **Jake's Steakhouse**

QUEENS: ASTORIA

- 26 | **Vesta**
- 25 | **Il Bambino**
- 23 | **Trattoria L'incontro**
- 23 | **Piccola Venezia**
- 22 | **Taverna Kyclades**
- 22 | **Agnanti**
- 22 | **Elias Corner**
- 22 | **Telly's Taverna**

QUEENS: FLUSHING

- 25 | **White Bear**
- 24 | **Biang!**
- 24 | **Spicy & Tasty**
- 23 | **Xi'an Famous Foods**
- 23 | **Pho Bang**
- 23 | **Sik Gaek**
- 22 | **Dumpling Galaxy**
- 22 | **Joe's Shanghai**

QUEENS: LONG ISLAND CITY

- 26 | **Casa Enrique**
- 26 | **Hibino**
- 26 | **LIC Market**
- 25 | **Manetta's**
- 24 | **Manducatis**
- 24 | **Mu Ramen**
- 24 | **M. Wells Steakhouse**
- 23 | **Sweetleaf**

QUEENS: OTHER AREAS

- 26 | **Don Peppe** (S. Ozone Park)
- 26 | **Caracas Rockaway** (Rkwy. Pk.)
- 26 | **Ayada** (Elmhurst)
- 26 | **Sripraphai** (Woodside)
- 26 | **Danny Brown** (Forest Hills)
- 25 | **Park Side** (Corona)
- 25 | **Press 195** (Bayside)
- 25 | **La Vigna** (Forest Hills)

STATEN ISLAND

- 26 | **Denino's**
- 26 | **Enoteca Maria**
- 26 | **Trattoria Romana**
- 25 | **Bocelli**
- 24 | **Beso**
- 24 | **Fushimi**
- 24 | **Bayou**
- 24 | **Defonte's**

BEST BETS

DESTINATIONS

BARCLAYS CENTER

Bark
Berlyn
Convivium Osteria
Habana Outpost
Miriam
Morgans BBQ
No. 7
Rose's
Shake Shack
Smoke Joint

BROOKLYN BRIDGE PARK
(North)

Atrium Dumbo
Gran Electrica
Grimaldi's

BEST BETS

DESTINATIONS

Jack the Horse
Jacques Torres Ice Cream
Juliana's
Luke's Lobster
Noodle Pudding
No. 7 Sub
Shake Shack

BROOKLYN BRIDGE PARK
(South)

Ample Hills
ChipShop
Colonie
Fornino
Hanco's
Luzzo's
Pok Pok Ny
Red Gravy
Smorgasburg
Teresa's

GRAND CENTRAL

Ammos
Cafe Centro
Capital Grille
Cipriani
La Fonda del Sol
Michael Jordan's
Oyster Bar
Pera
Shake Shack
Sushi Yasuda

HIGH LINE *(Gansevoort St. Exit)* / WHITNEY MUSEUM

Bubby's
Dos Caminos
El Colmado Butchery
Fig & Olive
Gansevoort Market
Santina
Serafina
Spice Market
Standard Grill
Untitled

HIGH LINE *(23rd St. Exit)*

Bottino
Co.
Cookshop
El Quinto Pino
Empire Diner
Ovest Pizzoteca
Red Cat
Tia Pol
Trestle on Tenth
Txikito

JURY DUTY *(Manhattan)*

Blaue Gans
Buddha Bodai
Excellent Dumpling
Great NY Noodle Town
Nha Trang
The Odeon
Peking Duck House
Red Egg
Takahachi
Xi'an Famous Foods

JURY DUTY *(Brooklyn)*

Bareburger
Ganso
Hanco's
Hill Country
Joya
Junior's
Mile End
Queen
Shake Shack
Teresa's

MADISON SQUARE GARDEN

Arno
David Burke Fabrick
Delmonico's Kitchen
Frankie & Johnnie's
Gaonnuri
Keens
Larb Ubol
Nick & Stef's
State Grill & Bar
Uncle Nick's

BEST BETS

DESTINATIONS

METROPOLITAN MUSEUM

Café Boulud
Café Sabarsky/Fledermaus
E.A.T.
Giovanni Venticinque
Grazie
Le Pain Quotidien
The Mark
Ristorante Morini
Sant Ambroeus
Serafina

MoMA

Benoit
Chevalier
China Grill
Circo
Fogo de Chão
La Bonne Soupe
Michael's
The Modern
PizzArte
21 Club

MUSEUM OF NATURAL HISTORY

Cafe Frida
Caffe Storico
Calle Ocho
Dovetail
Isabella's
Luke's Lobster
Nice Matin
Ocean Grill
Shake Shack
Spring Natural Kitchen

9/11 MEMORIAL

Beaubourg
El Vez
Harry's Italian
Hudson Eats
Le District
North End Grill
One Dine
P.J. Clarke's
Shake Shack

ROCKEFELLER CENTER

Bouchon Bakery
Brasserie Ruhlmann
Del Frisco's Grille
Fogo de Chão
Limani
NYY Steak
Oceana
Rock Center Café
Sea Grill
Wu Liang Ye

THEATER DISTRICT DELUXE

Aureole
Charlie Palmer at the Knick
db Bistro Moderne
Esca
Gabriel Kreuther
Hunt & Fish Club
Lambs Club
STK
Strip House
Wolfgang's Steakhouse

THEATER DISTRICT FAMILY-FRIENDLY

Carmine's
City Kitchen
5 Napkin Burger
John's Pizzeria
Junior's
Ruby Foo's
Schnipper's
Shake Shack
Tony's Di Napoli
Virgil's

THEATER DISTRICT OLD-SCHOOL

Barbetta
Chez Josephine
Chez Napoleon
Frankie & Johnnie's

BEST BETS

DESTINATIONS

Joe Allen
Landmark Tavern
Le Rivage

Orso
Patsy's
Sardi's

OCCASIONS & SITUATIONS

ANNIVERSARY-WORTHY

Del Posto
Gabriel Kreuther
The House
Il Buco
Lambs Club
One if by Land
The Place
Rainbow Room
River Café
Water's Edge

Egg
Lafayette
Little Park
Maison Kayser
Norma's
The Odeon
Veselka

BAR SCENES

Arlington Club
The Clocktower
East Pole
Gato
Hunt & Fish Club
Javelina
Margaux
Rosie's
Salvation Taco
Upland

BRIDAL/BABY SHOWERS

Alice's Tea Cup
Anassa
Beauty & Essex
Bobo
Kings' Carriage House
Laduree
Lady Mendl's
Mari Vanna
Palm Court
Sarabeth's

BEER STANDOUTS

Berg'n
Birreria
Cafe d'Alsace
Cannibal
DBGB
Eleven Madison Park
Gramercy Tavern
Jacob's Pickles
Jimmy's No. 43
Luksus

BRUNCH (Downtown)

ABC Kitchen
Cafe Cluny
Clinton St. Baking Co.
Estela
Jack's Wife Freda
Locanda Verde
Northern Spy
Prune
Rosemary's
Russ & Daughters

BRUNCH (Midtown)

Artisanal
db Bistro Moderne
44 & X
Lavo
Má Pêche
Penelope
Rainbow Room

BREAKFAST

Balthazar
Buvette
Cookshop

BEST BETS

OCCASIONS & SITUATIONS

Salvation Taco
The Smith
Upland

BRUNCH *(Uptown)*

Barney Greengrass
Cafe d'Alsace
Cafe Luxembourg
The Cecil
Jacob's Pickles
Nice Matin
Penrose
Pizza Beach
Ristorante Morini
The Smith

BRUNCH *(Brooklyn)*

Aita
Allswell
Buttermilk Channel
Colonie
Delaware & Hudson
Egg
Five Leaves
River Café
Roberta's
Rose Water
Stone Park Café

BUSINESS DINING
(Financial District)

Beaubourg
Bobby Van's
Capital Grille
Cipriani
Delmonico's
Harry's Cafe
MarkJoseph Steakhouse
Morton's
North End Grill
P.J. Clarke's on the Hudson

BUSINESS DINING *(Midtown)*

Casa Lever
Del Frisco's
Four Seasons

Gabriel Kreuther
Jean-Georges
Le Bernardin
Le Cirque
Marea
Michael's
21 Club

BYO

Azuri Cafe
Gazala's Place
Kuma Inn
Lucali
Phoenix Garden
Poke
Queens Comfort
Taci's Beyti
Tartine
Zaytoons *(Carroll Gdns./Clinton Hill)*

CHILD-FRIENDLY

Alice's Tea Cup
Brooklyn Farmacy
Bubby's
Cowgirl
L&B Spumoni
Ninja
Otto
Peanut Butter & Co.
Ruby Foo's
Serendipity 3

CHILDREN'S MENUS

Blue Ribbon Brooklyn
Blue Smoke
Buttermilk Channel
DBGB
Dinosaur Bar-B-Que
Han Dynasty
Isabella's
Kefi
Landmarc
Rosa Mexicano

OCCASIONS & SITUATIONS

COCKTAIL STARS

Atera
Dead Rabbit
Decoy
Grand Army
Mayahuel
NoMad Bar
Oleanders
Porchlight
Santina
Tijuana Picnic

HOT DATES

Cafe Clover
Charlie Bird
The Clocktower
Dirty French
Gemma
Polo Bar
Reynard
Santina
Upland
Zenkichi

DESIGN STANDOUTS

Chevalier
The Clocktower
Gabriel Kreuther
Lafayette
Limani
Lincoln
Maison Premiere
Marea
NoMad Bar
Polo Bar

OLD NY VIBE

Bamonte's
Ferrara
Keens
Landmark Tavern
Minetta Tavern
Morgan Dining Room
Oyster Bar
Peter Luger
21 Club
Waverly Inn

GROUP DINING

Beauty & Essex
Buddakan
Decoy
Kang Ho Dong Baekjeong
Mission Chinese
Otto
Tao
Tavern on the Green
Tijuana Picnic
Toro

PATIOS/GARDENS

Aurora (Williamsburg)
Barbetta
Brasserie Ruhlmann
Bryant Park Grill
Ladurée
New Leaf
Salinas
Santina
Tavern on the Green
The Vine

HAPPY HOURS

Burger & Lobster
The Clam
El Colmado
FishTag
Fonda
Keens
Maialino
Mermaid Inn
Red Rooster
Rye

SOCIALITE CENTRAL

Amaranth
Beautique
Elio's
Harlow
Le Bilboquet
Leopard at des Artistes
Polo Bar
Ristorante Morini
Sant Ambroeus
Swifty's

BEST BETS

THANKSGIVING

Blue Hill
Breslin
Cookshop
Gramercy Tavern
Mas (Farmhouse)
One If By Land
Tavern on the Green
Telepan
21 Club
Waverly Inn

24/7

BCD Tofu House
Cafeteria
Coppelia
Gray's Papaya
Kang Suh
Kunjip
New Wonjo
Sanford's
Sarge's Deli
Veselka

VIEWS

Asiate
Gaonnuri
Michael Jordan's
The Modern
One Dine
Riverpark
Robert
Sea Grill
Stella 34
The View

WATERSIDE

Boathouse
Brooklyn Crab
Hudson Eats
Industry Kitchen
Pier A Harbor House
River Café
River Dock Cafe
Shi
Water Club
Water's Edge

WINE BARS

Aldo Sohm
Bacaro
Casellula
Corkbuzz
Danny Brown
El Quinto Pino
Fifty Paces
Il Buco Alimentari
June
Upholstery Store

WINE: CONNOISSEUR PICKS

Babbo
Bâtard
Charlie Bird
Daniel
Eleven Madison Park
Gabriel Kreuther
Jean-Georges
Le Bernardin
Pearl & Ash
Per Se

WINE: UNUSUAL LISTS

All'onda
Birds & Bubbles
Estela
The Gander
Marta
M. Wells Steakhouse
O Ya
Racines
Rebelle
Wildair

BEST UNDER $40

40 UNDER $40: FULL-MEAL WINNERS

27 Paulie Gee's	26 Sripraphai
27 Totonno's	26 Taverna Kyclades
27 Olea	26 Bar Chuko
26 Vesta	26 Taci's Beyti
26 Il Bambino	26 Pure Thai Cookhouse
26 Lucali	25 Clinton St. Baking Co.
26 Di Fara	25 Mill Basin Deli
26 Russ & Daughters	25 White Bear
26 Denino's Pizzeria	25 Ducks Eatery
26 Fette Sau	25 Ribalta
26 San Matteo	25 Hometown
26 Emily	25 David's Brisket House
26 Javelina	25 Motorino
26 Juliana's	25 Momofuku Noodle Bar
26 Roberta's	25 Speedy Romeo
26 Hibino	25 Barney Greengrass
26 Caracas Arepa Bar	25 Northeast Kingdom
26 Chuko	25 Brooklyn Star
26 LIC Market	25 Five Leaves
26 Ayada	25 Katz's

20 UNDER $20: QUICK-BITE WINNERS

27 Alidoro	24 Dumpling Man
27 Los Tacos	24 Defonte's
26 Taïm	24 Mimi Cheng's Dumplings
25 Untamed Sandwiches	24 Banh Mi Saigon
25 Biang!	23 Ali's Roti
25 Burger Joint	23 Mamoun's
24 Shanghai Cafe	23 Kung Fu Ramen
24 Prosperity Dumpling	23 Tasty Hand-Pulled Noodles
24 Joe's Pizza	23 B & H Dairy
24 Leo's Latticini	23 Arepas Café

BY CUISINE

FRENCH	SEAFOOD
23 Café Henri	26 Taverna Kyclades
22 Cafe Gitane	25 Telly's Taverna
22 Tartine	24 Lobster Joint
21 Cafe Luluc	24 Luke's Lobster
20 Bar Tabac	24 Red Hook Lobster Pound
20 Au Za'atar	23 Littleneck

BEST UNDER $40

BY CUISINE

SOMETHING DIFFERENT

- 25 **Ducks**
- 23 **Han Dynasty**
- 23 **Jeepney**
- 22 **Madiba**
- 22 **Maharlika**
- 22 **Amazing 66**

SUSHI

- 26 **Hibino**
- 25 **Momo Sushi Shack**
- 23 **Samurai Mama/Papa**
- 23 **Poke**
- 23 **Yuka**
- 21 **Kouzan**

BY DESTINATION

COLUMBUS CIRCLE

- 24 **Kashkaval Garden**
- 22 **Bouchon Bakery**
- 21 **Bareburger**
- 21 **Mooncake Foods**
- 18 **Le Pain Quotidien**

MUSEUM MILE

- 22 **El Paso**
- 22 **Shake Shack**
- 21 **Brick Lane Curry House**
- 20 **Sarabeth's**
- 18 **Le Pain Quotidien**

MADISON SQUARE GARDEN

- 23 **Cho Dang Gol**
- 23 **Kati Roll Company**
- 22 **Friedman's**
- 22 **Larb Ubol**
- 21 **Mooncake Foods**

THEATER DISTRICT

- 25 **Ootoya**
- 24 **Wu Liang Ye**
- 24 **Luke's Lobster**
- 23 **Sake Bar Hagi**
- 23 **John's Pizzeria**

BY SPECIAL FEATURE

BUZZING SCENE
(Manhattan)

- 26 **Javelina**
- 26 **Ducks**
- 25 **Momofuku Noodle Bar**
- 23 **Miss Lily's**
- 23 **Yuca Bar**
- 21 **Meatball Shop**

BUZZING SCENE
(Brooklyn)

- 26 **Roberta's**
- 26 **Chuko**
- 25 **Hometown BBQ**
- 25 **Brooklyn Star**
- 25 **Gran Electrica**
- 23 **The Commodore**

CHEAP DATE
(Manhattan)

- 26 **Taverna Kyclades**
- 24 **Murray's Cheese Bar**
- 24 **Barrio Chino**
- 23 **Emporio**
- 22 **Gnocco**
- 20 **Gotham West Market**

CHEAP DATE
(Brooklyn)

- 27 **Olea**
- 26 **Emily**
- 26 **Bar Chuko**
- 25 **Northeast Kingdom**
- 25 **Five Leaves**
- 24 **Aita**

NOTABLE PRIX FIXES

LUNCH

$24	**Philippe**
$25	**Tamarind**
$28	**Milos**
$28	**Osteria Morini**
$28	**Perry St**
$28	**Spice Market**
$29	**Asiate**
$29	**Benoit**
$29	**The NoMad**
$29	**Tocqueville**
$30	**Beaubourg**
$30	**Tao** (Uptown)
$32	**db Bistro Moderne**
$32	**Mercer Kitchen**
$34	**21 Club**
$35	**Felidia**
$35	**Oceana**
$36	**Del Frisco's**
$36	**Gotham Bar & Grill**
$37	**Café Boulud**
$38	**Aureole**
$38	**Jean-Georges' Noug.**
$47	**Marea**
$49	**Babbo**
$49	**Del Posto**
$55	**Bouley**
$58	**Jean-Georges**
$65	**La Grenouille**
$76	**The Modern**
$80	**Le Bernardin**

DINNER

$24	**Becco**
$29	**Le Relais de Venise**
$45	**Sushi Dojo**
$54	**Delaware & Hudson**
$55	**Bâtard**
$55	**Empellón Cocina**
$67	**Contra**
$75	**Scalini Fedeli**
$79	**Aldea**
$80	**Recette**
$82	**Dovetail**
$85	**Colicchio & Sons**
$85	**Semilla**
$92	**Gramercy Tavern**
$95	**Betony**
$98	**Gabriel Kreuther**
$115	**Luksus**
$120	**River Café**
$120	**Sushi Nakazawa**
$120	**Take Root**
$135	**Daniel**
$135	**Shuko**
$140	**Le Bernardin**
$175	**Momofuku Ko**
$195	**Blanca**
$225	**Eleven Madison Park**
$235	**Atera**
$306	**Chef's Table/Brooklyn Fare**
$310	**Per Se**
$450	**Masa**

RESTAURANT
DIRECTORY

	FOOD	DECOR	SERVICE	COST

Abboccato *Italian*
21 | 18 | 21 | $56

West 50s | Blakely Hotel | 136 W. 55th St. (bet. 6th & 7th Aves.) | 212-265-4000 | www.abboccato.com
It boasts "convenient" coordinates – near both City Center and Carnegie Hall – and this Midtown Italian "sleeper" follows through with "dependably good" eats, "prompt" service and "intimate" environs; the $38 dinner prix fixe is a "bargain" vis-à-vis the otherwise "higher-end" tabs.

ABC Cocina *Pan-Latin*
25 | 24 | 22 | $61

Flatiron | ABC Carpet & Home | 38 E. 19th St. (bet. B'way & Park Ave. S.) | 212-677-2233 | www.abccocinanyc.com
"Another winner" from Jean-Georges Vongerichten, this "hip" Pan-Latin in ABC Carpet & Home earns a spot on the "repeat list" with "inventive", "well-executed" tapas and "fabulous" cocktails; bills can get "pricey" and the "rustic" digs can be a "little loud" (especially in the "lively" bar area), but it remains one "tough" ticket.

ABC Kitchen *American*
26 | 25 | 23 | $66

Flatiron | ABC Carpet & Home | 35 E. 18th St. (bet. B'way & Park Ave. S.) | 212-475-5829 | www.abckitchennyc.com
Jean-Georges Vongerichten's "bustling" Flatiron American is "all it's cracked up to be", pairing a "first-rate" "market-driven" menu with "unbelievable" cocktails in "charming, unstuffy" surrounds "popular" with the "see-and-be-seen" set; be ready to pay, and "plan ahead" since snagging a rez is a "project in and of itself."

Abigael's *Eclectic/Kosher*
21 | 19 | 20 | $54

West 30s | 1407 Broadway (bet. 38th & 39th Sts.) | 212-575-1407 | www.abigaels.com
A menu spanning "short ribs to sushi" gives kosher cuisine an "upscale" gloss at this double-decker Garment District Eclectic overseen by "creative" chef Jeffrey Nathan; "bland" atmospherics detract, but it remains a "staple" for observant folks.

Abraço Espresso *Coffee*
24 | 15 | 21 | $7

East Village | 86 E. Seventh St. (bet. 1st & 2nd Aves.) | no phone | www.abraconyc.com
They have "espresso down proper" at this East Village "standout", a seatless "hole-in-the-wall" where the "cool" baristas purvey "top-notch coffee" (drips included) and nibbles like the "tantalizing olive cake"; "there's often a line", but its "cult following" is "happy to wait."

Aburiya Kinnosuke *Japanese*
24 | 18 | 21 | $62

East 40s | 213 E. 45th St. (bet. 2nd & 3rd Aves.) | 212-867-5454 | www.aburiyakinnosuke.com
The "real deal" in East Midtown, this "classic izakaya" transports you to Japan with a "top-notch", sushi-free lineup featuring grilled robata bites and housemade tofu; since course after course can do some "damage to your wallet", bargain-hunters opt for lunch.

Acappella *Italian*
23 | 20 | 23 | $81

TriBeCa | 1 Hudson St. (Chambers St.) | 212-240-0163
Dining is "an event" at this "old-world" TriBeCa Northern Italian renowned for "delicious" food, *Godfather* opulent" decor and "warm"

staffers who "treat you like gold"; "try not to faint when you get the check" or you'll miss out on the complimentary grappa.

Acme *American*
20 | 20 | 19 | $62

NoHo | 9 Great Jones St. (Lafayette St.) | 212-203-2121 | www.acmenyc.com

The "Downtown vibe" hits the acme of "cool" at this "jumping" NoHo New American, where the "satisfying" dishes take on "dynamic" Nordic accents courtesy of chef Mads Refslund; the "loud", "see-and-be-seen" crowd and lower-level "cocktail den" set a tone that's "hip but not tragically so."

Acqua at Peck Slip *Italian*
21 | 19 | 22 | $46

South Street Seaport | 21 Peck Slip (Water St.) | 212-349-4433 | www.acquarestaurantnyc.com

"Away from the touristy Seaport places", this "simple", rustic Italian is praised for its housemade pastas and "interesting" selection of boutique wines; despite "reasonable" prices, "attentive" service and "lovely" out-door seating on a cobblestone street, there's "never a long wait" here.

Adrienne's Pizzabar *Pizza*
24 | 16 | 18 | $27

Financial District | 54 Stone St. (Old Slip) | 212-248-3838 | www.adriennespizzabarnyc.com

Brace yourself for "lunchtime madness" when "Wall Street suits" and "casual passersby" descend on this FiDi pizzeria for its "outstand-ing" thin-crust pies; "adequate" service and "nonexistent decor" are part of the package, making it best enjoyed at an alfresco seat on "picturesque Stone Street."

Afghan Kebab House *Afghan*
21 | 13 | 18 | $30

East 70s | 1345 Second Ave. (71st St.) | 212-517-2776
West 50s | 764 Ninth Ave. (bet. 51st & 52nd Sts.) | 212-307-1612

"Mouthwatering" kebabs get skewered at these "authentic" Afghans hailed for "flavorful", "substantial" grub for "bargain-basement" dough; service is "efficient", and if the "simple" settings "don't look like much", they're still "good for a quick meal."

Agave *Southwestern*
19 | 18 | 20 | $42

West Village | 140 Seventh Ave. S. (bet. Charles & 10th Sts.) | 212-989-2100 | www.agaveny.com

Sure, the chow is "decent" enough, but according to this Village South-westerner's "young" fan base it's the "killer margaritas" that "keep the place buzzing"; though service skews "slow", time is on your side during the "popular" all-you-can-drink (aka "boozy") weekend brunch.

Agnanti *Greek*
25 | 17 | 21 | $34

Astoria | 19-06 Ditmars Blvd. (19th St.) | Queens | 718-545-4554 | www.agnantimeze.com

A "notch above the typical Astorian", this "tried-and-true" Hellenic tav-erna rolls out "delicious", "reasonably priced" meals that conjure up the "Greek isles"; the decor is on the "forgettable" side, so regulars request seats on the "wonderful" patio facing Astoria Park and the East River.

Agora Taverna *Greek*

20 | 19 | 20 | $37

Forest Hills | 70-09 Austin St. (70th Ave.) | Queens | 718-793-7300 | www.agorataverna.com

"They know how to grill fish" at this Forest Hills taverna, whose "varied menu" ups the local ante for "traditional Greek dishes"; it can get "noisy", but it's "amiable" if you're "not in the mood to go to Astoria."

Ai Fiori *Italian*

26 | 25 | 25 | $91

West 30s | Langham Place Fifth Avenue Hotel | 400 Fifth Ave. (bet. 36th & 37th Sts.) | 212-613-8660 | www.aifiorinyc.com

"High standards" are a given at Michael White's "swanky" showcase in the Langham Place Fifth Avenue Hotel, where "discreet" servers set down "swoon-worthy", Riviera-inspired cuisine led by "exceptional pastas" in a sanctum of "ultrasleek" luxury made for "celebrating something special"; the prices are predictably "splurge"-worthy, yet its "upscale" clientele has "no complaints."

Aita *Italian*

24 | 24 | 23 | $35

Clinton Hill | 132 Greene Ave. (Waverly Ave.) | Brooklyn | 718-576-3584
Crown Heights | 798 Franklin Ave. (bet. Lincoln Pl. & Service Rd.) | Brooklyn | 917-966-2670
www.aitarestaurant.com

These "homey" trattorias produce "excellent" pasta-centric Italian fare highlighting ingredients "straight from the farmer's market"; the "intimate" Clinton Hill original is a "neighborhood favorite" also known for its "must-try" brunch, while the newer Crown Heights sequel shows "great potential."

Aji Sushi *Japanese*

21 | 16 | 19 | $29

Murray Hill | 519 Third Ave. (bet. 34th & 35th Sts.) | 212-686-2055 | www.ajisushinyc.com

Maybe it's "just a standard sushi spot", but Murray Hill locals swear by this "reliable" Japanese "staple" for its "good variety" and "value" tabs; "swift delivery" seems the preferred way to go, what with the "bland" atmosphere.

Akdeniz *Turkish*

23 | 13 | 20 | $33

West 40s | 19 W. 46th St. (bet. 5th & 6th Aves.) | 212-575-2307 | www.akdenizturkishusa.com

It's all about "value" at this Midtown Turk offering a "can't-be-beat" dinner prix fixe that's a showstopper for theatergoers; the "tiny", "unmemorable" setting can feel a bit "claustrophobic", but the grub's "tasty" and the service "accommodating."

A La Turka *Turkish*

20 | 15 | 19 | $40

East 70s | 1417 Second Ave. (74th St.) | 212-744-2424 | www.alaturkarestaurant.com

A "reliable neighborhood place", this Upper Eastsider "always delivers" ("just like the mailman") with "solid" Turkish fare; okay, when it's "crowded" the "pleasant" service can be a bit "lacking", and the space could use a "makeover", but "totally reasonable" tabs save the day.

Alberto *Italian*

24 | 20 | 22 | $59

Forest Hills | 98-31 Metropolitan Ave. (bet. 69th & 70th Aves.) | Queens | 718-268-7860 | www.albertorestaurant.com

A "Forest Hills find", this "marvelously old-fashioned" Italian remains a "steady" neighborhood "institution" (since '73) thanks to "well-prepared classics" and a "staff and owners who greet you like family"; indeed, the "high prices" and "romantic", fireplace-equipped room suggest "special occasion."

Al Bustan *Lebanese*   21 | 20 | 20 | $54

East 50s | 319 E. 53rd St. (bet. 1st & 2nd Aves.) | 212-759-5933 | www.albustanny.com

"Hidden" on an East Midtown side street, this upscale double-decker delivers "succulent" Lebanese classics in a "modern", chandeliered room; although the "big space" is "rarely busy" at the dinner hour, at least it's "comfortable" and you can "hear yourself speak."

Alcala Restaurant *Spanish*   24 | 19 | 23 | $46

East 40s | 246 E. 44th St. (2nd Ave.) | 212-370-1866 | www.alcalarestaurant.com

For a taste of "Spain in Manhattan", this "fixture" near the U.N. fits the bill, offering a "variety"-filled menu highlighted by "excellent" tapas and "tempting" entrees; "attentive" service and "cozy" confines are other reasons it's a "nice neighborhood place."

Aldea *Mediterranean*   24 | 21 | 23 | $103

Flatiron | 31 W. 17th St. (bet. 5th & 6th Aves.) | 212-675-7223 | www.aldearestaurant.com

After a refresh, George Mendes' "cool and classy" Flatiron Mediterranean now offers his "standout" Portuguese-inspired fare in two prix fixe formats, with à la carte options being offered in the expanded bar area; "refined" surroundings and "impeccable" service further justify the "expensive" tabs.

Al Di La *Italian*   26 | 19 | 24 | $52

Park Slope | 248 Fifth Ave. (Carroll St.) | Brooklyn | 718-783-4565 | www.aldilatrattoria.com

This "rustic" Park Slope "star" draws a "devoted clientele" with its "brilliant" Venetian dishes and "20th-century prices"; blame the no-reservations policy for al di "long lines", though the attached wine bar "helps pass the time" and "you can avoid waiting" altogether at lunch.

Aldo Sohm Wine Bar *French*   21 | 23 | 24 | $52

West 50s | 151 W. 51st St. (bet. 51st & 52nd Sts.) | 212-554-1143 | www.aldosohmwinebar.com

Le Bernardin's master sommelier, Aldo Sohm, brings "vaunted wine expertise" to his nearby Midtown namesake, where "wonderful" vintages complement light lunches and "creative", French-informed small plates at dinner; with a "well-versed" staff manning the "smart-casual" space (think "upscale living room"), it's "buzzy" and "reasonably priced" – aldo "not cheap."

Al Forno Pizzeria *Pizza*   20 | 14 | 19 | $28

East 70s | 1484 Second Ave. (bet. 77th & 78th Sts.) | 212-249-5103 | www.alfornopizzeria77.com

This "no-frills" Yorkville "standby" churns out "quality" brick-oven pizzas on the "quick" for low dough; "typical" Italian pastas and salads are also on offer, but given "lots of kids" and little atmosphere, delivery may be the way to go.

	FOOD	DECOR	SERVICE	COST

Alfredo 100 *Italian*

21 | 19 | 21 | $75

East 50s | 7 E. 54th St. (bet. 5th & 6th Aves.) | 212-688-1999 |
www.alfredo100.com

Spun off from an Italy-based original, this Midtowner provides
"generous portions" of "pretty good" Roman cooking (including the
trademark fettuccini) via a "cordial staff"; with Al Hirschfeld prints
lining the "spacious" room, it caters to corporate sorts with the lire to
settle "expensive" tabs.

Ali Baba *Turkish*

21 | 15 | 18 | $36

East 40s | 862 Second Ave. (46th St.) | 212-888-8622 |
www.alibabasterrace.com
Murray Hill | 212 E. 34th St. (bet. 2nd & 3rd Aves.) | 212-683-9206 |
www.alibabaturkishcuisine.com

Ottoman expats say these "convivial" Turks "taste like home", then
up the ante with "generous portions" at real-"value" tabs; proponents
praise Second Avenue's "lovely roof deck", though the "nothing-fancy"
decor is another story.

Alice's Tea Cup *Teahouse*

20 | 21 | 19 | $28

East 60s | 156 E. 64th St. (Lexington Ave.) | 212-486-9200
East 80s | 220 E. 81st St. (bet. 2nd & 3rd Aves.) | 212-734-4832
West 70s | 102 W. 73rd St. (bet. Amsterdam & Columbus Aves.) |
212-799-3006
www.alicesteacup.com

"Heaven for little girls (and big ones too)", these "darling" tearooms with
"whimsical" *Alice in Wonderland* decor serve a "staggering" selection
of brewed pots and "scrumptious" scones with an actual side of "fairy
dust"; not even "long lines", "rushed" service or "cramped" quarters can
break the "enchanting" spell.

Alidoro *Italian/Sandwiches*

27 | 16 | 19 | $16

NEW Murray Hill | 18 E. 39th St. (bet. 5th & Madison Aves.) |
646-692-4330
SoHo | 105 Sullivan St. (bet. Prince & Spring Sts.) | 212-334-5179 |
www.alidoronyc.com

Boasting "Italian sandwiches that rival any", these cash-only take-out
niches (with limited seating in Murray Hill) dispense "a wide variety"
of "massive" two-handers stuffed with "mouthwatering" ingredients;
paesani "put up" with "brusque" counter service (it's "not a place for the
indecisive") and "a bit of a wait" because "it's worth it."

Ali's Roti *Caribbean*

23 | 12 | 18 | $15

Wakefield | 4220 White Plains Rd. (E. 233rd St.) | Bronx | 718-655-2178
Bedford-Stuyvesant | 1267 Fulton St. (Arlington Pl.) | Brooklyn |
718-783-0316
Crown Heights | 337 Utica Ave. (Carroll St.) | Brooklyn | no phone
Prospect Lefferts Gardens | 589 Flatbush Ave. (bet. Midwood St. &
Rutland Rd.) | Brooklyn | 718-462-1730

"Mouthwatering" rotis with "fresh dough" and meaty fillings ("ask for
them spicy") bring the "Trini flavor" to NYC at these low-cost Trinidadi-
ans; despite "no-frills" setups and sparse seating, expect a "line of loyal
customers" at prime times.

	FOOD	DECOR	SERVICE	COST

All'onda *Italian*
23 | 20 | 22 | $67

Greenwich Village | 22 E. 13th St. (bet. 5th Ave. & University Pl.) | 212-231-2236 | www.allondanyc.com

"Expert renderings of Venetian cuisine" heightened by chef Chris Jaeckle's Japanese touches yield the "enticing" likes of "showstopper" uni pasta ("not what my mama made") at this bi-level Villager; the "cool interior" and "efficient service" clinch an all-around "memorable time."

Allswell *American*
23 | 20 | 20 | $41

Williamsburg | 124 Bedford Ave. (10th St.) | Brooklyn | 347-799-2743 | www.allswellnyc.tumblr.com

"Very Brooklyn", this rustic Williamsburg pub is well regarded for "innovation" thanks to a "rotating menu" of "flavorful" American grub with "complex" farm-to-table ingredients; occupying "casual" quarters with an "appropriately hipsterized" staff and clientele, it's especially "popular at brunch."

Alma *Mexican*
20 | 22 | 19 | $39

Columbia Street Waterfront District | 187 Columbia St., 2nd fl. (Degraw St.) | Brooklyn | 718-643-5400 | www.almarestaurant.com

"Mind-altering" Manhattan skyline views from a "year-round" rooftop are the bait at this Columbia Street Waterfront District Mexican where the chow is as "solid" as the margaritas are "strong"; an "off-the-beaten-path" address "not close to public transportation" makes "walking shoes" the footwear of choice.

NEW Almanac *American*
26 | 26 | 27 | $81

West Village | 28 Seventh Ave. S. (St. Lukes Pl.) | 212-255-1795 | www.almanacnyc.com

"Prepare to be amazed" at chef Galen Zamarra's "pricey" West Village "triumph", which replaces Mas (la grillade) in an "intimate" duplex where the "inspired" American tasting menus are built upon "the freshest" hyper-seasonal ingredients; with "on-point" service, "killer" wines and an à la carte option, "this place has it all."

Almayass *Armenian/Lebanese*
24 | 22 | 22 | $54

Flatiron | 24 E. 21st St. (bet. B'way & Park Ave. S.) | 212-473-3100 | www.almayassnyc.com

For a "delicious" introduction to Lebanese-Armenian cooking, this "lovely" Flatiron branch of a Beirut-based chain offers a share-worthy menu offering an "amazing range" of cold and hot meze; the "enjoyable" scene includes a room "spacious" enough to "go with a few people so you can try more", plus there's an adjacent bar/lounge for grabbing a drink.

Almond *French*
20 | 20 | 20 | $47

Flatiron | 12 E. 22nd St. (bet. B'way & Park Ave. S.) | 212-228-7557
NEW TriBeCa | 186 Franklin St. (bet. Greenwich & Hudson Sts.) | 212-431-0606
www.almond.nyc

"Honest" French dishes are "well prepared" and "decently priced" at these "enjoyable" bistros, which branch out from a Bridgehampton original; "reliable" fallbacks "if you're in the 'hood", they're "spacious" and "cheerful" but "busy busy" (brunch is especially "packed") and "a bit loud."

Alobar *American*

20 | 21 | 21 | $41

Long Island City | 46-42 Vernon Blvd. (47th Ave.) | Queens | 718-752-6000 | www.alobarnyc.com

An "intelligent" take on "farm-to-table" cuisine showcased in rustic-chic accommodations sets this LIC American abuzz with local foodies; the "quality" offerings can make for spendy tabs, but the consensus is it's "cool and bold" for the 'hood.

Alta *Mediterranean*

25 | 23 | 21 | $58

Greenwich Village | 64 W. 10th St. (bet. 5th & 6th Aves.) | 212-505-7777 | www.altarestaurant.com

Small plates are "full of big flavors" at this Village Med, which stays "on its game" serving "premier" tapas and "awesome sangria" in "warm" bi-level surroundings helmed by a "welcoming" crew; prices are "fair", but they can still "add up", as with the "super-fun" $460 "everything-on-the-menu" deal.

Altesi Ristorante *Italian*

22 | 22 | 22 | $63

East 60s | 26 E. 64th St. (Madison Ave.) | 212-759-8900 | www.altesinyc.com

"Chic yet warm", this all-day Italian in an UES brownstone takes diners "to the Amalfi Coast" with its "beautifully prepared" plates served by a "lovely" staff; the "contemporary" setting includes a "gem" of a back garden, and "pricey" tariffs just come with the territory.

Amali *Mediterranean*

25 | 22 | 24 | $59

East 60s | 115 E. 60th St. (Park Ave.) | 212-339-8363 | www.amalinyc.com

"Classic Mediterranean flavors" with "farm-to-table" sensibilities are an "inspired" mix at this Periyali sib tucked away near Bloomie's, which also "surprises" Midtowners with a "biodynamic wine list"; "warm" service and rustically "stylish" decor help justify the "high" price tag.

Amaranth *Mediterranean*

21 | 19 | 20 | $63

East 60s | 21 E. 62nd St. (bet. 5th & Madison Aves.) | 212-980-6700 | www.amaranthrestaurant.com

Aka "air-kissing central", this "buzzy" Madison Avenue–area Med is the kind of place where the "better-than-average" food is accompanied by even better "people-watching"; service is generally "attentive" (especially if you've got a "European title"), and "expensive" pricing is part of the deal.

Amarone *Italian*

22 | 18 | 22 | $51

West 40s | 686 Ninth Ave. (47th St.) | 212-245-6060 | www.amaroneristorantenyc.com

A "perfect choice" pre-theater, this Hell's Kitchen trattoria delivers "solid" Italian fare via "convivial" staffers sure to "get you out in time" for the show; "modest" digs mean it's "nothing fancy", but that just makes it a "go-to staple" kind of place.

Amazing 66 *Chinese*

22 | 14 | 16 | $24

Chinatown | 66 Mott St. (bet. Bayard & Canal Sts.) | 212-334-0099 | www.amazing66.com

"Genuine" Cantonese cooking comes at "reasonable prices" at this C-town storefront where the encyclopedic menu includes "some real gems" for "adventurous" eaters and the lunch specials are "unbelievable"; just know that service is "quick" ("don't expect to linger") and the decor "pretty much nonexistent."

American Cut Steak

 24 | 25 | 24 | $89

TriBeCa | 363 Greenwich St. (bet. Franklin & Harrison Sts.) | 212-226-4736 | www.americancutsteakhouse.com
Chef Marc Forgione's "jazzed-up riff on a classic steakhouse", this "trendy" TriBeCa redo of an Atlantic City meatery makes the cut with "imaginative" preparations of "superb" beef; "impeccable" servers manning "sleek" surrounds with "art deco accents" round out "a real winner" where "satisfaction overcomes the very high prices."

Amma Indian

25 | 18 | 24 | $48

East 50s | 246 E. 51st St. (bet. 2nd & 3rd Aves.) | 212-644-8330 | www.ammanyc.com
Count on "a few twists" at this "cut-above" East Midtowner, where "expertly" crafted Northern Indian dishes highlighting "distinct" regional flavors are "graciously served" in "cozy" (if "tight") quarters; the "high quality" is "not inexpensive", though "value"-seekers cite the "popular" lunch specials.

Ammos Greek/Seafood

22 | 21 | 22 | $64

East 40s | 52 Vanderbilt Ave. (bet. 44th & 45th Sts.) | 212-922-9999 | www.ammosnewyork.com
This "business standard" near Grand Central turns out "mouthwatering" Greek fare in a "pretty" white-tablecloth setting with an "active" (read: "noisy") bar scene; "close-together" tables are "not for the claustrophobic", and tabs trend "high", especially if you go with the "excellent" whole fish option.

Amor Cubano Cuban

21 | 18 | 21 | $37

East Harlem | 2018 Third Ave. (111th St.) | 212-996-1220 | www.amorcubanonyc.com
Giving Miami a run for its money, this "hopping" East Harlem Cuban doles out "tasty, traditional" chow right out of "pre-Castro Havana", paired with "amazing" mojitos; live music via a "loud band" adds "authenticity" and distracts from the just "OK" ambiance.

Amorina Italian/Pizza

 ▽ 22 | 17 | 21 | $25

Prospect Heights | 624 Vanderbilt Ave. (Prospect Pl.) | Brooklyn | 718-230-3030 | www.amorinapizza.com
When in the mood for "delicious" Roman-style pizzas and pastas, all at "low, low prices", locals turn to this Prospect Heights Italian; the "small", red-checkered-tablecloth setting exudes a "homey" vibe and is overseen by a "hard-working" staff.

Amorino Ice Cream

25 | 20 | 21 | $9

Chelsea | 162 Eighth Ave. (18th St.) | 212-255-6471
Greenwich Village | 60 University Pl. (bet. 10th & 11th Sts.) | 212-253-5599
www.amorino.com
Some of the most "fabulous" gelato "outside of Italy" can be found at these "small" links in a European chain offering "bold" flavors in "flower-

shaped" scoops plus "divine" macaron sandwiches too; since you can "get as many flavors as you'd like", the kinda "hefty" prices are easier to take.

Ample Hills Creamery *Ice Cream*   27 | 19 | 23 | $8

NEW **West 40s** | 600 11th Ave. (bet. 44th & 45th Sts.) | 212-582-7940
Brooklyn Heights | 334 Furman St. (Joralemon St.) | Brooklyn | 347-240-3926
Gowanus | 305 Nevins St. (Union St.) | Brooklyn | 347-725-4061
Prospect Heights | 623 Vanderbilt Ave. (St. Marks Ave.) | Brooklyn | 347-240-3926
www.amplehills.com

"Nirvana" say fans of the "seriously good" housemade scoops at these "packed" ice cream "meccas" where ultra-"imaginative" flavors include favorites like the "addictive" salted crack caramel; the lines are "long", but they "move fast", and a "lovely" rooftop awaits in the "supersized" Gowanus locale.

Amsterdam Burger Company *Burgers*   24 | 17 | 19 | $29

West 90s | 654 Amsterdam Ave. (92nd St.) | 212-362-0700 | www.amsterdamburger.com

The burgers are "excellent" and "they're kosher" too exalt the observant of the "enormous, juicy, perfectly seasoned" patties at this UWSider; "prompt" service is another plus, and while the "laid-back" digs might be nothing special, they're still often "packed."

Amy Ruth's *Soul Food*   23 | 14 | 19 | $28

Harlem | 113 W. 116th St. (bet. Lenox & 7th Aves.) | 212-280-8779 | www.amyruths.com

Those jonesing for a taste of "classic Harlem" head to this low-budget soul-food "stalwart" for "hearty" cooking highlighted by "amazing" chicken and waffles; regulars "ignore the decor" and "spotty" service, and get there early "before the tourist buses arrive."

Anassa Taverna *Greek*   21 | 19 | 18 | $50

East 60s | 200 E. 60th St (3rd Ave.) | 212-371-5200 | www.anassataverna.com
A "lively" Avra sibling "convenient to Bloomie's", this UES Greek "hits the spot" with a lineup of seafood and other staples that's "pretty solid" if "a little pricey"; the "casual", split-level setting emits "feel-good vibes", though at peak hours it can be "quite noisy."

Andanada 141 *Spanish*   22 | 21 | 22 | $56

West 60s | 141 W. 69th St. (bet. B'way & Columbus Ave.) | 646-692-8762 | www.andanada141.com

This "lovely" Upper Westsider serves tapas and other Spanish classics "done with modern flair" in "sleek", graffiti-mural-adorned digs; the vibe is "lively but allows for conversation", and its location is tailor-made for the "pre–Lincoln Center" set.

Añejo *Mexican*   22 | 20 | 20 | $43

TriBeCa | 301 Church St. (Walker St.) | 212-920-6270 | www.anejotribeca.com
West 40s | 668 10th Ave. (47th St.) | 212-920-4770 | www.anejonyc.com
Angelo Sosa's "interesting" Mexican small plates are perfect for "trying a multitude of items" at these "hip" cantinas where an "excellent" tequila lineup and "inventive" combinations make for "fabulous" cocktails; if the digs get a bit "noisy" at prime times, sidewalk patios can help; P.S. the TriBeCa locale has a downstairs speakeasy called Abajo.

	FOOD	DECOR	SERVICE	COST

Angelica Kitchen   *Vegan/Vegetarian*

23 | 18 | 20 | $27

East Village | 300 E. 12th St. (2nd Ave.) | 212-228-2909 |
www.angelicakitchen.com

A longtime vegan "standard-bearer", this "go-with-the-flow" East Village mainstay is a "wholesome" destination for "your-body-as-a-temple" dining at a "reasonable", cash-only cost; though the decor is "spartan" and the service "loose", there's "always a line for a table"; news flash: it now serves wine and beer.

Angelina's   *Italian*

24 | 24 | 22 | $69

Tottenville | 399 Ellis St. (Arthur Kill Rd.) | Staten Island | 718-227-2900 |
www.angelinasristorante.com

"Fine dining" comes to Tottenville at this "highly recommended" Italian offering "fabulous" food and "professional" service in a "stunning" tri-level mansion on the water; sure, it's "expensive" for SI and the crowd can be a bit "Jersey Shore", but to most it's a bona fide "special-occasion" hub.

Angelo's of Mulberry Street   *Italian*

23 | 18 | 22 | $50

Little Italy | 146 Mulberry St. (bet. Grand & Hester Sts.) | 212-966-1277 |
www.angelosofmulberryst.com

It doesn't get more "old-school" than this circa-1902 Little Italy "favorite" that stays popular thanks to "consistently delicious" Neapolitan cooking and "attentive" service; maybe the "stereotypical" decor could use "a little touching up", but otherwise fans "feel the love" – "maybe the tourists know something" after all.

Angelo's Pizzeria   *Pizza*

21 | 14 | 18 | $28

East 50s | 1043 Second Ave. (55th St.) | 212-521-3600 |
www.angelospizzany.com
West 50s | 1697 Broadway (bet. 53rd & 54th Sts.) | 212-245-8811 |
www.angelosnyc.com
West 50s | 117 W. 57th St. (bet. 6th & 7th Aves.) | 212-333-4333 |
www.angelospizzany.com

These "family-friendly" Midtown pizzerias turn out "worthy" brick-oven pies with "generous" toppings for "economical" dough; OK, "ambiance is not their strong point", ditto the "hit-or-miss" service, but regulars say a "glass of wine always helps."

Angus Club Steakhouse   *Steak*

25 | 24 | 24 | $81

East 50s | 135 E. 55th St. (Lexington Ave.) | 212-588-1585 |
www.angusclubsteakhouse.com

You can "cut the meat with your fork" at this Midtown East chophouse pairing "top-notch" dry-aged Angus beef (natch) with "properly done" sides and "exceptional" wines; "attentive" servers preside over the "lovely" bi-level setting where it's "calm" enough to "enjoy conversation."

Annabel   *Italian/Pizza*

21 | 21 | 19 | $38

West 50s | 809 Ninth Ave. (bet. 53rd & 54th Sts.) | 212-245-2209 |
www.annabelnyc.com

"Lively" crowds, "delicious" wood-fired pizzas and reliable service all "come together" at this "cozy" Hell's Kitchen Italian; pastas and salads round out the menu, while "inventive" cocktails and loads of craft beers help fuel a "vibrant bar scene."

	FOOD	DECOR	SERVICE	COST

Ann & Tony's *Italian*
22 | 17 | 22 | $42

Arthur Avenue/Belmont | 2407 Arthur Ave. (bet. 187th & 188th Sts.) | Bronx | 718-933-1469 | www.annandtonysonline.com

Talk about "classic" – this circa-1927 "Arthur Avenue mainstay" remains a steady "favorite" thanks to its "healthy portions" of "old-fashioned" Italiana served by a "treat-you-like-family" crew; "great prices" mean most don't notice the "decor from the '70s."

Annisa *American*
27 | 24 | 26 | $99

West Village | 13 Barrow St. (bet. 7th Ave. S. & W. 4th St.) | 212-741-6699 | www.annisarestaurant.com

Star chef Anita Lo "never ceases to dazzle" at this "phenomenal" West Village "oasis", where American cuisine crafted with "exquisite" Asian "flair" is presented by a "smooth" staff; set in "serene" quarters with "understated" decor, it's "about as good as it gets" for a high-end "special occasion."

Antica Pesa *Italian*
24 | 23 | 23 | $67

Williamsburg | 115 Berry St. (bet. 7th & 8th Sts.) | Brooklyn | 347-763-2635 | www.anticapesa.com

"One of the posher" options in Williamsburg, this American branch of a Rome stalwart puts forth "cooked-to-perfection pastas" and other Italian classics delivered by a "welcoming" staff; the space breaks from the nabe's shabby-chic norm, offering instead an "elegant" fine-dining vibe and a salonlike, fireplace-equipped lounge.

Antique Garage *Mediterranean*
19 | 24 | 19 | $49

SoHo | 41 Mercer St. (Grand St.) | 212-219-1019 | www.antiquegaragesoho.com

It's all about the "charming" decor at this "repurposed" SoHo auto-body shop that's been turned into a Med eatery where the "cool" antique furnishings are for sale; the cooking is "creative" enough, and frequent live jazz is another plus.

Antonucci Cafe *Italian*
23 | 17 | 21 | $62

East 80s | 170 E. 81st St. (bet. Lexington & 3rd Aves.) | 212-570-5100 | www.antonuccicafe.com

In a "neighborhood filled with Italian restaurants", this "nice-and-easy" UES trattoria holds its own with "consistently good" fare highlighted by especially "excellent pastas"; seating is "tight" and tabs "pricey for every day", but "warm" vibes and "unhurried" service help compensate.

A.O.C. L'aile ou la Cuisse *French*
20 | 18 | 18 | $45

West Village | 314 Bleecker St. (Grove St.) | 212-675-9463 | www.aocnyc.com

"You just might be in Paris" at this "Frenchy French" West Village bistro, supplier of "unfussy but tasty" staples in a "throwback" setting with a "sweet petite garden"; the "everyday" style means sometimes "sloppy" service, but for a Gallic "hankering" it'll do "in a pinch."

Ápizz *Italian*
24 | 21 | 22 | $55

Lower East Side | 217 Eldridge St. (bet. Rivington & Stanton Sts.) | 212-253-9199 | www.apizz.com

One of the "coziest" joints in town, this "sexy" LES Italian purveys "excellent" pizza and other "melt-in-your-mouth" dishes straight from a "wood-burning oven"; despite "quality" service, "accessible" rates and "intimate", "rustic" digs, it remains something of a "hidden gem" – maybe because of the "tucked-away" location.

Applewood *American*

24 | 21 | 22 | $54

Park Slope | 501 11th St. (bet. 7th & 8th Aves.) | Brooklyn | 718-788-1810 | www.applewoodny.com

"Inventively prepared farm-fresh ingredients" lure "locals and foodies" to this "charming" New American that's "like going to the country without leaving Park Slope"; sure, it's "a tad pricey", but "welcoming" service, "cozy" atmospherics and a "fabulous brunch" compensate.

Aquagrill *Seafood*

27 | 20 | 23 | $68

SoHo | 210 Spring St. (6th Ave.) | 212-274-0505 | www.aquagrill.com

A seafood "mecca", this "consistently terrific" SoHo longtimer is known for "exceptionally good" oysters and fish "so fresh" you can almost "feel the sea breeze"; "upscale yet still homey", it's presided over by a "warm" crew, and the brunch is "one of the best scenes" around.

Aquavit *Scandinavian*

26 | 25 | 25 | $111

East 50s | 65 E. 55th St. (bet. Madison & Park Aves.) | 212-307-7311 | www.aquavit.org

After more than 25 years, this "elegant, but low-key" Midtown "fixture" is still "pushing the envelope", turning out "innovative" Scandinavian tasting menus of the "highest level"; the "sleek" space is matched by "top-notch" service, and while prices are "steep", sampling from its "huge" aquavit selection will have you thinking "you're dining in Denmark."

Areo *Italian*

24 | 19 | 21 | $56

Bay Ridge | 8424 Third Ave. (bet. 84th & 85th Sts.) | Brooklyn | 718-238-0079

"Fuhgeddaboudit" – this "busy" Bay Ridge "staple" continues to "stand the test of time" as a supplier of "wonderful" Italiana and "old-world" service; assuming "you can handle the noise", its "lively scene" and "local color" are an all-around "hoot."

Arepa Lady *S American*

▽ 25 | 15 | 22 | $14

Elmhurst | 77-02 Roosevelt Ave. (enter on 77th St.) | Queens | 347-730-6124

After plying her "fabulous" mozzarella-stuffed corn cakes from an "insanely popular" cart, Maria Cano is now doing her thing at this "small" Elmhurst storefront where fans say "the lady's still got it"; the digs "aren't much to look at", but with "friendly" service and "reason-able" prices, "who cares?"

Arepas Café *Venezuelan*

23 | 15 | 20 | $18

Astoria | 33-07 36th Ave. (bet. 33rd & 34th Sts.) | Queens | 718-937-3835

Arepas Grill *Venezuelan*

Astoria | 21-19 Broadway (bet. 21st & 23rd Sts.) | Queens | 718-355-9686 www.arepascafe.com

"Flavors straight out of Caracas" are stuffed into "fluffy", affordable arepas at these "something-different" Astoria Venezuelans; the bite-size Cafe original sports a "diner atmosphere" that suggests "takeout", but the Grill offshoot is roomier, with a broader menu that includes Caribbean and Med dishes.

Aretsky's Patroon *American* | 23 | 21 | 24 | $78 |

East 40s | 160 E. 46th St. (bet. Lexington & 3rd Aves.) | 212-883-7373 | www.aretskyspatroon.com

Ken Aretsky's "polished" East Midtown "business" "oasis" remains a place to "impress clients" with "solid" American fare and "first-class service" in "men's club" digs done up with "classic photos"; "especially nice" are the private rooms and roof bar, but just "watch out for those prices."

Arirang Hibachi Steakhouse *Japanese* | 23 | 21 | 23 | $41 |

Bay Ridge | 8814 Fourth Ave. (bet. 88th & 89th Sts.) | Brooklyn | 718-238-9880

Great Kills | 23 Nelson Ave. (Locust Pl.) | Staten Island | 718-966-9600

www.partyonthegrill.com

Food and entertainment go "hand in hand" at these "family-friendly" Japanese outposts where "funny" hibachi chefs perform "tricks" while cooking "tender" steaks and other "flavorful" fare tableside; it's not inexpensive and can get "noisy", but it's a "blast" with a group.

Arlington Club *Steak* | 21 | 22 | 20 | $75 |

East 70s | 1032 Lexington Ave. (bet. 73rd & 74th Sts.) | 212-249-5700 | www.arlingtonclubny.com

A "steady" UES choice, this "upscale" steakhouse supplies "pricey" cuts alongside modern American fare in a "busy" setting sporting a "vaulted ceiling" and hardwood aplenty; the "over-the-top" scene is popular with locals "of a certain age" who've "removed their wedding rings" at the "cougarville" bar.

Armani Ristorante *Italian* | 23 | 24 | 22 | $82 |

East 50s | 717 Fifth Ave., 3rd fl. (56th St.) | 212-207-1902 | www.armaniristorante.com

"A terrific find" say "fashionistas" of this "suave" and "sleek" Italian "charmer" in Giorgio Armani's Midtown flagship, where the "solid" fare is prepared with the "surest hand"; while the "trendy" lunch crowd makes way for "quiet", "pleasant" dinners, tabs stay "expensive."

Arno *Italian* | 22 | 19 | 23 | $54 |

West 30s | 141 W. 38th St. (B'way) | 212-944-7420 | www.arnoristorante.com

A "go-to place" in Midtown's Garment District, this "old-fashioned" Northern Italian is targeted to the "garmento" business-lunch trade; the "down-to-earth" cooking is "reliable" and the service "friendly", but the decor seems a bit "plain" given the tabs.

Aroma Kitchen & Winebar *Italian* | 22 | 19 | 21 | $45 |

NoHo | 36 E. Fourth St. (bet. Bowery & Lafayette St.) | 212-375-0100 | www.aromanyc.com

For a "big surprise" in a "tight" but "delightful" space, sniff out this NoHo "hideaway" where "well-prepared" Italian plates are matched with "nicely picked" wines and delivered by "friendly" staffers; it's convenient to the Public Theater, and its private party rooms are perfect for an "intimate get-together."

Artichoke Basille's Pizza *Pizza* | 22 | 11 | 16 | $15 |

Chelsea | 114 10th Ave. (17th St.) | 212-792-9200

East Village | 328 E. 14th St. (bet. 1st & 2nd Aves.) | 212-228-2004

continued

Greenwich Village | 111 MacDougal St. (bet. Bleecker & 3rd Sts.) | 646-278-6100

NEW **Park Slope** | 59 Fifth Ave. (St Marks Ave.) | Brooklyn | 347-763-1975

NEW **Astoria** | 22-56 31st St. (bet. Ditmars Blvd. & 23rd Ave.) | Queens | 718-215-8100

www.artichokepizza.com

This "no-frills" mini-chain "will change the way you see pizza" with its "goopy", "super-filling" slices slathered with "deliciously creamy" artichoke dip that leaves fans "yearning for more"; although not much on looks, it's a "beacon" for bar-crawlers given its "late-night" hours.

Artie's *Seafood/Steak*   21 | 17 | 22 | $54

City Island | 394 City Island Ave. (Ditmars St.) | Bronx | 718-885-9885 | www.artiesofcityisland.com

"Actual City Island residents" eat at this "been-there-forever" surf 'n' turfer offering a "retro" Italian-accented menu; true, it's "not on the water", still "unhurried" service and fair pricing keep locals "happy as clams."

Artisanal *French*   21 | 20 | 19 | $61

Murray Hill | 2 Park Ave. (bet. 32nd & 33rd Sts.) | 212-725-8585 | www.artisanalbistro.com

It's all about the "heavenly" cheese at this "classic" Midtown "standby" where a "crazy variety" (including "unbeatable" fondues) is offered alongside "solid" French brasserie dishes in a "soaring" Parisian-style space; "high prices", "spotty service" and "noisy" conditions to one side, most say it's still "*très bien*."

Arturo's Pizzeria *Pizza*   23 | 16 | 20 | $33

Greenwich Village | 106 W. Houston St. (Thompson St.) | 212-677-3820 | www.arturoscoaloven.com

"Old Greenwich Village" endures at this 1957-vintage pizzeria where a "slice of the past" comes via "delicious, no-nonsense" pies "straight out of the coal oven"; a live jazz combo and an "unpretentious" mood compensate for decor that's somewhere between "faded" and "dingy."

A Salt & Battery *British*   22 | 13 | 19 | $20

West Village | 112 Greenwich Ave. (bet. 12th & 13th Sts.) | 212-691-2713 | www.asaltandbattery.com

Fish 'n' chips fanciers say this "cleverly named" West Village "hole-in-the-wall" does a "jolly good" rendition of the British staple for an "affordable" sum; "anti-health food" treats like "deep-fried candy bars" fill out the "greasy" bill, but since there's "no decor" and seating's just a "few stools", most get the goods to go.

NEW **Asia de Cuba** *Asian/Cuban*   23 | 23 | 23 | $69

Greenwich Village | 415 Lafayette St. (4th St.) | 212-726-7755 | www.asiadecuba.com

The former *Sex and the City*–era hot spot in the Morgans Hotel is reborn Downtown via this Greenwich Village fusion spot for "delicious" and "inventive" Asian-Latin plates and "creative" cocktails; it ain't cheap, but leather banquettes and an "active" scene make it "great with a group."

	FOOD	DECOR	SERVICE	COST

Asiate *American/Asian*

24 | 28 | 25 | $124

West 50s | Mandarin Oriental Hotel | 80 Columbus Circle, 35th fl. (B'way) | 212-805-8881 | www.mandarinoriental.com

Dine "on top of the world" at the Mandarin Oriental's "transcending" Asian–New American aerie, where "magnificent" Central Park views and "totally elegant" surroundings set a "serene" scene for "exquisite" prix fixe menus served by a "polished" team; all this "indulgence" comes at "astronomical prices", but "if you're going to splurge, this is the place to do it."

Astor Room *American*

21 | 23 | 22 | $44

Astoria | 34-12 36th St. (bet. 35th & 36th Aves.) | Queens | 718-255-1947 | www.astorroom.com

It "feels like the 1920s" at this "throwback" spot inside Kaufman Astoria Studios, supplying American eats to "TV and movie" industry types; "speakeasy" looks, a "great bar" mixing "vintage" drinks and frequent "live jazz" complete the "old-school" vibe.

Atera *American*

24 | 23 | 24 | $259

TriBeCa | 77 Worth St. (bet. B'way & Church St.) | 212-226-1444 | www.ateranyc.com

"Revelations abound" at this ultra-"intimate" TriBeCa American, where tasting menus produced at the chef's counter by a "choreographed" kitchen reach "the height of experimental cuisine"; if you're "ready to spend" the $225 set price, the experience is "memorable" "unlike any other"; P.S. Danish chef Ronny Emborg is now manning the burners following the departure of founding chef Matthew Lightner.

Atlantic Grill *Seafood*

23 | 20 | 21 | $59

East 70s | 1341 Third Ave. (bet. 76th & 77th Sts.) | 212-988-9200
West 60s | 49 W. 64th St. (bet. B'way & CPW) | 212-787-4663
www.atlanticgrill.com

"Tried-and-true", these "big", "bustling" seafooders can be counted on for "something-for-everyone" menus, including "first-rate" fish, "dependable" turf and a "go-to" brunch; manned by a "smart staff", they're "not cheap" and can be "awfully noisy" but remain "perennial favorites" for a reason.

Atrium Dumbo *French*

23 | 25 | 21 | $44

Dumbo | 15 Main St. (bet. Plymouth & Water Sts.) | Brooklyn | 718-858-1095 | www.atriumdumbo.com

An "airy, modernist-rustic space" and "refined" "locavore" fare "with flair" have locals declaring this "*très* chic" French "so completely Dumbo"; the "lively" downstairs bar presents a sophisticated drinks list, and a "magnificent wall of live green plants" further boosts the mood.

August *American*

21 | 21 | 22 | $59

East 60s | 791 Lexington Ave. (bet. 61st & 62nd Sts.) | 212-935-1433 | www.augustny.com

A former Downtowner migrated to the UES, this "cozy" "oasis" augurs well thanks to an "impressive" menu of American comfort fare devised "with creativity" in mind; the "attentive" service and "classy bistro vibe" help distract from "big prices."

	FOOD	DECOR	SERVICE	COST

Aureole *American*

25 | 24 | 25 | $91

West 40s | 135 W. 42nd St. (bet. B'way & 6th Ave.) | 212-319-1660 |
www.charliepalmer.com

Offering a "classy meal bar none", Charlie Palmer's "sophisticated" New
American flagship near Times Square maintains "high standards" with
"exceptional" food, "perfect wine matches" and "polished service"; while
the "handsome" main room's prix fixes come at a "whopping" cost ("invite
your banker"), dining à la carte in the bar is "more casual" and affordable.

Aurora *Italian*

24 | 22 | 21 | $51

SoHo | 510 Broome St. (bet. Thompson St. & W. B'way) | 212-334-9020 |
www.aurorasoho.com
Williamsburg | 70 Grand St. (Wythe Ave.) | Brooklyn | 718-388-5100 |
www.aurorabk.com

At these "quaint" Williamsburg and SoHo Italians, the "delectable" rustic
cooking is a match for the "Tuscan countryside" settings, complete with
a "lovely garden" at the Brooklyn original; "hip" crowds, midrange prices
and "helpful" service ensure "enjoyable" repasts.

Au Za'atar *French/Mideastern*

20 | 16 | 18 | $34

East Village | 188 Ave. A (12th St.) | 212-254-5660 | www.auzaatar.com
"A French slant" animates the "flavorful" Middle Eastern eats at this all-
day East Villager, where the "deep menu" includes Lebanese meze with
"many vegetarian options"; "homey" digs with "wood everywhere" keep
the focus on the food, which leaves the majority "satisfied."

A Voce *Italian*

23 | 23 | 23 | $71

Flatiron | 41 Madison Ave. (26th St.) | 212-545-8555
West 50s | Time Warner Ctr. | 10 Columbus Circle (bet. 58th & 60th
Sts.) | 212-823-2523
www.avocerestaurant.com

The "creative flourishes" are a "breath of fresh air" at these "classy"
Italians, where the "carefully prepared" contemporary cuisine (notably "excellent pastas"), "outstanding" wines and "solicitous" service
are "worth every penny"; Flatiron's "refined" setting allows for "quiet
conversation", while the "convivial" Columbus Circle follow-up enjoys
"knockout views of Central Park."

Avra *Greek/Seafood*

26 | 22 | 22 | $67

East 40s | 141 E. 48th St. (bet. Lexington & 3rd Aves.) | 212-759-8550 |
www.avrany.com

A "mainstay" for East Midtown "suits", this "buzzing" "upscale taverna"
beckons with "unforgettable" grilled fish and other "terrific Greek seafood" items dispatched by a "helpful" team; the by-the-pound selections
can be quite "expensive", though the "tight", "loud" quarters can be
sidestepped by snagging a "great" outdoor table.

Awadh *Indian*

24 | 20 | 20 | $49

West 90s | 2588 Broadway (98th St.) | 646-861-3604 | www.awadhnyc.com
"A far cry" from your average Indian outfit, this "contemporary" UWS
duplex showcases "high-end" Awadhi cuisine "innovatively prepared"
with "complex" flavors; service ranges from "prompt" to "spotty", but it's
still hailed as a "gem" whose "flair" is "no longer a secret."

	FOOD	DECOR	SERVICE	COST

Awash *Ethiopian*

21 | 13 | 17 | $30

East Village | 338 E. Sixth St. (bet. 1st & 2nd Aves.) | 212-982-9589
West 100s | 947 Amsterdam Ave. (bet. 106th & 107th Sts.) | 212-961-1416
Cobble Hill | 242 Court St. (bet. Baltic & Kane Sts.) | Brooklyn | 718-243-2151
www.awashny.com

"Different experience" seekers tout these "unsung", utensil-free Ethiopians where "delectable" stews are scooped up with injera flatbread; "decidedly relaxed" service and settings that "need sprucing up" come with the territory, but at least you'll walk out awash with cash.

Ayada *Thai*

26 | 15 | 20 | $24

Elmhurst | 77-08 Woodside Ave. (bet. 77th & 78th Sts.) | Queens | 718-424-0844 | www.ayadathaiwoodside.com

"Behind a nondescript storefront", this "authentic" Elmhurst Thai supplies "exceptional" takes on all the favorites "without breaking the bank" – just "don't order 'spicy' unless you mean it"; service is "efficient", but "crowds" form in the "smallish" space now that "the secret is out."

Azuri Cafe *Israeli/Kosher*

∇ 23 | 7 | 12 | $19

West 50s | 465 W. 51st St. (bet. 9th & 10th Aves.) | 212-262-2920 | www.azuricafe.com

Falafel "from heaven" and other "cheap", "delicious" Israeli eats offset the "dumpy" decor at this Hell's Kitchen "hole-in-the-wall"; just "don't expect a warm welcome" – the "short-tempered" owner is the neighborhood's "favorite curmudgeon."

NEW Baba's Pierogies *E European*

— | — | — | I

Gowanus | 295 Third Ave. (Carroll St.) | Brooklyn | 718-222-0777 | www.babasbk.com

Inspired by grandma's recipes, this cash-only Gowanus eatery specializes in pierogi, with traditional Eastern European fillings (cheese, potato) as well as some modern variations (jalapeño, bacon-cheese), and also offers soups, salads and sandwiches; its simple counter-service space is outfitted with a tiled counter, lots of reclaimed wood and a few light-wood tables.

Babbo *Italian*

26 | 23 | 24 | $89

Greenwich Village | 110 Waverly Pl. (bet. MacDougal St. & 6th Ave.) | 212-777-0303 | www.babbonyc.com

The "original jewel" in the Batali-Bastianich empire, this "energetic" Village Italian in a "quaint" carriage house "lives up to the hype" with "sublime" pastas and other "transcendent" dishes delivered by a "gracious" crew; "wrangling" a reservation is "hard" and you'll need a "full wallet", but it's "legendary" for a reason.

NEW Babu Ji *Indian*

— | — | — | E

East Village | 175 Ave. B (11th St.) | 212-951-1082 | www.babujinyc.com

An offshoot of an Indian restaurant in Australia, this East Villager offers a pricey-for-the-genre menu that mixes the expected curries and naan with more unusual street food–inspired snacks; the corner space eschews tapestries and urns for a streamlined, modern look with playful artwork and a grab-it-yourself display case of canned craft beers.

	FOOD	DECOR	SERVICE	COST

Baby Bo's Cantina *Mexican*   21 | 17 | 19 | $28

Murray Hill | 627 Second Ave. (bet. 34th & 35th Sts.) | 212-779-2656 | www.babyboscantinanyc.com

A "real find", this Murray Hill "hole-in-the-wall" delivers with "crave-worthy" Mexican comfort food and "excellent" margaritas; year-round Christmas lights and "funky" Day of the Dead decor keep the "cramped" digs "festive", while "value" prices keep it "packed."

Bacaro *Italian*   21 | 25 | 20 | $57

Lower East Side | 136 Division St. (bet. Ludlow & Orchard Sts.) | 212-941-5060 | www.bacaronyc.com

There's a "sultry", "wine-cellar vibe" in play at this "gorgeous" LES basement offering "delicious" Venetian small plates (and particularly "wonderful" pastas) to a crowd of "hipsters, artists and the Uptowners who love them"; "flickering candles" keep things seriously "romantic", so it's "perfect for a date."

Bacchanal *American*   22 | 20 | 21 | $56

Little Italy | Sohotel | 146 Bowery (Broome St.) | 646-355-1840 | www.bacchanalnyc.com

True to its name, this Bowery New American in the Sohotel is an "indulgent" place to "chill" over "well-presented" Med-accented plates matched with a "dazzling" drinks list; an "inviting" wraparound bar dominates the roomy space, and a basement lounge, Bacchanal Downstairs, keeps the party going till late.

Bacchus *French*   21 | 20 | 20 | $44

Downtown Brooklyn | 409 Atlantic Ave. (bet. Bond & Nevins Sts.) | Brooklyn | 718-852-1572 | www.bacchusbistro.com

Francophiles tout the "classic French bistro" fare at this "charming little" Downtown Brooklyn wine bar/eatery; "reasonable" rates, "no pretension" and a "beautiful" back garden lend "lazy-day" appeal, even if a few Francophobes feel it has "no particular distinction."

Baci & Abbracci *Italian*   23 | 19 | 22 | $35

Williamsburg | 204 Grand St. (Driggs Ave.) | Brooklyn | 718-599-6599 | www.baciny.com

There's lots of neighborhood love for the "delicious" Italian "basics" served at this Williamsburg joint; "value" tabs, "friendly" staffers and a "lovely" garden are other reasons it's a "charming" pick.

Back Forty West *American*   21 | 19 | 20 | $40

SoHo | 70 Prince St. (Crosby St.) | 212-219-8570 | www.backfortynyc.com

"Convenient for hungry fashionistas", farm-to-table maven Peter Hoffman's "laid-back" SoHo New American furnishes a "well-prepared" all-day lineup boasting "a super burger" and a "go-to" brunch; the rates are "affordable", though on weekends the smallish space "can feel crammed."

Back Room at One57 *American*   24 | 25 | 25 | $70

West 50s | Park Hyatt Hotel | 157 W. 57th St., 3rd Fl. (7th Ave.) | 212-897-2188 | www.thebackroomone57.com

The "beautiful" setting "enhances the class" at this American grill in Midtown's Park Hyatt Hotel, a "calming" haven for "delicious", steak-oriented fare from a "welcoming" team; "immediately relaxing" vibes even temper the "expense-account" pricing.

Bagatelle *French*

18 | 24 | 19 | $83

Meatpacking District | 1 Little W. 12th St. (9th Ave.) | 212-488-2110 | www.bagatellenyc.com

"Hot and cool at the same time", this Meatpacking jet-setter central bolsters its splurgy but "better-than-average" French fare with an exuberant "funday mentality"; its infamous "party brunch" featuring "expensive champagne", "throbbing Euro house" sounds and "dancing on the tables" is "not for the faint of heart" (or wallet).

Bahari Estiatorio *Greek*

24 | 16 | 21 | $36

Astoria | 31-14 Broadway (32nd St.) | Queens | 718-204-8968 | www.bahariestiatorio.com

"Excellent" Hellenic "home cooking" served "with a smile" explains why this Astoria "neighborhood" joint is usually "packed"; the spare storefront space may be "a little tight", but given the "authentic" eats and "bargain prices", no one minds.

Baker & Co. *Italian*

24 | 22 | 22 | $41

West Village | 259 Bleecker St. (Cornelia St.) | 212-255-1234 | www.bakernco.com

A neighborhood "standout" for "delightful" dining in a "low-key setting", this West Villager offers "interesting takes" on Italiana (e.g. "incredible fresh pastas") at "affordable prices"; "on-point" staffers oversee a stripped-down space noted for the "gorgeous patio" out back.

Bakeri *Bakery/European*

26 | 25 | 24 | $12

Greenpoint | 105 Freeman St. (Franklin St.) | Brooklyn | 718-349-1542
Williamsburg | 150 Wythe Ave. (8th St.) | Brooklyn | 718-388-8037
www.bakeribrooklyn.com

From the "amazing" sweet and savory pastries to the "delicious" Euro-accented breads and "delectable" cookies, there's "little you can go wrong with" at these bakery/cafes also known for their "divine" coffee; the "rustic" digs are "darling", but "tight" quarters make it tough to snag a seat.

Balaboosta *Mediterranean/Mideastern*

25 | 19 | 22 | $54

NoLita | 214 Mulberry St. (Spring St.) | 212-966-7366 | www.balaboostanyc.com

Med-Mideastern "comfort food" gets an "imaginative" and "delicious" boost at this "homey" NoLita "favorite" from the Taïm team; the "understated" space may seem "cramped", but the "welcoming" staff and relatively "affordable prices" help keep it a "player."

Balade *Lebanese*

24 | 20 | 23 | $36

East Village | 208 First Ave. (bet. 12th & 13th Sts.) | 212-529-6868 | www.baladerestaurants.com

"Hidden away" in the East Village, this "traditional" Lebanese outfit is lauded for "mouthwatering" meals (the "meze are a must") at "reasonable prices"; with a "friendly" staff manning the "low-key" quarters, "addicted" followers keep "coming back."

	FOOD	DECOR	SERVICE	COST

Balkanika *Mediterranean*

20 | 14 | 18 | $38

West 40s | 691 Ninth Ave. (bet. 47th & 48th Sts.) | 212-974-0300 | www.balkanikany.com

"Something different" in Hell's Kitchen, this "well-priced" Mediterranean wine bar offers a "tasty" "tour of the Balkans" encompassing meze, grilled meats and vinos to match; with "super-friendly" service and a "cozy hangout vibe", it's a welcome "alternative" for pre-theater types.

Balthazar *French*

24 | 23 | 21 | $62

SoHo | 80 Spring St. (Crosby St.) | 212-965-1414 | www.balthazarny.com

"Keith McNally has a perennial winner" in this "splashy" SoHo brasserie, supplying "delectable" French fare (including "delish breakfasts" and a "fabulous" bread basket) in a "Left Bank"–style space perpetually "abuzz" with "tourists, natives" and "famous" folks; despite "shoehorned" seating and "challenging" acoustics, it "has an electricity of its own" that "never gets old."

Baluchi's *Indian*

21 | 15 | 17 | $32

East 80s | 1724 Second Ave. (bet. 89th & 90th Sts.) | 212-996-2600 | www.brooklynbaluchis.com
Murray Hill | 329 Third Ave. (25th St.) | 212-679-3434 | www.baluchisnewyork.com

This "Americanized" Indian chain is popular for its "good, basic" food and "economical" tabs (lunch is a particular "bargain"); but critics citing "conventional" cooking, "mundane" settings and unremarkable service say "don't expect nirvana."

Bamonte's *Italian*

23 | 18 | 23 | $51

Williamsburg | 32 Withers St. (bet. Lorimer St. & Union Ave.) | Brooklyn | 718-384-8831

"Red sauce is king" at this "long-established" (since 1900) Williamsburg Italian, which remains "the ultimate old-school Brooklyn" joint for "belly-bustin'" standards "like grandma made"; it's "not fancy", but the "tuxedoed waiters" and assorted "characters" (e.g. "wise guys") are "wildly entertaining."

B & H Dairy *Deli/Vegetarian*

23 | 12 | 21 | $17

East Village | 127 Second Ave. (bet. 7th St. & St. Marks Pl.) | 212-505-8065

This "hole-in-the-wall" East Village "patch of history" has been filling bellies with veggie borscht-and-blintz fare (aka "Jewish soul food") since the 1940s; talk about kickin' it "old school" – the "diner" ambiance "hasn't changed since your grandpa ate there" way back when.

Banh Mi Saigon *Sandwiches/Vietnamese*

24 | 9 | 16 | $11

Little Italy | 198 Grand St. (bet. Mott & Mulberry Sts.) | 212-941-1541 | www.banhmisaigonnyc.com

"Super-delicious" Vietnamese sandwiches with "crusty" French bread and "flavorful" pork are the eponymous specialty at this cash-only Little Italy storefront; "dirt-cheap prices" make it "popular with the lunch crowd", though spare seating at "countertops with stools" encourages takeout.

Bann *Korean*

22 | 20 | 21 | $45

West 50s | 350 W. 50th St. (bet. 8th & 9th Aves.) | 212-582-4446 | www.bannrestaurant.com

"Classy" Korean barbecue is no oxymoron at this Theater District "change of pace" where the smokeless tabletop grills and "modern" setting impress do-it-yourselfers; maybe the tabs skew "upscale", but the food's "exciting", the service "caring" and the overall experience "satisfying."

The Bao *Chinese* 23 | 16 | 16 | $31

East Village | 13 St. Marks Pl. (bet. 2nd & 3rd Aves.) | 212-388-9238
"Not-to-be-missed" signature soup dumplings lead the multiregional menu at this East Village Chinese, also appreciated for its "unbeatable" prices; the modest digs get "packed" and "loud", but the "delicious" grub "more than makes up for all of that."

Baoburg *Eclectic* ∇ 25 | 22 | 25 | $40

Williamsburg | 126 N. Sixth St. (Berry St.) | Brooklyn | 718-782-1445 | www.baoburgnyc.com
This Williamsburg nook from a Jean-Georges alum baos in with an "amazing" Eclectic lineup featuring "innovative" mash-ups of French, Spanish and Thai influences; it's a "tiny" setup with a single table and counter seats, but the culinary experience "could not be better."

BaoHaus *Taiwanese* 23 | 14 | 16 | $14

East Village | 238 E. 14th St. (bet. 2nd & 3rd Aves.) | 646-669-8889 | www.baohausnyc.com
The "savory" Taiwanese steamed buns are "seriously delicious" at Eddie Huang's East Villager, whose "fast-food vibe" gets a boost from "blaring hip-hop music"; despite "teenage" service and "no decor to speak of", "cheap" checks keep its "college" crowd content.

NEW Bara *French/Japanese* – | – | – | M

East Village | 58 E. First St. (bet. 1st & 2nd Aves.) | 917-639-3197 | www.bararestaurantnyc.com
A Momofuku alum brings together influences from French and Japanese bar culture at this simple East Villager, offering a daily changing menu plus wines, beers and creative cocktails; the small, minimalist space keeps the focus on the food, and there's also a tiny bar in the back.

Bar Americain *American* 23 | 22 | 23 | $67

West 50s | 152 W. 52nd St. (bet. 6th & 7th Aves.) | 212-265-9700 | www.baramericain.com
A "big, bold" Bobby Flay "hit", this Midtown brasserie stands out with "creative" New American plates served in a "dramatic, soaring" space by a "diligent" team; a "boisterous" bar lures the after-work set, and it's also "popular" with pre-theater types despite the "expense-account" price tags.

BarBacon *American* 20 | 15 | 18 | $32

West 50s | 836 Ninth Ave. (bet. 54th & 55th Sts.) | 646-362-0622 | www.barbacon.com
"Life is better with bacon in it", and this Midtown American gastropub is a "popular" place to "pig out" on "quality" cured swine "in all forms", "spectacular" bacon flights included; "willing" staffers also decant a lengthy whiskey list in the "simple", "loud" setting.

Barbès *French/Moroccan* 21 | 18 | 20 | $45

Murray Hill | 21 E. 36th St. (bet. 5th & Madison Aves.) | 212-684-0215 | www.barbesrestaurantnyc.com
An "exotic escape from *la vie ordinaire*", this Midtown "sure thing"

purveys "toothsome" French-Moroccan vittles in a setting akin to an "Algerian bistro in Marseilles"; it may be "cramped" and "noisy", but "pleasant" service and "value" pricing help to distract.

Barbetta *Italian* 22 | 23 | 23 | $69

West 40s | 321 W. 46th St. (bet. 8th & 9th Aves.) | 212-246-9171 | www.barbettarestaurant.com

Dating to 1906, this Theater District "grande dame" turns back the clock with "polite waiters" setting down "well-prepared" Northern Italian dishes in a "lovely old" setting that includes a "beautiful", "vacation"-like back garden; just be aware that this "throwback to a different time" has distinctly up-to-date pricing.

NEW Bar Bolinas *American* — | — | — | M

Clinton Hill | 455 Myrtle Ave. (Washington Ave.) | Brooklyn | 718-935-9333 | www.barbolinas.com

The Allswell team is behind this low-key Clinton Hill American, whose seasonal, seafood-heavy cooking is inspired by the Northern California coast; the compact space features exposed-brick walls, beachy white beams and a leafy back patio, plus a redwood bar pouring a pared-down drinks selection.

Bar Bolonat *Israeli/Mideastern* 25 | 20 | 22 | $64

West Village | 611 Hudson St. (W. 12th St.) | 212-390-1545 | www.barbolonatny.com

Chef Einat Admony (Balaboosta, Taim) takes Israeli cuisine to "new levels" at this West Village "standout", where her "inspired" dishes "showcase the Middle East's best flavors"; "tiny" digs and "not-so-tiny" prices are offset by "helpful" service and an "upscale" yet "relaxed" vibe.

Bar Boulud *French* 24 | 20 | 22 | $68

West 60s | 1900 Broadway (bet. 63rd & 64th Sts.) | 212-595-0303 | www.barboulud.com

A "more relaxed" showcase for Daniel Boulud's "artistry", this "vibrant" French bistro/wine bar in a "hard-to-beat" address opposite Lincoln Center serves "magic" charcuterie and other "sophisticated dishes" at "fair" prices; if the "sleek", "narrow" quarters seem "too close", there's always fun alfresco "people-watching" from the sidewalk tables.

Barbounia *Mediterranean* 21 | 23 | 20 | $54

Flatiron | 250 Park Ave. S. (20th St.) | 212-995-0242 | www.barbounia.com

"Stylish" and "upbeat", this "cacophonous" Flatiron Med lures "see-and-be-seen" "Gen-X" types with a "tasty", "something-for-everyone" menu (and one "crazy brunch"); still, it's the "beautiful", "airy" setting – replete with vaulted ceilings – that's the star of the show here.

Barbuto *Italian* 24 | 19 | 22 | $60

West Village | 775 Washington St. (bet. Jane & W. 12th Sts.) | 212-924-9700 | www.barbutonyc.com

A "repurposed garage" is the "cool" backdrop for Jonathan Waxman's "sophisticated" yet "approachable" Italian menu (notably that "astonishing" roast chicken) at this "inviting" West Villager; though the "lively" crowd can kick up "deafening" decibels, warmer months are mellower when the doors "open to the street."

| | FOOD | DECOR | SERVICE | COST |

Bar Chuko *Japanese*
26 | 21 | 23 | $37

Prospect Heights | 565 Vanderbilt Ave. (Pacific St.) | Brooklyn | 347-425-9570 | www.barchuko.com

An offshoot of Chuko Ramen on the next block, but with a roomier space and a full bar, this Prospect Heights izakaya turns out "wonderful, inventive" Japanese small plates that make for "elevated" grazing; "efficient" service "transfers over" from the original, but here there's "usually a shorter wait."

Bar Corvo *Italian*
25 | 20 | 22 | $46

Prospect Heights | 791 Washington Ave. (bet. Lincoln & St Johns Pls.) | Brooklyn | 718-230-0940 | www.barcorvo.com

A "real winner", this Prospect Heights Al Di La "offspring" fields a "well-curated menu" of "delicious" Italian dishes in "cozy" quarters run by an "attentive" team; "reasonable" prices ensure it "does fill up", though a patio helps stretch the space.

Bareburger *Burgers*
21 | 17 | 19 | $24

Chelsea | 153 Eighth Ave. (bet. 17th & 18th Sts.) | 212-414-2273
East 70s | 1370 First Ave. (73rd St.) | 212-510-8559
East 80s | 1681 First Ave. (87th St.) | 212-390-1344
East Village | 85 Second Ave. (5th St.) | 212-510-8610
NEW **Financial District** | 155 William St. (Ann St.) | 646-657-0388
Greenwich Village | 535 Laguardia Pl. (bet. 3rd St. & Washington Square Vill.) | 212-477-8125
Murray Hill | 514 Third Ave. (bet. 34th & 35th Sts.) | 212-679-2273
West 40s | 366 W. 46th St. (9th Ave.) | 212-673-2273
West 50s | 313 W. 57th St. (8th Ave.) | 212-685-2273
NEW **West 90s** | 795 Columbus Ave. (bet. 97th & 100th Sts.) | 646-398-7177
Cobble Hill | 149 Court St. (Pacific St.) | Brooklyn | 347-529-6673
Park Slope | 170 Seventh Ave. (bet. 1st St. & Garfield Pl.) | Brooklyn | 718-768-2273
Astoria | 23-01 31st St. (23rd Ave.) | Queens | 718-204-7167
Astoria | 33-21 31st Ave. (34th St.) | Queens | 718-777-7011
Long Island City | 48-19 Vernon Blvd. (49th Ave.) | Queens | 718-937-2273
www.bareburger.com

A "relatively guilt-free" option for "getting your nom on", this "wholesome" burger chain "stands out" with organic, natural patties (beef, veggie or "outside-of-the-box" game meats) "personalized" with a "plethora of toppings"; the "green" pedigree costs a "few extra bucks", but that barely dents its "popularity."

Bar Eolo *Italian*
23 | 16 | 20 | $57

Chelsea | 190 Seventh Ave. (bet. 21st & 22nd Sts.) | 646-225-6606 | www.eolonewyork.com

There's "intelligent life in the kitchen" of this Sicilian "contender" offering "off-the-beaten-recipe-path" dishes paired with "exceptional wines"; the "nondescript" trattoria setting may be at odds with the "Chelsea prices", perhaps why there are "no struggles to get a table."

Bar Italia *Italian*
21 | 20 | 20 | $61

East 60s | 768 Madison Ave. (66th St.) | 917-546-6676 | www.baritaliamadison.com

"Wanna-be-seen" Euros flock to this "fashion-forward" Madison Avenue

Italian where the "better-than-expected" cooking takes a backseat to the "sleek" white setting and *Real Housewives* people-watching; expect serious tabs and lots of "air-kissing."

Bar Jamón *Spanish*

24 | 19 | 20 | $49

Gramercy Park | 125 E. 17th St. (Irving Pl.) | 212-253-2773 | www.casamononyc.com

Mario Batali's "convivial" Gramercy tapas bar–cum–"holding pen" for his 'round-the-corner Casa Mono puts out "top-of-the-line" Spanish small plates paired with an "extensive" wine list; it's a "tight squeeze" and the tabs are "not cheap", but most don't mind given the "sexy-time" mood.

Bark *Hot Dogs*

20 | 17 | 18 | $19

NEW **Greenwich Village** | 155 Bleecker St. (Thompson St.) | 718-789-1939
Park Slope | 474 Bergen St. (bet. 5th & Flatbush Aves.) | Brooklyn | 718-789-1939
www.barkhotdogs.com

When "hipsters" have "the munchies", these "creative" pit stops supply "snappy" "designer dogs" with locavore origins (along with "noteworthy side dishes") in settings sporting a "relaxed rustic look"; the prices may "bite your wallet", but most give franks for a "quick meal" "done well."

BarKogi *Chicken/Korean*

22 | 16 | 17 | $29

East 50s | 957 Second Ave. (51st St.) | 212-308-8810 | www.barkogi.com
"Habit-forming" is the verdict on the "out-of-sight" Korean fried chicken with "crispy, parchmentlike skin" dispensed at this international chain outpost in Midtown East; since the birds are cooked to order, expect "forever" waits, not to mention "slipshod" service, "no decor" and just- "decent" prices.

Barney Greengrass *Deli*

25 | 10 | 17 | $30

West 80s | 541 Amsterdam Ave. (bet. 86th & 87th Sts.) | 212-724-4707 | www.barneygreengrass.com

A circa-1908 "throwback", this "renowned" Upper Westsider "brings back memories" with "classic Jewish" deli fare and "unsurpassed smoked fish" slung by a "gruff but efficient" staff; cash-only tabs and "functional" decor don't deter the perpetual "crowds on the weekend."

Barn Joo *Korean*

22 | 22 | 20 | $39

Flatiron | 893 Broadway (bet. 19th & 20th Sts.) | 646-398-9663 | www.barnjoo.com

Korean fare takes an "interesting twist" at this "barn-esque" gastropub in the Flatiron's Hotel Verite, which matches "delicious" small plates (e.g. the "flavorful" fried chicken specialty) with "quality" cocktails in a sprawling, wood-lined space; while "not exactly authentic", it's "reason-ably priced" and can be a "crowded" scene.

Barosa *Italian*

23 | 21 | 23 | $44

Rego Park | 62-29 Woodhaven Blvd. (62nd Rd.) | Queens | 718-424-1455 | www.barosas.com

"Tasty" red-sauce fare "like mom used to make" is available for a "good price" at this "neighborhood favorite" Rego Park Italian; its "upscale" ambitions are apparent in the "polite" service, while "fantastic specials" seal the deal.

	FOOD	DECOR	SERVICE	COST

Bar Pitti *Italian*
23 | 15 | 18 | $46

Greenwich Village | 268 Sixth Ave. (bet. Bleecker & Houston Sts.) | 212-982-3300

Home to "many a celeb sighting", this "jet-set" Village Italian is best known for its "excellent people-watching", even if the "easygoing" fare is pretty "delicious" as well; no reservations, no plastic, "no discernible decor" and "far-from-friendly" service don't faze its "paparazzi"-ready patrons.

Bar Primi *Italian*
24 | 21 | 21 | $48

East Village | 325 Bowery (2nd St.) | 212-220-9100 | www.barprimi.com

Fans swear the "undeniably fresh" pastas are "worth going off Paleo" for at Andrew Carmellini's "lively" Bowery Italian; the "rustic" double-decker space can feel a "bit cramped" (upstairs has "better flow"), and a few gripe about "small portions", but "fair pricing" wins the day.

Barrio Chino *Mexican*
24 | 20 | 19 | $39

Lower East Side | 253 Broome St. (bet. Ludlow & Orchard Sts.) | 212-228-6710 | www.barriochinonyc.com

A "total hipster joint", this LES cantina serves "flavorful" Mexican fare in a "microscopic" setting; it's still "something of a scene" after more than a decade, maybe because of its "highly affordable" price point and "lay-you-out-flat" tequila list.

Bar Tabac *French*
20 | 20 | 19 | $37

Cobble Hill | 128 Smith St. (Dean St.) | Brooklyn | 718-923-0918 | www.bartabacny.com

A "Parisian bistro transplanted" to Cobble Hill, this "hip" Gallic eatery has plenty of "good energy", especially during its "tasty" brunch; "tight" seating and occasionally "lackadaisical" service aside, it's a neighborhood "favorite" and late-night "staple."

Bassanova Ramen *Japanese/Noodle Shop*
21 | 15 | 16 | $22

Chinatown | 76 Mott St. (bet. Bayard & Canal Sts.) | 212-334-2100 | www.bassanovanyc.com

Noodle bowls via Tokyo are the "tasty" stock in trade at this subterranean Chinatown niche, known for dispensing pork-based "twists" on ramen like the "superior" green curry specialty; slurpers say the "portions aren't huge" but still "pretty filling" all the same.

Basso56 *Italian*
22 | 18 | 23 | $59

West 50s | 234 W. 56th St. (bet. B'way & 8th Ave.) | 212-265-2610 | www.basso56.com

A "reliable" Carnegie Hall "resource", this Midtown Italian features a "nicely-put-together menu" with "modern flair" ferried by an "accommodating" team; some sniff at the "narrow", "nothing-fancy" setting, but admit the prices are "reasonable for the quality."

Basta Pasta *Italian*
23 | 17 | 20 | $50

Flatiron | 37 W. 17th St. (bet. 5th & 6th Aves.) | 212-366-0888 | www.bastapastanyc.com

"Japanese-style Italian food" begs the question "where else but NY?" – and this "unusual" Flatiron "change of pace" comes through with "interesting" dishes led by a signature "pasta tossed in a Parmesan wheel"; if the decor's getting "dated", the "hospitable" service is fine as is.

Bâtard *American*

FOOD	DECOR	SERVICE	COST
27	22	24	$101

TriBeCa | 239 W. Broadway (bet. Walker & White Sts.) | 212-219-2777 | www.batardtribeca.com

Restaurateur Drew Nieporent scores "another hit" with this "sophisticated" TriBeCa New American, which takes a "modern approach" to fine dining with its "ambitious" customizable tasting menus, "beautifully cooked" dishes and "excellent" wines, all offered in "relaxed", "minimalist" surrounds; it'll cost you, but it's considered a "relative deal" compared to its peers.

Battersby *American*

FOOD	DECOR	SERVICE	COST
26	19	25	$78

Boerum Hill | 255 Smith St. (bet. Degraw & Douglass Sts.) | Brooklyn | 718-852-8321 | www.battersbybrooklyn.com

"Endlessly inventive" flavor combinations make for "inspired" New American meals at this "outstanding" Smith Street "shoebox"; "friendly" service helps distract from the "elbow-to-elbow" setup, but since reservations are only taken for the "memorable" tasting menu, "be prepared to wait."

Battery Gardens *American/Continental*

FOOD	DECOR	SERVICE	COST
19	22	19	$72

Financial District | SW corner of Battery Park (State St.) | 212-809-5508 | www.batterygardens.com

The "harbor is at your feet" at this "shoreline" Battery Park bastion where the "peerless" views of the harbor and Lady Liberty are matched with "better-than-expected" American-Continental fare; tabs skew high, but for the most "priceless" experience, go for "outdoor cocktails at sunset."

Bayou *Cajun*

FOOD	DECOR	SERVICE	COST
24	23	23	$44

Rosebank | 1072 Bay St. (bet. Chestnut & St. Marys Aves.) | Staten Island | 718-273-4383 | www.bayounyc.com

"Ragin' Cajun" cooking and "real Southern hospitality" come to Staten Island via this Rosebank "favorite" where the "tasty" cooking is as "true" to N'Awlins as the "Big Easy" decor; "affordable" tabs and "designated-driver-recommended" drinks ratchet up the "festive" vibrations.

Baz Bagel *Bakery/Jewish*

FOOD	DECOR	SERVICE	COST
▽ 21	18	19	$16

Little Italy | 181 Grand St. (bet. Baxter & Mulberry Sts.) | 212-335-0609 | www.bazbagel.com

"Delicious" hand-rolled bagels and "all the toppings" (lox, whitefish, schmear) are the focus of this Little Italy cafe from Barney Greengrass and Rubirosa alums; classic Jewish staples round out the menu, and it's all on offer in a narrow space with an old-school coffee-shop vibe.

B. Café *Belgian*

FOOD	DECOR	SERVICE	COST
20	16	20	$43

East 70s | 240 E. 75th St. (bet. 2nd & 3rd Aves.) | 212-249-3300
West 80s | 566 Amsterdam Ave. (bet. 87th & 88th Sts.) | 212-873-0003
www.bcafe.com

"Classic" Belgian fare is yours at these "satisfying" crosstown "reliables" offering "consistently fine" mussels and frites washed down with "high-test" brews; OK, the "railroad" settings are a bit "drab" and "squashed", but the staff "tries its best" and you do get "lots for your money."

BCD Tofu House *Korean*

FOOD	DECOR	SERVICE	COST
23	15	17	$27

West 30s | 5 W. 32nd St. (bet. B'way & 5th Ave.) | 212-967-1900 | www.bcdtofu.com

Home to "legit" "Korean comfort food", this 24/7 K-town link in an LA-based chain is "popular" for "rich" tofu hot pots tailored to "your level of spiciness"; the "decor is blah" and service is "functional", but you "can't go wrong" for "what you're paying."

Beatrice Inn *American*
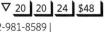
21 | 23 | 18 | $77

West Village | 285 W. 12th St. (bet. 4th & Hudson Sts.) | 917-566-7400 | www.thebeatriceinn.com

This "grown-up" destination from editor Graydon Carter inhabits a storied West Village basement, where the New American fare is considered "good" enough, but it's the cocktails and clubby "mystique" that people "love"; it's equally suited "for a group of friends or date night", though plan on "upscale" pricing.

NEW Beaubourg *French*
▽ 20 | 20 | 24 | $48

Battery Park City | 230 Vesey St. (West St.) | 212-981-8589 | www.ledistrict.com

Set in Battery Park's Le District food hall, this "simple" but "elegant" French bistro offers solid Gallic fare with seasonal touches, as well as a raw bar and daily prix fixe lunch options; thanks to seasonal terrace seating and Hudson River views, it's a "beautiful spot to sit outside."

Beautique *American/French*
20 | 23 | 20 | $75

West 50s | 8 W. 58th St. (bet. 5th & 6th Aves.) | 212-753-1200 | www.beautiquedining.com

This "stylish underground boîte" neighboring Midtown's Paris Theatre is a "sexy, upscale" enclave where the French-influenced American fare is "unexpectedly good", though the premium pricing is less of a surprise; "nothing special" to a few, it's still an "it" place for "beautiful" people who stay for "late nights" in the back lounge.

Beauty & Essex *American*
23 | 26 | 21 | $63

Lower East Side | 146 Essex St. (bet. Rivington & Stanton Sts.) | 212-614-0146 | www.beautyandessex.com

Behind an "extra-cool" hidden entrance in a pawn shop, this "vibrant" LES resto-lounge draws a "glam crowd" to "splurge" on "imaginative" New American bites in a bi-level space that "truly is a beauty"; if you "don't mind a bit of shameless trendiness" (free champagne in the ladies' room is a "nice touch"), it "does impress."

Becco *Italian*
23 | 18 | 21 | $51

West 40s | 355 W. 46th St. (bet. 8th & 9th Aves.) | 212-397-7597 | www.becco-nyc.com

Continuing its "hit run" on Restaurant Row, this Joe and Lidia Bastianich "phenomenon" provides "super" "homestyle Italian" meals via an "unlimited pasta deal" and a "tough-to-beat" $29 wine list; it sure "packs them in", but "punctual" servers get you "out the door in plenty of time" to make the curtain.

Beccofino *Italian*
24 | 20 | 23 | $40

Riverdale | 5704 Mosholu Ave. (bet. Fieldston Rd. & Spencer Ave.) | Bronx | 718-432-2604 | www.beccofinorestaurant.com

Pretty "happening" for Riverdale, this "traditional" Italian offers "Manhattan-quality" red-sauce cooking at Bronx prices; its "neighborly atmosphere" draws huzzahs, but no reservations and "small" dimensions mean you must "come early or be prepared to wait."

Beecher's Cellar *American*

23 | 21 | 20 | $38

Flatiron | 900 Broadway (20th St.) | 212-466-3340 |
www.beechershandmadecheese.com

It's "all about" the "power of cheese" at this "subterranean" Flatiron hideout, a "cool" lounge/eatery under Beecher's artisanal fromage factory, which it draws on for "creative" American nibbles led by "heavenly" mac 'n' cheese; take note, when the "young crowd" descends it can be "quite a scene."

Bella Blu *Italian*

22 | 17 | 20 | $58

East 70s | 967 Lexington Ave. (bet. 70th & 71st Sts.) | 212-988-4624 |
www.baraondany.com

"Well-to-do" Upper Eastsiders "get happy" at this "popular" Italian serving a "high-quality" menu led by "fantastic" pizzas; granted, it's "pricey", the seating's "cheek-by-jowl" and service depends on "how familiar you look", but "superior people-watching" saves the day.

Bella Via *Italian*

23 | 19 | 21 | $34

Long Island City | 47-46 Vernon Blvd. (48th Ave.) | Queens |
718-361-7510 | www.bellaviarestaurant.com

"Funky" Long Island City is home to this "reliable" Italian known for its pastas and "standout" coal-fired pizzas at prices that "won't break the bank"; set in a big-windowed storefront, it features "simple" decor that contributes to its "pleasant" mien.

Bell Book & Candle *American*

22 | 20 | 20 | $50

West Village | 141 W. 10th St., downstairs (bet. Greenwich Ave. &
Waverly Pl.) | 212-414-2355 | www.bbandcnyc.com

Best known for an aeroponic roof garden that supplies most of its produce, this "cozy-chic" West Villager is appreciated for its "delicious" seasonal American menu; the "dark" basement setting has "great date" potential, and it's also "worth checking out" for its "awesome happy-hour" deals.

Ben & Jack's Steak House *Steak*

24 | 20 | 23 | $71

NoMad | 255 Fifth Ave. (bet. 28th & 29th Sts.) | 212-532-7600 |
www.benandjackssteakhouse.com

Among the "best of the Luger's imitators", this NoMad carnivorium features "cooked-to-perfection" steaks and "man-size" sides; "boys'-club" looks and "friendly" staffers offset the typically "expensive" tabs.

Benares *Indian*

21 | 17 | 20 | $39

TriBeCa | 45 Murray St. (bet. B'way & Church St.) | 212-766-4900
West 50s | 240 W. 56th St. (bet. B'way & 8th Ave.) | 212-397-0707
www.benaresnyc.com

The "flavorful" Indian menu includes dishes "not often found" at these "upscale" venues where the wide-ranging choices ("veggie-friendly" options are a focus) are presented in "comfortable", modern surrounds; the Midtown branch's buffet lunch "steal" is matched by a prix fixe option in TriBeCa.

Benchmark *American/Steak*

23 | 21 | 21 | $54

Park Slope | 339 Second St. (bet. 4th & 5th Aves.) | Brooklyn |
718-965-7040 | www.benchmarkrestaurant.com

Nestled in an "intimate" carriage house, this "somewhat overlooked" Park Slope steakhouse offers "quality" cuts as well as "quite-good"

American accompaniments; fans admire its "calm" mood and midrange tabs, while a "lovely patio" allows it to "double in size" in good weather.

Benjamin Steak House *Steak*   27 | 24 | 26 | $85

East 40s | Dylan Hotel | 52 E. 41st St. (bet. Madison & Park Aves.) | 212-297-9177 | www.benjaminsteakhouse.com

You can "eat like a man" at this "first-class" chop shop in the Dylan Hotel, supplying "perfectly prepared" beef and "top-shelf" service in "clubby" quarters with a "soaring ceiling" and "massive fireplace"; it's certainly "not cheap", but then again this "sublime experience" is always "memorable."

Benoit Bistro *French*   23 | 22 | 21 | $66

West 50s | 60 W. 55th St. (bet. 5th & 6th Aves.) | 646-943-7373 | www.benoitny.com

"As French as could be", this durable Midtown bistro from Alain Ducasse turns out "well-done" traditional dishes (e.g. "killer roast chicken") in "bright, lively" digs that channel the City of Light; ever the "worthy destination", it's on the "expensive" side but certainly "worth the cost."

Ben's Best *Deli/Kosher*   23 | 12 | 17 | $26

Rego Park | 96-40 Queens Blvd. (bet. 63rd Dr. & 64th Rd.) | Queens | 718-897-1700 | www.bensbest.com

For an "authentic artery-clogging experience", look no further than this circa-1945 Rego Park Jewish deli known for "old-time" kosher fare "and lots of it"; the "oy!" decor is "just what you'd expect", but "Queens prices" and "OK service" compensate.

Ben's Kosher Deli *Deli/Kosher*   19 | 13 | 17 | $27

West 30s | 209 W. 38th St. (bet. 7th & 8th Aves.) | 212-398-2367
Bayside | 211-37 26th Ave. (Bell Blvd.) | Queens | 212-398-2367
www.bensdeli.net

These "retro" delis cater to the "masses" with "colossal" sandwiches and other kosher staples; purists protest the "pedestrian" eats, "so-so" service and "run-down" "Miami Beach decor", but they're "accessible" enough in a pinch.

Bergen Hill *Seafood*   ∇ 27 | 21 | 24 | $75

Carroll Gardens | 387 Court St. (1st Pl.) | Brooklyn | 718-858-5483 | www.bergenhill.com

"Innovative twists" on seafood courtesy of a former Le Cirque chef will "knock your socks off" at this ultra-"cozy" Carroll Gardens sleeper, where the "beautifully composed" small plates and "killer cocktails" come via a "kind" staff; it's that much more "memorable" if you sit at the chef's counter, but "expensive" tabs may help explain why it's still "under the radar."

Berg'n *Food Hall*   23 | 20 | 18 | $21

Crown Heights | 899 Bergen St. (bet. Classon & Franklin Aves.) | Brooklyn | 718-857-2337 | www.bergn.com

"Super Brooklynized fun" is on tap at this all-day Crown Heights beer hall from the Smorgasburg crew, offering a "large" list of microbrews, as well as cocktails and "interesting" grub from an "eclectic" array of vendors; though not for the "hipster"-averse, the "industrial" digs and "long picnic tables" work for a "boozy weekend afternoon."

	FOOD	DECOR	SERVICE	COST

Berlyn *German* | 21 | 19 | 19 | $49

Fort Greene | 25 Lafayette Ave. (Ashland Pl.) | Brooklyn | 718-222-5800 | www.berlynrestaurant.com

"Handy for BAM" given its right-across-the-street location, this Fort Greene German takes a "refined" approach with a "well-prepared", meat-centric menu; the "laid-back", banquette-lined space and all-seasons garden area add incentive pre- or post-performance.

Beso *Spanish* | 24 | 22 | 22 | $45

St. George | 11 Schuyler St. (Richmond Terr.) | Staten Island | 718-816-8162 | www.besonyc.com

A "short walk from the ferry", this St. George Spaniard rolls out "terrific" tapas and sangria in a "relaxed" setting that "feels very far away from Staten Island"; admirers "wish it were bigger", though the "reasonable" rates and staff that "never misses a beat" are fine as is.

Best Pizza *Pizza* | 22 | 14 | 19 | $13

Williamsburg | 33 Havemeyer St. (bet. 7th & 8th Sts.) | Brooklyn | 718-599-2210 | www.best.piz.za.com

Though it "looks like your typical corner pizza shop", this Williamsburg joint "doesn't shirk" from its "bold" name, turning out "quality" brick-oven pies with "inventive" toppings plus a handful of Italian subs; the "small, crowded" space with paper-plate decor does the job for "a quick bite."

Betony *American* | 25 | 23 | 24 | $124

West 50s | 41 W. 57th St. (bet. 5th & 6th Aves.) | 212-465-2400 | www.betony-nyc.com

You're in for a "fancy" "foodie experience" at this Midtown New American where "impressive" and "complex" tasting menus are paired with "carefully crafted" cocktails; a "polished" staff watches over the "civilized" bi-level space – just "bring your expense account" as bills run "high."

Beyoglu *Turkish* | 21 | 16 | 17 | $37

East 80s | 1431 Third Ave. (81st St.) | 212-650-0850

A "lively crowd" descends on this UES Turkish "standby" to graze on "irresistible meze" at an "oh-so-reasonable" cost; it can be "rushed", "cramped" and "loud", but the upstairs room is "quieter" and come summer the sidewalk seats are a "big draw."

Bianca *Italian* | 25 | 20 | 22 | $36

NoHo | 5 Bleecker St. (Bowery) | 212-260-4666 | www.biancanyc.com

The "wow"-worthy Emilia-Romagna dishes are "clearly made with love" and a "fabulous bargain" to boot, making this cash-only NoHo Italian "gem" well worth the "tight squeeze"; no reservations means there's "definitely a wait", which those in the know spend "next door at the wine bar."

Biang! *Chinese/Noodle Shop* | 25 | 20 | 19 | $19

Flushing | 41-10 Main St. (bet. 41st Ave. & 41st Rd.) | Queens | 718-888-7713 | www.biang-nyc.com

"Bold, spicy flavors" mark this cash-only Flushing scion of Xi'an Famous Foods, where the "extraordinary" Western Chinese lineup stars the "all-time freshest" hand-pulled noodles and "super-tasty" skewers; the full-service setup is "laid-back", and you can't beat that "bang for the buck."

	FOOD	DECOR	SERVICE	COST

Big Gay Ice Cream Shop *Ice Cream* 25 | 18 | 22 | $9

East Village | 125 E. Seventh St. (bet. Ave. A & 1st Ave.) | 212-533-9333
West Village | 61 Grove St. (7th Ave. S.) | 212-414-0222
www.biggayicecream.com

The name's as "hard to resist" as the "heavenly" licks at these soft-serve ice cream parlors, famed for creating "cool" cones with "campy" handles (e.g. the "life-changing" Salty Pimp); most agree the "long lines" are a "small price to pay" for the "sweet finish."

Big Wong *Chinese* 22 | 6 | 13 | $16

Chinatown | 67 Mott St. (bet. Bayard & Canal Sts.) | 212-964-0540 |
www.bigwongking.com

Known for roast meats and "excellent congee", this cash-only "Chinatown favorite" is ever "reliable" for "real" Cantonese grub; it's also known for "bustling" crowds, "revolving-door" service and "zero decor", but given the "outstanding value", "who cares?"

Bill's Food & Drink *American/Steak* 18 | 20 | 18 | $60

East 50s | 57 E. 54th St. (bet. Madison & Park Aves.) | 212-518-2727 |
www.bills54.com

Prohibition-era speakeasy Bill's Gay Nineties reboots as this Midtown American grill, where chef John DeLucie (The Lion) focuses on "juicy" steaks; a townhouse setting replete with vintage artwork and a "great piano bar" recalls '20s Gotham, though some wonder if retro chic is "too cool" for this turf.

Birch Coffee *Coffee* 25 | 22 | 23 | $10

East 60s | 134 ½ E. 62nd St. (Lexington Ave.) | 212-840-1444
NEW Murray Hill | 432 Third Ave. (30th St.) | 212-686-1444
NoMad | 21 E. 27th St. (Madison Ave.) | 212-686-1444
West 90s | 750 Columbus Ave. (bet. 96th & 97th Sts.) | 212-665-1444
West Village | 56 Seventh Ave. (bet. 13th & 14th Sts.) | 212-929-1444
Long Island City | 40-35 23rd St. (bet. 40th & 41st Aves.) | Queens |
212-686-1444
www.birchcoffee.com

They sure "know their coffee" at this rapidly growing Manhattan-based chain where "personable" baristas pour "strong and flavorful" brews made from thoughtfully sourced beans; snacks like breakfast sandwiches and pastries are "excellent" too, and the "relaxed" vibe is just right for a "leisurely afternoon."

NEW Birds & Bubbles *Southern* 21 | 17 | 19 | $52

Lower East Side | 100 Forsyth St. (bet. Broome & Grand Sts.) |
646-368-9240 | www.birdsandbubbles.com

The "name says it all" at this "hip" LES Southerner where "tender" fried chicken and other "elevated" comfort fare pairs with a "thoughtful" champagne list; an "adorable patio" gives the "small", brick-walled quarters some breathing room when things feel "tight."

Birreria *Italian* 21 | 23 | 18 | $41

Flatiron | Eataly | 200 Fifth Ave. (bet. 23rd & 24th Sts.) | 212-937-8910 |
www.eataly.com

"Hard to beat on a nice summer" day, this "beer-lover's garden" atop Eataly is an all-seasons, retractable-roofed "experience" dispensing an "excellent" selection of cask ales soaked up with "light" Italian bites (mostly cheeses and salumi); the place is "hopping" from lunch till late, so "to actually gain access, go early."

Bistango *Italian*
21 | 17 | 22 | $42

East 50s | 145 E. 50th St. (bet. Lexington & 3rd Aves.) | 212-888-4121
Murray Hill | 415 Third Ave. (29th St.) | 212-725-8484
www.bistangonyc.com

With a "plethora" of "classic" Italian dishes prepared gluten-free (if requested), these neighborhood standbys deliver "goodness that all can enjoy"; "reasonable" pricing and "warm" service (with a "sweetheart" host at the Kips Bay original) come with the territory.

Bistro Cassis *French*
20 | 17 | 18 | $49

West 70s | 225 Columbus Ave. (bet. 70th & 71st Sts.) | 212-579-3966 | www.bistrocassis.com

For a serving of "old Paris on the UWS", this French bistro can be counted on for "traditional", "satisfying" dishes at a relatively "reasonable price"; the "intimate" atmosphere and "expeditious" service make it "good pre-Lincoln Center", an "easy walk" away.

Bistro Chat Noir *French*
21 | 19 | 21 | $68

East 60s | 22 E. 66th St. (bet. 5th & Madison Aves.) | 212-794-2428 | www.bistrochatnoir.com

A "low-key fave" in a "chic" address off Madison Avenue, this Gallic East-sider caters to "fashionable" folk with "Parisian intimacy" and "quite good" French bistro fare dispensed in a "snug" setting; tabs are "expensive", but a "fantastic" owner and "convivial staff" keep customers satisfied.

Bistro Les Amis *French*
22 | 19 | 23 | $47

SoHo | 180 Spring St. (Thompson St.) | 212-226-8645 | www.bistrolesamis.com

Bringing a soupçon of the "Left Bank" to SoHo, this seasoned French bistro lures fans with its "comforting" cooking vs. cost ratio; OK, there's "no scene" going on, but sidewalk seats provide prime people-watching and the "*charmant*" staff lives up to the promise of its name.

Bistro Vendôme *French*
22 | 20 | 22 | $57

East 50s | 405 E. 58th St. (1st Ave.) | 212-935-9100 | www.bistrovendomenyc.com

"Sutton seniors" gather at this "upscale bistro" for French fare dispatched by "Gallic-accented staffers" who are as "charming" as the tri-level town-house setting; the less-impressed shrug "nothing special", but those who love the "particularly pretty" terrace call it a "neighborhood jewel."

NEW BKB *Seafood*
∇ 23 | 22 | 22 | $71

East 70s | 321 E. 73rd St. (bet. 1st & 2nd Aves.) | 212-861-1038 | www.bkbrestaurant.com

This "cool, casual" East Hampton-bred fish house makes a splash on the UES with Med-tinged "sea-to-table" fare in a "clean-lined" setting that's amply "spaced for civilized conversation"; prices can drift upmarket, but early adopters pronounce it a "definite winner."

| | FOOD | DECOR | SERVICE | COST |

Black Ant *Mexican*

24 | 22 | 21 | $50

East Village | 60 Second Ave. (bet. 3rd & 4th Sts.) | 212-598-0300 | www.blackantnyc.com

"Be prepared for the unexpected" at this "innovative" East Village Mexican whose "foodie"-friendly menu showcases actual ants (and grasshoppers too) in "delicious", "nuanced" plates; "amazing" agave-based cocktails fuel a "lively crowd" having "fiesta fun" in the "dark" "lounge"-like surrounds.

Black Forest Brooklyn *German*

▽ 20 | 21 | 20 | $26

Fort Greene | 733 Fulton St. (Elliott Pl.) | Brooklyn | 718-935-0300 | www.blackforestbrooklyn.com

A "Brooklyn-esque take on the beer hall", this indoor Fort Greene biergarten taps Bavarian brews and does "justice" to "traditional German" grub; given a roomy, rustic setup with skylights and "long wooden tables", it's no surprise the "demo skews young."

Black Iron Burger *Burgers*

23 | 16 | 19 | $20

East Village | 540 E. Fifth St. (Ave. B) | 212-677-6067 | www.blackironburger.com

"Pretty damn good" "no-frills" burgers paired with draft pints "go down easy" at this East Village "hole-in-the-wall"; though the "earthy" setting's on the "small" side, the staff is "fun", the tabs "reasonable" and the late-night hours a bonus.

NEW Black Tap *Burgers*

20 | 18 | 20 | $32

SoHo | 529 Broome St. (bet. Sullivan & Thompson Sts.) | 917-639-3089 | www.blacktapnyc.com

A "delicious" burger is the main event at this "friendly" SoHo spot, where the creative patties comprise the likes of chorizo, lamb, bison and Wagyu beef; the bar pours an "unbelievable" selection of craft brews, and the tiny dinerlike space has a front counter as well as a few booths.

Black Whale *American*

21 | 19 | 21 | $35

City Island | 279 City Island Ave. (Hawkins St.) | Bronx | 718-885-3657 | www.theblackwhalefb.wix.com

The "offbeat" nautical decor conjures up "Cape Cod in the Bronx" at this "cute" City Island vet where the "inexpensive" New American menu includes some notably "decadent desserts"; fans find the "terrific" Sunday brunch and "lovely" back patio equally "memorable."

Blanca *American*

▽ 26 | 21 | 25 | $254

Bushwick | 261 Moore St. (Bogart St.) | Brooklyn | 347-799-2807 | www.blancanyc.com

An "epic food adventure" awaits at this loft annex of the Bushwick phenom Roberta's, which presents chef Carlo Mirarchi's "unbelievable" New American tasting menu at a 12-seat counter fronting a pristine kitchen; the $195 set price may mean "dumping out your whole wallet", but the payoff is a "one-of-a-kind" dining experience.

Blaue Gans *Austrian/German*

22 | 18 | 21 | $56

TriBeCa | 139 Duane St. (B'way) | 212-571-8880 | www.kg-ny.com

"First-rate" Wiener schnitzel heads the list of "hearty" Austro-German dishes at Kurt Gutenbrunner's "down-to-earth" neighborhood TriBeCan, abetted by "wonderful" Teutonic brews; the "artsy poster-clad" room is "simple" but "cool", while "fair prices" and "pleasant" staffers add to the "gemütlich" mood.

Blenheim *American*
<u>20</u> <u>21</u> <u>19</u> <u>$75</u>

West Village | 283 W. 12th St. (4th St.) | 212-243-7073 | www.blenheimhill.com

"Innovation is key" at this West Village "farm-to-table experience", where "high ambitions" often produce "flavorful" American dishes featuring ingredients from the namesake Catskills grange; the "comfortable" space has "homey" accents, and while it's "a little pricey", there's "always a welcome surprise on the menu."

Blossom *Vegan/Vegetarian*
<u>25</u> <u>18</u> <u>21</u> <u>$34</u>

Chelsea | 187 Ninth Ave. (bet. 21st & 22nd Sts.) | 212-627-1144
NEW **West 80s** | 507 Columbus Ave. (bet. 84th & 85th Sts.) | 212-875-2600
West Village | 41 Carmine St. (bet. Bedford & Bleecker Sts.) | 646-438-9939
www.blossomnyc.com

Blossom du Jour *Vegan/Vegetarian*

Chelsea | 259 W. 23rd St. (bet. 7th & 8th Aves.) | 212-229-2595
West 40s | 617 Ninth Ave. (bet. 43rd & 44th Sts.) | 646-998-3535
West 60s | 165 Amsterdam Ave. (bet. 67th & 68th Sts.) | 212-799-9010
NEW **West 80s** | 449 Amsterdam Ave. (bet. 81st & 82nd Sts.) | 212-712-9822
www.blossomdujour.com

The food's "completely vegan" but "you wouldn't know" at these "earthy" organic "havens", whose "impressive" fare makes healthy almost seem "hedonistic"; "efficient" service and "relaxed" surroundings add to the overall "solid" feel, while the du Jour outlets offer a "quick" fix to go.

BLT Prime *Steak*
<u>26</u> <u>24</u> <u>25</u> <u>$86</u>

Gramercy Park | 111 E. 22nd St. (bet. Lexington Ave. & Park Ave. S.) | 212-995-8500 | www.bltprime.com

"They know their way around a cow" at this "chic" Gramercy steakhouse touted for "perfectly cooked" chops and "light-as-a-feather" popovers; "stellar" wines, "solicitous" service and "sleek" decor add to the overall "special experience" and help explain tabs that may "leave your credit card smoking."

BLT Steak *Steak*
<u>25</u> <u>22</u> <u>24</u> <u>$84</u>

East 50s | 106 E. 57th St. (bet. Lexington & Park Aves.) | 212-752-7470 | www.bltsteak.com

East Midtown "power brokers" mix "business and pleasure" at this "classy" cow palace featuring "spot-on" "quality" via its famed "melt-in-your-mouth" popovers and "beautifully prepared" steaks; a "stylish", "modern" enclave tended by a "professional" team, "it ain't cheap" but "you get what you pay for."

Blue Bottle Coffee *Coffee*
<u>24</u> <u>19</u> <u>20</u> <u>$8</u>

Chelsea | 450 W. 15th St. (10th Ave.) | 510-653-3394
West 40s | Gotham West Mkt. | 600 11th Ave. (bet. 44th & 45th Sts.) | 212-582-7945
West 40s | 1 Rockefeller Plaza (bet. 48th & 49th Sts.) | 510-653-3394
NEW **West 40s** | 54 W. 40th St. (6th Ave.) | 510-653-3394

continued

Boerum Hill | 85 Dean St. (bet. Hoyt & Smith Sts.) | Brooklyn | 510-653-3394

Williamsburg | 160 Berry St. (bet. 4th & 5th Sts.) | Brooklyn | 718-387-4160
www.bluebottlecoffee.com

Every hipster's "favorite way to start the day", these Bay Area imports are known for their "marvelous" slow-drip coffee (including a "showstopper" New Orleans–style iced brew) and "intense", freshly roasted blends; "knowledgeable baristas" do the honors, but "the line's often long" – "and deservedly so."

Blue Fin *Seafood*　　　　22 | 20 | 20 | $59

West 40s | W Hotel Times Sq. | 1567 Broadway (47th St.) | 212-918-1400 | www.bluefinnyc.com

Broadway "buzz" is in full swing at this Times Square seafood "staple" supplying "delish" fish via "aim-to-please" servers in "slick, modern" surrounds; "high prices" are the only catch; P.S. plans to turn part of the space into a Dos Caminos are underway.

Blue Ginger *Japanese*　　　　22 | 18 | 19 | $45

Chelsea | 106 Eighth Ave. (15th St.) | 212-352-0911

Handy for a "quick bite before a show" at the nearby Joyce Theater, this "fun" Chelsea Japanese slices sushi that's "pleasing to the eye" and also offers "mouthwatering" cooked items, all "well priced"; "friendly" staffers take your mind off the "typical" decor.

Blue Hill *American*　　　　28 | 23 | 27 | $103

Greenwich Village | 75 Washington Pl. (bet. MacDougal St. & 6th Ave.) | 212-539-1776 | www.bluehillfarm.com

Defining the "farm-to-table ethos", this "intimate" Village American from chef Dan Barber is a shrine to "spectacular" seasonal dining where "ultrafresh" ingredients and "loving preparation" yield "nuanced" cuisine "that excites"; overseen by an ever-"hospitable" staff, it's a definite "splurge", but also an "utterly unforgettable experience."

Blue Ribbon *American*　　　　25 | 19 | 23 | $56

SoHo | 97 Sullivan St. (Spring St.) | 212-274-0404
Blue Ribbon at Brooklyn Bowl *American*
Williamsburg | 61 Wythe Ave. (12th St.) | Brooklyn | 718-963-3369
Blue Ribbon Bakery *American*
West Village | 35 Downing St. (Bedford St.) | 212-337-0404
Blue Ribbon Brooklyn *American*
Park Slope | 280 Fifth Ave. (bet. 1st St. & Garfield Pl.) | Brooklyn | 718-840-0404
www.blueribbonrestaurants.com

The Bromberg brothers "consistently get it right" at these "beloved" New Americans where "down-home" cooking ("wonderful" matzo ball soup, "ballin'" fried chicken) and a "myriad" of choices make for "comfort-food heaven"; the original SoHo "standby" is a late-night "haunt for off-duty chefs", while the Bakery Kitchen has "intoxicating" smells of baking bread, and though they're not inexpensive, they remain "perennial favorites."

	FOOD	DECOR	SERVICE	COST

Blue Ribbon Fried Chicken *Chicken*

21 **14** **18** **$21**

East Village | 28 E. First St. (2nd Ave.) | 212-228-0404 |
www.blueribbonfriedchicken.com

Offering over-the-counter access to the "super-tasty", Southern-style
fried chicken served at some of the Bromberg brothers' other restaurants, this "functional" East Villager vends its "well-seasoned" poultry
by the piece along with shakes and sides, plus beer and wine; OK, so
it's "a little pricey for fast food", but late hours mean it's a good option
"after your night out."

Blue Ribbon Sushi *Japanese*

25 **20** **22** **$66**

Battery Park City | Hudson Eats | 230 Vesey St. (West St.) | 212-417-7000
SoHo | 119 Sullivan St. (bet. Prince & Spring Sts.) | 212-343-0404

Blue Ribbon Hi-Bar *Japanese*

West 50s | 6 Columbus Hotel | 308 W. 58th St. (bet. 8th & 9th Aves.) |
212-397-0404

Blue Ribbon Sushi Bar & Grill *Japanese*

West 50s | 6 Columbus Hotel | 308 W. 58th St. (bet. 8th & 9th Aves.) |
212-397-0404

Blue Ribbon Sushi Izakaya *Japanese*

Lower East Side | Sixty LES Hotel | 187 Orchard St. (bet. Houston &
Stanton Sts.) | 212-466-0404
www.blueribbonrestaurants.com

"First-class" fish in "creative and classic" combos makes for "dazzling"
sushi at these Japanese "go-tos" by the brothers Bromberg; you'll also
find brasserie favorites (like "surprisingly good fried chicken") at some
locales, and while the SoHo original is more "minimalist" than the rest
(minus the Hudson Eats counter), all will cost you a "chunk of change."

Blue Smoke *BBQ*

22 **18** **21** **$46**

Battery Park City | 255 Vesey St. (bet. North End Ave. & West St.) |
212-889-2005
Murray Hill | 116 E. 27th St. (bet. Lexington Ave. & Park Ave. S.) |
212-447-7733
www.bluesmoke.com

"Meat fiends" have a "grand time" at Danny Meyer's "smokin'", "family-
friendly" BBQ joints, where "up-tempo" staffers supply "fall-off-the-bone
ribs" and other "honest" staples; a "fine selection of bourbons" (and
"cool" sounds at the Kips Bay flagship's downstairs Jazz Standard)
should cure any "pseudo-Texas-atmosphere" blues.

Blue Water Grill *Seafood*

24 **22** **22** **$62**

Union Square | 31 Union Sq. W. (16th St.) | 212-675-9500 |
www.bluewatergrillnyc.com

Expect a "class operation" at this "upbeat" Union Square "favorite" that
owes its "staying power" to "superb" seafood, "smart" service and an
"expansive" former bank setting with a "lovely" marbled interior and
"delightful" wraparound terrace; add a "jazz room downstairs", and its
"good-looking" clientele doesn't mind the "high sticker price."

Boathouse *American*

18 **25** **19** **$58**

Central Park | Central Park Lake, enter on E. 72nd St. (Park Dr. N.) |
212-517-2233 | www.thecentralparkboathouse.com

It's all about the "unbeatable location" at this lakeside American, where "the decor is Central Park" and watching the rowboats drift by "feels like being on vacation"; the menu's "not overly exciting" and the service just "so-so", but for tourists and natives alike, this "must-have" NYC experience truly "sells itself."

Bobby Van's Steakhouse *Steak*

23 | 20 | 22 | $75

East 40s | 230 Park Ave. (46th St.) | 212-867-5490
East 50s | 131 E. 54th St. (bet. Lexington & Park Aves.) | 212-207-8050
Financial District | 25 Broad St. (Exchange Pl.) | 212-344-8463
JFK Airport | JFK Airport, Terminal 8 | JFK Access Rd. (JFK Expy.) |
Queens | 718-553-2100

Bobby Van's Steakhouse & Grill *Steak*

West 40s | 120 W. 45th St. (bet. 6th & 7th Aves.) | 212-575-5623
West 50s | 135 W. 50th St. (bet. 6th & 7th Aves.) | 212-957-5050
www.bobbyvans.com

A "safe bet" for "suits" entertaining clients over lunch, these "straight-forward" chop shops feature career waiters ferrying "well-executed" slabs of beef in "masculine", "clubby" environs (including a "really cool" bank-vault setting at the FiDi branch); expect "no surprises", right down to the "hefty" check.

Bobo *French*

23 | 24 | 23 | $58

West Village | 181 W. 10th St. (7th Ave. S.) | 212-488-2626 |
www.bobonyc.com

At this West Village "standby", a "professional" staff delivers "solid" French cooking in a "civilized" townhouse space spanning an upstairs dining room, "lively" lower-level bar area and "cute" back garden; it's "romantic" enough for a date, but "equally great" for just "meeting with friends."

Bocca *Italian*

22 | 20 | 22 | $53

Flatiron | 39 E. 19th St. (bet. B'way & Park Ave. S.) | 212-387-1200 |
www.boccanyc.com

It "feels like Rome" at this "enjoyable" Cacio e Pepe sibling in the Flatiron known for its "expert" Italian cooking, "appealing" modern look and "friendly" service; regulars say "pasta is the thing to eat" here, notably its "cool" signature dish tossed tableside in a wheel of pecorino.

Bocelli *Italian/Seafood*

25 | 23 | 24 | $58

Old Town | 1250 Hylan Blvd. (Parkinson Ave.) | Staten Island |
718-420-6150 | www.bocellirest.com

With "delicious" seafood specialties, "professional" service and "pretty elegant" Tuscan decor, this Old Town Italian "definitely stands out" among its Staten Island peers; despite Manhattan-style pricing, "reservations are a must" on weekends.

Bodega Negra *Mexican*

22 | 23 | 21 | $64

Chelsea | Dream Downtown Hotel | 355 W. 16th St. (bet. 8th & 9th Aves.) | 212-229-2336 | www.bodeganegranyc.com

The "young and trendy" tout this Serge Becker sequel to a buzzy London original, furnishing "inventive" Mexicana in "hip", rancho-style quarters inside Chelsea's Dream Downtown Hotel; there's "people-watching" aplenty, with "*muy delicioso*" margaritas to help make it "a blast" – though the front cafe is a mellower alternative.

Bodrum *Mediterranean/Turkish*

21 | 15 | 20 | $37

West 80s | 584 Amsterdam Ave. (bet. 88th & 89th Sts.) | 212-799-2806 | www.bodrumnyc.com

"Small and cozy", this UWS neighborhood Med is the "real deal" for "inexpensive" dining on "stellar" Turkish meze and "tasty thin-crust pizza"; though service is "speedy", it's often "crowded and cramped", so insiders flee to the "outside tables."

Bogota Latin Bistro *Pan-Latin*
24 | 19 | 21 | $36

Park Slope | 141 Fifth Ave. (St. Johns Pl.) | Brooklyn | 718-230-3805 | www.bogotabistro.com

"It's always a party" at this "hyper-popular" Park Slope Pan-Latin, where the "awesome", "Colombian-style" eats and "exotic drinks" whisk you to "Bogotá"; "decent prices" and an "incredible staff" help keep the "good times" and "noise level" going strong.

Bohemian *Japanese*

27 | 24 | 25 | $78

NoHo | 57 Great Jones St. (bet. Bowery & Lafayette St.) | no phone

"You'll need a reservation" and a referral (there's "no listed phone number") to access this "exclusive" NoHo Japanese hidden "behind a butcher shop", where the "exceptional" food and cocktails are presented by "truly wonderful people"; an "intimate", denlike room furnished with "low couches" is perfect for conversation, and while prices run "steep", it will leave a "lasting memory."

The Boil *Seafood*
23 | 14 | 20 | $49

Lower East Side | 139 Chrystie St. (bet. Broome & Delancey Sts.) | 212-925-8815 | www.theboilny.com

"Don't wear your best clothes" to this "down-and-dirty" LES seafooder, where the "super-messy", "Louisiana-style" shellfish boils come with "addictive" sauces plus wet naps and gloves; the "busy", no-reservations setup often means "long" waits, but "what fun it is" in the end.

Bo-Ky *Noodle Shop*
22 | 6 | 12 | $13

Chinatown | 80 Bayard St. (bet. Mott & Mulberry Sts.) | 212-406-2292
Little Italy | 216 Grand St (Elizabeth St.) | 212-219-9228
www.bokynyc.com

One of the few "good things about jury duty" is the chance to lunch at these Chinatown–Little Italy noodle shops churning out "authentic" Chinese and Vietnamese soups for ultra-"cheap" coin; "dreary" decor, "busy" atmospherics and "poor" (albeit "quick") service come with the territory.

BonChon *Chicken*
23 | 13 | 16 | $22

Financial District | 104 John St. (Cliff St.) | 646-692-4660
Murray Hill | 325 Fifth Ave. (bet. 32nd & 33rd Sts.) | 212-686-8282
West 30s | 207 W. 38th St. (bet. 7th & 8th Aves.) | 212-221-3339
NEW Astoria | 25-30 Broadway (29th St.) | Queens | 917-860-4770
Bayside | 45-37 Bell Blvd. (bet. 45th Dr. & 45th Rd.) | Queens | 718-225-1010
www.bonchon.com

"Habit-forming" is the verdict on the "out-of-sight" Korean fried chicken with "crispy, parchmentlike skin" sold at this international chain; since the birds are cooked to order, expect "forever" waits, not to mention "slipshod" service, "no decor" and just-"decent" prices.

	FOOD	DECOR	SERVICE	COST

Bond 45 *Italian/Steak*
19 | 18 | 19 | $60

West 40s | 154 W. 45th St. (bet. 6th & 7th Aves.) | 212-869-4545 |
www.bond45.com

Shelly Fireman's "cavernous", "vibrant" trattoria in Times Square's old
Bond clothing store presents a "straight-up", "something-for-everybody"
Italian steakhouse menu in a "well-decorated barn" of a setting; "service
with alacrity" suits theatergoers, though "loud" acoustics and kinda
"high" prices are less well received.

Bond St *Japanese*
25 | 22 | 22 | $75

NoHo | 6 Bond St. (bet. B'way & Lafayette St.) | 212-777-2500 |
www.bondstrestaurant.com

"They've still got it" at this NoHo Japanese "knockout", where the "work-
of-art" sushi and "swanky" space with a "cool" downstairs lounge deliver
both "style and substance"; "beautiful" people out "to see and be seen"
readily bond with the "trendy vibe", less so with the "expensive" tabs.

Bonnie's Grill *Burgers*
21 | 13 | 17 | $25

Park Slope | 278 Fifth Ave. (bet. 1st St. & Garfield Pl.) | Brooklyn |
718-369-9527 | www.bonniesgrill.com

Park Slopers refuel at this "short-order joint" slinging "damn-good burgers" and other basics in "classic diner" digs; it's "fun sitting at the counter" and the grub's "well priced", but since the dimensions are "slim",
"good luck getting a seat on the weekend."

Boqueria *Spanish*
23 | 20 | 20 | $49

NEW East 70s | 1460 Second Ave. (76th St.) | 212-343-2227
Flatiron | 53 W. 19th St. (bet. 5th & 6th Aves.) | 212-255-4160
SoHo | 171 Spring St. (bet. B'way & Thompson St.) | 212-343-4255
www.boquerianyc.com

"Graze your way" through "top-class tapas" at these "happening",
"no-room-to-spare" Spaniards with a "transported-to-Barcelona" feel;
"well-priced" wines offset tabs that can "add up pretty quickly" – though
groups of six or more can go for the "value" tasting menu that's a "nonstop parade of fabulous" little bites.

Bosie Tea Parlor *Teahouse*
21 | 19 | 20 | $26

West Village | 10 Morton St. (bet. Bleecker St. & 7th Ave. S.) |
212-352-9900 | www.bosienyc.com

This "quiet" West Village teahouse offers "exotic" brews and "delicate"
nibbles (including "delish" French macarons) in a "quaint" cafe setting; fans
say this "delightful oasis" makes for a "truly relaxing" dining experience.

Bottega *Italian*
20 | 18 | 21 | $50

East 70s | 1331 Second Ave. (bet. 70th & 71st Sts.) | 212-288-5282 |
www.bottegany.com

A "nice neighborhood place", this UES trattoria turns out "accessible"
Italian staples in a "pleasant" atmosphere; other pluses include a "large,
comfortable" setting with a "busy bar" and "terrific outdoor" seating, as
well as "personable" service.

Bottino *Italian*
20 | 17 | 19 | $48

Chelsea | 246 10th Ave. (bet. 24th & 25th Sts.) | 212-206-6766 |
www.bottinonyc.com

Convenient to West Chelsea's gallery district and the High Line, this "all-around pleasant" Tuscan "pioneer" delivers "solid" meals at "moderate-to-a-bit-expensive" prices; the "unhurried" pace suits its "arty" constituents, though the "charming", "spacious" garden is bound to please everyone.

Bouchon Bakery *American/French*

22 | 16 | 18 | $28

West 40s | Rockefeller Ctr. | 1 Rockefeller Plaza (bet. 48th & 49th Sts.) | 212-782-3890
West 50s | Time Warner Ctr. | 10 Columbus Circle, 3rd fl. (60th St. at B'way) | 212-823-9363

You can "treat yourself" to "quality" bites at Thomas Keller's French-inspired bakery/take-out counters, where the "distinctive" macarons, "first-rate pastries", "mouthwatering breads" and sandwiches are "worth the guilt"; they can be "frenetic" and "costly", but the Time Warner Center original's "wonderful view" of Columbus Circle is "certainly an added value."

Bouley *French*

29 | 28 | 28 | $141

TriBeCa | 163 Duane St. (bet. Hudson St. & W. B'way) | 212-964-2525 | www.davidbouley.com

A "wow by any standard", David Bouley's "glorious" TriBeCa flagship is an "icon of fine dining", where the "masterful" French cuisine is "a revelation" brought on by an "exemplary" staff in a "gorgeous formal" setting (jackets are required); tabs for such a "bucket-list" experience are unsurprisingly *"très cher"*, but the $55 prix fixe lunch is "a terrific deal."

Boulton & Watt *American*

21 | 19 | 20 | $36

East Village | 5 Ave. A (1st St.) | 646-490-6004 | www.boultonandwattnyc.com

Gastropub grub gets "kicked up a couple of notches" at this "barlike" East Village American offering updated comfort fare, "inventive" drinks (including "must-try" picklebacks) and an "especially awesome" brunch; "fair prices" help compensate for "noisy" conditions, so it's a "safe bet" for the "young crowd."

Boulud Sud *Mediterranean*

25 | 23 | 24 | $78

West 60s | 20 W. 64th St. (bet. B'way & CPW) | 212-595-1313 | www.bouludsud.com

"Lincoln Center–goers never had it so good" thanks to Daniel Boulud's "grown-up" Mediterranean "treat", where "engaging" staffers serve "glorious" cuisine in "spacious", "comfortable-chic" surroundings; it's simultaneously "expensive" and right "on the money", but its "high-end" fan base can handle the rates.

Bourgeois Pig *French*

∇ 23 | 22 | 21 | $30

Greenwich Village | 127 MacDougal St. (3rd St.) | 212-475-2246 | www.bourgeoispigny.com

"Quirky but cool", this "dimly lit" wine bar now occupies "cozy" Greenwich Village quarters, where the cheese board–led small bites "hit the spot" and "fondue enthusiasts" can dip into savory or sweet varieties; better still, the tabs leave its youngish fans "pleasantly surprised."

NEW Bowery Meat Co. *Steak*
25 | 23 | 23 | $95

East Village | 9 E. First St. (Bowery) | 212-460-5255 |
www.bowerymeatcompany.com
Restaurateur John McDonald (Burger & Barrel, Lure) "brings innovation"
to his East Village steakhouse, offering a menu that goes "far beyond"
the usual with "interesting" choices as well as "quality" chops; a retro
'60s vibe gives the space an "inviting" feel, and while tabs are predictably
"pricey", it still offers many reasons to "return again and again."

Brasserie *French*
22 | 21 | 22 | $58

East 50s | Seagram Bldg. | 100 E. 53rd St. (bet. Lexington & Park Aves.) |
212-751-4840 | www.patinagroup.com
A "tried-and-true" "crowd-pleaser", this sunken brasserie in the Seagram
Building remains a "go-to" for "delicious" French bites and "unpretentious" service in a "stylish", "futuristic space"; steadfast supporters keep
it "happening" (and "noisy") despite the "steep-ish prices."

Brasserie Cognac *French*
18 | 18 | 19 | $53

West 50s | 1740 Broadway (55th St.) | 212-757-3600 |
www.cognacrestaurant.com

Brasserie Cognac East *French*

East 70s | 963 Lexington Ave. (70th St.) | 212-249-5100 |
www.cognaceast.com
"Homesick Parisians" feel at home at these "debonair" brasseries where
"simple, tasty" standards come at "reasonable" prices; the West 50s
original is "convenient to Carnegie Hall" and City Center, but both locations are deemed "attractive" enough for a "romantic" tête-à-tête.

Brasserie 8½ *French*
22 | 23 | 22 | $64

West 50s | 9 W. 57th St. (bet. 5th & 6th Aves.) | 212-829-0812 |
www.patinagroup.com
Make an "entrance" down a "sweeping stairway" at this subterranean Midtown brasserie that provides "delicious" French fare and "cordial" service in
"charming" environs with "fine art on display"; it's a "decorous" nexus for
"conversational dining", albeit with a "busy" post-work bar scene.

Brasserie Ruhlmann *French*
18 | 20 | 20 | $60

West 50s | Rockefeller Ctr. | 45 Rockefeller Plaza (bet. 50th & 51st Sts.) |
212-974-2020 | www.brasserieruhlmann.com
"Hobnob with the NBC crowd" and others "happily expensing their
meals" at Laurent Tourondel's "heart-of-Rock-Center" brasserie providing a "sumptuous art deco" setting for "good" (if "not spectacular")
French cooking; the "fascinating people-watching" from its "amazing"
patio supplies added "fun."

Bread *Italian/Sandwiches*
21 | 17 | 18 | $32

NoLita | 20 Spring St. (bet. Elizabeth & Mott Sts.) | 212-334-1015 |
www.bread-nolita.com

Bread To Go *Italian/Sandwiches*

West Village | 450 Hudson St. (bet. Barrow & Morton Sts.) |
212-929-1015 | www.bread-togo.com
"Simple" Italian fare (including "must-try" tomato soup) makes for "simply good" meals at these "unassuming" all-day stops; both are tiny, but

the NoLita original has "just enough romantic appeal" for a "casual" date, while the West Village counter has a handful of back tables.

Brennan & Carr *Sandwiches*   22 | 11 | 18 | $19

Sheepshead Bay | 3432 Nostrand Ave. (Ave. U) | Brooklyn | 718-646-9559

More than 75 years old, this cash-only Sheepshead Bay "tradition" still "rocks" thanks to "outrageous" double-dipped roast beef sandwiches "drowned in au jus"; it's something of a "dive" with "table-mat menus", but enthusiasts of "old-fashioned goodness" keep returning "with the new generation in tow."

The Breslin *British*   22 | 20 | 20 | $54

NoMad | Ace Hotel | 16 W. 29th St. (bet. B'way & 5th Ave.) | 212-679-1939 | www.thebreslin.com

"Haute comfort food" reigns at April Bloomfield and Ken Friedman's "NY version of an English pub" in the Ace Hotel, dishing up "elevated", "unapologetically hearty" fare to the "über-hip throngs"; despite no reservations (except for hotel guests) and surplus "attitude", most find it "worth" the "steep" bill.

Bricco *Italian*   20 | 18 | 21 | $52

West 50s | 304 W. 56th St. (bet. 8th & 9th Aves.) | 212-245-7160 | www.bricconyc.com

This Midtown Italian hideaway is a "steady" source of "well-prepared" pasta and wood-oven pizza delivered by the "nicest staff"; "reasonable rates" and "warm" atmospherics (check out the lipsticked kisses on the ceiling) buttress its "reliable" rep.

Brick Cafe *Italian*   21 | 22 | 21 | $33

Astoria | 30-95 33rd St. (31st Ave.) | Queens | 718-267-2735 | www.brickcafe.com

Astorians assemble at this "neighborhood standby" for "tasty" Italian eats served in rustic digs so atmospheric it's "hard to believe you're in Queens"; "reasonable" rates, "can't-be-beat" alfresco tables and a sepa-rate bar area are other marks in its favor.

Brick Lane Curry House *Indian*   21 | 15 | 18 | $31

East 50s | 235 E. 53rd St. (bet. 2nd & 3rd Aves.) | 212-339-8353 | www.bricklanetoo.com
East 90s | 1664 Third Ave. (bet. 93rd & 94th Sts.) | 646-998-4440 | www.bricklane93rd.com
East Village | 99 Second Ave. (6th St.) | 212-979-2900 | www.bricklanecurryhouse.com

There's "no need to go to London – let alone India" – thanks to this curry-savvy East Side mini-chain purveying "real-deal" dishes with heat levels ranging from "mild to crazy hot" (the "fiery phaal" requires "extra napkins to wipe away the sweat and tears"); like the decor, the tabs are distinctly "low budget."

NEW Bricolage *Vietnamese*   – | – | – | M

Park Slope | 162 Fifth Ave. (Degraw St.) | Brooklyn | 718-230-1835 | www.bricolage.nyc

Alums from San Francisco's famed Slanted Door are behind this arrival to Park Slope's Fifth Avenue strip, offering a modern Vietnamese menu heavy on appetizers and an ambitious beer, wine and cocktail list; the brick-walled space has a low-key gastropub vibe, with candlelit tables, an open kitchen and a front bar area, plus a back patio.

Brindle Room   *American*   24 | 18 | 20 | $33

East Village | 277 E. 10th St. (Ave. A) | 212-529-9702 | www.brindleroom.com

It's all about the "worth-a-trip" burger at this compact but "cozy" East Villager that also features a "small" menu of "delicious" American dishes; some complain about "sitting on high stools", but at least the service and pricing are "accommodating."

Brioso   *Italian*   24 | 20 | 21 | $56

New Dorp | 174 New Dorp Ln. (9th St.) | Staten Island | 718-667-1700 | www.briosoristorante.com

A "vast" menu of "delectable" Italian dishes (plus lots of nightly specials) arrives in a white-tablecloth setting at this "rustic" Staten Island standby; some find the "festive" atmosphere verges on "noisy", but others say the "pro" service helps justify the pricey tabs.

BrisketTown   *BBQ*   24 | 15 | 20 | $30

Williamsburg | 359 Bedford Ave. (bet. 4th & 5th Sts.) | Brooklyn | 718-701-8909 | www.delaneybbq.com

Pitmaster Daniel Delaney is the mind behind this "destination" Williamsburg joint smoking "melt-in-your-mouth" BBQ – notably "unequaled" brisket – at "great prices"; a "friendly" counter crew and "rustic, old-wood" decor are also part of the package – just know it "can be crazy" at prime times, and when they run out of meat, it's closing time.

Brooklyn Crab   *Seafood*   20 | 19 | 19 | $44

Red Hook | 24 Reed St. (bet. Conover & Van Brunt Sts.) | Brooklyn | 718-643-2722 | www.brooklyncrab.com

From the owners of Alma, this "casual" Red Hook triplex fields a "solid" menu of fish-shack classics and raw bar snacks that taste even better given its "to-die-for" views of the harbor; additional perks like "fun" mini-golf and plenty of "outdoor seats" offset the "ridiculous" waits and "slow" service.

Brooklyn Farmacy   *Ice Cream*   24 | 27 | 23 | $16

Carroll Gardens | 513 Henry St. (Sackett St.) | Brooklyn | 718-522-6260 | www.brooklynfarmacy.blogspot.com

"Nostalgia" and seasonal, locally sourced ice cream add up to "a lot of fun" at this Carroll Gardens homage to "old-school soda shops", where the sundaes, egg creams and such – plus "simple, satisfying" diner staples – are "expertly" dispensed by "friendly" staffers; housed in a "beautiful" restored apothecary, it's "retro" to the core.

The Brooklyn Star   *Southern*   25 | 20 | 23 | $35

Williamsburg | 593 Lorimer St. (Conselyea St.) | Brooklyn | 718-599-9899 | www.thebrooklynstar.com

"Come hungry" to this "excellent" Williamsburg Southerner where "interesting takes" on "good ol'" American food are served up in "plentiful" portions; though it's "perennially packed" for brunch, the "reasonable" bills, "jovial" staff and "homey" vibe all add up to one "lucky find."

	FOOD	DECOR	SERVICE	COST

Brucie *Italian*
21 | **19** | **20** | **$40**

Cobble Hill | 234 Court St. (Baltic St.) | Brooklyn | 347-987-4961 |
www.brucienyc.com

Local foodies laud this Cobble Hill Italian "keeper" for its "always-changing" menu of "inventive" fare, served in "informal", rustic environs; talk about taking the "neighborhood restaurant" concept to the next level – drop off a pan and they'll bake you a take-home lasagna.

Brushstroke *Japanese*
26 | **26** | **26** | **$152**

TriBeCa | 30 Hudson St. (Duane St.) | 212-791-3771
Ichimura at Brushstroke *Japanese*
TriBeCa | 30 Hudson St. (Duane St.) | 212-791-3771
www.davidbouley.com

At this "Zen-like" TriBeCa Japanese from David Bouley and Osaka's Tsuji Culinary Institute, "little works of art" make up the "incredible" kaiseki menus, while the "brilliant" à la carte offerings include sushi so "extraordinary" it's akin to a "religious experience"; yes, it's "shockingly expensive", but those who manage a seat at "maestro" Eiji Ichimura's 12-person omakase "heaven" deem it "worth every yen."

Bryant Park Grill/Cafe *American*
18 | **21** | **19** | **$56**

West 40s | 25 W. 40th St. (bet. 5th & 6th Aves.) | 212-840-6500 |
www.bryantparkgrillnyc.com

"Primo" Bryant Park scenery is the main "selling point" of these American eateries, where "location, location, location" trumps the "pricey" tabs and rather "average" food and service; the Grill's the more "handsome" of the pair with both indoor and outdoor seats, while the alfresco-only Cafe is more of a "tourist magnet."

Bubby's *American*
21 | **17** | **18** | **$34**

TriBeCa | 120 Hudson St. (Moore St.) | 212-219-0666
Bubby's High Line *American*
Meatpacking District | 71 Gansevoort St. (bet. Greenwich & Washington Sts.) | 212-206-6200
www.bubbys.com

"Put your diet aside" for "hearty portions of comfort classics" at these "down-to-earth" Americans, home to "breakfast all day" and "mayhem" at brunch; the longtime TriBeCa original serves round-the-clock on weekends, while its Meatpacking sib boasts an "old-fashioned" soda fountain.

Buddakan *Asian*
25 | **26** | **22** | **$75**

Chelsea | 75 Ninth Ave. (bet. 15th & 16th Sts.) | 212-989-6699 |
www.buddakannyc.com

"Stunning" decor lends a "dark, sexy" backdrop to the "trendy" scene at Stephen Starr's Chelsea multilevel "mega room", a "bigger-than-life experience" where the "energetic" crowd is "blown away" by "flavorful" Asian dishes; just "bring earplugs" and sufficient funds to cover the "splurge."

Buddha Bodai *Chinese/Kosher*
22 | **10** | **17** | **$25**

Chinatown | 5 Mott St. (Worth St.) | 212-566-8388 |
www.chinatownvegetarian.com

"It may be fake meat", but the "sheer variety" and "excellent quality" of the "inventive" kosher vegetarian options "blow your mind" at this

Chinatown dim sum dojo; an "eclectic" following also feels blessed that it's so "reasonably priced."

Buenos Aires *Argentinean/Steak*   23 | 17 | 21 | $54

East Village | 513 E. Sixth St. (bet. Aves. A & B) | 212-228-2775 | www.buenosairesnyc.com

Beef eaters convene at this East Village Argentine steakhouse for "mouthwatering", chimichurri-slathered chops that you can "cut with a fork" and wash down with a "great selection of Malbecs"; forget the "don't-judge-a-book-by-its-cover" decor: "super" service and "gentle" tabs make this often-crowded spot a "keeper."

Bukhara Grill *Indian*   24 | 17 | 20 | $41

East 40s | 217 E. 49th St. (bet. 2nd & 3rd Aves.) | 212-888-2839 | www.bukharany.com

They "spice it up" at this "authentic" North Indian near the U.N., where the cooking's "tasty" and the service "courteous"; if it seems a bit "pricey" given the "nothing-to-write-home-about" digs, at least the lunch buffet is a "terrific bargain."

Bull & Bear *Steak*   21 | 22 | 22 | $84

East 40s | Waldorf-Astoria Hotel | 540 Lexington Ave. (bet. 49th & 50th Sts.) | 212-872-1275 | www.bullandbearsteakhouse.com

"Time travel" to *Mad Men* days at this circa-1960 Waldorf-Astoria steakhouse where "professional" servers ply *Wall Street Journal* subscribers with "quality" cuts ("strong" cocktails gratify those on a "liquid diet"); it's a NYC "tradition", assuming one can "bear what they charge" for those bulls.

Bun-Ker Vietnamese *Vietnamese*   ▽ 26 | 15 | 21 | $36

Ridgewood | 46-63 Metropolitan Ave. (bet. Onderdonk & Woodward Aves.) | Queens | 718-386-4282 | www.bunkervietnamese.com

A "delicious adventure" awaits at this way "out-of-the-way" Ridgewood Vietnamese, which renders "high-quality" street-food staples in a "hipsterish" "hole-in-the-wall" setting; since it won't cost a bundle many find it "well worth the trip."

Bunna Cafe *Ethiopian/Vegan*   ▽ 25 | 21 | 22 | $21

Bushwick | 1084 Flushing Ave. (Porter Ave.) | Brooklyn | 347-295-2227 | www.bunnaethiopia.net

"Interesting" takes on traditional Ethiopian cuisine result in "big flavors" at this cash-only Bushwick vegan, which also hosts live music and a tra-ditional coffee ceremony ("so cool"); the prices suit "shallow pockets", especially since "you won't leave hungry."

Burger & Barrel *Burgers/Pub Food*   22 | 20 | 19 | $42

SoHo | 25 W. Houston St. (bet. Greene & Mercer Sts.) | 212-334-7320 | www.burgerandbarrel.com

"Trendy" burgers, "barrel beers" and "wine on tap" collide in a "high-en-ergy" setting at this "happy" SoHo gastropub from the Lure Fishbar folks; sure, it's "loud", with "lighting so low you can barely see your food", but its "cool", cost-conscious crowd doesn't care.

NEW Burger & Lobster *American*

24 | 20 | 22 | $34

Flatiron | 39 W. 19th St. (bet. 5th & 6th Aves.) | 646-833-7532 |
www.burgerandlobster.com

"It's easy to decide what to eat" at this "no-muss-no-fuss" Flatiron American, a British import with a "simple" formula: a choice of lobster roll, steamed lobster or burger, "all well prepared" and a "complete steal"; staffers are "upbeat", and the "huge" setup is perfect for "large groups."

Burger Bistro *Burgers*

22 | 15 | 21 | $22

East 80s | 1663 First Ave. (bet. 86th & 87th Sts.) | 646-368-1134
Bay Ridge | 7217 Third Ave. (bet. 72nd & 73rd Sts.) | Brooklyn | 718-833-5833
Park Slope | 177 Fifth Ave. (bet. Berkeley & Lincoln Pls.) | Brooklyn |
718-398-9800
www.theburgerbistro.com

"So many options to choose from" is the hallmark of this born-in-Brooklyn "build-your-own-burger" chainlet offering "perfectly cooked" patties accessorized with "every topping imaginable"; "friendly" service and "cute", casual setups help keep 'em "busy."

Burger Joint *Burgers*

25 | 15 | 16 | $19

Greenwich Village | 33 W. Eighth St. (bet. 5th & 6th Aves.) | 212-432-1400
West 50s | Le Parker Meridien | 119 W. 56th St. (bet. 6th & 7th Aves.) |
212-708-7414
www.burgerjointny.com

"Daunting" lines through the Parker Meridien's "gorgeous lobby" lead to the "hidden" entry of this "down-and-dirty" dispensary of "superior burgers", where the service is "no-nonsense" and "getting a table is a contact sport"; the "quieter" Village offshoot features "plenty of seating" and "awesome boozy milkshakes."

Burke & Wills *Australian*

23 | 22 | 23 | $60

West 70s | 226 W. 79th St. (B'way) | 646-823-9251 |
www.burkeandwillsny.com

At this UWS "surprise" you'll find "beautifully done" fare off an "interesting" Australian menu that's "kangaroo inclusive" ("check out the 'roo burger"); its white-tiled bar and "greenhouse"-like dining area are "cool" places to hang, and there's also an upstairs speakeasy, Manhattan Cricket Club.

Bustan *Mediterranean*

23 | 20 | 21 | $56

West 80s | 487 Amsterdam Ave. (bet. 83rd & 84th Sts.) | 212-595-5050 |
www.bustannyc.com

A neighborhood "favorite", this "warm" Upper Westsider supplies "shockingly good" dishes from "all around the Mediterranean" (including "beyond-delicious" bread) via a "welcoming" staff; while the arty interior can be "crowded" and "noisy", the "sweet garden" is "a real draw."

Butcher Bar *BBQ*

24 | 19 | 19 | $29

Astoria | 37-08 30th Ave. (bet. 37th & 38th Sts.) | Queens |
718-606-8140 | www.butcherbar.com

Grass-fed local beef from the in-house organic butcher yields "absolutely awesome" BBQ (e.g. the "ethereal burnt ends") at this "friendly" Astoria smokehouse; now occupying "bigger and better" digs, it's still "nothing fancy" and still "packed" with 'cue hounds "coming back for more."

Butcher's Daughter *Vegan* `21` `21` `19` `$32`

NoLita | 19 Kenmare St. (Elizabeth St.) | 212-219-3434 |
www.thebutchersdaughter.com

Fans "feel healthier just entering" this all-day NoLita vegan cafe/juice
bar, a "hot spot" for "delicious" (if "pretty expensive") soups, sandwiches
and salads; the "rustic" white-tiled space exudes a sunny vibe, and
there's a take-out shop next door.

Butter *American* `23` `23` `20` `$72`

West 40s | Cassa Hotel | 70 W. 45th St. (bet. 5th & 6th Aves.) |
212-253-2828 | www.butterrestaurant.com

"Still hot" since its move to Midtown, this "upscale" New American from
Alex Guarnaschelli offers "creatively prepared" dishes in a "striking"
subterranean space; the "bustling" scene is "cool" for the area, even if
the "beautiful people" have mostly given way to a "business" crowd.

The Butterfly *American* `19` `16` `19` `$49`

TriBeCa | 225 W. Broadway (bet. Franklin & White Sts.) | 646-692-4943 |
www.thebutterflynyc.com

You're "transported back to the '50s" at this "retro" TriBeCa American,
where chef Michael White produces "comfort food with some style";
meanwhile, those who "expected better" still flutter by for "old-fash-
ioned-with-a-twist cocktails", swearing the "drinks are king."

Buttermilk Channel *American* `26` `21` `23` `$45`

Carroll Gardens | 524 Court St. (Huntington St.) | Brooklyn |
718-852-8490 | www.buttermilkchannelnyc.com

"Still going strong", this "sunny" Carroll Gardens "stalwart" supplies
"killer" fried chicken and other "excellent" New American comfort food
at the hands of a "gracious" crew; while often "busy", it's a "madhouse"
at brunch when limited reservations make for "long waits."

Buvette *French* `25` `23` `20` `$47`

West Village | 42 Grove St. (bet. Bedford & Bleecker Sts.) | 212-255-3590 |
www.ilovebuvette.com

"Ooh-la-la!", this West Village "godsend" "oozes charm" thanks to chef-
owner Jody Williams' "glorious" French small-plate fare served in "cute",
"pint-size" quarters by an "easygoing" crew; the "upbeat" vibe includes
"chairs bumping" at peak hours, but in warm weather there's always the
"lovely" (but equally "tiny") back garden.

BXL Cafe *Belgian* `20` `14` `18` `$33`

West 40s | 125 W. 43rd St. (6th Ave.) | 212-768-0200
BXL East *Belgian*
East 50s | 210 E. 51st St. (3rd Ave.) | 212-888-7782
BXL Zoute *Belgian*
Flatiron | 50 W. 22nd St. (6th Ave.) | 646-692-9282
www.bxlcafe.com

"Moules frites done right" chased with "awesome beers" explain the
"crush" at these "friendly" Belgian pubs; they're "nothing fancy" and can
be "way too noisy" at prime times, but the "price is right", particularly
the "endless mussel" special on Sunday and Monday nights.

	FOOD	DECOR	SERVICE	COST

Cabana *Nuevo Latino*
22 | 18 | 19 | $40

East 60s | 1022 Third Ave. (bet. 60th & 61st Sts.) | 212-980-5678
Forest Hills | 107-10 70th Rd. (bet. Austin St. & Queens Blvd.) | Queens | 718-263-3600
www.cabanarestaurant.com

It "always feels like a party" at these "casual", "colorful" Nuevo Latinos where "nicely spiced" chow and "rocket-fuel" mojitos make for a "happening" vibe; the "noise factor" and "erratic" service may be sore points, but at least the tabs are "reasonable."

Cacio e Pepe *Italian*
22 | 16 | 21 | $42

East Village | 182 Second Ave. (bet. 11th & 12th Sts.) | 212-505-5931 | www.cacioepepe.com

The "titular" signature pasta served in a "massive round" of pecorino is the star of the "traditional Roman" menu at this "sweet" East Village Italian; "pleasant" service and "fair prices" keep things "bustling", so regulars take "respite" in the "pretty" back garden.

Cafe Asean *SE Asian*
23 | 14 | 20 | $36

West Village | 117 W. 10th St. (bet. Greenwich & 6th Aves.) | 212-633-0348 | www.cafeasean.com

"Modest" looks belie the "well-crafted" Southeast Asian lineup purveyed at this "tiny" West Villager where the "inexpensive", cash-only menu "takes you further East with every bite"; an "easy vibe", "accommodating" service and a "serene" garden round out this "offbeat find."

Café Boulud *French*
27 | 24 | 26 | $90

East 70s | Surrey Hotel | 20 E. 76th St. (bet. 5th & Madison Aves.) | 212-772-2600 | www.cafeboulud.com

A "quintessential UES" fixture, Daniel Boulud's "civilized" "oasis" "hasn't skipped a beat" crafting "flawless" French fare that's "impeccably served" by a "professional staff" in a "charming" setting; well-to-do regulars "expect to pay" for the "extreme pleasure", though the lunch prix fixe is "a great deal for what you get."

Cafe Centro *French/Mediterranean*
22 | 20 | 22 | $53

East 40s | MetLife Bldg. | 200 Park Ave. (45th St.) | 212-818-1222 | www.patinagroup.com

An "escalator ride" from Grand Central, this "reliable" bistro offers "well-prepared" French-Med fare via an "efficient" crew in "classy" surrounds with an art deco bar and a sidewalk patio; at lunch it's "buzzing" with a "business crowd", but it "settles down" during the evening.

Cafe China *Chinese*
24 | 18 | 18 | $37

Murray Hill | 13 E. 37th St. (bet. 5th & Madison Aves.) | 212-213-2810 | www.cafechinanyc.com

Fans praise the "authentically spicy Sichuan" fare at this "inviting" Midtown Chinese that offers "outstanding" specialties in a setting recalling a "circa-1930 Shanghai teahouse"; "moderate" prices make some amends for sometimes "spotty service."

Cafe Clover *American*
24 | 23 | 22 | $63

West Village | 10 Downing St. (6th Ave.) | 212-675-4350 | www.cafeclovernyc.com

Health-conscious fare in a "chic" setting is the "refreshing" spin at this West

Village New American, where the cutting-edge locavore menu features "ultrafresh" vegetables in "creatively prepared" plates; "inviting" vibes and seasonal cocktails further help account for the "lively atmosphere."

Cafe Cluny *American/French*
23 | 21 | 22 | $52

West Village | 284 W. 12th St. (4th St.) | 212-255-6900 | www.cafecluny.com

A "wonderful vibe" has evolved at this "cute" West Village bistro, a once-"trendy" joint that's now a bona fide "neighborhood favorite" thanks to "terrific" Franco-American cooking served in a "charming", "sun-filled" space; since the weekend brunch can be a "free-for-all", regulars say "arrive early."

Café d'Alsace *French*
21 | 18 | 19 | $47

East 80s | 1695 Second Ave. (88th St.) | 212-722-5133 | www.cafedalsace.com

This "unpretentious" Yorkville brasserie is a "bustling" standby for "stick-to-your-ribs" Alsatian fare paired with an epic beer menu that merits its own sommelier; given the "too-close" quarters and "high decibels", many opt to sit outside, weather permitting.

Cafe El Presidente *Mexican*
20 | 20 | 20 | $30

Flatiron | 30 W. 24th St. (bet. 5th & 6th Aves.) | 212-242-3491 | www.cafeelpresidente.com

A "colorful" follow-up to Tacombi at Fonda NoLita, this "buzzy" Flatiron Mexican vends "tasty" tacos and street food in a "big" mercado-style space featuring a taqueria plus an on-site tortilleria and counters for coffee, juice and cocktails; with plenty of "super-casual" seating, it's a "popular" stop for "cheapish" eats.

Cafe Espanol *Spanish*
21 | 17 | 20 | $40

Greenwich Village | 172 Bleecker St. (Sullivan St.) | 212-505-0657 | www.cafeespanol.com

When you "don't want to spend much" on "traditional" Spanish fare, this "been-there-forever" Villager provides "satisfying" basics doled out in "generous", "paella-for-days" portions; sure, the space is "tight" and "hokey", but the sangria "always calls you back."

Cafe Evergreen *Chinese*
20 | 15 | 19 | $36

East 70s | 1367 First Ave. (bet. 73rd & 74th Sts.) | 212-744-3266 | www.cafeevergreenchinese.com

Upper Eastsiders who "don't want to schlep to Chinatown" depend on this "reliable" vet for "tasty" dim sum and other "solid" Chinese classics dished up by "pleasant" servers; the decor gets mixed responses, but there's always "speedy delivery."

Cafe Fiorello *Italian*
20 | 18 | 19 | $57

West 60s | 1900 Broadway (63rd St.) | 212-595-5330 | www.cafefiorello.com

"Convenience to Lincoln Center" makes this Italian vet a "swift"-paced "default" for "satisfying" staples like its "fresh antipasti bar" and "super pizza"; the interior gets "ridiculously crowded" and "chaotic" pre-performance, so "don't forget the outdoor seating."

	FOOD	DECOR	SERVICE	COST

Café Frida *Mexican*

20 | 16 | 18 | $42

West 70s | 368 Columbus Ave. (77th St.) | 212-712-2929 |
www.cafefrida.com

For a "Mexican fix", this UWS "staple" is a "steady" source of old-school fare and "standout" margaritas served amid "Hollywood backlot" decor; "reliable if not exciting", it's "popular" with the locals and "can get crowded."

Cafe Gitane *French/Moroccan*

22 | 19 | 17 | $33

NoLita | 242 Mott St. (Prince St.) | 212-334-9552
West Village | Jane Hotel | 113 Jane St. (bet. Washington & West Sts.) |
212-255-4113
www.cafegitanenyc.com

The food's a match for the "trendy vibe" at these "fashionable" French-Moroccan lairs where "affordable" bites like "fabulous" couscous are dispensed by a "gorgeous" staff; the NoLita original is on the "tight" side, but the more spread-out Jane Hotel spin-off is just as "energetic."

Café Habana *Cuban/Mexican*

23 | 19 | 17 | $24

NoLita | 17 Prince St. (Elizabeth St.) | 212-625-2001 | www.cafehabana.com

Habana Outpost *Cuban/Mexican*

Fort Greene | 757 Fulton St. (Portland Ave.) | Brooklyn | 718-858-9500 |
www.habanaoutpost.com

Habana To Go *Cuban/Mexican*

NoLita | 229 Elizabeth St. (Prince St.) | 212-625-2002 | www.cafehabana.com
NEW **Fort Greene** | 690 Fulton St. (Portland Ave.) | Brooklyn |
718-858-9500 | www.habanatogo.com

"Must-have" grilled corn, "addicting" Cuban sandwiches and "strong" margaritas are highlights on the "tasty, affordable" menu at these "buzzy" Cuban-Mexican kitchens with sister to-go outlets; the "tiny" "dinerlike" NoLita original is "usually packed" with a "young" crowd, while "it's all about the garden" at the seasonal, solar-powered Fort Greene outpost.

Café Henri *French*

23 | 17 | 17 | $26

Long Island City | 10-10 50th Ave. (Vernon Blvd.) | Queens |
718-383-9315 | www.henrinyc.com

"Quaint" and "always inviting", this all-day "slice of Paris" in LIC supplies "delicious" crêpes and other "simple" French bites at an agreeable "quality-to-price ratio"; it's "relaxed" *jour et nuit* "if you need a place to chat."

Cafe Katja *Austrian*

25 | 21 | 23 | $37

Lower East Side | 79 Orchard St. (bet. Broome & Grand Sts.) |
212-219-9545 | www.cafekatja.com

"Genuine" Austrian "classics" like wursts and schnitzel are "produced with a deft hand" at this Lower Eastsider, a "local hot spot" run by a "hospitable" team; the "homey" quarters, "excellent beer selection" and "companionable clientele" all play a part in the "gemütlichkeit."

Cafe Lalo *Coffee/Dessert*

18 | 20 | 15 | $27

West 80s | 201 W. 83rd St. (Amsterdam Ave.) | 212-496-6031 |
www.cafelalo.com

Famously "featured in *You've Got Mail*", this veteran UWS "sweetery" is ever a "tempting" rendezvous for "decadent desserts"; despite "wall-to-wall" tourists and "can't-be-bothered" service, it still makes fans "fall in love with NYC all over again."

Cafe Loup *French*

20 | 19 | 22 | $50

West Village | 105 W. 13th St. (6th Ave.) | 212-255-4746 | www.cafeloupnyc.com

Long a West Village "neighborhood standby", this "timeless" bistro is a "grown-up" nexus for "fairly priced" French fare "like *grand-mère* used to make" dispatched by a "personable" crew; the room may need "updating", but loyalists attest it's "worth repeating", especially for "Sunday jazz brunch."

Cafe Luluc *French*

21 | 17 | 19 | $30

Cobble Hill | 214 Smith St. (bet. Baltic & Butler Sts.) | Brooklyn | 718-625-3815

An "easy way to feel Parisian", this cash-only Cobble Hill bistro offers "satisfying" French food served "sans attitude" at "Brooklyn prices"; just "be ready to wait" on weekends – it's a renowned "brunch destination", flipping some of the "world's best pancakes."

Cafe Luxembourg *French*

21 | 19 | 21 | $58

West 70s | 200 W. 70th St. (bet. Amsterdam & West End Aves.) | 212-873-7411 | www.cafeluxembourg.com

By "now a neighborhood landmark", this "perennial favorite" brings a "touch of glamour" to the UWS with its "arty", "adult" crowd, Parisian atmosphere and "jolly" mood; the "simple" French cooking is "delicious" enough, but the "stargazing" and "eavesdropping" are even better.

Cafe Mogador *Moroccan*

24 | 19 | 20 | $35

East Village | 101 St. Marks Pl. (bet. Ave. A & 1st Ave.) | 212-677-2226
Williamsburg | 133 Wythe Ave. (bet. 7th & 8th Sts.) | Brooklyn | 718-486-9222
www.cafemogador.com

Popular with the "tattooed, leathered" set, this "go-to" East Village Moroccan and its indoor-garden-equipped Williamsburg sequel "have it down to a science", providing "memorable" tagines for "super-affordable" dough; to avoid "long waits" for the "delicious" brunch, go for "early dinner."

Cafe Orlin *American*

22 | 16 | 20 | $28

East Village | 41 St. Marks Pl. (2nd Ave.) | 212-777-1447 | www.cafeorlin.com

Something of a "neighborhood institution", this East Villager's "satisfying" American basics (with some Middle Eastern accents) are dished up in "mellow" confines; it's a "brunch hot spot", so "get there early" to avoid the line – and even earlier to snag a "coveted" outdoor seat.

Café Sabarsky *Austrian*

22 | 23 | 20 | $44

East 80s | Neue Galerie | 1048 Fifth Ave. (86th St.) | 212-288-0665
Café Fledermaus *Austrian*
East 80s | Neue Galerie | 1048 Fifth Ave., downstairs (86th St.) | 212-288-0665
www.kg-ny.com

Kurt Gutenbrunner's "civilized" Neue Galerie cafes transport you to "fin de siècle Vienna", with "exquisite pastries" and "vonderful" Austrian

| | | | FOOD | DECOR | SERVICE | COST |

savories dispensed in "glorious", "old-worldy" settings; Sabarsky is the "prettier" of the pair while Fledermaus is "easier to get into", but both are "pretty expensive."

Cafe Tallulah *French/Mediterranean*   20 | 21 | 20 | $52

West 70s | 240 Columbus Ave. (71st St.) | 212-209-1055 | www.cafetallulah.com

"Big and vibrant", this brasserielike Upper Westsider rates "all-around enjoyable" for "satisfying" French-Med plates and "carefully crafted" cocktails; the "comfortable" digs boast an "expansive" zinc bar and a "cool" downstairs lounge, and as extra incentive, it's "not astronomically priced."

Cafeteria *American*   20 | 19 | 18 | $34

Chelsea | 119 Seventh Ave. (17th St.) | 212-414-1717 | www.cafeteriagroup.com

With a 24/7 open-door policy, this longtime Chelsea "after-the-clubs" spot serves "dressed-up" American comfort classics to a crowd that "clearly expects to be watched"; though it's lost the "allure of years past", it's reassuring to know that it's there when you feel like "meatloaf and a Cosmopolitan at 3 AM."

Caffe e Vino *Italian*   22 | 16 | 21 | $40

Fort Greene | 112 DeKalb Ave. (bet. Ashland Pl. & St. Felix St.) | Brooklyn | 718-855-6222 | www.caffeevino.com

"Delightful", "rustic" Italian food is the thing at this "tiny but terrific" Fort Greene trattoria near BAM; the "unpretentious" setting (complete with "requisite brick wall") can be "cramped", but the "attentive" servers will "get you out well-fed" before curtain time.

Caffe Storico *Italian*   21 | 21 | 20 | $50

West 70s | NY Historical Society | 170 CPW (77th St.) | 212-485-9211 | www.caffestorico.com

"A lovely little secret", Stephen Starr's "charming" UWS Italian within the New-York Historical Society furnishes "artful" fare with Venetian leanings via "courteous" servers; "ladies who lunch" applaud a "bright, sunny" space that's "tastefully decorated" with china selected from the museum.

Calexico *Mexican*   21 | 17 | 19 | $24

Lower East Side | 153 Rivington St. (bet. Clinton & Suffolk Sts.) | 646-590-4172
Columbia Street Waterfront District | 122 Union St. (bet. Columbia & Hicks Sts.) | Brooklyn | 718-488-8226
Greenpoint | 645 Manhattan Ave. (Bedford Ave.) | Brooklyn | 347-763-2129
Park Slope | 278 Fifth Ave. (1st St.) | Brooklyn | 347-254-7644
www.calexico.net

Mexican food fans "all abuzz" over these "rough-and-ready" street-cart spin-offs call out their "outstanding", "Cali-inspired" tacos, tortas and burritos; "fabulous prices" and "fast service" offset the "simple" "hole-in-the-wall" settings; P.S. "make sure to get the 'crack' sauce on anything you order."

| | FOOD | DECOR | SERVICE | COST |

Calle Ocho *Nuevo Latino*

21 | 21 | 21 | $48

West 80s | Excelsior Hotel | 45 W. 81st St. (bet. Columbus Ave. & CPW) | 212-873-5025 | www.calleochonyc.com

The "gourmet aspirations" are still "interesting" and the "fabulous mojitos" still flowing at this Upper West Side Nuevo Latino vet situated in "attractive" Excelsior Hotel digs; weekends the "party" picks up during the "unlimited sangria brunch" (just "bring a designated driver").

Campagnola *Italian*

24 | 18 | 23 | $73

East 70s | 1382 First Ave. (74th St.) | 212-861-1102 | www.campagnolany-hub.com

All eyes are on the "floor show" at this "old-school" UES veteran where the stellar people-watching is on par with the "excellent", "garlicky" Italian cooking and "all-business" service; for best results, "go with somebody they know" – it's much "better if you're a regular" – and better yet if you bring "someone else's expense account."

Candle Cafe *Vegan/Vegetarian*

24 | 20 | 23 | $40

East 70s | 1307 Third Ave. (bet. 74th & 75th Sts.) | 212-472-0970
Candle Cafe West *Vegan/Vegetarian*

West 80s | 2427 Broadway (bet. 89th & 90th Sts.) | 212-769-8900 www.candlecafe.com

Candle 79's crosstown cousins lure "Gwyneth Paltrow wannabes" with "intriguing" vegan eats "prepared with love"; though the low-key East Side locale is "cramped", things are more "upscale" if you head west – either way the cooking is "right-on" at both.

Candle 79 *Vegan/Vegetarian*

26 | 23 | 24 | $50

East 70s | 154 E. 79th St. (bet. Lexington & 3rd Aves.) | 212-537-7179 | www.candle79.com

"Tasting is believing" at this UES vegan "fine-dining" "phenom" that "sets the standard" with "quality-sourced", "distinctive" organic dishes and wines delivered by "enthusiastic" servers in "intimate", "classic" digs; a "pleasant departure from meaty fare", it's "so worth" the "premium price."

The Cannibal *Belgian*

22 | 15 | 20 | $43

Murray Hill | 113 E. 29th St. (bet. Lexington & Park Aves.) | 212-686-5480
West 40s | Gotham West Mkt. | 600 11th Ave. (bet. 44th & 45th Sts.) | 212-582-7947
www.thecannibalnyc.com

You can feed "your inner carnivore" at these Resto offshoots where "meat-centric" Belgian gastropub fare pairs with a "phenomenal" beer list; the "so-small" Murray Hill original draws "endless crowds" and has a "noisy" "social" scene, while the Gotham West counter is pretty "lively" too.

The Capital Grille *Steak*

25 | 23 | 24 | $77

East 40s | 155 E. 42nd St. (bet. Lexington & 3rd Aves.) | 212-953-2000
Financial District | 120 Broadway (Pine St.) | 212-374-1811
West 50s | 120 W. 51st St. (bet. 6th & 7th Aves.) | 212-246-0154 | www.thecapitalgrille.com

"Power brokers seal deals" while others mark "special occasions" at these steakhouses known for "top-notch" beef "prepared with care" and "impressive" wines delivered by "pro" staffers in "refined", "contemporary" rooms; the Chrysler Center locale is particularly "splendid", but they're all a "splurge."

Caracas Arepa Bar *Venezuelan*　　26 | 18 | 20 | $20

East Village | 93½ E. Seventh St. (bet. Ave. A & 1st Ave.) | 212-529-2314

Caracas Brooklyn *Venezuelan*

Williamsburg | 291 Grand St. (bet. Havemeyer & Roebling Sts.) | Brooklyn | 718-218-6050

Caracas Rockaway *Venezuelan*

Rockaway Park | 106-01 Shore Front Pkwy. (Beach 106th St.) | Queens | 718-474-1709

Caracas to Go *Venezuelan*

East Village | 91 E. Seventh St. (1st Ave.) | 212-228-5062 www.caracasarepabar.com

Vending "real-deal" arepas with "piping-hot" fillings so "addictive" you'll "want to try them all", these "cheerful" Venezuelans "hit the spot" "for little money"; if the East Village "shoebox" is a bit "squished" (nearby To Go is "great for takeaway"), the patio-equipped Williamsburg site is "more low-key" and there's always "watching the surf" in Rockaway.

Cara Mia *Italian*　　21 | 16 | 20 | $43

West 40s | 654 Ninth Ave. (bet. 45th & 46th Sts.) | 212-262-6767 | www.caramianyc.com

"Not fancy but plenty comfortable", this "red-sauce" Italian is a Theater District "standby" for homemade pasta and "spot-on" service; granted, it's "space-challenged" and "crazy busy" pre-curtain, but at least you can mangia "without paying an arm and a leg."

Caravaggio *Italian*　　25 | 25 | 25 | $88

East 70s | 23 E. 74th St. (bet. 5th & Madison Aves.) | 212-288-1004 | www.caravaggioristorante.com

More than "just dining out", this "refined" UES Italian is a "special-occasion" nexus owing to its "sophisticated" cooking, "flawless" service and "exquisite" modern setting; "money is no object" for most of its "mature" fan base, though frugal folks find the prix fixe lunch quite "enticing."

Caravan of Dreams *Kosher/Vegan*　　23 | 17 | 20 | $30

East Village | 405 E. Sixth St. (1st Ave.) | 212-254-1613 | www.caravanofdreams.net

A dream come true for "healthy food" fanatics, this East Village vet offers "transformative" kosher vegan fare in "mellow", "bohemian" quarters; fair prices and occasional "live music" enhance its "aura of peace and satisfaction", making followers "feel good inside and out."

Carbone *Italian*　　24 | 22 | 23 | $99

Greenwich Village | 181 Thompson St. (bet. Bleecker & Houston Sts.) | 212-254-3000 | www.carbonenewyork.com

An "homage" to "traditional Italian-American cuisine", this "lively" Village "hit" from the Torrisi team (Dirty French, Parm) turns out "huge portions" of "delectable" dishes (including a "divine veal parm") for a beyond-"hefty" price; the mood is "Rat Pack", the soundtrack classic "Motown" and the "maroon-tuxedoed waiters" recall the days when "service came first" – no wonder it's "nearly impossible" to get reservations, but "so worth trying."

	FOOD	DECOR	SERVICE	COST

The Carlyle Restaurant *French*   24 | 27 | 25 | $87

East 70s | Carlyle Hotel | 35 E. 76th St. (Madison Ave.) | 212-570-7192 |
www.thecarlyle.com

"Synonymous with class", this "old-world" room in the Carlyle Hotel
holds "fond memories" for a "blue-blood" fan base in thrall to its
"refined" New French fare, "royal-treatment" service and "Dorothy
Draper"–esque digs; plan to wear your "finest baubles" (jackets required
for dinner), and be prepared for "super-premium prices."

Carmine's *Italian*   22 | 18 | 20 | $45

West 40s | 200 W. 44th St. (bet. 7th & 8th Aves.) | 212-221-3800
West 90s | 2450 Broadway (bet. 90th & 91st Sts.) | 212-362-2200
www.carminesnyc.com

Built for "group feasting", these "boisterous", "fast-paced" Italians
offer "whirlwind experiences in family-style dining" via "large platters"
of "red-sauce" cooking with a "punch of garlic"; granted, the Times
Square outlet may be too "touristy" for some, but overall "you can't beat
it for taste and value."

Carnegie Deli *Deli*   23 | 12 | 16 | $31

West 50s | 854 Seventh Ave. (55th St.) | 212-757-2245 |
www.carnegiedeli.com

"Sandwiches large enough to fill Carnegie Hall" set the "oversized" mood
at this "iconic" all-day Midtowner that's been dishing out "scrumptious"
deli (and "lots of leftovers") to "loud" crowds since 1937; despite "plain"
looks, "famously surly" service and "elbow-to-elbow" seating, the experience is "always entertaining", starting with the "starry-eyed tourists"
looking for "Woody Allen"; P.S. closed at press time.

Carol's Cafe *Eclectic*   ∇ 24 | 18 | 21 | $63

Todt Hill | 1571 Richmond Rd. (bet. 4 Corners Rd. & Garretson Ave.) |
Staten Island | 718-979-5600 | www.carolscafe.com

"Thoughtful", "Manhattan-quality" cooking via chef Carol Frazzetta is
yours at this "pretty" Eclectic standby in Staten Island's Todt Hill; maybe
the tabs run "a little high" for these parts, but "perfect-ending" desserts
and weekly "cooking lessons" sweeten the pot.

Casa Enrique *Mexican*   26 | 18 | 22 | $40

Long Island City | 5-48 49th Ave. (bet. 5th St. & Vernon Blvd.) | Queens |
347-448-6040 | www.henrinyc.com

A "fresh take on Mexican", this LIC sib to Cafe Henri is a "hidden" local
"favorite" for "incredible" regional cooking crafted with a "complex",
Chiapas-style "twist" and "served with a smile" for "reasonable" pesos; if
the cantinalike quarters seem "sparse", well "it's not about the decor."

Casa Lever *Italian*   22 | 23 | 22 | $80

East 50s | Lever House | 390 Park Ave. (53rd St.) | 212-888-2700 |
www.casalever.com

Luring Park Avenue "power" players, this Midtown Milanese from the
Sant Ambroeus team offers "delicious" chow delivered by an "attentive" crew; set in the "historic" Lever House, the "modernist" room lined
with "wall-to-wall Warhols" is so "fashionable" that many say you're
"paying for the style" here.

	FOOD	DECOR	SERVICE	COST

Casa Mono *Spanish* 25 | 18 | 21 | $62

Gramercy Park | 52 Irving Pl. (17th St.) | 212-253-2773 |
www.casamononyc.com

"Inspired" tapas and an "encyclopedic" selection of Spanish vintages
pack the house nightly at this "standout" Gramercy tapas bar from Mario
Batali; sure, it's "like eating in a phone booth", and tabs "can mount up",
but "who cares when the grub's this good?"

Casa Nonna *Italian* 22 | 21 | 21 | $52

West 30s | 310 W. 38th St. (bet. 8th & 9th Aves.) | 212-736-3000 |
www.casanonna.com

A "perfect place to unwind" near the Javits Center, this Italian has its "act
together" offering "creative glosses" on Roman-Tuscan standards served
with "quick" "professionalism"; it's a "relaxing" option in a "lacking" dining zone, with well-spaced tables allowing for "private conversations."

Cascabel Taqueria *Mexican* 19 | 15 | 16 | $30

East 80s | 1556 Second Ave. (81st St.) | 212-717-8226
West 100s | 2799 Broadway (108th St.) | 212-665-1500
www.nyctacos.com

"Ay caramba", these "popular" taquerias are about as "legitimate" as
you'll find in these parts, slinging "above-average" tacos in "funky" quarters; "bargain" tabs and "downtown" vibes keep them "overwhelmingly
busy", so expect service that's "cheerful" but "not very polished."

Casellula *American* 25 | 19 | 21 | $44

West 50s | 401 W. 52nd St. (bet. 9th & 10th Aves.) | 212-247-8137 |
www.casellula.com

"First-date" places don't get much more "cute" than this rustic Hell's
Kitchen cheese specialist where the "never-ending" wine and fromage
list is available nightly till 2 AM; the "little sliver" of a setting is "cozy" to
some, "tight" to others, but the "bustling" mood speaks for itself.

Cata *Spanish* ∇ 22 | 22 | 20 | $55

Lower East Side | 245 Bowery (bet. Rivington & Stanton Sts.) |
212-505-2282 | www.catarestaurant.com

"Taking tapas to the next level", this "low-key" Bowery Spaniard from
the Alta crew offers both "creative and traditional" small plates in a
"relaxed", brick-lined room outfitted with a dining counter and communal
tables; regulars recommend "working your way" through its "extensive
gin-and-tonic selection", 23 versions at last count.

Catch *Seafood* 23 | 22 | 19 | $75

Meatpacking District | 21 Ninth Ave. (bet. Little W. 12th & 13th Sts.) |
212-392-5978 | www.emmgrp.com

"Beautiful people" and random "Kardashians" populate this "trendy"
Meatpacking "scene" where the "fresh" seafood is dispensed by
"Abercrombie model"–like staffers in a sprawling, "pumping" duplex
with a rooftop lounge; reservations can be somewhat hard to catch
despite the "expensive" tabs.

Catfish *Cajun* 22 | 20 | 21 | $26

Crown Heights | 1433 Bedford Ave. (bet. Park & Prospect Pl.) | Brooklyn |
347-305-3233 | www.catfishnyc.com

Like a "trip up the bayou" in Crown Heights, this "friendly" neighborhood joint features Cajun faves like catfish po' boys and shrimp 'n' grits "done right" and "reasonably priced"; "theme-appropriate" drinks boost the "New Orleans vibe", and there's a popular "patio in the back."

Ça Va *French*

21 | 20 | 21 | $59

West 40s | InterContinental Hotel Times Sq. | 310 W. 44th St. (bet. 8th & 9th Aves.) | 212-803-4545 | www.cavatoddenglish.com

"Above the norm" for the Theater District, Todd English's "sleek" hotel brasserie delivers a "varied" menu of "reliable" French eats; despite somewhat "steep" tabs, the "convenient" locale and "attractive" enough space make it "a good bet" for a "leisurely" pre-show meal.

Caviar Russe *American*

24 | 23 | 21 | $110

East 50s | 538 Madison Ave., 2nd fl. (bet. 54th & 55th Sts.) | 212-980-5908 | www.caviarrusse.com

The "decadent experience" at this Midtown New American "conjures up tsars" as patrons are "pampered" with "exquisite caviar" and crudo from "knowledgeable" staffers in "deluxe" digs suitable for an "illicit affair"; prices are predictably "astronomical", but big spenders urge "indulge in this when you can."

Cávo *Greek*

20 | 24 | 18 | $45

Astoria | 42-18 31st Ave. (bet. 42nd & 43rd Sts.) | Queens | 718-721-1001 | www.cavoastoria.com

A "cool-looking", "spacious" setting is the lure at this "upscale" Astoria Greek offering "solid" Hellenic fare that's upstaged by its "spectacular", waterfall-equipped garden; just be aware it "can get pricey" and "loud" – as the evening progresses, it becomes "more of a nightclub."

Cebu *Continental*

22 | 19 | 19 | $38

Bay Ridge | 8801 Third Ave. (88th St.) | Brooklyn | 718-492-5095 | www.cebubrooklyn.com

"Large" and "busy", this "reasonably priced" Continental brings a bit of "Manhattan chic" to Bay Ridge via an "enjoyable" menu, "on-the-ball" service and night-owl noshing; "younger" folks with "fake tans" keep the bar scene "buzzing."

The Cecil *American/Eclectic*

23 | 22 | 21 | $58

Harlem | 210 W. 118th St. (St. Nicholas Ave.) | 212-866-1262 | www.thececilharlem.com

"A top choice in Harlem", this "inviting" hot spot "doesn't miss a note" as chef Alexander Smalls' "inventive and delicious" Afro-Asian-American "mélange" is presented by a "hospitable staff" in a "vibrant" space that's "brimming with energy"; it can get "crowdy" and "expensive", but the experience is "always a treat."

Celeste *Italian*

23 | 11 | 16 | $37

West 80s | 502 Amsterdam Ave. (bet. 84th & 85th Sts.) | 212-874-4559 | www.celestenewyork.com

"Celestial" Neapolitan cooking, "wonderful" cheese plates and "tough-to-beat" tabs make for "crammed" conditions at this UWS "winner", whose engaging owner is "part of the experience"; despite "no rezzies", no credit cards and "little ambiance", "long lines" are the norm here.

	FOOD	DECOR	SERVICE	COST

Cellini *Italian*

| 22 | 18 | 21 | $57 |

East 50s | 65 E. 54th St. (bet. Madison & Park Aves.) | 212-751-1555 | www.cellinirestaurant.com

A "staple" for "entertaining clients", this "expense-account" Midtowner draws a "chatty lunch crowd" with "authentic", "sure-bet" Italian standards served in a "not-so-fancy" setting; it's more subdued come suppertime, but you can expect "comfortable, grown-up" dining at any hour.

'Cesca *Italian*

| 22 | 20 | 20 | $64 |

West 70s | 164 W. 75th St. (Amsterdam Ave.) | 212-787-6300 | www.cescanyc.com

Seekers of "civilized" surrounds "pack" this "comfortable" UWS "standby" for "consistently solid" Italian fare at "slightly-above-average" prices; if it's lost some former "pizzazz", the "vibrant" (if "noisy") front bar and "accommodating" staff still keep many returning to it "like an old friend."

Cha An *Japanese/Teahouse*

| 22 | 23 | 21 | $27 |

East Village | 230 E. Ninth St. (bet. 2nd & 3rd Aves.) | 212-228-8030 | www.chaanteahouse.com

A "hideaway" from East Village "hustle and bustle", this "tranquil" second-story "sanctuary" offers "quality" Japanese teas, "delicate bites" and "inventive" desserts; though the "traditional" environs can get "busy", at least credit cards are now accepted.

Chadwick's *American*

| 24 | 19 | 24 | $50 |

Bay Ridge | 8822 Third Ave. (89th St.) | Brooklyn | 718-833-9855 | www.chadwicksbrooklyn.com

On the Bay Ridge scene since '87, this American "stroll down memory lane" bats out a "solid" menu dispatched by "old-time waiters" who "treat you right"; the decor may "need a little uplift", but the "value" is intact, notably its "early-bird specials" Monday–Thursday.

Chalk Point Kitchen *American*

| 24 | 22 | 22 | $53 |

SoHo | 527 Broome St. (Thompson St.) | 212-390-0327 | www.chalkpointkitchen.com

"Creative" and "delicious" sums up the fare at this SoHo American where a "fresh-from-the-farm" menu includes "tons" of "vegetable-centric" options; reclaimed wood and exposed brick keep the "comfortable" space casual, and there's also a "cool" downstairs lounge, the Handy Liquor Bar.

Charlie Bird *American*

| 23 | 20 | 21 | $69 |

SoHo | 5 King St. (6th Ave.) | 212-235-7133 | www.charliebirdnyc.com

The "scene buzzes" at this SoHo "destination" for "thinsters glamming it up" over "spot-on" American fare with Italian "twists" and an "incredible" wine list; flaunting "hip-hop inspiration" with boom-box prints and "loud beats in the background", it's "too cool for school", which is why it's a "hot" ticket.

NEW Charlie Palmer at The Knick *American*

| ▽ 27 | 27 | 25 | $92 |

West 40s | Knickerbocker Hotel | 6 Times Sq. (bet. B'way & 42nd St.) | 855-865-6425 | www.theknickerbocker.com

Charlie Palmer "raises the bar" in Times Square with this "expensive" Knickerbocker Hotel dining room, serving "impressive" upscale Ameri-

| | FOOD | DECOR | SERVICE | COST |

can fare in contemporary surrounds done up in soothing hues; add the adjacent lounge with a roving martini cart, and it's a natural for "delightful" pre- and post-theater "repasts."

Charlie Palmer Steak *Steak*
24 | 22 | 23 | $81

East 50s | 3 E. 54th St. (5th Ave.) | 646-559-8440 | www.charliepalmer.com

A "classic" steakhouse menu highlighted by "well-prepared" chops and "step-above" sides make this outpost of Charlie Palmer's chophouse franchise a "nice addition to Midtown"; "yes, expensive" tabs are part of the deal, but so are "attentive" service and a "classy" modern setting.

Chavela's *Mexican*
24 | 24 | 23 | $25

Crown Heights | 736 Franklin Ave. (Sterling Pl.) | Brooklyn | 718-622-3100 | www.chavelasnyc.com

This Crown Heights Mexican "shines" with "fantastic" cuisine, a "quick" staff and prices that "don't hurt"; sure, "there's always a wait" to get in, but the reward – at least according to margarita drinkers – is a "permanent smile on your face."

Chef Ho's Peking Duck Grill *Chinese*
22 | 14 | 19 | $35

East 80s | 1720 Second Ave. (bet. 89th & 90th Sts.) | 212-348-9444 | www.chefho.com

De-ho-tees say the "crispy, juicy" Peking duck is some of the "best" around at this "old-school" Yorkville Chinese, a "neighborhood favorite" also lauded for its "above-average" cooking, "below-average" tabs and "efficient" service; fans say it's so good that there's "no need to go to Chinatown."

NEW Chefs Club by Food & Wine *American*
∇ 24 | 26 | 22 | $88

NoLita | Puck Bldg. | 275 Mulberry St. (Jersey St.) | 212-941-1100 | www.chefsclub.com

"Get in while you still can" say fans of this "under-the-radar" NoLita showcase from *Food & Wine* magazine, where the seasonal New American menu includes "exciting" dishes designed by notable chefs and some of F&W's 'Best New Chefs' prepare "sublime" tasting menus a few nights a month; a sizable open kitchen makes the "beautiful" loft space even more "cool."

Chef's Table at Brooklyn Fare *French*
26 | 19 | 25 | $332

Downtown Brooklyn | Brooklyn Fare | 200 Schermerhorn St. (bet. Bond & Hoyt Sts.) | Brooklyn | 718-243-0050 | www.brooklynfare.com

"Dinner as theater" comes alive at this "king of all chef's tables", an 18-seat counter in a Downtown Brooklyn kitchen, where "inventive" chef César Ramirez unveils a 15-plus-course tasting menu of "sophisticated", Japanese-influenced French plates; it makes for "unique" communal dining, and while it's "impossible to get in" – and quite expensive – word is this "amazing experience" is "absolutely" worth it.

Cherche Midi *French*
22 | 21 | 22 | $66

NoLita | 282 Bowery (Houston St.) | 212-226-3055 | www.cherchemidiny.com

You can "take a quick trip to Paris" courtesy of Keith McNally's upscale Bowery French where a "caring" team delivers "well-prepared" bistro

	FOOD	DECOR	SERVICE	COST

classics including "must-try" prime rib and an "unbelievable" burger; filled with "flattering light", the "carefully distressed" space is often "bustling" and perfect for "people-watching."

Cherry *Japanese*
22 | 23 | 19 | $63

Chelsea | Dream Downtown Hotel | 355 W. 16th St. (bet. 8th & 9th Aves.) | 212-929-5800

Cherry Izakaya *Japanese*

Williamsburg | 138 N. Eighth St. (Berry St.) | Brooklyn | 347-889-6300 | www.cherrynyc.com

This "sexy" basement burrow in Chelsea's Dream Hotel and its Williamsburg izakaya follow-up deliver "deliciously innovative" Japanese fusion cuisine ("inventive" sushi included); the original's "bordello"-like red-and-black interior provides "perfect date ambiance" (and more "expensive" bills), while the Tokyo-inspired sequel is a "cool" place to hang.

NEW Chevalier *French*
▽ 22 | 23 | 21 | VE

West 50s | Baccarat Hotel | 30 W. 53rd St. (bet. 5th and 6th Aves.) | 212-790-8869 | www.baccarathotels.com

A "lovely", "roomy" setting with comfortably spaced tables, leather banquettes and chandeliers galore provides the backdrop for a "small" but "exciting" menu of "beautifully prepared" French dishes at this posh brasserie in Midtown's Baccarat Hotel; "over-the-top" prices aren't unexpected given the "high-end" experience.

Chez Jacqueline *French*
20 | 18 | 21 | $52

Greenwich Village | 72 MacDougal St. (bet. Bleecker & Houston Sts.) | 212-505-0727 | www.chezjacquelinerestaurant.com

This "unassuming", "been-there-forever" Village bistro has a "winning way" thanks to "satisfying" traditional French fare served by a "charming" staff that "keeps the vin rouge flowing"; maybe you "won't be surprised by any of the dishes", but most report "pleasant times" here.

Chez Josephine *French*
22 | 24 | 23 | $57

West 40s | 414 W. 42nd St. (bet. Dyer & 9th Aves.) | 212-594-1925 | www.chezjosephine.com

They "hit the right notes" at this "stalwart" Theater District "tribute to Josephine Baker", an "old-style Parisian" boîte featuring "capable" French bistro fare from a "welcoming" staff (though "sui generis" host Jean-Claude "will be missed"); colorful "boudoir" decor and a pianist "tinkling the ivories" boost the "theatrical vibe."

Chez Lucienne *French*
22 | 19 | 20 | $48

Harlem | 308 Lenox Ave. (bet. 125th & 126th Sts.) | 212-289-5555 | www.chezlucienne.com

"Parisian soul" is the thing at this French bistro on a happening stretch of Harlem's Lenox Avenue, where the midpriced Gallic grub is as "genuine" as the "accommodating" service; it's a "great alternative" to Red Rooster next door, and sidewalk seats supply "people-watching" galore.

Chez Napoléon *French*
22 | 16 | 23 | $52

West 50s | 365 W. 50th St. (bet. 8th & 9th Aves.) | 212-265-6980 | www.cheznapoleon.com

"Vérité" could be the motto of this circa-1960 Theater District "relic" where an "old-school" crew dispatches "time-stood-still" French bistro classics à la escargot, frogs' legs and calf's brains; the "tiny" setting exudes "faded elegance", but prices are "moderate" and you're "there to eat, not sightsee."

ChikaLicious *Dessert*

25 | 15 | 20 | $18

East Village | 203 E. 10th St. (bet. 1st & 2nd Aves.) | 212-475-0929
East Village | 204 E. 10th St. (bet. 1st & 2nd Aves.) | 212-475-0929
NEW **ChikaLicious Dessert Club** *Dessert*
West Village | 27 Bedford St. (Downing St.) | 212-691-2426
www.chikalicious.com

For desserts so "delicious" they'll "knock you over", these "charming" sweets bars are a "must", offering "imaginative" tasting menus and wine pairings too; the "tiny" East Village original is joined by an across-the-street bakery for "creative" treats to go, while the West Village offshoot offers both the prix fixe option and a counter for takeout.

Chimichurri Grill *Argentinean/Steak*

24 | 17 | 22 | $56

West 40s | 609 Ninth Ave. (bet. 43rd & 44th Sts.) | 212-586-8655 | www.chimichurrigrill.com

"Well-cooked" Argentine steaks topped with the namesake sauce thrill carnivores at this "tiny" Hell's Kitchen hideout; "efficient" staffers and "reasonable" pricing make it a natural for the "pre-theater" crowd, who only "wishes it had more tables."

China Grill *Asian*

22 | 22 | 21 | $59

West 50s | 60 W. 53rd St. (bet. 5th & 6th Aves.) | 212-333-7788 | www.chinagrillmgt.com

Long a bastion of "upmarket chic", this Midtown "powerhouse" offers "fancy takes" on Asian cuisine served in "dark", airy digs with an "'80s James Bond" vibe; it's "deafeningly loud" and "definitely not a bargain", but "business" types still belly up for its "fun bar scene."

ChipShop *British*

20 | 16 | 20 | $26

Brooklyn Heights | 129 Atlantic Ave. (bet. Clinton & Henry Sts.) | Brooklyn | 718-855-7775 | www.chipshopnyc.com

The "fried goodness" "hits the spot" at this Brooklyn Heights British pub and "cardiac alert zone", where Anglophiles scarf staples like "scrumptious" fish 'n' chips and deep-fried candy bars; set to a "child-of-the-'80s" soundtrack, it's a "true English experience" that "can easily become habit-forming."

Chocolate Room *Dessert*

25 | 20 | 22 | $21

Cobble Hill | 269 Court St. (bet. Butler & Douglass Sts.) | Brooklyn | 718-246-2600
Park Slope | 51 Fifth Ave. (bet. Bergen St. & St. Marks Ave.) | Brooklyn | 718-783-2900
www.thechocolateroombrooklyn.com

"Paradise" for the "chocolate lover", these "welcoming" Brooklyn dessert cafes specialize in indulgences like sundaes, floats and "life-changing" cakes; there are also wine, bubbles and even cocoa-based stouts, so it's got all of the ingredients for a "great date place."

	FOOD	DECOR	SERVICE	COST

Cho Dang Gol *Korean*
23 | 14 | 16 | $33

West 30s | 55 W. 35th St. (bet. 5th & 6th Aves.) | 212-695-8222 |
www.chodanggolny.com

"Real-deal" Korean cooking is offered at this "step-above" K-town joint
that's famous for its "luscious" homemade tofu; "low prices", "utilitarian"
decor and "typical" service are all part of the package, along with a "full
house" at prime times.

Chola *Indian*
23 | 15 | 19 | $43

East 50s | 232 E. 58th St. (bet. 2nd & 3rd Aves.) | 212-688-4619 |
www.cholamidtowneast.com

"Spices abound" at this "delectable" Indian on East 58th Street's sub-
continental strip, supplying a "wide-ranging" roster of "complex" dishes;
tariffs are generally "moderate", but for "quality and selection" the buffet
lunch provides true "value for the money."

NEW Chomp Chomp *Singaporean*
— | — | — | M

West Village | 7 Cornelia St. (4th St.) | 212-929-2888 |
www.chompchompnyc.com

Devoted to Singaporean hawker fare, this West Villager by chef-owner
Simpson Wong (Café Asean) serves noodles, rice dishes and snacks;
the thoughtfully designed space incorporates whitewashed brick walls,
ornate Chinese doors and an open kitchen, plus the unexpected touch of
classroom-style wooden chairs.

Christos Steak House *Steak*
24 | 19 | 22 | $74

Astoria | 41-08 23rd Ave. (41st St.) | Queens | 718-777-8400 |
www.christossteakhouse.com

"Fabulous" cuts of meat plus apps and sides with a "Greek twist" are
"cheerfully served" at this Astoria "neighborhood steakhouse"; it's "not
cheap" for these parts and the space "could be fixed up", but hey, the
valet parking's a "real winner."

Chuko *Japanese/Noodle Shop*
26 | 20 | 22 | $25

Prospect Heights | 552 Vanderbilt Ave. (Dean St.) | Brooklyn |
718-576-6701 | www.barchuko.com

Acclaimed as the "ramen of choice", this cash-only Prospect Heights
Japanese doles out "exceptional" pork or vegetarian "slurpers" that
merge "full-bodied" broths with "pliant" noodles known for "just the
right chew"; space is "tight" and reservations aren't taken, so "expect
to wait" with "the masses."

Churrascaria Plataforma *Brazilian/Steak*
24 | 21 | 23 | $82

West 40s | 316 W. 49th St. (bet. 8th & 9th Aves.) | 212-245-0505 |
www.churrascariaplataforma.com

Brace yourself for a "food coma" after dining at this Brazilian rodizio
all-you-can-eat "extravaganza" in the Theater District, where "skewer-
bearing" waiters bring on a "nonstop" barrage of "cooked-to-perfection"
meats; since it's "kinda expensive", gluttons "try not to fill up" at the
"bountiful" salad bar.

Cibo *American/Italian*
20 | 20 | 22 | $50

East 40s | 767 Second Ave. (41st St.) | 212-681-1616 |
www.cibonyc.com

A "grown-up" favorite in the land of "limited" options around Tudor City, this "comfortable" Tuscan–New American offers a seasonal "something-for-everyone" menu in a "spacious", "white-tablecloth" milieu; "reasonably priced" bills are another reason it's "worth coming back to."

Cilantro *Southwestern*   21 | 17 | 20 | $34

East 70s | 1321 First Ave. (71st St.) | 212-537-4040
West 80s | 485 Columbus Ave. (83rd St.) | 212-712-9090
www.cilantronyc.com
"Ample portions" and "low prices" keep these "solid" Southwesterns enduringly "popular" with twentysomethings on a budget; "gigantic" margaritas help blot out the "excessive noise" and "fake adobe" decor.

Cipriani *Italian*   23 | 22 | 22 | $75

East 40s | 89 E. 42nd St. (Park Ave.) | 212-973-0999
Cipriani Club 55 *Italian*
Financial District | 55 Wall St., 2nd fl. (William St.) | 212-699-4096
Cipriani Downtown *Italian*
SoHo | 376 W. Broadway (bet. Broome & Spring Sts.) | 212-343-0999
www.cipriani.com
"Air kisses" abound at these "posh" Italians where "pretty people", "billionaires" and those wanting to "feel powerful" go for "well-prepared" Italian dishes at "absurdly expensive" tabs; all offer "chic" surrounds, including a columned terrace over Wall Street and a "spectacular" perch above Grand Central's concourse.

Circo *Italian*   22 | 23 | 22 | $68

West 50s | 120 W. 55th St. (bet. 6th & 7th Aves.) | 212-265-3636 | www.circonyc.com
Exhibiting its "Le Cirque DNA", this "big-top" Midtowner from the Maccioni family purveys "wonderful Tuscan fare" in a "playful" room festooned with "circus-themed decor"; given the "high-end" price tags, the "prix fixe deals" draw bargain-hunters, especially "pre- or post-City Center."

City Bakery *Bakery*   23 | 14 | 16 | $19

Flatiron | 3 W. 18th St. (bet. 5th & 6th Aves.) | 212-366-1414 | www.thecitybakery.com
It's beloved for its "ever-so-rich" hot chocolate, "one-of-a-kind" pretzel croissants and "scrumptious" sweets, but this Flatiron bakery also wins favor with its "wholesome" salad and juice bars; maybe prices are "out of whack" given the "mess-hall" decor and "unhelpful service", but that doesn't faze the "crazed" lunch crowds.

City Hall *Seafood/Steak*   22 | 22 | 22 | $60

TriBeCa | 131 Duane St. (bet. Church St. & W. B'way) | 212-227-7777 | www.cityhallnyc.com
"Politicos" and "power" players rub elbows at Henry Meer's TriBeCa "mainstay" where "attentive" staffers ferry "dependable" surf 'n' turf in a "lofty", "sophisticated" setting that feels like "old NY"; bonuses include "space between tables" and "lovely private rooms" downstairs.

City Island Lobster House *Seafood*   22 | 16 | 19 | $50

City Island | 691 Bridge St. (City Island Ave.) | Bronx | 718-885-1459 | www.cilobsterhouse.com
Fans commend this "basic" City Island "throwback" as a "fine and dandy" option for "abundant", satisfying seafood; sure, it offers "not much

decor", but alfresco dining "overlooking Long Island Sound" gives it "staycation" status.

NEW City Kitchen *Food Hall* ▽ 25 | 21 | 21 | $28

West 40s | 700 Eighth Ave. (bet. 44th & 45th Sts.) | 646-863-0901 | www.citykitchen.nyc

A "welcome oasis" in Times Square, this "bright and open" food hall offers "something for everyone" with "wonderful" vendors like Dough, Luke's Lobster and ilili Box alongside counters for tacos, sushi, burgers and more; add cafe seating for the "hopping" crowds, and perusers are "pleasantly surprised."

City Lobster & Steak *Seafood/Steak* 20 | 18 | 19 | $63

West 50s | 121 W. 49th St. (6th Ave.) | 212-354-1717 | www.citylobster.com

For "standard" surf 'n' turf with "no surprises", this "convenient" harbor is a "good all-around" performer in the "touristy" turf around Rock Center; some crab about shelling out for "nothing special", but then again the pre-theater prix fixes are a "best buy."

The Clam *Seafood*   25 | 21 | 23 | $58

West Village | 420 Hudson St. (St. Lukes Pl.) | 212-242-7420 | www.theclamnyc.com

Yep, you'll find "all things clam" ("pizza, sliders, chowder") at this "charming" West Village seafooder where "interesting" preparations elevate classic dishes to "excellent" levels; "welcoming" staffers and a "grown-up" atmosphere make it a "slam dunk" for both a "hot date" or dinner with "your parents."

Claudette *French* 21 | 23 | 21 | $60

Greenwich Village | 24 Fifth Ave. (9th St.) | 212-868-2424 | www.claudettenyc.com

It's like "stepping into a restaurant in Provence" at this "breezy" Village bistro on lower Fifth, where a "charming" "French country" setting provides the backdrop for "tasty" Provençal cuisine; "dim lighting" lends "date"-night appeal, but the "noise averse" should "go early."

Clement Restaurant & Bar *American* 25 | 25 | 25 | $89

West 50s | 700 Fifth Ave. (55th St.) | 212-903-3918 | www.peninsula.com

One of Midtown's "best-kept secrets", this high-end New American "gem" set on The Peninsula's mezzanine furnishes "excellent" food and "impeccable" service in "chic, modern" surrounds overlooking Fifth Avenue; its "spaciously" arranged layout makes it "comfortable" for a "quiet meal" or "conversation" – just be ready for an "expensive" bill.

Clinton St. Baking Company *American*   25 | 13 | 18 | $29

Lower East Side | 4 Clinton St. (bet. Houston & Stanton Sts.) | 646-602-6263 | www.clintonstreetbaking.com

"Bring *War and Peace*" to pass the time in the "brunch line" at this "tiny" LES bakery/cafe where the "ridiculous" waits pay off when homespun Americana "made with love" (especially those "divine pancakes") arrives; insiders hint "dinner is just as good" – and "you can get in"; P.S. a next-door expansion is in the works.

NEW The Clocktower *American* ▽ 24 | 24 | 21 | E

Flatiron | Edition Hotel | 5 Madison Ave., 2nd Fl. (24th St.) |
212-413-4300 | www.theclocktowernyc.com
Restaurateur Stephen Starr teams up with London chef Jason Atherton
at this sceney Madison Square New American on the second floor of the
posh Edition Hotel (the former Metropolitan Life tower); expect artfully
plated high-end dishes served in an expansive, clubby milieu comprising
three dining rooms, a bar and a pool table–equipped lounge.

Club A Steak House *Steak* 26 | 23 | 25 | $92

East 50s | 240 E. 58th St. (bet. 2nd & 3rd Aves.) | 212-688-4190 |
www.clubasteak.com
Set in the "lesser known" area near the Queensboro Bridge, this bi-level
steakhouse draws "older" locals with "A-1" chops, "top-notch" service
and a fireplace-equipped setting; the "relaxed" mood comes in handy
when it's time to pay the bill.

Clyde Frazier's Wine & Dine *American* 21 | 22 | 22 | $45

West 30s | 485 10th Ave. (bet. 37th & 38th Sts.) | 212-842-1110 |
www.clydefraziers.com
In an otherwise "lacking" area near the Javits Center, this Hell's Kitchen
American from the storied Knicks star draws a "lively" crowd to a sprawling, TV-filled space (the indoor half-court is "an amazing add") for a pub
menu that shoots "above expectations"; it's a slam dunk "if you want to
watch a game", and "Clyde himself is frequently there."

Co. *Pizza* 23 | 16 | 18 | $33

Chelsea | 230 Ninth Ave. (24th St.) | 212-243-1105 | www.co-pane.com
It's all about the "love of dough" at this Chelsea pizzeria where "bread
guru" Jim Lahey serves "gourmet" pies flaunting "innovative toppings"
and crust that "hits the magic spot between crispy and pillowy"; just
don't expect much "elbow room" – this baby is "always busy."

Coco Roco *Chicken/Peruvian* 21 | 15 | 17 | $31

Park Slope | 392 Fifth Ave. (bet. 6th & 7th Sts.) | Brooklyn |
718-965-3376 | www.cocorocorestaurant.com
"Juicy-crisp" rotisserie chicken is the signature of this Park Slope
Peruvian known for "substantial portions" of "hearty" grub that
"won't empty your wallet"; "no atmosphere" leads some to fly the
coop via takeout or delivery.

Cocoron *Japanese* 23 | 14 | 19 | $27

Lower East Side | 61 Delancey St. (Allen St.) | 212-925-5220
NoLita | 37 Kenmare St. (Elizabeth St.) | 212-966-0800 |
www.cocoron-soba.com
For "amazingly delicious" soba "done right", fans command you "go
immediately" to these tiny noodle shops set in "unpretentious digs" just
like "you'll find in Japan"; while the staff is "friendly", be prepared "for
long waits at peak time"; P.S. the NoLita outpost's next-door sib, Goemon
Curry, focuses on Japanese curry.

Cocotte *French* 23 | 19 | 22 | $64

SoHo | 110 Thompson St. (bet. Prince & Spring Sts.) | 212-965-9100 |
www.cocotte-ny.com
"Dark" and moody, this tiny, wine-focused SoHo French offers up a

"refined" small-plates menu with Basque accents, all spelled out on the chalkboard walls; though the "portions are tapas size" and the prices "main-course size", "cozy" atmospherics and "solicitous" service more than compensate.

Coffee Shop *American/Brazilian*   17 | 14 | 14 | $33 ✓

Union Square | 29 Union Sq. W. (16th St.) | 212-243-7969 | www.thecoffeeshopnyc.com

One of NY's "quintessential" late-night scenes, this longtime American-Brazilian rolls out a "diner-esque menu" delivered by a "leggy" staff that's "more attractive than you" – and "less hardworking" too; since the chow's just "so-so" and the decor "tired", regulars take sidewalk seats to "watch Union Square pass by."

Colicchio & Sons *American*   26 | 26 | 26 | $89

Chelsea | 85 10th Ave. (bet. 15th & 16th Sts.) | 212-400-6699 | www.craftrestaurantsinc.com

"Another triumph" from *Top Chef*'s Tom Colicchio, this Chelsea "winner" hits all the marks with its "spectacular" American fare, "serious" wine selection and "gorgeous", "grown-up" setting overseen by a "polished" team; OK, it's "not cheap by any means", but the "more casual" Tap Room offers the "same quality and service" at a gentler price.

Colonia Verde *Latin American*   – | – | – | M

Fort Greene | 219 Dekalb Ave. (bet. Adelphi St. & Clermont Ave.) | Brooklyn | 347-689-4287 | www.coloniaverdenyc.com

Remodeled and reopened after a fire, this Fort Greene follow-up to Cómodo carries on producing grilled Latin American fare with modern twists; a front bar serves light bites, while the greenhouse-style dining area is complete with a choice backyard.

Colonie *American*   25 | 25 | 24 | $49

Brooklyn Heights | 127 Atlantic Ave. (bet. Clinton & Henry Sts.) | Brooklyn | 718-855-7500 | www.colonienyc.com

"Vibrant atmosphere meets inspired menu" at this Brooklyn Heights New American, where a seasonal lineup of "exceptional locavore" dishes pairs with "top-notch" service in a space sporting a "lush garden" wall; it's an acknowledged "keeper", though the "lively" crowds and "tight" quarters can make it "hard to snag a table."

The Commodore *Southern*   23 | 17 | 15 | $24

Williamsburg | 366 Metropolitan Ave. (Havemeyer St.) | Brooklyn | 718-218-7632

It "looks and acts like a dive bar", but this Williamsburg standby houses "some of the finest fried chicken and biscuits" going, along with other "revisited" Southern fare and "fabulous cocktails"; its "'70s den" look-alike digs are predictably "packed on weekends", and the "order-your-food-at-the-bar system isn't ideal", but "super-cheap" tabs and an overall "chill vibe" go a long way.

Community Food & Juice *American*   23 | 17 | 19 | $33

Morningside Heights | 2893 Broadway (bet. 112th & 113th Sts.) | 212-665-2800 | www.communityrestaurant.com

"Beloved by its own community", this "buzzy" Morningside Heights New American is a "healthy" haven in "Columbialand" for "nourishing" eats

with "locavore-ish" leanings; exuding "good vibes" all day, it's "wildly popular" for brunch, thus there's "always a line."

Cómodo *Latin American*   ▽ 25 | 20 | 24 | $54

SoHo | 58 MacDougal St. (bet. Houston & King Sts.) | 646-580-3866 | www.comodonyc.com

It's "always a pleasure" dining at this candlelit, brick-lined SoHo "date spot" where a "gracious" staff serves "unique" Latin dishes drawn from Mexican, Spanish and South American recipes; despite the "tiny" dimensions, fans dig the "romantic", "relaxing" atmosphere.

Congee Bowery *Chinese*   21 | 14 | 15 | $24

Lower East Side | 207 Bowery (bet. Rivington & Spring Sts.) | 212-766-2828 | www.congeebowerynewyork.com

Congee Village *Chinese*

Lower East Side | 100 Allen St. (bet. Broome & Delancey Sts.) | 212-941-1818 | www.congeevillagerestaurants.com

You "can't go wrong" with the namesake porridge at these kinda "tacky" Lower Eastsiders, which also ply a laundry list of "pleasing" Cantonese plates; "major miscommunication" with staffers isn't uncommon, but the "congeenial" (read: "oh-so-cheap") pricing draws plenty of bargain-hunters.

Contra *American*   25 | 21 | 22 | $87

Lower East Side | 138 Orchard St. (bet. Delancey & Rivington Sts.) | 212-466-4633 | www.contranyc.com

"Inventiveness and originality" are hallmarks of this LES American, where the nightly tasting menu uses seasonal ingredients to craft "exciting" dishes that are "delicious in every way"; the "spare" setting is "totally unpretentious", and though not cheap, prices are considered "fair for the quality."

Convivium Osteria *Mediterranean*   26 | 23 | 24 | $58

Park Slope | 68 Fifth Ave. (bet. Bergen St. & St. Marks Ave.) | Brooklyn | 718-857-1833 | www.convivium-osteria.com

"Superb cooking" and "ambiance to burn" define this Park Slope Mediterranean "date-night" nexus featuring an "intimate" mood and service that "shines"; a "quality" wine list, "fantastic" garden and "particularly romantic" cellar are additional bonuses, and if that's not enough, it's an "easy walk to Barclays Center."

Cookshop *American*   23 | 20 | 21 | $52

Chelsea | 156 10th Ave. (20th St.) | 212-924-4440 | www.cookshopny.com

"Fresh-from-the-farm" fare served by an "informed" crew in a "gallery-chic" setting makes for an "energetic" scene at this "consistently good" American near the High Line; since the "airy" dining room is usually "full" and "loud", insiders opt for the "great outdoor seating" or perhaps a "quiet midweek breakfast."

Coppelia *Diner/Pan-Latin*   23 | 16 | 20 | $31

Chelsea | 207 W. 14th St. (bet. 7th & 8th Aves.) | 212-858-5001 | www.coppelianyc.com

An "interesting" spin on a Cuban diner, this "hopping" Chelsea luncheonette slings "accomplished" Pan-Latin comfort chow in "colorful" confines; the "low tabs", "no-rush atmosphere" and 24/7 open-door policy make it a hit with early-risers and "all-nighters" alike.

	FOOD	DECOR	SERVICE	COST

Coppola's *Italian*   20 | 16 | 20 | $48

Murray Hill | 378 Third Ave. (bet. 27th & 28th Sts.) | 212-679-0070
West 70s | 206 W. 79th St. (bet. Amsterdam Ave. & B'way) |
212-877-3840
www.coppolas-nyc.com

"Like an old friend", these longtime Southern Italians are "relaxing",
"reliable" fallbacks for "comfort" chow heavy on the "red sauce"; maybe
the "homey" settings are becoming "outdated", but "plentiful" portions,
"courteous" service and "moderate" prices compensate.

Corkbuzz *Eclectic*   20 | 21 | 22 | $52

Chelsea | Chelsea Mkt. | 75 Ninth Ave. (bet. 15th & 16th Sts.) |
646-237-4847
Greenwich Village | 13 E. 13th St. (bet. 5th Ave. & University Pl.) |
646-873-6071
www.corkbuzz.com

Like the name suggests, wine is "the star" at these "lively" enotecas,
where "inventive" Eclectic nibbles provide "thoughtful" pairings for
"interesting" pours dispensed by "knowledgeable" staffers (aka "wine
Jedis"); the "warm, relaxed" atmosphere makes for a "perfect date spot."

Cornelia Street Cafe *American*   18 | 17 | 19 | $38

West Village | 29 Cornelia St. (bet. Bleecker & W. 4th Sts.) |
212-989-9319 | www.corneliastreetcafe.com

"Old-school" West Village dining thrives at this circa-1977 "charmer"
with a "yoga vibe", offering "perfectly acceptable" New American fare
and a "cheap and cheerful" brunch; although "starting to show its age", it
gets "bonus" points for the "cool" performance space downstairs.

Corner Bistro *Burgers*   23 | 13 | 16 | $21

West Village | 331 W. Fourth St. (Jane St.) | 212-242-9502
Long Island City | 47-18 Vernon Blvd. (47th Rd.) | Queens | 718-606-6500
www.cornerbistrony.com

"Memorable", "messy" burgers dished out on paper plates in "sticky
booths" make for classic "slumming" at this "dingy" Village perennial
(with a slightly "nicer" LIC spin-off); "cheap beer", "long waits" and
"student crowds" are all part of the timelessly "cool" experience.

Cosme *Mexican*   25 | 23 | 23 | $83

Flatiron | 35 E. 21st St. (bet. B'way & Park Ave. S.) | 212-913-9659 |
www.cosmenyc.com

"Renowned" chef Enrique Olvera shows how "mind-blowingly delicious"
contemporary Mexican cooking can be at this "much-hyped" Flatiron
locale; the "sleek", "cavernous" space reads either "sexy" or "boring",
and the bill "adds up quickly", but it's still one of the most "impossible
reservations" to get.

Costata *Italian/Steak*   23 | 21 | 23 | $84

SoHo | 206 Spring St. (bet. 6th Ave. & Sullivan St.) | 212-334-3320 |
www.costatanyc.com

"Delicious" steaks and "even better" pastas make for a "great combo" at
Michael White's Italian steakhouse set in a SoHo triplex; the space is "inviting but not clubby", and while the cost is "in the clouds", the first-floor
tavern room is a more affordable option.

Cotta *Italian*
20 | 17 | 17 | $41

West 80s | 513 Columbus Ave. (bet. 84th & 85th Sts.) | 212-873-8500 | www.cottanyc.com

"Busy and lively", this "rustic" UWS "neighborhood" Italian puts forth "delicious" pizza and tapas-style plates in a ground-floor wine bar or "cozy" mezzanine (watch out for those "candles on the stairs"); it's "perfect for a casual date", with equally casual tabs to match.

The Counter *Burgers*
20 | 14 | 17 | $22

West 40s | 1451 Broadway (41st St.) | 212-997-6801 | www.thecounterburger.com

"Near-infinite" burger options are the draw at this Times Square link of the "build-it-yourself" national chain, where diners customize their orders "from bun to patty to toppings"; some shrug "nothing stellar", but most agree it's an "easy, cheap pre-theater bite."

Covo *Italian*
23 | 22 | 20 | $35

Hamilton Heights | 701 W. 135th St. (12th Ave.) | 212-234-9573 | www.covony.com

"Solid" is the word on this "tucked-away" Hamilton Heights Italian supplying "tasty" pizza and pastas for "bang-for-the-buck" tabs in a "spread-out", brick-walled setting; "caring" servers distract from the "ear-ringing" noise, but night owls tout the "upstairs lounge."

Cowgirl *Southwestern*
17 | 16 | 17 | $33

West Village | 519 Hudson St. (W. 10th St.) | 212-633-1133 | www.cowgirlnyc.com

Cowgirl Sea-Horse *Southwestern*

South Street Seaport | 259 Front St. (Dover St.) | 212-608-7873 | www.cowgirlseahorse.com

"Down-to-earth" says it all about this West Village Southwesterner slinging "decent" chow in a "kitschy", "retro rodeo" setting that's "kid-friendly" by day and a "high-octane" margaritaville after dark; the Seaport satellite gets a "fishy spin" with a seafood focus.

Craft *American*
25 | 24 | 25 | $89

Flatiron | 43 E. 19th St. (bet. B'way & Park Ave. S.) | 212-780-0880 | www.craftrestaurant.com

"Still inventive, still exciting", this "grown-up" Flatiron American from *Top Chef* star Tom Colicchio offers "simply yet expertly prepared" food that's "perfect for group sharing", served in "warm, modern" digs by a "terrific" team; though the "one-percenter" pricing suggests "special occasions", it's a "worthy splurge" at any time.

Craftbar *American*
22 | 20 | 22 | $57

Flatiron | 900 Broadway (20th St.) | 212-461-4300 | www.craftrestaurantsinc.com

"More affordable" and thus "more accessible" than Tom Colicchio's Craft, this "casually elegant" Flatiron American plates "quality" fare in a "dark", "relaxed" setting patrolled by an "attentive" team; its "young, noisy" crowd labels it a "go-to for weekend brunch."

	FOOD	DECOR	SERVICE	COST

Crave Fishbar *Seafood* 24 | 19 | 21 | $56

East 50s | 945 Second Ave. (bet. 50th & 51st Sts.) | 646-895-9585 |
www.cravefishbar.com

Bringing some "much needed" "cool" to Midtown East, this "friendly"
seafood specialist delivers "delicious" ocean fare in a "casual", coastal-
rustic setting; relatively "reasonable" rates and "$1 oysters during happy
hour" are further lures.

Crema *Mexican* 23 | 18 | 21 | $47

Chelsea | 111 W. 17th St (bet. 6th & 7th Aves.) | 212-691-4477 |
www.cremarestaurante.com

French techniques give an "innovative" lift to the modern Mexican
cooking at chef Julieta Ballesteros' "tucked-away" Chelsea "sleeper"; it's
a "relaxed" enclave for "elevated" eating and "energetic" service – and
"affordable" enough for *fanáticos* to "go back again and

Crif Dogs *Hot Dogs* 22 | 14 | 17 | $13

East Village | 113 St. Marks Pl. (bet. Ave. A & 1st Ave.) | 212-614-2728
Williamsburg | 555 Driggs Ave. (7th St.) | Brooklyn | 718-302-3200
www.crifdogs.com

"Spunky", "deep-fried" hot dogs are a "guilty pleasure" at these "gritty"
joints famed for their "fun toppings" (like bacon, avocado and cream
cheese); they're a natural for "cheap", "late-night munchies", and the
East Village original houses the famed "speakeasy" bar PDT, accessed
through a phone booth.

NEW Crimson & Rye *American* ▽ 20 | 19 | 20 | $61

East 50s | 198 E. 54th St. (3rd Ave.) | 212-687-6692 |
www.crimsonandrye.com

Anchoring Midtown's Lipstick Building, this "cool" lounge from Charlie
Palmer specializes in "creative" craft cocktails but also offers a "limited"
lineup of "well-executed" American bites; it's "suitable for business" or
"clandestine dates" – if you can swing "way-high" tabs.

Crispo *Italian* 25 | 21 | 22 | $55

West Village | 240 W. 14th St. (bet. 7th & 8th Aves.) | 212-229-1818 |
www.crisporestaurant.com

Fans are "blown away" by this "favorite" West Village trattoria purveying
"gratifying" Northern Italiana led by a signature spaghetti carbonara that
"has no rivals"; its "popularity" results in "loud, cramped" conditions, so
insiders head for the "all-seasons garden."

Cuba *Cuban* 24 | 19 | 21 | $42

Greenwich Village | 222 Thompson St. (bet. Bleecker & 3rd Sts.) |
212-420-7878 | www.cubanyc.com

Everyone's "Havana great time" at this "high-energy" Village supplier
of "authentic" Cuban standards and "heavenly" mojitos "charmingly"
served in "funky" Latin digs; live bands, "relatively affordable" tabs and a
"cigar-rolling man" lend a "vacation" vibe to the proceedings.

Cubana Café *Cuban* 21 | 18 | 20 | $28

Park Slope | 80 Sixth Ave. (St. Marks Ave.) | Brooklyn | 718-398-9818 |
www.cubanacafenyc.com

An "enjoyable little spot", this "bright, cheery" Cuban on the Park Slope-

Prospect Heights border offers up "solid" standards and "really good mojitos" at "even better prices"; just be aware there's "not much elbow room", service is "casual" and the payment's cash only.

Cull & Pistol *Seafood*
24 | 18 | 20 | $51

Chelsea | Chelsea Mkt. | 75 Ninth Ave. (bet. 15th & 16th Sts.) | 646-568-1223 | www.cullandpistol.com

Brought to you by the folks behind Chelsea Market's Lobster Place, this "bustling" next-door adjunct is a "sit-down" affair offering "super-fresh" seafood and raw-bar items in "tiny" but "friendly" digs; bargain-hunters report the "best bet" here is the "one-dollar-oyster" weekday happy hour.

Da Andrea *Italian*
23 | 16 | 22 | $41

Greenwich Village | 35 W. 13th St. (bet. 5th & 6th Aves.) | 212-367-1979 | www.daandreanyc.com

"Delicious" housemade pastas and other Emilia-Romagna standards are a "steal" at this "cozy", "unpretentious" Villager; with "warm", "friendly" staffers keeping the vibe copacetic, it's no wonder "neighborhood" denizens come back "time after time."

Dafni Greek Taverna *Greek*
21 | 15 | 20 | $36

West 40s | 325 W. 42nd St. (bet. 8th & 9th Aves.) | 212-315-1010 | www.dafnitaverna.com

Set on a "no-man's-land" block opposite Port Authority, this "genuine" Greek comes across with "satisfying" fare like "yia-yia used to make"; "convenience to the theater", a short trip to Jersey and "affordability" are its trump cards, though the "nothing-special" decor needs work.

Daisy May's BBQ *BBQ*
22 | 9 | 15 | $28

West 40s | 623 11th Ave. (46th St.) | 212-977-1500 | www.daisymaysbbq.com

"Fall-off-the-bone" ribs and other "darn-good" BBQ allow patrons to "get in touch with the caveman within" at this Hell's Kitchen 'cue hut; despite "cafeteria-style" service, decor "best left undescribed" and a "nearly-in-the–Hudson River" address, fans feel "lucky to have it."

Da Nico *Italian*
21 | 18 | 19 | $42

Little Italy | 164 Mulberry St. (bet. Broome & Grand Sts.) | 212-343-1212
Tottenville | 7324 Amboy Rd. (bet. Sleight & Sprague Aves.) | Staten Island | 718-227-7200
www.danicoristorante.com

A "Mulberry Street staple" for more than 20 years, this "traditional" Italian and its Staten Island sequel roll out "gargantuan" portions of "tasty" vittles; "welcoming" service and "nominal" prices (plus a "beautiful" back garden at the original) complete the overall "comfortable" picture.

Daniel *French*
29 | 28 | 29 | $176

East 60s | 60 E. 65th St. (bet. Madison & Park Aves.) | 212-288-0033 | www.danielnyc.com

"Perennially at the top of its game", Daniel Boulud's "incomparable" UES "pamperville" delivers "life-changing" New French prix fixes with the "pomp and circumstance" of "white-glove service" and a "magnificent", jackets-required setting; the main room is the "epitome" of fine dining, but the bar area is also "lovely" for à la carte bites with a side of "people-watching" – either way, be ready to "call your broker" when the bill comes.

Danji Korean
25 | 19 | 21 | $49

West 50s | 346 W. 52nd St. (bet. 8th & 9th Aves.) | 212-586-2880 | www.danjinyc.com

"Fantastic, elegant" cooking and a "lively, energetic" vibe mean this "upscale" Midtown Korean tapas specialist remains a "tough table to get" (brace for an "interminable wait"); a pleasant "pared-down" setting and capable – if slightly "indifferent" – service help ensure it's a "fun place to be."

Danny Brown Wine Bar & Kitchen European
26 | 20 | 24 | $58

Forest Hills | 104-02 Metropolitan Ave. (71st Dr.) | Queens | 718-261-2144 | www.dannybrownwinekitchen.com

"Rivaling any place in Manhattan", this Forest Hills "gem" is a "low-key" neighborhood retreat that's beloved for its "excellent" European fare, "fabulous" wine list and "on-the-mark" service, all offered at "Queens prices"; if that's not enough, there's a "can't-be-beat" prix fixe deal on Tuesday and Wednesday nights.

Da Noi Italian
22 | 18 | 21 | $53

East 40s | 214 E. 49th St. (bet. 2nd & 3rd Aves.) | 212-754-5710
Shore Acres | 138 Fingerboard Rd. (Tompkins Ave.) | Staten Island | 718-720-1650
Travis-Chelsea | 4358 Victory Blvd. (Crabbs Ln.) | Staten Island | 718-982-5040
www.danoinyc.com

"Old-world" "red-sauce" cooking "like nonna's" draws fans to these "congenial" Italians where "generous portions" turn somewhat "pricey" tabs into "money well spent"; the crowd's right out of a "scene from *The Godfather*", while the sound level's a bit on "da noisy" side.

Darbar Indian
21 | 16 | 18 | $35

East 40s | 152 E. 46th St. (bet. Lexington & 3rd Aves.) | 212-681-4500 | www.darbarny.com

Darbar Grill Indian

East 50s | 157 E. 55th St. (bet. Lexington & 3rd Aves.) | 212-751-4600 | www.darbargrill.com

These East Midtown Indians offer a "standard repertoire" of "well-prepared" dishes served by a "gracious" team in "comfortable" (if a "bit threadbare") confines; even better, there's "no sticker shock", particularly at the "can't-be-beat" lunch buffet.

Da Silvano Italian
21 | 17 | 20 | $75

Greenwich Village | 260 Sixth Ave. (bet. Bleecker & Houston Sts.) | 212-982-2343 | www.dasilvano.com

The "glitterati" draw the "paparazzi" to this ever-"trendy" Villager where "celeb-spotting" is the "main course", though the Tuscan eats are almost as "delicious"; it costs "wads of cash" and the staff can be "snooty" to outsiders, so for best results, bring "George Clooney" – and get him to pick up the check.

Da Umberto *Italian*

`25` `21` `23` `$73`

Chelsea | 107 W. 17th St. (bet. 6th & 7th Aves.) | 212-989-0303 |
www.daumbertonyc.com

"Still a classic", this longtime Chelsea "favorite" rolls out "serious" Northern Italian cuisine with "vibrant" flavors in a "simple" space where the white-tablecloth "elegance" is matched by "impeccable" service; "costly" tabs aside, it fits the bill for a "romantic" or otherwise "special" occasion.

David Burke Fabrick *American*

`24` `22` `22` `$64`

West 30s | Archer Hotel | 47 W. 38th St. (bet. 5th & 6th Aves.) |
212-302-3838 | www.davidburkefabrick.com

David Burke's trademark "creativity" is on display at this Midtown American in the Archer Hotel, where the "bold" fare focuses on "wittily" conceived share plates (e.g. "candied bacon on a clothesline"); "solicitous" staffers oversee a "modern" setting that's "upscale yet relaxed", while an attached lounge offers light fare and patio seats.

David Burke Fishtail *Seafood*

`24` `22` `23` `$71`

East 60s | 135 E. 62nd St. (bet. Lexington & Park Aves.) | 212-754-1300 |
www.fishtaildb.com

"Fish so fresh you can smell the sea" earns kudos at David Burke's "class-act" UES seafooder, where the "creative" preparations are dispensed by an "informative" crew; its "lovely" townhouse setting includes a "busy" downstairs bar and a "quieter", "more formal" upper dining room, but no matter where you sit, the dining's "delicious" (and "pricey").

David Burke Kitchen *American*

`25` `23` `23` `$59`

SoHo | James Hotel | 23 Grand St., downstairs (6th Ave.) |
212-201-9119 | www.davidburkekitchen.com

"Fit for foodies", this "farm-to-fork" option from David Burke matches "inventive" New Americana with "on-point" service and a "semi-subterranean" setting in SoHo's James Hotel; the "charming" Treehouse Bar upstairs adds an extra dimension to the "inviting" package.

David's Brisket House *Deli*

`25` `12` `21` `$20`

Bay Ridge | 7721 Fifth Ave. (78th St.) | Brooklyn | 718-333-5662
Bedford-Stuyvesant | 533 Nostrand Ave. (Herkimer Pl.) | Brooklyn |
718-789-1155
www.davidsbriskethouseinc.com

Catering to Brooklynites with a "big taste" for "lots of meat", these delis turn out "perfectly prepared" sandwiches stuffed with "phenomenal" pastrami, brisket and other staples; they're "nothing special to look at", but are "one of the musts" in the neighborhood.

Dawat *Indian*

`24` `18` `22` `$55`

East 50s | 210 E. 58th St. (bet. 2nd & 3rd Aves.) | 212-355-7555 |
www.dawatrestaurant.com

East Midtown's Indian "pioneer" (since 1986) "still pleases", thanks to actress/chef Madhur Jaffrey's "high-caliber" cooking, "graciously served" in a "quiet", "contemporary" room that's "conducive to conversation"; it may look a little "tired", but loyalists avow the tabs are "worth the extra cost."

db Bistro Moderne *French*

24 | 22 | 23 | $71

West 40s | City Club Hotel | 55 W. 44th St. (6th Ave.) | 212-391-2400 | www.dbbistro.com

"Elevated bistro fare" (e.g. that "decadent" burger stuffed with foie gras) is "well prepared" at Daniel Boulud's "bustling" Theater District French that comes in "handy" for pre-curtain dining; the "modern" room exudes "New York cool", service is "sharp" and "hefty" bills come with the territory.

DBGB *French*
22 | 22 | 21 | $55

East Village | 299 Bowery (bet. 1st & Houston Sts.) | 212-933-5300 | www.dbgb.com

"Astonishingly good" housemade sausages, "amped-up" burgers and a "massive" craft beer selection define Daniel Boulud's Bowery French; "more relaxed" than its brethren, the "casual" space includes a some-what "spacious" dining room and "convivial" front bar area, making it a solid "anytime" pick.

Dead Rabbit *Pub Food*
22 | 24 | 23 | $44

Financial District | 30 Water St. (bet. Pearl & Water Sts.) | 646-422-7906 | www.deadrabbitnyc.com

While this Irish-inspired FiDi duplex boasts a "well-deserved" rep as a "cocktail mecca" with a "Bible" of "enviable" craft drinks, its "well-pre-pared" pub fare is "not just an afterthought"; manned by an "excellent" staff, the saloonish digs "get busy quickly" and "just need more elbow room" when it hops.

Decoy *Chinese*
26 | 17 | 21 | $80

West Village | 529½ Hudson St., downstairs (bet. Charles & W. 10th Sts.) | 212-691-9700 | www.decoynyc.com

"Insanely good" Peking duck is the "raison d'être" of this Chinese nook downstairs from the West Village's RedFarm, where "over-the-top" prix fixe feasts also include "inventive" sides; the "bare-bones" digs with one "long" communal table can feel "crowded", but there's also a bar for "artisanal" cocktails and à la carte ordering.

Dee's *Pizza*
23 | 20 | 23 | $31

Forest Hills | 107-23 Metropolitan Ave. (74th Ave.) | Queens | 718-793-7553 | www.deesnyc.com

Dee-votees depend on this "homey" Forest Hills outlet for "especially good" brick-oven pizzas, Mediterranean "comfort" classics and other grill items; "fair prices", a "huge" space and "ample seating" bolster the "amicable", "family-friendly" mood.

Defonte's *Sandwiches*
24 | 11 | 21 | $16

Red Hook | 379 Columbia St. (Luquer St.) | Brooklyn | 718-625-8052
Stapleton | 95 Water St. (bet. Beach & Canal Sts.) | Staten Island | 718-285-4310
www.defontesofbrooklyn.com

"Don't eat for a week" before attacking the "two-handed" "Dagwood" sand-wiches at these "lip-smacking" Italian sub shops; the '20s-era Red Hook original "used to feed the longshoremen" and still exudes a whiff of "old-fashioned Brooklyn", while its Staten Island outpost continues the tradition.

	FOOD	DECOR	SERVICE	COST

DeGrezia *Italian*
24 | 22 | 24 | $69

East 50s | 231 E. 50th St. (bet. 2nd & 3rd Aves.) | 212-750-5353 |
www.degreziaristorante.com

A "hidden jewel" below street level, this East Midtowner is a model of
"old-world elegance", offering "first-rate" Italian food, "experienced"
service and a "civilized" milieu where "one can actually talk"; though a
"bit costly", it's "worth it for special occasions" and "business lunches."

Degustation *American*
25 | 19 | 22 | $87

East Village | 239 E. Fifth St. (bet. 2nd & 3rd Aves.) | 212-979-1012 |
www.degustation-nyc.com

"Anticipation" is in the air as chefs prepare "sublime" American small
plates with "meticulous attention to detail" and a heavy Franco-Spanish
accent at this "tiny" East Village tasting bar courtesy of Grace and Jack
Lamb; even though the tabs may "pinch your wallet", the other payoffs
are "caring" service and that "courtside" counter-seating experience.

🆕 Delaware & Hudson *American*
26 | 21 | 25 | $70

Williamsburg | 135 N. Fifth St. (Bedford Ave.) | Brooklyn | 718-218-8191 |
www.delawareandhudson.com

A "constantly changing" prix fixe menu "honors the seasons" at this
Williamsburg American where "elevated" takes on mid-Atlantic comfort
food are "delicious" and "well presented" by an "accommodating" crew;
the "warm, cozy" surrounds fill up fast, and though not cheap, you get
some serious "bang for the buck."

Del Frisco's *Steak*
25 | 23 | 24 | $85

West 40s | 1221 Sixth Ave. (bet. 48th & 49th Sts.) | 212-575-5129 |
www.delfriscos.com

Del Frisco's Grille *Steak*

West 50s | Rockefeller Ctr. | 50 Rockefeller Plaza (51st St.) |
212-767-0371 | www.delfriscosgrille.com

"A hit all around", these "energetic" Midtown steakhouses hum like "a
well-oiled machine" as an "engaged" staff sets down "premium" beef
in "sprawling" surrounds with "urbane" vibes and a "power bar scene";
they're perpetually "packed" with "suits" wielding the "corporate Amex"
to cover the "splurge"; P.S. "definitely try the lemon cake."

Delicatessen *American*
23 | 22 | 22 | $36

NoLita | 54 Prince St. (Lafayette St.) | 212-226-0211 |
www.delicatessennyc.com

NoLita is home to this "cool" spot slinging "solid" American comfort food
with an "upscale twist" (including "really good" mac 'n' cheese); the "relaxed" digs are outfitted with retractable walls for "great people-watching on a nice day", and the "good-looking" staff is "friendly" enough.

Dell'anima *Italian*
24 | 20 | 22 | $64

West Village | 38 Eighth Ave. (Jane St.) | 212-366-6633 |
www.dellanima.com

Ever "jam-packed" thanks to its "*delizioso*" rustic Italian fare
(including "the best housemade pastas"), this "cozy" West Villager
features a chef's counter where you can watch the "magic" happen;
"reservations are a must", or be prepared for a "long wait" in its adjacent
wine bar, Anfora.

	FOOD	DECOR	SERVICE	COST

Delmonico's *Steak*
24 | 23 | 24 | $78

Financial District | 56 Beaver St. (William St.) | 212-509-1144 |
www.delmonicosny.com

Delmonico's Kitchen *Steak*

West 30s | 207 W. 36th St. (bet. 7th & 8th Aves.) | 212-695-5220 |
www.delmonicosrestaurantgroup.com

One of America's "most historic" restaurants, this FiDi steakhouse rolls
out "gold-standard" chops along with "classic dishes" actually invented
here (e.g. baked Alaska, lobster Newburg), all dispensed by an "attentive" staff in "old-world" digs; its Midtown spin-off is a fine "oasis" near
Penn Station and shares the "big bills" of the mother ship.

Del Posto *Italian*
27 | 27 | 27 | $134

Chelsea | 85 10th Ave. (bet. 15th & 16th Sts.) | 212-497-8090 |
www.delposto.com

"You'll be transported" to Italy at this "mind-blowing" Chelsea "masterpiece", where the Batali-Bastianich "empire" offers "the ultimate" in
Italian dining with "superbly realized" cuisine and "exceptional" wines
served by a "stellar" team in a "grand space" resembling a "stately"
"villa"; diners "pay dearly" for the "luxurious experience", though the
set-price lunch "is a fabulous deal."

Denino's Pizzeria *Pizza*
26 | 13 | 21 | $22

Elm Park | 524 Port Richmond Ave. (bet. Hooker Pl. & Walker St.) | Staten
Island | 718-442-9401 | www.deninos.com

"Always a contender for Staten Island's best", this circa-1937 Elm Park
pizzeria turns out "phenomenal" pies with "the most remarkable" crispy
crusts (not to mention "out-of-this-world" fried calamari); it's cash-only
and the space is "no-frills" to put it mildly, but "bargain" tabs help keep it
perennially packed.

Deux Amis *French*
20 | 17 | 22 | $50

East 50s | 356 E. 51st St. (1st Ave.) | 212-230-1117 | www.deuxamisnyc.com

The "warm" owner and "agreeable staff" lend a "feel-at-home" air to
this East Midtown bistro, an approximation of "side-street-Paris" dining
featuring "solid" French country cuisine; the interior's *plaisant* if "a bit
close", so some find it's "best sitting outside."

Dhaba *Indian*
23 | 15 | 17 | $32

Murray Hill | 108 Lexington Ave. (bet. 27th & 28th Sts.) | 212-679-1284 |
www.dhabanyc.com

"Delicious and different", this "simple" Curry Hill Indian turns out "impressive", "pungently spiced" specialties – even "'regular' is hot, hot, hot"
– at "terrific-value" tabs; there's "always a line" at the "sliver" of a space
for the "bargain" lunch buffet.

Di Fara *Pizza*
26 | 6 | 10 | $19

Midwood | 1424 Ave. J (15th St.) | Brooklyn | 718-258-1367 |
www.difara.com

Pizzaiolo "legend" Dom DeMarco is "a master plying his art" at this 1964
Midwood "institution", where his "lovingly handmade" pies are "a must
for the pizza addicted"; despite "unappealing" digs, "interminable waits"
and service with "zero sense of urgency", it's "thronged" with those who
urge "patience – it's worth it."

Dimes *American*

▽ 23 | 19 | 19 | $29

Lower East Side | 49 Canal St. (Orchard St.) | 212-240-9410 | www.dimesnyc.com

Now relocated to the LES, this "super-hip" all-day eatery retains its "LA vibe" and "fresh", Californian-inspired American menu (think grain bowls and chia pudding); the streamlined quarters are roomier than before, but they still don't take reservations so "come early", especially at brunch.

Dim Sum Go Go *Chinese*

21 | 11 | 15 | $26

Chinatown | 5 E. Broadway (bet. Catherine St. & Chatham Sq.) | 212-732-0797 | www.dimsumgogo.com

"Cheap", "tasty" dim sum ordered off a menu rather than snagged from a trolley makes this "utilitarian" Chinese "less chaotic" than the typical C-town outfits; however, traditionalists "miss the ladies schlepping the carts" and report "perfunctory service" and "run-of-the-mill" decor.

Diner *American*

25 | 22 | 22 | $42

Williamsburg | 85 Broadway (Berry St.) | Brooklyn | 718-486-3077 | www.dinernyc.com

The "daily changing", locally sourced New Americana – "far from diner fare" – is as "tops as the crowd" at this "cool, laid-back" Williamsburg pioneer; its "blast-from-the-past" 1927 dining car digs are a "snug fit", but the helpful staff ("don't be afraid to ask for direction") and "good wine/cocktail list" help keep the mood copacetic.

Dinosaur Bar-B-Que *BBQ*

22 | 17 | 18 | $34

Morningside Heights | 700 W. 125th St (12th Ave.) | 212-694-1777
Gowanus | 604 Union St. (4th Ave.) | Brooklyn | 347-429-7030
www.dinosaurbarbque.com

"Funky" is the word on these "high-volume" Gowanus and Morningside Heights smoke joints where the BBQ is "tender" and "juicy", and the settings "loud, crowded" and "great for groups"; it's "welcoming to both bikers and families" alike, but be prepared for "hectic" atmospheres and "long lines."

Dirt Candy *Vegetarian*

25 | 20 | 24 | $58

Lower East Side | 86 Allen St. (Broome St.) | 212-228-7732 | www.dirtcandynyc.com

"Genius" chef-owner Amanda Cohen takes vegetarian fare to "amazing heights" with a "playful" menu of "wildly creative" dishes at this LES "must-visit"; it remains a "difficult reservation" despite moving to much larger digs, but at least the administrative fee (no tipping) is a "refreshing change."

Dirty French *French*

24 | 23 | 22 | $81

Lower East Side | Ludlow Hotel | 180 Ludlow St. (bet. Houston & Stanton Sts.) | 212-254-3000 | www.dirtyfrench.com

The Torrisi folks "fire on all cylinders" at this LES "hot spot", where staffers "put on the whole performance" delivering "dreamy" French fare "reimagined" with Moroccan, Cajun and Southeast Asian influences; a "sexy" brasserie setup that draws a "buzzy" (read: "loud") crowd, it's a "tough" reservation and you're "definitely going to pay for what you get."

	FOOD	DECOR	SERVICE	COST

Distilled *American*

FOOD 20 | DECOR 17 | SERVICE 20 | COST $46

TriBeCa | 211 W. Broadway (bet. Franklin & White Sts.) | 212-601-9514 | www.distilledny.com

"Epic wings" are a menu standout at this "spacious" TriBeCan offering American public-house fare "taken to another level" and washed down with "original" cocktails and NY-made meads; it might be a tad "expensive", but it's an overall "fun" hang serviced by an "aim-to-please" staff.

Docks Oyster Bar *Seafood*

FOOD 21 | DECOR 20 | SERVICE 20 | COST $58

East 40s | 633 Third Ave. (40th St.) | 212-986-8080 | www.docksoysterbar.com

"Reliable" fish and bivalves galore reel in the masses at this "cavernous" seafood standby near Grand Central; "briskly professional" servers tend to schools of "biz lunchers" and "after-work" revelers who dive in for its "active" happy hour and high-octane "social" scene.

Do Hwa *Korean*

▽ FOOD 23 | DECOR 17 | SERVICE 20 | COST $50

West Village | 55 Carmine St. (bet. Bedford St. & 7th Ave.) | 212-414-1224 | www.dohwanyc.com

"Authentic" eats packing "lots of spice" chased with "creative" cocktails fuel the "cool vibe" at this "hip" West Village Korean, a slightly "upscale" take on the "traditional" with grill-equipped tables on hand for hands-on types; sure, it may cost "a little more than K-town", but it's a much "sexier" experience.

Dominick's *Italian*

FOOD 22 | DECOR 11 | SERVICE 19 | COST $45

Arthur Avenue/Belmont | 2335 Arthur Ave. (bet. 184th & 187th Sts.) | Bronx | 718-733-2807

Patrons have been filling the communal tables of this "iconic" Arthur Avenue Italian since 1962, despite no decor, "no menus" ("you eat what they're cooking"), "no checks" ("trust the waiter") and no reservations or credit cards; "off-the-charts" food and "cost performance" make the "daunting waits" bearable, but to save time, go early.

Dominique Ansel Bakery *Bakery/French*

FOOD 25 | DECOR 16 | SERVICE 17 | COST $15

SoHo | 189 Spring St. (bet. Sullivan & Thompson Sts.) | 212-219-2773 | www.dominiqueansel.com

Pastry chef "extraordinaire" Dominique Ansel and his "cult-status" Cronuts draw "crazy morning lines" to this SoHo "fantasy land of desserts" where you'll also find other "transcendent innovations" plus "exceptional" French classics too; the counter crew can be "slow" and the "small" space gets "super packed", but if you head to the back garden, "it's like leaving the city."

NEW Dominique Ansel Kitchen *Bakery/French*

FOOD – | DECOR – | SERVICE – | COST I

West Village | 137 Seventh Ave. S. (bet. Charles & 10th Sts.) | 212-242-5111 | www.dominiqueanselkitchen.com

Dominique Ansel brings his inventive take on French *classiques* to this Cronut-free West Village bakery where desserts prepared à la minute join viennoiserie favorites and savory items; tiny with limited bleacher seats, the airy space also has a walk-up window for gourmet ice cream and a second floor called U.P. for themed dessert tasting menus (reservations through a ticketing system).

	FOOD	DECOR	SERVICE	COST

Don Antonio *Pizza* 23 | 17 | 19 | $33

West 50s | 309 W. 50th St. (bet. 8th & 9th Aves.) | 646-719-1043 | www.donantoniopizza.com

Fans ascend to "pie heaven" via the dozens of varieties built on "light, flaky" crusts (its flash-fried rendition is especially "scrumptious") at this "excellent" Midtown Neapolitan; the setting can be "cramped" and "hectic", yet in the end those "tasty" wood-fired pizzas "overcome all."

Don Coqui *Puerto Rican* 22 | 22 | 20 | $50

City Island | 565 City Island Ave. (Cross St.) | Bronx | 718-885-2222 | www.doncoqui.nyc

"Go hungry" to this City Island outpost of a family-run chainlet, which serves "well-sized portions" of "tasty" Puerto Rican classics in a "fancy" bayside space with "water views"; salsa enthusiasts can "stay for some dancing" when it morphs into a Latin "party" by night.

Donovan's *American* 21 | 19 | 21 | $30

Bayside | 214-16 41st Ave. (Bell Blvd.) | Queens | 718-423-5178 | www.donovansofbayside.com
Woodside | 57-24 Roosevelt Ave. (58th St.) | Queens | 718-429-9339 | www.donovansny.com

"Something-for-everyone" menus draw the "family" trade to these separately owned Queens Americans lauded for "perfect" hamburgers along with "solid", "Irish-tinged" pub grub; "bargain" tabs and "pleasant" service come with the territory.

Don Peppe *Italian* 26 | 13 | 19 | $54

South Ozone Park | 135-58 Lefferts Blvd. (149th Ave.) | Queens | 718-845-7587

An "old-school", cash-only red-sauce joint "unburdened by pretension", this circa-1968 South Ozone Park Italian is home to "marvelous" meals that end with "sacks of leftovers"; the house wines might have been "made yesterday" and the digs "could use redecorating", but it's hard to find a more authentic "NY experience."

Do or Dine *Eclectic* 25 | 18 | 21 | $40

Bedford-Stuyvesant | 1108 Bedford Ave. (bet. Lexington Ave. & Quincy St.) | Brooklyn | 718-684-2290 | www.doordinebk.com

"Weird and wonderful", this Bed-Stuy Eclectic excels with "all kinds of crazy dishes and drinks" ("the foie gras donuts are a highlight") delivered by a "friendly staff"; the come-as-you-are space featuring a skull-and-bones mosaic, disco ball and "hip-hop" soundtrack can "get a little crowded", but most are too busy "having fun" to care.

Dos Caminos *Mexican* 19 | 19 | 19 | $45

East 50s | 825 Third Ave. (bet. 50th & 51st Sts.) | 212-336-5400
Meatpacking District | 675 Hudson St. (bet. 13th & 14th Sts.) | 212-699-2400
Murray Hill | 373 Park Ave. S. (bet. 26th & 27th Sts.) | 212-294-1000
SoHo | 475 W. Broadway (bet. Houston & Prince Sts.) | 212-277-4300
www.doscaminos.com

"Signature margaritas" and "delicious" tableside guacamole are menu standouts at these "lively" Mexicans fielding "standard fare done well"; "cheerful" service and stellar "people-watching" are other incentives, though some say the "party" atmospheres overshadow the food.

	FOOD	DECOR	SERVICE	COST

Dos Toros *Mexican*

22 | 13 | 17 | $16

Battery Park City | Hudson Eats | 230 Vesey St. (West St.) | 212-786-0392
NEW **East 40s** | 465 Lexington Ave. (bet. 45th & 46th Sts.) | 347-394-3844
East 70s | 1111 Lexington Ave. (bet. 77th & 78th Sts.) | 212-535-4658
NEW **Gramercy Park** | 295 Park Ave. S. (23rd St.) | 347-946-6225
Greenwich Village | 137 Fourth Ave. (13th St.) | 212-677-7300
West Village | 11 Carmine St. (bet. Bleecker St. & 6th Ave.) | 212-627-2051
Williamsburg | 189 Bedford Ave. (bet. N. 6th & 7th Sts.) | Brooklyn | 718-384-8833
www.dostoros.com

"Legitimate" Mexican fare by way of the Bay Area is the specialty of these "cheap, fab" taquerias, "eco-friendly" stops luring both bullish burrito buffs and Cali transplants; there's "always a line and never a table", but "fast delivery" is an option at most outlets.

Dover *American*

26 | 18 | 25 | $78

Carroll Gardens | 412 Court St. (bet. 1st & 2nd Pls.) | Brooklyn | 347-987-3545 | www.doverbrooklyn.com

"Wow" is the word on this Carroll Gardens American where the "innovative", ambitious American fare is "remarkably good" (ditto the "first-rate" cocktails) and service is "super attentive"; its "simple" (some say "stark") surrounds may be an "odd match" for the "fine-dining" fare, but the "pricey" tabs are right in line.

Dovetail *American*

25 | 23 | 24 | $107

West 70s | 103 W. 77th St. (Columbus Ave.) | 212-362-3800 | www.dovetailnyc.com

After a revamp, John Fraser's "sophisticated" UWS New American has gone prix fixe only, offering his "cut-above" "haute cuisine" in "inventive" (and "pricey") customizable tasting menus; the redone space has a lighter look, though the "relaxed" vibe remains, as does the "great-deal" 'Sunday suppa.'

Ducks Eatery *Eclectic*

25 | 20 | 22 | $36

East Village | 351 E. 12th St. (1st Ave.) | 212-432-3825 | www.duckseatery.com

Cafe on weekdays and resto-bar by night, this "cool" East Villager "wows" with "excellent, exotic" dishes like "succulent" smoked meats (chicken wings, duck, goat) with "huge" Asian, Creole and Southern flavors; "interesting" drinks are another reason the small, "hipster"-friendly space is "crowded at peak hours."

Due *Italian*

22 | 17 | 22 | $55

East 70s | 1396 Third Ave. (bet. 79th & 80th Sts.) | 212-772-3331 | www.duenyc.com

Locals tout the "simple", "satisfying" Northern Italian cooking and "feel-at-home" atmosphere at this longtime "low-profile" Upper Eastsider; "rustic" looks and "warm" service enhance its "unpretentious" air, and fair prices seal the deal.

| | FOOD | DECOR | SERVICE | COST |

DuMont Burger *Burgers*   23 | 15 | 19 | $26

Williamsburg | 314 Bedford Ave. (bet. 1st & 2nd Sts.) | Brooklyn |
718-384-6127 | www.dumontnyc.com

Williamsburg's "burger aficionados" insist the "prime" patties at this
"hip" hideaway are "definitely high up there", especially matched with
"amazing" boozy shakes; the "very small" space has limited counter
seating, but it "hits the spot for a greasy craving."

Dumpling Galaxy *Chinese*   22 | 14 | 15 | $24

Flushing | 42-35 Main St. (Franklin Ave.) | Queens | 718-461-0808 |
www.dumplinggalaxy.com

The "rich and juicy" dumplings really are "out of this world" at this
mall-based Flushing Chinese, a Tianjin Dumpling satellite whose
"mind-boggling" selection includes plenty of "unusual options"; it's
a "no-frills venue", but given "speedy service" and "great prices", "it
makes kitschy work."

Dumpling Man *Chinese*   24 | 13 | 20 | $16

East Village | 100 St. Marks Pl. (bet. Ave. A & 1st Ave.) | 212-505-2121 |
www.dumplingman.com

Steamed or seared, the "scrumptious dumplings" at this East Village
Chinese make for a "super-cheap", cash-only snack that's handmade
"right in front of you" (a "show in itself"); many prefer to "stuff themselves" on the run since the premises "aren't much to look at."

The Dutch *American*   22 | 21 | 20 | $60

SoHo | 131 Sullivan St. (Prince St.) | 212-677-6200 |
www.thedutchnyc.com

"Just what one hopes for in SoHo", this "happening" American presents chef Andrew Carmellini's "well-crafted plates" in an "attractive"
"retro setting" where "downtown" types can "see and be seen"; skeptics
say it's "noisy" and "expensive for what it is", but expect "bustling"
business "at all times."

E&E Grill House *Steak*   21 | 18 | 21 | $50

West 40s | 233 W. 49th St. (bet. B'way & 8th Ave.) | 212-505-9909 |
www.eegrillhouse.com

"Darn-good steaks" and seafood are the headliners at this "heart-of-
Times Square" chophouse where a minimalist, "modern" setting and "eager-to-please" staffers set a "delightful" mood; throw in tabs that "won't
break the bank", and showgoers say this baby's got star "potential."

East End Kitchen *American*   20 | 17 | 18 | $45

East 80s | 539 E. 81st St. (bet. East End & York Aves.) | 212-879-0450 |
www.eastendkitchennyc.com

A "wonderful asset" in "sleepy" Yorkville, this neighborhood haunt trades
in "homey" Americana, with "casual" brunching and a seasonal grab-
and-go espresso bar as additional pluses; the "Hamptons"-esque decor
is "stylish", but critics wish the servers would "get their act together."

The East Pole *American/British*   23 | 20 | 20 | $66

East 60s | 133 E. 65th St. (bet. Lexington & Park Aves.) | 212-249-2222 |
www.theeastpolenyc.com

"Downtown moves Uptown" via this Fat Radish offshoot that's "enchanting" Upper Eastsiders with its "farm-to-table-done-right", British-

accented New American fare and "original" cocktails served in airy, "hip" quarters; despite "pricey" tabs, it's generally "crowded" – especially at the "fantastic brunch."

E.A.T. *American* | 19 | 12 | 15 | $45 |

East 80s | 1064 Madison Ave. (bet. 80th & 81st Sts.) | 212-772-0022 | www.elizabar.com

Before "Madison Avenue shopping" or hitting the Museum Mile, "East Side ladies" and others drop by Eli Zabar's "high-style" American for "tastefully prepared" sandwiches and salads; despite "money-is-no-object" tabs, "rushed" service and "glamorized deli" digs, it's "always busy."

Eataly *Food Hall/Italian* | 24 | 20 | 18 | $43 |

Flatiron | 200 Fifth Ave. (bet. 23rd & 24th Sts.) | 212-229-2560 | www.eataly.com

"Wonderment" awaits at the Batali-Bastianich crew's "massive" Flatiron food hall, a "phenomenal" gustatory "playground" where "chaotic" throngs "ramble and graze" among counters vending "top-shelf", all-Italian eats from pasta and pizza to fish and veggies; also housing the full-service ristorante Manzo and rooftop Birreria, it's "spendy" and "tough to get a table" but "deserves to be experienced."

Eatery *American* | 19 | 15 | 18 | $38 |

West 50s | 798 Ninth Ave. (53rd St.) | 212-765-7080 | www.eaterynyc.com

"Comfort food with a trendy twist" is the calling card of this Hell's Kitchen American where the midpriced chow arrives in "minimalist", "diner-chic" digs; "be-seen" types like the "gay-friendly" people-watching and tolerate the high-volume "hustle and bustle."

Ecco *Italian* | 22 | 19 | 21 | $65 |

TriBeCa | 124 Chambers St. (bet. Church St. & B'way) | 212-227-7074 | www.eccorestaurantny.com

"Still going strong", this "old-school" TriBeCan turns out "true-to-its-roots" Italian fare in mahogany-paneled "publike" surrounds with a "bustling bar"; "friendly" staffers add to the "classic" neighborhood vibe, making "Uptown prices" the only kink.

Eddie's Sweet Shop *Ice Cream* | 25 | 22 | 22 | $12 |

Forest Hills | 105-29 Metropolitan Ave. (72nd Rd.) | Queens | 718-520-8514

Around since "before they invented calories", this "throwback" Forest Hills soda shop still makes its own ice cream, toppings and fountain drinks to the "highest standards"; indeed, its "candy-store" decor and "old-fashioned service" recall a "kinder era of simple pleasures."

The Eddy *American* | 26 | 23 | 24 | $71 |

East Village | 342 E. Sixth St. (bet. 1st & 2nd Aves.) | 646-895-9884 | www.theeddynyc.com

This "charming" East Village New American "nails it" with "exciting" plates (including "fancy" tater tots) "executed with perfect flavors" plus some of the "most creative" cocktails around; despite "expensive" tabs and an "itty-bitty" space that can feel a "bit tight", most still "can't say enough great things."

	FOOD	DECOR	SERVICE	COST

Edi & The Wolf *Austrian*

22 | 22 | 20 | $50

East Village | 102 Ave. C (bet. 6th & 7th Sts.) | 212-598-1040 |
www.ediandthewolf.com

"Unique" is the word on this "funky" East Village Austrian offering "rich",
"authentic" fare paired with super suds and wines; the hipster "cozy-cot-
tage" design seems straight out of a fractured fairy tale, while the "cute"
garden is a quiet alternative to the "loud" goings-on inside.

Ed's Chowder House *Seafood*

20 | 20 | 20 | $61

West 60s | Empire Hotel | 44 W. 63rd St. (bet. B'way & Columbus Ave.) |
212-956-1288 | www.chinagrillmgt.com

"Civilized dining by Lincoln Center" is alive and well at this "sophisticated" seafooder in the Empire Hotel where the "skillfully prepared" catch
is dispatched by a staff that "gets you out on time" for the show; "nicely
spaced" tables and overall "convenience" make the rather "pricey"
tabs more palatable.

Ed's Lobster Bar *Seafood*

25 | 17 | 21 | $40

NEW **Meatpacking District** | Gansevoort Mkt. | 52 Gansevoort St.
(Greenwich St.) | 212-242-1701
SoHo | 222 Lafayette St. (bet. Broome & Spring Sts.) | 212-343-3236
www.lobsterbarnyc.com

A "seafood bonanza" awaits at this "tiny" SoHo fish house (with a
Gansevoort Market offshoot), where "consistently fresh" fare includes
a "loaded" lobster roll that "tops the charts"; space is "tight" in the
"beachy" room, but the front bar can be quite "pleasant."

Egg *Southern*

24 | 17 | 18 | $28

Williamsburg | 109 N. Third St. (bet. Berry St. & Wythe Ave.) | Brooklyn |
718-302-5151 | www.eggrestaurant.com

Known for "one of the best brunches in town", this Williamsburg
daytimer packs 'em in for "very good", "simple" Southern dishes made
with ingredients from its own upstate farm; a move to larger digs means
"more space", but there's still an "enormous wait" on weekends.

Egg Shop *American*

24 | 20 | 20 | $26

NoLita | 151 Elizabeth St. (Kenmare St.) | 646-666-0810 |
www.eggshopnyc.com

"Creative" egg dishes are "on point" at this all-day NoLita American
supplying "Instagram-friendly" sandwiches and bowls alongside "divine"
biscuits and "very good" cocktails; seating's limited in the "sunny-side-
up" space, so weekend wait times are an "investment", but the "good
price point" helps.

83.5 *Italian*

22 | 17 | 23 | $53

East 80s | 345 E. 83rd St. (1st Ave.) | 212-737-8312 |
www.eighty-threeandahalf.com

This "charming" UES "hideaway" puts a "creative" modern spin on
classic Italian fare with its "flavorful" dishes (including "to-die-for"
Brussels sprouts) and "enticing" specials; "gracious" staffers preside
over the "intimate" space, where an open kitchen allows a glimpse of
"the chefs at work."

	FOOD	DECOR	SERVICE	COST

Eisenberg's Sandwich Shop *Sandwiches*
20 | 10 | 17 | $18

Flatiron | 174 Fifth Ave. (22nd St.) | 212-675-5096 |
www.eisenbergsnyc.com

A "bygone" ode to the "greasy spoon", this circa-1929 Flatiron luncheonette is known for "basics" like tuna sandwiches and "old-style" egg creams; modernists may moan about "shabby" decor and "rickety" service, but for many, this remains a "sentimental" favorite.

Élan *American*
23 | 20 | 23 | $80

Flatiron | 43 E. 20th St. (bet. B'way & Park Ave. S.) | 646-682-7105 |
www.elannyc.com

Chef David Watluck's "welcome return" after shuttering Chanterelle, this Flatiron American earns its name with "imaginative", "well-prepared" French-influenced dishes including "old favorites" like the "luscious" seafood sausage; "understated" with "warm" service and a "hip bar", it's "a bit pricey" but "promising."

El Centro *Mexican*
23 | 19 | 22 | $34

West 50s | 824 Ninth Ave. (54th St.) | 646-763-6585 |
www.elcentro-nyc.com

This "upbeat" Midtown Mexican throws a "hip", "loud" fiesta ramped up by "awesome" margaritas and, oh yeah, "decently priced" south-of-the-border bites; the "quirky", "kitschy" setting is "always packed", though regulars wish the "music could be lowered a few decibels."

El Charro Espanol *Spanish*
▽ 24 | 15 | 23 | $50

West Village | 4 Charles St. (bet. Greenwich & 7th Aves.) | 212-242-9547 |
www.el-charro-espanol.com

Tucked away in a West Village brownstone basement, this circa-1925 Spaniard fields "first-rate" tapas, large plates and deadly sangria; the "generic decor" is "quaint" to some, "dated" to others, but everyone likes the "warm" service.

El Colmado *Spanish*
▽ 19 | 13 | 16 | $41

West 40s | Gotham West Mkt. | 600 11th Ave. (bet. 44th & 45th Sts.) |
212-582-7948

NEW El Colmado Butchery *Spanish*

Meatpacking District | 53 Little W. 12th St. (bet. 10th Ave. &
Washington St.) | 212-488-0000
www.elcolmadonyc.com

"Tasty and quick", these informal Spaniards pair Tertulia chef Seamus Mullen's "interesting" tapas with "decently priced" Iberian vinos; the Gotham West Market setup is "just a counter", and the Meatpacking site's tiny, table-service quarters double as a butcher shop.

Eleven Madison Park *American*
28 | 28 | 28 | $293

Flatiron | 11 Madison Ave. (24th St.) | 212-889-0905 |
www.elevenmadisonpark.com

"This one goes to 11" cheer fans of Daniel Humm's "transcendent" New American housed in a soaring, "spectacular" art deco space on Madison Square Park, where the "exciting" tasting menu is "full of discoveries", the wine pairings "heighten the experience" and it's all delivered by an "impeccable" staff; sure, you'll "drop big bucks", but it's a "culinary event" that will "leave you breathless" ("wowzers!") – "what more can one ask?"

	FOOD	DECOR	SERVICE	COST

Eliá *Greek* ▽ 26 | 21 | 24 | $57

Bay Ridge | 8611 Third Ave. (bet. 86th & 87th Sts.) | Brooklyn | 718-748-9891 | www.eliarestaurant.com

Bringing Bay Ridge an "exceptional" "taste of the Mediterranean", this Greek neighborhood fixture produces "perfectly cooked" whole fish and other "innovative" specials; sure, it's a "splurge", but the staff is "hospitable" and there are bonus "outdoor seats" on the garden deck.

Elias Corner *Greek/Seafood* 25 | 9 | 16 | $41

Astoria | 24-02 31st St. (24th Ave.) | Queens | 718-932-1510 | www.eliascorner.com

Grilled fish so fresh it tastes like it was "caught an hour ago" is the specialty of this "no-frills" Astoria Greek with not much decor and "no menus" (just check out the "cold case" and point); though it only accepts cash and service is "so-so", the tabs are sure "hard to beat."

Elio's *Italian* 25 | 19 | 23 | $71

East 80s | 1621 Second Ave. (bet. 84th & 85th Sts.) | 212-772-2242

A magnet for "media" moguls, "Page Six regulars" and "monied" UES types, this "old-school" Italian dispenses food "delectable" enough to justify the "through-the-nose" tabs; expect the "cold shoulder" if you're not a "member of the club", but at least the "cheek-to-jowl" seating bolsters the chance of rubbing elbows with "Matt Lauer."

NEW Eli's Table *American* 22 | 16 | 18 | $62

East 80s | 1413 Third Ave. (80th St.) | 212-717-9798 | www.elistablenyc.com

"There's a lot to like" at this modern UES American from Eli Zabar, where "fine-tuned" sourcing from the neighboring gourmet shop informs a "market-driven" menu (brunch included) matched with "very good wines"; if it's "not drawing big crowds", pocket-watchers point to "high prices."

El Parador Cafe *Mexican* 22 | 18 | 21 | $53

Murray Hill | 325 E. 34th St. (bet. 1st & 2nd Aves.) | 212-679-6812 | www.elparadorcafe.com

A "devoted clientele" gets its "paella fix" at this '59-vintage Murray Hill vet that's known for "true-to-its-roots", "old-world" Mexican cooking; obscured by Midtown Tunnel traffic, it's a "hidden gem" – polished by "cordial" servers – that insiders want to keep "secret."

El Paso *Mexican* 22 | 16 | 21 | $31

East 90s | 64 E. 97th St. (bet. Madison & Park Aves.) | 212-996-1739
East Harlem | 1643 Lexington Ave. (104th St.) | 212-831-9831
www.elpasony.com

Eastsiders count on these "solid", unpretentious Uptown Mexicans for "terrific" tacos and other standards ("try the aguas frescas") made "fresh" with "quality ingredients"; "tight quarters" and "so-so" service are offset by "unbelievable-value" prices.

El Porrón *Spanish* 22 | 18 | 21 | $50

East 60s | 1123 First Ave. (bet. 61st & 62nd Sts.) | 212-207-8349 | www.elporronnyc.com

Tapas "like you'd find in Barcelona" make for "real-thing" dining at this UES Spaniard sporting a "something-for-everyone" menu; "winning "wine" arrives in the namesake pitcher, and the crowd's a mix of "lively" types who "come hungry, thirsty and often."

El Pote *Spanish*
22 | 15 | 22 | $42

Murray Hill | 718 Second Ave. (bet. 38th & 39th Sts.) | 212-889-6680 | www.elpote.com

"Home away from home" for Murray Hill amigos since '77, this Spanish stalwart keeps business brisk with "fantastic paella" and other "first-rate" Iberian standards; maybe it's looking a bit "shabby", but locals count themselves "lucky" to have it.

El Quijote *Spanish*
22 | 16 | 20 | $49

Chelsea | 226 W. 23rd St. (bet. 7th & 8th Aves.) | 212-929-1855 | www.elquijoterestaurant.com

"Old-school to the hilt", this "colorful" Chelsea octogenarian may be "faded" but is still "memorable" for Spanish food plated in "gut-buster portions"; the decor lies somewhere between "tacky" and "kitschy", but the prices are "decent" and that "lobster deal can't be beat."

El Quinto Pino *Spanish*
23 | 17 | 21 | $49

Chelsea | 401 W. 24th St. (bet. 9th & 10th Aves.) | 212-206-6900 | www.elquintopinonyc.com

Little plates "go a long way" at Alex Raij's "tiny", "adorable" Chelsea tapas bar, where the "rich" Spanish bites – including that "nothing-like-it-on-this-planet" uni panini – pair well with the "solid" wines and "romantic" vibe; fans say the "super-chill" atmosphere alone makes it a "come-back-to" kind of place.

NEW El Rey Coffee Bar & Luncheonette *American*
▽ 25 | 25 | 24 | $21

Lower East Side | 100 Stanton St. (Ludlow St.) | 212-260-3950 | www.elreynyc.com

"Cute and cozy" during the day for "healthy and delicious" bites, this vegetarian-friendly Lower Eastsider is also "killing it" at night with ambitious New American small plates; the compact space can be a "zoo" during brunch, but there's always draft beer and "interesting" wines to help distract.

El Toro Blanco *Mexican*
21 | 19 | 20 | $55

West Village | 257 Sixth Ave. (bet. Bedford & Downing Sts.) | 212-645-0193 | www.eltoroblanconyc.com

Elevating classic Mexican eats to "gourmet" levels, Josh Capon's slick West Villager delivers dishes that "burst with flavor" amid a scene of "trendy" "hustle and bustle"; though service can be "spotty", "potent" drinks provide another reason to "come back."

El Vez *Mexican*
20 | 21 | 20 | $42

Battery Park City | 259 Vesey St. (bet. North End Ave. & West St.) | 212-233-2500 | www.elveznyc.com

The Battery Park City outpost of a Philly original, this "spacious" Mexican provides "big flavors" via a classic menu with "modern" twists served amid "quirky" cantina decor; given a "busy bar" pouring "well-mixed" drinks with a "preponderance of mezcal", "expect suits after work" – and during the day at the burrito bar.

	FOOD	DECOR	SERVICE	COST

Emilia's *Italian*

 24 | 18 | 23 | $41

Arthur Avenue/Belmont | 2331 Arthur Ave. (Crescent Ave.) | Bronx | 718-367-5915 | www.emiliasrestaurant.com

"In the heart of" Arthur Avenue's "food mecca", this longtime Italian "mainstay" proffers "delicious" "red-sauce standards" in "generous portions", including "wonderful daily specials"; happily there's "minimal frenzy" within its "cozy", nothing-fancy digs, which are presided over by a "friendly" staff.

Emilio's Ballato *Italian*

▽ 26 | 18 | 23 | $62

NoLita | 55 E Houston St. (Mott St.) | 212-274-8881

The "food sings" at this "back-in-the-day" NoLita "red-sauce" joint that "looks like an Italian farmhouse hallway" and is "one of the last of a breed" (it's been around since 1956); owner Emilio is "always there", and his presence "makes the evening complete."

Emily *Pizza*

26 | 20 | 24 | $30

Clinton Hill | 919 Fulton St. (bet. Clinton & Waverly Aves.) | Brooklyn | 347-844-9588 | www.pizzalovesemily.com

The "buzz is warranted" at this Clinton Hill pie parlor wowing "true pizza fanatics" with "creative but not wacky" Neapolitan rounds boasting a "standout" thin crust and "addictive" toppings; an "amazing" burger, solid cocktails and "personable" service also explain why "word is getting out", so the "tiny" quarters are typically "jam-packed."

NEW Empellón al Pastor *Mexican*

▽ 19 | 18 | 17 | $30

East Village | 132 St. Marks Pl. (Ave. A) | 646-833-7039 | www.empellon.com

"Fun for a pit stop" when you're in the East Village, this "lively" counter-service Mexican specializes in tacos al pastor featuring spit-roasted pork shoulder and housemade tortillas; there are other "creative" options and "seriously good" drinks too, plus graffiti art lends a "trendy" feel to the "no-nonsense" digs.

Empellón Cocina *Mexican*

 23 | 19 | 20 | $60

East Village | 105 First Ave. (bet. 6th & 7th Sts.) | 212-780-0999 | www.empellon.com

Mexican cooking gets "adventurous" at this "lively" East Villager where "high-end" tacos and other "wow"-worthy plates are "perfect for sharing" and the drinks are "delish"; recently renovated, the lightened-up space now has an open kitchen, fewer seats and a small chef's counter for prix fixe meals.

Empellón Taqueria *Mexican*

 22 | 19 | 19 | $53

West Village | 230 W. Fourth St. (W. 10th St.) | 212-367-0999 | www.empellon.com

"First-rate" ingredients in "imaginative" combinations make for some seriously "haute" tacos at this "trendy" West Village Mexican where the "strong" margaritas are just as "creative"; "slightly upscale" pricing doesn't deter those who keep its "barlike" space "crowded and noisy."

	FOOD	DECOR	SERVICE	COST

Empire Diner *Diner*
19 | 18 | 18 | $35

Chelsea | 210 10th Ave. (bet. 22nd & 23rd Sts.) | 212-596-7523 |
www.empire-diner.com

Occupying an art deco metal diner that's a Chelsea icon, this "updated"
take on the "traditional" formula offers "tasty" spins on comfort "classics"
with plenty of "retro-chic" appeal; the "funky", made-over interior fills up
fast, so don't be surprised if "service varies" and seating's "squished."

Empire Steakhouse *Steak*
22 | 19 | 21 | $76

West 50s | 237 W. 54th St. (bet. B'way & 8th Ave.) | 212-586-9700 |
www.empiresteakhousenyc.com

Fans are "pleasantly surprised" by the "quality" preparation at this Midtown
chop shop convenient to Rock Center and the Theater District, where the
steaks are "cooked exactly as ordered"; "efficient" service and "nothing-
special" decor complete the overall "old-world steakhouse" picture.

Emporio *Italian*
23 | 21 | 21 | $39

NoLita | 231 Mott St. (bet. Prince & Spring Sts.) | 212-966-1234 |
www.emporiony.com

Aurora alums are behind this *"bellissimo"* NoLita trattoria, a "sublime"
option for "authentic" Neapolitan pizzas and "homemade pastas" served
in a rustic-industrial setting; when the front room gets too "tight", regulars head for the "greenhouse"-like back room.

EN Japanese Brasserie *Japanese*
25 | 26 | 22 | $73

West Village | 435 Hudson St. (Leroy St.) | 212-647-9196 | www.enjb.com
"Excellent" Japanese cuisine – including "amazing" housemade tofu and
"wow"-worthy kaiseki menus – served within "beautiful" digs have made
a "favorite" of this "upscale" West Villager; a "tremendous sake list" and
"earnest" service are other reasons it's spot on for "date night."

Enoteca Maria *Italian*
26 | 17 | 22 | $56

St. George | 27 Hyatt St. (Central Ave.) | Staten Island | 718-447-2777 |
www.enotecamaria.com

A cast of "rotating nonnas" in the kitchen "lovingly" prepare "fabulous"
regional Italian specialties at this "convivial" Staten Island enoteca where
a "strong selection" of affordable wines and "blasting rock 'n' roll" con-
tribute to the "warm, appealing" atmosphere; though "seating is tight",
supporters swear the food is "worth any discomfort."

Enzo's *Italian*
25 | 20 | 23 | $45

Morris Park | 1998 Williamsbridge Rd. (Neill Ave.) | Bronx |
718-409-3828 | www.enzosbronxrestaurant.com

Enzo's of Arthur Avenue *Italian*
Arthur Avenue/Belmont | 2339 Arthur Ave. (bet. 184th & 187th Sts.) |
Bronx | 718-733-4455 | www.enzosofarthuravenue.com

These separately owned "blue-ribbon" "red-sauce palaces" in the Bronx
dish out "down-home" Italian standards in mammoth portions and toss in
some "old-school charm" on the side; the "unpretentious" staff "treats you
like family", so embrace the "time warp" – and "don't fill up on the bread."

Erawan *Thai*
24 | 21 | 22 | $42

Bayside | 42-31 Bell Blvd. (bet. 42nd & 43rd Aves.) | Queens |
718-428-2112 | www.erawanthaibayside.com

Bayside locals tout this "go-to Thai" for its "aromatic" offerings with

	FOOD	DECOR	SERVICE	COST

"interesting modern twists", abetted by "gentle" service and a "Manhattan atmosphere"; though prices lie on the "premium" side for the genre, it's ever "crowded" at prime times.

Erminia *Italian*
24 | 24 | 25 | $71

East 80s | 250 E. 83rd St. (bet. 2nd & 3rd Aves.) | 212-879-4284 | www.erminiaristorante.com

If you're looking for "romance", try this "transporting" UES Roman boîte where a "cavelike", candlelit setting sets the mood for "knockout" Italian cooking, while "attentive" service and a "leisurely" pace do the rest; sure, it's "expensive", but there are "only a few tables", lending exclusivity to this "special experience."

Esca *Italian/Seafood*
25 | 20 | 22 | $79

West 40s | 402 W. 43rd St. (bet. 9th & 10th Aves.) | 212-564-7272 | www.esca-nyc.com

"Like eating on the Positano coast", this "high-end" Hell's Kitchen fish specialist from the Batali-Bastianich-Pasternack team fields "impeccable" Italian seafood and pastas, paired with a "terrific" wine list; "knowledgeable" staffers, an "unpretentious" setting and a "hefty" check are all part of the "glorious" package.

NEW Esme *American*
▽ 23 | 22 | 22 | $41

Greenpoint | 999 Manhattan Ave. (Huron St.) | Brooklyn | 718-383-0999 | www.esmebk.com

Updated American classics deliver "big taste" at this relaxed Greenpoint bistro, whose understated style features reclaimed church pews and subdued hues; craft (and draft) cocktails are mixed at a wooden-ceilinged bar under exposed-filament bulbs that create a soft, "romantic" glow.

Estela *American/Mediterranean*
27 | 19 | 22 | $70

NoLita | 47 E. Houston St. (bet. Mott & Mulberry Sts.) | 212-219-7693 | www.estelanyc.com

"Paradise for adventurous eaters", this "spectacular" Med-influenced American from Isa alum Ignacio Mattos "lives up to the hype" with "clever but not overwrought" small plates and "interesting" wines in a compact NoLita space; sure, it's "crowded and noisy", and seating is "cramped", but this doesn't seem to faze its "young, sophisticated" following one bit.

Etcetera Etcetera *Italian*
23 | 19 | 22 | $54

West 40s | 352 W. 44th St. (bet. 8th & 9th Aves.) | 212-399-4141 | www.etcetcnyc.com

"Casual" but "lively", this Midtown Italian features a "modern" menu that's a match for its "contemporary" looks; "splendid", "get-you-to-the-theater-on-time" service makes up for "noisy" acoustics, though regulars say it's "quieter upstairs."

Ethos *Greek/Seafood*
22 | 17 | 18 | $51

East 50s | 905 First Ave. (51st St.) | 212-888-4060
Murray Hill | 495 Third Ave. (bet. 33rd & 34th Sts.) | 212-252-1972 | www.ethosrestaurants.com

continued

Ethos Meze   *Greek/Seafood*
Murray Hill | 542 Third Ave. (36th St.) | 212-686-0372 |
www.ethosmeze.com

"Generous" plates of "well-prepared" catch are the lure at these Greek
seafooders along with "polite" if "slow" service and "affordable" tabs; the
Murray Hill branches are more "dinerlike", while the separately owned Sutton Place locale is "airy" with "energetic" (read: "noisy") atmospherics.

NEW Eugene & Company   *American*   — | — | — | M
Bedford-Stuyvesant | 397 Tompkins Ave. (Jefferson Ave.) | Brooklyn |
718-443-2223 | www.eugeneandcompany.com

A corner spot with exposed brick, big windows and a wraparound
banquette, this Bed-Stuy arrival offers seasonal New American fare by a
Le Bernardin alum; classic cocktails, draft beers and global vinos up the
appeal as does a small late-night menu.

Excellent Dumpling House   *Chinese*   22 | 7 | 12 | $19
Chinatown | 111 Lafayette St. (bet. Canal & Walker Sts.) | 212-219-0212 |
www.excellentdumplinghouse.com

There's "no false advertising" at this Chinatowner where the "name-says-it-all" dumplings are served with equally "worthwhile" Shanghainese
plates; true, there's "no atmosphere" and service is of the "rush-you-out"
variety, but "at these prices, who cares?"

Extra Fancy   *Seafood*   23 | 21 | 22 | $36
Williamsburg | 302 Metropolitan Ave. (Roebling St.) | Brooklyn |
347-422-0939 | www.extrafancybklyn.com

Ironic moniker to the contrary, this Williamsburg seafooder is "nothing
too fancy", both in its "reasonably priced", "delicious" New England–inspired eats and clam-shack looks; "friendly, prompt" service, an impressive craft beer and cocktail list and a big backyard are other draws.

Extra Virgin   *Mediterranean*   22 | 18 | 20 | $48
West Village | 259 W. Fourth St. (Perry St.) | 212-691-9359 |
www.extravirginrestaurant.com

The "young" and "glamorous" hobnob at this "fashionable" West Villager
over "dependable" Med fare that "won't break the bank"; although the
place is usually "crowded" and the no-rez policy leads to "waits", amusing "people-watching" helps pass the time.

F & J Pine Restaurant   *Italian*   23 | 21 | 22 | $40
Van Nest | 1913 Bronxdale Ave. (bet. Matthews & Muliner Aves.) |
Bronx | 718-792-5956 | www.fjpine.com

"Gigantic portions" are the name of the game at this "doggy bag"–guaranteed Van Nest Italian ladling out "loads of red sauce" for fans of "old-time" carbo-loading; "checkered" tablecloths, "old Yankee" memorabilia
and Bronx Bomber sightings are all part of the "colorful" package here.

Farm on Adderley   *American*   23 | 20 | 21 | $37
Ditmas Park | 1108 Cortelyou Rd (bet. Stratford & Westminster Rds.) |
Brooklyn | 718-287-3101 | www.thefarmonadderley.com

With its "inventive" New American fare showcasing "farm-fresh" ingredients, this "quaint" Ditmas Park "favorite" is something of an "oasis" in the "wilds of Brooklyn"; it "gets super crowded" ("and with reason") during weekend brunch, but summer brings access to a "gorgeous" backyard.

NEW Faro *Italian*

— | — | — | E

Bushwick | 436 Jefferson St. (bet. St. Nicholas & Wyckoff Aves.) | Brooklyn | 718-381-8201

This Bushwick Italian in a renovated warehouse space offers housemade pastas and wood-fired dishes based around personally sourced ingredients; rustic woods and gleaming tiles define the room, while counter seats offer the best view of the action.

The Fat Radish *American*

22 | 22 | 20 | $54

Lower East Side | 17 Orchard St. (bet. Canal & Hester Sts.) | 212-300-4053 | www.thefatradishnyc.com

"Veggie fanatics" get the royal treatment at this "trendy" Lower Eastsider that "oozes cool" with its "creative", locavore-oriented New American cooking and "hiptastic" "art-crowd" following; sure, it's a "tad pricey" and can feel "cramped", but thanks to "friendly" servers and "interesting cocktails", it "doesn't matter."

Fatty Crab *Malaysian*

21 | 14 | 18 | $52

Meatpacking District | 643 Hudson St. (bet. Gansevoort & Horatio Sts.) | 212-352-3592 | www.fattycrabnyc.com

"Sticky-salty-sweet" Malaysian street eats make for "delectable" dining at this "buzzy" Meatpacking joint that's a magnet for "adventurous" "heat"-seekers; still, it's "not for the faint of heart" given the "doing-you-a-favor" service, "pounding music" and "steadily climbing bills."

Fatty Fish *Asian*

20 | 14 | 18 | $47

East 60s | 406 E. 64th St. (bet. 1st & York Aves.) | 212-813-9338 | www.fattyfishnyc.com

Upper Eastsiders are hooked on this Asian-fusion practitioner boasting "surprisingly creative" cooking (and sushi) served by "solicitous" staffers who just "keep smiling"; a "Zen-like" mood and "beautiful" enclosed garden distract from the "small" dimensions.

Fedora *American/French*

22 | 22 | 22 | $65

West Village | 239 W. Fourth St., downstairs (bet. Charles & W. 10th Sts.) | 646-449-9336 | www.fedoranyc.com

Gabe Stulman's "low-key chic" West Village basement earns a tip of the cap for its "interesting" Franco-American menu, "tasty cocktails" and "beautiful neon sign"; blending a "speakeasy vibe" with some "Wisconsin hospitality", it's "an all around win", except perhaps for the cost.

Felice *Italian*

21 | 19 | 21 | $48

East 60s | 1166 First Ave. (64th St.) | 212-593-2223 | www.felice64.com
East 80s | 1593 First Ave. (83rd St.) | 212-249-4080 | www.felice83.com
Financial District | 15 Gold St. (Platt St.) | 212-785-5950 | www.felice15goldstreet.com

These "moderately hip" wine bars spice up "date nights" with "affordable", "well-chosen" vinos paired with "tasty" Italian small plates; the "gracious" service and "sexy" ambiance "appeal to multiple generations", though they mainly draw "younger" folks.

	FOOD	DECOR	SERVICE	COST

Felidia *Italian*
25 | 21 | 24 | $87

East 50s | 243 E. 58th St. (bet. 2nd & 3rd Aves.) | 212-758-1479 | www.felidia-nyc.com

A "classy gem" from cuisine queen Lidia Bastianich, this "memorable" East Midtown Italian is touted for its "silky" pastas and overall "stellar" fare "cooked to perfection" and complemented by "accommodating" service and a "lovely" (if "conservative") townhouse setting; while you'll "spend a bundle" for dinner, the prix fixe lunch is a "bargain by any standard."

Ferrara *Bakery*
24 | 18 | 18 | $23

Little Italy | 195 Grand St. (bet. Mott & Mulberry Sts.) | 212-226-6150 | www.ferraracafe.com

Open 120-plus years "and counting", this Little Italy bakery is a "legend" famed for its "heaven-on-a-plate" cannoli and "pick-me-up" espresso; "crowds of tourists" and "expensive"-for-what-it-is tabs draw some complaints, yet most agree this NYC relic "still has charm."

Fette Sau *BBQ*
26 | 18 | 17 | $32

Williamsburg | 354 Metropolitan Ave. (bet. Havemeyer & Roebling Sts.) | Brooklyn | 718-963-3404 | www.fettesaubbq.com

It's the "quintessential Williamsburg experience" to "join the hipsters" at this "serious foodie" "heaven" for "awesome" dry-rub, by-the-pound BBQ paired with "artisanal" beers and bourbons; no rezzies means "crazy lines" for "cafeteria-style" service in a "former garage" outfitted with "communal picnic tables" – but to most it's so "worth it."

15 East *Japanese*
27 | 22 | 24 | $114

Union Square | 15 E. 15th St. (5th Ave.) | 212-647-0015 | www.15eastrestaurant.com

"The real deal" for "pristine" sushi, this Union Square Japanese "maintains high standards" to rival "the big hitters" with its "incredible" food, "array" of sakes and "flawless" service; the "stylish", "Zen-like atmosphere" even softens the blow of "over-the-top pricing."

NEW Fifty Paces *American*

∇ 22 | 22 | 25 | $41

East Village | 413 E. 12th St. (bet. Ave. A & 1st Ave.) | 646-602-1300 | www.fiftypaces.restauranthearth.com

Marco Canora has turned Terroir into this "great little" East Village wine bar, a "lower-key" extension of Hearth, where the "delicious" New American bites include broth bowls, charcuterie and some heartier plates; "romantic" enough "to bring a date", it's also simply a "fun place to hang", with "helpful" service to boot.

57 Napoli Pizza e Vino *Pizza*
24 | 20 | 22 | $32

East 50s | 120 E. 57th St., upstairs (bet. Lexington & Park Aves.) | 212-750-4586 | www.57napoli.com

OK, the obscure second-floor address may be "easy to miss", but this East Midtown pizzeria is worth seeking out for "tasty" Neapolitan pies fired in a wood-burning oven; there's not much decor save for a floor-to-ceiling window "with a good view of 57th Street", but service is "friendly" and the tabs "affordable."

| | FOOD | DECOR | SERVICE | COST |

Fig & Olive *Mediterranean*

21 | 21 | 20 | $56

East 50s | 10 E. 52nd St. (bet. 5th & Madison Aves.) | 212-319-2002
East 60s | 808 Lexington Ave. (bet. 62nd & 63rd Sts.) | 212-207-4555
Meatpacking District | 420 W. 13th St. (bet. 9th Ave. & Washington St.) |
212-924-1200
www.figandolive.com

"Small plates with big flavors" are the draw at these "upbeat" Mediterraneans that also roll out fun "olive oil flights"; the big Meatpacking branch has a "high-energy", "nightclub" atmosphere, while its East Side siblings are a natural for "client lunches" and the après-Bloomingdale's set.

NEW The Finch *American*

22 | 21 | 23 | $51

Clinton Hill | 212 Greene Ave. (bet. Cambridge Pl. & Grand Ave.) |
Brooklyn | 718-218-4444 | www.thefinchnyc.com

A Gramercy Tavern alum "flies high" with "imaginative" seasonal American dishes that "pack a wallop of flavor" at this Clinton Hill brownstoner, overseen by a "friendly" team; though "small"-ish portions come at "Manhattan" prices, the "minimalist" space with a marble bar exudes "neighborhood charm."

Fiorentino's *Italian*

20 | 12 | 19 | $39

Gravesend | 313 Ave. U (bet. McDonald Ave. & West St.) | Brooklyn |
718-372-1445 | www.fiorentinosristorante.com

"Old-school Brooklyn" endures at this "bustling" Gravesend Italian best known for "grandma"-style Neapolitan food plated in "tremendous" portions; its *Goodfellas*-esque crowd doesn't mind the "no-frills" decor, "noisy" decibels and no-rez rule given the "astonishingly cheap" tabs.

Firenze *Italian*

21 | 20 | 23 | $58

East 80s | 1594 Second Ave. (bet. 82nd & 83rd Sts.) | 212-861-9368 |
www.firenzeny.com

Candlelight and exposed-brick walls set a "romantic" mood at this longtime UES Italian that evokes Florence with "solid" Tuscan cooking delivered by a "couldn't-be-nicer" crew; the "small" confines can feel "cramped" or "cozy" depending on who you ask, but everyone agrees it's a neighborhood "favorite."

Fish *Seafood*

23 | 15 | 20 | $45

West Village | 280 Bleecker St. (Jones St.) | 212-727-2879 |
www.fishrestaurantnyc.com

Like the "simpleton name" implies, there's "nothing fancy" going on at this West Village seafood shack, just "truly good" catch proffered with great shuck for your buck (check out the $9 oyster special); trade-offs include "funky" looks and "tight-squeeze" seating.

FishTag *Greek/Seafood*

22 | 17 | 21 | $51

West 70s | 222 W. 79th St. (bet. Amsterdam Ave. & B'way) |
212-362-7470 | www.fishtagrestaurant.com

Bringing a "downtown" vibe to the UWS, Michael Psilakis' "relaxed" Greek is a "breath of fresh air" for "delectable" fish dispatched in "nice-looking" digs by "enthusiastic" staffers; "decoding the menu" may require repeat visits, if you can abide the "din" and the "pricey" check.

	FOOD	DECOR	SERVICE	COST

5 & Diamond *American*
21 | 18 | 21 | $42

Harlem | 2072 Frederick Douglass Blvd. (112th St.) | 917-860-4444 |
www.5anddiamondrestaurant.com

A "neighborhood gem", this Harlem "charmer" furnishes "addictive"
New American comfort cooking via a "two-steps-ahead" staff; the
modest interior may "feel a bit crowded" (especially during the "lively
brunch"), but that hardly detracts from the "pleasant surprise."

Five Leaves *American*
25 | 22 | 20 | $38

Greenpoint | 18 Bedford Ave. (Lorimer St.) | Brooklyn | 718-383-5345 |
www.fiveleavesny.com

A "must-try" "signature burger" and "excellent pancakes" star on the
"fab" all-day New American menu at this "informal" Greenpoint bistro;
its "casual" quarters get "packed", especially during weekend brunch,
when the wait can be "tough" – though "friendly" service and "fair"
prices compensate.

5 Napkin Burger *Burgers*
21 | 16 | 18 | $29

Greenwich Village | 150 E. 14th St. (bet. 3rd & 4th Aves.) | 212-228-5500
West 40s | 630 Ninth Ave. (45th St.) | 212-757-2277
West 80s | 2315 Broadway (84th St.) | 212-333-4488
www.5napkinburger.com

"Good thing there isn't a five-napkin limit" given the "mammoth",
"messy" and "super-tasty" patties (and assortment of sushi, hurrah!)
proffered at this "family-oriented" burger chain; the faux "butcher"-shop
settings are often "congested", but it's still a "solid" standby – if you
"could only hear yourself eat."

Flatbush Farm *American*
21 | 18 | 16 | $44

Park Slope | 76 St. Marks Ave. (Flatbush Ave.) | Brooklyn | 718-622-3276 |
www.flatbushfarm.com

"Farm-to-table" bounties are the draw at this affordable Park Slope
American where the "solid" menu is assembled from "wholesome" local
ingredients; the less-enthused cite "uneven" service, but it wins kudos
for a "super brunch" and a "little-piece-of-heaven" garden.

Fletcher's Brooklyn Barbecue *BBQ*
22 | 16 | 18 | $28

Gowanus | 433 Third Ave. (bet. 7th & 8th Sts.) | Brooklyn | 347-763-2680
Roxbury | Riis Park Bazaar, Gateway National Recreation Area |
157 Rockaway Beach Blvd. (Beach Channel Dr.) | Queens | 347-763-2680
www.fletchersbklyn.com

There's "real BBQ" in store at this locavore-friendly Gowanus joint smoking the classics (St. Louis ribs, brisket) as well as more "unique items";
the "super-casual" setup features "friendly" counter service, by-the-
pound pricing and communal seating.

Flex Mussels *Seafood*
23 | 18 | 20 | $47

East 80s | 174 E. 82nd St. (bet. Lexington & 3rd Aves.) | 212-717-7772
West Village | 154 W. 13th St. (bet. 6th & 7th Aves.) | 212-229-0222
www.flexmussels.com

"Steamy pots of mussels" are served with "exotic sauces" and "crusty
bread" at these "fast-moving" seafooders also touted for their "standout"
donuts and "won't-break-the-bank" tabs; not much decor and "noisy",
"highly social" scenes come with the territory.

	FOOD	DECOR	SERVICE	COST

Flinders Lane *Australian* ▽ 25 | 20 | 24 | $51

East Village | 162 Ave. A (bet. 10th & 11th Sts.) | 212-228-6900 |
www.flinderslane-nyc.com

A "rare find" in the East Village outback, this "approachable" Australian
produces "well-prepared" dishes with a "burst of Asian flair"; "sweet"
service lends a "welcoming" vibe to "intimate" digs that get bigger when
floor-to-ceiling windows open and it feels like "you're dining outdoors."

Flor de Mayo *Chinese/Peruvian* 23 | 11 | 19 | $26

West 100s | 2651 Broadway (bet. 100th & 101st Sts.) | 212-663-5520 |
www.flordemayo.com

"Divine" rotisserie chicken draws "believers" to this "consistent" UWS
stalwart where "homestyle" Peruvian-Chinese fare comes at "value"
prices; the "nothing-fancy" surrounds are "not for date night", but its
"mixed crowd" digs the "true New York" experience.

NEW Florian *Italian* 22 | 22 | 22 | $59

Gramercy Park | 225 Park Ave. S. (18th St.) | 212-869-8800 |
www.floriannyc.com

Owner Shelly Fireman (Trattoria Dell'Arte, Brooklyn Diner) brings a little
flash down to Gramercy with this upscale Italian where menu highlights
include "excellent" housemade mozzarella and "simple" pastas "done
well"; the "cavernous" space is either "beautiful" or "over the top" depending on who you ask, but most agree it's a "welcome addition."

Fogo de Chão *Brazilian* 25 | 24 | 23 | $72

West 50s | 40 W. 53rd St. (bet. 5th & 6th Aves.) | 212-969-9980 |
www.fogo.com

An all-you-can-eat "meat extravaganza" awaits at this big Brazilian churrascaria near Rock Center offering "positively delicious"
skewers (along with a "vast" salad bar) in a "beautiful" triplex setting;
true, the tabs are "not inexpensive", but it's "paradise" for those bent
on "protein overload."

Fonda *Mexican* 23 | 17 | 20 | $43

Chelsea | 189 Ninth Ave. (bet. 21st & 22nd Sts.) | 917-525-5252
East Village | 40 Ave. B (3rd St.) | 212-677-4096
Park Slope | 434 Seventh Ave. (bet. 14th & 15th Sts.) | Brooklyn |
718-369-3144
www.fondarestaurant.com

"Upscale Mexican food with a down-home feel" is yours at these "energetic" joints where the "creative" dishes feature "new flavors" and the
cocktails are "killer"; "tight quarters in Park Slope (bonus: there's a back
patio) and "noisy" conditions at all are offset by a "terrific" happy hour.

Foragers City Table *American* 22 | 18 | 19 | $51

Chelsea | 300 W. 22nd St. (8th Ave.) | 212-243-8888 |
www.foragersmarket.com

"You can really taste the difference" in "creative" farm-to-table fare that
"bursts with freshness" at this Chelsea New American, an "informal"
eatery and locally sourced grocer spun off from a Dumbo market; it's an
"easy" dinner option and "good for brunch", though some find it "a little
pricey for what you get."

	FOOD	DECOR	SERVICE	COST

Forcella *Pizza*   23 | 15 | 19 | $31

Murray Hill | 377 Park Ave. S. (bet. 26th & 27th Sts.) | 212-448-1116
Williamsburg | 485 Lorimer St. (bet. Grand & Powers Sts.) | Brooklyn | 718-388-8820
www.forcellaeatery.com

An "experience straight from Italy", these separately owned pizzerias are the "real-deal" for "light-as-air" Neapolitan pies, many of which are "flash-fried", then oven-finished in brightly tiled stoves; the digs might not impress and the service "could be more attentive", but at least they're "lively" and "affordable."

Fornino *Pizza*   24 | 19 | 19 | $23

Brooklyn Heights | Brooklyn Bridge Park Pier 6 (Joralemon St.) | Brooklyn | 718-422-1107
Greenpoint | 849 Manhattan Ave. (bet. Milton & Noble Sts.) | Brooklyn | 718-389-5300
Williamsburg | 187 Bedford Ave. (7th St.) | Brooklyn | 718-384-6004
www.forninopizza.com

In the eternal "NY pizza wars", these Brooklyn "favorites" are "strong players" thanks to "decadent" toppings and "perfectly done" wood-fired crusts; "price-is-right" tabs enhance their "can't-go-wrong" reputations.

Fort Defiance *American*   23 | 18 | 21 | $39

Red Hook | 365 Van Brunt St. (bet. Coffey & Dikeman Sts.) | Brooklyn | 347-453-6672 | www.fortdefiancebrooklyn.com

Named for a Revolutionary War fort that once stood nearby, this "funky" Red Hook haunt dishes up "solid" American food, including a "great" brunch, washed down with "terrific" classic cocktails; OK, the menu is "small", but "excellent-value" pricing makes it a "home base" for locals.

Forty Four *American*   ▽ 22 | 21 | 22 | $50

West 40s | Royalton Hotel | 44 W. 44th St. (bet. 5th & 6th Aves.) | 212-944-8844 | www.morganshotelgroup.com

The Royalton Hotel's "elegant" decor is the backdrop for a "pretty great" meal at this Theater District lobby lounge offering a "focused" New American menu; especially known for "business lunches", it also hosts an "after-work scene" fueled by craft cocktails and "people-watching."

44 & X *American*   23 | 21 | 22 | $50

West 40s | 622 10th Ave. (bet. 44th & 45th Sts.) | 212-977-1170 | www.44andx.com
44½ *American*
West 40s | 626 10th Ave. (bet. 44th & 45th Sts.) | 212-399-4450 | www.44andahalf.com

"Gaiety abounds" at these Hell's Kitchen "go-to" spots where "well-toned" waiters in "tight, witty" T-shirts serve "consistently delicious" American fare with "theatrical flair"; "inviting" havens in an area with "limited" options, they host a "popular" brunch and "fit the bill" before or after a play at the nearby Signature Theatre complex.

Four & Twenty Blackbirds *Bakery*   25 | 18 | 21 | $15

Gowanus | 439 Third Ave. (8th St.) | Brooklyn | 718-499-2917

continued

Prospect Heights | Brooklyn Public Library | 10 Grand Army Plaza
(Plaza St.) | Brooklyn | 718-230-2100
www.birdsblack.com

The "pies are nothing less than magic" at this Gowanus cafe and shop
(with a spin-off counter in the Brooklyn Public Library), where "inventive"
fillings make it "hard to choose" from the rotating lineup of "fantastic"
by-the-slice offerings; a "laid-back" setting and "friendly peeps" are more
reasons there's "no need to bake anymore."

456 Shanghai Cuisine *Chinese*
23 | 14 | 18 | $22

Chinatown | 69 Mott St. (bet. Bayard & Canal Sts.) | 212-964-0003 |
www.456shanghaicuisine.com

"Wonderful" soup dumplings are the draw at this busy Chinatown "find"
that's also a "reliable" source for "ample portions" of "authentic Shanghainese" chow; the "tight quarters" sport "minimal" decor, but prices are
so "reasonable" that no one minds.

Four Seasons *American*
26 | 28 | 27 | $112

East 50s | Seagram Bldg. | 99 E. 52nd St. (bet. Lexington & Park Aves.) |
212-754-9494 | www.fourseasonsrestaurant.com

As "iconic" as it gets, Alex von Bidder and Julian Niccolini's "storied"
Midtown New American provides a "first-class dining experience from
every angle", with "flawless" staffers ferrying "impressive" fare in "gorgeous" Philip Johnson–designed surrounds voted No. 1 for Decor in NYC;
the Pool Room is "incomparable" for a "romantic" dinner, while the Grill
Room hosts the "ultimate power lunch", and though both require "serious cash" (and jackets), it's "one of the all-time greats"; P.S. a relocation
is in the works for 2016.

The Fourth *American*
20 | 19 | 20 | $53

Greenwich Village | Hyatt Union Sq. Hotel | 132 Fourth Ave. (13th St.) |
212-432-1324 | www.thefourthny.com

From the Tocqueville team, this all-day American brasserie in the
Hyatt Union Square offers "quality" food in "upbeat", "high-ceilinged"
environs (including a cafe and more formal dining room); it's "not
inexpensive", but the "value is high" – especially at Sunday brunch
when there's "live music."

Fragole *Italian*
24 | 17 | 21 | $37

Carroll Gardens | 394 Court St. (bet. Carroll St. & 1st Pl.) | Brooklyn |
718-522-7133 | www.fragoleny.com

This veteran Carroll Gardens Italian remains a "neighborhood favorite" for
its "solid" cooking "with an eye toward authenticity", "quality wine list"
and overall "charm"; "affordable" tabs keep it filled with "happy" customers – but as it's "small", be "prepared to wait" for a table at prime times.

Franchia *Korean*
24 | 21 | 21 | $38

Murray Hill | 12 Park Ave. (bet. 34th & 35th Sts.) | 212-213-1001 |
www.franchia.com

"Innovative" vegan cuisine is the hallmark of this Midtown Korean
"favorite" where the "wonderful, filling" offerings ("I didn't miss meat at
all") are complemented by "friendly" service and a "Zen-like ambiance"

that suffuses the "jewel-box" teahouse setting; thanks to "value" pricing, it's an "affordable oasis."

Francisco's Centro Vasco *Seafood/Spanish*   22 | 14 | 19 | $59

Chelsea | 159 W. 23rd St. (bet. 6th & 7th Aves.) | 212-645-6224 | www.franciscoscentrovasco.com

"Monster-size" lobsters at "fair prices" are the highlight of this longtime Chelsea Spaniard that also offers "wonderful paella" and "potent sangria"; "dumpy" digs and "noisy, crowded" conditions don't deter fans who feel it's "cheaper to come here than to cook your own."

Frank *Italian*   23 | 15 | 18 | $39

East Village | 88 Second Ave. (bet. 5th & 6th Sts.) | 212-420-0202 | www.frankrestaurant.com

This cash-only East Villager is a longtime standby for "da best" Italian "home cooking" at "solid-value" prices; it's a "jam-packed", no-frills joint with a "no-rez policy" that spells waits at prime times, but you can always pass the time at its next-door Vera Bar.

Frankie & Johnnie's *Steak*   21 | 16 | 21 | $73

West 30s | 32 W. 37th St. (bet. 5th & 6th Aves.) | 212-947-8940
West 40s | 269 W. 45th St., 2nd fl. (8th Ave.) | 212-997-9494
www.frankieandjohnnies.com

To experience "days long past", try this circa-1926 Theater District "throwback" accessed via "rickety stairs" and known for "delectable" steaks, "career" waiters and "rough-around-the-edges" decor; its 37th Street sibling (set in John Barrymore's former townhouse) is similarly "old-fashioned", though prices are decidedly up to date.

Frankies Spuntino *Italian*   25 | 20 | 22 | $46

West Village | 570 Hudson St. (11th St.) | 212-924-0818
Carroll Gardens | 457 Court St. (bet. 4th Pl. & Luquer St.) | Brooklyn | 718-403-0033
www.frankiesspuntino.com

"Special local places", these "homey" Italians serve "delicate" dishes with a "modern spin", including "main-attraction" meatballs, at prices that won't "break the bank"; no-rez policies create "long waits", but Carroll Gardens' "enchanting" patio is a summer "plus."

Franny's *Italian/Pizza*   23 | 17 | 19 | $44

Park Slope | 348 Flatbush Ave. (bet. 8th Ave. & Sterling Pl.) | Brooklyn | 718-230-0221 | www.frannysbrooklyn.com

"Out-of-this-world" wood-fired pizzas, pastas and other dishes built around "wonderful local ingredients" plus "fantastic" wines and cocktails mean you "can't lose" at this Park Slope Italian "go-to"; yes, the "hip", "rustic" space gets "noisy" (especially at "kid-friendly" brunch), but at least they're now taking reservations.

Fraunces Tavern *Pub Food*   18 | 23 | 19 | $39

Financial District | 54 Pearl St. (Broad St.) | 212-968-1776 | www.frauncestavern.com

Have a side of "history" with dinner at this FiDi "landmark" where George Washington bid farewell to his troops in 1783; today, it's a "refurbished" tavern serving "decent" pub grub and "diverse" beers in a "faux-Revolutionary" setting; cynics snipe it's "all about the building – not the food."

	FOOD	DECOR	SERVICE	COST

Fred's at Barneys NY *American/Italian*

| 20 | 19 | 19 | $55 |

East 60s | Barneys NY | 660 Madison Ave., 9th fl. (61st St.) | 212-833-2200 | www.barneys.com

"Shopping is hard work" and "sustenance is necessary", so "well-Botoxed" types unwind and "pick at a salad" at this "chichi" department-store canteen in Barneys; the "consistently good" Italian-American fare may be "pricey for what it is", but no one cares – it's "fun to be chic" here.

Freemans *American*

| 22 | 25 | 21 | $51 |

Lower East Side | Freeman Alley (off Rivington St., bet. Bowery & Christie St.) | 212-420-0012 | www.freemansrestaurant.com

"Hidden" down a Lower East Side alley, this "homey" American feels like a "hunting-lodge wonderland" with its "curiosity-cabinet" decor ("embrace the taxidermy"); "hearty" cooking, "killer" cocktails and an "especially great" brunch are all popular with the "cool kids" who keep it "totally fun" (and "crowded").

French Louie *American/French*

| 25 | 23 | 25 | $52 |

Boerum Hill | 320 Atlantic Ave. (bet. Hoyt & Smith Sts.) | Brooklyn | 718-935-1200 | www.frenchlouienyc.com

This "sophisticated" Boerum Hill sib to Buttermilk Channel delivers "excellent" farm-to-table French-American fare via a "gracious" crew in "Parisian bistro" surrounds with a "gorgeous" backyard and a petite front bar; even with "high prices" it gets "crowded" – though now that reservations are taken it's "a much better experience."

Fresco by Scotto *Italian*

| 22 | 19 | 20 | $66 |

East 50s | 34 E. 52nd St. (bet. Madison & Park Aves.) | 212-935-3434 | www.frescobyscotto.com

Fresco on the Go *Italian*

East 50s | 40 E. 52nd St. (bet. Madison & Park Aves.) | 212-754-2700 | www.frescoonthego.com

For "delicious", "dependable" Tuscan fare with *Today Show* people-watching on the side, try this "friendly" longtime Midtowner via the "dedicated" Scotto family; it's "pricey", and "always packed" for lunch, but there's "super-fast" takeout from the to-go outlet.

Friedman's *American*

| 22 | 18 | 20 | $28 |

Chelsea | Chelsea Mkt. | 75 Ninth Ave. (bet. 15th & 16th Sts.) | 212-929-7100

NEW **Morningside Heights** | 1187 Amsterdam Ave. (118th St.) | 212-932-0600

West 30s | 132 W. 31st St. (bet. 6th & 7th Aves.) | 212-971-9400

NEW **West 30s** | 450 10th Ave. (35th St.) | 212-268-1100

www.friedmansrestaurant.com

"Inventive" touches and seasonal ingredients make for "higher-end" takes on "consistently good" comfort food at these "reasonably priced" Americans also known for "excellent" gluten-free options; the simple digs can get "pretty packed", especially during the "madhouse" lunches, but "accommodating" servers are another reason many "dig" 'em.

	FOOD	DECOR	SERVICE	COST

Friend of a Farmer *American*

19 | 18 | 17 | $35

Gramercy Park | 77 Irving Pl. (bet. 18th & 19th Sts.) | 212-477-2188 | www.friendofafarmerny.com

Bringing a "Vermont" feel to Gramercy Park, this "quaint" American "country kitchen" has crowds crowing about its "farm-fresh" fare and "hippie" air; citified pricing, "slow service" and weekend brunch "lines down the block" come with the territory.

NEW Fuku *Chicken/Sandwiches*

– | – | – | I

East Village | 163 First Ave. (10th St.) | no phone | www.momofuku.com

David Chang's Momofuku empire gets a fast-casual addition with this East Village instant hit specializing in spicy fried chicken sandwiches – given the gourmet treatment, of course; it also offers chicken fingers and a couple of sides with more menu items on the way, and though it's standing room only, it also serves booze.

Fung Tu *American/Chinese*

25 | 21 | 24 | $58

Lower East Side | 22 Orchard St. (bet. Canal & Hester Sts.) | 212-219-8785 | www.fungtu.com

"Adventurous" eaters say it's "not your mama's egg roll" at this "artful" LES Chinese-American where the "unexpected", "completely original" dishes are "excellent" and matched with "well-chosen" wines and "delicious" cocktails; "nicely timed" service and "understated-chic" decor complete the "upscale" picture.

Fushimi *Japanese*

24 | 25 | 22 | $46

Bay Ridge | 9316 Fourth Ave. (bet. 93rd & 94th Sts.) | Brooklyn | 718-833-7788

Williamsburg | 475 Driggs Ave. (bet. 10th & 11th Sts.) | Brooklyn | 718-963-2555

Grant City | 2110 Richmond Rd. (bet. Colfax & Lincoln Aves.) | Staten Island | 718-980-5300
www.fushimigroup.com

These "sexy" Japanese standouts are "an experience" complete with "sleek" settings, "fun atmospheres", "city-quality" sushi and "inventive" cocktails"; maybe tabs are "not the cheapest", but then again these are "not your regular around-the-corner sushi" joints.

NEW Gabriel Kreuther *French*

– | – | – | VE

West 40s | 41 W. 42nd St. (bet. 5th & 6th Aves.) | 212-257-5826

At this chic locale facing Bryant Park, chef Gabriel Kreuther (ex The Modern) puts together a sophisticated French tasting menu that honors his Alsatian roots; the elegant, lofty surrounds feature salvaged beams from a Vermont barn and Alsace-inspired stork decor.

Gabriel's *Italian*

21 | 18 | 22 | $67

West 60s | 11 W. 60th St. (bet. B'way & Columbus Ave.) | 212-956-4600 | www.gabrielsbarandrest.com

"Caring" service overseen by "natural host" Gabriel Aiello sets the "classy" tone at this "even-keeled" Columbus Circle Italian known for "delicious" cooking, a "comfortable" setting and proximity to Lincoln Center; given the rather "hefty" tabs, "media" types from nearby CBS and CNN prefer it for lunch.

	FOOD	DECOR	SERVICE	COST

Gallaghers *Steak* — 23 | 20 | 21 | $80

West 50s | 228 W. 52nd St. (bet. B'way & 8th Ave.) | 212-586-5000 |
www.gallaghersnysteakhouse.com

Longtime fans still find the "real deal" at this "premier" Theater District
steakhouse that's been around since 1927 and "beautifully restored" to
its "former glory"; "succulent" chops, "amiable" service and "expensive"
price tags are all part of this "old-style" experience.

Galli *Italian* — 24 | 22 | 23 | $41

NEW **Lower East Side** | 98 Rivington St. (Ludlow St.) | 212-966-9288
SoHo | 45 Mercer St. (bet. Broome & Grand Sts.) | 212-966-9288
www.gallirestaurant.com

"Absolutely delicious" Italian comfort classics – "simple" pastas, "excellent" parms – make for "happy bellies" at these "homey" joints also
known for their gluten-free options (a "major plus"); an "inviting" vibe
and "not-too-expensive" tabs round out the overall "charm."

The Gander *American* — 20 | 20 | 21 | $64

Flatiron | 15 W. 18th St. (bet. 5th & 6th Aves.) | 212-229-9500 |
www.thegandernyc.com

Recette chef Jesse Schenker fields an "inventive menu" at this "expansive" Flatiron entry, where an "adult" clientele deems the "well-executed"
New American fare (and "exciting array" of bar snacks) "worth the cost";
run by "efficient" staffers, the banquette-bordered space is "unpretentious" and "calmer than you'd expect."

NEW **Gansevoort Market** *Food Hall* — – | – | – | M

Meatpacking District | 52 Gansevoort St. (bet. Greenwich & Washington
Sts.) | no phone | www.gansmarket.com

Set in a historic building in the Meatpacking District, this all-day food
hall brings together popular vendors including Ed's Lobster Bar, Sushi
Dojo, Tacombi and many more. Vines cover the exposed-brick walls of
the sky-lit space, where there are plenty of seats for noshers to take a
load off and refuel.

Ganso *Japanese/Noodle Shop* — 21 | 18 | 21 | $26

Downtown Brooklyn | 25 Bond St. (Livingston St.) | Brooklyn |
718-403-0900 | www.gansonyc.com

"Truly addictive" noodles are what it's about at this Downtown Brooklyn
Japanese, which slings an "interesting" ramen-bowl selection and other
quick bites ("you can't go wrong with the wings"); a streamlined setup
with a "friendly" "hipster staff", it's "much needed in the neighborhood."

NEW **Ganso Yaki** *Japanese* — – | – | – | M

Downtown Brooklyn | 515 Atlantic Ave. (3rd Ave.) | Brooklyn |
646-927-0303 | www.gansonyc.com

An offshoot of the nearby ramen shop, this Downtown Brooklyn Japanese
features "delicious" street-food classics including skewers, grilled meats
and other comfort fare; "amiable" staffers, reasonable prices and a
slightly roomier space built around an open kitchen complete the picture.

Gaonnuri *Korean* — 19 | 26 | 20 | $62

West 30s | 1250 Broadway (32nd St.) | 212-971-9045 |
www.gaonnurinyc.com

Its "biggest appeal" is the "stellar" panoramic Midtown vistas from its "chic", 39th-floor space, but this "upmarket" player on the K-town scene also "holds its own" with "stylishly prepared" Korean fare, including "traditional" tabletop BBQ; service is variable and you "pay for the view", but that "sunset over the Hudson" is more than "worth it."

NEW Gardenia *Mediterranean* — | — | — | M

West Village | 64 Downing St. (7th Ave.) | 212-604-0500 | www.gardenianyc.com

The team behind Ofrenda and Black Ant turns its attention to Mediterranean fare at this West Village entry offering a modern, Latin-accented menu designed for sharing; creative cocktails feature sophisticated ingredients, and the bright, airy setting also includes a bar.

Gargiulo's *Italian* 23 | 20 | 22 | $53

Coney Island | 2911 W .15th St. (bet. Mermaid & Surf Aves.) | Brooklyn | 718-266-4891 | www.gargiulos.com

After a "swim at the beach", have a "swim in red sauce" at this circa-1907 Coney Island "time warp", a "catering hall"–size arena for good "old-fashioned" Neapolitan cooking ferried by "tuxedo-clad" waiters; the "colorful" crowd feels its "reputation is deserved", while a nightly raffle means "you could eat for free."

Gato *Mediterranean* 26 | 24 | 24 | $73

NoHo | 324 Lafayette St. (bet. Bleecker & Houston Sts.) | 212-334-6400 | www.gatonyc.com

Bobby Flay "hits the nail on the head" at this "happening" NoHo Med where his "wonderfully creative" dishes "burst" with "bold flavors"; a "downtown sceney" crowd keeps the "industrial" digs feeling "cool", and a large front bar area is a "nice alternative" if you can't "snag" a coveted rez.

Gazala's *Mideastern* 22 | 10 | 17 | $28

West 40s | 709 Ninth Ave. (bet. 48th & 49th Sts.) | 212-245-0709 | www.gazalaplace.com

"Dependably good" Druze fare at "value" prices makes this "tiny" Hell's Kitchen BYO a "reliable" standby; the "humble" digs "lack atmosphere" and seating is tight ("prepare to get cozy with your neighbor"), but the grub "more than makes up" for all that.

NEW Gelso & Grand *Italian* ▽ 18 | 19 | 18 | $47

Little Italy | 186 Grand St. (Mulberry St.) | 212-226-1600

Italian staples like "super-fresh" housemade pastas get a contemporary boost from a Bouley and Momofuku vet at this sprawling Little Italy locale; the "rustic" setting also includes sidewalk seats, and though tabs can be a little "steep", at least it's "perfectly comfortable."

Gemma *Italian* 21 | 23 | 20 | $49

East Village | Bowery Hotel | 335 Bowery (bet. 2nd & 3rd Sts.) | 212-505-7300 | www.theboweryhotel.com

Primo "people-watching" abounds at this "fun", all-day Bowery Hotel Italian that lures "scenesters" with a "romantic", "country-chic" setting festooned with "hundreds of candles"; "tasty" fare, "attentive service" and "fair prices" make the "no-rez" policy (except for hotel guests) less of a drag.

	FOOD	DECOR	SERVICE	COST

Gennaro *Italian* | 24 | 15 | 20 | $43 |

West 90s | 665 Amsterdam Ave. (bet. 92nd & 93rd Sts.) | 212-665-5348 | www.gennaronyc.com

Be ready for a "long line" at this "durable" UWS Italian that takes no reservations and no plastic but does provide "wonderful", "hearty" fare for "nongourmet prices"; even after a "third expansion", it's still "difficult to get a table after 7 PM."

GG's *American/Pizza* ∇ 22 | 19 | 20 | $36 |

East Village | 511 E. Fifth St. (bet. Aves. & B) | 212-687-3641 | www.ggsnyc.com

"Delicious", "innovation"-prone pizzas (the grandma pie is a "revelation") lead a roster running from pastas to burgers at this East Village American; a "neighborhood joint" with a marble bar furnishing "awesome drinks", it's a "go-to" for a "quality" meal that's "not super-expensive."

Gigino at Wagner Park *Italian* | 21 | 19 | 20 | $53 |

Battery Park City | 20 Battery Pl. (Little West St.) | 212-528-2228 | www.gigino-wagnerpark.com

Gigino Trattoria *Italian*

TriBeCa | 323 Greenwich St. (Duane St.) | 212-431-1112 | www.gigino-trattoria.com

It almost "feels like Florence" at this "affordable" TriBeCa Tuscan featuring "above-average" food, "friendly" service and a "high-ceilinged", "farmhouselike" setting; outdoor dining with a "one-of-a-kind view" of the harbor and Statue of Liberty is the thing at its "off-the-beaten-path" sibling in Battery Park.

Gino's *Italian* | 24 | 18 | 22 | $37 |

Bay Ridge | 7414 Fifth Ave. (bet. Bay Ridge Pkwy. & 74th St.) | Brooklyn | 718-748-1698 | www.ginosbayridge.com

A neighborhood "staple" since 1964, this ever-"crowded" Bay Ridge Italian serves up "generous portions" of "terrific" classics "just like mom makes", in "casual" environs; "get ready to wait in line" at prime times, but the all-around "enjoyable" experience and "reasonable" tab ensure it's "well worth it."

Giorgio's of Gramercy *American/Italian* | 22 | 19 | 22 | $53 |

Flatiron | 27 E. 21st St. (bet. B'way & Park Ave. S.) | 212-477-0007 | www.giorgiosofgramercy.com

The epitome of a "true sleeper", this longtime Italian-American "class act" in the Flatiron features "consistently good" cooking that suggests "unsung talent in the kitchen"; "gracious" service and "cozy" surrounds that are "never overcrowded" are other incentives.

Giovanni Rana Pastificio & Cucina *Italian* | 23 | 20 | 20 | $47 |

Chelsea | 75 Ninth Ave. (16th St.) | 212-370-0975 | www.rananyc.com

The "fresh-cut" pastas "justify the carb hit" at this Chelsea Market eatery from a Boot-based pasta maker, offering "darn tasty" Italiana for on-site dining alongside a carry-away market; a "rustic", roomy space with "hanging pots and pans" complements the "real homemade" style.

	FOOD	DECOR	SERVICE	COST

Giovanni Venticinque *Italian*   25 | 20 | 24 | $69

East 80s | 25 E. 83rd St. (bet. 5th & Madison Aves.) | 212-988-7300 |
www.giovanniventicinque.com

"Excellent" Tuscan fare and a "gracious" staff keep this UES Italian popular with a "neighborhood" crowd; "intimate" and "hushed" enough for
"real conversation", it boasts "proximity to the Met" and an "unbeatable"
lunch prix fixe that offsets otherwise "pricey" tabs.

Glady's *Caribbean*   ▽ 24 | 23 | 21 | $32

Crown Heights | 788 Franklin Ave. (Lincoln Pl.) | Brooklyn | 718-622-0249 |
www.gladysnyc.com

"Like going back to your roots" say fans of the "delicious" "homestyle"
fare off a well-edited menu at this "affordable" Crown Heights Caribbean; tropical drinks, rum flights and a turquoise palette add to the
"cool" island feel.

Glasserie *Mediterranean*   ▽ 25 | 24 | 21 | $44

Greenpoint | 95 Commercial St. (bet. Box St. & Manhattan Ave.) |
Brooklyn | 718-389-0640 | www.glasserienyc.com

"Imaginative" and "delicious" sum up the fare at this "hip" Greenpoint
Mediterranean where a "small but complete" seasonal menu gets an as-
sist from "well-balanced" cocktails; the "comfortable", vintage-industrial
space jibes with its glass-factory past, and the neighborhood's skyline
views are another reason it's "worth the trek."

Glass House Tavern *American*   20 | 19 | 21 | $47

West 40s | 252 W. 47th St. (bet. B'way & 8th Ave.) | 212-730-4800 |
www.glasshousetavern.com

Something "calming" in the "hectic" Theater District, this "solid performer" provides New Americana that tastes even better when Broadway
"stars" are seated alongside you; "reasonable" rates and "cordial" service
also draw applause, though conversationalists advise "eat upstairs."

Gnocco *Italian*   22 | 18 | 19 | $39

East Village | 337 E. 10th St. (bet. Aves. A & B) | 212-677-1913 |
www.gnocco.com

"Authentic Emilian fare" is the focus of this all-day East Village Italian
praised for its "tasty pizza", "lengthy wine list" and "excellent" namesake
dish; the "most prized tables" are in its "lovely", all-seasons garden,
though "modest" pricing and "helpful" service are available throughout.

NEW Goemon Curry *Japanese*   – | – | – | I

NoLita | 29 Kenmare St. (Elizabeth St.) | 212-226-1262

Next door to its soba-making sib, Cocoron, this humble NoLita spot
with group tables and wooden benches specializes in Japanese curry;
the dishes have a spicy, gravy-style sauce with rice, and can be ordered
with a variety of toppings.

Golden Shopping Mall *Chinese*   22 | 8 | 10 | $13

Flushing | 41-36 Main St. (41st Rd.) | Queens | no phone

An "adventure" for the "intrepid", this bi-level Flushing food court offers
a "variety" of "tasty" Chinese "delights" from vendors like "terrific"
dumpling shops and the original Xi'an Famous Foods; it's "crazy" "crowded" with "no ambiance", but never mind – the eats are "really cheap."

	FOOD	DECOR	SERVICE	COST

Golden Unicorn *Chinese*
21 | 14 | 15 | $28

Chinatown | 18 E. Broadway (Catherine St.) | 212-941-0911 |
www.goldenunicornrestaurant.com
"Mobbed and noisy" is a given at this "huge" C-town Cantonese featuring
"endless carts" stocked with "heavenly" dim sum; "hurried", English-
challenged service and "basic Chinatown wedding party decor" are
forgiven since it's a lot "cheaper than flying to Hong Kong."

Good *American*
21 | 16 | 20 | $40

West Village | 89 Greenwich Ave. (bet. Bank & W. 12th Sts.) |
212-691-8080 | www.goodrestaurantnyc.com
"Should be named 'great'" say supporters of this West Village American "respite" that's still something of a "hidden gem" despite "simple",
"hearty" cooking and "kind service"; some may find the decor "boring",
but there's always a "weekend line" for its "amazing brunch."

Good Enough to Eat *American*
19 | 15 | 16 | $31

West 80s | 520 Columbus Ave. (85th St.) | 212-496-0163 |
www.goodenoughtoeat.com
This "great-value" UWS "favorite" offers all-day dining à la "Vermont" via
a "simple" American comfort-food menu; the "no-frills" setting exudes
farmhousey vibes and also offers outdoor seating, although "painful
waits" are the norm at weekend brunch.

Good Fork *American*
25 | 20 | 24 | $50

Red Hook | 391 Van Brunt St. (bet. Coffey & Van Dyke Sts.) | Brooklyn |
718-643-6636 | www.goodfork.com
"Hidden away" in Red Hook, this "funky" New American maintains a
"loyal following" for its "excellent", Korean-influenced cooking dispensed
in "cozy" digs with an "amazing" back garden; "warm" service and a
"small but fine" drinks list are other reasons reservations are a "must."

The Gorbals *Eclectic*
▽ 25 | 24 | 24 | $46

Williamsburg | 98 N. Sixth St. (Wythe Ave.) | Brooklyn | 718-387-0195 |
www.thegorbalsbk.com
"Inventive is the word" at this Williamsburg Eclectic inside Space Ninety
8, where *Top Chef* winner Ilan Hall's "adventurous" preparations are
"freakin' delicious" and the "carefully crafted" drinks score points too;
spacious surroundings up its "group" appeal, and the "rooftop is tops."

Gotham Bar & Grill *American*
28 | 26 | 27 | $91

Greenwich Village | 12 E. 12th St. (bet. 5th Ave. & University Pl.) |
212-620-4020 | www.gothambarandgrill.com
Chef Alfred Portale has "excellence down to a science" at this longtime
Village "champ" known for "expertly prepared", "stunningly presented"
New American fare dispatched by a "high-caliber" crew in "elegant" sur-
rounds; the "top-flight" experience will cost you, but the "killer" prix fixe
lunch is one of the "best deals" in town.

Gotham West Market *Food Hall*
20 | 15 | 16 | $25

West 40s | 600 11th Ave. (bet. 44th & 45th Sts.) | 212-582-7940 |
www.gothamwestmarket.com
Some of the city's best-regarded chefs – including Seamus Mullen and
Ivan Orkin – whip up "everything from burgers to tapas to noodles" at

this "industrial-chic" Hell's Kitchen food hall offering both counter and communal table seating; it's perfect for "grazing" and definitely "worth the trip to 11th Avenue."

Gradisca *Italian* 24 | 18 | 22 | $52

West Village | 126 W. 13th St. (bet. 6th & 7th Aves.) | 212-691-4886 | www.gradiscanyc.com

"Superb pastas" hand-rolled by the owner's mama are the "main attraction" at this "low-key" West Village Italian, but other "savory" dishes and a "strong wine list" further secure its standing as an area "favorite"; some say it's a bit "pricey" considering the "small portions" and "casual ambiance", but "friendly" service adds value.

Graffiti *Eclectic* 28 | 23 | 27 | $58

East Village | 224 E. 10th St. (bet. 1st & 2nd Aves.) | 212-464-7743 | www.graffitinyc.com

An "inventive original" from "truly awesome" chef Jehangir Mehta, this "teensy" East Villager's "sublime" Eclectic plates highlight "exotic", Indian-inspired flavors, matched with a remarkably affordable wine list and served with "gracious hospitality"; the shared seating is undeniably "tight", but "an unforgettable meal" at these rates is "a rare treat."

Gramercy Tavern *American* 28 | 26 | 27 | $120

Flatiron | 42 E. 20th St. (bet. B'way & Park Ave. S.) | 212-477-0777 | www.gramercytavern.com

A "landmark" that "never wavers", Danny Meyer's "exemplary" Flatiron New American remains "totally on point" thanks to chef Michael Anthony's "phenomenal" menu, "off-the-charts" service and a "vibrant" setting adorned with "fanciful flowers"; prix fixe-only at dinner, the dining room is "high-end" but "not stuffy", while going à la carte in the "less formal" front tavern is "not too eye-popping" pricewise.

NEW Grand Army *Seafood* ∇ 22 | 21 | 21 | $49

Downtown Brooklyn | 338 State St. (Hoyt St.) | Brooklyn | 718-422-7867 | www.grandarmybar.com

"The spot to be", this "lively" Downtown Brooklyn hangout from Noah Bernamoff (Mile End) and crew pairs an "imaginative" seafood-centric menu featuring "excellent" oysters with craft cocktails and a "killer" wine list; "snagging a table" in the airy space can be difficult but seats at the vintage bar provide another option.

Grand Sichuan *Chinese* 21 | 10 | 16 | $30

Chelsea | 229 Ninth Ave. (24th St.) | 212-620-5200 | www.grandsichuan.com
Chelsea | 172 Eighth Ave. (bet. 18th & 19th Sts.) | 212-243-1688 | www.grandsichuaneasternnyc.com
East 50s | 1049 Second Ave. (bet. 55th & 56th Sts.) | 212-355-5855 | www.grandsichuaneasternnyc.com
East Village | 19-23 St. Marks Pl. (bet. 2nd & 3rd Aves.) | 212-529-4800 | www.ordergrandsichuan.com
West 40s | 368 W. 46th St. (bet. 8th & 9th Aves.) | 212-969-9001 | www.thegrandsichuan.com
West 70s | 307 Amsterdam Ave. (bet. 74th & 75th Sts.) | 212-580-0277 | www.grandsichuan74.com

continued

West Village | 15 Seventh Ave. S. (bet. Carmine & Leroy Sts.) | 212-645-0222 | www.grandsichuannyc.com

"Hot stuff" seekers tout the "mouth-numbing" Sichuan fare served at this all-over-town mini-chain where the "huge" plates are on par with the "extensive" menu; service is "perfunctory" and there's "no ambiance", but otherwise it's "fast", "reliable" and "doesn't hurt the wallet."

Grand Tier *American*

 21 | 26 | 23 | $94

West 60s | Metropolitan Opera House | 30 Lincoln Center Plaza (65th St.) | 212-799-3400 | www.patinagroup.com

Those long performance nights have a "delightful" prelude at this Lincoln Center New American (open during opera season only to all ticket-holders), where the "tasty" if "limited" menu is served in a "dramatic", chandeliered setting overlooking the Met foyer; tabs are "expensive", but payoffs include "efficiency" and "dessert at intermission."

Gran Electrica *Mexican*

25 | 25 | 24 | $38

Dumbo | 5 Front St. (Old Fulton St.) | Brooklyn | 718-852-2700 | www.granelectrica.com

"Simple but super-delicious", the Mexican eats at this "pleasant" Dumbo taqueria pair well with its extensive list of mezcals, tequilas and "killer" margaritas; Day of the Dead–inspired wallpaper adds to the "festive" vibrations, while the "fun patio" provides a "civilized respite from the noisy interior."

Gray's Papaya *Hot Dogs*

21 | 5 | 15 | $8

West 70s | 2090 Broadway (72nd St.) | 212-799-0243 | www.grayspapayanyc.com

This 24/7 UWS hot dog stand vends "surprisingly good" wieners washed down with "frothy" papaya drinks; "quick" turnaround and "chump-change" tabs offset the "gruff" service, "what-a-dump" decor and lack of seats at this "quintessential" NY "institution."

Grazie *Italian*

20 | 17 | 20 | $49

East 80s | 26 E. 84th St. (Madison Ave.) | 212-717-4407 | www.grazienyc.com

With its "dignified" townhouse setting and "quite creditable" Italian cooking, this veteran UES duplex off Museum Mile is a "restful" respite "before, after or instead of the Met"; maybe it's "a bit pricey", but the set-price lunch is a "bargain considering the neighborhood."

Great Jones Cafe *Cajun*

21 | 15 | 19 | $32

NoHo | 54 Great Jones St. (bet. Bowery & Lafayette St.) | 212-674-9304 | www.greatjones.com

"No-frills" says it all about this "friendly" NoHo Cajun where the "solid" grub arrives in a "dumpy", verging on "campy" setting; 30-plus years on, the crowd's still "local", the vibe "downtown" and the jukebox as "great" as ever.

Great NY Noodle Town *Noodle Shop*

24 | 6 | 14 | $20

Chinatown | 28 Bowery (Bayard St.) | 212-349-0923 | www.greatnynoodletown.com

"Surrender to the crowd experience" and "sit with strangers" at this "chaotic" C-town noodle shop known for "dirt-cheap" Cantonese eats

	FOOD	DECOR	SERVICE	COST

(and notable salt-baked seafood) served into the wee hours; not so great is "no decor", no credit cards and "difficult" service.

Greek Kitchen *Greek*
21 | 16 | 20 | $34

West 50s | 889 10th Ave. (58th St.) | 212-581-4300 | www.greekkitchennyc.com

"Tasty", "economical" eats make this "real Greek" a "staple" on the edge of Hell's Kitchen, a location "convenient to Lincoln Center"; there's "no decor" to speak of and service is "hit-or-miss", but the servings are "generous" and they "never rush you" out.

Grey Dog *American*
22 | 18 | 18 | $20

Chelsea | 242 W. 16th St. (8th Ave.) | 212-229-2345
Greenwich Village | 90 University Pl. (E. 12th St.) | 212-414-4739
NoLita | 244 Mulberry St. (bet. Prince & Spring Sts.) | 212-966-1060
West Village | 49 Carmine St. (Bedford St.) | 212-462-0041
www.thegreydog.com

Folks find a "sweet throwback" to what neighborhood coffee stops "used to be" in these "comfortable" hangouts for "relaxing" and "people-watching" over "inexpensive", "above-average" java and American comfort fare; yes, "brunch lines" can be "over the top", but staffers "know how to work the crowd."

Grifone *Italian*
24 | 17 | 24 | $66

East 40s | 244 E. 46th St. (2nd Ave.) | 212-490-7275

A "tried-and-true" East Side option since '85, this "old-line" Northern Italian near the U.N. fields an "extensive" menu of "outstanding" dishes; "dated" decor and "captains-of-industry" price tags detract, but its mature following digs the "discreet" service and "calm, quiet" mien.

Grimaldi's *Pizza*
22 | 14 | 16 | $24

Flatiron | Limelight Mktpl. | 656 Sixth Ave. (bet. 20th & 21st Sts.) | 646-484-5665
Coney Island | 1215 Surf Ave. (bet. Stillwell Ave. & 12th St.) | Brooklyn | 718-676-2630
Dumbo | 1 Front St. (bet. Dock & Old Fulton Sts.) | Brooklyn | 718-858-4300
Douglaston | 242-02 61st Ave. (Douglaston Pkwy.) | Queens | 718-819-2133
www.grimaldis-pizza.com

Brace yourself for "endless crowds" at this Dumbo pizzeria–cum–"tourist" magnet where the payoff is "excellent" "thin-crust", coal-fired pies; the other branches can usually be accessed "without the wait", but they share the mother ship's no-plastic, no-reservations, no-slices rules.

Grom *Ice Cream*
25 | 14 | 18 | $10

West 50s | 1796 Broadway (58th St.) | 212-974-3444
West Village | 233 Bleecker St. (Carmine St.) | 212-206-1738
www.grom.it

"Some of the best gelato around" (plus "outrageously rich" hot chocolate too) is found at these artisanal gelaterias whose "heavenly" product incorporates ingredients imported from Italy, including the water for its sorbets; despite *molto* grumbling about "long lines", "small" portions and "exorbitant prices", most agree it's "worth the extra bucks."

	FOOD	DECOR	SERVICE	COST

Guantanamera *Cuban*
23 | 18 | 21 | $46

West 50s | 939 Eighth Ave. (bet. 55th & 56th Sts.) | 212-262-5354 |
www.guantanameramy.com

"Jumping" is the word on this "fun" Midtown Cuban where the "tasty",
"authentic" chow is nearly overwhelmed by the "amazing mojitos" and
"ridiculously loud live music"; "reasonable" rates and hand-rolled cigars
on Friday and Saturday nights supply extra "oomph."

Gyu-Kaku *Japanese*
21 | 18 | 20 | $43

East 40s | 805 Third Ave., 2nd fl. (bet. 49th & 50th Sts.) | 212-702-8816
Greenwich Village | 34 Cooper Sq. (bet. Astor Pl. & 4th St.) | 212-475-2989
West 40s | 321 W. 44th St. (bet. 8th & 9th Aves.) | 646-692-6297
www.gyu-kaku.com

"Novelty"-seekers hype this "delicious, do-it-yourself" Japanese yakiniku
franchise where you cook your own BBQ on tabletop charcoal braziers;
since the "small portions" can add up to "pricey" tabs, bargain-hunters
show up for the happy-hour specials.

Hakata Tonton *Japanese*
22 | 13 | 18 | $44

West Village | 61 Grove St. (7th Ave. S.) | 212-242-3699
You'll feel "instantly transported" at this West Village Japanese where
the "refreshing" menu of "obscure" small plates is heavy on "fantastic"
pork dishes ("try the pig's feet"); the "warm" staff is "eager to educate"
first-timers, though, and "reasonable" tabs are a plus.

Hakkasan *Chinese*
24 | 25 | 22 | $86

West 40s | 311 W. 43rd St. (bet. 8th & 9th Aves.) | 212-776-1818 |
www.hakkasan.com

"Beautiful" Shanghai-chic decor sets the "glitzy" mood at this "luxe"
Theater District outpost of the London-based chain turning out "high-
quality" Cantonese-inspired dishes with Western accents; ornate
latticework partitions make the "massive" space feel more intimate, but
the "gargantuan" tabs are harder to disguise.

The Halal Guys *Mideastern*
22 | 11 | 18 | $17

Gramercy Park | 307 E. 14th St. (2nd Ave.) | 347-527-1505
NEW **West 90s** | 722 Amsterdam Ave. (95th St.) | no phone
www.thehalalguysny.com

After servicing Midtown lunchers and late-night eaters for years, the
popular food cart guys go brick-and-mortar with these "simple and
quick" Middle Easterns offering "addicting" fare like gyros and chicken
and rice platters "doused" in their "deservedly famous" white sauce;
"generous" portions and "cheap" prices further bump up the appeal.

NEW Haldi Indian Cuisine *Indian*
19 | 16 | 18 | $30

Murray Hill | 102 Lexington Ave. (27th St.) | 212-213-9615 |
www.haldinyc.com

"Well-spiced" Bengali specialties and dishes influenced by Calcutta's
Jewish population make for a "different" dining experience at this "casual" Murray Hill Indian; the "bright" space is on the "narrow" side, but
"moderate" prices "make the curry go down smoothly."

Hampton Chutney Co. *Indian*
22 | 12 | 16 | $17

SoHo | 143 Grand St. (bet. Crosby & Lafayette Sts.) | 212-226-9996

continued

West 80s | 464 Amsterdam Ave. (bet. 82nd & 83rd Sts.) | 212-362-5050
www.hamptonchutney.com

"Crispy and light", the "delicious" dosas with "nonconventional" fillings add up to "exotic", "affordable" eating at these "casual" Indian standbys; it's a "cool concept", but the "basic" counter-service setups have many turning to them mostly for takeout.

Hanco's *Vietnamese* 20 | 10 | 15 | $14

Brooklyn Heights | 147 Montague St. (bet. Clinton & Henry Sts.) | Brooklyn | 347-529-5054
Cobble Hill | 134 Smith St. (bet. Bergen & Dean Sts.) | Brooklyn | 718-858-6818
Park Slope | 350 Seventh Ave. (10th St.) | Brooklyn | 718-499-8081
www.hancosny.com

"Addictive" banh mi sandwiches washed down with "excellent" bubble teas (plus pho in Park Slope and Brooklyn Heights) ensure these Vietnamese storefronts are "always busy"; "no-frills" sums up both the decor and service, but few mind given the price.

Han Dynasty *Chinese* 23 | 12 | 17 | $31

Greenwich Village | 90 Third Ave. (bet. 12th & 13th Sts.) | 212-390-8685
NEW **West 80s** | 215 W. 85th St. (B'way) | 212-858-9060
www.handynasty.net

"Hot in just the right way", these "awesome Philly transplants" offer "unapologetically spicy" Sichuan dishes including "knockout" dan dan noodles; the Villager draws "long lines" while the newer UWS offshoot is much more "spacious", and though both are "no-frills", "value" prices mean most still "can't get enough."

Hangawi *Korean/Vegetarian* 24 | 24 | 23 | $51

Murray Hill | 12 E. 32nd St. (bet. 5th & Madison Aves.) | 212-213-0077 | www.hangawirestaurant.com

A "wonderful respite" in "honky-tonk" K-town, this "transporting" Korean provides "exotic" vegetarian fare that tastes even better in its "calm atmosphere"; "polite" service is also part of the "relaxing" package, but be prepared to "check your shoes at the door" – it's a "requirement" here.

Hanjan *Korean* 24 | 20 | 20 | $50

Flatiron | 36 W. 26th St. (bet. B'way & 6th Ave.) | 212-206-7226 | www.hanjan26.com

On a "booming stretch" of the Flatiron lies this upscale gastropub (a Danji sibling), where "inspired" Korean small plates pair well with "awesome" rice beer and "exotic cocktails"; the "simple", "minimalist" space might not be fancy but has an overall "good vibe", and night owls say its "late-night ramen hits the spot."

Harlem Shake *Burgers* 20 | 17 | 17 | $18

Harlem | 100 W. 124th St. (Lenox Ave.) | 646-396-3040 | www.harlemshakenyc.com

"Excellent smash-griddled burgers" are the signature of this all-day Harlem patty palace with "malt-shop-meets-*Jet*-magazine" decor and a neighborhood-centric "wall of fame"; "sidewalk seating" and "affordable" tabs add to its popularity.

Harlow *Seafood* — 20 | 25 | 20 | $77

East 50s | Lombardy Hotel | 111 E. 56th St. (bet. Lexington & Park Aves.) | 212-935-6600 | www.harlownyc.com

"Glamorous" is the word for this East Midtown seafooder from restaurateur Richie Notar (Nobu), where the "gorgeous" setting and "beautiful" crowd are in keeping with its "pricey" catch; service is equally "upscale", though some find the "bar scene better than the cuisine."

Harry Cipriani *Italian* — 24 | 22 | 22 | $82

East 50s | Sherry-Netherland Hotel | 781 Fifth Ave. (bet. 59th & 60th Sts.) | 212-753-5566 | www.cipriani.com

"Vanderbilts" and other "VIPs" feel "right at home" at this "sophisticated" Sherry-Netherland "landmark" modeled after the Venice original; the "on-point" Italian fare and fan-"favorite" Bellinis arrive in "classy" surrounds, and as for the "over-the-top" tabs – it's "worth the bucks" just to see "who might walk in."

Harry's Cafe & Steak *Steak* — 23 | 20 | 21 | $60

Financial District | 1 Hanover Sq. (bet. Pearl & Stone Sts.) | 212-785-9200 | www.harrysnyc.com

Long "Wall Street's go-to eatery", this FiDi "throwback" beneath the historic India House attracts "captains of industry" with "mouthwatering" steaks and more backed by one of the best wine cellars in the city; it's "busy" for lunch, quieter at dinner and "expense account"–worthy all the time.

Harry's Italian *Italian* — 20 | 17 | 19 | $32

Battery Park City | 225 Murray St. (West St.) | 212-608-1007
Financial District | 2 Gold St. (Platt St.) | 212-747-0797
West 50s | 30 Rockefeller Plaza, Concourse Level (bet. 49th & 50th Sts.) | 212-218-1450
www.harrysitalian.com

"Sterling" pizzas are standouts on the menu of "standard Italian favorites" at these "welcoming" fallbacks from the Harry's Cafe folks; "ample portions" and "reasonable pricing" cement their "go-to" status for "less-than-formal lunches" at the Downtown locations or eats on the move from the "busy", takeout-only Rock Center outlet.

Haru *Japanese* — 21 | 17 | 18 | $44

East 70s | 1329 Third Ave. (76th St.) | 212-452-2230
Financial District | 1 Wall Street Ct. (Pearl St.) | 212-785-6850
Union Square | 220 Park Ave. S. (18th St.) | 646-428-0989
West 40s | 229 W. 43rd St. (bet. 7th & 8th Aves.) | 212-398-9810
West 80s | 433 Amsterdam Ave. (bet. 80th & 81st Sts.) | 212-579-5655
www.harusushi.com

This "consistent" Japanese mini-chain is a "default" choice for many, thanks to "big pieces" of "solid" sushi for fairly "modest" sums; though "nothing special" in terms of service or ambiance, it perpetually draws "young" types who call out its "excellent" happy hour.

Hatsuhana *Japanese* — 25 | 17 | 21 | $58

East 40s | 17 E. 48th St. (bet. 5th & Madison Aves.) | 212-355-3345 | www.hatsuhana.com

"Serious", "old-school sushi" is the lure at this "long-established" Midtown Japanese where the "artful presentation" begins with "aim-to-please" service; "bland" decor that "needs refreshing" seems at odds with the rather "pricey" tabs, but you don't last this long without doing something right.

Havana Alma de Cuba   *Cuban*   23 | 17 | 21 | $37
West Village | 94 Christopher St. (bet. Bedford & Bleecker Sts.) | 212-242-3800 | www.havananyc.com
"Loyal to its Cuban roots", this "upbeat" West Villager dispenses "authentic" grub with the "right mix of flavors and seasonings" alongside mojitos and pitchers of sangria; live music, "reasonable" rates and a "lovely rear garden" keep things "bustling", so be prepared for "noise" and "chair-bumping."

Havana Central   *Cuban*   22 | 20 | 19 | $39
West 40s | 151 W. 46th St. (bet. 6th & 7th Aves.) | 212-398-7440 | www.havanacentral.com
A "festive" pick for "entertaining friends", this Midtown Cuban "escape" offers "well-prepared" food and "delicious" drinks in a "tropical" setting where "Desi Arnaz" would feel at home; too bad the "enthusiastic" service and "spirited" live music can make for "jet-airplane" noise levels.

Haveli   *Indian*   23 | 18 | 22 | $34
East Village | 100 Second Ave. (bet. 5th & 6th Sts.) | 212-477-5956 | www.haveliny.com
Former "down-the-block" neighbor Banjara has been "transplanted" to this longtime East Village Indian's "comfortable, informal" bi-level space; those who find the new arrangement "splendid" cite the "well-seasoned" dishes off a "goes-on-forever" menu plus "attentive" service and "reasonable" bills.

Hearth   *American/Italian*   25 | 22 | 24 | $72
East Village | 403 E. 12th St. (1st Ave.) | 646-602-1300 | www.restauranthearth.com
Bringing "fine dining to the East Village", this Tuscan-American from chef Marco Canora offers "delectable" fare from a "farm-to-table menu", complemented by an "interesting" wine list; granted, such "locavore goodness doesn't come cheap", but "sincere" service and a "warm", "bustling" atmosphere help ensure it's "worth the splurge."

Hecho en Dumbo   *Mexican*   22 | 18 | 18 | $47
NoHo | 354 Bowery (bet. 4th & Great Jones Sts.) | 212-937-4245 | www.hechoendumbo.com
"Inventive" Mexican small plates are "served with a side of hipster" at this "sceney", "sex-Mex" standout that's a prime example of the "Bowery renaissance"; sure, "service could be better", but tabs are "pretty reasonable" and insiders say the tasting menu–only "chef's table is the way to go."

Heidelberg   *German*   19 | 17 | 18 | $42
East 80s | 1648 Second Ave. (bet. 85th & 86th Sts.) | 212-628-2332 | www.heidelbergrestaurant.com
When it comes to "classic", "stick-to-your-ribs" Germanica, this vintage-1936 Yorkville "time capsule" fields a "heavy", "no-apologies" menu washed down with "boots of beer"; "costumed" staffers and a "kitschy", "oompah-pah" setting are part of the "fun" package.

✓ **Hell's Kitchen** *Mexican* 23 | 18 | 20 | $48

West 50s | 754 Ninth Ave. (51st St.) | 212-977-1588 | www.hellskitchen-nyc.com

"Tasty modern" Mexican food draws "big crowds" to this "high-concept" Hell's Kitchen cantina where the "margaritas keep flowing" as the "noise" levels rise; even "thoughtful service" can't ease the "pre-theater crush", yet the overall experience is "closer to heaven" than the name suggests.

Henry Public *Pub Food* 23 | 22 | 20 | $35

Cobble Hill | 329 Henry St. (Pacific St.) | Brooklyn | 718-852-8630 | www.henrypublic.com

"Trendy in a late-1800s sort of way", this "olde-timey" Cobble Hill pub serves a "limited" menu anchored by an "off-the-charts" turkey-leg sandwich; "cool", "suspendered" bartenders shake "sophisticated" cocktails, leaving the cash-only, no-rez rules as the only downsides.

Henry's End *American* 25 | 17 | 25 | $52

Brooklyn Heights | 44 Henry St. (bet. Cranberry & Middagh Sts.) | Brooklyn | 718-834-1776 | www.henrysend.com

"As good as the day it opened" in 1973, this "distinctive" Brooklyn Heights destination remains a "sentimental favorite" due to "inventive" New American cooking, including its seasonal wild-game festival bringing "exotic critters" to the table; a "small-town" atmosphere and "efficient" service make the "sardine seating" feel almost "cozy."

Hibino *Japanese* 26 | 19 | 22 | $36

Cobble Hill | 333 Henry St. (Pacific St.) | Brooklyn | 718-260-8052 | www.hibino-brooklyn.com

Long Island City | 10-70 Jackson Ave. (bet. 49th & 50th Aves.) | Queens | 718-392-5150 | www.hibino-lic.com

"Fresh-as-one-can-get" sushi vies for the spotlight with the "daily changing" obanzai (small plates) and "compelling" housemade tofu at these "unusual", Kyoto-style Japanese eateries; "budget-friendly" tabs and "unobtrusive" service embellish the "subdued" ambiance.

Hide-Chan *Japanese/Noodle Shop* 23 | 15 | 17 | $23

East 50s | 248 E. 52nd St., 2nd fl. (bet. 2nd & 3rd Aves.) | 212-813-1800 | www.hidechanramen.com

The sound of diners "noisily slurping" "cooked-to-perfection" noodles swimming in "flavorful" broth provides the background music at this "authentic" East Midtown Japanese ramen joint; alright, the service can be "a bit rushed" and the setting "cramped", but "low costs" keep the trade brisk.

Hill Country *BBQ* 22 | 16 | 17 | $34

Flatiron | 30 W. 26th St. (bet. B'way & 6th Ave.) | 212-255-4544 | www.hillcountryny.com

Downtown Brooklyn | 345 Adams St. (bet. Fulton & Johnson Sts.) | Brooklyn | 718-885-4608 | www.hillcountrybk.com

"Hip BBQ" is yours at these "cafeteria-style" joints where patrons order the "messy", "smoky" 'cue from a counter, then find a communal table and dig in; "toe-tapping" live music, a "good bourbon selection" and "friendly" vibrations make it the "next best thing to being in Austin."

	FOOD	DECOR	SERVICE	COST

Hill Country Chicken *Chicken/Southern*   21 | 15 | 16 | $22

Flatiron | 1123 Broadway (25th St.) | 212-257-6446
Downtown Brooklyn | 345 Adams St. (bet. Fulton & Johnson Sts.) |
Brooklyn | 718-885-4609
www.hillcountrychicken.com

"Crispy-crunchy" fried chicken (including a "fabulous" skinless version)
and "decent sides" make it hard to "save room for pie" at these low-budget
Southerners; regulars ignore the "service hiccups" and "groan-inducing",
"rec-room" decor, since the desserts are "nothing short of spectacular."

Hillstone *American*   22 | 20 | 21 | $48

East 50s | 153 E. 53rd St. (enter on 3rd Ave. & 54th St.) | 212-888-3828
NoMad | 378 Park Ave. S. (27th St.) | 212-689-1090
www.hillstone.com

"Corporate crowds" like these "busy" Americans serving "well-executed"
food (including a "must-have" spinach-artichoke dip) in "dark", "modern" digs that work equally well for everything from "business lunches"
to "date nights"; just be ready for "crowded", "noisy" bar scenes,
particularly "after work."

Home Restaurant *American*   21 | 15 | 21 | $48

West Village | 20 Cornelia St. (bet. Bleecker & 4th Sts.) | 212-243-9579 |
www.homerestaurantnyc.com

A West Village "find", this under-the-radar vet serves up "comfort"-
oriented Americana at a "fair price"; its "tiny" digs are "cozy" ("just like
the name implies"), but "tables on top of each other" have many trying
for seats in the "nice garden that takes you out of the city" for a while.

Hometown BBQ *BBQ*   25 | 19 | 18 | $33

Red Hook | 454 Van Brunt St. (Reed St.) | Brooklyn | 347-294-4644 |
www.hometownbarbque.com

"Real-deal" Texas-style BBQ with a Brooklyn edge awaits at this Red
Hook "find", a mammoth affair with a walk-up counter offering "seriously
good" 'cue ("divine" brisket, "incredibly delicious" pastrami bacon), craft
beers and an array of whiskeys; its "first-come, first-served" policy can
make for "long lines", but "hipster-watching" can help pass the time.

Hope & Anchor *Diner*   ▽ 20 | 16 | 20 | $22

Red Hook | 347 Van Brunt St. (Wolcott St.) | Brooklyn | 718-237-0276 |
www.hopeandanchorredhook.com

A "little bit of everything for everyone" is what's on offer at this
Red Hook diner with a "friendly, small-town vibe" and a "rockabilly
sensibility"; the "great brunch" is a draw on weekends, while "good
value" is a pull at all times.

Hop Kee *Chinese*   22 | 7 | 15 | $24

Chinatown | 21 Mott St., downstairs (bet. Chatham Sq. & Mosco St.) |
212-964-8365 | www.hopkeenyc.com

This "old-guard", cash-only Chinatown cellar has been slinging "traditional" Cantonese food – "and plenty of it" – since 1968; the "dank" decor
and "zombie" service are offset by "late"-night hours, "rock-bottom" tabs
and an "Anthony Bourdain" endorsement.

Houdini Kitchen Laboratory *Pizza*

▽ 25 | 23 | 23 | $28

Ridgewood | 1563 Decatur St. (Wyckoff Ave.) | Queens | 718-456-3770 | www.houdinikitchenlaboratoryridgewood.com

"Far off any tourist map", this "cool" Ridgewood pizzeria turns out a "fantastic" array of "fancy" wood-fired pies alongside Italian-leaning apps; set in a former brewery, the "charmingly renovated" space maintains an "industrial" feel and there's also a "pleasant" back patio.

The House *American*

▽ 24 | 25 | 23 | $63

Gramercy Park | 121 E. 17th St. (bet. Irving Pl. & Park Ave. S.) | 212-353-2121 | www.thehousenyc.com

This tri-level Gramercy standout proffers "solid" New American cooking but "even better ambiance" given its "romantic", "candlelit" setting in a "gorgeous" 1854 carriage house; factor in "attentive" service, and you've got a "perfect" date place – though you'll pay to "impress" here.

NEW Houseman *American*

– | – | – | E

Hudson Square | 508 Greenwich St. (Spring St.) | 212-641-0654 | www.housemanrestaurant.com

Opened by a veteran of Prune, this Hudson Square American offers a daily one-page dinner menu of surf, turf and veggie selections; the room is furnished with tables made from salvaged bowling-alley wood, along with a zinc bar providing a tight list of cocktails, wines and beers.

Hudson Clearwater *American*

25 | 23 | 22 | $54

West Village | 447 Hudson St. (Morton St.) | 212-989-3255 | www.hudsonclearwater.com

Set in a "quasi-hidden" West Village space, this New American "date spot" delivers "well-prepared, well-presented" plates to a "trendy" clientele; a "beautiful" back patio comes in handy when the "cozy" confines get a bit too "lively" – and is another reason it's a real "find."

Hudson Eats *Food Hall*

19 | 18 | 16 | $23

Battery Park City | Brookfield Pl. | 230 Vesey St. (West St.) | 212-417-7000 | www.brookfieldplaceny.com

There's "something for everyone" at this "fancy food court" in Battery Park City's Brookfield Place, where the "substantial" variety includes local vendors like Mighty Quinn's BBQ, Blue Ribbon Sushi and Num Pang; sure, it's "packed at lunch", but the "modern" space has "lots of seats."

NEW Hudson Garden Grill *American*

– | – | – | M

Bronx Park | 2900 Southern Blvd. (Bronx Park Rd.) | Bronx | 646-627-7711 | www.nybg.org

With an open kitchen, whitewashed walls and arched windows looking out to the arboretum, this polished New American by Stephen Starr is a full-service first for the New York Botanical Garden; offering lunch and light bites with ingredients from local farms, the restaurant is open to both garden visitors and the general public.

Huertas *Spanish*

25 | 22 | 24 | $64

East Village | 107 First Ave. (bet. 6th & 7th Sts.) | 212-228-4490 | www.huertasnyc.com

After initially launching as two separate concepts, this "hip" East Village "up-and-comer" now serves one "interesting" Basque menu featuring "wildly delicious" pintxos and larger "flavor-packed" plates; "approachable" wines and "creative" vermouth cocktails help fuel a "lively" bar scene, while "knowledgeable" service adds to its overall "charm."

NEW Hugo & Sons *Italian*   ▽ 23 | 19 | 21 | $55

Park Slope | 367 Seventh Ave. (11th St.) | Brooklyn | 718-499-0020
Occupying a prominent corner space on Park Slope's Seventh Avenue strip, this packed-from-the-start Italian twofer includes an airy, bistro-ish front dining room serving "interesting" housemade pastas, creative salads and a few French classics; around back is the pizzeria, where "very tasty" pies come out of a wood-burning oven, and in summer there's patio seating.

Hu Kitchen *Health Food*   24 | 18 | 18 | $20

Greenwich Village | 78 Fifth Ave. (bet. 13th & 14th Sts.) | 212-510-8919 | www.hukitchen.com
A "paleo paradise", this organic-leaning Villager delivers "high-quality" gluten-free grub all day, including "interesting" veggie-based dishes; the "cafeteria-style" setup with prepackaged snacks and a smoothie bar makes it "perfect" for "grab-and-go", though the "cool" second floor has "lots of space" to sit.

Hummus Place *Israeli/Kosher/Vegetarian*   22 | 12 | 19 | $21

West 70s | 305 Amsterdam Ave. (bet. 74th & 75th Sts.) | 212-799-3335
West Village | 71 Seventh Ave. S. (bet. Barrow & Bleecker Sts.) | 212-924-2022
www.hummusplace.com
Those who like their hummus "silky" and their pita bread "fresh" and "warm" kvell over the kosher vegetarian offerings at these "popular" Israelis; though decor is nearly "nonexistent", service is "pleasant", the grub "filling" and the tabs "terrific."

Hundred Acres *American*   21 | 21 | 21 | $53

SoHo | 38 MacDougal St. (Prince St.) | 212-475-7500 | www.hundredacresnyc.com
"Farm-fresh" New American "home cooking" arrives in an appropriately "country-road" setting at this SoHo charmer that's kin to Cookshop; its "cult following" commends its "delicious brunch" and "awesome" garden room, only wishing there were "more menu options."

NEW Hunt & Fish Club *Steak*   19 | 24 | 20 | $80

West 40s | 125 W. 44th St. (bet. 6th & 7th Aves.) | 212-575-4949 | www.hfcnyc.com
"Sleek and sexy", this marbled, mirrored Times Square chophouse offers "solid" steaks, seafood and game to a "Page Six"–worthy crowd of "heavy hitters" – and "wannabes" – who don't mind the "big price tags"; adding to the "glamour" is an "impressive" bar scene swarming with "see-and-be-seen" types.

Il Bambino *Italian/Sandwiches*   26 | 18 | 22 | $21

Astoria | 34-08 31st Ave. (bet. 34th & 35th Sts.) | Queens | 718-626-0087 | www.ilbambinonyc.com
Panini addicts rave about the "beyond-crispy" bread and "fantastic ingredients" in the "bargain"-priced pressed sandwiches at this "rustic" Astoria Italian; factor in "impeccable service" with "zero pretense" and a

"cozy" back garden, and it's a neighborhood "must-try"; P.S. a Manhattan offshoot is in the works.

Il Buco *Italian/Mediterranean* 25 | 23 | 23 | $74

NoHo | 47 Bond St. (bet. Bowery & Lafayette St.) | 212-533-1932 | www.ilbuco.com

"Marvelous" *"cucina rustica"* pairs with a "well-crafted" wine list in "intimate farmhouse-inspired" surrounds that'll "transport" you to a "Tuscan home" at this NoHo Med-Italian; if it gets "loud", the downstairs wine cellar is a "beautiful" alternative, though it's "not cheap" no matter where you sit.

Il Buco Alimentari e 24 | 21 | 21 | $65
Vineria *Italian/Mediterranean*

NoHo | 53 Great Jones St. (bet. Bowery & Lafayette St.) | 212-837-2622 | www.ilbucovineria.com

"Unpretentious" but with a "pure NY vibe", this Il Buco spin-off is a "go-to" for "simple yet refined" Italian-Med fare – "especially the pastas" and "ridiculously good" short ribs – in a "homey" NoHo setup with a front market area/coffee bar; communal seats and somewhat "pricey" tabs aside, it's "comfortable" for just about "every occasion."

Il Cantinori *Italian* 24 | 24 | 23 | $73

Greenwich Village | 32 E. 10th St. (bet. B'way & University Pl.) | 212-673-6044 | www.ilcantinori.com

"Top-of-the-line" Tuscan cooking is the draw at this "classy" Village "favorite", "still going strong" after more than three decades; it's known as a "celebrity hangout" with a concordant "price factor", but "genuine" hospitality and "gorgeous flowers" make it a "special-occasion" destination for mere mortals.

Il Cortile *Italian* 23 | 20 | 22 | $60

Little Italy | 125 Mulberry St. (bet. Canal & Hester Sts.) | 212-226-6060 | www.ilcortile.com

"Buongusto is an understatement" at this "memory-lane" Italian, a "good bet on Mulberry" since 1975 thanks to its "hearty" food served by waiters who have "been there forever"; though it's "a bit pricey" for the area, regulars report a seat in the "delightful" garden atrium is "worth the trip" alone.

NEW Il Falco *Italian* ∇ 24 | 22 | 26 | $53

Long Island City | 21-50 44th Dr. (23rd St.) | Queens | 718-707-0009 | www.ilfalcolic.com

"First-rate" service adds to the "classy" feel of this "great surprise" in Long Island City, where the "delicious" Italian dishes come courtesy of two Il Mulino alums; the "cozy" white-tablecloth surrounds have a "comfortable" vibe, so it's "enjoyable" all around.

Il Gattopardo *Italian* 24 | 21 | 23 | $80

West 50s | 13-15 W. 54th St. (bet. 5th & 6th Aves.) | 212-246-0412 | www.ilgattopardonyc.com

"Formal dining in the European manner" comes via a "terrific" Southern Italian menu, "smooth" service and an "elegant" townhouse setting at this Midtown "gem"; its atrium is especially "lovely" for a "unique" brunch or lunch, but be prepared for "hold-on-to-your-wallet" tabs.

	FOOD	DECOR	SERVICE	COST

Ilili *Lebanese*
24 | 23 | 22 | $58

NoMad | 236 Fifth Ave. (bet. 27th & 28th Sts.) | 212-683-2929 | www.ililinyc.com

"Modern takes" on "traditional" Lebanese cooking come with "creative enhancements" at this NoMad "scene", where the cocktails are equally "inventive"; the "cathedral-sized", wood-lined space is made for "big groups", but its "nightclub vibe" has "noise" to match (upstairs nooks are "more sedate").

Il Laboratorio del Gelato *Ice Cream*
25 | 15 | 19 | $8

Lower East Side | 188 Ludlow St. (Houston St.) | 212-343-9922 | www.laboratoriodelgelato.com

It's the "best thing to come out of a lab since penicillin" say fans of the "silky smooth" artisanal gelato served at this LES gelateria-cum-re-search facility; with "so many flavors, so little time", routinely "long lines" and upmarket pricing, there's only one sensible strategy: "skip dinner and go right to it."

Il Mulino *Italian*
25 | 20 | 23 | $87

Greenwich Village | 86 W. Third St. (bet. Sullivan & Thompson Sts.) | 212-673-3783 | www.ilmulino.com

Il Mulino Uptown *Italian*

East 60s | 37 E. 60th St. (bet. Madison & Park Aves.) | 212-750-3270 | www.ilmulino.com

Trattoria Il Mulino *Italian*

Flatiron | 36 E. 20th St. (bet. B'way & Park S.) | 212-777-8448 | www.trattoriailmulino.com

At least once, "everyone should experience" this "old-time" Village Italian where "huge portions" of *magnifico* fare (including "a ton of free appe-tizers") are dispatched by "old-world waiters" in "tight", "crowded" quar-ters; there's "modern" decor at the UES offshoot and a "casual" vibe at the Flatiron trattoria, but whichever you choose, "bring loads of money."

Il Mulino Prime *Italian/Steak*
25 | 22 | 23 | $96

SoHo | 331 W. Broadway (Grand St.) | 212-226-0020 | www.ilmulino.com

Carnivores declare this SoHo Italian steakhouse an "outstanding addition" to the Il Mulino mini-empire, presenting "feasts" of hefty chops, pastas and more ("bring your appetite") in minimalist, white-on-white environs; factor in "friendly" pro service, and the "only downside" is the price tag.

Il Postino *Italian*
24 | 20 | 23 | $77

East 40s | 337 E. 49th St. (bet. 1st & 2nd Aves.) | 212-688-0033 | www.ilpostinony.com

Waiters inhale, then recite a "huge list of daily specials" at this "old-world" U.N.-area Italian that will also "cook anything you want"; an "intimate" "opera"-enhanced space further boosts the "wonderful dining experience", but value-seekers avoid the "reliably expensive" tabs by going for the lunchtime prix fixe.

Il Riccio *Italian*
21 | 16 | 21 | $53

East 70s | 152 E. 79th St. (Lexington Ave.) | 212-639-9111 | www.eatilriccionyc.com

UESiders "of a certain age" patronize this "clubby" Italian for its "above-average" Amalfi Coast food served in a "friendly", "white-tablecloth" room; if the compact main room gets "tight", there's a "lovely" "little" enclosed garden in back.

Il Tinello *Italian*

| 24 | 20 | 24 | $79 |

West 50s | 16 W. 56th St. (bet. 5th & 6th Aves.) | 212-245-4388 | www.iltinellony.com

"Serenity" reigns at this Midtown "grande dame" exuding "senior appeal" and patrolled by "conscientious" waiters in "black tie"; everyone agrees that the Northern Italian cooking is "superb", but given the "corporate-checkbook" tabs, many save it for "special occasions."

Il Vagabondo *Italian*

| 19 | 15 | 19 | $53 |

East 60s | 351 E. 62nd St. (bet. 1st & 2nd Aves.) | 212-832-9221 | www.ilvagabondo.com

"Old-school" Italian fans find "all the favorites" at this 1965-vintage Upper Eastsider, where the food "sticks to your ribs" and the waiters have "been there for centuries"; the decor may be "nothing to write home about", but the "unique" indoor bocce court is.

Inakaya *Japanese*

| 24 | 22 | 21 | $62 |

West 40s | NY Times Bldg. | 231 W. 40th St. (bet. 7th & 8th Aves.) | 212-354-2195 | www.inakayany.com

It's always "showtime" at this "high-drama" Japanese robatayaki specialist in the NY Times building, where "friendly" staffers dish out "grilled delights" (plus "swanky sushi") while engaging in ritualized "yelling and screaming"; however, all the "fun" – which is most intense at the robata counter – can add up to "big bucks."

Indochine *French/Vietnamese*

| 23 | 22 | 21 | $59 |

Greenwich Village | 430 Lafayette St. (bet. Astor Pl. & 4th St.) | 212-505-5111 | www.indochinenyc.com

Ever "sexy" – even "timeless" – this "'80s hot spot" opposite the Public Theater still lures "attractive thin" folk with "on-target" French-Vietnamese fare served in "exotic" digs à la 1930s Saigon; perhaps its "elegance is slightly worn", but the "people-watching" is as stellar as ever.

NEW Industry Kitchen *American*

| – | – | – | M |

Financial District | 70 South St. (Maiden Ln.) | 212-487-9600 | www.industry-kitchen.com

This sprawling South Street Seaport New American offers plenty to look at, from the water view to the open kitchen turning out a diverse menu highlighting wood-fired pizzas; both the island bar and the communal tables lend it a sociable feel, while the outdoor seating is a further plus.

Indus Valley *Indian*

| 22 | 15 | 18 | $35 |

West 90s | 2636 Broadway (100th St.) | 212-222-9222 | www.indusvalleyny.com

A "neighborhood standby", this UWS Indian "does the trick" thanks to "tasty" standards and a "plentiful" weekend lunch buffet; sure, it gets "noisy" and "crowded", but with "reasonable" prices and "friendly" service", it's still a "go-to."

	FOOD	DECOR	SERVICE	COST

Injera *Ethiopian*

▽ 23 | 21 | 23 | $30

West Village | 11 Abingdon Sq. (8th Ave.) | 212-206-9330 |
www.injeranyc.com

The spongy namesake bread serves as the only utensil for "flavorful" berbere-spiced Ethiopian meats and greens at this dark sliver of a restaurant on Abingdon Square; the "cool" decor includes zebra-print walls and hanging tribal masks, with "lovely" service boosting the "warm" vibe.

Ipanema *Brazilian/Portuguese*
20 | — | 18 | $43

West 40s | 43 W. 46th St. (bet. 5th & 6th Aves.) | 212-730-5848 |
www.ipanemanyc.com

Under the radar "in the middle of Little Brazil", this "friendly" West 40s "stalwart" has been churning out "tasty" Brazilian-Portuguese dishes for more than a quarter-century; a recent relocation to roomier digs nearby may alleviate the "cramped" conditions, but luckily the "better-than-fair" prices remain.

Ippudo *Japanese/Noodle Shop*
25 | 21 | 21 | $32

Greenwich Village | 65 Fourth Ave. (bet. 9th & 10th Sts.) | 212-388-0088
West 50s | 321 W. 51st St. (bet. 8th & 9th Aves.) | 212-974-2500
www.ippudony.com

"Rich", "category-defining" ramen and "incredible" pork buns make for "ridiculously long waits" and "insanely packed" conditions at these Japanese joints; digs are "more spacious" in Midtown, while the Village original is "darker" with "interesting" Asian-inspired decor, but expect a "warm", "shouted" greeting at both.

Isabella's *American/Mediterranean*
20 | 19 | 20 | $48

West 70s | 359 Columbus Ave. (77th St.) | 212-724-2100 |
www.isabellas.com

"Convenient" for a "post–Museum of Natural History" meal, this "UWS staple" delivers "dependable" American-Mediterranean fare for "reasonable" sums; "go early" if you want a seat on the "large" sidewalk patio, because the "light, airy" interior can feel a bit "frantic", especially during brunch.

Island Burgers & Shakes *Burgers*
21 | 12 | 17 | $20

West 50s | 766 Ninth Ave. (bet. 51st & 52nd Sts.) | 212-307-7934
West 80s | 422 Amsterdam Ave. (80th St.) | 212-877-7934
www.islandburgersandshakes.com

"Huge burgers" on "big buns" accessorized with "every topping known to man" are the raisons d'être of these funky West Side joints that "finally sell fries" too; "spoon-licking shakes" sweeten the sour taste left by "sparse seating and service."

Isle of Capri *Italian*
20 | 18 | 22 | $58

East 60s | 1028 Third Ave. (61st St.) | 212-223-9430 |
www.isleofcapriny.com

A "little slice of Italy" near Bloomingdales, this "throwback" Italian has been serving "classic" red-sauce fare via "old-world" staffers since 1955; OK, so it's "nothing exciting", but the "rustic" trattorialike setting is "cozy", and it has a "loyal following" for "good reason."

I Sodi *Italian*

25 | 18 | 22 | $68

West Village | 105 Christopher St. (bet. Bleecker & Hudson Sts.) | 212-414-5774 | www.isodinyc.com

Like a "little bit of Florence" in the West Village, this "small" Italian supplies "generously sized" portions of "first-tier" Tuscan fare lubricated by a "substantial wine list" and signature Negronis; "charming" service makes the "tight squeeze" seem delightfully "intimate", even "romantic."

Ithaka *Greek/Seafood*

20 | 15 | 20 | $56

East 80s | 308 E. 86th St. (bet. 1st & 2nd Aves.) | 212-628-9100 | www.ithakarestaurant.com

"Neighborhood tavernas" don't get much more "relaxed" than this "quiet" Yorkville Greek where the "honest" food and "wonderful grilled fish" channel Santorini – or at least "Astoria"; maybe the whitewashed setting could be "spiffed up", but thankfully the tables are "far enough apart" and service is "attentive."

I Trulli *Italian*

23 | 22 | 23 | $61

Murray Hill | 122 E. 27th St. (bet. Lexington & Park Ave. S.) | 212-481-7372 | www.itrulli.com

"Rustic but sophisticated", this Kips Bay Southern Italian purveys a trulli "special" Puglian menu paired with "outstanding" wines via its adjoining enoteca; an "expansive" garden and "roaring" fireplace are seasonal draws, though "helpful" service and "costly" tabs are part of the package year-round.

Ivan Ramen *Japanese/Noodle Shop*

22 | 15 | 18 | $27

Lower East Side | 25 Clinton St. (bet. Houston & Stanton Sts.) | 646-678-3859

Ivan Ramen Slurp Shop *Japanese/Noodle Shop*

West 40s | Gotham West Mkt. | 600 11th Ave. (bet. 44th & 45th Sts.) | 212-582-7942
www.ivanramen.com

"Master" chef Ivan Orkin "brings Tokyo to NYC" with his "hyped" slurp shops where "interesting" takes on traditional ramen feature "complex" flavors and "soul-satisfying" bowls; the LES flagship is "small but comfortable" with "funky" Japanese pop decor and a back patio, while the Hell's Kitchen counter has communal tables, but both are typically "jam-packed."

Jackson Diner *Indian*

23 | 12 | 18 | $25

Bellerose | 256-01 Hillside Ave. (256th St.) | Queens | 718-343-7400
Jackson Heights | 37-47 74th St. (bet. 37th Ave. & 37th Rd.) | Queens | 718-672-1232
www.jacksondinerny.com

Jackson Heights' Little India is home to this 30-plus-year-old "landmark" (with a Bellerose offshoot) that's "still the champion" for "spicy", "real-deal" grub; the decor is "pure diner", but the prices "low" and the service "laid-back" – and regulars say the lunchtime buffet is "the way to go."

Jackson Hole *Burgers*

20 | 13 | 18 | $24

East 60s | 232 E. 64th St. (bet. 2nd & 3rd Aves.) | 212-371-7187
Murray Hill | 521 Third Ave. (35th St.) | 212-679-3264
West 80s | 517 Columbus Ave. (85th St.) | 212-362-5177
Bayside | 35-01 Bell Blvd. (35th Ave.) | Queens | 718-281-0330

continued

East Elmhurst | 69-35 Astoria Blvd. (70th St.) | Queens | 718-204-7070
www.jacksonholeburgers.com

Whether the burgers at this mini-chain are "quite tasty" or merely "run-of-the-mill", everyone agrees that their "manhole"-cover size makes them "reasonable values"; those who find the "old-time" diner decor "outdated" are relieved that the staff gets them in and out "fast."

Jack's Wife Freda *American*   23 | 19 | 20 | $32

SoHo | 224 Lafayette St. (Spring St.) | 212-510-8550
NEW **West Village** | 50 Carmine St. (Bedford St.) | 646-669-9888
www.jackswifefreda.com

"Simple but delicious" American fare gets a "modern" and often "Mediterranean spin" at these "well-priced" bistros; a "pretty-people" favorite, they're especially "sceney" at brunch ("if you can get in, you have made it in life") when the "cozy" digs fill up fast.

Jack the Horse Tavern *American*   24 | 21 | 22 | $44

Brooklyn Heights | 66 Hicks St. (Cranberry St.) | Brooklyn | 718-852-5084 |
www.jackthehorse.com

A "cozy, taverny" vibe, "terrific cocktails" and "upscale" American comfort fare delivered by a "cheerful" crew make a "neighborhood go-to" of this Brooklyn Heights "hideaway"; some find the menu "limited" and "slightly pricey", but all welcome the next-door Oyster Room dispensing bivalves and small plates.

Jacob's Pickles *Southern*   22 | 19 | 20 | $36

West 80s | 509 Amsterdam Ave. (bet. 84th & 85th Sts.) | 212-470-5566 |
www.jacobspickles.com

An UWS "den of decadence", this "country-meets-city" tavern keeps 'em coming with "fantastic fried chicken" and other well-priced "Southern comfort" faves (including, yes, "divine pickles") dished up in "casual" surrounds; it all goes down well with suds from the "amazing" beer list that helps you forget the "long line" to get in.

Jacques *French*   20 | 18 | 19 | $45

East 80s | 206 E. 85th St. (bet. 2nd & 3rd Aves.) | 212-327-2272 |
www.jacquesbrasserie.com
NoLita | 20 Prince St. (bet. Elizabeth & Mott Sts.) | 212-966-8886 |
www.jacques1534.com

The "fabulous" mussels are the standout dish at these "traditional" French brasseries; though a few find the settings "old-fashioned" and "noisy", the "reasonable" pricing is fine as is; P.S. the NoLita branch has a downstairs cocktail bar called Shorty.

Jacques Torres Ice Cream *Ice Cream*   26 | 17 | 20 | $13

East 40s | 89 E. 42nd St. (Vanderbilt Ave.) | 212-983-7353
Dumbo | 62 Water St. (Front St.) | Brooklyn | 718-875-1269
www.mrchocolate.com

From Mr. Chocolate himself, this "cute, little" Dumbo parlor and its Grand Central spin-off dishes out the namesake chocolatier's "gourmet" scoops in an "amazing" array of "intense" flavors; the ice cream also comes sandwiched between his "delicious" signature cookies for the ultimate "decadent" treat.

Jaiya *Thai*

| 23 | 18 | 17 | $40 |

East 80s | 1553 Second Ave. (bet. 80th & 81st Sts.) | 212-717-8877
Murray Hill | 396 Third Ave. (28th St.) | 212-889-1330
www.jaiya.com

Whether you prefer "spicy" or "incendiary", these East Side Thais offer "authentic" Siamese food running the gamut from standard classics to "challenging, take-no-hostages" dishes; "decent" price points trump the "noisy" settings and less-than-stellar service.

Jake's Steakhouse *Steak*

| 24 | 19 | 22 | $60 |

Fieldston | 6031 Broadway (242nd St.) | Bronx | 718-581-0182 | www.jakessteakhouse.com

"Scenic views" of Van Cortlandt Park make the "Manhattan-quality" steaks taste even juicier at this Fieldston chophouse where the service is "professional" and the beer selection "vast"; although "expensive", it's "cheaper than the city", and there's "valet parking" to boot.

James *American*

| 24 | 21 | 21 | $46 |

Prospect Heights | 605 Carlton Ave. (St Marks Ave.) | Brooklyn | 718-942-4255 | www.jamesrestaurantny.com

"Creative" Americana with a "local" focus match with an "awesome" drink list at this "charming" Prospect Heights haunt, quartered in "welcoming" whitewashed-brick digs; it's "convenient to BAM" and the Barclays Center, but also a local brunch magnet.

NEW Jams *Californian*

| — | — | — | M |

West 50s | 1 Hotel Central Park | 1414 Sixth Ave. (58th St.) | 212-703-2001 | www.1hotels.com

Jonathan Waxman revives his '80s-era farm-to-table pioneer with this modern dining room in Midtown's 1 Hotel Central Park, where the very of-the-moment menu reflects his signature Californian style. Natural colors and large windows give the striking space an airy feel, while the bar is lined with vintage glassware from the original locale.

Jane *American*

| 22 | 19 | 20 | $41 |

Greenwich Village | 100 W. Houston St. (bet. LaGuardia Pl. & Thompson St.) | 212-254-7000 | www.janerestaurant.com

"Young" types head to this "upbeat" Village American for "quite tasty" cooking, with "moderate" tabs, "austere" decor and "generally good service" on the side; though "insanely busy", the weekend brunch is the scene to make, provided you can stomach "loud" decibels on top of your "hangover."

Japonica *Japanese*

| 23 | 16 | 21 | $50 |

Greenwich Village | 90 University Pl. (12th St.) | 212-243-7752 | www.japonicanyc.com

An "old friend" since '78, this Village Japanese (recently relocated to its original digs) "never gets old" thanks to "enormous portions" of "super-fresh", "delicate" sushi; a "smaller" space means it gets "crowded" quickly, and if not exactly cheap, tabs feel "reasonable" given the "quality."

NEW Javelina *Tex-Mex*

| 26 | 22 | 23 | $37 |

Gramercy Park | 119 E. 18th St. (bet. Irving Pl. & Park Ave.) | 212-539-0202 | www.javelinatexmex.com

Packed since day one, this "real-deal" Gramercy Park joint is a "happy place" for Tex-Mex fans thanks to "sizzling" fajitas, "addictive" queso and other "awesome" staples; its narrow space has a "modern Southwestern aesthetic" and a "super-fun" vibe, and if it's "noisy", the "trendy" crowd is too into the "strong" drinks to notice.

Jean-Georges *French*   28 | 28 | 28 | $166

West 60s | Trump Int'l Hotel | 1 Central Park W. (61st St.) | 212-299-3900 | www.jean-georgesrestaurant.com

Jean-Georges Vongerichten's "superlative" CPW namesake "pulls out all the stops" for a "rarefied dining experience", with "heavenly" New French "culinary artistry" bolstered by a "top wine list", "orchestrated" service and "civilized" surroundings; just "dress up" (jackets are required), "forget the mortgage this month" and prepare to be "wowed."

Jean-Georges' Nougatine *French*   27 | 23 | 26 | $76

West 60s | Trump Int'l Hotel | 1 Central Park W. (61st St.) | 212-299-3900 | www.jean-georgesrestaurant.com

While "not as opulent" as the adjacent Jean-Georges, this "appealing" front room (plus a "beautiful terrace") delivers the "same excellence" thanks to an "impressive" New French lineup and service that "goes the extra mile"; though it's "surprisingly affordable" all day, the lunch prix fixe stands out as a "shockingly good value."

Jeepney *Filipino*   23 | 18 | 22 | $39

East Village | 201 First Ave. (bet. 12th & 13th Sts.) | 212-533-4121 | www.jeepneynyc.com

You can "be as adventurous (or as cautious) as you want" at this "dope" East Village gastropub offering "equal parts daring and gourmet" takes on traditional Filipino comfort food; a "knowledgeable" crew can help guide "neophytes" through the menu, and the colorful decor (e.g. pin-up photos) keeps the space "interesting."

Jeffrey's Grocery *American*   23 | 21 | 21 | $53

West Village | 172 Waverly Pl. (Christopher St.) | 646-398-7630 | www.jeffreysgrocery.com

There's "Wisconsin" in the air at Gabe Stulman's "hip" West Village American, a "homey", all-day thing where the "tasty" menu is as limited as the square footage; "divine oysters" and "attention to detail" offset the "not-Midwestern prices", though a few feel it's "more scene than place to eat."

Jewel Bako *Japanese*   24 | 23 | 22 | $90

East Village | 239 E. Fifth St. (bet. 2nd & 3rd Aves.) | 212-979-1012 | www.jewelbakosushi.com

"Casually elegant" and "expensively" priced, this bamboo-lined East Village Japanese slices a "flawless symphony" of "incredibly fresh fish"; for best results, insiders "sit at the sushi bar" and go the omakase route, though no matter where you land, owners Jack and Grace Lamb "really take care of you."

J.G. Melon *Pub Food*   22 | 14 | 17 | $31

East 70s | 1291 Third Ave. (74th St.) | 212-744-0585
NEW **Greenwich Village** | 89 MacDougal St. (Bleecker St.) | 212-460-0900

"Old-school preppies" and modern-day "bros" catch up over "frosty mugs", "juicy" burgers and "awesome" cottage fries at this "always-packed" Upper East Side "institution" that recalls "old-time", circa-1972 NY right down to its cash-only policy; the new Village offshoot is separately owned, but offers the same menu plus desserts from Magnolia.

Jimmy's No. 43 *SE Asian*
▽ 20 | 19 | 19 | $34

East Village | 43 E. Seventh St. (2nd Ave.) | 212-982-3006 | www.jimmysno43.com

A "destination for the beer lover", this "relaxed" East Village "basement" pairs its "impressive" suds selection with ciders, craft whiskeys and Filipino-Thai street eats from chef King Phojanakong (Kuma Inn); the "tavern"-like space is nothing fancy, but it's still a "cozy" hang for the "'in' crowd."

Jing Fong *Chinese*
21 | 14 | 14 | $25

Chinatown | 20 Elizabeth St. (bet. Bayard & Canal Sts.) | 212-964-5256 | www.jingfongny.com

Set in a "football field–size" hall, this "bustling" C-town Cantonese rolls out "delectable" dim sum "à la Hong Kong" on "quickly moving carts" propelled by "brusque" staffers; it's "crowded at peak hours", a "hectic madhouse" on weekends and "affordable" all the time.

Jin Ramen *Japanese/Noodle Shop*
23 | 16 | 18 | $23

Morningside Heights | 3183 Broadway (bet. 125th St. & Tiemann Pl.) | 646-559-2862

NEW **West 80s** | 462 Amsterdam Ave. (82nd St.) | 646-657-0755 www.jinramen.com

"Slurp-alicious" bowls of hand-pulled noodles will "warm you up" at these "inexpensive" ramen shops where the "limited" menu is dispatched by an "attentive" team; the wood-lined spaces are "cute" but "cramped", so there might be a "wait at peak times."

Joe *Coffee*
21 | 15 | 21 | $8

Chelsea | 405 W. 23rd St. (9th Ave.) | 212-206-0669
Chelsea | 131 W. 21st St. (bet. 6th & 7th Aves.) | 212-924-7400
East 40s | 44 Grand Central Terminal (Lexington Ave.) | 212-661-8580
East 70s | 1045 Lexington Ave. (75th St.) | 212-988-2500
Greenwich Village | 9 E. 13th St. (bet. 5th Ave. & University Pl.) | 212-924-3300
Greenwich Village | 37 E. Eighth St. (University Pl.) | 212-466-2800
Morningside Heights | 550 W. 120th St. (B'way) | 212-851-9101
West 60s | 187 Columbus Ave. (68th St.) | 212-877-0244
West 80s | 514 Columbus Ave. (85th St.) | 212-875-0100
West Village | 141 Waverly Pl. (Gay St.) | 212-924-6750
www.joetheartofcoffee.com

"Cheerful" baristas whip up "high-quality" coffee drinks at this growing mini-chain that also serves a "small selection of nice pastries"; the "unassuming" settings are pleasantly "unpretentious", while the Joe Pro Shop in the Flatiron offers classes and the chance to sample "beans from guest roasters."

Joe Allen *American*
18 | 18 | 21 | $47

West 40s | 326 W. 46th St. (bet. 8th & 9th Aves.) | 212-581-6464 | www.joeallenrestaurant.com

Known for its "posters of Broadway bombs" and "serviceable" American grub, this "timeless" Theater District joint is still a magnet for "showbiz" types and those who love them; après-theater "star-gazing" – "yes, that's who you think it is in that dark corner" – lends "glamour" to the proceedings.

Joe & Pat's *Italian/Pizza*   24 | 12 | 16 | $23

Castleton Corners | 1758 Victory Blvd. (bet. Manor Rd. & Winthrop Pl.) | Staten Island | 718-981-0887 | www.joeandpatspizzany.com

It's all about the "deliciously thin, crispy" pizzas at this Castleton Corners "staple" that's been dishing up "delicious" Italian family meals for "generations" of Staten Island folks; there's "not much atmosphere" to speak of, but "fast" service and modest tabs go a long way.

Joe's Ginger *Chinese*   20 | 10 | 14 | $22

Chinatown | 25 Pell St. (Mott St.) | 212-285-0999 | www.joeginger.com

"Slightly slicker" and "less crazy" than its nearby sibling, Joe's Shang-hai, this C-town contender features the "same great soup dumplings", "rushed service" and lack of decor; "individual tables" and "less waiting on line" are additional benefits.

Joe's Pizza *Pizza*   24 | 9 | 16 | $10

Greenwich Village | 150 E. 14th St. (bet. Irving Pl. & 3rd Ave.) | 212-388-9474

West Village | 7 Carmine St. (bet. Bleecker St. & 6th Ave.) | 212-366-1182

NEW Williamsburg | 216 Bedford Ave. (5th St.) | Brooklyn | 718-388-2216

www.joespizzanyc.com

"Iconic for a reason", this circa-1975 West Village original and its offshoots deliver "reliably excellent" "old-school" slices "straight from the oven"; "divey" surroundings and "stand-up" tables mean it's best for "on the go", but when you want "classic NY pizza", it's a "quintessential" choice.

Joe's Shanghai *Chinese*   22 | 10 | 15 | $27

Chinatown | 9 Pell St. (bet. Bowery & Doyers St.) | 212-233-8888

West 50s | 24 W. 56th St. (bet. 5th & 6th Aves.) | 212-333-3868

Flushing | 136-21 37th Ave. (bet. Main & Union Sts.) | Queens | 718-539-3838

www.joeshanghairestaurants.com

"Delicate, savory and fun to eat", the "signature" soup dumplings at these Chinese "staples" are "justly famous"; trade-offs include "long lines", "perfunctory service" and "no atmosphere", yet they're "always packed for a reason."

John Brown Smokehouse *BBQ*   22 | 15 | 19 | $25

Long Island City | 10-43 44th Dr. (bet. 10th & 11th Sts.) | Queens | 347-617-1120 | www.johnbrownseriousbbq.com

"No-nonsense" BBQ (including "awesome burnt ends") is the specialty of this Kansas City–style joint in Long Island City that also provides "plentiful sides" and a "great craft beer selection"; it's a "simple setup", i.e. you "order at the counter and pick up your tray when it's ready."

John Dory Oyster Bar *Seafood*   21 | 17 | 18 | $61

NoMad | Ace Hotel | 1196 Broadway (29th St.) | 212-792-9000 | www.thejohndory.com

Set in the Flatiron's Ace Hotel, this "airy" seafooder from April Bloomfield and Ken Friedman offers everything from "succulent oysters" to "inspired" small plates; "hefty" tabs for "guppy-size portions" are offset by the "happening vibe", kitschy-"cool" digs and those "sublime" Parker House rolls.

John's of 12th Street *Italian*   22 | 17 | 21 | $33

East Village | 302 E. 12th St. (2nd Ave.) | 212-475-9531 | www.johnsof12thstreet.com

"Upholding the art of Italian cooking" since 1908, this East Village "institution" endures thanks to "no-nonsense" red-sauce meals (plus some vegan selections), all at "fair prices"; no credit cards and "nothing-fancy" decor – think Chianti bottles and "melted candle wax" – add to the "time-warp" vibe.

John's Pizzeria *Pizza*   23 | 16 | 18 | $25

West 40s | 260 W. 44th St. (bet. 7th & 8th Aves.) | 212-391-7560 | www.johnspizzerianyc.com
West Village | 278 Bleecker St. (Jones St.) | 212-243-1680 | www.johnsbrickovenpizza.com
Arthur Avenue/Belmont | 2376 Arthur Ave. (186th St.) | Bronx | 718-220-0000 | www.johnspizzerianyc.com

"True" NY-style pizza emerges from the coal-fired brick ovens of these separately owned "bang-for-the-buck" pie joints; the cash-only West Village "institution" is "worth the wait in line" ("forget the decor"), while the "big" Theater District outlet is set in an old church with "beautiful" stained-glass windows.

JoJo *French*   24 | 21 | 23 | $72

East 60s | 160 E. 64th St. (bet. Lexington & 3rd Aves.) | 212-223-5656 | www.jojorestaurantnyc.com

The French fare is "delectable" at this UES "jewel" in the Jean-Georges Vongerichten "crown", backed up by an "excellent" wine list and a "lovely townhouse setting", whose "intimate" rooms prompt "romance aplenty"; the feeling of "magic" in the air "makes the prices easier to swallow."

Jones Wood Foundry *British*   20 | 20 | 19 | $42

East 70s | 401 E. 76th St. (bet. 1st & York Aves.) | 212-249-2700 | www.joneswoodfoundry.com

Bringing a bit of "jolly old England" to Yorkville, this wood-paneled British pub dispenses "wonderful fish 'n' chips" and other "simple" classics washed down with an "impressive" suds selection; the "cool, low-key" ambiance is also "what sells this place", along with "helpful" service and a "lovely garden."

Jordans Lobster Dock *Seafood*   22 | 9 | 13 | $33

Sheepshead Bay | 3165 Harkness Ave. (Plumb 2nd St.) | Brooklyn | 718-934-6300 | www.jordanslobster.com

Locals "pretend they're in Maine" at this longtime Sheepshead Bay seafooder where live lobsters in "big tanks" make for ultra-"fresh" eating; sure, the "decor's as minimal as the service", but tabs aren't high and an on-site retail market means you can "eat your goodies at home."

Joseph Leonard *American*   24 | 22 | 23 | $59

West Village | 170 Waverly Pl. (Grove St.) | 646-429-8383 | www.josephleonard.com

"Original", "deeply satisfying" takes on New American standards draw "super-cool" folks to Gabe Stulman's West Village "hot spot" that ups the ante with open-all-day hours; the "hiply rustic", "lumberjacky" setting is so "tiny" that "crowded" conditions and long "waits" are a given.

Joya *Thai*   22 | 19 | 21 | $25

Cobble Hill | 215 Court St. (bet. Warren & Wyckoff Sts.) | Brooklyn | 718-222-3484

Scenes don't get much more "boisterous" or "fun" than at this Cobble Hill Thai where a mix of "solid" food, "cheap" tabs and "sleek" design attracts "young, hip" throngs; "dance-club" acoustics send regulars to the "more peaceful" back garden, but there's no sidestepping the cash-only rule.

Jubilee *French*   21 | 18 | 20 | $56

East 50s | 948 First Ave. (bet. 52nd & 53rd Sts.) | 212-888-3569 | www.jubileeny.net

A "clientele of a certain age" touts this "longtime" Sutton Place-area bistro as a haven of "relaxed sophistication" that's like a "quick trip to Paris"; it's "not noisy" and the seafood-oriented French fare (including "claim-to-fame" moules) is "tasty", so it's no wonder "reservations for dinner" are recommended.

Juliana's *Pizza*   26 | 18 | 21 | $27

Dumbo | 19 Old Fulton St. (bet. Front & Water Sts.) | Brooklyn | 718-596-6700 | www.julianaspizza.com

"The king of pizza", aka Patsy Grimaldi, tosses "thin-crust perfection" at his parlor under the Brooklyn Bridge where "consistently tops" coal-fired pies are the "real deal"; "fast" service comes in handy when there's a line "snaking outside", but you also might find "no wait" at all.

NEW June Wine Bar *American*   20 | 22 | 20 | M

Cobble Hill | 231 Court St. (Baltic St.) | Brooklyn | 917-909-0434 | www.junebk.com

A long, dramatically lit space with big booths and a marble bar, this "charming" Cobble Hill hangout pours natural European wines (plus beers, cocktails and digestifs) alongside a "short and sweet" New American menu of "inventive" seasonal small plates; the "intimate" vibe ups its "date"-night appeal.

Jungsik *Korean*   26 | 25 | 26 | $200

TriBeCa | 2 Harrison St. (Hudson St.) | 212-219-0900 | www.jungsik.kr

They "take Korean food up a notch or two" at this TriBeCa "find", where a "discreet" team brings on "extraordinary" contemporary cuisine and the tasting menus "are events"; the understated white-tablecloth setting rates just as high, but "excellence comes at a price" so count on a "hefty tab."

Juni *American*   27 | 25 | 28 | $134

Murray Hill | Chandler Hotel | 12 E. 31st St. (bet. 5th & Madison Aves.) | 212-995-8599 | www.juninyc.com

"Genius" chef Shaun Hergott delivers a "simply extraordinary" experience at this New American in Murray Hill's Chandler Hotel, where his "sublime" tasting menus feature an "ongoing parade" of "precisely-put-together" dishes that look like "fine art"; though "impeccable" service and "luxe" decor are in keeping with the high tabs, the prix fixe lunch is a total "steal."

	FOOD	DECOR	SERVICE	COST

Junior's *Diner*

19 | 13 | 17 | $30

East 40s | Grand Central | 89 E. 42nd St., Lower Dining Concourse (Vanderbilt Ave.) | 212-983-5257
West 40s | 1515 Broadway (45th St.) | 212-302-2000
Downtown Brooklyn | 386 Flatbush Ave. Extension (Dekalb Ave.) | Brooklyn | 718-852-5257
www.juniorscheesecake.com

"World famous" for its "stupendous" cheesecakes, this Downtown Brooklyn "icon" and its Midtown offshoots also sling a "huge menu" of "decent" American diner fare, served in "gigantic portions" by "swift" staffers; sure, the atmosphere's "frenetic" and the decor "bland", but the "fair prices" alone make it "worth a visit."

Junoon *Indian*

24 | 25 | 24 | $66

Flatiron | 27 W. 24th St. (bet. 5th & 6th Aves.) | 212-490-2100 | www.junoonnyc.com

You can "dine like a prince" at this "upmarket" Flatiron "oasis" offering "innovative" Indian food with "rich, complex flavors" in a "gorgeous" front lounge and main dining room; tabs are "higher than average", but "precise" service and a sommelier who "knows his stuff" up the appeal.

Kafana *E European*

∇ 24 | 19 | 19 | $34

East Village | 116 Ave. C (bet. 7th & 8th Sts.) | 212-353-8000 | www.kafananyc.com

"Traditional, old-school" Serbian cooking that's like a "trip to Belgrade" is the draw at this "unusual" East Village option where the "hedonistic" menu is a "must-try for meat lovers"; the servers are "knowledgeable", and the "warm", brick-lined space is studded with photos reflecting the "Eastern European" mood.

Kajitsu *Japanese/Vegetarian*

24 | 20 | 25 | $115

Murray Hill | 125 E. 39th St. (bet. Lexington & Park Aves.) | 212-228-4873 | www.kajitsunyc.com

This wood-lined, "Zen"-like Japanese vegetarian in Murray Hill is a "hushed" oasis for "excellent" ancient Buddhist shojin cuisine, served kaiseki-style at dinner by an "impeccable" staff (and priced "as if it were Harry Winston jewels"); the more casual first-floor adjunct goes by the name Kokage, and offers non-vegetarian, à la carte dishes for lunch and dinner.

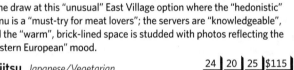 NEW Kang Ho Dong Baekjeong *Korean*

23 | 17 | 20 | $44

Murray Hill | 1 E. 32nd St. (5th Ave.) | 212-966-9839

"Packed" since day one, this "modern" K-town branch of a South Korea-based BBQ chain is known for "fantastic-quality" beef and pork grilled tableside by a "fast"-moving staff; the waits are "long", but they'll "take your number and call when a table's available."

Kang Suh *Korean*

18 | 13 | 15 | $39

West 30s | 1250 Broadway (bet. 31st & 32nd Sts.) | 212-564-6845 | www.kangsuhnyc.com

"After-hours" types tout this 30-plus-year-old Garment Center Korean for its "authentic" BBQ, low tabs and "24/7" open-door policy; since it's "not much to look at" and "you'll smell like it when you leave", maybe it's good that the staff "rushes you through your meal."

	FOOD	DECOR	SERVICE	COST

Kanoyama *Japanese*
24 | 16 | 21 | $63

East Village | 175 Second Ave. (bet. 11th & 12th Sts.) | 212-777-5266 |
www.kanoyama.com

"Artfully arranged" sushi, including "varieties you don't often see",
is the hook at this East Village Japanese "adventure" that seals the deal
with tabs that are "reasonable" vis-à-vis the "high quality"; maybe the
place "doesn't look like much", but an adjacent sake/oyster bar allows
room to spread out.

NEW Kao Soy *Thai*
∇ 21 | 16 | 17 | M

Red Hook | 283 Van Brunt St. (Pioneer St.) | Brooklyn | 718-875-1155
The namesake noodle dish is a "must" at this simple Red Hook stop
specializing in "spicy" Northern Thai fare highlighted by "bold" flavors;
"small" digs mean there may be a wait during peak hours, but at least
prices are "reasonable."

NEW Kappo Masa *Japanese*
∇ 25 | 25 | 22 | $150

East 70s | 976 Madison Ave. (76th St.) | 212-906-7141 |
www.kappomasanyc.com

You're "in the hands of a master" at chef Masa Takayama's "serene"
UES Japanese below Gagosian Gallery, where "delicate" sushi made from
the "freshest-quality" fish is offered alongside a diverse array of cooked
dishes; "painfully expensive" tabs are no surprise given the "elegant"
surrounds and ritzy zip code.

Kashkaval Garden *Mediterranean*
24 | 19 | 21 | $30

West 50s | 852 Ninth Ave. (bet. 55th & 56th Sts.) | 212-245-1758 |
www.kashkavalgarden.com

A "good first-date place", this "casual" Midtown Med offers a "wide
selection" of "terrific" tapas (plus some "quality" fondues), all for
"reasonable" dough; an "inviting" interior and a small, "under-the-radar"
back garden are other reasons it's a "local favorite."

Kati Roll Company *Indian*
23 | 11 | 15 | $13

East 50s | 229 E. 53rd St. (bet. 2nd & 3rd Aves.) | 212-888-1700
Greenwich Village | 99 MacDougal St. (Bleecker St.) | 212-420-6517
West 30s | 49 W. 39th St. (bet. 5th & 6th Aves.) | 212-730-4280
www.thekatirollcompany.com

"Grab-and-go" Indian street food is the concept at these counter-service
joints specializing in "mouthwatering" kati wraps stuffed with "fragrant
ingredients"; "exceptional value" keeps them as "busy as Bombay" at
lunchtime, "no-decor" settings notwithstanding.

Katsu-Hama *Japanese*
22 | 14 | 17 | $29

East 40s | 11 E. 47th St. (bet. 5th & Madison Aves.) | 212-758-5909
West 50s | 43-45 W. 55th St. (bet. 5th & 6th Aves.) | 212-541-7145
www.katsuhama.com

"Deep-fried comfort food" in pork-cutlet form is the specialty of these
Midtown Japanese tonkatsu parlors where the goods are "tender and
juicy" and "most of the customers speak the language"; "easy-on-the-
pocketbook" tabs trump "not much decor" and "indifferent" service.

	FOOD	DECOR	SERVICE	COST

Katz's Delicatessen *Deli*
25 | 12 | 15 | $27

Lower East Side | 205 E. Houston St. (Ludlow St.) | 212-254-2246 |
www.katzsdelicatessen.com

A "legendary" LES landmark since 1888, this cash-only "bucket lister"
remains the "gold standard" for "sky-high" pastrami sandwiches and
other "real-deal" Jewish deli eats; resembling a "high school cafeteria", the "crowded, hectic" space is "nothing to talk about", but for a
"classic NYC" experience it still has many joining *When Harry Met Sally*
fans in shouting "yes, yes, yes!"

Keens Steakhouse *Steak*
26 | 25 | 25 | $87

West 30s | 72 W. 36th St. (bet. 5th & 6th Aves.) | 212-947-3636 |
www.keens.com

The "granddaddy of all NYC steakhouses", this circa-1885 Midtown
"temple to meat" remains "rock solid", with "sinful" *"Flintstones-*
sized" mutton chops and other "succulent" slabs of beef in "masculine" "museum"-like surrounds with "lines upon lines" of antique
pipes on the ceiling; it's "not for the weak of wallet", but "welcoming" service and an "endless" scotch selection are other reasons you
"won't regret splurging."

Kefi *Greek*
22 | 17 | 19 | $42

West 80s | 505 Columbus Ave. (bet. 84th & 85th Sts.) | 212-873-0200 |
www.kefirestaurant.com

For "generous" portions of "well-prepared" Greek comfort food at
"über-reasonable prices", locals head to this "relaxed" UWS "staple";
while service can seem "bewildered" and the "too-close-for-comfort"
main room can get "noisy" (downstairs is "quieter"), most still
think it's "very good indeed."

Kellari Taverna *Greek/Seafood*
22 | 21 | 21 | $56

West 40s | 19 W. 44th St. (bet. 5th & 6th Aves.) | 212-221-0144 |
www.kellariny.com

"Mouthwatering" displays of "fresh fish on ice" beckon at this "sophisticated" Midtown Greek seafooder offering "next-flight-to-Athens"-quality
cooking; though some menu items are "pricey", the pre-theater prix fixe
is a "steal" – and "efficient" staffers "make sure you make your curtain."

Keste Pizza e Vino *Pizza*
23 | 14 | 18 | $31

West Village | 271 Bleecker St. (Morton St.) | 212-243-1500 |
www.kestepizzeria.com

"Blow-you-away" Neapolitan pizzas ("oh, that crust!") with "fresh,
flavorful toppings" are the draw at this "popular", "no-frills" West Village
pizzeria; but while the goods may be "hard to beat", trade-offs include
"so-so service", "super-cramped" digs and "indulgence" pricing.

Khe-Yo *Laotian*
24 | 20 | 21 | $55

TriBeCa | 157 Duane St. (bet. Hudson St. & W. B'way) | 212-587-1089 |
www.kheyo.com

The "underexposed, underappreciated" cuisine of Laos gets its due at
this Marc Forgione–backed TriBeCan where the "helpful" staff guides diners through the "bold", "adventurous" menu; the brick- and wood-lined
space exudes "hip" vibrations, and there's a daytime cafe, Khe-Yosk, that
serves banh mi sandwiches.

	FOOD	DECOR	SERVICE	COST

NEW Kiin Thai *Thai*
▽ 22 | 18 | 20 | $29

Greenwich Village | 36 E. Eighth St. (University Pl.) | 212-529-2363 | www.kiinthaieatery.com

"Interesting and delicious", the classic Central and Northern Thai dishes served up at this bright, casual Greenwich Villager make a "wonderful change from the typical"; toss in "decent" prices and a "warm staff" and you have a "great addition" to the neighborhood.

NEW King Bee *Cajun/French*
▽ 21 | 22 | 22 | $55

East Village | 424 E. Ninth St. (bet. Ave. A & 1st Ave.) | 646-755-8088 | www.kingbeenyc.com

Fans of New Orleans cuisine find some familiar flavors at this "welcoming" East Village Acadian, where "interesting" and "delicious" seasonal offerings are served alongside "innovative" cocktails and "eclectic" wines; the subterranean space has a farmhouselike feel, and there's a raw bar too.

Kings' Carriage House *American*
23 | 25 | 24 | $65

East 80s | 251 E. 82nd St. (bet. 2nd & 3rd Aves.) | 212-734-5490 | www.kingscarriagehouse.com

Best known for its "lovely setting", this Upper East Side "hidden treasure" is nestled in a "romantic" duplex suggesting an "English country house"; the prix fixe–only New American menu is also "quite good", with "gracious" service, "quiet" decibels and "dainty" afternoon tea as bonuses.

Kin Shop *Thai*
25 | 16 | 21 | $51

West Village | 469 Sixth Ave. (bet. 11th & 12th Sts.) | 212-675-4295 | www.kinshopnyc.com

"Taking Thai in new directions", chef Harold Dieterle's "ambitious" West Villager "gives your taste buds a workout" via "fantastic" dishes delivered by a "helpful" team; loyalists insist the "creative" flavors trump the "serene" but somewhat "pedestrian" setting.

Ki Sushi *Japanese*
24 | 19 | 22 | $47

Cobble Hill | 122 Smith St. (bet. Dean & Pacific Sts.) | Brooklyn | 718-935-0575

This "intimate" Cobble Hill Japanese serves "memorable signature rolls" made with "high-quality fish" in a "typical", "low-key" setting; with "knowledgeable" service thrown into the mix, it's a "reliable" neighborhood favorite.

Kitchenette *Southern*
20 | 16 | 17 | $26

Morningside Heights | 1272 Amsterdam Ave. (bet. 122nd & 123rd Sts.) | 212-531-7600 | www.kitchenetterestaurant.com

Southern "comfort" cooking is the specialty of this "kitschy" "country farmhouse"–inspired standby in Morningside Heights where both the menu and the portions are "big"; the "cutesy", "small-town" decor earns mixed response, but all agree on the "rushed" service and low tabs.

Knickerbocker Bar & Grill *American*
21 | 19 | 21 | $53

Greenwich Village | 33 University Pl. (9th St.) | 212-228-8490 | www.knickerbockerbarandgrill.com

"Time warps" don't get more "lovable" than this 1977-vintage Villager, an "old-school" source of "no-surprises" Americana that's "solid" but "won't knock your socks off"; though the room's a tad "tattered", "warm" service and "surprisingly good" weekend jazz make this one a keeper.

Koi *Japanese* — 24 | 23 | 21 | $67

Hudson Square | Trump Soho Hotel | 246 Spring St. (bet. 6th Ave. & Varick St.) | 212-842-4550

West 40s | Bryant Park Hotel | 40 W. 40th St. (bet. 5th & 6th Aves.) | 212-921-3330

www.koirestaurant.com

"Fashionistas" and other "trendy" types nibble "Japanese delicacies" (including "designer" sushi) at these "plush" hotel retreats; the "LA vibe" and "wonderfully snooty" service are a "bit too Beverly Hills" for some, but even enthusiasts agree it's best to "avoid getting stuck with the bill."

NEW Korilla *Korean/Mexican* — ∇ 23 | 15 | 21 | $14

East Village | 23 Third Ave. (St. Marks Pl.) | 646-823-9423 | www.korillabbq.com

"Delight your taste buds" with an "awesome" Korean-meets-Mexican mash-up at this East Village brick-and-mortar outlet from the namesake BBQ truck, known for build-your-own burritos and bowls in "gut-busting" portions; the counter-serve setup is "minimalist", but no one cares given the "affordable" rates.

Ko Sushi *Japanese* — 20 | 13 | 19 | $35

East 70s | 1329 Second Ave. (70th St.) | 212-439-1678

East 80s | 1619 York Ave. (85th St.) | 212-772-8838

www.newkosushi.com

These "no-frills", separately owned Japanese Upper Eastsiders furnish a "neighborhood" following with "tasty" raw fish that's "priced right"; "quick" service makes the "cafeteria"-like settings more palatable, though aesthetes recommend the "reliable delivery."

NEW Kottu House *Sri Lankan* — – | – | – | M

Lower East Side | 250 Broome St. (Ludlow St.) | 646-781-9222 | www.kottuhouse.com

Specializing in the Sri Lankan street food it's named after, this Lower Eastsider offers the roti-based dish in a number of preparations alongside small bites and sides; tiny with only a handful of tables and barstools, the brick-walled space is as modest as the tabs.

Kouzan *Japanese* — 21 | 18 | 19 | $35

West 90s | 685 Amsterdam Ave. (93rd St.) | 212-280-8099 | www.kouzanjapanese.com

Starting with its "dim lighting" and "serene" feeling, this "pretty" Upper West Side Japanese "raises expectations" that are met by "quality" sushi and cooked items, all delivered by a "bend-over-backwards" team; throw in tabs geared to the "99%" and no wonder it's such a "neighborhood asset."

Kristalbelli *Korean* — 25 | 22 | 24 | $56

West 30s | 8 W. 36th St. (bet. 5th & 6th Aves.) | 212-290-2211 | www.kristalbelli.com

A "classy" yet "hip" vibe matches the "high-end" Korean cuisine offered at this "Rolls-Royce"-esque K-town restaurant/lounge where the "refined" dishes include meats that diners barbecue on "cool", smoke-free crystal grills; "attentive" staffers help distract from the "pricey" tabs.

Krupa Grocery *American* ▽ 25 | 21 | 22 | $39

Windsor Terrace | 231 Prospect Park W. (Windsor Pl.) | Brooklyn | 718-709-7098 | www.krupagrocery.com

This "terrific" "neighborhood find" in Windsor Terrace supplies "can't-go-wrong" American fare breakfast through dinner (plus a "creative brunch") in an "unassuming" space with a back patio; with the "smart staff" also dispensing "tasty" cocktails, it's a "local secret" where those in the know "keep coming back."

Kuma Inn *Filipino/Thai* ▽ 23 | 12 | 19 | $40

Lower East Side | 113 Ludlow St., 2nd fl. (bet. Delancey & Rivington Sts.) | 212-353-8866 | www.kumainn.com

One of NYC's "best hidden gems", this "obscure" Filipino-Thai accessed up a flight of LES stairs puts out an "avant-garde" small-plates menu "exploding with flavor"; the "hole-in-the-wall" digs are "tight", but the "price is right" and "BYO makes it even better."

Kum Gang San *Korean* 21 | 13 | 15 | $39

Flushing | 138-28 Northern Blvd. (bet. Bowne & Union Sts.) | Queens | 718-461-0909 | www.kumgangsan.net

This 24/7 "kitsch" palace in Flushing slings Korean BBQ in a "cavernous" setting equipped with a waterfall and piano; the "traditional" food is "solid", the decor "age-worn" and the service "rush-rush", but it's still "good for first-timers" and "out-of-towners."

Kung Fu Ramen *Noodle Shop* 23 | 7 | 16 | $18

West 40s | 811 Eighth Ave. (49th St.) | 917-388-2555 | www.nykungfuramen.com

"Definitely no-frills", this Midtown West "hole-in-the-wall" "surprises in the best way", supplying "hand-pulled" noodles, "satisfying" soups and "wonderful" dumplings on the "cheap"; trade-offs include "perfunctory service" and "chaotic" lunchtime crowds, but hey, it "should win an award for its name alone."

Kunjip *Korean* 21 | 14 | 16 | $31

West 30s | 9 W. 32nd St. (5th Ave.) | 212-216-9487 | www.kunjip.net

Always open and "always crowded", this "popular" 24/7 K-town venue plies an "extensive menu" of "traditional" Korean cooking in a "no-frills" atmosphere; while seating's "cramped" and servers "rush you out the door", the "solid" chow largely redeems all.

Kurumazushi *Japanese* ▽ 24 | 13 | 17 | $121

East 40s | 7 E. 47th St., 2nd fl. (bet. 5th & Madison Aves.) | 212-317-2802 | www.kurumazushi.com

The "ethereal, next-level" sushi "couldn't be fresher or more delicious" at chef Toshihiro Uezu's pioneering Midtown eatery, perched in a "peaceful", second-floor space; tabs may be "extravagant", but the prices are "warranted" for a "traditional experience" on par with "high-end places in Japan."

Kyochon Chicken *Chicken*

21 | 17 | 17 | $24

Murray Hill | 319 Fifth Ave. (bet. 32nd & 33rd Sts.) | 212-725-9292
Flushing | 156-50 Northern Blvd. (bet. 156th & 157th Sts.) | Queens |
718-939-9292
www.kyochonus.com

Fried chicken gets an "oh-so-spicy" Korean spin – and some "soy-garlic"
inflections – at these "addictive" satellites of the global poultry chain;
"modern" food-court design distracts from the "small portions" and tabs
that are "a bit pricey for wings."

Kyo Ya *Japanese*

26 | 23 | 25 | $98

East Village | 94 E. Seventh St., downstairs (1st Ave.) | 212-982-4140
The "complex" Kyoto-style dishes "take you to Japan" at this "hidden"
East Villager where the "incredible" seasonal cuisine is best showcased
via multicourse kaiseki spreads (by reservation only); with "personal"
service and a "blessedly quiet" subterranean setting, it's a "high-end"
dining "adventure" that's worth "saving up for."

La Baraka *French*

23 | 19 | 25 | $46

Douglaston | 255-09 Northern Blvd. (2 blocks east of Little Neck Pkwy.) |
Queens | 718-428-1461 | www.labarakarest.com
Renowned for the "hospitality" of "lovely hostess" Lucette, this long-
standing Douglaston venue follows through with "terrific" Tunisian-
accented French fare; though the decor "needs an update", tabs are
"reasonable" and the overall mood definitely "enjoyable."

La Bergamote *Bakery/French*

24 | 18 | 20 | $35

Chelsea | 177 Ninth Ave. (20th St.) | 212-627-9010
West 50s | 515 W. 52nd St. (bet. 10th & 11th Aves.) | 212-586-2429
www.labergamotenyc.com

These "buttery" patisserie/cafes supply "dynamite" French pastries that
are "gorgeous to look at and just as delicious to taste", along with other
savory "light meals"; "neighborhoody" vibes and "easy-on-the-wallet"
pricing make up for the "spare seating."

La Boîte en Bois *French*

20 | 16 | 20 | $62

West 60s | 75 W. 68th St. (bet. Columbus Ave. & CPW) | 212-874-2705 |
www.laboitenyc.com

A longtime "pre-theater favorite" near Lincoln Center, this "tiny" French
boîte turns out "classic" bistro dishes in a "congenial" setting overseen by
"fast-moving" staffers; "sardine"-can dimensions, "old-fashioned" decor
and kinda "pricey" tabs come with the territory.

La Bonne Soupe *French*

19 | 14 | 17 | $34

West 50s | 48 W. 55th St. (bet. 5th & 6th Aves.) | 212-586-7650 |
www.labonnesoupe.com

"Serviceable" enough for a "quick bite", this longtime Midtown "pinch
hitter" is best known for its "divine onion soup", though the rest of its
French bistro menu is certainly "reliable"; "brusque" service, "crowded"
conditions and "no-frills" looks are blunted by good "value."

La Colombe Torrefaction *Coffee*

25 | 20 | 19 | $8

NEW **Greenwich Village** | 400 Lafayette St. (4th St.) | 212-677-5834
NEW **Hudson Square** | 75 Vandam St. (Hudson St.) | 212-929-9699
SoHo | 270 Lafayette St. (Prince St.) | 212-625-1717

continued
TriBeCa | 319 Church St. (Lispenard St.) | 212-343-1515
www.lacolombe.com

"Fantastic coffee" with the power of "rocket fuel" is the draw at these
java joints imported from Philly; "yummy pastries" are also on offer,
and while there's often a "long line", "knowledgeable" baristas work
to ensure it moves quickly.

Ladurée *Bakery/French*   22 | 24 | 19 | $43

SoHo | 398 W. Broadway (bet. Broome & Spring Sts.) | 646-392-7868 |
www.ladureeus.com

"Glorious excess reigns" at this SoHo outpost of the luxury French
bakery, with an up-front patisserie showcasing "phenomenal" macarons
abetted by a "candy-box" rear dining room offering "quite-good" Gallic
fare; *bien sûr*, it's "pricey", but payoffs include a knockout back garden.

Lady Mendl's *Teahouse*   21 | 24 | 22 | $59

Gramercy Park | Inn at Irving Pl. | 56 Irving Pl. (bet. 17th & 18th Sts.) |
212-533-4600 | www.ladymendls.com

Ladies live it up à la *Downton Abbey* at this "mahvelous" Gramercy
tearoom where "excellent" servers present "tasty" sandwiches and
sweets along with "wonderful" brews in an "elegant" Victorian setting;
it's "pricey" whether "your boyfriend" comes or not, but a "pampered
afternoon" is the reward.

La Esquina *Mexican*   23 | 21 | 19 | $44

SoHo | 114 Kenmare St. (bet. Cleveland Pl. & Lafayette St.) |
646-613-7100 | www.esquinanyc.com
Cafe de la Esquina *Mexican*

Williamsburg | 225 Wythe Ave. (3rd St.) | Brooklyn | 718-393-5500 |
www.esquinabk.com

"Straight-up *delicioso*" describes both the food and the scene at this
ever-"trendy" SoHo Mexican comprised of a "dive"-like taqueria, casual
indoor/outdoor cafe and "ultracool", hard-to-access underground grotto;
the Williamsburg spin-off set in a "futuristic retro diner" comes equipped
with a moody back room and "huge outdoor patio."

Lafayette *French*   22 | 24 | 21 | $62

NoHo | 380 Lafayette St. (Great Jones St.) | 212-533-3000 |
www.lafayetteny.com

A "gorgeous", "expansive" space with "plenty of room to breathe" lures
"beautiful people" to this "bustling" all-day NoHo cafe that's a showcase
for Andrew Carmellini's "hearty" French cooking; insiders say it "shines
best at breakfast", though the front bakery is a "great pit stop" for "delicious bread" and "delectable" pastries any time.

La Follia *Italian*   23 | 18 | 20 | $39

Gramercy Park | 226 Third Ave. (19th St.) | 212-477-4100 |
www.lafollianyc.com

Whether you land in the up-front enoteca or the rear dining room, the
same "terrific" Italian small plates and pastas are available at this "casual" Gramercy "neighborhood place"; fans like the "sincere" service and
"affordable" rates, the "no-reservations policy" not so much.

	FOOD	DECOR	SERVICE	COST

La Fonda del Sol *Spanish*   22 | 21 | 21 | $59

East 40s | 200 Park Ave. (enter on 44th St. & Vanderbilt Ave.) |
212-867-6767 | www.patinagroup.com
Conveniently sited above Grand Central, this reincarnation of a "classic" '60s Spaniard offers both a "lively after-work bar" serving "upscale tapas" and a "soothing", more "sophisticated" back room; it's "a bit high-priced", but at least the service is "professional."

NEW La Gamelle *French*   — | — | — | M

Lower East Side | 241 Bowery (Stanton St.) | 212-388-0052 |
www.lagamellenyc.com
Taking over where Bowery Diner left off, this LES French brasserie near the New Museum offers a menu of Gallic classics augmented by a variety of charcuterie platters; the atmospheric, Balthazar-lite setting features the requisite zinc bar, tiled floors and globe lights.

La Grenouille *French*   27 | 28 | 28 | $129

East 50s | 3 E. 52nd St. (bet. 5th & Madison Aves.) | 212-752-1495 |
www.la-grenouille.com
The "charm remains" at this *"magnifique"* Midtown "grande dame" offering a "sublime" selection of "refined" French fare dispatched by "faultless" staffers in an "opulent" room festooned with "heavenly" floral arrangements; granted, all this "elegance" comes at a price, but it's "worth every franc" – and the requisite jacket.

La Lanterna di Vittorio *Italian*   20 | 24 | 20 | $35

Greenwich Village | 129 MacDougal St. (bet. 3rd & 4th Sts.) |
212-529-5945 | www.lalanternacaffe.com
It's all about the "romantic feel" at this Village Italian "slice of heaven" purveying "enjoyable", "affordable" light bites in "quaint" quarters lit by a fireplace and "lantern-filled" garden; "live jazz" in the adjoining bar adds further "first-date" appeal.

La Lunchonette *French*   23 | 14 | 19 | $46

Chelsea | 130 10th Ave. (18th St.) | 212-675-0342
"It hasn't changed much in all these years, and that's a good thing" say supporters of this "quirky", "fair-priced" West Chelsea French bistro; its "divey charm" is just the thing post–"High Line" – and on Sunday night there's a "chanteuse/accordionist" – but go soon, as it's slated to close at the end of 2015.

La Mangeoire *French*   22 | 19 | 21 | $64

East 50s | 1008 Second Ave. (bet. 53rd & 54th Sts.) | 212-759-7086 |
www.lamangeoire.com
If you "can't get to Provence", check out this next-best-thing East Midtowner offering "imaginative takes on traditional country French dishes"; its longevity (since 1975) may be due to the "warm" service and "transporting" South-of-France decor.

La Masseria *Italian*   24 | 20 | 23 | $65

West 40s | 235 W. 48th St. (bet. B'way & 8th Ave.) | 212-582-2111 |
www.lamasserianyc.com

continued

NEW Masseria dei Vini *Italian*

West 50s | 887 Ninth Ave. (bet. 57 & 58th Sts.) | 212-315-2888 |
www.masseriadeivini.com

Showgoers tout this "quick-pace" Times Square–area Italian for its
"hearty" cooking, "sweet farmhouse" setting and "fast" service that
"gets you to the theater on time"; its new "upscale" Hell's Kitchen sibling
sports a more "modern" look and an added focus on wine.

Lambs Club *American*   21 | 24 | 21 | $78

West 40s | Chatwal Hotel | 132 W. 44th St. (bet. 6th & 7th Aves.) |
212-997-5262 | www.thelambsclub.com

You'll be "looking around for Nick and Nora Charles" given the "red-
leather" deco decor at Geoffrey Zakarian's "sophisticated" Theater
Districter; the New American food is just as "fabulous", ditto the service,
and in winter the fireplace is "roaring", but "steep" tabs have some going
for cocktails in the upstairs lounge instead.

La Mela *Italian*   20 | 13 | 19 | $34

Little Italy | 167 Mulberry St. (bet. Broome & Grand Sts.) | 212-431-9493 |
www.lamelarestaurant.com

"Belly-busting, multicourse" meals are the backbone of this "old-school
Little Italy" vet where the "solid" Southern Italian cooking can be ordered
either à la carte or in family-style prix fixes; maybe the decor "leaves
much to be desired", but service is "prompt" and the pricing "fair."

L&B Spumoni Gardens *Ice Cream/Pizza*   24 | 12 | 17 | $25

Gravesend | 2725 86th St. (bet. W. 10th & 11th Sts.) | Brooklyn |
718-449-1230 | www.spumonigardens.com

This circa-1939 Gravesend "icon" is beloved for its "twin legends" –
Sicilian square pizza that "rules" and spumoni in portions big enough to
feed "all the families in your building"; there's a "dated" dining room, but
in summer most opt to order at the window and eat outside with the
"neighborhood characters."

Landmarc *French*   19 | 19 | 18 | $56

TriBeCa | 179 W. Broadway (bet. Leonard & Worth Sts.) | 212-343-3883
West 50s | Time Warner Ctr. | 10 Columbus Circle, 3rd fl. (60th St. at
B'way) | 212-823-6123
www.landmarc-restaurant.com

"Safe bets" for dining at "pleasing price points", Marc Murphy's
"popular" French bistros offer "hearty" Gallic fare paired with especially
economical wine lists; the TriBeCa original is more of a "neighborhood
destination", while the "big", "loud" TWC offshoot is a "godsend" for
"shoppers" and the "stroller" set.

Landmark Tavern *Pub Food*   19 | 19 | 20 | $40

West 40s | 626 11th Ave. (46th St.) | 212-247-2562 |
www.thelandmarktavern.org

Around since 1868, this "off-the-beaten-path" Hell's Kitchen tavern is
deemed "worth the detour" for its "cozy olde NY" atmosphere alone;
grab a pint and some "standard" pub grub delivered by a "caring" crew –
"they don't make 'em like this anymore."

	FOOD	DECOR	SERVICE	COST

Land Thai Kitchen *Thai*
22 | 14 | 18 | $28

West 80s | 450 Amsterdam Ave. (bet. 81st & 82nd Sts.) | 212-501-8121 | www.landthaikitchen.com

"Big on flavor" but not in decor or size, this UWS "neighborhood Thai" dispenses "delicious" standards "quick" at "wallet-friendly" rates; since "waits" are the norm at peak times, many elect for "takeout/delivery."

L & W Oyster Co. *Seafood*
20 | 16 | 19 | $54

NoMad | 254 Fifth Ave. (bet. 28th & 29th Sts.) | 212-203-7772 | www.landwoyster.com

A "find" near Madison Square Park, this NoMad seafooder dispenses "informal beach-style" favorites (fresh oysters, a lobster BLT) in airy, urban-clam-shack environs; solid service and an overall "fun atmosphere" have most plotting to "go back again" soon.

Lan Larb *Thai*
▽ 21 | 14 | 19 | $27

Little Italy | 227 Centre St. (Grand St.) | 646-895-9264
Murray Hill | 637 Second Ave. (35th St.) | 212-889-1769
www.lanlarb.com

These "affordable" spin-offs of Larb Ubol specialize in "adventurous" Isan cuisine from northeastern Thailand, with an emphasis on "delicious" larbs (spicy ground-meat salads) as well as more "predictable" curries and pad Thai; although "takeout"-friendly, the storefront settings do offer plenty of space to sit and linger.

NEW L'Antagoniste *French*
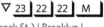
▽ 23 | 22 | 22 | M

Bedford-Stuyvesant | 238 Malcolm X Blvd. (Hancock St.) | Brooklyn | 917-966-5300 | www.lantagoniste.com

A "surprise" in Bed-Stuy, this Le Philosophe sibling is a "lovely hideaway" matching "high-quality", "reasonably priced" renditions of French classics with fine wines in a simple space adorned with a black-and-white photo mural; far from antagonized, Francophiles wonder "who could resist?"

La Palapa *Mexican*
22 | 18 | 20 | $40

East Village | 77 St. Marks Pl. (bet. 1st & 2nd Aves.) | 212-777-2537 | www.lapalapa.com

"High-class Mexican" cuisine "cooked with love" is offered "cheap" and served with "courtesy" at this East Village cantina; the "luscious margaritas" that pack "plenty of punch" take your mind off "scrunched" seating, but "bring ear protection" at peak times.

L'Apicio *Italian*
23 | 21 | 22 | $60

East Village | 13 E. First St. (bet. Bowery & 2nd Ave.) | 212-533-7400 | www.lapicio.com

A bona fide "hit" with "fashionable" folk, this "wonderful" East Village Italian from the Dell'anima/L'Artusi team offers a "refined", pasta-centric menu in a big, "glam" room; "appreciative" service, an "amazing bar scene" and a "bustling" mood complete the "trendy" picture.

La Pizza Fresca *Italian/Pizza*
24 | 19 | 19 | $46

Flatiron | 31 E. 20th St. (bet. B'way & Park Ave. S.) | 212-598-0141 | www.lapizzafresca.com

It was a "granddaddy of the artisanal pizza trend", and this Flatiron "favorite" continues to turn out "superior" Neapolitan pies along with "terrific pasta"; "attentive" staffers with "smiles on all faces" help maintain the "relaxed" mood.

Larb Ubol *Thai* ▽ 22 | 12 | 18 | $28

West 30s | 480 Ninth Ave. (37th St.) | 212-564-1822 | www.larbubol.com

It's the "real deal" say supporters of this "tasty" Hell's Kitchen Thai supplying Isan specialties from the country's northeast region that pack an "incendiary punch"; the bare-bones space jibes with the wallet-friendly tabs, while "friendly" servers add to the overall "pleasant" vibe.

La Rivista *Italian* 20 | 16 | 20 | $52

West 40s | 313 W. 46th St. (bet. 8th & 9th Aves.) | 212-245-1707 | www.larivistanyc.com

"Conveniently located on Restaurant Row", this Theater District "standby" offers "reliable" Italian basics at "sensible" tabs for those who "want to be sure to make their curtain"; some say the decor "could use updating", but others like the "old-school" vibe and occasional piano playing.

L'Artusi *Italian* 27 | 23 | 24 | $71

West Village | 228 W. 10th St. (bet. Bleecker & Hudson Sts.) | 212-255-5757 | www.lartusi.com

"Impeccably executed" modern Italian fare pairs with an "impressive" wine list at this "busy", date-worthy West Villager where "cordial" staffers ratchet up the "class" factor; what's "upbeat" to some is "loud" to others, but the majority feels it ultimately "hits all the marks."

La Sirène *French* 24 | 17 | 21 | $63

Hudson Square | 558½ Broome St. (Varick St.) | 212-925-3061 | www.lasirenenyc.com

"Decadent" preparations of "traditional" French cuisine shuttled by "charming" staffers are the lures at this "small" Hudson Square bistro; though seating is "tight", loyalists call it "cozy" and all agree on the "exceptional" service.

La Superior *Mexican* ▽ 25 | 18 | 20 | $20

Williamsburg | 295 Berry St. (bet. 2nd & 3rd Sts.) | Brooklyn | 718-388-5988 | www.lasuperiornyc.com

Connoisseurs of "authentic Mexican" street food say the "menu is a winner" at this cash-only Williamsburg hangout where "amazing" mini-tacos lead a "very reasonably priced" lineup; though the setting is admittedly "small", it's "perfect for socializing" and the food makes it "worth waiting for seats."

La Tarte Flambee *French* 20 | 13 | 20 | $30

East 90s | 1750 Second Ave. (91st St.) | 212-860-0826

Murray Hill | 153 E. 33rd St. (bet. Lexington & 3rd Aves.) | 917-261-2070 www.latarteflambee.com

Alsatian-style thin-crust flatbreads – think "France's answer to pizza" – are the specialty of these "nice changes from the ordinary" on the East Side; toppings range from sweet (fruit, chocolate) to savory (bacon, cheese, veggies), while "hospitable" service and "moderate price points" make them all the more "welcome."

	FOOD	DECOR	SERVICE	COST

Lattanzi *Italian*

| 22 | 20 | 22 | $63 |

West 40s | 361 W. 46th St. (bet. 8th & 9th Aves.) | 212-315-0980 | www.lattanzinyc.com

Something "special" on Restaurant Row, this "better-than-average" Italian separates itself from the pack with an unusual post-theater menu of Roman-Jewish specialties; otherwise, it's a strictly "old-guard" experience with "gracious" service and a "charming" setting featuring lots of "dining nooks and crannies."

Laut *Malaysian/Thai*

| 22 | 14 | 18 | $32 |

Union Square | 15 E. 17th St. (bet. B'way & 5th Ave.) | 212-206-8989 | www.lautnyc.com

Southeast Asia's "vast variety of flavors" gets its due at this Union Square purveyor of "authentic", "delicious" dishes from Malaysia, Thailand and beyond; there's "no ambiance" to speak of, but "affordable" tabs and "friendly" service keep things copacetic.

Lavagna *Italian*

| 24 | 19 | 22 | $49 |

East Village | 545 E. Fifth St. (bet. Aves. A & B) | 212-979-1005 | www.lavagnanyc.com

At this "unassuming" yet "polished" Alphabet City "gem", "terrific" Tuscan cooking, "attentive" staffers and "cozy, brick-walled" digs work "romantic" wonders; factor in "affordable" prices, and it's no wonder the "tight" digs are "always crowded."

La Vara *Spanish*

| 27 | 20 | 23 | $55 |

Cobble Hill | 268 Clinton St. (bet. Verandah Pl. & Warren St.) | Brooklyn | 718-422-0065 | www.lavarany.com

"Delicious", "unique combinations" of "sophisticated" Moorish- and Jewish-inspired tapas are the draw at this "relaxed" Cobble Hill Spaniard where "helpful" staffers guide diners through the "original" menu; the "cozy", brick-walled space opens onto a "little patio", and regulars highly "recommend reservations."

La Vigna *Italian*

| 25 | 20 | 24 | $47 |

Forest Hills | 100-11 Metropolitan Ave. (70th Ave.) | Queens | 718-268-4264 | www.lavignany.com

Forest Hills locals "can't say enough about" this Italian charmer that enjoys a "well-earned reputation" for "authentic", "premium-quality" cooking; the "cozy", brick-walled quarters and "thoughtful" service add to its "dependable" reputation.

La Villa Pizzeria *Pizza*

| 24 | 18 | 21 | $29 |

Mill Basin | 6610 Ave. U (66th St.) | Brooklyn | 718-251-8030
Park Slope | 261 Fifth Ave. (bet. 1st St. & Garfield Pl.) | Brooklyn | 718-499-9888
Howard Beach | 8207 153rd Ave. (82nd St.) | Queens | 718-641-8259
www.lavillaparkslope.com

These "basic neighborhood red-sauce" joints dish out "first-rate" pizzas along with a "lengthy" roster of "comfort" Italian items; nondescript settings and "loud" acoustics are offset by "modest" tabs.

| | FOOD | DECOR | SERVICE | COST |

Lavo *Italian*
20 | 18 | 18 | $65

East 50s | 39 E. 58th St. (bet. Madison & Park Aves.) | 212-750-5588 | www.lavony.com

It's one "crazy" scene at this "pricey" Midtown Italian that rivals nearby sibling Tao as a "meet-and-mingle" hub for the "Botox-and-high-heels" set and the "expense-account suits" who love them; just bring "earplugs" and an appetite – the "garlicky" fare is "surprisingly good" – and then "go party" in the "thumping" downstairs club.

Le Bernardin *French/Seafood*
29 | 28 | 29 | $182

West 50s | 155 W. 51st St. (bet. 6th & 7th Aves.) | 212-554-1515 | www.le-bernardin.com

"Nothing comes close" to this "widely acclaimed" Midtown exercise in "luxury" from Maguy Le Coze and chef Eric Ripert, providing "absolute bliss" in the form of "ethereal" French seafood and a "mind-blowing wine list" dispatched in a "calming", "opulent" milieu by "read-your-mind" servers; its prix fixe–only format, starting at $140, will put a "substantial dent in your wallet" (lunch is cheaper), yet it has garnered No. 1 honors for Food, Service and Popularity in NYC for a reason – this "sine qua non" dining experience remains "the best splurge in town."

Le Bilboquet *French*
22 | 21 | 19 | $75

East 60s | 20 E. 60th St. (bet. Madison & Park Aves.) | 212-751-3036

"One does not go for the meal alone" to this "see-and-be-seen" UES French bistro that functions as a clubhouse for "power" types, "Euro locals" and "Park Avenue dowagers"; the food's "consistently good" and the service "rude" if you're not a regular, but the "outrageous" pricing extends to all.

Le Cirque *French*
24 | 26 | 25 | $102

East 50s | 151 E. 58th St. (bet. Lexington & 3rd Aves.) | 212-644-0202 | www.lecirque.com

"Impressive" is the word for this "iconic" destination in the Bloomberg Tower, where Sirio Maccioni and his "gracious" staff deliver "outstandingly prepared" French fare with a side of "VIP treatment"; while the "astronomical" prices befit Adam Tihany's "spectacular", circus-themed main dining room, neither a "lotto win" nor a jacket and tie are required in the more casual cafe.

Le Colonial *French/Vietnamese*
22 | 23 | 21 | $68

East 50s | 149 E. 57th St. (bet. Lexington & 3rd Aves.) | 212-752-0808 | www.lecolonialnyc.com

At this "gorgeous" East Midtowner, you'll be "transported to an exotic place" where the spirit of 1920s "colonial Indochine" is in the air and on the plate in the form of "terrific" French-Vietnamese fare; the "old Saigon" sensibility extends to a "comfortable upstairs lounge", though prices are strictly modern day.

NEW Le District *Food Hall/French*
– | – | – | M

Battery Park City | 230 Vesey St. (West St.) | 212-981-8588 | www.ledistrict.com

The Eataly model gets a Gallic spin at this Battery Park City food hall in Brookfield Place vending a wide range of French goods, everything from bread, cheese, coffee and charcuterie to fish, produce and rotisserie meats; although the complex is mostly geared toward takeout (or counter snacking), a sit-down, fine-dining brasserie, Beaubourg, anchors the space.

Left Bank *American*   25 | 23 | 26 | $54

West Village | 117 Perry St. (Greenwich St.) | 212-727-1170 | www.leftbanknewyork.com
"Impeccably prepared" New American fare with European influences is paired with a "terrific wine selection" at this "relaxed" West Village "home away from home"; "outstanding" service and a "quiet, cozy" ambiance further burnish this "neighborhood gem."

Le Gigot *French*   25 | 18 | 24 | $66

West Village | 18 Cornelia St. (bet. Bleecker & 4th Sts.) | 212-627-3737 | www.legigotrestaurant.com
A little piece of the "Left Bank" in the West Village, this "lovely" French bistro offers "beautifully cooked" Provençal dishes, a "superb" wine list and "warm" service; the "petite" space can feel "tight", but "flattering lighting" adds to the "romantic" appeal.

Le Marais *French/Kosher/Steak*   23 | 19 | 20 | $60

West 40s | 150 W. 46th St. (bet. 6th & 7th Aves.) | 212-869-0900 | www.lemarais.net
"If you're a kosher carnivore", this Theater District French "staple" comes across with "excellent steaks" that pass muster with the highest authority; maybe the service "doesn't match" the food quality and the surrounds are "forgettable", but it's generally "packed" all the same.

Lemon Ice King of Corona *Ice Cream*   26 | 7 | 17 | $6

Corona | 52-02 108th St. (52nd Ave.) | Queens | 718-699-5133 | www.thelemonicekingofcorona.com
A "delicious" way to "cool off" since the 1940s, this Corona "landmark" draws "long lines" with its "vast assortment" of "real-deal" Italian ices that loyalists dub the "city's best"; there's no seating, so regulars head for nearby Flushing Meadows Park.

Leopard at des Artistes *Italian*   21 | 25 | 23 | $85

West 60s | 1 W. 67th St. (bet. Columbus Ave. & CPW) | 212-787-8767 | www.theleopardnyc.com
Dining amid "sumptuous" Howard Chandler Christy murals always lifts the spirits at this "nicely done" Café des Artistes "reincarnation" near Lincoln Center; with a "breathtaking" space, "genuine" Italian fare and "personalized attention", it has a "luxury" that justifies the "bruises to your credit card."

Leo's Latticini *Italian/Sandwiches*   ∇ 24 | 12 | 20 | $19

Corona | 46-02 104th St. (46th Ave.) | Queens | 718-898-6069
Mama's of Corona *Italian/Sandwiches*
Willets Point | Citi Field | 12301 Roosevelt Ave. (behind the scoreboard) | Queens | no phone
"Nobody makes a sandwich" like this Corona "old-school Italian deli" where the subs are "fit for royalty" and the mozz is among the "best in the boroughs"; its Citi Field stand services Mets fans on game days, but, unfortunately, without those "adorable ladies" behind the counter.

Le Pain Quotidien *Bakery/Belgian*

	FOOD	DECOR	SERVICE	COST
	18	15	15	$25

Chelsea | 52 Ninth Ave. (bet. 14th & 15th Sts.) | 646-350-4789
East 60s | 1270 First Ave. (bet. 68th & 69th Sts.) | 212-988-5001
East 60s | 833 Lexington Ave. (bet. 63rd & 64th Sts.) | 646-762-2209
East 70s | 252 E. 77th St. (bet. 2nd & 3rd Aves.) | 212-249-8600
East 80s | 1131 Madison Ave. (bet. 84th & 85th Sts.) | 212-327-4900
Flatiron | 931 Broadway (bet. 21st & 22nd Sts.) | 646-395-9926
Greenwich Village | 10 Fifth Ave. (8th St.) | 212-253-2324
NoHo | 65 Bleecker St. (Crosby St.) | 646-797-4922
SoHo | 100 Grand St. (Mercer St.) | 212-625-9009
West 40s | 70 W. 40th St. (6th Ave.) | 212-354-5224
West 50s | 922 Seventh Ave. (58th St.) | 212-757-0775
West 60s | 60 W. 65th St. (bet. B'way & CPW) | 212-721-4001
West 70s | 50 W. 72nd St. (bet. Columbus Ave. & CPW) | 212-712-9700
West 90s | 2463 Broadway (91st St.) | 212-769-8879
Brooklyn Heights | 121 Montague St. (Henry St.) | Brooklyn | 718-858-3078
www.lepainquotidien.com
Additional locations throughout the NY area

For an "unfussy" "coffee-shop alternative", try this "quickie" Belgian bakery/cafe chain patronized for its "easy" menus (with "many organic choices") served in "rustic" rooms at "elbow-to-elbow" communal tables; "predictability" and "disorganized" service are a pain, but "inexpensive" tabs and "all-around-town" locations compensate.

Le Parisien *French*

	FOOD	DECOR	SERVICE	COST
	22	15	20	$47

Murray Hill | 163 E. 33rd St. (bet. Lexington & 3rd Aves.) | 212-889-5489 | www.leparisiennyc.com

"Teleport" to the "banks of the Seine" via this "cozy" Murray Hill French bistro offering "excellent", "well-priced" renditions of "all the classics"; "charming" staffers compensate for "tiny" dimensions and help seal its standing as a local "winner."

Le Perigord *French*

	FOOD	DECOR	SERVICE	COST
	25	22	25	$86

East 50s | 405 E. 52nd St. (bet. FDR Dr. & 1st Ave.) | 212-755-6244 | www.leperigord.com

"White glove" all the way, this Sutton Place "bastion of civility" has been a "treat for adults" since 1964 thanks to a menu of "exquisite" French classics and an "impeccable" wine list, "served with grace" by an "old-school" staff; *bien sûr,* it's a "splurge", but still less costly than a "trip to Paris."

Le Philosophe *French*

	FOOD	DECOR	SERVICE	COST
	22	16	20	$64

NoHo | 55 Bond St. (bet. Bowery & Lafayette St.) | 212-388-0038 | www.lephilosophe.us

"Delicious", age-old Gallic dishes – think frogs' legs, lobster Thermidor, duck à l'orange – turn up at this NoHo bistro that's a hit with "locals" who like its wall mural of famed French philosophers; "tiny" dimensions can make getting a table here "a challenge."

Le Relais de Venise L'Entrecôte *French/Steak*

	FOOD	DECOR	SERVICE	COST
	20	17	19	$45

East 50s | 590 Lexington Ave. (52nd St.) | 212-758-3989 | www.relaisdevenise.com

It's all about "value" at this "unique" East Midtown French brasserie where the "one-trick-pony" menu consists only of steak frites and salad for a $29 fixed price; fans find it "quick and easy", though the no-reservations rule can make for waits at prime times.

Le Rivage *French*
21 | 17 | 21 | $52

West 40s | 340 W. 46th St. (bet. 8th & 9th Aves.) | 212-765-7374 | www.lerivagenyc.com

"Old-school" French dining is alive and well at this circa-1958 Restaurant Row survivor where the "middle-of-the-road" Gallic offerings are "consistent" and the staff "understands curtain time"; the digs may be "dated", but the post-theater $29 prix fixe is quite the "deal."

Les Halles *French/Steak*
20 | 18 | 18 | $46

Financial District | 15 John St. (bet. B'way & Nassau St.) | 212-285-8585
Murray Hill | 411 Park Ave. S. (bet. 28th & 29th Sts.) | 212-679-4111
www.leshalles.net

Ever "popular", these "vibrant" French brasseries are known for their "first-rate" steak frites, "dark" lighting and "noisy" decibels; though the "people-watching" can be "fun", "don't count on seeing" long-gone chef-at-large Anthony Bourdain.

Le Veau d'Or *French*
19 | 15 | 20 | $58

East 60s | 129 E. 60th St. (bet. Lexington & Park Aves.) | 212-838-8133

"Forgotten" French bistro classics work their "throwback" magic on loyal patrons of this circa-1937 Eastsider; though it's "had a full life" – and it shows – here's hoping it'll "continue forever."

Le Zie *Italian*
21 | 15 | 21 | $45

Chelsea | 172 Seventh Ave. (bet. 20th & 21st Sts.) | 212-206-8686 | www.lezie.com

"High-end in quality but not in price" sums up the Venetian cuisine at this "lively" Chelsea Italian; regulars suggest the "back room" if quiet dining is preferred, and say "beware" the "daily specials" that sell for "much more" than the regular fare.

The Library at the Public *American*
19 | 22 | 20 | $50

Greenwich Village | 425 Lafayette St. (bet. Astor Pl. & 4th St.) | 212-539-8777 | www.thelibraryatthepublic.com

"Hidden away" upstairs at the Public Theater is this "gem" providing "pricey" American fare from chef Andrew Carmellini in "dark", "clubby" quarters with a "vibrant" bar scene; opinions are mixed on the food ("terrific" vs. "nothing special"), but all agree it "couldn't be easier before the show."

LIC Market *American*
26 | 21 | 24 | $32

Long Island City | 21-52 44th Dr. (23rd St.) | Queens | 718-361-0013 | www.licmarket.com

LIC denizens feel "lucky to have" this rustic American "gem" providing "lick-your-plate" good farm-to-table fare and "personable service" at a "reasonable" price point; since it's both "small" and "popular", seating can be "scarce" – particularly for the "delicious" brunch.

Lido *Italian*
23 | 20 | 21 | $39

Harlem | 2168 Frederick Douglass Blvd. (117th St.) | 646-490-8575 | www.lidoharlem.com

Harlem denizens declare you "don't need to go Downtown for first-rate

Italian food" thanks to this "solid" Uptown player; its "skillfully prepared" dishes are served in "relaxed" environs by "friendly" staffers, with no letup in "quality" during the popular "bottomless-mimosa" brunch.

Liebman's Delicatessen *Deli/Kosher*
24 | 13 | 21 | $24

Riverdale | 552 W. 235th St. (Johnson Ave.) | Bronx | 347-227-0776 | www.liebmansdeli.com

For a "corned beef on rye, hold the cardiogram", check out this "quint-essential" kosher Jewish deli that's been a "Riverdale landmark" for "delicious", "stacked-high" sandwiches since 1953; it "hasn't changed in years" – as evidenced in the "faded" decor and "slapdash" service – but to fans it "never disappoints."

Lil' Frankie's Pizza *Italian/Pizza*
23 | 16 | 19 | $33

East Village | 19 First Ave. (bet. 1st & 2nd Sts.) | 212-420-4900 | www.lilfrankies.com

Really "solid" Italian fare "without frills" at an "affordable price" is the signature of this "casual", cash-only East Villager, a sibling of Frank, Sauce and Supper; it offers "standout" Neapolitan pizzas, late hours and a "garden room", so it's no wonder it gets way-"crowded" at peak times.

NEW Limani *Mediterranean*
23 | 25 | 24 | $71

West 50s | 45 Rockefeller Plaza (5th Ave.) | 212-858-9200 | www.limani.com

Spun off from the Long Island original, this "impressive" Rock Center Mediterranean offers a "high-quality", seafood-focused menu dispatched by an "engaging" team; granted, it's rather "expensive", but compensations include "great-deal" prix fixes and a "gorgeous" white-on-white setting, complete with its own "reflecting pool."

Lincoln *Italian*
25 | 27 | 25 | $90

West 60s | Lincoln Ctr. | 142 W. 65th St. (bet. Amsterdam Ave. & B'way) | 212-359-6500 | www.lincolnristorante.com

A "calm oasis" on the Lincoln Center campus, Jonathan Benno's Italian "showstopper" rolls out a "marvelous" menu in a "sleek", glass-walled space built around a "gleaming" open kitchen; "polished" service and ultra-"proximity" to the various concert halls are part of the "superb" package, but be prepared to spend "many Lincolns" for the privilege.

NEW Lincoln Square Steak *Steak*
20 | 20 | 21 | $86

West 70s | 208 W. 70th St. (Amsterdam Ave.) | 212-875-8600 | www.lincolnsquaresteak.com

A "high-end steakhouse" comes to the Upper West Side via this "wel-coming" venue where "charming" servers set down "juicy" prime cuts in a "well-spaced" room with a "colorful" mural, barside pianist and "bordellolike" crimson walls; sure, the tabs skew "pricey", but it gives rivals "a run for their money."

The Lion *American*
18 | 20 | 18 | $70

Greenwich Village | 62 W. Ninth St. (bet. 5th & 6th Aves.) | 212-353-8400 | www.thelionnyc.com

Chef-owner John DeLucie conjures up "old-school" NY at this "fashion-able" Village American where a "huge skylight, eclectic art and photos" provide an apt backdrop for the "handsome, affluent crowd"; the "homey-yet-upscale" fare takes a backseat to the "stimulating" scene, but it's just as "delicious."

Little Beet *American*   22 | 17 | 18 | $40

West 50s | 135 W. 50th St. (7th Ave.) | 212-459-2338 | www.thelittlebeet.com

NEW Little Beet Table *American*

Murray Hill | 333 Park Ave. S. (bet. 24th & 25th Sts.) | 212-466-3330 | www.thelittlebeettable.com

"Proving that healthy can be delicious", these "busy", veggie-centric Americans offer "beautifully presented" gluten-free menus sensitive to "dietary constraints"; the full-service Park Avenue South outpost is a magnet for "loud" girls'-night-out groups, while the Midtown branch is more of a "grab-and-go" affair with "brutal" lunchtime lines.

Littleneck *Seafood*   23 | 21 | 21 | $34

Gowanus | 288 Third Ave. (bet. Carroll & President Sts.) | Brooklyn | 718-522-1921

Littleneck Outpost *Seafood*

Greenpoint | 128 Franklin St. (Milton St.) | Brooklyn | 718-363-3080 www.littleneckbrooklyn.com

"Terrific" New England–style seafood washes up at these cash-only clam shacks where the "well-priced" roster ranges from "always-fresh" raw bar items to steamers and rolls; a "mean brunch", "great-deal" happy-hour oysters and "cozy", marine-themed digs keep its "hipster" crowd content.

Little Owl *American/Mediterranean*   26 | 20 | 24 | $59

West Village | 90 Bedford St. (Grove St.) | 212-741-4695 | www.thelittleowlnyc.com

A definite "bucket-list" candidate, this "tiny" but "stellar" West Villager offers chef Joey Campanaro's "elevated" Med–New American cuisine served by an "expert" team in "extremely tight quarters"; reservations remain "ever-elusive" even a month in advance, but wised-up admirers just "keep trying."

NEW Little Park *American*   26 | 24 | 24 | $67

TriBeCa | Smyth Hotel | 85 W. Broadway (Chambers St.) | 212-220-4110 | www.littlepark.com

"Big on unique flavors", this all-day TriBeCa American from chef Andrew Carmellini (Locanda Verde, The Dutch) boasts a seasonal roster of "masterfully done" small and large plates spotlighting "gourmet vegetarian options"; look for a "responsive" staff and mellow "modern decor" at this "grown-up oasis", where the "rather steep" bill is decidedly "worth it."

Little Poland *Diner/Polish*   21 | 9 | 16 | $23

East Village | 200 Second Ave. (bet. 12th & 13th Sts.) | 212-777-9728

"Heaping portions" of "filling" Polish "diner food" comes "cheap as can be" at this "old-time" East Village "greasy spoon"; "drab" the interior may be, but wait till you taste those "perfect pierogi" – you couldn't do better in Gdansk.

	FOOD	DECOR	SERVICE	COST

Little Prince *French* 22 | 18 | 18 | $50

SoHo | 199 Prince St. (bet. MacDougal & Sullivan Sts.) | 212-335-0566 | www.littleprincesoho.com

"Take a Francophile" to this "charming" SoHo bistro, where the "well-executed takes" on Gallic classics "pack a punch" – especially the "acclaimed French Onion Soup Burger"; the "cool crowd", "playful staff" and banquette-lined digs "straight out of the Left Bank" complete the "memorable" rendezvous.

Lobster Joint *New England/Seafood* 24 | 16 | 18 | $31

Greenpoint | 1073 Manhattan Ave. (bet. Dupont & Eagle Sts.) | Brooklyn | 718-389-8990 | www.lobsterjoint.com

"Lobster fresher than a Brooklyn waiter" is the lure at this "laid-back" Greenpoint seafood shack that furnishes "quality" New England–style fare and "no-nonsense" cocktails "without cleaning out your wallet"; come summer, a "picnic-table backyard" expands the "simple" setup.

Locanda Verde *Italian* 25 | 23 | 22 | $70

TriBeCa | Greenwich Hotel | 377 Greenwich St. (N. Moore St.) | 212-925-3797 | www.locandaverdenyc.com

"Energetic" is the word on chef Andrew Carmellini's "grand-slam" TriBeCa Italian offering a "delectable", all-day menu to a "swinging" clientele basking in its "trendiness factor"; despite an "overcrowded", somewhat "frantic" scene at prime times, reservations are still "hard to get."

Locanda Vini & Olii *Italian* 26 | 24 | 24 | $46

Clinton Hill | 129 Gates Ave. (bet. Cambridge Pl. & Grand Ave.) | Brooklyn | 718-622-9202 | www.locandavinieolii.com

The "former pharmacy" setting lends "old-fashioned but stylish appeal" to this "refreshingly distinctive" Clinton Hill Northern Italian, home to "expertly prepared" pastas and other "top-quality" fare delivered by a "hands-on" staff; it's a bona fide "hidden gem" where regulars "leave full and happy."

NEW Loi Estiatorio *Greek* ▽ 25 | 21 | 23 | $103

West 50s | 132 W. 58th St. (6th Ave.) | 212-713-0015 | www.loiestiatorio.com

Chef Maria Loi is the mind behind this "upscale" Midtown Greek where "adroit" takes on seafood and other "authentic" "homestyle" dishes make for a "wonderful culinary experience"; chicly understated digs and "superb service" are more reasons why fans see lots of "potential" here.

NEW Lolo's Seafood Shack *Caribbean/Seafood* ▽ 25 | 20 | 23 | $22

Harlem | 303 W. 116th St. (Frederick Douglass Blvd.) | 646-649-3356 | www.lolosseafoodshack.com

This "tiny" Harlem seafooder rolls out "delectable" takes on Caribbean street eats, offering "sloppy-casual" dishes like conch fritters, steampots with an array of sauces and plenty of veggie-centric sides; while the counter-order space is simple, with patio seating out back, service is "bubbly."

Lombardi's *Pizza* 24 | 15 | 17 | $28

NoLita | 32 Spring St. (bet. Mott & Mulberry Sts.) | 212-941-7994 | www.firstpizza.com

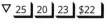

This 1905-vintage NoLita pizza "shrine", which claims to be America's

first pizzeria, still draws throngs with its "real-deal" coal-fired pies; it doesn't take plastic or reservations, and you may have to "tussle with the tourists to get a table", but it's a true "slice of NY" – even though it "doesn't do slices."

London Lennie's *Seafood*

24 | 19 | 21 | $51

Middle Village | 63-88 Woodhaven Blvd. (bet. Fleet Ct. & Penelope Ave.) | Queens | 718-894-8084 | www.londonlennies.com

It's been in operation since 1959 and this Middle Village seafooder "hasn't lost its touch", putting forth a "wide selection" of "fresh", "unfussy" shore fare in "big", "nothing-fancy" digs; "fast" service and "fair prices" are two more reasons it's "always crowded."

Lorenzo's *Italian*
∇ 22 | 24 | 21 | $51

Bloomfield | 1100 South Ave. (Lois Ln.) | Staten Island | 718-477-2400 | www.lorenzosdining.com

"Food and entertainment" go hand in hand at this Staten Island Italian in Bloomfield, where the "weekend cabarets" and "jazz brunch" are big hits with "locals" looking for a "classy" outing "without city hassles"; service also rates high, but grumbles about "uneven" cuisine persist.

Los Tacos *Mexican*
27 | 13 | 18 | $13

Chelsea | Chelsea Mkt. | 75 Ninth Ave. (bet. 15th & 16th Sts.) | 212-256-0343 | www.lostacos1.com

For a "real-deal" Mexican fix, this simple Chelsea Market counter supplies a "limited but expertly executed" lineup of "crave-worthy tacos" and quesadillas on the "cheap"; instant, "well-deserved popularity" means you'll probably have to "wait in line", however, and be aware there's "no place to sit."

Loukoumi Taverna *Greek*
23 | 18 | 21 | $40

Astoria | 45-07 Ditmars Blvd. (bet. 45th & 46th Sts.) | Queens | 718-626-3200 | www.toloukoumi.com

"Excellent", "authentic" taverna fare leads the charge at this "warm, inviting" Astoria Greek; it's located "a bit away" from the main neighborhood action, but "affordable" tabs and a back garden clinch the "good-on-all-counts" endorsement.

Lucali *Pizza*

26 | 20 | 21 | $28

Carroll Gardens | 575 Henry St. (bet. Carroll St. & 1st Pl.) | Brooklyn | 718-858-4086 | www.lucali.com

"Something to write home about", this Carroll Gardens storefront fields "phenomenal pizzas" and "glorious calzones" straight from a brick oven; a cash-only policy, no-rezzie rule and "ridiculous" waits are part of the package, but there's a "bonus" BYO policy.

Lucien *French*
24 | 18 | 22 | $55

East Village | 14 First Ave. (1st St.) | 212-260-6481 | www.luciennyc.com

"Charming" owner Lucien Bahaj's East Village French "favorite" presents "first-rate bistro" classics in "convivial" quarters that will "take you to Paris in a flash"; OK, it's on the "cramped" side, but tell that to its regulars who "leave with a smile every time."

	FOOD	DECOR	SERVICE	COST

Luke's Lobster *Seafood*

	24	12	17	$24

East 40s | 685 Third Ave. (bet. 43rd & 44th Sts.) | 646-657-0066
East 80s | 242 E. 81st St. (bet. 2nd & 3rd Aves.) | 212-249-4241
East Village | 93 E. Seventh St. (bet. Ave. A & 1st Ave.) | 212-387-8487
Financial District | 26 S. William St. (bet. Beaver & Broad Sts.) | 212-747-1700
NEW West 40s | City Kitchen | 700 Eighth Ave. (bet. 44th & 45th Sts.) | 917-338-0928
West 50s | Plaza Food Hall | 1 W. 59th St. (5th Ave.) | 646-755-3227
West 80s | 426 Amsterdam Ave. (bet. 80th & 81st Sts.) | 212-877-8800
Dumbo | 11 Water St. (bet. New Dock & Old Fulton Sts.) | Brooklyn | 917-882-7516
NEW Park Slope | 237 Fifth Ave. (Carroll St.) | Brooklyn | 347-457-6855
www.lukeslobster.com

"Quintessential lobster rolls" await at these "no-fuss" seafood outlets where purists willingly shell out for a "lightly dressed" rendition loaded with "abundant", "consistently fresh" meat and no filler; the "stripped-down" digs being "nothing to look at", most "opt for takeout."

Luksus *American*

	▽ 25	21	24	$150

Greenpoint | 615 Manhattan Ave. (bet. Driggs & Nassau Aves.) | Brooklyn | 718-389-6034 | www.luksusnyc.com

They "keep your palate entertained" at this Greenpoint New American (set in the "intimate back room" at Tørst), where an open kitchen turns out an "incredible", Scandinavian-inspired tasting menu for a $115 set price; an "original" beer pairing option and an "amazing show put on by the chef" make it a natural for a foodie "special occasion."

Lupa *Italian*

	25	19	22	$64

Greenwich Village | 170 Thompson St. (bet. Bleecker & Houston Sts.) | 212-982-5089 | www.luparestaurant.com

A "casual" destination that "never gets old", this "earthy" Village trattoria from Mario Batali offers "marvelous" Roman cooking and an "incredible wine list" at a relatively "affordable" price point; the staffers turn on the "friendly charm", although the "lack of space" keeps it "tightly packed" and "crazy in the evening."

NEW Lupulo *Portuguese*

	–	–	–	M

Chelsea | 835 Sixth Ave. (29th St.) | 212-290-7600 | www.lupulonyc.com

Portuguese comfort dishes – with a focus on seafood – is the concept at this laid-back Chelsea tavern via Aldea's George Mendes that also offers a roster of unusual specialty beers (the name translates as 'hops'); a large, U-shaped bar made for drinking and dining is the focal point of the rustic, tiled-lined space, and an open kitchen with a wood-fired grill anchors the rear.

Lure Fishbar *Seafood*

	25	24	22	$66

SoHo | 142 Mercer St. (Prince St.) | 212-431-7676 | www.lurefishbar.com

It's "quite the scene" at this "packed" SoHo cellar seafooder where the "fresh" catch is "perfectly cooked" and on par with the "classy", "cruise-ship" decor; though tabs are steep and the "ebullient", "mixed-age" crowd can kick up a racket, most consider it an "all-around winner."

	FOOD	DECOR	SERVICE	COST

Lusardi's *Italian*
24 | 19 | 23 | $67

East 70s | 1494 Second Ave. (bet. 77th & 78th Sts.) | 212-249-2020 |
www.lusardis.com

"Friendly" owners oversee the "vintage poster"–lined room at this long-time UES "institution" where the Tuscan food is as "terrific" as the "gracious" service and "old-fashioned style"; its "adult", "well-heeled crowd" doesn't mind the "expensive" checks, given that it has "maintained its quality over the years."

Luzzo's *Pizza*
24 | 15 | 19 | $30

East Village | 211-13 First Ave. (bet. 12th & 13th Sts.) | 212-473-7447
Brooklyn Heights | 145 Atlantic Ave. (bet. Clinton & Henry Sts.) |
Brooklyn | 718-855-6400
www.luzzospizza.com

Fans "thank the pizza gods" for these "no-frills" joints, where "superior" Neapolitan-style pies emerge from coal-fired ovens with enough "authenticity" to "make an Italian grandma proud"; they're kinda "dumpy" and often "jammed", but the Brooklyn Heights follow-up to the East Village original boasts a back patio.

Lychee House *Chinese*
21 | 13 | 19 | $43

East 50s | 141 E. 55th St. (bet. Lexington & 3rd Aves.) | 212-753-3900 |
www.lycheehouse.com

Ranking a "notch above most", this East Midtown Chinese offers a "wide variety" of "well-prepared", midpriced dishes, plus "inventive dim sum", backed by libations from a full bar; although it's "tiny in size", fans feel it's "big in heart."

Mable's Smokehouse *BBQ*

23 | 17 | 19 | $26

Williamsburg | 44 Berry St. (11th St.) | Brooklyn | 718-218-6655 |
www.mablessmokehouse.com

Get your "BBQ fix" at this "spacious", "laid-back" Williamsburg joint where the "plentiful" ribs, brisket and pulled pork pack "robust" flavors and are "priced just right"; "cafeteria-style ordering" and "shared tables" bolster the "transports-you-to-Tennessee" vibe.

Macao Trading Co. *Chinese/Portuguese*
22 | 24 | 19 | $59

TriBeCa | 311 Church St. (bet. Lispenard & Walker Sts.) | 212-431-8750 |
www.macaonyc.com

Channeling a 1940s "Macao gambling parlor", this "dazzling", bi-level TriBeCan offers plentiful "eye candy" to go with its Chinese-Portuguese chow; late-night, it turns "club"-like – "loud and crowded" with uneven service – but most are having too much "fun" to care.

Macelleria *Italian/Steak*

22 | 20 | 19 | $70

Meatpacking District | 48 Gansevoort St. (bet. Greenwich & Washington Sts.) | 212-741-2555 | www.macelleria.com

"When you want some pasta with your steak", try this "buzzy" Meatpacking Italian chophouse whose "unadorned" fare "doesn't disappoint" but also "doesn't come cheap"; it boasts a "witty butcher theme" indoors, while alfresco sidewalk seats afford prime "MPD crowd"–watching.

	FOOD	DECOR	SERVICE	COST

Machiavelli *Italian*

21 | 22 | 20 | $51

West 80s | 519 Columbus Ave. (85th St.) | 212-724-2658 |
www.machiavellinyc.com

"Dine like a prince" at this "elegant", all-day UWS Italian, where cande-
labras, plush upholstered chairs and "gorgeous" "Renaissance"-inspired
murals – not to mention live music most nights – set a "romantic" tone;
the "pricey", "carefully prepared" Northern Italian food is somewhat
more down to earth (think pastas, pizzas).

Macondo *Pan-Latin*

19 | 18 | 15 | $39

Lower East Side | 157 E. Houston St. (bet. Allen & Eldridge Sts.) |
212-473-9900
NEW **West Village** | 2 Bank St. (Greenwich Ave.) | 212-463-0090
www.macondonyc.com

These "lively" crosstown joints "transport you to urban Latin America"
with "flavor-packed", street food–inspired small plates washed down
with "strong" tropical cocktails; given the *muy* "happening" bar scenes,
be ready for "crowds and noise."

Madangsui *Korean*

▽ 22 | 14 | 19 | $45

West 30s | 35 W. 35th St. (bet. 5th & 6th Aves.) | 212-564-9333 |
www.madangsui.com

Koreatown cognoscenti "head straight for the BBQ" at this "authentic"
Seoul-fooder where the meat hits the grill at your table and an "efficient"
crew keeps the proceedings on track; there's "not much" in the way of
decor, but then the "long waits" on weekends aren't for the scenery.

Madiba *S African*

22 | 22 | 22 | $35

NEW **Harlem** | 46 W. 116th St. (bet. 5th Ave. & Malcom X Blvd.) |
646-738-3043 | www.madibaharlem.com
Fort Greene | 195 DeKalb Ave. (bet. Adelphi St. & Carlton Ave.) |
Brooklyn | 718-855-9190 | www.madibarestaurant.com

For a "real taste of South Africa", hit these "unassuming, relaxed" hangouts
that feel "like a vacation" thanks to "cool", eclectic looks, "comforting", "affordable" grub and "warm" service (just "don't be in a rush"); regulars say
it's just the ticket for "watching futbol and World Cup games."

Madison Bistro *French*

21 | 16 | 21 | $49

Murray Hill | 238 Madison Ave. (bet. 37th & 38th Sts.) | 212-447-1919 |
www.madisonbistro.com

"Every neighborhood should have a local bistro" like this Murray Hill
"sleeper" that's appreciated for its "quality" French cooking and prix fixe
deals; "well-behaved" locals are drawn to its "friendly" vibe and "relaxing" (if "generic") dining room that's "conducive to conversation."

Madison's *Italian*

20 | 18 | 21 | $38

Riverdale | 5686 Riverdale Ave. (bet. 258th & 259th Sts.) | Bronx |
718-543-3850

"One of the more upscale" options on Riverdale's "main drag",
this "popular" Italian fallback features "fresh, well-prepared" fare
delivered by an "attentive" crew; those who "don't want to go" to
Manhattan call it a "safe" bet.

| | FOOD | DECOR | SERVICE | COST |

Maharlika *Filipino* | 22 | 18 | 21 | $33

East Village | 111 First Ave. (bet. 6th & 7th Sts.) | 646-392-7880 |
www.maharlikanyc.com
Filipino food gets "redefined" at this "hip" East Villager that jump-
starts the "not-mainstream" cuisine with some modern "twists"
(Spam fries, anyone?); its "enthusiastic audience" happily overlooks
the kinda "tight" conditions given the overall "cozy" mood, "warm"
service and bargain tabs.

Maialino *Italian* | 25 | 23 | 24 | $74

Gramercy Park | Gramercy Park Hotel | 2 Lexington Ave. (21st St.) |
212-777-2410 | www.maialinonyc.com
"Danny Meyer does Italian" at this Gramercy "standout", a "handsome"
Roman trattoria where the "first-rate" rustic menu (led by a "fabulous
roast suckling pig") and "top-drawer" service are "consistently satisfying"; the "buzzy", "well-put-together" crowd confirms it "gets everything
right", but brace for a "tough reservation."

Maison Harlem *French* | ▽ 22 | 20 | 21 | $41

Manhattanville | 341 St. Nicholas Ave. (127th St.) | 212-222-9224 |
www.maisonharlem.com
Like a little "chunk of Paris" transported to NYC, this all-day bistro "gem"
on the Harlem/Manhattanville border supplies "solid" French classics in
"super-cozy" quarters with a "vintage" vibe; it's a "bustling scene" that
expands out onto the sidewalk in warmer months.

Maison Kayser *Bakery/French* | 21 | 16 | 17 | $30

East 70s | 1294 Third Ave. (74th St.) | 212-744-3100
East 80s | 1535 Third Ave. (74th St.) | 212-348-8400
Flatiron | 921 Broadway (21st St.) | 212-979-1600
NEW TriBeCa | 355 Greenwich St. (Harrison St.) | no phone
West 40s | 8 W. 40th St. (bet. 5th & 6th Aves.) | 212-354-2300
West 50s | 1800 Broadway (bet. CPS & 58th St.) | 212-245-4100
www.maison-kayser-usa.com
"Irresistible breads and pastries" are the calling cards of these all-day
patisserie/cafes, "handy" links of a Parisian chain offering "tasty" French
fare; to avoid "hectic" crowds, "elbow-to-elbow" seating and "bring-a-
megaphone" noise, insiders "go at off hours."

Maison Premiere *Seafood* | 26 | 28 | 25 | $50

Williamsburg | 298 Bedford Ave. (1st St.) | Brooklyn | 347-335-0446 |
www.maisonpremiere.com
"NOLA meets Brooklyn" at this "convivial" Williamsburg seafooder, cel-
ebrated for its "robust selection" of oysters and "complicated" cocktails
(notably the absinthe-based variety); the Big Easy–style "old-world"
setting adds some "intoxicating elegance", while a "beautiful garden"
expands the typically "crowded" quarters.

Malatesta Trattoria *Italian* | 24 | 16 | 21 | $35

West Village | 649 Washington St. (Christopher St.) | 212-741-1207 |
www.malatestatrattoria.com
"Wonderful" trattoria staples at "reasonable", cash-only rates make this
"friendly", "popular" way West Village Italian well "worth" the "waits" at

More on zagat.com

prime times; the "simple" interior gets "crowded and noisy", but in the summertime, "sidewalk dining" offers a bit more elbow room.

Malecon *Dominican*   23 | 12 | 18 | $22

Washington Heights | 4141 Broadway (175th St.) | 212-927-3812
West 90s | 764 Amsterdam Ave. (bet. 97th & 98th Sts.) | 212-864-5648
Kingsbridge | 5592 Broadway (231st St.) | Bronx | 718-432-5155
www.maleconrestaurants.com

When "you're looking for a fix" of "super-good" "traditional" Dominican fare, it's "hard to beat" these "favorites" known especially for their "mmm" rotisserie chicken slathered in "garlicky goodness"; "huge portions" at "bargain" prices mean most don't mind if the settings are on the "tacky" side.

Maloney & Porcelli *Steak*   25 | 22 | 25 | $83

East 50s | 37 E. 50th St. (bet. Madison & Park Aves.) | 212-750-2233 |
www.maloneyandporcelli.com

"High quality all around" marks Alan Stillman's Midtown "classic", a *Mad Men*-ish cow palace where "marvelous" "old-school" servers ferry "extraordinary steaks", "superb" crackling pork shank and "killer martinis"; the "mighty expensive" tabs are somewhat eased by the nightly $79 wine dinner.

Mamajuana Cafe *Dominican/Nuevo Latino*   22 | 22 | 19 | $36

Inwood | 247 Dyckman St. (Seaman Ave.) | 212-304-0140
Woodside | 33-15 56th St. (B'way) | Queens | 718-565-6454
www.mamajuana-cafe.com

Admirers advise "go hungry" to these "inviting" Dominican–Nuevo Latino cafes serving "huge portions" of "delish" fare with "modern flair"; a "lively" scene fueled by "fantastic" sangria makes for "fun times", especially during summer in the outdoor seats.

NEW Maman *American/French*   ∇ 20 | 21 | 18 | $16

Little Italy | 239 Centre St. (bet. Broome & Grand Sts.) | 212-226-0770 |
www.mamannyc.com

Bringing that "you're-in-Paris" feel to Little Italy, this "cozy" bakery/cafe furnishes "tasty" French and American bites for breakfast and lunch, plus sweet stuff à la its "famous chocolate chunk cookie"; it's a "busy" niche with "limited" seating, so many opt for "takeout."

NEW Mamo *Italian*   — | — | — | E

SoHo | 323 W. Broadway (bet. Canal & Grand Sts.) | 646-964-4641 |
www.mamonyc.com

Spun off from the celeb favorite in Antibes – a longtime staple for Cannes Film Festival attendees – this slick duplex aims to lure the jet set to SoHo with pricey Italian standards as well as a luxe burger gussied up with truffles and fois gras; the chic digs channel the French Riviera with white-washed brick walls, vintage movie posters and a la dolce vita-esque vibe.

Mamoun's *Mideastern*   23 | 10 | 18 | $10

East Village | 22 St. Marks Pl. (bet. 2nd & 3rd Aves.) | 212-387-7747
Greenwich Village | 119 MacDougal St. (bet. Minetta Ln. & W. 3rd St.) |
212-674-8685
www.mamouns.com

"Tasty and hasty" sums up these cross-Village Middle Eastern "favorites", whose "awesome" falafel and shawarma "can't be beat" for "cheap, filling eats" served into the "wee hours"; "bare-bones" digs with a serious "space crunch" don't keep them from "bustling."

Mandoo Bar   *Korean*   22 | 13 | 17 | $27

West 30s | 2 W. 32nd St. (bet. B'way & 5th Ave.) | 212-279-3075 | www.mandoobarnyc.com

"Man oh mandoo" – the "freshest", "fast and fab" dumplings made right in front of you are the main event at this "reliable" K-town Korean; its "no-decor" digs are "small" and "often crowded", but "cheap" prices compensate.

Manducatis   *Italian*   24 | 18 | 23 | $47

Long Island City | 13-27 Jackson Ave. (47th Ave.) | Queens | 718-729-4602 | www.manducatis.com

Manducatis Rustica   *Ice Cream/Pizza*

Long Island City | 46-33 Vernon Blvd. (bet. 46th & 47th Sts.) | Queens | 718-937-1312 | www.manducatisrustica.com

"You expect Tony Bennett to arrive" any minute at this "warm", "family-run" LIC Italian supplying "wonderful" "homestyle" fare and wines from a "deep" list (plus there's the "scaled-down" Rustica offshoot focusing on pizza and gelato); yes, the look may be "dated", but loyalists say that only "adds to the charm."

Manetta's   *Italian*   25 | 17 | 21 | $41

Long Island City | 10-76 Jackson Ave. (11th St.) | Queens | 718-786-6171 | www.manettaslic.com

"Go with family" to this LIC "favorite", a "friendly" "neighborhood staple" offering "excellent" wood-fired brick-oven pizza and "everyday Italian" eats likened to "mom's cooking"; while rather "dated" in the decor department, it's "affordable" and has a fireplace that's perfect on a "cold winter's night."

Manzo   *Italian/Steak*   25 | 18 | 22 | $68

Flatiron | Eataly | 200 Fifth Ave. (bet. 23rd & 24th Sts.) | 212-229-2180 | www.eataly.com

A "walled-off oasis" amid the "flurry of Eataly", this full-service Italian steakhouse within the Batali-Bastianich food hall shows a "nice range" with "terrific" chops bolstered by "excellent" pastas and an "extensive wine list"; the venue's upmarket pricing carries over, but most report being "well fed" for the money.

Maoz Vegetarian   *Mideastern/Vegetarian*   22 | 10 | 16 | $13

Central Park | Fifth Ave. at 106th St. | no phone
Greenwich Village | 59 E. Eighth St. (bet. B'way & University Pl.) | 212-420-5999
Union Square | 38 Union Sq. E. (bet. 16th & 17th Sts.) | 212-260-1988
West 30s | 558 Seventh Ave. (bet. 39th & 40th Sts.) | 212-777-0820
West 40s | 683 Eighth Ave. (43rd St.) | 212-265-2315
West 70s | 2047 Broadway (71st St.) | 212-362-2622
www.maozusa.com

"Quick and easy" is the word on this Mideastern-vegetarian franchise where the falafel is "respectable", the tabs "economical" and the salads customizable at a "self-serve topping bar"; little decor and service lead many to reserve it "strictly for takeout."

Má Pêche *American*

23 | 17 | 19 | $57

West 50s | Chambers Hotel | 15 W. 56th St. (bet. 5th & 6th Aves.) | 212-757-5878 | www.momofuku.com

With the "welcome" addition of "dim sum–style" plates to complement its "delightful" shared dishes, David Chang's "upbeat" Midtown New American maintains its rep for "creativity"; sure, the "sparse" setting "could be cozier", but there's nothing wrong with the group-friendly large-format spreads and "rich" sweets from Milk Bar upstairs.

Mapo Korean B.B.Q. *Korean*

∇ 24 | 16 | 20 | $46

Flushing | 149-24 41st Ave (149th Pl.) | Queens | 718-886-8292

It's all about the tabletop barbecue at this "tasty" Flushing Korean, where the "meats are everything" and grilled over lump charcoal (insiders "go for the fabulous marinated kalbi"); maybe it "needs improvement" in the decor department, but at least the staff is "patient" and the pricing modest.

Marc Forgione *American*

26 | 24 | 24 | $85

TriBeCa | 134 Reade St. (bet. Greenwich & Hudson Sts.) | 212-941-9401 | www.marcforgione.com

This TriBeCa "charmer" from "talented" Iron Chef Marc Forgione "excels in every way" with "superlative" New American cooking and "warm", "knowledgeable" service in a "rustic" space with "romantic" vibes; it's usually "mobbed" despite "platinum-card" pricing, so reservations are a foregone conclusion.

Marcony *Italian*

24 | 21 | 22 | $77

Murray Hill | 184 Lexington Ave. (bet. 31st & 32nd Sts.) | 646-837-6020 | www.marconyusa.com

When an "Italian vacation" isn't in the cards, there's always this Murray Hill "standout" whose "fantastic" classic dishes with "service to match" arrive in "Capri-comes-to-NY" digs (including "sidewalk seating"); given the "all-around wonderful" experience, fans don't blink at the "pricey" tab and "out-of-the-way" locale.

Marco Polo *Italian*

22 | 20 | 22 | $59

Carroll Gardens | 345 Court St. (Union St.) | Brooklyn | 718-852-5015 | www.marcopoloristorante.com

"Old-school Italian in every respect", this Carroll Gardens vet presents "upscale red-sauce" fare in a "warm" space complete with fireplace and murals; "treat-you-like-family" service and an "amazing happy hour" are two more reasons locals keep coming.

Marea *Italian/Seafood*

27 | 26 | 26 | $119

West 50s | 240 Central Park S. (bet. B'way & 7th Ave.) | 212-582-5100 | www.marea-nyc.com

"First class all the way", this "civilized" Central Park South Italian shows off chef Michael White's "culinary mastery" with "dream-worthy" seafood and housemade pastas delivered by a "cosseting" team in "stylish" contemporary quarters; it caters to a "moneyed crowd" with "prices for the one percent", but for wallet-watchers the lunch menu remains a "fiscal possibility."

	FOOD	DECOR	SERVICE	COST

Margaux *French/Mediterranean* ▽ 18 | 20 | 18 | $57

Greenwich Village | Marlton Hotel | 5 W. Eighth St. (bet. 5th & 6th Aves.) | 212-321-0111 | www.marltonhotel.com

Breakfast through dinner, this Village cafe in the Marlton Hotel fields an "original" roster of seasonal French-Med fare served "with no drama" in "comfortable", faux-Parisian surrounds; while the food's just "OK", the "lively" bar is apt to be "jammed with hip sippers."

Maria Pia *Italian* 21 | 17 | 21 | $46

West 50s | 319 W. 51st St. (8th Ave.) | 212-765-6463 | www.mariapianyc.com

"Geared to the pre-theater crowd", this "reliable" Hell's Kitchen "red-sauce" Italian keeps 'em coming back with "quick" service, a "charming garden" and "reasonable" rates (especially the $27 dinner prix fixe); non-showgoers hit it "off-hours" to avoid the "noisy" crush.

Mario's *Italian* 21 | 16 | 21 | $45

Arthur Avenue/Belmont | 2342 Arthur Ave. (bet. Crescent Ave. & 184th St.) | Bronx | 718-584-1188 | www.mariosrestarthurave.com

A Neapolitan "home away from home" on the Arthur Avenue "tourist strip", this "iconic red-sauce" joint is nearly a century old and still "never steers you wrong"; "friendly" waiters working the "bustling", "no-pretense" digs ensure regulars remain in their "comfort zone."

Mari Vanna *Russian* 20 | 24 | 21 | $66

Flatiron | 41 E. 20th St. (bet. B'way & Park Ave. S.) | 212-777-1955 | www.marivanna.ru

Like "stepping into your grandmother's house in Moscow" – but with a "party" vibe fueled by "flowing vodka" – this "fabulous" Flatiron magnet for "expats" and "beautiful young things" serves up "hearty" Russian staples; "attentive" service and a "unique-in-NY" experience help justify the "pricey" tab.

The Mark *American* 23 | 25 | 22 | $84

East 70s | Mark Hotel | 25 E. 77th St. (bet. 5th & Madison Aves.) | 212-744-4300 | www.themarkrestaurantnyc.com

"Another dining coup" by Jean-Georges Vongerichten, this "very UES" enclave is "always on the mark" with "top-notch" New American fare and "deferential" service at predictably "high prices"; since the "lovely" dining room is usually on the "quiet" side, go-getters head for the "vibrant bar."

Market Table *American* 23 | 20 | 22 | $57

West Village | 54 Carmine St. (Bedford St.) | 212-255-2100 | www.markettablenyc.com

A "solid farm-to-table" approach makes for "engaging dishes" at this West Village New American, a corner outfit with "big picture windows", "warm" service and an "unpretentious" vibe; it "continues to amaze" a wide following, meaning it's on the "crowded" and "loud" side at prime times.

MarkJoseph Steakhouse *Steak* 24 | 20 | 24 | $86

South Street Seaport | 261 Water St. (bet. Dover St. & Peck Slip) | 212-277-0020 | www.markjosephsteakhouse.com

Pack a "huge appetite" and a "corporate card" to best enjoy this chop shop "on the fringe of the Financial District", where "lunch is a better value"; "no-frills", "standard steakhouse" digs put the focus on the "outstanding" beef (and "even better" bacon appetizer) delivered by "friendly pro" staffers.

Markt *Belgian*
20 | 17 | 18 | $40

Flatiron | 676 Sixth Ave. (21st St.) | 212-727-3314 | www.marktrestaurant.com

There's "nothing fishy" about this "busy", all-day Flatiron brasserie, just "mussels in excelsis" and other "simple", "tasty" Belgian staples backed up by a "gazillion excellent beers"; the acoustics are "loud" and service can be "hurried", but that's just part of the "fun" package.

Marlow & Sons *American*
23 | 21 | 18 | $45

Williamsburg | 81 Broadway (Berry St.) | Brooklyn | 718-384-1441 | www.marlowandsons.com

"Pitch-perfect", "farm-fresh" New American fare from a "limited", "daily changing" lineup (including oysters from the raw bar) is the lure at this all-day Williamsburg pioneer that still packs plenty of "hipster" cred; the "dark", micro-size confines can be "cramped", so many angle to "sit outside."

Marseille *French/Mediterranean*
21 | 20 | 21 | $50

West 40s | 630 Ninth Ave. (44th St.) | 212-333-2323 | www.marseillenyc.com

"Like being in Paris – but with better service" – this Theater District French-Med brasserie serves a "well-priced", "quality" menu in a rather "hectic" room that suggests "Casablanca"; its trump card is "convenience" to Broadway shows, and they know how to "get you out in time for your curtain."

The Marshal *American*
24 | 17 | 21 | $51

West 40s | 628 10th Ave. (bet. 44th & 45th Sts.) | 212-582-6300 | www.the-marshal.com

The "farm-to-table philosophy" comes to Hell's Kitchen via this "welcoming" arrival offering an ever-evolving menu of "terrific" New American fare matched with a "thoughtful" list of "NY beers and wines"; its "tiny" space can get "cramped and loud", but "friendly" staffers help keep the mood "relaxed."

Marta *Italian/Pizza*
24 | 21 | 23 | $50

NoMad | Martha Washington Hotel | 29 E. 29th St. (bet. Madison & Park Aves.) | 212-651-3800 | www.martamanhattan.com

"Yet another hit" from Danny Meyer, this NoMad Italian in the Martha Washington Hotel rolls out "ultra-thin-crust" Roman pizza and equally "scrumptious" grilled fare, all served by a "well-versed" staff; the "spacious", open kitchen–equipped setting is "loud and buzzy", populated by folks who are "clearly enjoying themselves."

Martha *American*
∇ 21 | 19 | 17 | $30

Fort Greene | 184 Dekalb Ave. (bet. Carlton Ave. & Cumberland St.) | Brooklyn | 718-596-4147 | www.marthabrooklyn.com

"An adventure that's not fussy", this "upbeat" Fort Greene entry offers a carefully sourced menu of "inventive", Asian-influenced New American plates that feel "exciting and comforting at the same time"; it's no surprise the "inviting", subway-tiled space gets "lively."

	FOOD	DECOR	SERVICE	COST

Maruzzella *Italian*

20 | 14 | 21 | $56

East 70s | 1483 First Ave. (bet. 77th & 78th Sts.) | 212-988-8877 |
www.maruzzellanyc.com

There's "nothing fancy" about this UES "quintessential neighborhood Italian", just "surprisingly good" cooking brought to table by "old-school" servers; "friendly owners" on the scene and "reasonable"-for-the-zip-code rates make the "modest" decor easy to overlook.

Mary's Fish Camp *Seafood*

24 | 15 | 20 | $52

West Village | 64 Charles St. (4th St.) | 646-486-2185 |
www.marysfishcamp.com

"Like a visit to Cape Cod", this "funky" West Village seafood shack is famed for its "kicking lobster rolls" served in a "primitive" room by a "heavily tattooed" crew; sinkers include "cramped" seats and a "no-reservations" rule that leads to "long waits", but ultimately the "hard-to-beat" catch triumphs.

Masa *Japanese*

26 | 24 | 25 | $585

West 50s | Time Warner Ctr. | 10 Columbus Circle (60th St. at B'way) |
212-823-9800 | www.masanyc.com

"If you don't mind spending", chef Masayoshi Takayama's omakase meals are mighty "delectable" at this "Zen-like" Japanese in the Time Warner Center that devotees dub a "once-in-a-lifetime" experience; the $450-and-up set price strikes most as "prohibitive", though à la carte tabs are somewhat more "tolerable" in the "less formal" bar.

Mas (Farmhouse) *American*

26 | 24 | 25 | $96

West Village | 39 Downing St. (Bedford St.) | 212-255-1790 |
www.masfarmhouse.com

"Impeccable from start to finish", this West Village American is a showcase for chef Galen Zamarra's "splendid" seasonal dishes served by "informed" staffers in a "romantic" room exuding "understated elegance"; sure, it's "expensive" and the seating a tad "tight", but ultimately this "special-occasion" nexus is "so worth it."

NEW Mastro's Steakhouse *Steak*

25 | 24 | 25 | $100

West 50s | 1285 Sixth Ave. (52nd St.) | 212-459-1222 |
www.mastrosrestaurants.com

The mood's "upbeat" at this Midtown outlet of the national chophouse chain, where "perfectly cooked" steaks and "plentiful" sides are delivered by "attentive" servers in "noisy" digs complete with live music upstairs ("downstairs is quieter"); the tabs are "not for the faint of heart", but most maintain you "get your money's worth."

Max Caffe *Italian*

21 | 16 | 18 | $27

Morningside Heights | 1262 Amsterdam Ave. (bet. 122nd & 123rd Sts.) |
212-531-1210

Max SoHa *Italian*

Morningside Heights | 1274 Amsterdam Ave. (123rd St.) |
212-531-2221
www.maxsoha.com

"Popular with the Columbia crowd", these "friendly", low-cost Upper Westsiders have two distinct personalities: cash-only SoHa offers "rustic"

Italian staples in a "cozy" space with the option to "eat outside", while the Caffe features "comfy couches and chairs for relaxing and eating."

Maya *Mexican*   22 | 20 | 20 | $53

East 60s | 1191 First Ave. (bet. 64th & 65th Sts.) | 212-585-1818 | www.richardsandoval.com

"Not your usual Mexican" cucina, this "elevated" Upper Eastsider supplies "exciting" cooking with "full flavor in every bite" via a "solicitous" staff; the "smart setting" (with a "vibrant" tequileria attached) "tends to get loud" and it runs "a little pricey", "but hey, you get what you pay for."

Mayahuel *Mexican*   ∇ 23 | 23 | 22 | $49

East Village | 304 E. Sixth St. (2nd Ave.) | 212-253-5888 | www.mayahuelny.com

The "drinks are the highlight" of this "mezcal lover's paradise" in the East Village where the "unbeatable" cocktails can be paired with "uncomplicated" yet "flavorful" Mexican small plates; a brick-walled, two-story setting exuding "exotic" vibes adds to its "distinctive" feel.

Mayfield *American*   25 | 24 | 22 | $37

Crown Heights | 688 Franklin Ave. (Prospect Pl.) | Brooklyn | 347-318-3643 | www.mayfieldbk.com

"A real find" in Crown Heights, this "comfortable" New American offers a "wonderful" lineup of "Southern-influenced" plates in charmingly "rough-and-tumble" digs; staffers who "know what they're doing" suit the happening neighborhood, but the "price point is vintage Brooklyn."

Maysville *American*   22 | 22 | 21 | $62

NoMad | 17 W. 26th St. (bet. B'way & 6th Ave.) | 646-490-8240 | www.maysvillenyc.com

"Cool" New American fare with "a touch of Southern influence" is matched by a "literal wall" of whiskeys at this NoMad follow-up to Brooklyn's Char No. 4; just "bring your earplugs" since the "energetic" crowds are "as loud as the Kentucky Derby on the home stretch."

Maze *French*   22 | 18 | 18 | $71

West 50s | London NYC Hotel | 151 W. 54th St. (bet. 6th & 7th Aves.) | 212-468-8889 | www.gordonramsay.com

This New French eatery proffers "simple, elegant" small plates in a "bustling" space off the lobby of Midtown's London NYC Hotel; "tired" decor and "so-so" service make it a "not memorable" experience for some, though fans recommend it for a "pre-theater" bite.

Maz Mezcal *Mexican*   21 | 18 | 21 | $40

East 80s | 316 E. 86th St. (bet. 1st & 2nd Aves.) | 212-472-1599 | www.mazmezcal.com

"Hits all the right spots" say Yorkville locals of this "family-owned" Mexican "standby" where a "lively neighborhood crowd" assembles for "tasty" classics; "reasonable prices" and "friendly" service are further reasons why it's "still packed after all these years."

Meadowsweet *American/Mediterranean*   ∇ 25 | 24 | 25 | $63

Williamsburg | 149 Broadway (bet. Bedford & Driggs Aves.) | Brooklyn | 718-384-0673 | www.meadowsweetnyc.com

The "successor to Dressler" overseen by its "first-rate" former chef, this "on-point" Williamsburg New American fields an "enticing" menu with a decided Mediterranean bent; fans are also sweet on its "lovely", retro-hip look and "lighthearted atmosphere."

Meatball Shop *Sandwiches*

21 | 17 | 18 | $26

Chelsea | 200 Ninth Ave. (bet. 22nd & 23rd Sts.) | 212-257-4363
East 70s | 1462 Second Ave. (bet. 76th & 77th Sts.) | 212-257-6121
Lower East Side | 84 Stanton St. (bet. Allen & Orchard Sts.) | 212-982-8895
West 80s | 447 Amsterdam Ave. (81st St.) | 212-422-1752
West Village | 64 Greenwich Ave. (11th St.) | 212-982-7815
Williamsburg | 170 Bedford Ave. (bet. N. 7th & 8th Sts.) | Brooklyn | 718-551-0520
www.themeatballshop.com

"Typical and not-so-typical combos" mean there's a meatball "for everyone" at these "cool" sandwich shops also favored for their "scrumptious" cocktails and "to-die-for ice cream sandwiches"; factor in "economical" pricing, and it's no wonder they're often "packed" with "young" types who don't blink at the "brutal lines."

Meat Hook Sandwich Shop *Sandwiches*

▽ 23 | 16 | 20 | $17

Williamsburg | 459 Lorimer St. (bet. Grand & Powers Sts.) | Brooklyn | 718-302-4665 | www.meathooksandwich.com

Locals "trust the quality" at this lunch-only Williamsburg "hipster" niche vending "meaty sandwiches" stacked with beef, pork and lamb sourced from locavore butcher The Meat Hook; true, it's "a little pricey", but the two-handers are so "generous" that you "get your money's worth."

Mehtaphor *Eclectic*

28 | 26 | 28 | $64

TriBeCa | Duane Street Hotel | 130 Duane St. (Church St.) | 212-542-9440 | www.mehtaphornyc.com

Chef Jehangir Mehta (Graffiti) "knows how to wow" patrons of this "intimate gem" in TriBeCa's Duane Street Hotel, where his "innovative" Eclectic small plates showcase "refined" Indian influences; "gracious" service and a "modern" setting further enhance this "culinary treat."

Meijin Ramen *Japanese/Noodle Shop*

22 | 19 | 18 | $23

East 80s | 1574 Second Ave. (82nd St.) | 212-327-2800

Upper Eastsiders "craving ramen" hail this Japanese joint's "flavorful" noodle bowls and izakaya-style small plates (a next-door annex offers desserts and cocktails); the seating's mostly "communal", but no one cares given the "reasonable" tabs and "hits-the-spot" cooking.

Melba's *American/Southern*

25 | 21 | 21 | $34

Harlem | 300 W. 114th St. (8th Ave.) | 212-864-7777 | www.melbasrestaurant.com

"Down-home" Southern dishes including a "fan-favorite" chicken 'n' waffles ensure this "comforting" Harlem American remains "loved by all"; indeed, the "friendly" atmosphere trumps the "tiny", "cramped" setting and "long waits" for its "to-die-for" brunch.

Melt Shop *Sandwiches*

22 | 13 | 17 | $14

Financial District | 111 Fulton St. (bet. Nassau & William Sts.) | 646-741-7910
NoMad | 55 W. 26th St. (bet. B'way & 6th Ave.) | 212-447-6358

continued

NEW **West 50s** | 877 Eighth Ave. (52nd St.) | 646-781-8400
West 50s | 135 W. 50th St. (bet. 6th & 7th Aves.) | 212-447-6358
www.meltshop.com
"Gooey yumminess" is the hallmark of these "affordable" sandwich
shops that turn out "indulgent" toasted creations that "aren't your
mama's grilled cheese"; the counter-service settings are low on frills,
but when it comes to "guilty pleasures", they're "quick and comforting."

Mémé *Mediterranean/Moroccan* | 23 | 17 | 22 | $48 |
West Village | 581 Hudson St. (Bank St.) | 646-692-8450 |
www.memeonhudson.com
It's the "Mediterranean on Hudson Street" at this "affordable"
West Villager dispensing "wonderful" small plates and entrees with "Moroccan flair"; "friendly" service and an appealing "bohemian" vibe will
"keep you returning", unless the "tight-packed tables" make you feel
like you're "flying coach."

Mercato *Italian* | 23 | 17 | 20 | $41 |
West 30s | 352 W. 39th St. (bet. 8th & 9th Aves.) | 212-643-2000 |
www.mercatonyc.com
A "pleasant surprise" in the restaurant-"barren" zone near Port Authority, this "well-kept secret" slings "genuine homestyle" Italian food in
a "cozy", "rustic" setting; factor in "reasonable" rates and to most it's
"worth seeking out" when in the area.

Mercer Kitchen *American/French* | 23 | 22 | 20 | $58 |
SoHo | Mercer Hotel | 99 Prince St. (Mercer St.) | 212-966-5454 |
www.themercerkitchen.com
Ever "chic", Jean-Georges Vongerichten's "still buzzy" SoHo vet in the
Mercer Hotel is touted for "enjoyable" Franco-American cooking offered
in "dimly lit" subterranean digs; given the "social" atmosphere and
servers who "don't rush you", it's "easy to talk and linger" here.

Mermaid Inn *Seafood* | 23 | 19 | 21 | $47 |
East Village | 96 Second Ave. (bet. 5th & 6th Sts.) | 212-674-5870
West 80s | 570 Amsterdam Ave. (bet. 87th & 88th Sts.) | 212-799-7400
Mermaid Oyster Bar *Seafood*
Greenwich Village | 79 MacDougal St. (bet. Bleecker & Houston Sts.) |
212-260-0100
www.themermaidnyc.com
Like dining "at the shore", these New England–inspired "standbys"
supply "spot-on" seafood highlighted by a most "worthy lobster roll";
trade-offs include "tight quarters" and "high decibels", especially when
the "unbeatable happy hour" rolls around with its "swell" oyster deals.

Mesa Coyoacan *Mexican* | 24 | 22 | 20 | $35 |
Williamsburg | 372 Graham Ave. (bet. Conselyea St. & Skillman Ave.) |
Brooklyn | 718-782-8171 | www.mesacoyoacan.com
There's "always something to discover" at this "upbeat" Williamsburg
Mexican, a dispenser of "sensational" Mexico City–style cuisine and
"absolutely killer margaritas" at an "affordable" cost; a "very cool" staff
and "creative" decor help keep the mood "warm" and "inviting."

	FOOD	DECOR	SERVICE	COST

Mexico Lindo *Mexican*
22 | **19** | **22** | **$41**

Murray Hill | 459 Second Ave. (26th St.) | 212-679-3665 |
www.mexicolindonyc.com

A Murray Hill "fixture" since 1972, this neighborhood "hidden gem"
is touted for its "truly authentic", "down-to-earth" Mexican cooking,
"friendly" service and "best-buy" prices; maybe it "needs a makeover",
but no one cares "after a margarita or two."

Mexicue *Mexican*
21 | **16** | **19** | **$21**

Chelsea | 345 Seventh Ave. (bet. 29th & 30th Sts.) | 212-244-0002
NEW **NoMad** | 225 Fifth Ave. (bet. 26th & 27th Sts.) | 646-922-7289
West 40s | 1440 Broadway (40th St.) | 212-302-0385
www.mexicue.com

It's the "popular food truck" gone "brick-and-mortar" at these Manhattan spin-offs offering the same "fresh", Mexican-meets-BBQ fare served
"quick" in colorful settings; "very reasonable prices" compensate for the
"just satisfactory" ambiance.

Mezzaluna *Italian*
20 | **15** | **20** | **$52**

East 70s | 1295 Third Ave. (74th St.) | 212-535-9600 |
www.mezzalunanyc.com

Despite the "tiniest" of dimensions, this 1984-vintage UES Italian
"staple" boasts a "strong" track record, "swiftly" sending out wood-oven
pizzas ("the highlight") and other "soulful" standards; despite "crowded"
conditions, regulars say it's "what a neighborhood place should be."

Michael Jordan's
The Steak House NYC *Steak*
21 | **21** | **20** | **$75**

East 40s | Grand Central | 23 Vanderbilt Ave. (42nd St.) | 212-655-2300 |
www.michaeljordansnyc.com

It's the "unusual location" – a balcony overlooking the "scurrying"
masses in Grand Central's Main Concourse – that's the hook at this "reliable" chophouse, where the beef is "aged" and the prices "high"; critics
find "nothing original" going on here, but to fans the"spectacular setting"
alone makes it a "slam dunk."

Michael's *Californian*
23 | **23** | **23** | **$75**

West 50s | 24 W. 55th St. (bet. 5th & 6th Aves.) | 212-767-0555 |
www.michaelsnewyork.com

"Media titans" ("did Diane really just say that?") collect at this "classy"
Midtowner that's known more for its breakfast and lunch "power" scenes
than its "fresh", "premium-priced" Californian fare and "pro" service; "relaxed" dinner comes "without the hot crowd", but the food's "very good"
and there's always the "lovely" room's "fresh flowers and art" to look at.

Mighty Quinn's Barbecue *BBQ*
25 | **14** | **17** | **$24**

Battery Park City | Hudson Eats | 230 Vesey St. (West St.) | 646-649-2777
East Village | 103 Second Ave. (6th St.) | 212-677-3733
West Village | 75 Greenwich Ave. (bet. Bank & 11th Sts.) | 646-524-7889
Crown Heights | Berg'n | 899 Bergen St. (bet. Classon & Franklin Aves.) |
Brooklyn | 718-857-2337
www.mightyquinnsbbq.com

"Hard to beat" for "true-blue" barbecue "melding Texas and Carolina
styles", this "no-nonsense" counter-serve outfit satisfies with "dynamite

brisket" and other "mad-good" staples; granted, the waits can be "agonizing", but mighty "decent" pricing is the payoff.

Mike's Bistro *American/Kosher*   ▽ 26 | 21 | 23 | $78

East 50s | 127 E. 54th St. (bet. Lexington & Park Aves.) | 212-799-3911 | www.mikesbistro.com

An "upscale" endeavor from a namesake chef-owner "who cares", this East Midtowner offers "creative" New American fare prepared with such "elegance" that you'd "never know it was kosher"; overseen by a "helpful" staff, it's typically "busy" despite the "high prices."

Mile End *Deli*   22 | 14 | 18 | $27

Boerum Hill | 97 Hoyt St. (bet. Atlantic Ave. & Pacific St.) | Brooklyn | 718-852-7510

Mile End Sandwich Shop *Sandwiches*

NoHo | 53 Bond St. (bet. Bowery & Lafayette St.) | 212-529-2990 www.mileenddeli.com

Prepare for a "different kind" of fress at these "hip, low-key" spots where the Montreal-style Jewish deli menu is highlighted by "killer" house-smoked meats; sure, the "bare-bones" settings can get a bit "cramped", but even purists admit they give the old guard "a run for their money."

Mill Basin Deli *Deli/Kosher*   25 | 18 | 21 | $28

Flatlands | 5823 Ave. T (bet. 58th & 59th Sts.) | Brooklyn | 718-241-4910 | www.millbasindeli.com

"Old-style deliciousness" lives on at this '70s-era deli on the Flatlands–Mill Basin border, home to Jewish "standard-bearers" like "overstuffed sandwiches" piled high with pastrami; a wall of paintings for sale lends "arty" appeal, and though costs skew "high", the "hearty" nosh leaves most "satisfied."

NEW Milling Room *American*   24 | 25 | 21 | $60

West 80s | 446 Columbus Ave. (bet. 81st & 82nd Sts.) | 212-595-0380 | www.themillingroom.com

A "wonderful" addition to the Upper West Side, this New American offers an "approachable" menu of "big flavors" served in a "beautiful", "cavernous" space topped by a skylight; fans of its "active bar scene" and "unpretentious" vibe "hope it sticks."

Milos *Greek/Seafood*   27 | 24 | 25 | $91

West 50s | 125 W. 55th St. (bet. 6th & 7th Aves.) | 212-245-7400 | www.milos.ca

"Pristine" seafood is the "heavenly" specialty of this "upscale" Midtown Greek, where "consummate professionals" oversee a "spacious", white-washed setting with a "classy" but "convivial" mien; while the by-the-pound pricing may "make your head spin", the lunch and pre-theater prix fixes win kudos for "outstanding value."

NEW The Milton *British*   ▽ 23 | 22 | 24 | $39

East 90s | 1754 Second Ave. (bet. 91st & 92nd Sts.) | 212-369-1900 | www.themiltonnyc.com

A "plus for the neighborhood", this "much-needed" UES gastropub plies "surprisingly good" takes on British standards plus "well-crafted cocktails" in "dimly lit", brick-lined digs with a "cozy" feel; "excellent service" rounds out the "pleasant surprise."

	FOOD	DECOR	SERVICE	COST

Mimi Cheng's Dumplings *Taiwanese*
24 | 15 | 18 | $18

East Village | 179 Second Ave. (12th St.) | no phone |
www.mimichengs.com

"Deliciously innovative", this "simple" East Village dumpling shop hand-
crafts a concise, "healthier" menu of "crowd-pleasers" with "traditional
Taiwanese-style preparation" and "the freshest" locavore ingredients; it's
a "popular" "quick fix" if you're "willing to pay a bit more for top quality."

Mimi's Hummus *Mideastern*
24 | 16 | 20 | $25

Ditmas Park | 1209 Cortelyou Rd. (bet. Argyle & Westminster Rds.) |
Brooklyn | 718-284-4444 | www.mimishummus.com

"Hummus-fueled nirvana" that's "hard to come by without a passport"
is on tap at this "cute" Ditmas Park nook where the "killer" namesake
(paired with "tender pita") is joined by other "terrific" Middle Eastern
fare; the "heady" flavors are easy on the wallet, but "matchbox"-size
digs mean many do "takeout."

Minca *Japanese/Noodle Shop*
24 | 11 | 17 | $21

East Village | 536 E. Fifth St. (bet. Aves. A & B) | 212-505-8001 |
www.newyorkramen.com

There are "no pretenses" at this "traditional" Japanese noodle shop
in the East Village, just the "charming simplicity" of "delicious" ramen
featuring "rich", "slurp-worthy" broth, plus gyoza "just like in Tokyo"; its
"tiny", "basic" space is "perpetually packed", but "fast", "friendly" servers keep things on track.

Minetta Tavern *French*
25 | 22 | 22 | $70

Greenwich Village | 113 MacDougal St. (Minetta Ln.) | 212-475-3850 |
www.minettatavernny.com

"Nostalgia trip" meets "trendiness" at Keith McNally's "energetic"
Village "standout" that revives a circa-1937 tavern with "vintage"
knickknacks, "snappy" service and "excellent" French fare including a
"mind-blowing" Black Label burger ("holy cow!"); the prospect of "famous" faces in the back room keeps it a "tough table", despite quarters
"more crowded than the subway."

Minton's *Southern*
21 | 24 | 21 | $68

Harlem | 206 W. 118th St. (St. Nicholas Ave.) | 212-243-2222 |
www.mintonsharlem.com

The "transporting" rebirth of a legendary '40s jazz venue, this "engaging"
Harlem supper club syncs up "very good" Southern cooking with "fantastic" live combos jamming onstage; hepcats dig its "throwback" mood and
"leisurely service", but feel that the "live music makes it special."

Miriam *Israeli/Mediterranean*
22 | 17 | 20 | $36

Park Slope | 79 Fifth Ave. (Prospect Pl.) | Brooklyn | 718-622-2250 |
www.miriamrestaurant.com

"Dinner is a pleasure" but Park Slopers flock to this "affordable" Israeli-
Mediterranean for its "really good" daily brunch; since it's usually
a "mob scene" on weekends, insiders "go at off times" for a calmer
taste of its "tasty" fare.

	FOOD	DECOR	SERVICE	COST

Mission Cantina *Mexican*   `21` `15` `17` `$34`

Lower East Side | 172 Orchard St. (Stanton St.) | 212-254-2233 |
www.missioncantinanyc.com

A "refreshing break" from the expected, this "interesting" LES follow-
up to Mission Chinese Food highlights chef Danny Bowien's "tasty"
twists on Mexican standards served in "fun" cantina digs; it earns
"lots of buzz" from the "scenester crowd", though ordinary folk shrug
"definitely a mixed bag."

Mission Chinese Food *Chinese*   `22` `18` `18` `$49`

Lower East Side | 171 E. Broadway (bet. Jefferson & Rutgers Sts.) | no
phone | www.missionchinesefood.com

Danny Bowien's "like-no-other" Lower Eastsider "challenges your
taste buds" with spins on Californian Sichuan cooking that "turns up
the spice" to "mouth-burning" degrees; now installed in a "bigger"
setting with "improved decor", it's a "heady success" that's "always
crowded", so "be prepared to wait."

Miss Korea BBQ *Korean*   `21` `18` `18` `$41`

West 30s | 10 W. 32nd St. (bet. B'way & 5th Ave.) | 212-594-7766 |
www.on3rd.misskoreabbq.com

"Highly recommended", this "second-floor" Korean BBQ specialist is
a "popular" pick for "delicious" classics; with its "spacious", Zen-like
space, it feels somewhat "higher-end" compared to others in K-town
"without being more expensive" – no wonder it's "always packed."

Miss Lily's *Jamaican*   `23` `21` `19` `$37`

Greenwich Village | 132 W. Houston St. (Sullivan St.) | 646-588-5375
Miss Lily's 7A Cafe *Jamaican*
East Village | 109 Ave. A (7th St.) | 212-812-1482
www.misslilys.com

Serge Becker's "sexy" Jamaican joints are set in "fun" rooms pulsing with
"hip" island tunes and overseen by "beautiful" staffers; the well-priced
Caribbean eats are "delectable", while next-door outposts of Melvin's
Juice Box vending "fresh, green" juices ice the cake.

Miss Mamie's *Soul Food/Southern*   `22` `12` `17` `$29`

West 100s | 366 W. 110th St. (Columbus Ave.) | 212-865-6744 |
www.spoonbreadinc.com

"Real Southern comfort food" in "tremendous portions" keeps the
crowds coming to this UWS soul-fooder; OK, the decor is "kind of plain"
and the "friendly" servers "can be slow", but no one minds given the
"tasty" eats and "fair prices."

The Modern *American/French*   `26` `26` `25` `$127`

West 50s | Museum of Modern Art | 9 W. 53rd St. (bet. 5th & 6th
Aves.) | 212-333-1220 | www.themodernnyc.com

A "work of art in its own right", Danny Meyer's French–New American "masterpiece" inside MoMA offers "enticing" prix fixe menus
"served with grace" to a "sophisticated" crowd in a "picture-perfect"
room overlooking a sculpture garden ; true, this "splurge" demands
"deep pockets", but "less expensive" small plates are on offer in the
"more relaxed" front bar.

	FOOD	DECOR	SERVICE	COST

Moim *Korean* ▽ 23 | 18 | 17 | $46

Park Slope | 206 Garfield Pl. (7th Ave.) | Brooklyn | 718-499-8092 |
www.moimrestaurant.com

"Nouveau Korean" is the specialty of this Park Sloper that's also appreciated for its "modern" decor and "lovely" garden; it's "not the big new
thing" anymore – it's even something of a "hidden secret" – meaning
"no more ridiculous waits" for a table.

Mojave *Mexican* 23 | 23 | 21 | $30

Astoria | 22-36 31st St. (bet. Ditmars Blvd. & 23rd Ave.) | Queens |
718-545-4100 | www.mojaveny.com

A place for "good times" with friends or family, this spacious Astorian
plies "flavorful" Mexican grub and "fabulous margaritas" in a "beautiful"
hacienda with a "wonderful" back patio; "affordable" prices and "welcoming" service cement its standing as a solid "neighborhood spot."

Mŏkbar *Korean/Noodle Shop* ▽ 26 | 19 | 22 | $22

Chelsea Mkt. | 75 Ninth Ave. (15th St.) | 646-964-5963 |
www.mokbar.com

This "unique" Chelsea Market noodle bar vends an "addictively delicious" lineup of "Korean soul food" items including "craft ramen",
"excellent" small plates and homemade kimchi; low tabs and "killer
soju cocktails" take the edge off all the "hustle and bustle."

Móle *Mexican* 21 | 19 | 20 | $39

East 80s | 1735 Second Ave. (bet. 89th & 90th Sts.) | 212-289-8226
West Village | 57 Jane St. (Hudson St.) | 212-206-7559
Williamsburg | 178 Kent Ave. (4th Pl.) | Brooklyn | 347-384-2300
www.molenyc.com

"Tasty", "authentic" Mexican food turns up at this "everyday" mini-
chain that seals the deal with "even better" margaritas; "tight"
confines, "loud music" and "hurried" service are trumped by fair prices
and a "good happy hour."

Molly's *Pub Food* 21 | 20 | 22 | $28

Gramercy Park | 287 Third Ave. (22nd St.) | 212-889-3361 |
www.mollysshebeen.com

A burger that "could vie for best in town" served by "lovely Colleens"
make this "step-back-in-time" Irish pub a Gramercy "favorite"; it's the
"real deal" with a "like-in-Dublin" feel that includes a "sawdust-covered
floor" and "wood-burning fireplace."

Molyvos *Greek* 23 | 20 | 21 | $64

West 50s | Wellington Hotel | 871 Seventh Ave. (bet. 55th & 56th Sts.) |
212-582-7500 | www.molyvos.com

An "oh-so-convenient location" to Carnegie Hall and City Center is one of
the draws at this "perennial favorite" that follows through with "delicious"
Greek grub and "amiable" service; "nice decor", "bearable" acoustics and a
"spacious-by-Manhattan-standards" setting complete the "solid" picture.

Momofuku Ko *American* 26 | 21 | 24 | $228

East Village | 8 Extra Pl. (1st. St.) | 212-203-8095 | www.momofuku.com
David Chang rolls out "dinner and a show" at this pioneering East Village
"culinary adventure" offering a "memorable" tasting menu of Asian-
inflected Americana at an "intimate", 23-seat chef's counter; a recent

move to "bigger", "more relaxing" digs – the barstools now have backs! – makes the "splurge"-worthy, $175 prix fixe tab more palatable, though it's still as "hard to get into" as ever.

Momofuku Noodle Bar *American*

25 | 17 | 20 | $34

East Village | 171 First Ave. (bet. 10th & 11th Sts.) | 212-777-7773 | www.momofuku.com

"Noodle bliss" awaits at this "lively" East Village American where "master" chef David Chang offers specialties like his "hallmark pork buns" and "complex" ramen bowls; "crammed" quarters and "long waits" detract, but the payoff is "awesome" eating "without breaking the bank."

Momofuku Ssäm Bar *American*

26 | 17 | 21 | $57

East Village | 207 Second Ave. (13th St.) | 212-254-3500 | www.momofuku.com

David Chang shows off his "talent" at this "fast-paced" East Village American, where the "distinctive", Asian-influenced menu is simply "super", especially if you "round up a group" for the large-format pork shoulder feast; a "plain", "frequently jammed" room means "you won't linger" at this "can't-go-wrong" destination.

Momo Sushi Shack *Japanese*

25 | 21 | 25 | $36

Bushwick | 43 Bogart St. (Moore St.) | Brooklyn | 718-418-6666 | www.momosushishack.com

Understated but "definitely not a shack", this cash-only Bushwick Japanese "go-to" serves "interesting, delicious" small plates and "unconventional" sushi (including lots of veggie options); its wooden communal tables "fill up fast" at prime times, so regulars "get there early."

Momoya *Japanese*

23 | 18 | 19 | $46

Chelsea | 185 Seventh Ave. (21st St.) | 212-989-4466
West 80s | 427 Amsterdam Ave. (bet. 80th & 81st Sts.) | 212-580-0007
www.momoyanyc.com

Sushiphiles head to these "unassuming" Japanese eateries for "generous portions" of "amazingly fresh" fish, plus "top-notch" cooked dishes, at "won't-break-the-bank" prices; "modern" decor and "helpful" service are other reasons they're "always bustling."

Monkey Bar *American*

20 | 25 | 21 | $75

East 50s | Elysée Hotel | 60 E. 54th St. (bet. Madison & Park Aves.) | 212-288-1010 | www.monkeybarnewyork.com

The "jazz-age ambiance" endures at Graydon Carter's "old-school" Midtown canteen lined with Ed Sorel's "wonderful" murals of 1920s-era celebs; its American grub is "better than it needs to be" and accompanied by "expertly crafted" cocktails, so even though the "see-and-be-seen" scene has cooled, it still works for a "special night out."

Mon Petit Cafe *French*

21 | 17 | 20 | $47

East 60s | 801 Lexington Ave. (62nd St.) | 212-355-2233 | www.monpetitcafe.com

A "bit of Paris in the shadow of Bloomingdale's", this "tiny" vet offers "homey French" staples that hit the spot especially during an "intense shopping day"; its tearoom-style space "may not meet the standards of the Designers Guild", but to fans it has a certain "charm."

Mont Blanc *Austrian/Swiss*
23 | 17 | 23 | $45

West 40s | 315 W. 48th St. (bet. 8th & 9th Aves.) | 212-582-9648 |
www.montblancrestaurant.com

Fondue freaks seek out this "cozy" Theater District "time capsule" that's
been serving "delicious" Swiss-Austrian staples since 1982; "gracious"
staffers overseen by a "charming" owner "get you to the show on time",
so it's a "win-win all around" – even if it "could use a face-lift."

Montebello *Italian*
22 | 19 | 22 | $55

East 50s | 120 E. 56th St. (bet. Lexington & Park Aves.) | 212-753-1447 |
www.montebellonyc.com

One of the "best-kept secrets in Midtown" is this "oasis of peace and
quiet" where "personalized" service and "fantastic" Northern Italian
fare keep its longtime "dedicated clientele" returning; it's "a bit on the
expensive side", but hey, at least "you can linger."

NEW Monte Carlo *French*
▽ 23 | 17 | 20 | $59

East 70s | 181 E. 78th St. (3rd Ave.) | 646-863-3465 |
www.monte-carlo.nyc

Classic French dishes are rendered "extremely well" at this "pleasant"
Upper Eastsider, a "noteworthy" new arrival with a simple, traditional
style; while "not overly ambitious", it's manned by a "friendly staff"
overseeing a "comfortable", white-tablecloth setting.

Montmartre *French*
19 | 18 | 20 | $53

Chelsea | 158 Eighth Ave. (18th St.) | 646-596-8838 |
www.montmartrenyc.com

"Escape the city" at this Chelsea French bistro from Gabe Stulman, a
"welcoming" haven for "flavorful" meals prepared "without a lot of frills";
"accommodating" staffers patrol the "casual" interior as well as the
"beautiful back garden."

Monument Lane *American*
24 | 23 | 23 | $49

West Village | 103 Greenwich Ave. (W. 12th St.) | 212-255-0155 |
www.monumentlane.com

The "care is clear" at this "charming" West Village tavern with a "rough-
hewn" "Old NY atmosphere" that sets the scene for "accomplished" New
American cooking that's "often sourced locally" and rendered "with little
fuss"; "super-warm" service adds appeal to this "not-so-well-kept secret."

Mooncake Foods *Pan-Asian*
21 | 10 | 18 | $20

Financial District | 111 John St. (Pearl St.) | 212-233-8808
SoHo | 28 Watts St. (bet. 6th Ave. & Thompson St.) | 212-219-8888
West 30s | 263 W. 30th St. (8th Ave.) | 212-268-2888
West 50s | 359 W. 54th St. (9th Ave.) | 212-262-9888
www.mooncakefoods.com

The "healthy cheap eats" come "quickly and without fuss" at these
"cool", cash-only Pan-Asians; they're "loud" and "crowded" with "nonexistent decor", but the "great value" inspires many to keep them "in the
rotation" – especially for delivery and takeout.

Morandi *Italian*
23 | 22 | 21 | $59

West Village | 211 Waverly Pl. (bet. Charles St. & 7th Ave. S.) |
212-627-7575 | www.morandiny.com

A somewhat under-the-radar "jewel in Keith McNally's crown", this all-day West Village trattoria offers a "terrific" Italian menu in "rustic", "perennially buzzy" confines; the "energy is contagious" – but if the "noise overwhelms", "sit out on the sidewalk and people-watch."

Morgan Dining Room *American*   23 | 24 | 23 | $42

Murray Hill | 225 Madison Ave. (bet. 36th & 37th Sts.) | 212-683-2130 | www.themorgan.org

For a "civilized" repast while taking in the "wonders of the Morgan Library", this lunch-only Murray Hill museum option offers "limited" but quite "good" American bites served in the "light-filled" atrium or J. Pierpont's "elegant" former dining room; it's all very "genteel" – with "prices to match."

Morgans BBQ *BBQ*   23 | 18 | 19 | $25

Prospect Heights | 267 Flatbush Ave. (St. Marks Ave.) | Brooklyn | 718-622-2224 | www.morgansbrooklynbarbecue.com

"Legit Texas BBQ" from a transplanted Austin pitmaster distinguishes this Prospect Heights smokehouse, where the "terrific" choices include brisket and pulled pork, plus sides like Frito pie; the no-frills interior is joined by a sidewalk seating area in summer, and the adjacent Elbow Room stall supplies "inventive" mac 'n' cheese.

Morgenstern's   26 | 22 | 21 | $8
Finest Ice Cream *Ice Cream*

Lower East Side | 2 Rivington St. (bet. Bowery & Chrystie St.) | 212-209-7684 | www.morgensternsnyc.com

A "stellar" variety "makes choosing a treat" at Nick Morgenstern's cash-only LES ice cream parlor, which scoops "small-batch" concoctions in flavors ranging from "classic" to "unique"; "cute" digs equipped with an "old-school" counter appeal to "families and drunk hipsters" alike.

Morimoto *Japanese*   26 | 26 | 24 | $91

Chelsea | 88 10th Ave. (bet. 15th & 16th Sts.) | 212-989-8883 | www.morimotonyc.com

"The guy's an Iron Chef", and Masaharu Morimoto's "high-class" West Chelsea Japanese upholds his rep with "mind-blowing" cuisine – including a "stunning" omakase option – delivered by "exceptional" servers in "glitzy" surroundings; sure, it's "very expensive", but admirers have only "one word: wow."

Morso *Italian*   25 | 22 | 24 | $61

East 50s | 420 E. 59th St. (bet. 1st Ave. & Sutton Pl.) | 212-759-2706 | www.morso-nyc.com

Pino Luongo "knows what he's doing" at this "classy" East Midtown "oasis", a "dependable" source of "marvelous" Italian cuisine served by staffers who "genuinely care"; the "contemporary" room features Pop Art on the walls and a "dramatic" view of the Queensboro Bridge from the outdoor terrace.

Morton's The Steakhouse *Steak*   23 | 22 | 23 | $82

East 40s | 551 Fifth Ave. (45th St.) | 212-972-3315
NEW Morton's Grille *Steak*

Gramercy Park | 233 Park Ave. S. (19th St.) | 212-220-9200 | www.mortonsgrille.com

continued

Financial District | 136 Washington St. (Albany St.) | 212-608-0171 |
www.mortons.com

"Go hungry" to these "corporate" chophouses where "huge" steaks with
"just the right char" arrive with bountiful sides; it's predictably "expensive", but "classy" service and "upmarket" confines keep its "expense-account" crowd content; P.S. the new Grille spin-off features scaled-down
menus and more accessible price points.

Moti Mahal Delux *Indian*   24 | 16 | 20 | $36

East 60s | 1149 First Ave. (63rd St.) | 212-371-3535 |
www.motimahaldelux.us

"Innovative" Indian tandoor cooking – including a "to-die-for" signature
butter chicken – is the specialty of this Upper Eastsider; although it's part
of an international chain, its "simple", "comfortable" setting possesses a
"friendly neighborhood vibe" bolstered by "efficient" service.

Motorino *Pizza*   25 | 17 | 19 | $28

East Village | 349 E. 12th St. (bet. 1st & 2nd Aves.) | 212-777-2644
Williamsburg | 139 Broadway (bet. Bedford & Driggs Aves.) | Brooklyn |
718-599-8899
www.motorinopizza.com

"Hard to equal" for "creative pizza", these cross-borough parlors turn out
"incredible" Neapolitan-style pies that wed a "perfectly charred", "wood
smoke–kissed" crust to "top-of-the-line ingredients" (e.g. the "awesome"
Brussels sprout–pancetta version); "squeezed" seating and "minimal"
service are the trade-offs.

Moustache *Mideastern*   22 | 16 | 19 | $26

East Harlem | 1621 Lexington Ave. (102nd St.) | 212-828-0030
East Village | 265 E. 10th St. (bet. Ave. A & 1st Ave.) | 212-228-2022
West Village | 90 Bedford St. (bet. Barrow & Grove Sts.) | 212-229-2220
www.moustachepitza.com

"Straightforward", "delicious" Middle Eastern staples come at a "low
price" at these "popular" places; service is "nonchalant" and the "no-
decor" setups tilt "tiny and cramped", but the minute that "just-baked
pita" arrives, "all is forgiven."

MP Taverna *Greek*   24 | 21 | 22 | $43

NEW **Williamsburg** | 470 Driggs Ave. (10th St.) | Brooklyn |
516-686-6486
Astoria | 31-29 Ditmars Blvd. (33rd St.) | Queens | 718-777-2187
www.michaelpsilakis.com

"Always-reliable" Michael Psilakis ventures "outside tradition" with
"new takes" on Greek standards at these "stylish", "well-run" tavernas;
"welcoming" service and "reasonable prices" are other reasons why
the pace remains "busy."

Mr. Chow *Chinese*   23 | 23 | 21 | $84

East 50s | 324 E. 57th St. (bet. 1st & 2nd Aves.) | 212-751-9030
Mr. Chow Tribeca *Chinese*
TriBeCa | 121 Hudson St. (Moore St.) | 212-965-9500
www.mrchow.com

"Upper-crust dining" endures at these swanky Chinese dining rooms offering a "delicious", "classic" menu; voters split on its buzz factor – "still

	FOOD	DECOR	SERVICE	COST

glamorous" vs. "lost its luster" – but there's agreement on the "elegant" settings and "high" price tags.

Mr. K's *Chinese*

23 | 24 | 24 | $67

East 50s | 570 Lexington Ave. (51st St.) | 212-583-1668 | www.mrksny.com
A pink art deco dining room is the "opulent" backdrop for "sumptuous" Chinese fare at this "posh" East Side "throwback" patrolled by a "ritzy, tuxedoed" staff; yes, prices run "high", but fans feel that "taste trumps budget" here.

NEW Mu Ramen *Japanese/Noodle Shop*

24 | 23 | 21 | $36

Long Island City | 12-09 Jackson Ave. (bet. 47th Rd. & 48th Ave.) | Queens | 917-868-8903 | www.muramennyc.com
"Transcendent slurping" lures noodle enthusiasts to this LIC cash-only ramen shop serving "amazing bowls" and "innovative" Japanese apps; unsurprisingly, the "tight" quarters are "often jam-packed", while the no-rezzie rule causes "daunting" waits.

Murray's Cheese Bar *American*

24 | 17 | 21 | $38

West Village | 264 Bleecker St. (bet. Leroy & Morton Sts.) | 646-476-8882 | www.murrayscheesebar.com
A "cheese heaven" spun off from the popular down-the-block shop, this West Village American offers a fromage-focused lineup from "amazing" flights and wine pairings to "fabulous" fondue and "heavenly grilled cheese"; granted, it's "busy" and "crowded" at prime times, but to most it's "charming" nonetheless.

Musket Room *New Zealand*

26 | 24 | 26 | $92

NoLita | 265 Elizabeth St. (bet. Houston & Prince Sts.) | 212-219-0764 | www.musketroom.com
A "wonderful" Down Under "experience", this NoLita "find" rates "excellent on all fronts" with "serious" New Zealand cuisine matched with a "Kiwi-focused wine list", dispatched by a "top-notch" team; fans of its "sophisticated" yet "comfy" style are "hooked" despite the "high prices."

M. Wells Dinette *Québécois*

22 | 18 | 19 | $47

Long Island City | MoMA PS1 | 22-25 Jackson Ave. (46th Ave.) | Queens | 718-786-1800 | www.magasinwells.com
French-Canadian chef Hugue Dufour and wife Sarah Obraitis deliver an "amazing experience" at this lunch-only cafeteria inside LIC's MoMA PS1 (museum admission is not required for entry); the "rich, delicious" Québécois fusion fare arrives in a "funky" former classroom complete with chalkboard menus and cubbyhole desks; in summer, there's a rooftop annex for drinks and snacks.

M. Wells Steakhouse *Steak*

24 | 22 | 23 | $79

Long Island City | 43-15 Crescent St. (bet. 43rd Ave. & 44th Rd.) | Queens | 718-786-9060 | www.magasinwells.com
Located in a LIC "converted auto-body shop", this Québécois-accented take on the classic steakhouse from Hugue Dufour and Sarah Obraitis presents "terrific" chops "as big as your head" from a "wood-burning grill" in the open kitchen (where there's also a live trout tank); a patio with its own bar only adds to the "unique" – and "pricey" – experience.

Nanni *Italian*

23 | 14 | 22 | $66

East 40s | 146 E. 46th St. (bet. Lexington & 3rd Aves.) | 212-697-4161 | www.nanninyc.com

"Loyal regulars" populate this "old-world" Northern Italian near Grand Central, where "excellent" classic dishes "like grandma's" are ferried by beloved, "been-there-forever" waiters; yes, it's "expensive" given the "ancient surroundings", but you "won't leave disappointed."

Naples 45 *Italian/Pizza*

19 | 16 | 18 | $38

East 40s | 200 Park Ave. (45th St.) | 212-972-7001 | www.naples45.com

This "handy", "commuter"-friendly venue near Grand Central knocks out a "solid", if "unspectacular", Southern Italian menu led by "authentic" Neapolitan pizza; relatively "inexpensive" tabs offset the "loud" acoustics and crazy "bustle" at lunchtime, when it fills up with "non-CEO" types; P.S. closed weekends.

Narcissa *American*

25 | 24 | 23 | $73

East Village | The Standard East Village Hotel | 25 Cooper Sq. (bet. 5th & 6th Sts.) | 212-228-3344 | www.narcissarestaurant.com

A "total winner", this "stimulating" New American in The Standard East Village Hotel highlights chef John Fraser's "artful cooking", including notable rotisserie dishes and "heavenly" vegetable preparations featuring produce from co-owner André Balazs' farm; "proactive" service and a "civilized" setting also keep its "happening" crowd "wowed."

Naruto Ramen *Japanese/Noodle Shop*

20 | 10 | 17 | $17

East 80s | 1596 Third Ave. (bet. 89th & 90th Sts.) | 212-289-7803
Park Slope | 276 Fifth Ave. (bet. 1st St. & Garfield Pl.) | Brooklyn | 718-832-1111
www.narutoramenex.com

These "no-nonsense" ramen joints in underserved nabes assemble "heartwarming" bowls of classic Japanese "comfort" soup for affordable rates; "have cash on hand" (that's all they accept) and a tolerance for "cramped" conditions.

The National *American*

20 | 19 | 19 | $52

East 50s | Benjamin Hotel | 557 Lexington Ave. (50th St.) | 212-715-2400 | www.thenationalnyc.com

"Crazy-busy for lunch, quieter and more relaxed at dinner", Geoffrey Zakarian's "business" nexus in East Midtown's Benjamin Hotel presents a "comfortable" setting for "solid", "simple" American cooking; noise levels are "loud" and the service "spotty", but the crowds keep coming.

Natsumi *Japanese*

22 | 19 | 20 | $51

West 50s | Amsterdam Court Hotel | 226 W. 50th St. (bet. B'way & 8th Ave.) | 212-258-2988 | www.natsuminyc.com

Amid the Theater District "madness" lies this Japanese "sleeper" that "exceeds expectations" with its "delectable sushi", "helpful" service and "reasonable" rates; other endearments include a "sleek" room "not filled to the brim with tourists" and a "tolerable noise level."

Navy *Seafood*

∇ 21 | 20 | 16 | $50

SoHo | 137 Sullivan St. (bet. Houston & Prince Sts.) | 212-533-1137 | www.navynyc.com

This SoHo seafooder from the crew that launched Smith & Mills showcases "solid" marine cuisine via a raw bar and a menu that "changes regularly"; the space merges a "charming" nautical look with snug dimensions that "make for intimacy."

Naya *Lebanese*   22 | 16 | 19 | $29

East 50s | 1057 Second Ave. (bet. 55th & 56th Sts.) | 212-319-7777 | www.nayarestaurants.com

Naya Express *Lebanese*

East 40s | 688 Third Ave. (43rd St.) | 212-557-0007
West 50s | 54 W. 56th St. (bet. 5th & 6th Aves.) | 212-944-7777
www.nayaexpress.com

Meze mavens dig into "marvelous" Lebanese dishes at this "classy" Eastsider where the "staff treats you like family", but the "striking", "all-white" interior feels more "futuristic railway car" than homey taverna; meanwhile, the "lunchtime lines" at the counter-service Express offshoots "say it all."

Neary's *Pub Food*   19 | 16 | 24 | $51

East 50s | 358 E. 57th St. (1st Ave.) | 212-751-1434

"Consummate host" Jimmy Neary and his "welcoming" "old-school staff" keep loyal "seniors" coming back to this "frozen-in-time" Midtown watering hole; it's a "cozy place" to relax and have a drink, with "dependable" Irish bar food playing a supporting role.

Negril *Caribbean/Jamaican*   23 | 21 | 21 | $51

Greenwich Village | 70 W. Third St. (bet. La Guardia Pl. & Thompson St.) | 212-477-2804 | www.negrilvillage.com

"Hot food, hot crowd" sums up this "modern" Village Caribbean-Jamaican where the "lively" scene is fueled by "phenomenal" cocktails and "flavorful", "dressed-up" fare; sure, other competitors are "less expensive", but you're paying for the "upscale" milieu here.

Nello *Italian*   18 | 18 | 17 | $98

East 60s | 696 Madison Ave. (bet. 62nd & 63rd Sts.) | 212-980-9099 | www.nello-hub.com

Money is no object at this one-of-a-kind UES Italian, famed for serving "nothing-out-of-this-world" food for "mortgage-the-house" sums; habitués jockey for the "sidewalk seats" on Madison Avenue ("*the* place to be seen"), where a "too-tan" crowd is tolerated by staffers who "think they're celebs."

Nerai *Greek*   24 | 26 | 23 | $70

East 50s | 55 E. 54th St. (bet. Madison & Park Aves.) | 212-759-5554 | www.nerainyc.com

"Elegant and quiet", this "upscale" Midtown Greek caters to "business" types with "thoughtfully prepared", seafood-focused fare delivered by an "accommodating" crew in "sleek", breezy digs; though it's not cheap, there's a prix fixe lunch to "provide value."

Neta *Japanese*   26 | 20 | 23 | $107

Greenwich Village | 61 W. Eighth St. (6th Ave.) | 212-505-2610 | www.netanyc.com

"Sublime sushi", "wonderful small plates" and "dazzling" omakase options net a loyal fan base for this "civilized" Village Japanese; the "nondescript space" is brightened by "knowledgeable" staffers and an "entertaining" sushi bar, and though "not cheap", it's "a great way to spoil yourself."

New Leaf   *American*

Inwood | 1 Margaret Corbin Dr. (Cabrini Blvd.) | 212-568-5323 | www.newleafrestaurant.com

No longer operated by Bette Midler's NY Restoration Project, this Fort Tryon Park destination has been taken over by the java chainlet Coffeed, which promises a New American menu with a focus on local ingredients; the 1930s-era structure has been lightly renovated, and its leafy surrounds remain as lush as ever.

New WonJo   *Korean*

24 | 15 | 19 | $38

West 30s | 23 W. 32nd St. (bet. B'way & 5th Ave.) | 212-695-5815 | www.newwonjo.com

"Korean awesomeness" 24/7 is the deal at this K-town vet whose "crave"-worthy specialties include tableside BBQ; you "gotta love" the charcoal grills (vs. more typical gas ones) – but "no atmosphere" and "long lines" at peak hours are also part of the package.

New World Mall   *Food Hall*

22 | 10 | 11 | $13

Flushing | 136-20 Roosevelt Ave. (Main St.) | Queens | 718-353-0551 | www.newworldmallny.com

For the "curious and adventuresome", this basement Flushing food hall is "like a mini-trip to Asia" with vendors turning out handmade dumplings, noodles, hot pots and other "amazing" "cheap bites"; it's "as real as being in Shanghai", particularly when you're "jostled around" in the "crazy" crowds.

New York Sushi Ko   *Japanese*

Lower East Side | 91 Clinton St. (Rivington St.) | 917-734-5857 | www.newyorksushiko.com

You may "never see sushi in the same way" after visiting this "tiny" LES Japanese for a "delicious", omakase-only spread via a "personable" chef who "knows what he's doing"; the $115-and-up set price is steep, but the "overall flow" at the 11-seat counter is "absolutely perfect."

Ngam   *Thai*

24 | 19 | 19 | $31

East Village | 99 Third Ave. (bet. 12th & 13th Sts.) | 212-777-8424 | www.ngamnyc.com

Chef Hong Thaimee is "usually on-site sharing the love" at this "small" East Village "charmer" known for its "imaginative" twists on Thai comfort classics; "interesting" cocktails and a "fun" rough-hewn space are additional reasons why it's an all-around "favorite."

Nha Trang   *Vietnamese*

22 | 9 | 16 | $21

Chinatown | 148 Centre St. (bet. Walker & White Sts.) | 212-941-9292
Chinatown | 87 Baxter St. (bet. Bayard & Canal Sts.) | 212-233-5948
www.nhatrangnyc.com

"Fantastic" pho and other "authentic" Vietnamese eats trump "institutional decor" and the "rushed service you'd expect" at these "hole-in-the-wall" Chinatown joints; the "incredibly reasonable" prices alone make them "worth a stop" even if you're not on jury duty.

	FOOD	DECOR	SERVICE	COST

Nice Green Bo *Chinese* | 21 | 6 | 13 | $20 |

Chinatown | 66 Bayard St. (bet. Elizabeth & Mott Sts.) | 212-625-2359 |
www.nicegreenbo.com

"Hungry hordes" hit this Chinatown "hole-in-the-wall" to nosh on "some
of NY's best soup dumplings" and other "first-rate, bargain-priced"
Shanghai specialties; too bad "dumpy" digs and "grumpy" staffers are
part of the experience.

Nice Matin *French/Mediterranean* | 19 | 17 | 18 | $52 |

West 70s | 201 W. 79th St. (Amsterdam Ave.) | 212-873-6423 |
www.nicematinny.com

"Always running full throttle", this all-day UWS "hive" doles out "reliable"
French-Med eats in a "casual" space channeling the "south of France",
complete with "sidewalk seating" to "watch the passing scene"; however,
given the prime-time "noise" and "crush", regulars say it's "best off-peak."

Nick & Stef's Steakhouse *Steak* | 22 | 19 | 21 | $76 |

West 30s | 9 Penn Plaza (bet. 7th & 8th Aves.) | 212-563-4444 |
www.patinagroup.com

"Incredibly convenient to MSG" – diners can even use a private arena entrance – this "comfortable" Penn Plaza steakhouse boasts "tasty" chops
served by a "fast" team; even if the decor seems "sort of a decade ago",
it's ultimately a "bright spot" in a dining-challenged nabe.

Nick & Toni's Cafe *Mediterranean* | 21 | 16 | 20 | $56 |

West 60s | 100 W. 67th St. (bet. B'way & Columbus Ave.) |
212-496-4000 | www.nickandtoniscafe.com

Just a "short walk" from Lincoln Center, this "low-key" offshoot of the
"popular" East Hampton standby plies "delicious pizzas" and other
"straightforward" Med fare; it's a good bet "pre-movie or -show", with
the bonus of possibly spotting "journalists from nearby ABC."

Nick's *Pizza* | 24 | 14 | 19 | $24 |

East 90s | 1814 Second Ave. (94th St.) | 212-987-5700 |
www.nicksnyc.com
NEW **Murray Hill** | 365 Third Ave. (bet. 26th & 27th Sts.) |
646-918-6553 | www.nickspizzabar.com
Forest Hills | 108-26 Ascan Ave. (bet. Austin & Burns Sts.) | Queens |
718-263-1126

A "step above your everyday pizza place", these "neighborhood joints"
specialize in "charred", thin-crust pies with "perfect sauce" and some
"gourmet flair"; true, the decor and service are strictly "no-frills", but
they fill the bill for "family"-friendly dining.

Nicola's *Italian* | 22 | 16 | 22 | $65 |

East 80s | 146 E. 84th St. (Lexington Ave.) | 212-249-9850 |
www.nicolasnyc.com

"Yes, it's like a private club" and that's fine with the "well-heeled" regulars
who seek out this "unhurried" Upper Eastsider for "scrumptious", "old-
time" Italian cooking and "warm welcomes"; it's "expensive" and "a wee bit
dated", but at least you can "develop membership status" with return visits.

	FOOD	DECOR	SERVICE	COST

Nicoletta *Italian/Pizza*   22 | 18 | 20 | $33

East Village | 160 Second Ave. (10th St.) | 212-432-1600 |
www.nicolettapizza.com

Sample big-shot chef Michael White's wares "without the usual price tag"
at this East Village pizzeria, home to thick-crust pies topped with intrigu-
ingly "different combinations"; the results earn a split decision ("amazing"
vs. "disappointing"), though most agree it's "sort of a no-frills place."

Nightingale 9 *Vietnamese*   ▽ 21 | 18 | 20 | $37

Carroll Gardens | 329 Smith St. (bet. Carroll & President Sts.) | Brooklyn |
347-689-4699 | www.nightingale9.com

"Different" from the norm, this Carroll Gardens Vietnamese fields
"modern" takes on street eats, showcasing "interesting tastes and
textures"; "refreshing" cocktails and a minimal but "pleasant" setting
burnish its "casual", "cozy" mood.

99 Miles to Philly *Cheesesteaks*   21 | 11 | 18 | $15

East 40s | 212 E. 45th St. (bet. 2nd & 3rd Aves.) | 646-476-6521
Greenwich Village | 94 Third Ave. (bet. 12th & 13th Sts.) | 212-253-2700
www.99milestophilly.com

The closest you'll get to Philly that "doesn't involve a Chinatown bus",
these cheesesteak palaces proffer a marquee sandwich that's a "solid",
"satisfying", "gooey mess"; late-night availability trumps "grungy" looks
and minimal seating, but aesthetes advise "get it to go."

Ninja *Japanese*   16 | 23 | 20 | $61

TriBeCa | 25 Hudson St. (bet. Duane & Reade Sts.) | 212-274-8500 |
www.ninjanewyork.com

Costumed staffers perform "roaming magic acts" at this "gimmicky"
TriBeCa theme joint done up like a feudal ninja village; sure, they really
"go all out" and the "theatrics" are "fun for kids", but grown-ups say
you'll "shell out" for only "so-so" Japanese eats.

Nino's *Italian*   21 | 20 | 21 | $56

East 70s | 1354 First Ave. (bet. 72nd & 73rd Sts.) | 212-988-0002 |
www.ninosnyc.com

Nino's Tuscany Steak House *Italian/Steak*

West 50s | 117 W. 58th St. (bet. 6th & 7th Aves.) | 212-757-8630 |
www.ninostuscany.com

"More than typical neighborhood Italians", these "civilized" standbys
exude "old-world charm" from the "comfortable" settings to the "delicious", "traditional" cooking; maybe they're "a little pricey", but "smiling"
servers always "enhance the experience."

Ninth Street Espresso *Coffee*   23 | 16 | 20 | $9

Chelsea | 75 Ninth Ave. (bet. 15th & 16th Sts.) | 212-228-2930
East 50s | 109 E. 56th St. (bet. Lexington & Park Aves.) | 646-559-4793
East Village | 341 E. 10th St. (Ave. B) | 212-777-3508
East Village | 700 E. 9th St. (Ave. C) | 212-358-9225
NEW Gowanus | 333 Douglass St. (4th Ave.) | Brooklyn | 212-358-9225
www.ninthstreetespresso.com

This pioneering "coffee-lover's coffeehouse" chainlet is a "go-to" for
"meticulously prepared", "damn good" java – notably "espresso that
packs some punch"; its spaces featuring a "simple aesthetic" are staffed
by "serious" yet "mellow" baristas.

	FOOD	DECOR	SERVICE	COST

Nippon *Japanese*   24 | 18 | 22 | $57

East 50s | 155 E. 52nd St. (bet. Lexington & 3rd Aves.) | 212-688-5941
"One of NYC's oldest" Japanese restaurants, this circa-1963 Midtown
"favorite" still turns out "delicious", "traditional" fare – including sushi –
with "no glitz, no glam", just "gracious" attention; maybe the decor's a bit
"tired", but nearly everyone likes its "quiet, pleasant" mien.

Nirvana *Indian*   ∇ 22 | 19 | 20 | $30

Murray Hill | 346 Lexington Ave. (bet. 39th & 40th Sts.) | 212-983-0000 |
www.nirvanany.com
"Perfectly seasoned" classics at moderate rates draw curryphiles to this
"upscale", lesser-known Murray Hill Indian where they "tailor the spice
to taste"; "attentive" staffers tend the "contemporary", brick-walled setting featuring a lively lounge and "inviting" upstairs dining room.

Nizza *Italian*   20 | 16 | 19 | $45

West 40s | 630 Ninth Ave. (bet. 44th & 45th Sts.) | 212-956-1800 |
www.nizzanyc.com
"Won't-break-the-bank" prices for "solid" classics from the Italian Riviera
(including "impressive" gluten-free options) ensure this "casual" Theater
District spot is plenty "popular" pre- or post-curtain; the noise level can
be "a bit much", but in warm weather there's always the sidewalk seating.

Nobu *Japanese*   27 | 23 | 24 | $89

TriBeCa | 105 Hudson St. (Franklin St.) | 212-219-0500
Nobu 57 *Japanese*
West 50s | 40 W. 57th St. (bet. 5th & 6th Aves.) | 212-757-3000
Nobu Next Door *Japanese*
TriBeCa | 105 Hudson St. (Franklin St.) | 212-334-4445
www.noburestaurants.com
A "perennial" "shining star", Nobu Matsuhisa's "magical" TriBeCa "posh
spot" is the "sine qua non" for "spectacular" Japanese-Peruvian fare that
"leaves you in a state of bliss" boosted by "top-class service" and David
Rockwell's "chic, modern" surrounds; joined by a "slightly less fancy"
next-door neighbor and a "supersized" Midtown satellite, its "flair" is
as "unforgettable" as the "astronomic prices."

Nocello *Italian*   23 | 18 | 22 | $51

West 50s | 257 W. 55th St. (bet. B'way & 8th Ave.) | 212-713-0224 |
www.nocello.net
"Enduring and endearing" – not to mention "convenient" if you're bound
for Carnegie Hall or City Center – this "cozy" Tuscan turns out "plentiful"
platefuls of "fine" "traditional" fare; "charming owners" add "warmth"
to the "unassuming" setting.

NoHo Star *American/Asian*   20 | 17 | 20 | $40

NoHo | 330 Lafayette St. (Bleecker St.) | 212-925-0070 |
www.nohostar.com
The "offbeat" menu "should just say 'everything, plus Chinese'" at this
"long-standing" NoHo "favorite" that "cheerfully" offers Asian specialties
side by side with "kicked-up" American eats; tabs "priced right" and a
"comfy" setting are other reasons this "star keeps shining."

	FOOD	DECOR	SERVICE	COST

The NoMad *American/European*   `26` `26` `25` `$97`

NoMad | NoMad Hotel | 1170 Broadway (28th St.) | 347-472-5660 | www.thenomadhotel.com

This "stylish" "trendsetter" in the NoMad Hotel draws a "chic crowd" that's "blown away" by Daniel Humm's "superb" American-European menu (the roast chicken is "one for the books"); "spot-on service" and a "beautifully designed" space spread out over several cozy rooms help distract from the "heavy" tabs.

The NoMad Bar *American* `25` `26` `24` `$67`

NoMad | NoMad Hotel | 10 W. 28th St. (B'way) | 347-472-5660 | www.thenomadhotel.com

Spun off from The NoMad around the corner, this "less formal" boîte specializes in "expertly crafted" cocktails – including group-friendly large-format punches – accompanied by an "abbreviated" menu of elevated bar bites; though the "masculine", double-height space is "stately" and airy, the bar's "trendy" rep makes for "crowded" conditions and "noisy" acoustics.

Nom Wah Tea Parlor *Chinese* `21` `13` `15` `$21`

Chinatown | 13 Doyers St. (bet. Chatham Sq. & Pell St.) | 212-962-6047 | www.nomwah.com

You may "need Google Maps" to find it, but it's worth seeking out this "time-warp" Chinatown vet (around since 1920) for "surprisingly good", "real-deal" dim sum at "bargain" rates; despite a "nondescript ambiance" and "no-frills" service, it's still a "favorite" – "go early or really late" to avoid a wait.

Noodle Pudding *Italian* `25` `18` `22` `$43`

Brooklyn Heights | 38 Henry St. (bet. Cranberry & Middagh Sts.) | Brooklyn | 718-625-3737

An "enduring favorite" that "never gets old", this Brooklyn Heights "winner" is a hit with locals thanks to its "sublime" traditional Italian cooking and "wonderful energy"; the "crowds never cease" and regulars "wish they took reservations", but "moderate" tabs are the payoff.

NEW Noreetuh *Hawaiian*   `—` `—` `—` `M`

East Village | 128 First Ave. (bet. 7th St. & St. Marks Pl.) | 646-892-3050 | www.noreetuh.com

The underrepresented cuisine of Hawaii gets a new showroom at this East Village Asian-fusion practitioner from Per Se vets, rolling out a sophisticated menu incorporating Aloha State staples like tofu, Spam and hearts of palm; the spare, Momofuku-esque setting is free of South Seas island kitsch, and in lieu of tiki drinks, there's a surprisingly robust wine list.

Norma's *American* `25` `20` `21` `$45`

West 50s | Le Parker Meridien Hotel | 119 W. 56th St. (bet. 6th & 7th Aves.) | 212-708-7460 | www.normasnyc.com

"Lavish" breakfasts and brunches are the specialty of this Midtown American in the Parker Meridien, where the "memorable" morning fare arrives in "large, easily shareable" portions; no kidding, the tabs are "out of this world" (e.g. that $1,000 frittata) and it's a "bit of a tourist factory", but it's still a "highly recommended" experience.

	FOOD	DECOR	SERVICE	COST

Northeast Kingdom *American*   25 | 23 | 22 | $32

Bushwick | 18 Wyckoff Ave. (Troutman St.) | Brooklyn | 718-386-3864 |
www.north-eastkingdom.com

This "cool little" Bushwick pioneer is a "solid" bet for real-deal "farm-to-table" American fare, where your meal might feature foraging finds from the husband-and-wife proprietors; its "warm", "unassuming" quarters include a fireplace-equipped downstairs den serving cocktails and snacks.

North End Grill *American/Seafood*   25 | 23 | 25 | $77

Battery Park City | 104 North End Ave. (bet. Murray & Vesey Sts.) |
646-747-1600 | www.northendgrillnyc.com

Battery Park City is home to this "smart, upscale" American via Danny Meyer, where the "outstanding" seafood-focused menu arrives via an "on-point" staff that's "really on its game"; the "civilized", "modern" space features a "lively" bar that's a magnet for "suits."

Northern Spy Food Co. *American*   21 | 18 | 20 | $45

East Village | 511 E. 12th St. (bet. Aves. A & B) | 212-228-5100 |
www.northernspyfoodco.com

This "wonderfully eccentric" East Village "locavore destination" turns out "savory", "farm-to-table" American food at "moderate" rates; "warm and fuzzy" service makes up for the "very small space" that's usually "crammed" at prime times.

North Square *American*   24 | 21 | 24 | $55

Greenwich Village | Washington Sq. Hotel | 103 Waverly Pl. (MacDougal St.) | 212-254-1200 | www.northsquareny.com

Although a "favorite" of "NYU profs" and other "Washington Square regulars", this "swell little neighborhood place" mostly flies under the radar; "superior" New American cuisine, "civilized" service and a "grown-up", "comfy" setting where you "can talk without going hoarse" keep it a "neighborhood standby."

No. 7 *American*   21 | 15 | 18 | $23

Fort Greene | 7 Greene Ave. (bet. Cumberland & Fulton Sts.) | Brooklyn | 718-522-6370 | www.no7restaurant.com

No. 7 North *Sandwiches*

Greenpoint | 931 Manhattan Ave. (bet. Java & Kent Sts.) | Brooklyn | 718-389-7775 | www.no7north.com

No. 7 Sub *Sandwiches*

West 50s | Plaza Food Hall | 1 W. 59th St., lower level (5th Ave.) | 646-755-3228

Dumbo | 11 Water St. (bet. New Dock & Old Fulton Sts.) | Brooklyn | 917-618-4399
www.no7sub.com

This "cool", BAM-handy Fort Greene number is a "local favorite" for "intriguing" New American innovations ("two words: broccoli tacos!"); its counter-serve outlets follow up with "can't-be-beat" sub sandwiches whose "quality ingredients" and "wacky combos" likewise venture "beyond the common herd."

	FOOD	DECOR	SERVICE	COST

Novitá *Italian*
25 | 21 | 23 | $62

Gramercy Park | 102 E. 22nd St. (bet. Lexington Ave. & Park Ave. S.) | 212-677-2222 | www.novitanyc.com

A true neighborhood "standby", this longtime Gramercy Northern Italian offers a "top-notch" menu dispatched by an "attentive" staff; despite "small" dimensions and "shoehorned" seating, the "crowds still come", drawn by the "pleasant" atmosphere.

Nucci's *Italian*
22 | 16 | 21 | $38

Tottenville | 4842 Arthur Kill Rd. (S. Bridge St.) | Staten Island | 718-967-3600
West Brighton | 616 Forest Ave. (Oakland Ave.) | Staten Island | 718-815-4882
www.nuccis.net

"Delicious pizza" and other Italian basics have locals "dining regularly" at these "reliable" Staten Islanders; "fair prices" and "make-you-feel-like-family" service trump "mediocre" atmospherics, so most consider them decent enough "neighborhood" fallbacks.

Numero 28 *Pizza*
22 | 14 | 17 | $30

East 70s | 1431 First Ave. (bet. 74th & 75th Sts.) | 212-772-8200
East Village | 176 Second Ave. (bet. 11th & 12th Sts.) | 212-777-1555
West 90s | 660 Amsterdam Ave. (92nd St.) | 212-706-7282
West Village | 28 Carmine St. (bet. Bedford & Bleecker Sts.) | 212-463-9653
NEW **Park Slope** | 137 Seventh Ave. (bet. Carroll St. & Garfield Pl.) | Brooklyn | 718-398-9198
www.numero28.com

"In a sea of neighborhood pizza joints", these "homey" outlets produce "crispy", real-deal Neapolitan pies fired up in "blazing", wood-fired brick ovens; the "unpretentious", cash-only style is more reason to be "pleasantly surprised by the quality."

Num Pang *Cambodian/Sandwiches*
23 | 11 | 15 | $14

Battery Park City | Hudson Eats | 230 Vesey St. (West St.) | 212-227-1957
Chelsea | Chelsea Market | 75 Ninth Ave. (bet. 15th & 16th Sts.) | 212-390-8851
East 40s | 140 E. 41st St. (bet. Lexington & 3rd Aves.) | 212-867-8889
Flatiron | 1129 Broadway (bet. 25th & 26th Sts.) | 212-647-8889
Greenwich Village | 21 E. 12th St. (bet. 5th Ave. & University Pl.) | 212-255-3271
West 40s | 148 W. 48th St. (bet. 6th & 7th Aves.) | 212-421-0743
www.numpangnyc.com

"Cambodia's answer" to the banh mi craze, this local chain dispenses "damn good" sandwiches "worth standing in line" for, with "more-than-fair" prices and "speedy service" to sweeten the deal; though the setups are "fast food"–style, most feel "you can't go wrong" here.

Nurnberger Bierhaus *German*
∇ 21 | 18 | 21 | $36

Randall Manor | 817 Castleton Ave. (Regan Ave.) | Staten Island | 718-816-7461 | www.nurnbergerbierhaus.com

Staten Islanders in the mood for Wiener schnitzel and beer turn up at this "festive" Randall Manor take on Bavaria, where the German grub is matched with "wonderful" brews on tap; it's "authentic" right down to the "hokey decor", dirndl-clad staff and back biergarten.

	FOOD	DECOR	SERVICE	COST

Nyonya *Malaysian* 23 | 14 | 15 | $25

Little Italy | 199 Grand St. (bet. Mott & Mulberry Sts.) | 212-334-3669
Bath Beach | 2322 86th St. (Bay 34th St.) | Brooklyn | 718-265-0888
Sunset Park | 5323 Eighth Ave. (54th St.) | Brooklyn | 718-633-0808
www.ilovenyonya.com

When you crave "exotic flavors", these "favorite" Malaysians fill the bill with "generous" servings of "delicious" standards at "ridiculously good" rates (just "bring cash"); "assembly-line" service and "packed", "no-frills" quarters are part of the experience.

NYY Steak *Steak* 24 | 25 | 24 | $81

West 50s | 7 W. 51st St. (bet. 5th & 6th Aves.) | 646-307-7910
Concourse/Downtown | Yankee Stadium | 1 E. 161st St., Gate 6 (River Ave.) | Bronx | 646-977-8325
www.nyysteak.com

There's "no other place like" this ticket holders–only chophouse within Yankee Stadium, where "solid" steaks served in a room "adorned with memorabilia" are a "grand slam" for pinstripe patrons who can swing the "high prices"; there's also a sprawling, all-seasons offshoot that pinch-hits in Rock Center.

Oaxaca *Mexican* 23 | 15 | 19 | $15

NEW **Murray Hill** | 152 E. 33rd St. (bet. Lexington & 3rd Aves.) | 212-684-4404
NEW **West 40s** | 405 W. 44th St. (9th Ave.) | 212-757-2957
West 80s | 424 Amsterdam Ave. (bet. 80th & 81st Sts.) | 212-580-4888
West Village | 48 Greenwich Ave. (bet. 10th & 11th Sts.) | 212-366-4488
Bedford-Stuyvesant | 1116 Bedford Ave. (Quincy St.) | Brooklyn | 718-230-8111
NEW **Downtown Brooklyn** | 75 Hoyt St. (bet. Atlantic Ave. & State St.) | Brooklyn | 718-855-5530
NEW **Fort Greene** | 10 Clermont Ave. (Flushing Ave.) | Brooklyn | 718-858-4442
Gowanus | 250 Fourth Ave. (bet. Carroll & President Sts.) | Brooklyn | 718-222-1122
NEW **Williamsburg** | 130 Grand St. (Berry St.) | Brooklyn | 718-388-8804
www.oaxacatacos.com

"Addictive", "legit" tacos for "cheap" sums keep folks coming to these "casual" Mexicans; "no-frills" settings and "don't-hold-your-breath" service mean most rely on them as "stop-by-on-your-way-home" kinds of places.

Obao *Asian* 20 | 17 | 18 | $26

East 50s | 222 E. 53rd St. (bet. 2nd & 3rd Aves.) | 212-308-5588
Financial District | 38 Water St. (Broad St.) | 212-361-6313
West 40s | 647 Ninth Ave. (45th St.) | 212-245-8880
www.obaony.com

"Elevated" Southeast Asian street food is the specialty at these "local go-to" joints that supply an "array" of small and large plates at "affordable prices"; the setups are informal, though the Hell's Kitchen locale "stands out" with its "cool", nightclubbish decor.

Obicà Mozzarella Bar *Italian* 23 | 19 | 19 | $48

East 50s | 590 Madison Ave. (56th St.) | 212-355-2217

continued

Flatiron | 928 Broadway (bet. 21st & 22nd Sts.) | 212-777-2754
www.obica.com

A "delicious sampling" of diverse mozzarellas "freshly flown in" from
Italy is the draw at these links of an international chain; the IBM atrium
counter offers Midtowners artfully prepared "quick bites", while the
full-service Flatiron branch adds "awesome pizza" to the mix in an
"industrial-sleek" space.

Oceana *American/Seafood*   25 | 23 | 23 | $86

West 40s | 120 W. 49th St. (bet. 6th & 7th Aves.) | 212-759-5941 |
www.oceanarestaurant.com

"Business folk" and "pre-theater" people alike gravitate to this "cavernous" Rock Center American seafooder for its "pristine fish", "gorgeous
raw bar" and "classy" service; the "upscale" environs complete with
outdoor seating help make it a "go-to" despite the "hefty" tab.

Ocean Grill *Seafood*   23 | 21 | 22 | $62

West 70s | 384 Columbus Ave. (bet. 78th & 79th Sts.) | 212-579-2300 |
www.oceangrill.com

"Still hopping after all these years", this UWS seafooder lures "big
crowds" for "tasty", "simply grilled" marine cuisine dished out in a
"white-tablecloth", "Hamptons-esque" setting; when the "noise level
gets too high", insiders escape to the "pleasant" sidewalk seats.

The Odeon *American/French*   21 | 19 | 20 | $53

TriBeCa | 145 W. Broadway (bet. Duane & Thomas Sts.) | 212-233-0507 |
www.theodeonrestaurant.com

"Historical hipness" clings to this "sexy-smart" TriBeCa bistro that's
enjoying something of a rebirth with the renaissance of the Financial District; "solid" Franco-American fare, a "vibrant" mood and the
addition of breakfast service are reasons why it "seems fresher" than
ever to its perpetually "cool crowd."

Ofrenda *Mexican*   24 | 19 | 19 | $42

West Village | 113 Seventh Ave. S. (bet. 4th & 10th Sts.) | 212-924-2305 |
www.ofrendanyc.com

"*Fabuloso*" Mexican fare – and "even better margaritas" – delivered by a
"terrific" staff makes this "bustling", "bar-esque" West Villager a "go-to
for neighborhood foodies"; "fun" outdoor seating and "amazing" happy-
hour specials seal the deal.

NEW Oiji *Korean*   – | – | – | M

East Village | 119 First Ave. (7th St.) | 646-767-9050 | www.oijinyc.com
Elevated takes on barbecue-free Korean fare turn up at this under-the-
radar East Villager where the creative small plates include honey butter
chips and a deconstructed version of bibimbop; equal parts of brick, slate
and reclaimed wood make up the decor in the surprisingly chic room.

Okeanos *Greek*   21 | 18 | 21 | $40

Park Slope | 314 Seventh Ave. (8th St.) | Brooklyn | 347-725-4162 |
www.okeanosnyc.com

A "find" for Greek eats with an "emphasis on seafood", this Park Slope
sleeper plies all the Hellenic hallmarks, notably the freshest catch

"cooked to perfection"; the "neighborhood" space is unremarkable but "peaceful", and regulars report they "don't rush you."

Okonomi/Yuji Ramen *Japanese* ∇ 25 | 22 | 24 | $39

Williamsburg | 150 Ainslie St. (bet. Leonard & Lorimer Sts.) | Brooklyn | no phone | www.okonomibk.com

"Talk about originality", this "tiny" Williamsburg Japanese from chef Yuji Haraguchi provides "traditional" ichiju-sansai set meals for breakfast and lunch, then segues into Yuji Ramen at night, offering "excellent" noodles; service is "attentive", but seats can be scarce in the "minimal" space.

Old Homestead *Steak* 25 | 19 | 22 | $88

Chelsea | 56 Ninth Ave. (bet. 14th & 15th Sts.) | 212-242-9040 | www.theoldhomesteadsteakhouse.com

"Old-style NY" dining doesn't get much more authentic than this steakhouse "original" that's been grilling "perfectly seared" chops in Chelsea since 1868; "huge" tabs don't faze its core crowd of "men spending too much", though "massive" portions leave them as "over-stuffed" as the furniture.

Old Tbilisi Garden *Georgian* ∇ 22 | 16 | 20 | $48

Greenwich Village | 174 Bleecker St. (Sullivan St.) | 212-470-6064

Fans of Georgian food – "the country, not the state" – seek out this "different" Villager, where the "tasty" khachapuri and other "hearty" dishes are served with "old-world charm"; if the "decor's nothing much", tabs are "reasonable" and there's a garden with a "funky" waterfall.

Olea *Mediterranean* 27 | 24 | 23 | $35

Fort Greene | 171 Lafayette Ave. (Adelphi St.) | Brooklyn | 718-643-7003 | www.oleabrooklyn.com

"On the keeper list" in Fort Greene, this BAM-area "favorite" features "delightful" Med plates (including notably "wonderful tapas") set down in "cozy", "colorful" digs by an "accommodating" crew; since "everyone in the neighborhood" knows about it, be ready for "bustling" crowds and "long waits", "especially for brunch."

NEW Oleanders *American* – | – | – | M

Williamsburg | McCarren Hotel | 160 N. 12th St. (Berry St.) | Brooklyn | 718-218-7500 | www.oleandersnyc.com

Replacing The Elm in Williamsburg's McCarren Hotel, this super-casual New American is a riff on a '70s fern bar, with throwback cuisine (lobster Thermador, beef Wellington) and cocktails (Harvey Wallbangers, piña coladas) from mix-master Dale DeGroff; the breezy interior is lined with plants galore and faux Tiffany light fixtures.

Omai *Vietnamese* 23 | 16 | 21 | $42

Chelsea | 158 Ninth Ave. (bet. 19th & 20th Sts.) | 212-633-0550 | www.omainyc.com

A longtime "solid" neighborhood "go-to", this "pleasant", "low-key" Chelsea Vietnamese serves up "delicious", "delicate" standards; "reasonable prices" and a location "close to the Joyce Theater" are pluses, though the "little" space is on the "tight" side.

	FOOD	DECOR	SERVICE	COST

Omonia Cafe *Coffee/Greek*

| 19 | 17 | 16 | $24 |

Bay Ridge | 7612 Third Ave. (bet. 76th & 77th Sts.) | Brooklyn | 718-491-1435
Astoria | 32-20 Broadway (33rd St.) | Queens | 718-274-6650
www.omoniacafe.com

A "mind-boggling array" of "heavenly" sweets awaits at these Greek coffeehouses also serving some savory bites, where "neon lights" and a "disco vibe" suit "teenagers" who "hang out and socialize" late-night; P.S. Astoria's Next Door adjunct dabbles in more experimental pastries (cheesecake baklava, anyone?).

🆕 One Dine *American*

| – | – | – | E |

Financial District | 1 WTC | 285 Fulton St., 101st fl. (Church St.) | no phone
The highest restaurant in the Western Hemisphere, this New American atop One World Trade Center offers an $84 prix fixe-only menu, with airplanelike views of Manhattan and New Jersey on the side; it's not especially large, so advance reservations are recommended, and be aware there's an additional $32-per-person charge to ascend to its 101st-floor observatory setting.

100 Montaditos *Sandwiches*

| 19 | 17 | 18 | $18 |

Greenwich Village | 176 Bleecker St. (bet. MacDougal & Sullivan Sts.) | 646-719-1713 | www.100montaditosny.com
An "endless" array of "tapas-sized sandwiches" is the "satisfying" draw at this Village outpost of a Spain-based "cheap-eats" chain; given "relaxed" vibes aided by beer and sangria from the "efficient" counter staff, it predictably "does well with the NYU crowd."

One if by Land, Two if by Sea *American*

| 23 | 26 | 24 | $124 |

West Village | 17 Barrow St. (bet. 4th St. & 7th Ave. S.) | 212-255-8649 | www.oneifbyland.com
"Steeped in history" and "romance", this "historic" Village "rendezvous" set in Aaron Burr's former carriage house offers "excellent" American cuisine delivered by staffers who "take their job seriously"; "mood-setting" touches – "candlelit rooms", four fireplaces, a piano bar – distract from the "special occasion"–level, prix fixe-only tabs.

1 or 8 *Japanese*

| 24 | 22 | 23 | $61 |

Williamsburg | 66 S. Second St. (Wythe Ave.) | Brooklyn | 718-384-2152 | www.oneoreightbk.com
Representing the "new cool" in Williamsburg, this Japanese "find" turns out "exceptional sushi" and other "original" "culinary creations" in an "inviting space" with all-white, "modern" decor; also touted for "telepathic service" and an "under-the-radar omakase" deal, it's "a real treat" for those in the know.

Ootoya *Japanese/Noodle Shop*

| 25 | 20 | 21 | $39 |

Flatiron | 8 W. 18th St. (bet. 5th & 6th Aves.) | 212-255-0018
Greenwich Village | 41 E. 11th St. (University Pl.) | 212-473-4300
West 40s | 141 W. 41st St. (bet. B'way & 6th Ave.) | 212-704-0833
www.ootoya.us
Turning out "Japanese comfort food" "at its best", these "nothing-fancy" branches of a Tokyo-based izakaya chain provide a "delicious" lineup of

"down-to-earth" favorites like yakitori, soba and soup bowls; given the "reasonable" pricing, the only hitch is the occasional "wait."

Oriental Garden *Chinese/Seafood*   23 | 14 | 17 | $33

Chinatown | 14 Elizabeth St. (bet. Bayard & Canal Sts.) | 212-619-0085 | www.orientalgardenny.com

"Don't let the drab decor fool you" at this C-town Cantonese vet, because its "wonderful" dim sum and seafood fresh "from the tanks" just might "knock your socks off"; the mood gets "manic" at prime times, but at least the "banquet" comes "without an insane price."

Original Crab Shanty *Italian/Seafood*   25 | 18 | 22 | $45

City Island | 361 City Island Ave. (Tier St.) | Bronx | 718-885-1810 | www.originalcrabshanty.com

They "pile it on" at this "informal" City Island vet where the "king-size" Italian seafood servings are both "tasty" and "affordable"; the catch is certainly "fresh", but the nautical decor may have been out of the water too long.

Orsay *French*   20 | 20 | 19 | $61

East 70s | 1057 Lexington Ave. (75th St.) | 212-517-6400 | www.orsayrestaurant.com

An UES facsimile of "bygone France" by way of "Balthazar", this French brasserie offers the "expected" dishes (at "unexpectedly high prices") to a "boisterous", "multigenerational" crowd; "indifferent" service and a "lovely" art nouveau setting cement the "classique" feel.

Orso *Italian*   23 | 19 | 23 | $61

West 40s | 322 W. 46th St. (bet. 8th & 9th Aves.) | 212-489-7212 | www.orsorestaurant.com

A "Theater District standard" for decades, this "crowded-but-convivial" Restaurant Row Italian still supplies "reliably delicious", "upscale" fare via a "quick" staff of "would-be actors"; it's on the "plain" side and "reserving way ahead is a must", but to fans it's "worth it" for the "Broadway star"–gazing alone.

Oslo Coffee Roasters *Coffee*   22 | 16 | 22 | $7

East 70s | 422 E. 75th St. (bet. 1st & York Aves.) | 718-782-0332
Williamsburg | 328 Bedford Ave. (S. 2nd St.) | Brooklyn | 718-782-0332
Williamsburg | 133 Roebling St. (4th St.) | Brooklyn | 718-782-0332
www.oslocoffee.com

"Reawaken the five senses" with "delicious" brews from roasted-in-house beans at these "cool" Williamsburg-born coffee bars; "plain-and-simple" setups staffed by "fun baristas", they're reliable neighborhood stops when you're "on the go."

Osteria al Doge *Italian*   21 | 18 | 20 | $52

West 40s | 142 W. 44th St. (bet. B'way & 6th Ave.) | 212-944-3643 | www.osteria-doge.com

Exuding "old-world charm", this Times Square duplex rolls out "tasty" Venetian standards at a "reasonable-for-Midtown" price; the space is "cozy" (even if some say it "could use a face-lift"), while the "speedy" staff "gets you to the theater on time."

Osteria Laguna *Italian*

22 | **19** | **20** | **$47**

East 40s | 209 E. 42nd St. (bet. 2nd & 3rd Aves.) | 212-557-0001 | www.osteria-laguna.com

Offering a "welcome" "neighborhood feel in a non-neighborhood area", this "busy" Italian parked between Grand Central and the U.N. serves "straight-ahead" Venetian eats at relatively "reasonable" rates; it's a "perfect lunch spot for on-the-go execs", with a "people-watching" bonus when the French doors are open.

Osteria Morini *Italian*

26 | **20** | **23** | **$62**

SoHo | 218 Lafayette St. (bet. Broome & Spring Sts.) | 212-965-8777 | www.osteriamorini.com

Chef Michael White "goes bohemian" at this "boisterous" SoHo Italian where the "rustic" Emilia-Romagna menu is highlighted by "sublime pastas"; it's "not cheap", and can feel "crammed" at prime times, but there's a reason why it's "always busy."

Otto *Italian/Pizza*

22 | **19** | **19** | **$43**

Greenwich Village | 1 Fifth Ave. (8th St.) | 212-995-9559 | www.ottopizzeria.com

"Energetic" to say the least, this "happening" enoteca/pizzeria from the Batali-Bastianich crew lures "lots of families" and "NYU students" with "fantastic" pizzas and pastas, a "huge wine list" and "decent prices"; it's a perennially "packed", "fun, loud" scene – especially in the "Italian train station"-themed front bar.

Ovelia *Greek*

23 | **18** | **19** | **$31**

Astoria | 34-01 30th Ave. (34th St.) | Queens | 718-721-7217 | www.ovelia-ny.com

A "go-to" for Astorians seeking "Greek chic", this bar/eatery offers "fresh" Hellenic specialties with a "modern twist", including housemade sausages; "hospitable" owners, modest tabs and a "casual", "pleasant" setting with outdoor seating help keep it "popular."

Ovest Pizzoteca *Pizza*

∇ **23** | **18** | **17** | **$34**

Chelsea | 513 W. 27th St. (bet. 10th & 11th Aves.) | 212-967-4392 | www.ovestnyc.com

"Fantastic" wood-oven pizza that tastes "like Naples" is the specialty of this West Chelsea "neighborhood" pie parlor, a cousin of Luzzo's that also offers pastas and panini; "appropriate" tabs and a "relaxed" vibe tempt regulars to "hang out" well into the night.

NEW O Ya *Japanese*

– | – | – | VE

Murray Hill | Park South Hotel | 120 E. 28th St. (Lexington Ave.) | 212-204-0200 | www.o-ya.restaurant

A much-acclaimed Boston favorite lands in Murray Hill's Park South Hotel via this new, big-ticket Japanese, where the set-price omakase menus start at $185 for an 18-course, two-hour-long extravaganza; the modern, wood-lined setting is an exercise in Zen, with exposed-brick walls, artful lighting and an extended sushi bar.

Oyster Bar *Seafood*

22 | **18** | **18** | **$52**

East 40s | Grand Central | 89 E. 42nd St., Lower Level (Park Ave.) | 212-490-6650 | www.oysterbarny.com

continued

Oyster Bar Brooklyn *Seafood*

Park Slope | 256 Fifth Ave. (bet. Carroll St. & Garfield Pl.) | Brooklyn |
347-294-0596 | www.oysterbarbrooklyn-hub.com

"Historic" is the word on this 1913-vintage seafood mecca in Grand
Central's lower level serving "divine" bivalves and "classic" pan roasts
in a "glorious" setting outfitted with arched tile ceilings, long counters
and an "old-school" rear saloon; surveyors find the 2013 Park Slope
replica rather "underwhelming" in comparison, though the menu is as
"pricey" as the mother ship.

Pachanga Patterson *Mexican*

▽ 24 | 20 | 22 | $34

Astoria | 33-17 31st Ave. (bet. 33rd & 34th Sts.) | Queens |
718-554-0525 | www.pachangapatterson.com

A "not-so-hidden gem" in Astoria, this "hip" Mexican from the Vesta
folks puts a "cool spin" on tacos and other classics – but some say the sophisticated cocktails are its real "strong suit"; "multicolored string lights
and candles" enliven its "low-key" interior, while the "sunny" backyard
is a warm-weather "find."

Pacificana *Chinese*

24 | 15 | 16 | $28

Sunset Park | 813 55th St. (8th Ave.) | Brooklyn | 718-871-2880 |
www.sunset-park.com

"Delicious" dim sum draws "throngs" to this 500-seat, "you're-in-Hong
Kong" Sunset Park banquet hall, where a well-priced Cantonese menu
backs up what's on the "rolling carts"; on weekends it's a "madhouse"
packed with "big, multigenerational parties", but "be patient" –
it's "worth the wait."

Pagani *Italian*

20 | 19 | 21 | $52

West Village | 289 Bleecker St. (7th Ave. S.) | 212-488-5800 |
www.paganinyc.com

"They know what they're doing" at this "unpretentious" West Village
Italian, where "helpful" servers deliver an "interesting array" of "well-
thought-out" pastas and small plates; since it's also "reasonably priced",
the "biggest issue" is "knowing when to stop ordering."

The Palm *Steak*

25 | 19 | 23 | $81

TriBeCa | 206 West St. (bet. Chambers & Warren Sts.) | 646-395-6393
West 50s | 250 W. 50th St. (bet. B'way & 8th Ave.) | 212-333-7256

Palm Too *Steak*

East 40s | 840 Second Ave. (bet. 44th & 45th Sts.) | 212-697-5198
www.thepalm.com

"Everything's outsized" at these "upscale" links of the national
steakhouse chain where "ginormous" chops and "huge lobsters"
are dispatched in "old-school", caricature-adorned digs by a "professional" team; although the tabs run "pricey", for most it's a "classic
NY experience" that "shouldn't be missed"; P.S. the 1926 original at
837 Second Avenue has closed.

Palma *Italian*

24 | 25 | 23 | $60

West Village | 28 Cornelia St. (bet. Bleecker & 4th Sts.) | 212-691-2223 |
www.palmanyc.com

Italian food made with "loving care" tastes like "nonna's" at this "charming" West Villager with a "like-you're-in-Italy" vibe; its "lovely garden" is a "summer favorite", the private party–only carriage house is "perfect for a special occasion" and there's also a next-door wine bar, Aperitivo Di Palma.

Palm Court *American*   23 | 25 | 23 | $77
West 50s | Plaza Hotel | 768 Fifth Ave. (59th St.) | 212-546-5300 | www.theplazany.com
"Pomp and circumstance" is alive and well at this "gracious classic" in the Plaza Hotel, where chef Geoffrey Zakarian offers breakfast, afternoon tea and nighttime cocktails and American snacks; regulars say the "opulent" decor – an elaborate skylight, potted palms, a new oval bar – is just as breathtaking as the "Gilded Age" pricing.

Pampano *Mexican/Seafood*   24 | 21 | 21 | $56
East 40s | 209 E. 49th St., 2nd fl. (bet. 2nd & 3rd Aves.) | 212-751-4545
Pampano Taqueria *Mexican*
East 40s | Crystal Pavilion | 805 Third Ave. (bet. 49th & 50th Sts.) | 212-751-5257
www.richardsandoval.com
Coastal Mexican cuisine "hits the high notes" at this "upscale" East Midtown seafooder from chef Richard Sandoval and tenor Plácido Domingo, set in a "modern", white-on-white duplex; in a nearby underground food court lies the semi-"secret" Taqueria, slinging tacos and guac at lunchtime.

Pam Real Thai Food *Thai*   23 | 8 | 16 | $28
West 40s | 404 W. 49th St. (bet. 9th & 10th Aves.) | 212-333-7500 | www.pamrealthaifood.com
"Real-deal" Thai food, "spiced to your taste", comes via a "speedy" staff at this cash-only Hell's Kitchen "favorite" that makes an "excellent pre-theater" choice; the interior is "kinda dumpy", but to most that's "worth tolerating" given pricing that's among the area's "best values."

Paola's *Italian*   24 | 19 | 22 | $70
East 90s | Wales Hotel | 1295 Madison Ave. (92nd St.) | 212-794-1890 | www.paolasrestaurant.com
As a "sophisticated" haunt for "ritzy" Upper Eastsiders, this "attractive" Carnegie Hill Italian wins favor with *delizioso* cuisine and "hospitality" via the "gracious" eponymous owner and her "tip-top" staff; wallet-watchers dub it "Payola's" – but it's "thriving" (and "loud") for a reason.

Papaya King *Hot Dogs*   22 | 8 | 15 | $10
East 80s | 179 E. 86th St. (3rd Ave.) | 212-369-0648
East Village | 3 St. Marks Pl. (bet. 2nd & 3rd Aves.) | 646-692-8482
www.papayaking.com
"Easier than a trip to Coney Island", these wiener wonderlands supply "happiness in a tube" via "damn fine" hot dogs and papaya drinks on the "cheap" (even for "fast food"); OK, you're "not going for the ambiance", but as an "only-in-NYC-baby" experience, "nothing beats" 'em.

Pappardella *Italian*   21 | 17 | 19 | $49
West 70s | 316 Columbus Ave. (75th St.) | 212-595-7996 | www.pappardella.com
This "inviting" UWS "neighborhood joint" is "long established" as a "not-too-expensive" fallback for "tasty pastas" and other "solid" Italian

standards; whether you "relax" indoors or sit outside and take in the Columbus Avenue scene, count on "no pressure."

🆕 Pardon My French *French* ▽ 27 | 27 | 26 | $41

East Village | 103 Ave. B (7th St.) | 212-358-9683 | www.pmf.nyc
A remake of Casimir by the same owners, this New Wave French bistro in the East Village is "just as good, if not better", offering "delicious" small plates and upscale entrees until the wee hours, as well as a bottomless weekend brunch; the "inviting", softly lit setting "oozes charm" and now includes a tiled communal table and spiffy cocktail bar.

Paris Cafe *Pub Food* ▽ 18 | 19 | 21 | $31

South Street Seaport | 119 South St. (Peck Slip) | 212-240-9797 | www.thepariscafenyc.com
Back following a "rebuild" necessitated by Hurricane Sandy, this long-standing Seaport remnant of "historic NY" (since 1873) "retains its character" as an "old faithful" Irish pub; the grub's "consistent", though a few say it has a "glorious past, but not much of a present."

The Park *Mediterranean* 19 | 24 | 17 | $39

Chelsea | 118 10th Ave. (bet. 17th & 18th Sts.) | 212-352-3313 | www.theparknyc.com
A "beautiful" multitiered setting is the draw at this Chelsea vet that's a "relaxing" stop "before or after the High Line" thanks to its "fantastic" year-round garden "dressed up like Central Park"; the Med fare is just "OK", but it's a relative "bargain" compared to "higher-priced neighbors."

Park Avenue Spring/Summer/ Autumn/Winter *American* 25 | 26 | 24 | $70

Flatiron | 360 Park Ave. S. (26th St.) | 212-951-7111 | www.parkavenyc.com
Set in an "airy" Flatiron space, this "smooth" New American "keeps things fresh" with an "inspiring menu" and "transporting", AvroKO-conceived decor that both change quarterly to reflect the four seasons; it's "not cheap", but compensations include a "first-rate" staff and a "thoughtful wine list."

Park Side *Italian* 25 | 20 | 23 | $53

Corona | 107-01 Corona Ave. (bet. 51st Ave. & 108th St.) | Queens | 718-271-9321 | www.parksiderestaurantny.com
"Local color" abounds at this "Corona landmark" beloved for its "old-school" Italian cooking and "energetic" following, from "politicians" to "goodfellas"; with "valet parking", "plentiful" portions and "classy" "waiters in tuxes", it "rivals Arthur Avenue" – down to the "bocce games in the park across the street."

Parlor Steakhouse *Steak* 21 | 20 | 21 | $57

East 80s | 1600 Third Ave. (90th St.) | 212-423-5888 | www.parlorsteakhouse.com
"One of the few decent options above 86th Street", this "much-needed" Carnegie Hill steakhouse serves "quality" surf 'n' turf in a "lovely" modern setting; a "hopping bar scene" and convenience to the 92nd Street Y compensate for the "pricey" tabs.

Parm *Italian/Sandwiches* 21 | 15 | 17 | $37

🆕 **Battery Park City** | 250 Vesey St. (North End Ave.) | 212-776-4927
NoLita | 248 Mulberry St. (bet. Prince & Spring Sts.) | 212-993-7189

continued

NEW West 70s | 235 Columbus Ave. (71st St.) | 212-776-4921
www.parmnyc.com

This Italian-American mini-chain from the Torrisi crew supplies a "limited", "Carbone-lite" menu highlighted by its "full-throttle" namesake, offered in chicken, meatball and eggplant iterations; "tight quarters" and "long waits" make planned spin-offs in Barclays Center and Williamsburg all the more welcome.

Parma *Italian*

21	14	21	$61

East 70s | 1404 Third Ave. (80th St.) | 212-535-3520 | www.parmanyc.com
This longtime UES Italian is a bastion of "hearty" cooking delivered by a seasoned staff that's clearly "there to please"; maybe it's "pricey" and "not much to look at", but it just "feels right" to loyal patrons.

Pascalou *French*

22	15	21	$46

East 90s | 1308 Madison Ave. (bet. 92nd & 93rd Sts.) | 212-534-7522 | www.pascalou.info
So long as you don't mind sitting "elbow-to-elbow", this UES vet is "dependable" for "authentic" French fare served in the "tiniest" space; a "welcoming" vibe and "cost-conscious" tabs – "especially the early-bird" – are additional bonuses.

Pasha *Turkish*

22	19	21	$45

West 70s | 70 W. 71st St. (bet. Columbus Ave. & CPW) | 212-579-8751 | www.pashanewyork.com
It's a bit like being "magically transported" to the "Bosphorus" at this "sedate" UWS retreat where "fine" Turkish staples are enhanced by "attentive" service and "civilized" surroundings; adherents applaud it as a "fairly priced" fallback near Lincoln Center.

Pasquale Rigoletto *Italian*

22	17	21	$43

Arthur Avenue/Belmont | 2311 Arthur Ave. (184th St.) | Bronx | 718-365-6644 | www.pasqualesrigoletto.com
For an "authentic Bronx experience", try this Arthur Avenue "landmark" offering "generous" helpings of "real Italian" classics seasoned with "a lot of local color"; it's a post-Yankee game "favorite", though it might be time for a decor "makeover."

Pastrami Queen *Deli/Kosher*

23	6	16	$27

East 70s | 1125 Lexington Ave. (78th St.) | 212-734-1500 | www.pastramiqueen.com
"Outstanding pastrami" is the claim to fame of this "terrific" UES deli that's the "real thing" for "overstuffed sandwiches" and other kosher "basics done right"; seating is "almost an afterthought" in its "cramped, dingy" space, so regulars say "takeout is best."

Patricia's *Italian*

23	19	21	$35

Morris Park | 1082 Morris Park Ave. (bet. Haight & Lurting Aves.) | Bronx | 718-409-9069 | www.patriciasnyc.com
Bronx-based boosters of this Morris Park Italian say it "satisfies" any hankering for "solid" "homestyle cooking" and "excellent" wood-fired pizzas; "comfortable, relatively quiet" environs, "friendly" service and good "bang for the buck" round out the "dependable" picture.

	FOOD	DECOR	SERVICE	COST

Patsy's *Italian* — 21 | 17 | 21 | $60

West 50s | 236 W. 56th St. (bet. B'way & 8th Ave.) | 212-247-3491 |
www.patsys.com

It "doesn't get more old-school" than this 1944-vintage Midtown "throw-back", a "favorite of Sinatra's" that still purveys "delicious" Neapolitan cooking and "quality service"; maybe it could stand a "refresh", but the "heaping" portions and Theater District proximity are fine as is.

Patsy's Pizzeria *Pizza* — 20 | 12 | 16 | $27

Chelsea | 318 W. 23rd St. (bet. 8th & 9th Aves.) | 646-486-7400 |
www.patsyspizzeria.us
East 40s | 801 Second Ave. (43rd St.) | 212-878-9600 |
www.patsyspizzeria.us
East 60s | 1279 First Ave. (69th St.) | 212-639-1000 |
www.patsyspizzerianewyork.com
East 60s | 206 E. 60th St. (bet. 2nd & 3rd Aves.) | 212-688-9707 |
www.patsyspizzerianewyork.com
East Harlem | 2287 First Ave. (bet. 117th & 118th Sts.) | 212-534-9783 |
www.thepatsyspizza.com
Greenwich Village | 67 University Pl. (bet. 10th & 11th Sts.) |
212-533-3500 | www.patsyspizzeria.us
West 70s | 61 W. 74th St. (bet. Columbus Ave. & CPW) | 212-579-3000 |
www.patsyspizzeria.us
NEW **Park Slope** | 450 Dean St. (Flatbush Ave.) | Brooklyn |
718-622-2268

"Long-standing in the NY pizza wars", the circa-1933 East Harlem pie parlor and its separately owned spin-offs continue to turn out "yummy, thin-crust" versions at "easy-on-the-wallet" prices; die-hard fans say "the original's best", though all locations share "generic" decor and barely "decent service."

Paul & Jimmy's *Italian* — 20 | 17 | 22 | $53

Gramercy Park | 123 E. 18th St. (Irving Pl.) | 212-475-9540 |
www.paulandjimmys.com

"They know what they're doing" at this "been-there-for-ages" Gramercy Italian where a "welcoming" crew delivers "solid", "old-school" staples; it's particularly "appreciated" by locals since the lunch and dinner prix fixes are quite the "deal."

Paulie Gee's *Pizza* — 27 | 22 | 22 | $28

Greenpoint | 60 Greenpoint Ave. (bet. Franklin & West Sts.) | Brooklyn |
347-987-3747 | www.pauliegee.com

"Stellar pizza" is the signature of this Greenpoint joint, where the "unique" wood-fired Neapolitan pies merge "slightly charred" crusts with "delectable" topping options fit for either "omnivores or vegans"; "Paulie's always making the rounds" in the "dark, cozy" setting.

Peacefood Café *Kosher/Vegan/Vegetarian* — 24 | 18 | 20 | $26

Greenwich Village | 41 E. 11th St. (bet. B'way & University Pl.) |
212-979-2288
West 80s | 460 Amsterdam Ave. (82nd St.) | 212-362-2266
www.peacefoodcafe.com

"Fresh, creative" (and kosher) "vegan deliciousness" – including "awesome chickpea fries" and "terrific baked goods" – keeps "health-conscious" types returning to these "relaxed" neighborhood joints;

though service may be "spacey", the "affordable" tabs and "guilt-free" feeling are fine as is.

<table>
<tr><td></td><td align="right">FOOD</td><td align="right">DECOR</td><td align="right">SERVICE</td><td align="right">COST</td></tr>
</table>

Peaches *Southern* | 24 | 20 | 20 | $28 |

Bedford-Stuyvesant | 393 Lewis Ave. (MacDonough St.) | Brooklyn | 718-942-4162

Peaches HotHouse *Southern*

Bedford-Stuyvesant | 415 Tompkins Ave. (Hancock St.) | Brooklyn | 718-483-9111

www.bcrestaurantgroup.com

Easier than keeping "granny in the kitchen all day", these Bed-Stuy "local beacons" win "three thumbs up" for their "delicious" Southern staples; whether for "delightful" platters at Peaches or "spicy" fried chicken at The HotHouse, they're "well worth" the frequent wait.

The Peacock *British* | 22 | 23 | 22 | $64 |

Murray Hill | William Hotel | 24 E. 39th St. (bet. Madison & Park Aves.) | 646-837-6776 | www.thepeacocknyc.com

The "old-money" ambiance is in keeping with the "proper" "upscale" British fare served at this "classy" space in Midtown's William Hotel; the setup includes two dining rooms plus an "old-school pub" experience downstairs at The Shakespeare.

Peanut Butter & Co. *Sandwiches* | 22 | 16 | 21 | $14 |

Greenwich Village | 240 Sullivan St. (bet. Bleecker & 3rd Sts.) | 212-677-3995 | www.ilovepeanutbutter.com

"Kitschy" is the word on this Village niche "celebrating peanut butter in all its glory" with sandwiches spanning the "classics" to "concoctions you'd never think of" ("the Elvis should be on everyone's bucket list"); it's "fun for the kids", though the "bare-bones" digs can be a bit of a "squeeze."

Pearl & Ash *American* | 24 | 19 | 21 | $76 |

NoLita | 220 Bowery (bet. Prince & Spring Sts.) | 212-837-2370 | www.pearlandash.com

While the "original" New American small plates are "exciting" (if a bit "sparse") at this "trendy" Bowery hideaway, the "true find" is its "jumbo" wine list with countless "back vintages" decanted by "personable" staffers; a "cool clientele" keeps the slender room "buzzy", so expect "moderate noise."

Pearl Oyster Bar *New England/Seafood* | 27 | 16 | 21 | $51 |

West Village | 18 Cornelia St. (bet. Bleecker & 4th Sts.) | 212-691-8211 | www.pearloysterbar.com

"Succulent lobster rolls" to "swoon" over lead the lineup of "primo" New England seafood at this ever-"popular" West Village "treasure" from Rebecca Charles; "small" dimensions and a no-reservations rule make it "hard to get in", so savvier sorts go early to beat the lines.

Pearl Room *Seafood* | ▽ 20 | 19 | 21 | $57 |

Bay Ridge | 8201 Third Ave. (82nd St.) | Brooklyn | 718-833-6666 | www.thepearlroom.com

"As fancy as it gets in Bay Ridge", this seafaring "surprise" provides "excellent preparations" of "fresh" marine cuisine served by an "attentive" crew; factor in a white-tablecloth setting suitable for "romantic" encounters and "celebrations", and it's no surprise the tab can skew "pricey."

	FOOD	DECOR	SERVICE	COST

Peasant *Italian*
24 | **24** | **21** | **$56**

NoLita | 194 Elizabeth St. (bet. Prince & Spring Sts.) | 212-965-9511 |
www.peasantnyc.com

From the "warm", rustic setting to the "fabulous", wood-fired cuisine,
this "unforgettable" Italian "outshines" many of its NoLita neighbors;
"romantic" types on a "dinner date" finish up the meal in the "civilized"
cellar wine bar for after-dinner drinks.

Peking Duck House *Chinese*
23 | **14** | **18** | **$47**

Chinatown | 28 Mott St. (bet. Chatham Sq. & Pell St.) | 212-227-1810
East 50s | 236 E. 53rd St. (bet. 2nd & 3rd Aves.) | 212-759-8260
www.pekingduckhousenyc.com

With its "juicy" meat and "savory, crispy skin", the signature Peking duck
carved tableside is a "real treat" at these "old-fashioned" Chinese eateries; decor and service may be somewhat "lacking", but "wine lovers"
applaud the BYO policy at the Chinatown location.

Pellegrino's *Italian*
24 | **19** | **22** | **$52**

Little Italy | 138 Mulberry St. (bet. Grand & Hester Sts.) | 212-226-3177 |
www.pellegrinosristorante.com

"High-quality" "red-sauce" cooking and "personal service" foster the
"happy ambiance" at this Little Italy "winner"; regulars prefer sitting
outside and taking in the only-in-NY Mulberry Street "scene."

Penelope *American*
22 | **18** | **18** | **$29**

Murray Hill | 159 Lexington Ave. (30th St.) | 212-481-3800 |
www.penelopenyc.com

Murray Hill locals tout this "adorable" neighborhood "favorite" for "fab",
"comfort"-oriented New Americana at a "reasonable cost" served in a
"country-cafe" setting; there's "high demand" for the "amazing brunch",
so bring "patience" to deal with the inevitable "waits."

The Penrose *American*
22 | **22** | **18** | **$34**

East 80s | 1590 Second Ave. (bet. 82nd & 83rd Sts.) | 212-203-2751 |
www.penrosebar.com

A "hip spot" in the "otherwise unhip Upper East Side", this "lively" gastropub lures "younger" types with a "trendy" scene fueled by "delicious
burgers" and other "enjoyable" American bar bites; a "Brooklyn vibe" and
"rustic" looks make it a "welcome alternative" in the neighborhood.

Pepe Giallo *Italian*
23 | **16** | **20** | **$25**

Chelsea | 253 Tenth Ave. (25th St.) | 212-242-6055 |
www.pepegiallo.com

Pepe Rosso Social *Italian*
Little Italy | 173 Mott St. (Broome St.) | 212-219-0019 |
www.peperossosocial.com

Pepe Rosso To Go *Italian*
SoHo | 149 Sullivan St. (Houston St.) | 212-677-4555 |
www.peperossotogo.com

For a "budget-conscious" "quick bite", these "friendly" Italians sling
"lotsa pasta" and other classic dishes that are "easy on the wallet"; just
be prepared for "totally unassuming" settings and so-so service.

	FOOD	DECOR	SERVICE	COST

Pepolino *Italian*

| 24 | 17 | 23 | $64 |

TriBeCa | 281 W. Broadway (bet. Canal & Lispenard Sts.) | 212-966-9983 |
www.pepolino.com

"Hiding in plain sight" on the fringes of TriBeCa, this "charming" trattoria delivers a "magic combination" of "savory" Tuscan farm cuisine and "attentive" service amid "rustic" surrounds; the experience is "not cheap", but given the "high quality", insiders still consider it a "deal."

Pera *Mediterranean*

| 21 | 22 | 19 | $53 |

East 40s | 303 Madison Ave. (bet. 41st & 42nd Sts.) | 212-878-6301 |
www.peranyc.com

SoHo | 54 Thompson St. (bet. Broome & Spring Sts.) | 212-878-6305 |
www.soho.peranyc.com

These "attractive" eateries make "civilized" choices for Turkish-accented Mediterranean fare – including a "lovely range" of meze – served in "modern" surrounds; the Midtown original is a "no-brainer for business", while the stylin' SoHo spin-off sports a "stunning outdoor deck."

Perilla *American*

| 24 | 19 | 22 | $65 |

West Village | 9 Jones St. (bet. Bleecker & W. 4th Sts.) | 212-929-6868 |
www.perillanyc.com

Harold Dieterle's first restaurant, this snug West Villager still "delivers on its star-chef reputation" with "creative" New American standards (witness the "glory that is the spicy duck meatball") served by a "polished" staff; an "intimate" feel and "reasonable" prices "for the quality" make it a "spot-on" choice.

Periyali *Greek*

| 24 | 20 | 23 | $60 |

Flatiron | 35 W. 20th St. (bet. 5th & 6th Aves.) | 212-463-7890 |
www.periyali.com

"Dependably rewarding" since 1987, this Flatiron "Greek classic" remains a "refined" refuge for "superb fresh fish" and "gracious service" in "soothing", "not-too-loud" surrounds; "upscale" admirers attest the "like-you're-in-Greece" experience is "worth the high price."

Perla *Italian*

| 23 | 20 | 21 | $68 |

Greenwich Village | 24 Minetta Ln. (bet. MacDougal St. & 6th Ave.) |
212-933-1824 | www.perlanyc.com

"Righteous" pastas and other "rustic" plates are a "pure delight" at this "cozy" Village Italian from restaurateur Gabe Stulman, now offering a lighter seasonal menu; a "charming" crew ratchets up the "warm feelings" at this "crazy-busy" scene, so it's "worth a try" to snag a table.

Perry St. *American*

| 26 | 25 | 26 | $79 |

West Village | 176 Perry St. (West St.) | 212-352-1900 |
www.perrystrestaurant.com

"Another Jean-Georges gem", this high-end West Villager sees chef Cedric Vongerichten continue the family legacy ("like father, like son") with "top-notch" New American cuisine served by a "pro" staff in a "modern" Richard Meier–designed space opposite the Hudson River; sure, it's "expensive and a little out of the way", but most feel this "memorable" experience is "well worth" it.

More on zagat.com

	FOOD	DECOR	SERVICE	COST

Per Se American/French
28 | 27 | 28 | $341

West 50s | Time Warner Ctr. | 10 Columbus Circle (bet. 58th & 60th Sts.) | 212-823-9335 | www.perseny.com

"Still over-the-top magnificent", Thomas Keller's French–New American "milestone" in the Time Warner Center offers an "incomparable" chance to savor an "exquisite" nine-course tasting menu along with "well-choreographed" service, "ultraplush decor" and "breathtaking" park views; while the $310 set price "will get your attention" ("ka-ching!"), the lounge provides "excellent" à la carte small plates at less astronomical rates.

Persepolis Persian
23 | 17 | 20 | $42

East 70s | 1407 Second Ave. (bet. 73rd & 74th Sts.) | 212-535-1100 | www.persepolisnewyork.com

A "standout" among the "few Persians" in town, this Upper Eastsider offers "interesting", "well-spiced" Iranian dishes (the signature "sour-cherry rice is a treat") in an "understated" milieu; given the "personal service" and overall "value", it's "easy to relax and enjoy" here.

Pescatore Italian
21 | 16 | 21 | $46

East 50s | 955 Second Ave. (51st St.) | 212-752-7151 | www.pescatorerestaurant.com

Eastsiders count on this "reliable" "local Italian" thanks to its "plentiful" portions of fish and pasta that are "surprisingly good for the price"; with its "pleasant" service, "homey" feel and sidewalk seats, some call it a "sleeper" date place.

Peter Luger Steak House Steak
28 | 17 | 22 | $88

Williamsburg | 178 Broadway (Driggs Ave.) | Brooklyn | 718-387-7400 | www.peterluger.com

Voted NYC's No. 1 steakhouse for the 32nd year in a row, this 1887-vintage Williamsburg chop shop remains a "long-standing Brooklyn tradition" thanks to its "sublime" steaks and "outstanding" sides; "no-nonsense" service and "German-beer-hall" decor ratchet up its "throwback" allure, but make sure to "bring plenty of cash" (it doesn't take plastic) and, above all, "never mention the words 'well done.'"

Petite Abeille Belgian
19 | 16 | 17 | $31

Flatiron | 44 W. 17th St. (bet. 5th & 6th Aves.) | 212-727-2989
Stuyvesant Town/Peter Cooper Village | 401 E. 20th St. (1st Ave.) | 212-727-1505
www.petiteabeille.com

"Tasty" moules frites and other "hearty" Belgian classics pair with a "vast" beer selection at these "unpretentious" "neighborhood" bistros that double as "favorite" brunch fallbacks; they're hard to beat for "casual, low-key" dining, "especially for the price."

Petrossian Continental/French
24 | 24 | 23 | $93

West 50s | 182 W. 58th St. (7th Ave.) | 212-245-2214 | www.petrossian.com

"Caviar is king" at this "formal" art deco "classic" near Carnegie Hall where the staff "never rushes you" and the "very expensive" French-Continental menu includes some "bargain prix fixe" options for the non–"hedge fund guys"; there's also a "little cafe next door" perfect for a "quick bite."

	FOOD	DECOR	SERVICE	COST

Philippe *Chinese*
22 | 19 | 20 | $66

East 60s | 33 E. 60th St. (bet. Madison & Park Aves.) | 212-644-8885 | www.philippechow.com

"Low-lit and high-class", this East Side Chinese channels "Mr. Chow" with "well-crafted" cuisine served to a "glamorous" crowd in digs that turn "cacophonous" when going full tilt (the back room's more "chill"); skeptics shrug the scene's "better than the food" and note that the $24 prix fixe lunch is one way around the "sky-high" tabs.

Pho Bang *Noodle Shop/Vietnamese*
23 | 9 | 14 | $15

Little Italy | 157 Mott St. (bet. Broome & Grand Sts.) | 212-966-3797
Elmhurst | 82-90 Broadway (bet. 45th & Whitney Aves.) | Queens | 718-205-1500
Flushing | 41-07 Kissena Blvd. (bet. Barclay & 41st Aves.) | Queens | 718-939-5520

"Just as the name says", these "no-nonsense" Vietnamese joints cater to "pho phans" with "delicious" soup bowls and a "big bang for the buck"; otherwise they're "dingy" setups where the staffers "could be a little more courteous."

Phoenix Garden *Chinese*
23 | 11 | 16 | $37

East 40s | 242 E. 40th St. (bet. 2nd & 3rd Aves.) | 212-983-6666 | www.phoenixgardennyc.com

"Solid" Cantonese cooking and the "added benefit" of a BYO policy make this "unassuming" Midtown vet a "real find" ("save yourself a trip to Chinatown"); fans overlook the "attitude", "dreary decor" and cash-only policy because you can't beat the "value."

Piccola Venezia *Italian*
26 | 18 | 24 | $63

Astoria | 42-01 28th Ave. (42nd St.) | Queens | 718-721-8470 | www.piccola-venezia.com

"You name it, they prepare it" at this venerable Astoria "charmer", where the "menu's only a suggestion" and the "traditional" Northern Italian dishes are "impeccably" rendered; it's "a little pricey" given the "dated" decor, but "personalized service" ensures everyone feels "like family."

Piccolo Angolo *Italian*
26 | 14 | 23 | $50

West Village | 621 Hudson St. (Jane St.) | 212-229-9177 | www.piccoloangolo.com

A longtime West Village "family operation" that still "holds its own", this "old-school" Northern Italian consistently "wows" with its "excellent homestyle" cooking and "mama-loves-you" service; the "close", "no-frills" quarters are "always crowded", so "definitely have a reservation."

Piccolo Cafe *Coffee/Italian*
 22 | 16 | 20 | $27

Gramercy Park | 157 Third Ave. (bet. 15th & 16th Sts.) | 212-260-1175
Murray Hill | 238 Madison Ave. (37th St.) | 212-447-4399
West 40s | 274 W. 40th St. (8th Ave.) | 212-302-0143
West 70s | 313 Amsterdam Ave. (bet. 74th & 75th Sts.) | 212-873-0962
www.piccolocafe.us

These "cheerful" cafes are linked to an Italy-based coffee roaster, so count on espresso from imported beans and "real Italian" bites including "delicious" pastas and panini; just don't expect much seating because, as the name implies, they're "teensy-weensy."

	FOOD	DECOR	SERVICE	COST

Picholine *French/Mediterranean* — 26 | 24 | 26 | $120

West 60s | 35 W. 64th St. (bet. B'way & CPW) | 212-724-8585 |
www.picholinenyc.com

For "fine dining at its finest" in a locale "handy to Lincoln Center", Terry Brennan's "civilized" French-Med "classic" is "top-tier" "from soup to nuts", as "meticulous" servers set down "exquisite" dishes winding up with a "one-of-a-kind" cheese course; it's a haven of "subtle elegance", but the privilege is "expensive, so be prepared."

NEW Pier A Harbor House *American* — ▽ 18 | 24 | 18 | $41

Battery Park City | 22 Battery Pl. (Little West St.) | 212-785-0153 |
www.piera.com

A repurposed, 1886-vintage pier in Battery Park City is now one of the city's "coolest new venues", a sprawling megaplex offering drinks and snacks on the street level and a warren of fine-dining rooms on the second floor; though the pricey New American "menu still needs work", there's nothing wrong with its "amazing views" of the FiDi and the harbor.

Pies-N-Thighs *Southern* — 24 | 17 | 19 | $25

NEW Lower East Side | 43 Canal St. (Ludlow St.) | 212-431-7437
Williamsburg | 166 S. Fourth St. (Driggs Ave.) | Brooklyn | 347-529-6090
www.piesnthighs.com

"Come hungry" to these "homey" pit stops for "crunchy", "moist" fried chicken, pies "like heaven" and other "scrumptious" Southern staples that may prompt you to "join a gym afterwards"; both the "cramped", "no-frills" Williamsburg original and its LES spin-off "get busy quickly", so "expect to wait awhile."

Pietro's *Italian/Steak* — 23 | 15 | 22 | $72

East 40s | 232 E. 43rd St. (bet. 2nd & 3rd Aves.) | 212-682-9760 |
www.pietrosnyc.com

In the Grand Central area since 1932, this "old-school" holdout rests its rep on "excellent steaks" and "superior" Italian basics served in "copious amounts" by a "gracious", "been-there-for-years" staff; the room's "not glamorous", but "loyal" regulars appreciate the "quiet" vibe – or more "lively" times at its "great bar."

Pig and Khao *SE Asian* — 26 | 16 | 21 | $40

Lower East Side | 68 Clinton St. (bet. Rivington & Stanton Sts.) |
212-920-4485 | www.pigandkhao.com

The "adventurous will be rewarded" at chef Leah Cohen's "offbeat" LES Southeast Asian where "tongue-tingling" Thai and Filipino flavors inspire an "innovative array" of pork-centric dishes (e.g. "mouthwatering sisig") that make for "happy sharing"; "good-deal" pricing helps keep the patio-equipped space "bustling."

Pig Heaven *Chinese* — 20 | 15 | 18 | $40

East 80s | 1420 Third Ave. (bet. 80th & 81 Sts.) | 212-744-4333 |
www.pigheavennyc.com

"If pig is what you want", this UES Chinese "favorite" run by "gracious" Nancy Lee is "heaven indeed" for "anything pork-related", with a lineup showcasing its "signature spareribs"; although it has moved a block away from its longtime original location, word is out, so expect "lots of company at the trough."

The Pines *American*

FOOD	DECOR	SERVICE	COST
25	18	22	$56

Gowanus | 284 Third Ave. (bet. Carroll & President Sts.) | Brooklyn | 718-596-6560 | www.thepinesbrooklyn.com

"Ambitious", somewhat "edgy" New American cuisine and creative cocktails draw a "hipster" crowd to this Gowanus nook that also offers a "brilliant" all-natural wine list; despite "a lot of hype", it exudes a "down-to-earth" vibe, starting with its reclaimed church pew seating.

Pine Tree Cafe *American*

FOOD	DECOR	SERVICE	COST
▽ 24	20	22	$33

Bronx Park | 2900 Southern Blvd. (Bronx Park Rd.) | Bronx | no phone | www.nybg.org

Nestled in the New York Botanical Garden, this glassed-in American cafe from Stephen Starr (Buddakan, Morimoto) supplies "quite good" sandwiches, salads, soups and such over the counter; outdoor tables make the most of the pine-enclosed real estate.

Ping's Seafood *Chinese/Seafood*

FOOD	DECOR	SERVICE	COST
22	13	15	$27

Chinatown | 22 Mott St. (bet. Chatham Sq. & Mosco St.) | 212-602-9988
Elmhurst | 8302 Queens Blvd. (Goldsmith St.) | Queens | 718-396-1238
www.pingsnyc.com

With "first-rate" seafood backed by "varied", "flavorful" dim sum, these Cantonese contenders stay "ping on target"; despite "simple" settings and "not-that-welcoming" service, they "pack 'em in", especially for that "madhouse" Sunday brunch.

Pio Pio *Chicken/Peruvian*

FOOD	DECOR	SERVICE	COST
23	15	18	$31

East 90s | 1746 First Ave. (bet. 90th & 91st Sts.) | 212-426-5800
Murray Hill | 210 E. 34th St. (bet. 2nd & 3rd Aves.) | 212-481-0034
West 40s | 604 10th Ave. (bet. 43rd & 44th Sts.) | 212-459-2929
West 90s | 702 Amsterdam Ave. (94th St.) | 212-665-3000
Mott Haven | 264 Cypress Ave. (bet. 138th & 139th Sts.) | Bronx | 718-401-3300
Jackson Heights | 84-02 Northern Blvd. (bet. 84th & 85th Sts.) | Queens | 718-426-4900
Jackson Heights | 84-21 Northern Blvd. (85th St.) | Queens | 718-426-1010
Middle Village | 62-30 Woodhaven Blvd. (bet. Dry Harbor Rd. & 62nd Dr.) | Queens | 718-458-0606
www.piopio.com

"Succulent" rotisserie chicken slathered with an "excellent" green sauce makes these "quick-and-easy" Peruvians a "popular" "go-to", particularly given the "modest price"; the "bustling" setups are "not terribly comfy" and the acoustics "abysmal", but hey, "you won't leave hungry."

Piora *American*

FOOD	DECOR	SERVICE	COST
25	24	24	$105

West Village | 430 Hudson St. (bet. Morton St. & St. Lukes Pl.) | 212-960-3801 | www.pioranyc.com

A "lovely" "find" that "buzzes with good energy", this "wonderfully inventive" New American "sleeper" in the West Village showcases Korean and Italian influences in its "perfection-on-a-plate" menu; "attentive but not intrusive" service and a "romantic" setting help distract from the "expensive" tariffs.

	FOOD	DECOR	SERVICE	COST

Piper's Kilt *Pub Food*
20 | **13** | **21** | **$28**

Inwood | 4946 Broadway (207th St.) | 212-569-7071 |
www.piperskiltofinwood.com

"Locals" gather for some of the "best burgers around" at this Inwood
"mainstay", where the "satisfying" pub fare is best chased with a "mug of
beer" or three; the "throwback" Irish bar setup accommodates "everyone
from toddlers to drunken Jets fans."

Pippali *Indian*
▽ **24** | **15** | **20** | **$35**

Murray Hill | 129 E. 27th St. (Lexington Ave.) | 212-689-1999 |
www.pippalinyc.com

Thanks to chef Peter Beck (ex Tamarind), this Curry Hill Indian
rises "a cut above" its rivals with a "terrific", "nonstandard menu" of
"regional specialties" spanning the subcontinent (and it will "adjust
the heat for the timid"); "helpful" service distracts from decor that's
the "usual" for the genre.

Pisticci *Italian*
24 | **20** | **22** | **$36**

Morningside Heights | 125 La Salle St. (B'way) | 212-932-3500 |
www.pisticcinyc.com

It "doesn't get much better for local Italian" than this "warm, homey"
Columbia-area "favorite" for "scrumptious" food at "reasonable prices"
and free "jazz on Sundays"; the "no-reservations" rule can be "a drag",
yet the "long lines" deter few.

NEW Pizza Beach *Pizza*
19 | **20** | **17** | **$39**

East 80s | 1426 Third Ave. (81st St.) | 646-666-0819 |
www.pizzabeachclub.com

Whitewashed brick, palm fronds and surfboards lend a "laid-back" SoCal
vibe to this "popular" Upper Eastsider from the brothers Martignetti
(East Pole); the health-forward menu showcases "tasty" pizzas topped
with everything from purple kale to Thai coconut curry, washed down
with a list of reasonably priced wines.

PizzArte *Pizza*
23 | **19** | **20** | **$38**

West 50s | 69 W. 55th St. (bet. 5th & 6th Aves.) | 212-247-3936 |
www.pizzarteny.com

"True" Neapolitan pizzas and "well-curated" artwork, all for sale, make
an "intriguing" combo at this Midtown Italian, also vending pastas and
more; its "modern", "bowling-lane-thin" duplex digs can feel "cramped",
but the location's hard to beat "before Carnegie Hall" or City Center.

Pizzetteria Brunetti *Pizza*
▽ **26** | **18** | **23** | **$39**

West Village | 626 Hudson St. (bet. Horatio & Jane Sts.) | 212-255-5699 |
www.pizzetteriabrunetti.com

"Wonderful" pizzas emerge from the brick oven of this West Village import from Westhampton Beach, where the "distinctive" Neapolitan pies
include a signature clam version; "warm, witty" staffers keep the mood at
the "casual", patio-equipped setting "totally relaxed."

P.J. Clarke's *Pub Food*
18 | **17** | **18** | **$43**

East 50s | 915 Third Ave. (55th St.) | 212-317-1616
P.J. Clarke's at Lincoln Square *Pub Food*
West 60s | 44 W. 63rd St. (Columbus Ave.) | 212-957-9700

continued

P.J. Clarke's on the Hudson *Pub Food*
Battery Park City | 4 World Financial Ctr. (Vesey St.) | 212-285-1500
Sidecar at P.J. Clarke's *Pub Food*
East 50s | 205 E. 55th St. (3rd Ave.) | 212-317-2044
www.pjclarkes.com

A bastion of "old NY coolness", this circa-1884 East Midtown saloon is beloved for its "first-rate" burgers and raw bar, "legendary bartenders" and all-around "fun scene"; while the newer spin-offs don't have the original's "historic" charm, Sidecar upstairs is a "speakeasy"-like "hideaway", Lincoln Center is perfect pre-show and Battery Park City boasts "lovely water views."

The Place *American/Mediterranean*   24 | 24 | 24 | $59
West Village | 310 W. Fourth St. (bet. Bank & W. 12th Sts.) | 212-924-2711 | www.theplaceny.com

"Nestled" below sidewalk level, this "quintessential West Village date spot" is "sure to impress" with its "romantic", fireplace-equipped setting, "decadent" Med–New American cooking and "warm" service; the only quibble is with the "boring name", which fans complain "doesn't do it justice."

Plaza Food Hall *Food Hall*   21 | 19 | 17 | $39
West 50s | Plaza Hotel | 1 W. 59th St., lower level (5th Ave.) | 212-986-9260 | www.theplazany.com

A "great way to graze", this "vibrant" "one-stop shop" below The Plaza provides "outstanding" Eclectic options via "varying food stations" issuing sushi, pizza, grill fare and much more; partly run by Todd English, it's plenty "popular" despite "so-so" service and "lunch counter–style" seating.

Pó *Italian*   25 | 17 | 22 | $54
West Village | 31 Cornelia St. (bet. Bleecker & 4th Sts.) | 212-645-2189 | www.porestaurant.com

Pocket-size but "charming", this "longtime" Villager remains an "absolute gem" furnishing "first-quality" Italian fare "without an ounce of pretense"; "repeat customers" confirm the "tight squeeze" is "so worth it" for "amazing" dining that "won't break the bank."

Poke *Japanese*   23 | 13 | 18 | $38
East 80s | 343 E. 85th St. (bet. 1st & 2nd Aves.) | 212-249-0569 | www.pokesushinyc.com

The "finest fish" lures UES sushiphiles to this cash-only Japanese BYO, a modest standby touted for its "creative" rolls and "off-menu" items; "affordable" rates ensure it's "always busy", even if critics take a poke at the "no-reservations policy" and "long lines."

Pok Pok NY *Thai*   26 | 17 | 21 | $41
Columbia Street Waterfront District | 117 Columbia St. (Kane St.) | Brooklyn | 718-923-9322 | www.pokpokny.com

"Every bite is a revelation" at Andy Ricker's Thai "tour de force" on the Columbia Street Waterfront, where the "delectable" regional dishes are "different from the ordinary" and "totally reasonable" costwise; it "thankfully now takes reservations", but since the place is "tiny" and very "popular", it still can be "difficult to get in."

	FOOD	DECOR	SERVICE	COST

Pok Pok Phat Thai *Thai*
▽ 25 | 16 | 20 | $33

Columbia Street Waterfront District | 127 Columbia St. (bet. Degraw & Kane Sts.) | Brooklyn | 718-923-9322 | www.pokpokny.com
A "truer"-than-usual "rendition of pad Thai" is the highlight of Andy Ricker's Columbia Street Waterfront offshoot of Pok Pok NY, which fields a "small but mighty" menu of "vibrant", noodle-centric dishes; a simple setup with garden seating, it's "more laid-back" and "less crowded" than the down-the-block sib.

NEW Polo Bar *American*
20 | 26 | 23 | $84

East 50s | 1 E. 55th St. (5th Ave.) | 212-207-8562 | www.ralphlauren.com
Designer Ralph Lauren extends his brand at this instant Midtown "scene", a magnet for "celebs", tycoons and other "fortunate" folk, who show up for the stellar "people-watching" (and "people-knowing"); the "clubby", polo-themed underground setting is quite "swellegant" even if the "expensive" American vittles are "nothing extraordinary", but it's the "exclusivity" quotient that makes snagging a reservation close to "impossible."

Pomodoro Rosso *Italian*
20 | 15 | 21 | $48

West 70s | 229 Columbus Ave. (bet. 70th & 71st Sts.) | 212-721-3009 | www.pomodororossonyc.com
It's like "mama's in the kitchen" cooking up "hearty" Italian classics at this "quaint" UWS vet near Lincoln Center that's run with "loving care"; the "quintessential neighborhood gem", it's "always busy", so make a reservation to dodge the "wait for a table."

Ponticello *Italian*
▽ 23 | 20 | 25 | $56

Astoria | 46-11 Broadway (bet. 46th & 47th Sts.) | Queens | 718-278-4514 | www.ponticelloristorante.com
Ever "reliable" since 1982, this Astoria Northern Italian boasts a "terrific" roster of "classics" served by seasoned waiters who ensure you'll be "well taken care of"; if it seems "slightly overpriced" for the "old-world" ambiance, habitués still "feel completely at home."

Ponty Bistro *African/French*
22 | 13 | 21 | $45

Gramercy Park | 218 Third Ave. (bet. 18th & 19th Sts.) | 212-777-1616
Harlem | 2375 Adam Clayton Powell Junior Blvd. (139th St.) | 212-234-6474
www.pontybistro.com
"Sparking your taste buds", this all-day Gramercy "find" offers "original" French-Senegalese dishes livened up with African spices and "charming" service; it's also "well priced" (notably the $25 early-bird), but word's "getting out" and the "narrow" room fills up fast.

Porchetta *Italian/Sandwiches*
22 | 9 | 16 | $18

East Village | 110 E. Seventh St. (bet. Ave. A & 1st Ave.) | 212-777-2151 | www.porchettanyc.com
Famed for its "crave-worthy" namesake – "divine" Italian-style roast pork sandwiches and platters – Sara Jenkins' "tiny" East Villager offers a few other options, including soup, beans and greens; the setup is "counter service with a few stools", so most do "takeout."

| | FOOD | DECOR | SERVICE | COST |

NEW Porchlight American

▽ 21 | 22 | 23 | $45

Chelsea | 271 11th Ave. (bet. 27th & 28th Sts.) | 212-981-6188 | www.porchlightbar.com

Danny Meyer's first stand-alone bar, this "happening" Way West Chelsea watering hole offers "refreshing" classic cocktails paired with "original" American bar bites; "welcoming" service lends warmth to the "spacious", industrial-chic setting, and though the snack portions may be "on the small side", it does offer full lunch service.

Pork Slope Pub Food
20 | 16 | 18 | $26

Park Slope | 247 Fifth Ave. (bet. Carroll St. & Garfield Pl.) | Brooklyn | 718-768-7675 | www.porkslopebrooklyn.com

"Elevated bar food is the idea" at chef Dale Talde's "laid-back" Park Slope saloon presenting a American pub menu with plenty of "satisfying" porky options; it also pours an "extensive" brown-liquor selection, but be aware that its roadhouselike room "gets crowded" in peak hours.

Porsena Italian
24 | 17 | 21 | $45

East Village | 21 E. Seventh St. (bet. 2nd & 3rd Aves.) | 212-228-4923 | www.porsena.com

The "knowing hand" of chef-owner Sara Jenkins elevates the "heavenly pastas" and other "delicious, straightforward" Italian staples at this "friendly" East Villager; it works as a "down-to-earth" "date spot", albeit one that's apt to be "busy" and "uninteresting" to look at.

Porter House New York Steak

26 | 26 | 26 | $95

West 50s | Time Warner Ctr. | 10 Columbus Circle (bet. 58th & 60th Sts.) | 212-823-9500 | www.porterhousenewyork.com

From "exceptional cuts of meat" to "interesting" sides, a "feast awaits" at Michael Lomonaco's Time Warner Center "destination steakhouse"; "impeccable" service helps justify the "expensive" tab, as do the "elegant" room's Central Park views that are as "impressive" as the food.

Posto Pizza

23 | 14 | 18 | $27

Gramercy Park | 310 Second Ave. (18th St.) | 212-716-1200 | www.postothincrust.com

The "thinnest", "winningest" crust is the hallmark of this Gramercy pizzeria, a "local hot spot" cranking out "splendid" pies at "accessible prices"; its "small", "publike" digs are usually "packed and noisy", so the to-go trade stays brisk.

Press 195 Sandwiches
25 | 19 | 20 | $24

Bayside | 4011 Bell Blvd. (bet. 40th & 41st Aves.) | Queens | 718-281-1950 | www.press195.com

The "hardest part is choosing" from the "extensive list" of "amazing panini" at this "casual" Bayside "favorite", but the "terrific" Belgian fries are a no-brainer; with a full bar, "fun patio" and some of the "best craft beers" in these parts, it's no wonder locals "love this place."

Prime Grill Kosher/Steak
23 | 20 | 19 | $89

East 50s | 550 Madison Ave. (bet. 55th & 56th Sts.) | 212-692-9292 | www.theprimegrill.primehospitalityny.com

"Buzzing" with a Midtown crowd, this "standard bearer" for kosher steak now in the Sony Building "impresses" with its "top-quality" beef and sushi, as well as its "beautiful" balconied setting; tabs run "expensive", but to most, the "client-worthy" experience is "worth the price."

Prime KO *Japanese/Kosher/Steak*   ▽ 22 | 20 | 19 | $79

West 80s | 217 W. 85th St. (B'way) | 212-496-1888 | www.primehospitalityny.com

Steaks "cooked to perfection" plus "delicious" sushi keep this "swank" kosher Japanese chophouse on the Upper West Side "crowded", even though the tabs are decidedly "not cheap"; service gets mixed marks, but most consider it a "fun venue", especially if you factor in "fancy cocktails."

Prime Meats *American/Steak*   24 | 21 | 21 | $58

Carroll Gardens | 465 Court St. (Luquer St.) | Brooklyn | 718-254-0327 | www.frankspm.com

The "name says it" all about this Carroll Gardens carnivore-oriented sibling of Frankies Spuntino, where "delicious", "German-inspired" American steakhouse fare arrives via a "whiskered", "über-hip" staff; the "cool, Prohibition-style" digs get "packed", so insiders "arrive early" or make advance reservations.

Primola *Italian*   22 | 17 | 20 | $71

East 60s | 1226 Second Ave. (bet. 64th & 65th Sts.) | 212-758-1775

No stranger to "Page Six" mentions, this "clubby" Italian satisfies its "moneyed UES" clientele with "dependable" pastas at "steep prices"; count on service "with a smile" if you're a regular, a "celebrity" or "wearing dark glasses", but for first-timers the "attitude" can be "intimidating."

Print *American*   24 | 24 | 23 | $62

West 40s | Ink48 Hotel | 653 11th Ave. (bet. 47th & 48th Sts.) | 212-757-2224 | www.printrestaurant.com

Way "out of the way" in West Hell's Kitchen, this "memorable" New American is a "first-rate" option for "locavoracious" fare and "smart" service in "stylish" environs; insiders have cocktails after dinner on the "rooftop lounge" with its drop-dead, 360-degree "skyline view."

Prosperity Dumpling *Chinese*   24 | 4 | 14 | $6

Lower East Side | 46 Eldridge St. (bet. Canal & Hester Sts.) | 212-343-0683 | www.prosperitydumpling.com

"Frugal foodies" find "awesome", "meaty dumplings" and other "tasty" items at this cash-only, good "bang-for-your-buck" LES Chinese; "long lines" and "haphazard" service in "utterly cramped" surrounds make the case for takeout.

NEW Prova *Pizza*   ▽ 24 | 21 | 21 | $33

Chelsea | 184 Eighth Ave. (19th St.) | 212-641-0977 | www.provanyc.com

Donatella Arpaia takes Neapolitan pizza "to the next level" at this Chelsea standout, offering "fabulous" brick-oven pies garnished with toppings so "tasty" you won't want to "leave the crusts behind"; the "energetic" space comes equipped with a state-of-the-art oven and a "secret bar" in the back.

	FOOD	DECOR	SERVICE	COST

Prune *American*

24 | 16 | 22 | $56

East Village | 54 E. First St. (bet. 1st & 2nd Aves.) | 212-677-6221 |
www.prunerestaurant.com

An "innovator that's stood the test of time", chef Gabrielle Hamilton's
East Village "standout" serves a "perfectly curated" menu of "exceptional" New American dishes in "unfailingly professional" style; the
only drawbacks are a "toooo small" room with seating "on top of your
neighbors" and long lines for the "fabulous brunch."

Public *Eclectic*

24 | 25 | 24 | $72

NoLita | 210 Elizabeth St. (bet. Prince & Spring Sts.) | 212-343-7011 |
www.public-nyc.com

"Still hot" after 10-plus years, this NoLita "mainstay" offers a "bold", "inventive" Eclectic menu that riffs on "Aussie and Kiwi cuisine", matched
with a "well-curated" wine list; its "unpretentious yet elegant" AvroKO-
designed space and "knowledgeable" staff ensure it works for everything
from brunches with friends to "romantic" dinners.

Pure Thai Cookhouse *Thai*

26 | 15 | 19 | $28

West 50s | 766 Ninth Ave. (bet. 51st & 52nd Sts.) | 212-581-0999 |
www.purethaishophouse.com

"Taste the essence of Thailand" at this "hole-in-the-wall" Hell's Kitchen
Thai that "stands out" thanks to the "bold flavors" of its "excellent noodle
dishes" and other "cheap" eats; the only downside is a "shoebox" space
with "backless stools" that's "always packed."

Purple Yam *Asian*

21 | 18 | 18 | $36

Ditmas Park | 1314 Cortelyou Rd. (bet. Argyle & Rugby Rds.) | Brooklyn |
718-940-8188 | www.purpleyamnyc.com

"Sophisticated" Pan-Asian fare with an emphasis on Filipino flavors – as
in the "signature chicken adobo" – is the "unusual", "totally approachable" specialty of this "cozy" Ditmas Park "gem"; "inexpensive" tabs are
one reason why it's generally "packed."

Pylos *Greek*

26 | 22 | 22 | $57

East Village | 128 E. Seventh St. (bet. Ave. A & 1st Ave.) | 212-473-0220 |
www.pylosrestaurant.com

"Not your run-of-the-mill Greek", this "more upscale" East Villager offers
"unbeatable" cuisine that's "lovingly prepared" and "well priced" for the
quality; with a "wonderful" team overseeing a "memorable" space boasting a ceiling lined with terra-cotta pots, it's a "real find."

Qi *Asian/Thai*

22 | 21 | 20 | $34

Flatiron | 31 W. 14th St. (bet. 5th & 6th Aves.) | 212-929-9917
West 40s | 675 Eighth Ave. (43rd St.) | 212-247-8992

Qi Thai Grill *Asian/Thai*

Williamsburg | 176 N. Ninth St. (bet. Bedford & Driggs Aves.) | Brooklyn |
718-302-1499
www.qirestaurant.com

Chef Pichet Ong delivers "well-prepared", "beautifully presented"
Asian-Thai dishes at these "trendy" contenders; "reasonable prices" belie their "glittery", "Buddhist temple"-meets-"nightclub" decor, especially
at the "hopping", "over-the-top" Theater District outlet done up in
"chandeliers and holograms."

	FOOD	DECOR	SERVICE	COST

Quality Italian *Italian/Steak*
24 | 23 | 23 | $74

West 50s | 57 W. 57th St. (6th Ave.) | 212-390-1111 |
www.qualityitalian.com

A "home run" from the folks at Quality Meats, this Midtown double-decker caters to big spenders with "memorable" steaks and Italian fare (notably the "epic chicken parm" that "looks like a pizza") served by an "accommodating" team; though the decibels in the "trendy industrial setting" are "not for an intimate meal", all that "high energy" suggests they're "doing something right" here.

Quality Meats *American/Steak*
26 | 24 | 25 | $87

West 50s | 57 W. 58th St. (bet. 5th & 6th Aves.) | 212-371-7777 |
www.qualitymeatsnyc.com

In a city populated by "classic" chop shops, this "sexy", "modern" Midtowner is a "breath of fresh air", teaming "skilled" service with a "creative" American steakhouse menu that runs the gamut from "fabulous" cuts of beef to "killer ice cream"; sure, it's something of a "splurge", but it certainly "lives up to its name."

Quantum Leap *Health Food/Vegetarian*
22 | 14 | 21 | $22

Greenwich Village | 226 Thompson St. (3rd St.) | 212-677-8050 |
www.quantumleaprestaurant.com

"One of the original" Greenwich Village health-food havens, this "small" '70s survivor supplies "tasty" vegetarian specialties and a few fish options; in keeping with the "low-key", "collegey" atmosphere, expect "laid-back" service and "affordable" tabs.

Quatorze Bis *French*
22 | 20 | 21 | $65

East 70s | 323 E. 79th St. (bet. 1st & 2nd Aves.) | 212-535-1414
"Steady" and "essential", this "longtime" UES French bistro remains a local "favorite" for its "delicious" "Left Bank menu" and "welcoming" atmosphere; it's "not cheap" and could "use a face-lift", but its "prosperous clientele" deems it a "pleasant experience" all the same.

Queen *Italian*
24 | 16 | 22 | $57

Brooklyn Heights | 84 Court St. (bet. Livingston & Schermerhorn Sts.) |
Brooklyn | 718-596-5955 | www.queenrestaurant.com

A circa-1958 "Brooklyn Heights institution" near the courthouses, this "homey" Italian continues its reign as an area "favorite" for "true red-sauce" fare minus culinary gimmicks; given the "gracious service" and "reasonable" tabs, most pardon the "dated" decor.

Queen of Sheba *Ethiopian*
23 | 16 | 17 | $29

West 40s | 650 10th Ave. (bet. 45th & 46th Sts.) | 212-397-0610 |
www.shebanyc.com

"Hidden" in Hell's Kitchen, this "real-thing" Ethiopian offers "flavorful" fare – "numerous" veggie dishes included – that's eaten with your hands and a "heap of injera" bread; even with "small" quarters and "slow" pacing, it's a "repeater" for the cost-conscious crowd.

Queens Comfort *Southern*
24 | 22 | 22 | $26

Astoria | 40-09 30th Ave. (bet. Steinway & 41st Sts.) | Queens |
718-728-2350 | www.queenscomfort.com

"Get your comfort on" at this Astoria joint dishing up Southern "pig-out" fare in "simple" digs with a "wacky", "chill" vibe; it's "cash-only but cheap and BYO" – no wonder there are "lines on weekends", especially for "brunch with a live DJ."

Queens Kickshaw *Coffee/Sandwiches*   23 | 21 | 21 | $24

Astoria | 40-17 Broadway (bet. 41st & Steinway Sts.) | Queens | 718-777-0913 | www.thequeenskickshaw.com

"Divine grilled cheese" taken "to the next level" and other "creative", fromage-focused eats are the specialty of this all-day, "all-vegetarian" Astoria "gem"; its "serious" coffee drinks and craft beers are a "huge plus", as are the "reasonable prices", late-night hours and "hip", "touch-of-Brooklyn" vibe.

Racines *French*   22 | 18 | 22 | $86

TriBeCa | 94 Chambers St. (bet. B'way & Church St.) | 646-644-6255 | www.racinesny.com

Linked to a Parisian wine-bar outfit, this industrial-chic TriBeCan offers a "limited" but "well-executed" lineup of French market fare accompanied by a "wine geek"–worthy vino list, featuring many "obscure" and biodynamic bottles; "down-to-earth" service and a "relaxed" ambiance distract from the "not-cheap" tariffs.

Radiance Tea House *Teahouse*   21 | 20 | 20 | $33

East 50s | 208 E. 50th St. (3rd Ave.) | 212-888-8060
West 50s | 158 W. 55th St. (bet. 6th & 7th Aves.) | 212-217-0442
www.radiancetea.com

Radiating "calm" amid the "Midtown madness", these "delightful" teahouses match a "huge" selection of "exotic" brews with an affordable menu of "light", Chinese-accented bites; the "very Zen" surroundings lend "spiritual quietude."

Rafele *Italian*   25 | 21 | 23 | $52

West Village | 29 Seventh Ave. S. (Bedford St.) | 212-242-1999 | www.rafele.com

This West Village "neighborhood" Italian "knocks it out of the park" with an "inspired" menu served by "welcoming" staffers at "reasonable" rates; even though the "inviting" rustic room can get "noisy", regulars still "want to move in."

Rainbow Room *American*   23 | 28 | 25 | $132

West 50s | Rockefeller Ctr. | 30 Rockefeller Plaza, 65th fl. | 212-632-5000 | www.rainbowroom.com

Following a hiatus, this "iconic" Rock Center supper club is back with its deco details and "unparalleled" 65th-floor vistas intact, and though mostly reserved for private parties, it is open to the public for a "decadent" Sunday brunch as well as New American prix fixe dining and entertainment on select evenings (call ahead); there's also a weeknights-only cocktail lounge, SixtyFive, equipped with a wraparound outdoor terrace.

Ralph's Famous Italian Ices *Ice Cream*   25 | 10 | 20 | $6

Murray Hill | 144 E. 24th St. (bet. Lexington & 3rd Aves.) | 212-533-5333
Bayside | 214-13 41st Ave. (Bell Blvd.) | Queens | 718-428-4578
Glen Oaks | 264-21 Union Tpke. (265th St.) | Queens | 718-343-8724
Whitestone | 12-48 Clintonville St. (12th Rd.) | Queens | 718-746-1456

continued

Arden Heights | 3285 Richmond Ave. (Gurley Ave.) | Staten Island | 718-967-1212

Elm Park | 501 Port Richmond Ave. (Catherine St.) | Staten Island | 718-273-3675

Eltingville | 4212 Hylan Blvd. (bet. Armstrong & Robinson Aves.) | Staten Island | 718-605-5052

New Dorp | 2361 Hylan Blvd. (Otis Ave.) | Staten Island | 718-351-8133

Prince's Bay | 6272 Amboy Rd. (Bloomingdale Rd.) | Staten Island | 718-605-8133

Prince's Bay | 890 Huguenot Ave. (bet. Amboy & Drumgoole Rds.) | Staten Island | 718-356-8133

www.ralphsices.com

There's "nothing better on a hot summer day" than the "ah-mazing" Italian ices in a "dizzying" array of flavors served at this "beloved" SI-based chain; you've gotta "stand in line" at the circa-1949 Elm Park original, but it "goes quickly" – fans only wish this "NY highlight" were "open all year."

NEW Ramen Lab *Japanese/Noodle Shop* ▽ 26 | 13 | 23 | $20

NoLita | 70 Kenmare St. (Mulberry St.) | 646-613-7522 | www.ramen-lab.com

Backed by Sun Noodle (a noodle maker with "well-deserved" cred), this "Tokyo-style" NoLita nook features a 10-seat counter where "ramen artists" dispense a "limited" but "super-authentic" choice of "robust", "affordable" bowls; since there's "always a wait" in the "tiny" space, be prepared to "eat and go."

Randazzo's *Seafood* 22 | 12 | 19 | $41

Sheepshead Bay | 2017 Emmons Ave. (21st St.) | Brooklyn | 718-615-0010 | www.randazzosclambar.com

A "real Brooklyn joint" – "packed" and "boisterous" with lotsa "local color" – this "iconic" Sheepshead Bay clam bar is beloved for its "simple", "fresh" seafood plus random "red-sauce" classics in "ginormous portions"; the "dinerlike" interior is strictly no-frills, but "sitting outside as the boats come in" is hard to beat.

Rao's *Italian* 23 | 19 | 23 | $84

East Harlem | 455 E. 114th St. (Pleasant Ave.) | 212-722-6709 | www.raos.com

It practically "takes an act of Congress" to score a "coveted table", but if you "get lucky", Frank Pellegrino's East Harlem Italian lives up to the "mystique" with its "terrific" cooking and "central-casting" crowd; short of VIP connections, ordinary folks can visit the "one in Las Vegas" or just "buy the sauce in jars."

Raoul's *French* 23 | 19 | 22 | $69

SoHo | 180 Prince St. (bet. Sullivan & Thompson Sts.) | 212-966-3518 | www.raouls.com

The "'it' factor" endures at this "classic", circa-1975 SoHo bistro that stays "true to itself" and its arty admirers with "surprisingly serious" French fare served in a "sexy" setting that includes a "beautiful", "lively" bar; though it can be "noisy and crowded", few rue its "popularity" or high price.

	FOOD	DECOR	SERVICE	COST

Rare Bar & Grill *Burgers*
20 | **17** | **18** | **$34**

Chelsea | Fashion 26 Hotel | 152 W. 26th St. (bet. 6th & 7th Aves.) | 212-807-7273
Murray Hill | Affinia Shelburne Hotel | 303 Lexington Ave. (37th St.) | 212-481-1999
www.rarebarandgrill.com

Given their "top-notch" burgers and french fry samplers, these "mid-scale" patty purveyors are rarely less than "bustling"; if the Murray Hill original is too "packed", the Chelsea spin-off has a "ton of space" – and "hoppin'" rooftop bars await at both.

Ravagh *Persian*
24 | **17** | **19** | **$36**

East 60s | 1237 First Ave. (bet. 66th & 67th Sts.) | 212-861-7900
NEW **East Village** | 125 First Ave. (St. Marks Pl.) | 212-335-0207
Murray Hill | 11 E. 30th St. (bet. 5th & Madison Aves.) | 212-696-0300
www.ravaghpersiangrill.com

Among "NYC's few" options for classic Persian cooking, these Eastsiders dish up "solid", "stick-to-your-ribs" fare including "succulent kebabs" and "delicious" rice dishes; "generous" portions and "value" prices offset the "lacking decor."

Raymi *Peruvian*
24 | **22** | **21** | **$56**

Flatiron | 43 W. 24th St. (bet. 5th & 6th Aves.) | 212-929-1200 | www.rayminyc.com

This Flatiron Peruvian "gem" features "tasty, innovative" dishes including "outstanding" ceviche, best accompanied by the bar's "fantastic pisco cocktails"; a "big, buzzy, beautiful" space and "warm service" help justify the "pricey" tabs.

Real Madrid *Spanish*
∇ **21** | **15** | **21** | **$40**

Mariners Harbor | 2703 Forest Ave. (Union Ave.) | Staten Island | 718-447-7885

"You get what you pay for" at this Spanish vet in Staten Island's Mariners Harbor that scores with lobster specials and other "dependable" dishes in "hungry man–size" helpings; "satisfying meals" at "decent prices" help realists disregard decor that seems to have been kicked around a bit.

NEW Rebelle *French*
∇ **18** | **16** | **20** | **$49**

NoLita | 218 Bowery (Rivington St.) | 917-639-3880 | www.rebellenyc.com
Brought to you by the Pearl & Ash team next door, this wine-focused Bowery dining room features a "satisfying", pared-down modern French menu that's in sharp contrast to its voluminous vino list (88 pages at last count); the cavernous setting is done up in a distressed industrial style – think concrete floors, exposed-brick walls – with a "fun-to-watch" open kitchen and chef's counter.

Recette *American*
23 | **19** | **22** | **$65**

West Village | 328 W. 12th St. (Greenwich St.) | 212-414-3000 | www.recettenyc.com

"Inspired", "adventurous" New American small plates (and "exceptional" multicourse tasting menus) keep this "pricey", "unfussy" West Villager "bustling" and "noisy"; some say the "pretty" but "beyond-tiny" room is "too squeezed", but to most it's a "fun", even "rather romantic" scene.

	FOOD	DECOR	SERVICE	COST

Red Bamboo *Asian/Vegetarian*

| 24 | 18 | 22 | $22 |

Greenwich Village | 140 W. Fourth St. (6th Ave.) | 212-260-7049 |
www.redbamboo-nyc.com

With a vegan/vegetarian menu "straddling soul food and Pan-Asian cuisines", this Villager specializes in "clever", "so-convincing" mock versions of meat and fish dishes, from "kickin'" Creole chicken to Thai beef curry; the no-frills setting is matched with "affordable" tabs.

Red Cat *American/Mediterranean*

| 23 | 18 | 22 | $60 |

Chelsea | 227 10th Ave. (bet. 23rd & 24th Sts.) | 212-242-1122 |
www.theredcat.com

The "Chelsea art-world vibe" thrives at this "lively" vet near the High Line that remains a "favorite" for "top-notch" Med-American fare; "solid service" and a "charming" (if "loud") ambiance keep its "gallery-hopping" clientele content despite kinda "pricey" tabs.

Red Egg *Chinese*

| 20 | 16 | 18 | $30 |

Little Italy | 202 Centre St. (Howard St.) | 212-966-1123 |
www.redeggnyc.com

"Not nearly as hectic" as the usual dim sum specialists, this "contemporary" Little Italy Chinese dispenses "high-quality" tidbits that are "made to order" and served by a "competent" crew with "no carts" in sight; despite the "lounge"-like setting, prices remain egg-ceptably "low."

Redeye Grill *American/Seafood*

| 21 | 20 | 21 | $66 |

West 50s | 890 Seventh Ave. (56th St.) | 212-541-9000 |
www.redeyegrill.com

Steadily "busy" for nearly two decades, Shelly Fireman's "classy" Midtowner puts forth a "dependable" American menu featuring "tons of seafood"; "prompt" service, a "dramatic" setting and "pretty-penny" pricing are all part of the "vibrant" experience – and that location directly opposite Carnegie Hall sure is "handy."

RedFarm *Chinese*

| 24 | 18 | 20 | $57 |

West 70s | 2170 Broadway (bet. 76th & 77th Sts.) | 212-724-9700
West Village | 529 Hudson St. (bet. Charles & W. 10th Sts.) |
212-792-9700
www.redfarmnyc.com

Ed Schoenfeld and Joe Ng are growing a mini-"dynasty" with these "bustling" boîtes offering "genius" greenmarket twists on Chinese cooking plus "original dim sum"; the "frantic" farmhouselike surrounds are "jammed all the time", and there's a no-rez policy, though the "psychedelic" cocktails help make the "waiting time fly by."

Red Gravy *Italian*

| 20 | 18 | 17 | $58 |

Brooklyn Heights | 151 Atlantic Ave. (bet. Clinton & Henry Sts.) |
Brooklyn | 718-855-0051 | www.redgravynyc.com

Saul Bolton "does it again" with this "neighborhood favorite" in Brooklyn Heights, whose "slightly different take on Italian" marries "old-country" flavors with a "gifted chef's panache"; factor in "warm", low-key digs and a "gracious" staff, and to most it's worth the slightly "pricey" tab.

The Redhead *Southern*   23 | 17 | 19 | $41

East Village | 349 E. 13th St. (bet. 1st & 2nd Aves.) | 212-533-6212 | www.theredheadnyc.com

The mood is "chill" at this East Village Southern bar/eatery slinging comfort faves like "killer fried chicken" and "fun drinks" at "relatively inexpensive" rates; sure, it's a "cramped" "hole-in-the-wall", but "courteous" service is another reason it's "worth the wait."

Red Hook Lobster Pound *Seafood*   24 | 11 | 17 | $27

East Village | 16 Extra Pl. (off 1st St., bet. Bowery & 2nd Ave.) | 212-777-7225
Red Hook | 284 Van Brunt St. (bet. Pioneer & Verona Sts.) | Brooklyn | 718-858-7650
www.redhooklobster.com

"Superb lobster rolls" stuffed with "tender" chunks of "super-fresh" meat from Maine is the "transporting" signature dish at these "destination" fish shacks; the Red Hook original has undergone a top-to-bottom renovation, and its expanded menu now includes "whole lobster shore dinners" that "hit the spot."

Red Rooster *American*   22 | 22 | 21 | $59

Harlem | 310 Lenox Ave. (bet. 125th & 126th Sts.) | 212-792-9001 | www.redroosterharlem.com

"A scene to say the least", Marcus Samuelsson's "jumping Harlem joint" provides "delicious" Southern-accented American fare and "wow" cocktails with a side of "superb" people-watching; maybe it's "expensive for the neighborhood", but nonetheless it's "always packed"; P.S. there's often live music downstairs at Ginny's Supper Club.

NEW Red Stixs *Chinese*   ▽ 20 | 21 | 21 | $73

East 40s | 216 E. 49th St. (bet. 2nd & 3rd Aves.) | 646-964-5878 | www.redstixs.com

Spun off from the Hamptons original, this "fancy Chinese" in East Midtown offers a roster of Beijing-style favorites (dumplings, satays, Peking duck) that's "good but not amazing"; the rather stark setting is in sharp contrast to the "crazy expensive" price tags.

Regency Bar & Grill *American*   ▽ 24 | 24 | 23 | $58

East 60s | Regency Hotel | 540 Park Ave. (61st St.) | 212-339-4050 | www.regencybarandgrill.com

Now operated by the Sant Ambroeus team, this UES bastion in the Loews Regency Hotel fields an "improved" New American menu – "the power breakfast is no longer the only thing to write home about" here; "accommodating" service, "rarefied" atmospherics and a "chic", "lively" bar scene distract from the predictably "high-end" tabs.

Remi *Italian*   22 | 22 | 21 | $66

West 50s | 145 W. 53rd St. (bet. 6th & 7th Aves.) | 212-581-4242 | www.remi-nyc.com

"Reliable" "all-around quality" marks this "upscale" Midtown Italian vet, where "outstanding" Venetian specialties are "served with panache" to "pre-theater" and "business" types; the "serene" space with its "impressive" Grand Canal mural is "pretty" enough to help you forget the "expense account"-ready prices.

	FOOD	DECOR	SERVICE	COST

Republic *Asian*

19 | 14 | 17 | $27

Union Square | 37 Union Sq. W. (bet. 16th & 17th Sts.) | 212-627-7172 | www.republicrestaurantnyc.com

Long a "Union Square standby", this Asian "mess hall" still "does the trick" with "filling" bowls of noodles and more at "bargain-basement prices"; the "communal-style" setup is "awkward" and "noisy as all get-out", but its "young" followers eat and exit "in a flash."

Reserve Cut *Kosher/Steak*

24 | 26 | 23 | $101

Financial District | The Setai Club & Spa Wall St. | 40 Broad St. (Exchange Pl.) | 212-747-0300 | www.reservecut.com

"Who knew that kosher could taste, look and feel glamorous?" marvel the observant of this "beautiful" Financial District steakhouse's "standout" beef, sushi and French fusion dishes; prices are "expense-account" level, but the staff makes sure you're "happy."

Resto *Belgian*

21 | 17 | 19 | $53

Murray Hill | 111 E. 29th St. (bet. Lexington & Park Aves.) | 212-685-5585 | www.restonyc.com

A "hedonist's delight", this "energetic" Murray Hill "favorite" provides the "refreshing" chance to chow down on "delicious, meat-centric" Belgian eats, backed by a "tremendous beer selection"; regulars report the "sublime hangover pasta" is the thing to get at weekend brunch.

Reynard *American*

23 | 24 | 23 | $55

Williamsburg | Wythe Hotel | 80 Wythe Ave. (11th St.) | Brooklyn | 718-460-8004 | www.reynardsnyc.com

This "vibrant" Williamsburg New American from Andrew Tarlow (Diner, Marlow & Sons) is a "trendsetter"-worthy scene that's also "deeply serious" about its "creative" seasonal food and drink; factor in a "fabulous" setting in the converted-1901-factory Wythe Hotel, and it's an all-around "wow" – with prices to match.

Ribalta *Italian*

25 | 20 | 22 | $35

Greenwich Village | 48 E. 12th St. (B'way) | 212-777-7781 | www.ribaltapizzarestaurant.com

A "true Italian experience", this "under-the-radar" Villager is "totally committed" to producing "authentic Neapolitan" pizza and other "high-quality" specialties from the Napoli region; run by a "helpful" crew, the airy, modern space is at its most "vibrant" during "giant-screen soccer-watching."

NEW The Ribbon *American*

— | — | — | M

West 70s | 20 W. 72nd St. (bet. Columbus Ave. & CPW) | 646-416-9080 | www.theribbonnyc.com

The Blue Ribbon empire expands to the Upper West Side via this New American opposite the Dakota, offering a wide-ranging menu featuring pastas, prime rib and its famed fried chicken (Sunday–Monday nights only); the spacious, rambling setting exudes retro vibes, and there's an open kitchen and a raw bar to boot.

Ricardo Steak House *Steak*

∇ 25 | 20 | 22 | $58

East Harlem | 2145 Second Ave. (bet. 110th & 111th Sts.) | 212-289-5895 | www.ricardosteakhouse.com

East Harlem has a "real gem" in this "well-done" steakhouse where "simply delicious" chops are served with "flair" to a crowd with "energy" to spare; its art-lined room and "quiet patio" also draw applause, not to mention the "value" pricing.

Risotteria *Italian*

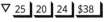

23 | 11 | 21 | $28

NEW **West 70s** | 375 Amsterdam Ave. (78th St.) | 212-362-8731
West Village | 270 Bleecker St. (Morton St.) | 212-924-6664
www.risotteria.com

A "celiac's delight", these West Side Italians work "gluten-free magic" with a "delish" menu showcasing the "art of risotto" plus wheatless pizza; the "crammed" settings may be "not much to look at", but fans would "squeeze in" for the "fair prices" alone.

Risotteria Melotti *Italian*

▽ 25 | 20 | 24 | $38

East Village | 309 E. Fifth St. (bet. 1st & 2nd Aves.) | 646-755-8939 | www.risotteriamelottinyc.com

"Heavenly risotto" via the owner's Verona rice fields is served in an "impressive" variety at this East Village Italian exemplar of "gluten-free" dining; "well-taken-care-of" regulars agree that the "authentic" cooking at a "good price" is worth the "tight quarters."

Ristorante Morini *Italian*

24 | 23 | 24 | $87

East 80s | 1167 Madison Ave. (bet. 85th & 86th Sts.) | 212-249-0444 | www.ristorantemorini.com

An "oasis on Madison Avenue", this "civilized" UES duplex from chef Michael White proffers "beautifully prepared" seasonal Italian fare headlined by "superb" handmade pastas; service is appropriately "white-glove", while happy hour at the downstairs bar offers an alternative to the otherwise "special-occasion" prices.

River Café *American*

26 | 28 | 27 | $156

Dumbo | 1 Water St. (bet. Furman & Old Fulton Sts.) | Brooklyn | 718-522-5200 | www.rivercafe.com

Renowned for "enchanting" Lower Manhattan views made for "popping the question", this riverfront Dumbo "classic" proves it's "all it's cracked up to be" as "anticipatory" servers set down "top-notch" New American plates in a "flower-bedecked" dining room; romantics vow the pricey prix fixe–only dinners are "worth the tariff" for an "indulgence" that "never fails to impress."

NEW River Dock Cafe *Seafood*

– | – | – | M

St. George | 1 Richmond Terr. (Ferry Terminal Viaduct) | Staten Island | 718-273-0809 | www.riverdockny.com

The view's the thing at this long-awaited seafooder off Staten Island's St. George Ferry Terminal, boasting drop-dead panoramas of Lower Manhattan and Lady Liberty from its spacious outdoor deck; its maritime menu highlights raw-bar items, steamed pots and chowders, while the crowd's a mix of tourists and commuters.

Riverpark *American*

26 | 27 | 26 | $69

Murray Hill | 450 E. 29th St. (1st Ave.) | 212-729-9790 | www.riverparknyc.com

"Out of the way and hard to find", this "serene" hideaway in a Murray Hill office park offers Tom Colicchio's "sophisticated" New American food showcasing "divine" seasonal dishes sourced from its own herb garden; the "special-occasion" pricing is offset by "free parking" and a "wonderful" East River view.

River Styx *American*

 ▽ 23 | 21 | 21 | $39

Greenpoint | 21 Greenpoint Ave. (Water St.) | Brooklyn | 718-383-8833 | www.riverstyxny.com

A bit "off the beaten path", this "funky" Greenpointer from the team behind Roebling Tea Room crafts New American dishes "with flair", including brick-oven offerings and a "delicious" brunch; "talented" bartenders and a "fun", wharf-chic setting are further pluses.

Rizzo's Fine Pizza *Pizza*

21 | 11 | 19 | $15

East 90s | 1426 Lexington Ave. (93rd St.) | 212-289-0500
Lower East Side | 17 Clinton St. (bet. Houston & Stanton Sts.) | 646-454-1262
Astoria | 30-13 Steinway St. (30th Ave.) | Queens | 718-721-9862
www.rizzosfinepizza.com

The thin, "tasty" square pies come with a "tangy sauce" at this enduring "local pizza joint" in Astoria, now joined by Carnegie Hill/LES annexes; the economical tabs are in line with the strictly functional setups.

Roast Kitchen *Health Food*

21 | 12 | 15 | $15

East 40s | 423 Madison Ave. (48th St.) | 212-753-6587
East 50s | 58 E. 56th St. (bet. Madison & Park Aves.) | 212-776-4395
Greenwich Village | 120 University Pl. (13th St.) | 212-776-4053
South Street Seaport | 199 Water St. (bet. Fulston & John Sts.) | 212-269-2590
West 40s | 740 Seventh Ave. (49th St.) | 212-399-9100

This "busy" health-food chain offers customizable hot and cold salads featuring a slew of trendy, upmarket ingredients (quinoa, kale), as well as your choice of fish, meat or roasted veggies (and "watching the prep is fun"); though service is "not so friendly", not many linger since the counter setups are geared toward takeout.

Robert *American*

21 | 25 | 22 | $69

West 50s | Museum of Art and Design | 2 Columbus Circle (bet. B'way & 8th Ave.) | 212-299-7730 | www.robertnyc.com

It's all about the "wondrous" Central Park views at this museum "aerie" high above Columbus Circle, though its "pricey" American fare is "fine" too – and live jazz on the weekend further boosts the "special" mood; insiders say the experience is just as "striking" over cocktails in the lounge, but either way, a window table is "key."

Roberta's *Italian/Pizza*

26 | 19 | 19 | $34

Bushwick | 261 Moore St. (Bogart St.) | Brooklyn | 718-417-1118 | www.robertaspizza.com

Despite "zero curb appeal", this "hipster-chic" Bushwick destination is a "real standout" thanks to "expertly crafted" pizzas and "seasonal" Italian dishes, enhanced by homegrown produce; perpetual "crowds" make for "massive" waits, so regulars head for the "outdoor beer tent" to pass the time.

Roberto's *Italian*

25 | 19 | 22 | $62

Arthur Avenue/Belmont | 603 Crescent Ave. (Hughes Ave.) | Bronx |
718-733-9503 | www.robertos.roberto089.com

Fans cheer this "real-deal" Bronx Italian where Roberto Paciullo turns
out "superb" housemade pastas and other "expertly prepared" dishes
in "convivial" surrounds; "splurge" pricing and "tough waits" due to the
no-reservations policy detract, but most agree it's "worth it."

Roc *Italian*

22 | 19 | 21 | $58

TriBeCa | 190 Duane St. (Greenwich St.) | 212-625-3333 |
www.rocrestaurant.com

"Year after year", this TriBeCa "standby" remains roc-"solid" for "fancy"
Italian classics courtesy of "delightful owners" who ensure that regulars
are "treated like family"; a "peaceful setting" with "outdoor seating"
distracts from prices that slant "expensive."

Rock Center Café *American*

18 | 21 | 19 | $60

West 40s | Rockefeller Ctr. | 20 W. 50th St. (bet. 5th & 6th Aves.) |
212-332-7620 | www.patinagroup.com

With its "rink-side" view of skaters during the winter and open-air tables
in front of the Prometheus statue in summer, this Rock Center American
is an "undeniable draw" for "tourists" and "holiday guests"; "only average" food proves that you're paying for "location, location, location."

Rocking Horse Cafe *Mexican*

22 | 18 | 20 | $44

Chelsea | 182 Eighth Ave. (bet. 19th & 20th Sts.) | 212-463-9511 |
www.rockinghorsecafe.com

"Handy" in the neighborhood, this "buoyant" Chelsea veteran "rocks
on" with "quality" Mexican staples and "fab" margaritas at "value" rates
(especially the "best-kept-secret" $16 brunch); the "lively scene" can get
"noisy", but in summer there's "terrific" sidewalk seating.

NEW Rocky Slims *Italian/Pizza*

∇ 21 | 19 | 19 | $33

Murray Hill | 338 Third Ave. (25th St.) | 212-889-4663 |
www.rockyslims.com

A Roberta's alum rocks "imaginative" wood-fired pizzas and "tasty"
Italian-American plates at this "welcome addition" to Murray Hill; adjoining the "hip", industrial-chic setting, there's an around-the-corner slice
shop for the take-out trade.

Roebling Tea Room *American*

∇ 24 | 25 | 19 | $42

Williamsburg | 143 Roebling St. (Metropolitan Ave.) | Brooklyn |
718-963-0760 | www.roeblingtearoom.com

"Don't let the name fool you" – though this "chill" Williamsburg hang
does pour "wonderful teas", it's more about the "inventive", "darn-good"
seasonal American fare (including "the best burger") and drinks list; the
"super-cute" setting opens to a roomy patio.

Rolf's *German*

15 | 24 | 14 | $48

Gramercy Park | 281 Third Ave. (22nd St.) | 212-473-8718 |
www.rolfsnyc.com

Best experienced "around the holidays", this circa-1968 Gramercy German
"time warp" is a "sight to see" when the "jaw-droppingly" "gaudy" Oktoberfest and Christmas decorations go up ("bring your sunglasses"); too
bad the "run-of-the-mill" food makes a case for just a "drink at the bar."

	FOOD	DECOR	SERVICE	COST

Roll-n-Roaster *Sandwiches*
22 | 13 | 17 | $15

Sheepshead Bay | 2901 Emmons Ave. (bet. Nostrand Ave. & 29th St.) | Brooklyn | 718-769-6000 | www.rollnroaster.com

"Retro fast-food" fans roll into this "busy" Sheepshead Bay "institution" to chow down on "bangin'" roast beef sandwiches and "must-have" cheese fries served into the wee hours; the aging digs are pretty "beat up", but "there's a reason why they've been in business" since 1970.

Roman's *Italian*
▽ 25 | 19 | 23 | $55

Fort Greene | 243 DeKalb Ave. (bet. Clermont & Vanderbilt Aves.) | Brooklyn | 718-622-5300 | www.romansnyc.com

Its "seasonally" attuned Italian menu "changes every day, but the quality doesn't" at this "hip", snug Fort Greene sibling of Marlow & Sons that's a "memorable" blend of culinary "passion" and "neighborhoody" vibes; no reservations means waits are "standard", providing time to size up the bar's "talented mixologists."

Room Service *Thai*
22 | 23 | 19 | $30

West 40s | 690 Ninth Ave. (bet. 47th & 48th Sts.) | 212-582-0999 | www.roomservicerestaurant.com

"Decked out with mirrors and chandeliers", this "eye-popping" Theater District Thai is a "jazzy" destination for "spot-on" cooking at a "fair price"; an "upbeat" vibe, "cool cocktails" and "fun-loving" crowd is all part of the "like-a-nightclub" milieu.

Root & Bone *Southern*
24 | 19 | 21 | $43

East Village | 200 E. Third St. (bet. Aves. A & B) | 646-682-7076 | www.rootnbone.com

Plying "delish" Southern-style plates like "delectable" fried chicken and waffles in a "rustic" setting, this "hip" East Villager is a "must-try"; sure, the "tiny" digs can get "cramped", but after a few "superb cocktails", it starts to feel "intimate."

Rosa Mexicano *Mexican*
22 | 21 | 21 | $52

East 50s | 1063 First Ave. (58th St.) | 212-753-7407
Flatiron | 9 E. 18th St. (bet. B'way & 5th Ave.) | 212-533-3350
West 60s | 61 Columbus Ave. (62nd St.) | 212-977-7700
www.rosamexicano.com

From the "terrific" tableside guacamole to the "habit-forming" pomegranate margaritas, the fare's "reliably delicious" at these "enjoyable", "upscale" Mexican cantinas; while tabs can be on the "pricey" side, "attentive" service and "lively" settings make dining here "feel like a party."

Rosanjin *Japanese*
▽ 25 | 22 | 25 | $187

TriBeCa | 141 Duane St. (bet. B'way & Church St.) | 212-346-0664 | www.rosanjintribeca.com

"Every dish is a work of art" at this TriBeCa Japanese kaiseki practitioner, where "superb" set menus and "excellent" sake pairings are delivered by an "informative" team in a "quiet", modern setting; sure, it will set you back a bundle, but "wow, what an experience."

Rosemary's *Italian*
22 | 22 | 20 | $49

West Village | 18 Greenwich Ave. (10th St.) | 212-647-1818 | www.rosemarysnyc.com

"Delicious yet light" Italian dishes are sourced "straight from the rooftop garden" at this "energetic", all-day West Village trattoria with a "sunny", "rustic" dining room; a no-reservations policy makes it "difficult to get a table" and the big "bar scene" pumps out "loud" decibels, so insiders say it's best "mid-afternoon."

NEW Rose's *American*

Prospect Heights | 295 Flatbush Ave. (Prospect Pl.) | Brooklyn | 718-230-0427 | www.rosesbklyn.com

This Prospect Heights remake of Marco's from the Franny's team is targeted to neighborhood types, offering a crowd-pleasing American bar-and-grill menu built around burgers and fries; the sports TV-equipped interior features repurposed high-school auditorium seats, while the back garden remains intact.

Rose Water *American*   26 | 21 | 24 | $49

Park Slope | 787 Union St. (bet. 5th & 6th Aves.) | Brooklyn | 718-783-3800 | www.rosewaterrestaurant.com

An enduring Park Slope "favorite", this "charming" New American offers a "beautiful representation of the seasons" via "excellent" locavore fare, including a "delicious" brunch; the "tight" environs are "worth squeezing into", and there's a "gorgeous" patio in the summertime.

NEW Rosie's *Mexican*   ∇ 24 | 23 | 25 | M

East Village | 29 E. Second St. (2nd Ave.) | 212-335-0114

The "cordial" Cookshop crew heads south of the border at this "vibrant" East Village Mexican turning out "delicious", market-driven fare matched with an array of tequilas, mezcals and beer; the "airy", glass-walled space (formerly Boukiés) is focused around a comal grill in the center of the room, where masa-based small bites are prepared.

Rossini's *Italian*   22 | 19 | 23 | $65

Murray Hill | 108 E. 38th St. (bet. Lexington & Park Aves.) | 212-683-0135 | www.rossinisrestaurant.com

The "good old days" endure at this 1978-vintage Murray Hill Italian touted for its "excellent" Tuscan fare and "seamless" service from "tuxedo"-attired staffers; the nightly piano player and live "opera music" on Saturdays help soothe any "sticker shock."

Rotisserie Georgette *French*   22 | 21 | 21 | $77

East 60s | 14 E. 60th St. (bet. 5th & Madison Aves.) | 212-390-8060 | www.rotisserieg.com

"Gracious" owner Georgette Farkas is the "heart and soul" of this "sophisticated" Upper Eastsider specializing in "delectable" rotisserie chicken "roasted to perfection" along with other "high-quality" French "comfort" dishes; the "guilt"-inducing tabs are countered by "professional" service and "warm" atmospherics.

Rouge et Blanc *French/Vietnamese*   25 | 21 | 24 | $60

SoHo | 48 MacDougal St. (bet. Houston & Prince Sts.) | 212-260-5757 | www.rougeetblancnyc.com

A SoHo bistro with "character", this "splendid" French-Vietnamese has "gracious" servers delivering "creative" cuisine with "punchy" accents and a "well-thought-out" wine list in an "Indochinese" setting; since it's somewhat "underappreciated", the vibe is "quiet" enough for conversation.

	FOOD	DECOR	SERVICE	COST

Rubirosa *Italian/Pizza* `26` `19` `21` `$41`

NoLita | 235 Mulberry St. (bet. Prince & Spring Sts.) | 212-965-0500 |
www.rubirosanyc.com

"Amazing" thin-crust pizzas and "to-die-for" meatballs are the fortes of
this "charming" NoLita Italian done up in "rustic-chic" style; "cozy" turns
"tight" during prime times, and reservations can be "a pain", but "cool"
vibes and "reasonable" tabs compensate.

Ruby Foo's *Asian* `18` `20` `18` `$48`

West 50s | 1626 Broadway (49th St.) | 212-489-5600 | www.rubyfoos.com

Theatergoers, tourist "throngs" and "kids galore" pile into this "fun",
"cavernous" Times Square Asian serving "better-than-expected" eats
with a side of "kitsch"; the "'50s Hollywood Chinese" decor and "spotty"
service lead some to sigh that "better choices abound."

Rucola *Italian* `25` `23` `22` `$45`

Boerum Hill | 190 Dean St. (Bond St.) | Brooklyn | 718-576-3209 |
www.rucolabrooklyn.com

There's "Brooklyn" in the air at this all-day "hipster Italian" on a "quiet
leafy street" in Boerum Hill offering "knockout" rustic fare served by a
"good-natured" team; since it's "crazy popular" and takes no reservations, expect to "rub elbows" in the "intimate" brick-and-plank space.

Rue 57 *French* `20` `19` `18` `$49`

West 50s | 60 W. 57th St. (6th Ave.) | 212-307-5656 | www.rue57.com

"Convenience is key" at this veteran brasserie that's "well located" on Bil-
lionaire's Row, turning out "reliable" if "not outstanding" French eats plus
sushi; despite "uneven" service, "noisy" decibels and a "tourist"-centric
crowd, it's usually "bustling" – verging on "hectic."

Runner & Stone *American/Bakery* `22` `19` `21` `$43`

Gowanus | 285 Third Ave. (bet. Carroll & President Sts.) | Brooklyn |
718-576-3360 | www.runnerandstone.com

"Outstanding breads" are the star at this "cute" all-day Gowanus bakery/
eatery from Smorgasburg vets; some find the simple New American fare
a bit "ordinary" compared to the "absolutely amazing" baked goods, but
it's still an "oasis" for a "quick bite" or drink at the bar.

Russ & Daughters Cafe *Jewish* `26` `19` `21` `$36`

Lower East Side | 127 Orchard St. (bet. Delancey & Rivington Sts.) |
212-475-4881 | www.russanddaughterscafe.com

Smoked "fish is the star of the show" at this "glorious" sit-down offshoot
of the "venerable" LES appetizing store, where the "creative" Jewish comfort fare (think halvah ice cream) reflects a "21st-century deli" sensibility;
the "streamlined" diner setting is "more refined" than the genre norm,
though "long" prime-time lines make fans "wish they took reservations."

Russian Samovar *Continental/Russian* `19` `20` `19` `$56`

West 50s | 256 W. 52nd St. (bet. B'way & 8th Ave.) | 212-757-0168 |
www.russiansamovar.com

"Home away from home" for "Russian-speakers", this "cheerful" Theater
District stalwart serves Russo-Continental staples amid live piano-led
"festivity" that gets louder as the night progresses; tasty "infused vod-
kas" distract from the kinda "cheesy" decor.

	FOOD	DECOR	SERVICE	COST

Russian Tea Room *Continental/Russian*   20 | 25 | 22 | $75

West 50s | 150 W. 57th St. (bet. 6th & 7th Aves.) | 212-581-7100 |
www.russiantearoomnyc.com

Its "glamorously ostentatious" decor intact, this "legendary" Russo-Continental stunner by Carnegie Hall still provides a "glitzy" czarist backdrop for "posh" noshing built around caviar and blini; "outrageous" prices for "so-so" food have fans lamenting its "former glory", but it's hard to top as a "theatrical experience" for "out-of-towners."

Russian Vodka Room *Continental/Russian*   18 | 17 | 18 | $47

West 50s | 265 W. 52nd St. (8th Ave.) | 212-307-5835 |
www.russianvodkaroom.com

Eastern Promises comes to the Theater District via this "boozy" Russian "martini heaven" that carries every "flavored vodka you can possibly think of – and many that you can't", along with "palatable" Russian grub; granted, the "masculine" setting "isn't very sexy", but don't worry – "you won't remember" it anyway.

Ruth's Chris Steak House *Steak*   25 | 22 | 24 | $79

West 50s | 148 W. 51st St. (bet. 6th & 7th Aves.) | 212-245-9600 |
www.ruthschris.com

"Melt-in-your-mouth" chops arrive with a butter-induced "sizzle" at this "high-end" Theater District steakhouse that's part of the New Orleans–born chain; fans like the "men's-club" decor and "eager-to-please" servers, adding that the food tastes even better when "you're not the one paying."

Rye *American*   25 | 22 | 21 | $49

Williamsburg | 247 S. First St. (bet. Havemeyer & Roebling Sts.) |
Brooklyn | 718-218-8047 | www.ryerestaurant.com

This "seemingly traditional" Williamsburg American offers up "quiet luxury" via "reliably delicious" cooking washed down with "spectacular cocktails" mixed at a vintage bar; augmenting the "comfy, romantic" vibe is an oak-paneled cellar (Bar Below Rye) and one of the "best happy hours" around.

Sachi *Asian*   ▽ 23 | 20 | 21 | $44

Murray Hill | 713 Second Ave. (38th St.) | 212-297-1883 |
www.sachinyc.com

Asian street food gets a "creative" rethinking at this Murray Hill bistro from Pichet Ong, whose "well-thought-out" dim sum and novel sushi rolls are paired with "delicious" cocktails; a "sexy" mix of dark woods and red leather banquettes makes the contemporary room a "great date spot."

Sacred Chow *Kosher/Vegan/Vegetarian*   23 | 16 | 19 | $30

Greenwich Village | 227 Sullivan St (bet. Bleecker & 3rd Sts.) |
212-337-0863 | www.sacredchow.com

The "delicious" organic, kosher and vegan offerings (think "exceptional fake meatballs") at this "quirky" Villager may just make carnivores "believe"; it's small in size and "popular" with the health-minded, so "definitely make a reservation."

Sahara *Turkish*   22 | 13 | 18 | $32

Sheepshead Bay | 2337 Coney Island Ave. (bet. Aves. T & U) | Brooklyn |
718-376-8594 | www.saharanewyork.com

It's "old-school at this point", but this durable Sheepshead Bay Turk is "hard to beat" for "seriously good" grilled fare ("kebab is king") at the right price; the "huge" space may be "short on ambiance", but that doesn't hurt its "popularity" with "groups and families."

Saju Bistro *French*

22 | 20 | 23 | $51

West 40s | Mela Hotel | 120 W. 44th St. (6th Ave.) | 212-997-7258 | www.sajubistro.com

A "slice of Paree" in Times Square, this "very French" bistro is "spot-on" for "traditional Provençal dishes" offered at "fair" prices; it's especially "convenient" pre-theater with an "engaging" staff to get you in and out.

Sakagura *Japanese*

25 | 22 | 21 | $57

East 40s | 211 E. 43rd St. (bet. 2nd & 3rd Aves.) | 212-953-7253 | www.sakagura.com

A "portal to Tokyo" "hidden away" beneath an "anonymous" office building near Grand Central, this Japanese izakaya couples "sophisticated" small plates with an "amazing array" of "superb" sakes in a "calm", bamboo-rich setting; given "dainty"-by-design portions, be prepared to "spend more than you expect."

Sake Bar Hagi *Japanese*

23 | 16 | 17 | $37

West 40s | 152 W. 49th St. (7th Ave.) | 212-764-8549 | www.sakebarhagi.com

Just off Times Square, this "underground" izakaya "fills up fast" with folks unwinding over "down-home" Japanese bar food and "plenty of booze on the cheap" – so get there soon after work or prepare to wait; there's "no decor" to speak of, but the crowd "lends atmosphere."

NEW Saki *Japanese*

– | – | – | M

Greenwich Village | 56 Third Ave. (bet. 10th & 11th Sts.) | 212-353-5088 | www.sakinyc.com

From the folks behind Sushi of Gari, this Village Japanese is a handy source of specialty sushi reinforced by a brief roster of entrees and served with no fuss; expect a stripped-down setting with low-key vibes and prices to match.

Sala One Nine *Spanish*

21 | 17 | 20 | $48

Flatiron | 35 W. 19th St. (bet. 5th & 6th Aves.) | 212-229-2300 | www.salaonenine.com

"Dependable" tapas and sangria fuel the "energetic" scene at this "inviting", "no-attitude" Flatiron Spaniard that works for "hanging out with friends" or going on a "fun date"; just be aware the "fantastic happy-hour" deals make for "crowded" conditions in the after-work hours.

Salinas *Spanish*

24 | 24 | 22 | $70

Chelsea | 136 Ninth Ave. (bet. 18th & 19th Sts.) | 212-776-1990 | www.salinasnyc.com

"Charmed" Chelsea dwellers hail this "creative" Spaniard for its "terrific tapas" and "unusually elegant" space complete with a "retractable roof" sheltering a "fabulous garden"; sure, it's on the "pricey" side, but this is "one to reckon with."

Salt & Fat *American/Asian*

 24 | 18 | 22 | $38

Sunnyside | 41-16 Queens Blvd. (bet. 41st & 42nd Sts.) | Queens | 718-433-3702 | www.saltandfatny.com

The name shows a "sense of humor", but they "take the food seriously" at this Sunnyside "rising star" where "inventive" small plates show-case a "delectable" blend of New American and Asian flavors, offered at "Queens prices"; "no reservations" and "tiny" dimensions mean "waits" at prime times.

Salvation Taco *Mexican*

20 | 21 | 17 | $39

Murray Hill | Pod 39 Hotel | 145 E. 39th St. (bet. Lexington & 3rd Aves.) | 212-865-5800 | www.salvationtaco.com

"Interesting" small plates with some "unusual" spins come courtesy of April Bloomfield and Ken Friedman (The Breslin, Spotted Pig) at this "sexy" Murray Hill Mexican where "after-work crowds" congregate for "tiny" but "full-of-flavor" tacos and snacks; an "awesome" rooftop bar also offers "killer" cocktails.

Sammy's Fishbox *Seafood*

23 | 17 | 19 | $43

City Island | 41 City Island Ave. (Rochelle St.) | Bronx | 718-885-0920 | www.sammysfishbox.com

"You will not leave hungry" could be the motto of this "huge" City Island vet, which has been churning out "generous" servings of seafood since 1966; though not cheap, it's something of a "tourist" magnet, so count on it being "crowded in summer months."

Sammy's Roumanian *Jewish*

19 | 10 | 17 | $60

Lower East Side | 157 Chrystie St. (Delancey St.) | 212-673-0330 | www.sammysroumanian.com

This LES "heartburn city" rolls out "old-fashioned" Jewish staples "covered in schmaltz" (and vodka in ice blocks) in a "grungy basement" setting where a keyboardist spouts "nonstop shtick"; like being in a "perpetual bar mitzvah", the clamorous "cavorting" could cause "cardiac arrest" – but it's a "great way to go."

Sammy's Shrimp Box *Seafood*

23 | 18 | 22 | $43

City Island | 64 City Island Ave. (Horton St.) | Bronx | 718-885-3200 | www.shrimpboxrestaurant.com

Docked "at the end of the strip" near its Fish Box forerunner, this "casual" City Islander dispenses "down-to-earth" fried seafood and "lots of it" at a "nice price"; it's a standard "hang in the summer", when you should expect "very crowded" conditions.

Samurai Mama *Japanese*

23 | 21 | 18 | $31

Williamsburg | 205 Grand St. (bet. Bedford & Driggs Aves.) | Brooklyn | 718-599-6161 | www.samuraimama.com

NEW Samurai Papa *Japanese*

Williamsburg | 32 Varet St. (Manhattan Ave.) | Brooklyn | 718-599-7171

"Craveable" udon soups, "crazy-good" dumplings and other "vibrant" Japanese classics are on offer at this Williamsburg "staple" (with a Varet Street offshoot specializing in "amazing" ramen); "warm wel-comes", "good prices" and a "special" setting evoking an "inn outside of Tokyo" are other pluses.

	FOOD	DECOR	SERVICE	COST

Sandro's *Italian*

23 | 16 | 21 | $91

East 80s | 306 E. 81st St. (bet. 1st & 2nd Aves.) | 212-288-7374 | www.sandrosnyc.com

Almost "better than a ticket to Rome", this "cozy" Upper Eastsider "rises above the ordinary" with "lovely" Italian cuisine via "mercurial" chef-owner Sandro Fioriti, who sometimes greets diners in his "pajama bottoms"; even if the "high prices" don't match the "simple setting", fans say it's "difficult to beat."

Sanford's *Diner*

23 | 20 | 21 | $28

Astoria | 30-13 Broadway (bet. 30th & 31st Sts.) | Queens | 718-932-9569 | www.sanfordsnyc.com

In business since 1922, this 24/7 Astoria "super-diner" serves "higher-caliber" American comfort food at "reasonable" rates; the formula is "deservedly popular", especially at brunch when the "only drawback is the wait."

San Matteo *Italian/Pizza*

26 | 14 | 22 | $29

East 80s | 1739 Second Ave. (90th St.) | 212-426-6943 | www.sanmatteopanuozzo.com

"Italian through and through", this "casual" UES niche turns out "exceptional" Neapolitan pies from a wood-burning oven and expands your "culinary vocabulary" with its "delicious" *panuozzi* (sandwiches); the ultracompact setting is "less than stellar", but "if you can get a seat, take it."

San Pietro *Italian*

24 | 21 | 24 | $97

East 50s | 18 E. 54th St. (bet. 5th & Madison Aves.) | 212-753-9015 | www.sanpietrorestaurant.us

"Filled with CEOs" and "older sophisticates" at lunch, this "top-notch" Southern Italian is a Midtown "class act" offering "sumptuous" cuisine and "treat-you-like-royalty" service; since its "money-is-no-object" tabs are "wildly costly", some reserve it for "special occasions."

Sant Ambroeus *Italian*

22 | 20 | 21 | $65

East 60s | Regency Hotel | 540 Park Ave. (61st St.) | 212-229-4050
East 70s | 1000 Madison Ave. (bet. 77th & 78th Sts.) | 212-570-2211
NoLita | 265 Lafayette St. (bet. Prince & Spring Sts.) | 212-966-2770
West Village | 259 W. Fourth St. (Perry St.) | 212-604-9254
www.santambroeus.com

"Sophisticated" sorts are drawn to these "Milano-in-NY" cafes where "chichi" Italian nibbles are served in a "civilized" milieu; the crowd runs the gamut from "past-due trophy wives" to "first-rate Eurotrash" who don't mind the "snooty" service and "splurge"-worthy tabs.

NEW Santina *Italian*

23 | 23 | 20 | $69

Meatpacking District | 820 Washington St. (Gansevoort St.) | 212-254-3000 | www.santinanyc.com

Coastal Italian cuisine comes to the Meatpacking via this slick entry under the High Line from team Torrisi, offering a "delicious", seafood-centric menu in "sexy" digs outfitted with glass walls and Murano chandeliers; "noisy" decibels, "lively" crowds – "all that's missing is a Kardashian" – and a vast outdoor patio are all part of the "über-trendy" package.

Sapphire Indian Cuisine *Indian*

21 | 19 | 20 | $45

West 60s | 1845 Broadway (bet. 60th & 61st Sts.) | 212-245-4444 |
www.sapphireny.com

This "quiet" Indian "retreat" off Columbus Circle is touted for its "reliable" kitchen, "courteous" service, "comfortable" quarters and convenience to Lincoln Center; though it's a tad "more expensive" than some, the $17 buffet lunch is a "bargain."

Sarabeth's *American*

20 | 18 | 19 | $39

Chelsea | 75 Ninth Ave. (bet. 15th & 16th Sts.) | 212-989-2424 |
www.sarabeth.com

East 90s | 1295 Madison Ave. (92nd St.) | 212-410-7335 |
www.sarabeth.com

Murray Hill | 381 Park Ave. S. (27th St.) | 212-335-0093 |
www.sarabeth.com

TriBeCa | 339 Greenwich St. (bet. Harrison & Jay Sts.) | 212-966-0421 |
www.sarabeth.com

West 30s | Lord & Taylor | 424 Fifth Ave., 5th fl. (bet. 38th & 39th Sts.) |
212-827-5068 | www.sarabeth.com

West 50s | 40 Central Park S. (6th Ave.) | 212-826-5959 |
www.sarabethscps.com

West 80s | 423 Amsterdam Ave. (bet. 80th & 81st Sts.) | 212-496-6280 |
www.sarabethswest.com

Longtime "favorites" for breakfast and brunch, these "charming" all-day eateries draw devotees with "hearty" American comfort food and baked goods; though the morning's "festive chaos" can be too "bracing" for some, at night a quieter, more "grown-up" vibe prevails.

Saraghina *Pizza*

▽ 23 | 19 | 19 | $28

Bedford-Stuyvesant | 435 Halsey St. (Lewis Ave.) | Brooklyn |
718-574-0010 | www.saraghinabrooklyn.com

A Bed-Stuy "hidden treasure", this "rustic" all-day "favorite" stands out with "wonderful" Neapolitan pizzas and other Italian dishes showcasing "top-quality ingredients"; cash-only and no-reservations policies are offset by a "cool backyard."

Saravanaa Bhavan *Indian/Vegetarian*

23 | 11 | 15 | $26

Murray Hill | 81 Lexington Ave. (26th St.) | 212-679-0204
West 70s | 413 Amsterdam Ave. (80th St.) | 212-721-7755
www.saravanaabhavan.com

"Packed" at prime times, these links of an international chain sling "delicious" South Indian veggie fare, including "crispy, buttery" dosas that are a "must-try"; "brusque" service and interiors that "need an upgrade" are offset by "interesting flavors" and "value" pricing.

Sardi's *Continental*

18 | 22 | 21 | $56

West 40s | 234 W. 44th St. (bet. 7th & 8th Aves.) | 212-221-8440 |
www.sardis.com

Sure, it's mainly a "tourist joint", but this circa-1921 "showbiz institution" is touted as a Theater District "must-experience" thanks to its celeb "caricatures" on the walls and "Broadway stargazing" in the seats; if its Continental fare and career waiters seem "passionately outdated", fans insist that's part of the "charm."

	FOOD	DECOR	SERVICE	COST

Sarge's Deli   *Deli/Sandwiches* — 23 | 12 | 19 | $28

Murray Hill | 548 Third Ave. (bet. 36th & 37th Sts.) | 212-679-0442 | www.sargesdeli.com

This 24/7 Murray Hill "staple" (since 1964) maintains its "across-the-board quality" with a "massive" roster of "traditional Jewish deli" favorites including corned beef and pastrami sandwiches "as big as your face"; its "nontouristy" following ignores the "tacky" diner decor and focuses on the "reasonable" price tags.

Sasabune   *Japanese* — 26 | 10 | 18 | $123

East 70s | 401 E. 73rd St. (1st Ave.) | 212-249-8583 | www.sasabunenyc.com

"Trust the chefs" at Kenji Takahashi's "outstanding" UES Japanese offering "delicate", "skillfully prepared" sushi in both à la carte and omakase formats; even though the digs are "cramped" and the service "rushed", devotees happily shell out "bank loan"–worthy sums for such a "high-quality" experience.

Sauce   *Italian* — 22 | 17 | 19 | $44

Lower East Side | 78 Rivington St. (Allen St.) | 212-420-7700 | www.saucerestaurant.com

"Comfortable and always crowded", this "booming" LES sibling of Lil' Frankie's and Supper provides "fresh, flavorful" Southern Italian eats in a "tight" setting, plus a few sidewalk seats; the pricing's moderate, and the BYO policy helps keep costs even more "reasonable."

Saul   *American* — 24 | 20 | 21 | $64

Prospect Heights | Brooklyn Museum | 200 Eastern Pkwy. (bet. Flatbush & Washington Aves.) | Brooklyn | 718-935-9842 | www.saulrestaurant.com

Sited in the Brooklyn Museum but "much more than a museum restaurant", Saul Bolton's eponymous New American furnishes "creative" cooking backed by "warm" service; despite debate over the decor ("art-worthy" vs. "sterile"), it's a "nice splurge", with an informal sidekick, The Counter, offering cafe-style lunches and brunches.

Saxon & Parole   *American* — 24 | 24 | 22 | $62

NoHo | 316 Bowery (Bleecker St.) | 212-254-0350 | www.saxonandparole.com

"Energetic" and "happening", this "stylish" NoHo "scene" from the AvroKO team "oozes cool", drawing deep-pocketed "beautiful people" into its equestrian-themed, "Ralph Lauren"–worthy digs; the "sophisticated" meat- and seafood-centric American menu is matched with "eye-opening cocktails."

Sazon   *Puerto Rican* — 23 | 20 | 21 | $44

TriBeCa | 105 Reade St. (bet. B'way & Church St.) | 212-406-1900 | www.sazonnyc.com

"High-class" Puerto Rican fare is the draw at this "sexy" TriBeCa spot, where the popular pernil is "as good as your *abuela*'s"; "upbeat" music and sangria with the "right amount of flair" ratchet up the "fun", "noisy" vibe.

Scaletta *Italian*

21 18 23 $56

West 70s | 50 W. 77th St. (bet. Columbus Ave. & CPW) | 212-769-9191 | www.scalettaristorante.com

Inventive it's not, but this "dependable" UWS "favorite" has been serving "solid", "old-style" Northern Italiana with "simple elegance" for more than a quarter century; the "spacious seating" and "blissful quiet" make conversation here a "pleasure", and "no one pushes you out the door."

Scalinatella *Italian*

24 17 22 $97

East 60s | 201 E. 61st St., downstairs (3rd Ave.) | 212-207-8280

"Exceptional" Capri-style dishes draw a moneyed crowd to this "private club"-like UES Italian, situated downstairs in an "intimate" grotto; service is as "impressive" as the "fabulous" food, but if your server steers you toward the specials, brace yourself for "sticker shock."

Scalini Fedeli *Italian*

26 24 25 $98

TriBeCa | 165 Duane St. (bet. Hudson & Staple Sts.) | 212-528-0400 | www.scalinifedeli.com

This TriBeCa class act from Michael Cetrulo matches "marvelous" Italian cuisine with "top-notch" service in a "lovely", "traditional" setting exuding "Old Europe" vibes; with prix fixe–only menus starting at $75, it's "not cheap", but "worth it for a special occasion."

Scalino *Italian*

23 16 22 $35

Greenpoint | 659 Manhattan Ave. (bet. Nassau & Norman Aves.) | Brooklyn | 718-389-8600 | www.scalinogp.com
Park Slope | 347 Seventh Ave. (10th St.) | Brooklyn | 718-840-5738 | www.scalinobrooklyn.com

It's "endearing" to be "treated like a regular" at these "small" but "proud" Brooklyn Italians serving "generous" plates of "simple", "earthy" pastas and other staples; "comfortable" and "no-frills", they deliver "value" – and naturally "fill up fast."

Scarlatto *Italian*

20 18 20 $50

West 40s | 250 W. 47th St. (bet. B'way & 8th Ave.) | 212-730-4535 | www.scarlattonyc.com

Expect "no gimmicks" at this "pleasant" Italian standby in the middle of the Theater District, just "tasty" standards delivered by a "prompt" crew; "reasonable"-for-the-neighborhood prices get even more so if you order the "bargain" prix fixe.

Scarpetta *Italian*

25 22 23 $78

Chelsea | 355 W. 14th St. (bet. 8th & 9th Aves.) | 212-691-0555 | www.scarpettanyc.com

"Heavenly" spaghetti is the highlight of the "expertly crafted" menu at this "classy" contemporary Italian on 14th Street, where "on-point" staffers ferry dishes that are "as good as advertised"; true, you'll "spend a pretty penny", but there's a reason why it's still so "popular" and "energetic."

Schiller's *Continental*

20 20 17 $46

Lower East Side | 131 Rivington St. (Norfolk St.) | 212-260-4555 | www.schillersny.com

Balthazar's younger, "lower-priced" cousin, this "cool" LES bistro from Keith McNally is an ever-"packed" nexus for "solid" Continental fare delivered by a "well-meaning" team; even though the "noisy" room is "a place to be seen, not heard", it remains a perennial Downtown "favorite."

Schnipper's Quality Kitchen *American*

| 19 | 13 | 15 | $18 |

East 50s | 570 Lexington Ave. (51st St.) | 212-826-8100
NEW Financial District | 1 New York Plaza (Broad St.) | 646-964-5409
Flatiron | 23 E. 23rd St. (bet. Madison & Park Ave. S.) | 212-233-1025
West 40s | 620 Eighth Ave. (41st St.) | 212-921-2400
www.schnippers.com

These "upscale fast-food joints" vend "tasty", "fair-priced" American staples – burgers and sandwiches, salads, "thick" shakes – in "cafeteria"-style settings; "place your order at the counter" and staffers deliver it to your table "quick", even when the scene's "hustle-bustle."

Scottadito Osteria Toscana *Italian*

| 23 | 21 | 22 | $40 |

Park Slope | 788 Union St. (bet. 6th & 7th Aves.) | Brooklyn | 718-636-4800 | www.scottadito.com

Whether for an "intimate dinner" or the "best brunch", this Park Sloper "steals hearts" with its "delicious" Northern Italian fare and "Tuscan farmhouse" setting ("sit by the fireplace"); "warm" service and a well-priced wine list complete the picture.

Sea *Thai*

| 23 | 26 | 20 | $34 |

Williamsburg | 114 N. Sixth St. (Berry St.) | Brooklyn | 718-384-8850 | www.seathainyc.com

It's all about the "awe-inspiring interior" at this "nightclub"-like Williamsburg Thai resembling a "dreamy temple" complete with a "huge Buddha"; "party" people swaying to the "techno" soundtrack report that the "served-fast" chow is as "delicious" as the "bargain" tab.

Sea Fire Grill *Seafood*

| 27 | 25 | 26 | $84 |

East 40s | 158 E. 48th St. (bet. Lexington & 3rd Aves.) | 212-935-3785 | www.theseafiregrill.com

Regulars feel "welcome and very well cared for" at this "outstanding" East Midtown seafooder offering "top-class" catch and "juicy" steaks paired with a "strong" wine list; a "civilized but not stuffy" setting equipped with a fireplace lends "warm" notes, leaving the "extravagant" price tags as the only sticking point.

Sea Grill *Seafood*

| 24 | 24 | 24 | $79 |

West 40s | Rockefeller Ctr. | 19 W. 49th St. (bet. 5th & 6th Aves.) | 212-332-7610 | www.theseagrillnyc.com

With a "prime setting" overlooking the skating rink and holiday Christmas tree, this "iconic" Rock Center seafooder is a "treat" that's "not just for tourists"; sure, the pricing is "special-occasion" level, but the "quality" fare and "exceptional" service are "worth the occasional splurge."

NEW Seamore's *Seafood*

| – | – | – | M |

Little Italy | 390 Broome St. (Mulberry St.) | 212-730-6005 | www.seamores.com

Inspired by Montauk fish shacks, this Little Italy eatery from the Meatball Shop founder spotlights sustainable seafood (including under-utilized local catch like monkfish and flounder) served in tacos, salads or customizable platters with a choice of sauce and sides; floor-to-ceiling windows and whitewashed woods lend beachy vibes to the proceedings.

	FOOD	DECOR	SERVICE	COST

Sea Shore *Seafood*
23 | 19 | 23 | $46

City Island | 591 City Island Ave. (Cross St.) | Bronx | 718-885-0300 |
www.seashorerestaurant.com

A City Island "place to be" since 1929, this "friendly" seafooder dishes
up "tastes-just-caught" catch in an "old-fashioned", shore-side setting;
it's "noisy", but the outdoor dining and marina views are compelling attractions for "families" and "weekend" visitors, likewise the
relatively moderate prices.

2nd Ave Deli *Deli/Kosher*
23 | 13 | 18 | $31

East 70s | 1442 First Ave. (75th St.) | 212-737-1700
Murray Hill | 162 E. 33rd St. (bet. Lexington & 3rd Aves.) | 212-689-9000
www.2ndavedeli.com

Comfort food "like Bubby used to make" – "insanely good" "overstuffed"
sandwiches, "healing" matzo ball soup, "unbelievable" knishes – are the
claim to fame of these traditional kosher "nosheries"; the setups are
"basic", the service "no-nonsense" and the tabs "not cheap", but for a
"true Jewish deli experience" they're real "crowd-pleasers."

 Semilla *American*
▽ 26 | 22 | 26 | $117

Williamsburg | 160 Havemeyer St. (2nd St.) | Brooklyn | 718-782-3474 |
www.semillabk.com

"Imaginative", "vegetable-focused" fare is the "delicious" trademark of this
"compact" Williamsburg "gem", offering seasonal New American plates
via a $75 set-price menu; its 18-seat counter features "entertaining"
kitchen views, while "delightful" service adds to the "warm experience."

Serafina *Italian*
19 | 16 | 17 | $45

East 50s | 38 E. 58th St. (bet. Madison & Park Aves.) | 212-832-8888
East 60s | 33 E. 61st St. (bet. Madison & Park Aves.) | 212-702-9898
East 70s | 1022 Madison Ave., 2nd fl. (79th St.) | 212-734-2676
Meatpacking District | 7 Ninth Ave. (Little W. 12th St.) | 646-964-4494
NEW Morningside Heights | 1260 Amsterdam Ave. (122nd St.) |
212-658-0226
West 40s | Time Hotel | 224 W. 49th St. (bet. B'way & 8th Ave.) |
212-247-1000
West 50s | Dream Hotel | 210 W. 55th St. (bet. B'way & 7th Ave.) |
212-315-1700
West 70s | On the Ave Hotel | 2178 Broadway (77th St.) | 212-595-0092
www.serafinarestaurant.com

Everyone from "families" to "fashionistas" turns up at this "easy" Italian
mini-chain that's renowned for its "super" thin-crust pizzas, backed up
with "satisfying" if "basic" pastas and salads; expect a "hectic" scene and
"rushed" service, but also a "good buy for your buck."

Serendipity 3 *Dessert*
19 | 20 | 17 | $33

East 60s | 225 E. 60th St. (bet. 2nd & 3rd Aves.) | 212-838-3531 |
www.serendipity3.com

"Must-try" frozen hot chocolate is the signature (the rest of the American
comfort offerings are mere "prelude") at this "whimsical", circa-1954 East
Side sweets 'n' gifts "institution"; despite "high prices", "sassy" service
and "crazy crowds", it's a magnet for "tourists" and "grandchildren" alike.

	FOOD	DECOR	SERVICE	COST

NEW Sessanta *Italian* — | — | — | M

SoHo | Sixty Hotel | 60 Thompson St. (Broome St.) | 212-219-8119 |
www.sessantanyc.com

Restaurateur John McDonald (Lure Fishbar) is the mind behind this chic
corner in SoHo's Sixty Hotel, fielding coastal Italian fare; the relaxed surrounds (formerly Kittichai) flaunt a midcentury-modern look by way of
La Dolce Vita, and there's a patio too.

Sette Mezzo *Italian*   23 | 15 | 21 | $83

East 70s | 969 Lexington Ave. (bet. 70th & 71st Sts.) | 212-472-0400
The "simple" Italian fare is "excellent" but almost beside the point at this
UES "cognoscenti" clubhouse, where "upscale" regulars get "house ac-
counts" and "personable" service, but for everyone else it's cash only and
"hurried" treatment; either way, expect "tight tables" and a "steep" tab.

Seva Indian Cuisine *Indian*   ▽ 24 | 11 | 19 | $24

Astoria | 30-07 34th St. (30th Ave.) | Queens | 718-626-4440 |
www.sevaindianrestaurant.com

Not your average curry house, this "small but cozy" Astoria standout
spotlights "flavorful" Northern Indian cuisine that can be made "as spicy
as you want"; everyone leaves "happily full", and the prix fixes and all-
you-can-eat weekend brunch supply amazing "bang for the buck."

Sevilla *Spanish*   24 | 16 | 22 | $48

West Village | 62 Charles St. (W. 4th St.) | 212-929-3189 |
www.sevillarestaurantandbar.com

"They know what they're doing" at this 1941-vintage West Village "garlic
haven" delivering "fabulous paellas" and other low-cost Spanish classics
via "efficient" staffers; maybe the decor's getting "worn", but patrons
downing "out-of-this-world sangria" are having too much "fun" to notice.

Sfoglia *Italian*   23 | 18 | 21 | $68

East 90s | 1402 Lexington Ave. (92nd St.) | 212-831-1402 |
www.sfogliarestaurant.com

An "oasis of class", this Carnegie Hill standby near the 92nd Street Y is
widely praised for its "authentic" Italian cooking, "knowledgeable" servers and "romantic" faux farmhouse digs; though "pricey", it's "worth the
money" – "getting a table" is the real problem.

Shabu-Shabu 70 *Japanese*   21 | 14 | 21 | $50

East 70s | 314 E. 70th St. (bet. 1st & 2nd Aves.) | 212-861-5635 |
www.shabushabu70.com

"Fun" shabu-shabu cooked at the table, plus "very good" sushi, are the
draws at this "casual" UES "neighborhood" Japanese; affordable rates
and "congenial" service are two more reasons it's been around for more
than three decades.

Shake Shack *Burgers*   22 | 14 | 16 | $17

Battery Park City | 215 Murray St. (bet. North End Ave. & West St.) |
646-545-4600
East 40s | Grand Central | 87 E. 42nd St. (bet. Lexington & Vanderbilt
Aves.) | 646-517-5804
East 80s | 154 E. 86th St. (bet. Lexington & 3rd Aves.) | 646-237-5035
Flatiron | Madison Square Park | 23rd St. (bet. B'way & Madison Ave.) |
212-889-6600

continued

NEW **Murray Hill** | 600 Third Ave. (40th St.) | 646-668-4880
West 40s | 691 Eighth Ave. (bet. 43rd & 44th Sts.) | 646-435-0135
West 70s | 366 Columbus Ave. (77th St.) | 646-747-8770
Downtown Brooklyn | Fulton Street Mall | 409 Fulton St. (Adams St.) |
Brooklyn | 718-307-7590
Dumbo | 1 Old Fulton St. (Water St.) | Brooklyn | 347-435-2676
Park Slope | 170 Flatbush Ave. (Pacific St.) | Brooklyn | 347-442-7721
Willets Point | Citi Field | 12301 Roosevelt Ave. (126th St.) | Queens |
no phone
www.shakeshack.com

"Addicting burgers" chased with "perfection-in-a-cup" shakes and
concretes are the calling cards of Danny Meyer's fast-food chain colos-
sus; though "daunting crowds" and "musical-chairs" seating come with
the territory, the lines "move quickly" and there's wine and beer too; P.S.
"amen for bringing back the crinkle fries."

Shalom Japan *Japanese/Jewish* ∇ 24 | 20 | 24 | $45

Williamsburg | 310 S. Fourth St. (Rodney St.) | Brooklyn | 718-388-4012 |
www.shalomjapannyc.com

If you think Jewish-Japanese food is a "strange concept", the "exciting"
"marriage of cuisines" at this cozy South Williamsburg standout may
"change your mind"; converts advise: reserve ahead, check out the chalkboard menu and "splurge" a little.

Shanghai Cafe *Chinese* 24 | 13 | 16 | $17

Little Italy | 100 Mott St. (bet. Canal & Hester Sts.) | 212-966-3988 |
www.shanghaicafenyc.com

This "tiny" Little Italy Chinese churns out its signature "succulent" soup
dumplings and other Shanghai treats "fast" and "dirt-cheap"; indeed,
the "flavorful" eats distract from the "barking" service and inauspicious
"Formica-and-fluorescent-light" decor.

Shi *Asian* 23 | 23 | 22 | $40

Long Island City | 4720 Center Blvd. (Vernon Blvd.) | Queens |
347-242-2450 | www.shilic.com

"Fantastic views of the NYC skyline" combine with "delicious" Pan-Asian
cuisine, "amazing cocktails" and a "lovely staff" for a winning overall
experience at this "upscale" LIC high-rise dweller; since it's "stronger
than most in the area", insiders advise reserving in advance.

Shorty's *Cheesesteaks* 21 | 13 | 16 | $22

East 80s | 1678 First Ave. (88th St.) | 212-348-2300
Financial District | 62 Pearl St. (bet. Broad St. & Coenties Slip) |
212-480-3900
NoMad | 66 Madison Ave. (bet. 27th & 28th Sts.) | 212-725-3900
West 40s | 576 Ninth Ave. (bet. 41st & 42nd Sts.) | 212-967-3055
www.shortysnyc.com

When "homesick for Philly", these "specialty" joints come in handy for
"darn good impersonations of classic cheesesteaks" washed down with
craft suds; just be aware they're "basically bars" that are particularly
"earsplitting" when Eagles games are on the tube.

	FOOD	DECOR	SERVICE	COST

NEW Shuko *Japanese*

26 | 24 | 24 | $196

Greenwich Village | 47 E. 12th St. (B'way) | 212-228-6088 |
www.shukonyc.com

This "tiny", "special-occasion" Village Japanese limits itself to
"phenomenal omakase", providing either "top-tier" sushi or traditional
kaiseki spreads at a "transporting" bar that takes diners "straight to
Tokyo"; options starting at $135 mean "it ain't cheap", but the payoff
is a real "wow experience."

Shun Lee Palace *Chinese*

23 | 22 | 23 | $64

East 50s | 155 E. 55th St. (bet. Lexington & 3rd Aves.) | 212-371-8844 |
www.shunleepalace.net

Michael Tong's "venerable" circa-1971 Eastsider remains a "grande
dame" of "fine Chinese dining", delivering "exceptional" dishes via
"outstanding" staffers in "elegant" environs; just bring a "fat wallet" –
it's among the "classiest" of its kind, and priced accordingly.

Shun Lee West *Chinese*

22 | 21 | 21 | $58

West 60s | 43 W. 65th St. (bet. Columbus Ave. & CPW) | 212-769-3888 |
www.shunleewest.com

At Michael Tong's UWS exemplar of "upscale" dining, "fancy" Chinese
food arrives in an "exotic", black-lacquered space festooned with gilded
dragons; sure, it's "high priced" and a bit "old-fashioned", but there's a
reason why it's been a neighborhood "cornerstone" since the '80s.

Sik Gaek *Korean*

23 | 18 | 17 | $46

Flushing | 161-29 Crocheron Ave. (162nd St.) | Queens | 718-321-7770
Sunnyside | 49-11 Roosevelt Ave. (50th St.) | Queens | 718-205-4555
www.sikgaekusa.com

Lovers of "super-fresh" Korean seafood crowd these "high-energy",
low-budget Queens standbys dishing up "authentic" specialties to
the tune of "blaring hip-hop"; though the sight of ocean critters "still
wriggling in the pot" can be "off-putting", it's "fun" for "big groups" and
high on "exotic excitement."

The Simone *French*

25 | 21 | 27 | $96

East 80s | 151 E. 82nd St. (bet. Lexington & 3rd Aves.) | 212-772-8861 |
www.thesimonerestaurant.com

Upper Eastsiders "can't rave enough about" this petite French "gem",
where "artful" classic cuisine and "wonderful" wines are "lovingly served" in
a "quiet, refined" setting catering to "grown-ups"; it's "up there on the cost
scale", but reservations for one of the 11 tables still "can be a challenge."

Sinigual *Mexican*

21 | 20 | 18 | $43

East 40s | 640 Third Ave. (41st St.) | 212-286-0250 |
www.sinigualrestaurants.com

"Delicious" Mexican standards and "potent margaritas" get a "modern
spin" at this "convivial" contender near Grand Central; the "cavernous"
space can get "noisy" (especially after work at the bar), but the "tableside guac" alone justifies the "price of admission."

Sip Sak *Turkish*

23 | 15 | 18 | $40

East 40s | 928 Second Ave. (bet. 49th & 50th Sts.) | 212-583-1900 |
www.sip-sak.com

"Fresh, deliciously spiced" Turkish specialties come at "fair" rates at this U.N.-area "standby"; the "Montparnasse-meets-the-Dardanelles" decor is "just OK", but the food and service shore up an overall "satisfying" experience.

Sirio *Italian*

21 | 21 | 23 | $88

East 60s | Pierre Hotel | 795 Fifth Ave. (61st St.) | 212-940-8195 | www.siriony.com

Legendary restaurateur Sirio Maccioni (Le Cirque) brings his brand of old-school sophistication to this UES venue in the Pierre Hotel, targeted to mature movers and shakers; expect "expensive", "delicious" Tuscan fare served in "elegant" Adam Tihany–designed confines.

Sistina *Italian*

25 | 19 | 23 | $87

East 80s | 1555 Second Ave. (bet. 80th & 81st Sts.) | 212-861-7660 | www.sistinany.com

Locals "feel pampered" at this "upscale" UES Italian, where "excellent food" pairs up with an "extensive wine list" and "crisp" service in a "warm" setting that's "like coming home"; cash-conscious types favor it for "special occasions" given the "expensive" tabs.

67 Burger *Burgers*

21 | 15 | 19 | $18

Fort Greene | 67 Lafayette Ave. (bet. Elliott Pl. & Fulton St.) | Brooklyn | 718-797-7150

Park Slope | 234 Flatbush Ave. (bet. Bergen St. & 6th Ave.) | Brooklyn | 718-399-6767

www.67burger.com

"Quick" and "affordable", these "low-key" Brooklynites purvey "tasty" burgers grilled to your specs with an "intriguing" array of toppings; the over-the-counter setups are "nothing fancy", but they're an "easy" option "before a Barclays event" or BAM.

S'MAC *American*

22 | 11 | 16 | $16

East Village | 345 E. 12th St. (bet. 1st & 2nd Aves.) | 212-358-7917

Murray Hill | 157 E. 33rd St. (bet. Lexington & 3rd Aves.) | 212-683-3900

www.smacnyc.com

"Fancy", "delicious" mac 'n' cheese is the specialty of these "affordable" "pleasure palaces" that offer vegan, gluten-free and customized variants in addition to the "ooey-gooey/crusty" classic; given "minimal seating" and kinda "cheesy" decor, many opt for the "take-and-bake" option.

Smashburger *Burgers*

20 | 15 | 19 | $16

NEW **Financial District** | 136 William St. (Fulton St.) | 646-568-5115

NEW **West 30s** | 10 W. 33rd St. (5th Ave.) | 646-692-6445

NEW **Kingsbridge** | 193 W. 237th St. (bet. B'way & Putnam Ave.) | Bronx | 718-618-4229

NEW **East New York** | 528 Gateway Dr. (Vandalia Ave.) | Brooklyn | 718-235-6900

Fort Greene | 80 Dekalb Ave. (bet. Hudson Ave. & Rockwell Pl.) | Brooklyn | 718-222-1101

www.smashburger.com

This Denver-based all-American burger chain offers "real-deal", made-to-order Angus beef patties with a bevy of toppings plus a variety of "tasty" french fry options; "standard service" and functional decor come with the territory.

	FOOD	DECOR	SERVICE	COST

The Smile *Mediterranean*

20 | 19 | 17 | $30

NoHo | 26 Bond St., downstairs (bet. Bowery & Lafayette St.) |
646-329-5836 | www.thesmilenyc.com

Smile to Go *Mediterranean*

SoHo | 22 Howard St. (bet. Crosby & Lafayette Sts.) | 646-863-3893 |
www.smiletogonyc.com

"Hidden beneath a NoHo side street", this "inviting" all-day cafe (with
a SoHo take-out adjunct) caters to the "quietly fashionable set" with its
"lovely, vegetable-forward" Med fare, "solid" coffee and "refreshing" drinks;
service is "just OK", but the moderate prices leave customers "pleased."

The Smith *American*

19 | 17 | 18 | $46

East 50s | 956 Second Ave. (bet. 50th & 51st Sts.) | 212-644-2700
East Village | 55 Third Ave. (bet. 10th & 11th Sts.) | 212-420-9800
West 60s | 1900 Broadway (63rd St.) | 212-496-5700
www.thesmithnyc.com

"Don't expect an intimate conversation" at this "million-decibel" mini-
chain that supplies "basic" but "appealing" American grub to "under-35"
throngs out to "eat and be merry"; "especially popular for brunch",
they're routinely "bustling" thanks to "good value" and "upbeat" vibes.

Smith & Wollensky *Steak*

24 | 21 | 23 | $83

East 40s | 797 Third Ave. (49th St.) | 212-753-1530 |
www.smithandwollenskynyc.com

"Get your year's quota" of "superior" beef at this "classic" East Midtown
steakhouse where "enormous", "juicy" cuts and "powerful" libations
arrive in a "boys'-club" setting packed with "chummy" suits "bonding
over business"; staffers "straight out of the '50s" run the show, delivering
checks best settled by "expense account."

Smoke Joint *BBQ*

20 | 13 | 16 | $24

Fort Greene | 87 S. Elliott Pl. (bet. Fulton St. & Lafayette Ave.) | Brooklyn |
718-797-1011 | www.thesmokejoint.com

BBQ fixes are sated at this "funky" Fort Greene standby offering "mouthwatering", "smoky" pit meats washed down with "top-shelf bourbons";
maybe it's a bit "rough around the edges", but factor in "budget" prices
and most will happily "eat while standing" – "'cuz it's so packed" (especially "pre-BAM and Barclays events").

Smorgasburg *Food Hall*

26 | 17 | 18 | $22

NEW **South Street Seaport** | 11 Fulton St. (Front St.) | no phone
NEW **Coney Island** | 1320 Bowery St. (15th St.) | Brooklyn | no phone
NEW **Prospect Park** | Breeze Hill | enter at Ocean Ave. & Lincoln Rd. |
Brooklyn | no phone
Williamsburg | East River Waterfront (bet. 6th & 7th Sts.) | Brooklyn |
no phone
NEW **Long Island City** | 43-29 Crescent St. (44th Rd.) | Queens |
no phone
www.smorgasburg.com

"Eat yourself silly sampling everything" at these seasonal "open-air" mar-
kets (Saturdays in LIC and Williamsburg, Sundays in Prospect Park, daily
in Coney Island and the Seaport), where "passionate vendors" showcase
the "best of the artisanal food scene"; "insane crowds" and "long lines"
don't dampen the overall "fun" experience.

Smorgas Chef *Scandinavian* | 20 | 16 | 17 | $40 |

Financial District | 53 Stone St. (William St.) | 212-422-3500
Murray Hill | Scandinavia House | 58 Park Ave. (bet. 37th & 38th Sts.) |
212-847-9745
www.smorgas.com

Fans would return "just for the meatballs", but these "low-key" Scandinavians also offer other "tantalizing" classics – many based on ingredients from the owners' own upstate farm – at prices that won't "break the bank"; the FiDi original is kinda "spare", but the Murray Hill spin-off within Scandinavia House is downright "elegant."

Snack *Greek* | 23 | 17 | 20 | $41 |

SoHo | 105 Thompson St. (bet. Prince & Spring Sts.) | 212-925-1040 |
www.snacksoho.com

Snack EOS *Greek*

West 30s | 522 Ninth Ave. (39th St.) | 646-964-4964 |
www.snackeos.com

Snack Taverna *Greek*

West Village | 63 Bedford St. (Morton St.) | 212-929-3499 |
www.snacktaverna.com

SoHo's "teeny" longtime "favorite" for "fresh, simple" Greek staples has begot spin-offs that are more of "a step up"; the 12-seat original's ideal for "grabbing lunch", while the all-day West Villager and "delightful" Hell's Kitchen "find" offer modern, "inventive" takes on Hellenic cuisine with a "farm-to-table" spin.

Soba Nippon *Japanese/Noodle Shop* ▽ 23 | 17 | 20 | $54 |

West 50s | 19 W. 52nd St. (bet. 5th & 6th Aves.) | 212-489-2525 |
www.sobanippon.com

They "grow their own buckwheat" to make the "fresh, tasty" noodles at this Midtown Japanese soba standout, whose "personal" service and "calm" atmosphere make it "perfect for stressed-out afternoons"; if the "simple" decor looks a bit "worn", no one seems to mind much.

Soba Totto *Japanese/Noodle Shop* | 23 | 16 | 18 | $45 |

East 40s | 211 E. 43rd St. (bet. 2nd & 3rd Aves.) | 212-557-8200 |
www.sobatotto.com

"Stunning" housemade soba and "fresh" yakitori (but no sushi) beckon Grand Central commuters to this "dimly lit" Midtown Japanese where it's a pleasure to "sit at the bar and watch the charcoal pros work their magic"; "great lunch specials" seal the deal.

Soba-ya *Japanese/Noodle Shop* | 23 | 18 | 20 | $30 |

East Village | 229 E. Ninth St. (bet. 2nd & 3rd Aves.) | 212-533-6966 |
www.sobaya-nyc.com

At this "low-key" East Village Japanese, the "perfectly made" soba features "refreshing broths" and "delicious noodles"; the no-reservations policy can cause "weekend waits", but "affordable" price tags and "pleasant" environs more than compensate.

Socarrat Paella Bar *Spanish* | 23 | 17 | 19 | $52 |

Chelsea | 259 W. 19th St. (bet. 7th & 8th Aves.) | 347-491-4236
East 50s | 953 Second Ave. (bet. 50th & 51st Sts.) | 212-759-0101

continued

NoLita | 284 Mulberry St. (bet. Houston & Prince Sts.) | 212-219-0101
www.socarratnyc.com

These "low-key" Spaniards dish up some of the best paella "this side
of Valencia", along with "hard-to-resist" tapas and "fantastic" sangria
choices; the Chelsea original is on the "cramped" side, but there's more
elbow room at the East Midtown and NoLita spin-offs.

Sojourn *American*　　　　　　23 | 19 | 20 | $47

East 70s | 244 E. 79th St. (bet. 2nd & 3rd Aves.) | 212-537-7745 |
www.sojournrestaurant.com

This "sexy" Upper Eastsider dispenses a "wide range" of "creative"
American small plates and "unusual beers" to an "attractive clientele";
the "dimly lit" setting exudes a "downtown" vibe and the staff is "knowledgeable", but "order carefully" or the bill may be a "shock."

Solera *Spanish*　　　　　　22 | 19 | 22 | $54

East 50s | 216 E. 53rd St. (bet. 2nd & 3rd Aves.) | 212-644-1166 |
www.solerany.com

"Civilized" is the word for this longtime East Midtown Spaniard where
"terrific" tapas, "plenty of paella" and Iberian wines are dispensed by a
"friendly" crew; prices are on the "high" side, but the payoff is a "comfortable" setting where "it's possible to converse."

Somtum Der *Thai*　　　　　　24 | 17 | 19 | $36

East Village | 85 Ave. A (bet. 4th & 6th Sts.) | 212-260-8570 |
www.somtumder.com

Presenting "nuanced" Thai flavors – "subtle" to "bold" to "knock-your-
socks-off-spicy" – this "terrific" East Village offshoot of a Bangkok eatery
specializes in "authentic" dishes from the Isan region; with "reasonable" prices and a "lively", "modern" interior, it's perfect for groups and
"sharing lots of plates."

Song *Thai*　　　　　　22 | 17 | 19 | $28

Park Slope | 295 Fifth Ave. (bet. 1st & 2nd Sts.) | Brooklyn |
718-965-1108

Park Slopers sing the praises of this "family-friendly" Joya sibling, where
the "delicious" Thai dishes are both "inexpensive" and "generously
portioned"; if the high "volume of music and chatter" inside rankles,
there's always the "rear garden."

Soto *Japanese*　　　　　　25 | 16 | 19 | $102

West Village | 357 Sixth Ave. (bet. 4th St. & Washington Pl.) |
212-414-3088

"Talented" (albeit "stern") chef Sotohiro Kosugi "does amazing things"
with fish in this West Village "uni heaven", crafting "highly creative"
sushi and other "unique" Japanese dishes; the space is "minimal" and the
prices maximal, but fans feel it's "worth every luscious bite."

Sotto 13 *Italian*　　　　　　23 | 21 | 22 | $54

West Village | 140 W. 13th St. (bet. 6th & 7th Aves.) | 212-647-1001 |
www.sotto13.com

"Solid in every aspect", this "hidden" West Village Italian "gem" fields
a small plate–centric menu stressing pasta and pizza; "friendly" service

| | FOOD | DECOR | SERVICE | COST |

and a "warm" setting topped by a "huge skylight" burnish its "cozy" feel, while a "boozy", "sceney" brunch and "terrific happy hour" seal the deal.

NEW Spaghetti Incident *Italian*

— | — | — | I

Lower East Side | 231 Eldridge St. (bet. Houston & Stanton Sts.) | 646-896-1446

A sibling of Malatesta, this LES Italian named after a Guns N' Roses LP specializes in, what else, spaghetti offered in iterations ranging from carbonara and Bolognese to kale pesto; the cash-only price tags are as modest as the setting, a compact space boasting the wittiest use of exposed brick in town.

Sparks Steak House *Steak*

25 | 21 | 24 | $93

East 40s | 210 E. 46th St. (bet. 2nd & 3rd Aves.) | 212-687-4855 | www.sparkssteakhouse.com

A "quintessential" "NY classic", this 1966-vintage Midtown "temple of beef" "still shines" with "huge" cuts of "mouthwatering" meats and an "exhaustive" wine list administered by an "experienced" team; "manly" - bordering on "stodgy" - surrounds and "power-lunch" prices are all part of its "old-world charm."

Speedy Romeo *Italian/Pizza*

25 | 20 | 22 | $30

Clinton Hill | 376 Classon Ave. (Greene Ave.) | Brooklyn | 718-230-0061 | www.speedyromeo.com

"Foodies" and "families" alike flock to this "upbeat" Clinton Hill Italian for "outstanding" wood-fired pizza and "inventive" grilled dishes served by a "courteous" crew; indeed, the "great name" and "comfy, yet hip" vibrations are so much "fun" that a LES spin-off is currently in the works.

Spice *Thai*

20 | 17 | 18 | $28

Chelsea | 199 Eighth Ave. (bet. 20th & 21st Sts.) | 212-989-1116
Chelsea | 236 Eighth Ave. (22nd St.) | 212-620-4585
East 70s | 1479 First Ave. (77th St.) | 212-744-6374
NEW East Village | 71 First Ave. (4th St.) | 212-253-2742
Greenwich Village | 39 E. 13th St. (bet. B'way & University Pl.) | 212-982-3758
SoHo | 177 Prince St. (bet. Sullivan & Thompson Sts.) | 212-254-7337
NEW West 100s | 975 Amsterdam Ave. (108th St.) | 212-864-4168
West 80s | 435 Amsterdam Ave. (81st St.) | 212-362-5861
Boerum Hill | 193 Smith St. (Warren St.) | Brooklyn | 718-722-7871
Park Slope | 61 Seventh Ave. (Lincoln Pl.) | Brooklyn | 718-622-6353
Long Island City | 47-45 Vernon Blvd. (48th Ave.) | Queens | 718-392-7888
www.spicethainyc.com

"Generous" helpings of "straightforward" Thai fare offered "cheap" keep this chain "popular" among "college" types and others "on a budget"; "noisy" decibels and "unenthusiastic" service are part of the package, but there's always "reliable" delivery.

Spice Market *SE Asian*

24 | 26 | 21 | $67

Meatpacking District | 403 W. 13th St. (9th Ave.) | 212-675-2322 | www.spicemarketnewyork.com

It's still "a scene" at this "exotic" Meatpacking District "crowd-pleaser" via Jean-Georges Vongerichten offering "intriguing" Southeast Asian street food and "inventive cocktails" in a "huge" duplex setting; its "dance-club" soundtrack is "festive" for some, too "loud" for others.

Spicy & Tasty Chinese

24 | 12 | 16 | $24

Flushing | 39-07 Prince St. (Roosevelt Ave.) | Queens | 718-359-1601 | www.spicyandtasty.com

The "name says it all" about this cash-only Flushing Chinese where the "hot, hot, hot" Sichuan cooking will "open your sinuses" but won't scorch your wallet; overlook the "nonexistent" decor, no-reservations rule and any "communication problems" with the staff – it's "all about the food" here.

Spiga Italian

23 | 17 | 20 | $61

West 80s | 200 W. 84th St. (bet. Amsterdam Ave. & B'way) | 212-362-5506 | www.spiganyc.com

Among the "best-kept secrets on the UWS", this "off-the-beaten-path" trattoria is a "tiny sanctuary" of "rich", "refined" Italian cooking; OK, the "romantic" setting skews "tight" and the tabs may be "a little pricey", but "gracious" service helps make up for it.

Spigolo Italian

22 | 16 | 20 | $60

East 70s | 1471 Second Ave. (bet. 76th & 77th Sts.) | 212-744-1100 | www.spigolonyc.com

An "easy choice" for "slightly upscale" dining, this UES trattoria remains a favorite for "interesting" (if "pricey") Italian classics delivered by a "congenial" crew; snagging a reservation can be "tough", but first-come, first-served outside seating eases the process in summer.

Spot Dessert Bar Dessert

24 | 18 | 19 | $16

East Village | 13 St. Marks Pl. (bet. 2nd & 3rd Aves.) | 212-677-5670
West 30s | 11 W. 32nd St. (5th Ave.) | 212-967-0269
www.spotdessertbar.com

"You'll want to try everything" at these "inventive" dessert parlors, where a "spot-on" mix of American and Asian ingredients yields "delectable" sweets crafted like "works of art"; even though they're "a bit expensive", most find them "hard to skip."

Spotted Pig European

24 | 20 | 19 | $54

West Village | 314 W. 11th St. (Greenwich St.) | 212-620-0393 | www.thespottedpig.com

A certified "hot spot", this West Village gastropub is a "proven winner" where nightly "throngs" convene for April Bloomfield's "mouthwatering" Modern European chow (including a "killer" burger) and sporadic "celeb sightings"; too bad the "tight quarters" are always "jammed" and the no-reservations policy makes for "really long waits."

S Prime Steakhouse Steak

23 | 22 | 21 | $81

Astoria | 35-15 36th St. (bet. 35th & 36th Aves.) | Queens | 718-707-0660 | www.sprimenyc.com

"Surprised to see this high-end steakhouse in Astoria", locals praise its "mouthwatering" dry-aged beef and extensive raw-bar offerings expertly served in "modern" digs with an "impressive wine cellar on display"; charging "city prices", it's still somewhat "undiscovered" and on the "quieter" side.

	FOOD	DECOR	SERVICE	COST

Spring Street Natural *Health Food*
20 | 17 | 19 | $36

SoHo | 62 Spring St. (Lafayette St.) | 212-966-0290 | www.springstreetnatural.com

Spring Natural Kitchen *Health Food*

West 80s | 474 Columbus Ave (83rd St.) | 646-596-7434 | www.springnaturalkitchen.com

"Not just for the granola crowd", these "affordable" health-food havens sling "wholesome" dishes featuring veggies, fish and fowl that suit everyone from "vegans to carnivores"; given the "relaxing" "hippie" ambiance, "you can sit forever and won't be bothered."

Spunto *Pizza*
22 | 14 | 19 | $27

West Village | 65 Carmine St. (7th Ave. S.) | 212-242-1200 | www.spuntothincrust.com

"Gorgeous thin-crust pizzas" crowned with "departure-from-the-usual" toppings are the calling card of this West Village member of the Gruppo/Posto/Vezzo family; the "relaxed" digs are small, so many try for the patio seating – or opt for "speedy" delivery.

Sripraphai *Thai*
26 | 14 | 17 | $29

Woodside | 64-13 39th Ave. (bet. 64th & 65th Sts.) | Queens | 718-899-9599 | www.sripraphairestaurant.com

Worth the "trek on the 7 train", this Woodside "holy grail of Thai food" offers an "enormous choice" of "memorable" dishes at varied heat levels ("make sure you really mean it if you ask for 'very spicy'"); although cash-only with "perfunctory" service and decor, it's also "super-cheap" and "out-of-this-world."

Stamatis *Greek*
23 | 14 | 19 | $37

Astoria | 29-09 23rd Ave. (bet. 29th & 31st Sts.) | Queens | 718-932-8596

"If you can't get to Greece", this "well-established", "family-oriented" Astoria taverna provides an "authentic" alternative with its "reliable" Hellenic cooking; maybe the "stark" decor is less transporting, but "reasonable prices" take the edge off.

Standard Grill *American*

21 | 21 | 21 | $57

Meatpacking District | The Standard Hotel | 848 Washington St. (bet. Little W. 12th & 13th Sts.) | 212-645-4100 | www.thestandardgrill.com

A "happening" crowd collects at this "festive" scene in the Meatpacking's Standard Hotel, drawn by its "reliably good" American bites, "fun people-watching" and front cafe "pickup scene"; still, "deafening" decibels and "shoulder-to-shoulder" crowds lead some to dub it a "place more to be seen than fed."

St. Anselm *American/Steak*

27 | 23 | 22 | $53

Williamsburg | 355 Metropolitan Ave. (4th St.) | Brooklyn | 718-384-5054

"Hipster" carnivores "leave smiling" from this "New Age" Williamsburg steakhouse supplying "mind-blowing" naturally raised beef and "excellent" sides in "rustic", brick-lined digs; "modest prices" make up for the "daunting" waits caused by the no-reservations policy, though regulars "kill time" at its neighboring "sister bar", Spuyten Duyvil.

	FOOD	DECOR	SERVICE	COST

Stanton Social *Eclectic*

23 | 22 | 20 | $66

Lower East Side | 99 Stanton St. (Ludlow St.) | 212-995-0099 |
www.thestantonsocial.com

"Young" things flock to this "energetic" Lower Eastsider to graze on
"delicious" Eclectic share plates and "yummy" cocktails in a "chic"
duplex setting; given the "extreme decibels" and "ridiculous waits",
its "bachelorette"-heavy crowd calls it "quite the scene", even if cynics
yawn it's "played out."

NEW State Grill & Bar *American*

▽ 25 | 23 | 23 | $45

West 30s | Empire State Bldg. | 350 Fifth Ave. (bet. 33rd & 34th Sts.) |
212-216-9693 | www.stategrillny.com

A new option in the Empire State Building, this all-day street-level American grill offers "very good" renditions of "classic dishes" prepared with
"nods to local purveyors" and dispatched in *Mad Men*"-esque surrounds
that "blend well" with the landmark locale; whether in the "lively bar" or
the "quieter dining room", it's a "winner."

Stella 34 *Italian*

22 | 20 | 20 | $48

West 30s | Macy's | 151 W. 34th St. (bet. B'way & 7th Ave.) |
212-967-9251 | www.stella34.com

"You forget you're in Macy's" while dining at this "stylish" Midtown
"respite" from the Patina Group offering "tasty" pastas, pizzas and other
upscale Italian fare (including "don't-miss" gelato) in "airy", "modern"
digs; "gorgeous" panoramic views of Herald Square "add to the charm."

STK *Steak*

23 | 24 | 21 | $80

Meatpacking District | 26 Little W. 12th St. (bet. 9th Ave. & Washington
St.) | 646-624-2444
West 40s | 1114 Sixth Ave. (bet. 42nd & 43rd Sts.) | 646-624-2455
www.stkhouse.com

Rolling a steakhouse and a nightclub into one "trendy" package, these
"sexy" "scenes" serve "surprisingly good" beef in "thumping", "lounge"-
like settings full of "beautiful people"; pricing is "steep", so "bring the
black card" and remember "you're paying for the vibe."

Stone Park Café *American*

25 | 20 | 23 | $53

Park Slope | 324 Fifth Ave. (3rd St.) | Brooklyn | 718-369-0082 |
www.stoneparkcafe.com

"Inventive" New American cooking in a "moderately upscale" milieu
earns "neighborhood favorite" status for this Park Sloper; a "wonderful"
staff, outdoor tables and a "fantastic brunch" are further enticements, so
if tabs are "a bit pricey", to most it's worth the "splurge."

Strand Smokehouse *BBQ*

20 | 19 | 16 | $32

Astoria | 25-27 Broadway (19th St.) | Queens | 718-440-3231 |
www.thestrandsmokehouse.com

"Solid" smokehouse eats are accompanied by craft suds at this "hip" Astoria BBQ where live bands on weekends provide a "raucous" soundtrack;
the sprawling, "counter-service" setting lies somewhere between a
"cafeteria" and a "glorified college beer hall."

NEW Streetbird *Chicken*

▽ | 18 | 21 | 20 | $37

Harlem | 2149 Frederick Douglass Blvd. (bet. 115th & 116th Sts.) | 212-206-2557 | www.streetbirdnyc.com

Top toque Marcus Samuelsson goes super-casual at this "kitschy" Harlem homage to rotisserie chicken, where the "tasty" signature bird is jazzed up with global inflections, and the menu's designed for both taking out or dining in; the "funky" setting celebrates '70s hip-hop culture, with graffiti-tagged walls, a boom-box tower and a salvaged neighborhood neon sign.

Strip House *Steak*

25 | 22 | 23 | $88

Greenwich Village | 13 E. 12th St. (bet. 5th Ave. & University Pl.) | 212-328-0000

West 40s | 15 W. 44th St. (bet. 5th & 6th Aves.) | 212-336-5454 www.striphouse.com

Strip House Next Door *Steak*

Greenwich Village | 11 E. 12th St., downstairs (bet. 5th Ave. & University Pl.) | 212-838-9197 | www.striphousegrill.com

Loyalists love the crimson "boudoir decor" that matches the "red meat" at these "energetic" chophouses, where "gracious" staffers serve up "magnificent" steaks, "high-quality" sides and "brilliant" cocktails; it's a "special night out" with an accordingly "expensive" price tag.

Stumptown Coffee Roasters *Coffee*

23 | 20 | 21 | $9

Greenwich Village | 30 W. Eighth St. (MacDougal St.) | 347-414-7802

NoMad | Ace Hotel | 18 W. 29th St. (B'way) | 855-711-3385 www.stumptowncoffee.com

Experience a "fine array" of "third-wave West Coast coffee" at these Portland outposts brewing "sublime" java from "meticulously selected", "freshly roasted" beans; sure, "endless crowds" come with the territory, but "talented" baristas keep the "line moving fast."

Sugar Freak *Cajun/Creole*

21 | 21 | 20 | $33

Astoria | 36-18 30th Ave. (37th St.) | Queens | 718-726-5850 | www.sugarfreak.com

A change of pace on the busy 30th Avenue strip, this "bit of N'Awlins in Astoria" traffics in "real-deal" Cajun-Creole favorites, "kickass cocktails" and "desserts that'll make a sugar freak out of anyone"; "kitschy-cute" decor with a "DIY feel" and "swift", "friendly" service seal the deal.

NEW Superiority Burger *Burgers*

─ | ─ | ─ | I

East Village | 430 E. Ninth St. (Ave. A) | 212-256-1192 | www.superiorityburger.com

The veggie burger gets some love at this instant-hit East Villager via chef Brooks Headley, where the limited menu includes the titular, quinoa-based patty as well as wraps, salads and a tofu sloppy joe; given just a handful of seats, the diminutive, white-tiled joint is primarily a take-out operation.

Supper *Italian*

26 | 19 | 22 | $41

East Village | 156 E. Second St. (bet. Aves. A & B) | 212-477-7600 | www.supperrestaurant.com

This "low-key" East Villager from the Frank crew is a perennial "favorite" thanks to "simple" Northern Italian fare offered at "low prices";

despite "tight" communal tables, "long waits" and a cash-only policy, the "rustic" digs are "always bustling."

Sushi Damo *Japanese*   21 | 17 | 20 | $46

West 50s | 330 W. 58th St. (bet. 8th & 9th Aves.) | 212-707-8609 | www.sushidamo.com

With "quality" sushi, "prompt" service and "median" prices, this "under-the-radar" Japanese standby near the Time Warner Center "ticks off all the boxes"; maybe the rather "stark" digs "could use an update", but ultimately it's "reliable" enough for an "easy" meal.

Sushiden *Japanese*   24 | 18 | 22 | $64

East 40s | 19 E. 49th St. (bet. 5th & Madison Aves.) | 212-758-2700
West 40s | 123 W. 49th St. (bet. 6th & 7th Aves.) | 212-398-2800
www.sushiden.com

"Catering to Japanese businessmen", these "no-frills" Midtown vets vend "exquisite" sushi and sashimi in "serene" settings; "attentive" service compensates for the "wallet-capturing" tabs, though they're decidedly cheaper than "going to Tokyo."

Sushi Dojo *Japanese*   25 | 17 | 23 | $88

East Village | 110 First Ave. (bet. 6th & 7th Sts.) | 646-692-9398 | www.sushidojonyc.com

NEW Sushi Dojo Express *Japanese*

Meatpacking District | Gansevoort Mkt. | 52 Gansevoort St. (Greenwich St.) | no phone | www.sushidojoexpress.com

From a Morimoto alum comes this "lively" East Village Japanese (with a counter spin-off in Gansevoort Market) that's making a name for itself with "melt-in-your-mouth" sushi and "affordable omakase", starting at $45; the slim setting has but 32 seats, so reservations are a must, and insiders say "sit at the bar" for a total "wow experience."

Sushi Nakazawa *Japanese*   27 | 23 | 26 | $184

West Village | 23 Commerce St. (bet. Bedford St. & 7th Ave. S.) | 212-924-2212 | www.sushinakazawa.com

"Sushi nirvana" awaits at this West Village Japanese "epiphany" from chef Daisuke Nakazawa (a protégé of "famous mentor" Jiro Ono), which "leaves you in awe" with "artfully crafted" omakase meals served by a "polished" team; even though it's "not cheap" (menus start at $120), getting a rezzie is a challenge both in the dining room and overlooking "the action" at the bar.

Sushi of Gari *Japanese*   26 | 15 | 21 | $98

East 70s | 402 E. 78th St. (bet. 1st & York Aves.) | 212-517-5340
TriBeCa | 130 W. Broadway (Duane St.) | 212-285-0130
West 40s | 347 W. 46th St. (bet. 8th & 9th Aves.) | 212-957-0046
Gari *Japanese*
West 70s | 370 Columbus Ave. (bet. 77th & 78th Sts.) | 212-362-4816
www.sushiofgari.com

"Omakase is a must" at these "exceptional" Japanese eateries from Gari Sugio, where avid fans "sit at the chef's bar" for a "thrilling" taste of "unique" sushi; though the settings are "tight", the decor "blah" and the price tags worthy of "two credit cards", the payoff is "memorable" dining that just might "blow your mind."

SushiSamba *Brazilian/Japanese*

 24 | 23 | 22 | $59

West Village | 87 Seventh Ave. S. (Barrow St.) | 212-691-7885 |
www.sushisamba.com

"Youthful" types favor this "fun", "upbeat" West Village standby for its
"interesting" Brazilian-Japanese fusion fare and "wonderful" libations
(if not their "premium prices"); its "bright and cheery" interior is usually
"bustling", plus the rooftop seating is a "treat."

Sushi Seki *Japanese*

26 | 15 | 20 | $93

Chelsea | 208 W. 23rd St. (bet. 7th & 8th Aves.) | 212-255-5988
East 60s | 1143 First Ave. (bet. 62nd & 63rd Sts.) | 212-371-0238
www.sushiseki.com

The "freshness of the fish shines through" in the "artful" omakase preparations by chef Seki at these "heavenly" Japanese venues; though they're
"pricey" with "not the best decor", "careful" service and "innovative"
output keep the crowd "happy."

Sushi Sen-nin *Japanese*

∇ 25 | 17 | 20 | $65

Murray Hill | 30 E. 33rd St. (bet. Madison & Park Aves.) | 212-889-2208 |
www.sushisennin.com

Although a "neighborhood favorite", this Midtown Japanese remains
an "under-the-radar" source for "some of the freshest sushi" around at
prices "accessible" enough for "semi-regular" dining; "smiling" service is
another plus, so never mind if the atmosphere is "less than impressive."

Sushi Yasuda *Japanese*

27 | 21 | 23 | $99

East 40s | 204 E. 43rd St. (bet. 2nd & 3rd Aves.) | 212-972-1001 |
www.sushiyasuda.com

Though "Mr. Yasuda has left the building", his "legacy lives on" at this
Grand Central–area destination for "sublime" sushi crafted by "chefs
who've devoted their lives to the art"; the space is "light and crisp", the
service "unparalleled" (there's no tipping) and, despite the "hit to your
wallet", ordering omakase at the bar delivers the "full experience."

Sushi Zen *Japanese*

25 | 21 | 23 | $77

West 40s | 108 W. 44th St. (bet. B'way & 6th Ave.) | 212-302-0707 |
www.sushizen-ny.com

It's "less touted" than some, but supporters say this Japanese "island of
calm" is "one of the Theater District's best" given its "pristine", "beautifully presented" sushi; "excellent" service and "small" but "Zen"-like digs
help justify the "expensive" tabs.

Sweet Chick *Southern*

24 | 21 | 22 | $29

Lower East Side | 178 Ludlow St. (Houston St.) | 646-657-0233
Williamsburg | 164 Bedford Ave. (N. 8th St.) | Brooklyn | 347-725-4793
www.sweetchicknyc.com

"Quirky", "delectable" takes on Southern staples – think "creative
chicken 'n' waffle combos" – and "seasonal" cocktails make these "drool-
worthy" eateries "excellent places to indulge"; they get "jam-packed" at
prime times, but "friendly" staffers help keep the feel "fun."

Sweetleaf *Coffee*

23 | 21 | 22 | $9

Williamsburg | 135 Kent Ave. (5th St.) | Brooklyn | 347-725-4862
Long Island City | 4615 Center Blvd. (46th Ave.) | Queens | 347-527-1038

continued

Long Island City | 10-93 Jackson Ave. (11th St.) | Queens | 917-832-6726 | www.sweetleaflic.com

A "mecca" for "local" javaphiles, these "favorite" espresso bars are touted for "amazing" premium pours (e.g. the "must-try" Rocket Fuel) and "friendly", "living room"-like settings; "free Wi-Fi" and "knowledgeable baristas" add to the "comfortable" ambiance.

Swifty's *American*   17 | 18 | 18 | $67

East 70s | 1007 Lexington Ave. (bet. 72nd & 73rd Sts.) | 212-535-6000 | www.swiftysnyc.com

"If you don't own a house in the Hamptons", you probably "won't feel at home" at this UES "neighborhood club" where "the elite meet for meatloaf" and other "flatline" American standards; outsiders are exiled to the front of the restaurant, but the choicest "social x-ray" people-watching is in the back room.

Sylvia's *Soul Food/Southern*   20 | 14 | 19 | $35

Harlem | 328 Malcolm X Blvd. (bet. 126th & 127th Sts.) | 212-996-0660 | www.sylviasrestaurant.com

A "true icon of Harlem", this circa-1962 soul-food "mainstay" warms hearts with "generous" helpings of Southern classics and a "fun" Sunday gospel brunch; old-timers opine it's "not what it used to be", but allow it's still "worth a visit", as the "tour buses out front" suggest.

Szechuan Gourmet *Chinese*   22 | 13 | 17 | $29

East 70s | 1395 Second Ave. (bet. 72nd & 73rd Sts.) | 212-737-1838 | www.szechuanchaletnyc.com
West 30s | 21 W. 39th St. (bet. 5th & 6th Aves.) | 212-921-0233 | www.szechuan-gourmet.com
West 50s | 242 W. 56th St. (bet. B'way & 8th Ave.) | 212-265-2226 | www.szechuangourmet56nyc.com
West 100s | 239 W. 105th St. (B'way) | 212-865-8808
Flushing | 135-15 37th Ave. (bet. Main & Prince Sts.) | Queens | 718-888-9388 | www.szechuangourmetnyc.com

"If you can take the heat", head for these "real Sichuans" where the "fiery" cuisine "beats the wontons off" typical Chinese joints; although the "brusque" service and "dumpy" decor aren't nearly as sizzling, "low prices" compensate.

Table d'Hôte *American/French*   22 | 15 | 21 | $57

East 90s | 44 E. 92nd St. (bet. Madison & Park Aves.) | 212-348-8125 | www.tabledhote.info

If you're "unable to take that trip to Paris", check out this Carnegie Hill "tradition" (since 1978) plying "delicious" French-American fare in "neighborly" confines; given the *très* "petite" dimensions, however, you might consider packing a "shoehorn."

Taboon *Mediterranean/Mideastern*   23 | 19 | 20 | $55

West 50s | 773 10th Ave. (52nd St.) | 212-713-0271 | www.taboononline.com
Taboonette *Sandwiches*
Greenwich Village | 30 E. 13th St. (bet. 5th Ave. & University Pl.) | 212-510-7881 | www.taboonette.com

"Different and delightful", this slightly "pricey" Hell's Kitchen "gem" delivers "knockout" Med–Middle Eastern dishes accompanied by "amazing" bread and "unique" cocktails in a "charming", "bustling" room; meanwhile, the "quick" Village outpost vending "excellent pita sandwiches" is a "real boon to the neighborhood."

Taci's Beyti *Turkish*   26 | 16 | 22 | $33

Sheepshead Bay | 1955 Coney Island Ave (bet. Ave. P & Quentin Rd.) | Brooklyn | 718-627-5750 | www.tacisbeyti.com

In a refreshingly "hipster-free corner of Brooklyn", this long-standing BYO Turk is a Sheepshead Bay "favorite" for "huge portions" of "delicious" classic dishes, including "juicy" kebabs; the staff "couldn't be nicer", ditto the prices, so never mind if the atmosphere is "nothing special."

Tacombi at Cafe El Presidente *Mexican*   24 | 25 | 19 | $32

Flatiron | Cafe El Presidente | 30 W. 24th St. (bet. 5th & 6th Aves.) | 212-242-3491

Tacombi at Fonda Nolita *Mexican*

NoLita | 267 Elizabeth St. (bet. Houston & Prince Sts.) | 917-727-0179

Tacombi at Gansevoort Market *Mexican*

Meatpacking District | Gansevoort Mkt. | 52 Gansevoort St. (Greenwich St.) | no phone
www.tacombi.com

"It feels like a beach stand" at this "laid-back" NoLita Mexican where "small", "delicious" tacos are served from a vintage VW van parked in a "big garage" space; the other outlets are equally "awesome", even if the food arrives at more mundane counters.

NEW Tacuba *Mexican*   20 | 21 | 20 | $37

Astoria | 35-01 36th St. (35th Ave.) | Queens | 718-786-2727 | www.tacubanyc.com

Chef Julian Medina (Toloache, Yerba Buena) takes a more casual turn with this spacious Astoria Mexican "hipster hacienda" done up in Day of the Dead style and specializing in "out-of-the-box" tacos (e.g. lobster, octopus and grasshopper varieties); "strong", "well-crafted" cocktails and "affordable" tabs complete the "pleasant" picture.

Taïm *Israeli/Vegetarian*   26 | 12 | 17 | $15

NoLita | 45 Spring St. (Mulberry St.) | 212-219-0600
West Village | 222 Waverly Pl. (bet. 11th & Perry Sts.) | 212-691-1287
www.taimfalafel.com

The "falafel to end all falafel" – plus "fresh, well-seasoned" salads and sides – is the claim to fame of these "modern" vegetarian Israelis from chef Einat Admony (Balaboosta); both are hard to beat for a "reasonably priced" "quick bite", but the West Village original is mostly "grab-and-go" given its "tiny" size.

Takahachi *Japanese*   24 | 19 | 23 | $48

East Village | 85 Ave. A (bet. 4th & 6th Sts.) | 212-505-6524
TriBeCa | 145 Duane St. (bet. B 'way & Church St.) | 212-571-1830
www.takahachi.net

"Creative sushi" and "tasty" Japanese home-cooking basics at a favorable "quality-to-price ratio" earn these neighborhood spots "favorite" status; a "helpful" staff adds warmth to the "nothing-fancy" setups, which "bustle" at prime times.

	FOOD	DECOR	SERVICE	COST

Takashi *Japanese*
26 | 20 | 22 | $63

West Village | 456 Hudson St. (bet. Barrow & Morton Sts.) |
212-414-2929 | www.takashinyc.com

"Adventurous" eaters head to this West Village Japanese to grill
"insanely good" classic meats on tabletop BBQs, along with some
"crazy" options (intestines, calf's brains); "vegetarians need not apply"
– the menu's "all beef" – and on weekends, it adds "out-of-this-world"
ramen to the mix.

Take Root *American*
∇ 23 | 20 | 24 | $156

Carroll Gardens | 187 Sackett St. (bet. Henry & Hicks Sts.) | Brooklyn |
347-227-7116 | www.take-root.com

Open Thursday–Saturday for one seating only, this "tiny" Carroll Gardens
American offers a "seasonally changing" tasting menu for a "special-
occasion" $120 set price; the simple, 12-seat space feels like an intimate
dinner party, albeit one that can be reserved 30 days in advance online.

Talde *Asian*
24 | 21 | 21 | $47

Park Slope | 369 Seventh Ave. (bet. 30th & 31st Sts.) | Brooklyn |
347-916-0031 | www.taldebrooklyn.com

A "seriously good" Pan-Asian menu with a "playful sensibility" (e.g. the
"fantastic" pretzel pork dumplings) makes Dale Talde's Park Slope namesake a "hip" neighborhood destination; given the no-reservations policy,
there's "usually a wait for a table", but no one minds after a few "nifty"
cocktails from the bar.

Tamarind *Indian*
26 | 25 | 24 | $65

TriBeCa | 99 Hudson St. (bet. Franklin & Harrison Sts.) | 212-775-9000 |
www.tamarindrestaurantsnyc.com

"First-class" across the board, this "exceptional" haute Indian in TriBeCa
presents "sublime" modern fare in a "soaring", white-tablecloth setting
overseen by a "gracious" staff; no surprise, all this "sophistication" comes
at a "premium" cost, but the $25 prix fixe lunch is an "amazing value."

Tang Pavilion *Chinese*
22 | 17 | 20 | $39

West 50s | 65 W. 55th St. (bet. 5th & 6th Aves.) | 212-956-6888 |
www.tangpavilionnyc.com

"Worthwhile" traditional Shanghai cooking makes this "sophisticated"
Midtown Chinese a "top choice" near City Center and Carnegie Hall;
some aesthetes note its once-"classy" decor is "getting a little frayed",
but the service remains "polished" as ever, and "reasonable prices" are
the crowning touch.

Tanoreen *Mediterranean/Mideastern*
26 | 21 | 24 | $43

Bay Ridge | 7523 Third Ave. (76th St.) | Brooklyn | 718-748-5600 |
www.tanoreen.com

Chef Rawia Bishara's "friendly table visits" add to the "charm" of this Bay
Ridge "institution" where the "carefully prepared" Med–Middle Eastern
menu is "consistently wonderful"; "spot-on service", "pretty" decor and
"fair prices" cement its "outstanding" rep.

Tanoshi Sushi *Japanese*
25 | 15 | 20 | $91

East 70s | 1372 York Ave. (bet. 73rd & 74th Sts.) | 917-265-8254 |
www.tanoshisushinyc.com

"Every bite's an adventure" at this "tiny", "no-nonsense" Yorkville Japanese where the "passionate chef" rolls out an "excellent", omakase-only menu at a "reasonable" market price; though the "atmosphere leaves a lot to be desired", the BYO policy makes it all the more affordable.

Tao *Asian*

| 24 | 27 | 21 | $66 |

East 50s | 42 E. 58th St. (bet. Madison & Park Aves.) | 212-888-2288 | www.taorestaurant.com

Tao Downtown *Asian*

Chelsea | Maritime Hotel | 92 Ninth Ave. (bet. 16th & 17th Sts.) | 212-888-2724 | www.taodowntown.com

It's still "quite a scene" at these "soaring" Pan-Asians, where "giant", "serene" Buddhas overlook the "dark", "exotic" confines and all the "action"; "flirty" service, "tasty" chow and "creative" drinks complete the "expensive", "party"-friendly package.

Tartine *French*

| 22 | 15 | 19 | $37 |

West Village | 253 W. 11th St. (4th St.) | 212-229-2611 | www.tartinecafenyc.com

At this cash-only West Village bistro, "delectable" French basics and a "could-be-in-Paris" vibe come at an "affordable" price, helped along by the BYO policy; the "tiny" space can be "tight", and "long waits" are a given, so regulars try for one of the sidewalk tables.

Tartinery *French/Sandwiches*

| 20 | 19 | 16 | $36 |

Battery Park City | Hudson Eats | 230 Vesey St. (West St.) | 646-755-8484
NoLita | 209 Mulberry St. (bet. Kenmare & Spring Sts.) | 212-300-5838
West 50s | Plaza Food Hall | 1 W. 59th St. (5th Ave.) | 646-755-3231
www.tartinery.com

The namesake open-faced French sandwiches are "tasty" and the look "modern" at these "no-frills" cafes exuding "Parisian cool"; despite "slow" service and "inflated" tabs, it still works as a casual "date place."

NEW Tasca Chino *Chinese/Spanish*

| ∇ 19 | 21 | 19 | $49 |

Gramercy Park | 245 Park Ave. S. (bet. 19th & 20th Sts.) | 212-335-2220 | www.tascachino.com

The marriage of Eastern and Western cuisines lives on at this Park Avenue South spot, previously the original home of SushiSamba; this time around, "creative chef" Alex Ureña (ex Rayuela) offers an "inventive" Spanish-Chinese mix, focusing on the bite-size favorites of both cultures – tapas and dim sum – served in a room decorated with paintings of bullfighters and Mao Zedong.

Tasty Hand-Pulled Noodles *Noodle Shop*

| 23 | 5 | 15 | $13 |

Chinatown | 1 Doyers St. (Bowery) | 212-791-1817 | www.tastyhandpullednoodlesnyc.com

Soups brimming with "springy, chewy" noodles and "excellent" dumplings are the stars at this tiny Chinatown "hole-in-the-wall"; "quick" service and "cheap" tabs – plus a view of the chefs at work "slamming and pulling" dough – help distract from the seriously "sketchy" decor.

Taverna Kyclades *Greek/Seafood*

| 26 | 13 | 20 | $39 |

East Village | 228 First Ave. (bet. 13th & 14th Sts.) | 212-432-0010
Astoria | 33-07 Ditmars Blvd. (33rd St.) | Queens | 718-545-8666
www.tavernakyclades.com

"Sublime", "simply prepared" seafood and "homey" Greek fare arrive in

	FOOD	DECOR	SERVICE	COST

"huge portions" at these "popular" tavernas; they take no reservations and the "nothing-fancy" digs are "always crowded", but you're "there for the food, not the ambiance."

Tavern on the Green *American*
15 | 23 | 19 | $65

Central Park | Central Park W. (bet. 66th & 67th Sts.) | 212-877-8684 | www.tavernonthegreen.com

Following a "beautiful restoration", this Central Park icon is back in business with its 700-seat, "ski chalet"–esque setting and sprawling alfresco courtyard intact; the "ordinary", "not inexpensive" American food "could be improved" and the crowd's as "touristy" as ever, but it's still hard to beat when in the mood for "quintessential NY" dining.

T-Bar Steak & Lounge *Steak*
21 | 18 | 20 | $63

East 70s | 1278 Third Ave. (73rd St.) | 212-772-0404 | www.tbarnyc.com

"Lively" and "welcoming", this "rock-steady" UES steakhouse via Tony Fortuna is *the* place to go" for "well-prepared" beef at "serious but acceptable prices"; just prepare for some "noise" and "watch out for the cougars at the bar."

Tea & Sympathy *Teahouse*
22 | 19 | 20 | $31

West Village | 108 Greenwich Ave. (Jane St.) | 212-989-9735 | www.teaandsympathynewyork.com

"Anglophiles and expat Brits" make a beeline for this "tiny" West Village teahouse where English comfort food arrives on "charmingly varied china"; "helpful"-but-"cheeky" service is a "hallmark", ditto the "long wait", but satisfied sippers say it's the "perfect place for afternoon tea."

Telepan *American*
26 | 22 | 25 | $80

West 60s | 72 W. 69th St. (Columbus Ave.) | 212-580-4300 | www.telepan-ny.com

For "adult" farm-to-table dining that "always impresses", Bill Telepan's Lincoln Center–area "winner" has "only improved with age" thanks to "top-rank" New Americana delivered in a "peaceful" milieu; service is "impeccable", and while dinner is a "splurge", the $28 prix fixe lunch is a "fabulous value."

Telly's Taverna *Greek/Seafood*
25 | 16 | 20 | $39

Astoria | 28-13 23rd Ave. (bet. 28th & 29th Sts.) | Queens | 718-728-9056 | www.tellystaverna.com

"Simple perfection" via the "freshest" grilled fish is yours at this "old-time" Astoria Greek taverna, where the "not-fancy" setting is "large", "relaxing" and overseen by a "friendly, never-rushed" staff; factor in "fair prices", and no wonder it's a hands-down local "favorite."

Tenzan *Japanese*
21 | 16 | 19 | $36

East 50s | 988 Second Ave. (bet. 52nd & 53rd Sts.) | 212-980-5900 | www.tenzanrestaurants.com
East 80s | 1714 Second Ave. (89th St.) | 212-369-3600 | www.tenzansushi89.com
West 70s | 285 Columbus Ave. (73rd St.) | 212-580-7300 | www.tenzanrestaurants.com
Bensonhurst | 7117 18th Ave. (72nd St.) | Brooklyn | 718-621-3238 | www.tenzanrestaurants.com

These "neighborhood staples" turn out "solid sushi" and other "basic but tasty" Japanese fare at a "bang-for-your-buck" price point; since the decor's "nothing to write home about", it's no surprise that they do a brisk "take-out and delivery" business.

Teodora *Italian*
21 | 15 | 20 | $55

East 50s | 141 E. 57th St. (Lexington Ave.) | 212-826-7101 | www.teodorarestaurant.com
It "almost gets lost" in the Midtown "hustle", but this "charming" Northern Italian can be counted on for "traditional", pasta-centric cooking; "aim-to-please" service and a "homey", "no-pretenses" setting make it a safe bet for a "quiet evening out."

Teresa's *Diner/Polish*
20 | 13 | 17 | $28

Brooklyn Heights | 80 Montague St. (Hicks St.) | Brooklyn | 718-797-3996
Just steps away from the Promenade, this longtime Brooklyn Heights "institution" lures locals with "hearty" diner staples (plus some Polish dishes) plated in "massive portions"; all appreciate the "value prices", though "standoffish" service and basic "coffee-shop" decor are the trade-offs.

Tertulia *Spanish*
24 | 20 | 21 | $52

West Village | 359 Sixth Ave. (Washington Pl.) | 646-559-9909 | www.tertulianyc.com
"Northern Spain" comes to "Nuevo York" via this West Villager from chef Seamus Mullen, dispensing "fabulous" tapas in "rustic", stone-walled digs; it's a "*muy caliente*" scene with "high prices" and "waits" at prime times, but fans insist it's "worth it."

Tessa *Mediterranean*
23 | 22 | 22 | $59

West 70s | 349 Amsterdam Ave. (bet. 76th & 77th Sts.) | 212-390-1974 | www.tessanyc.com
A "well-conceived" menu of "beautifully prepared" grilled dishes and "scrumptious pastas" ferried by "personable" servers lures Upper Westsiders to this "buzzy" Mediterranean; though the "dark", industrial-chic dining room can be "noisy", locals dub it a "keeper."

Testaccio *Italian*
22 | 23 | 22 | $40

Long Island City | 47-30 Vernon Blvd. (47th Rd.) | Queens | 718-937-2900 | www.testacciony.com
"Well worth the trip to LIC", this brick-walled, multilevel Italian serves "authentic" Roman cuisine in a "snazzy" former warehouse space manned by "attentive" staffers; the "sophisticated" ambiance and "nice wine list" make it a natural for "date night."

Texas de Brazil *Brazilian/Steak*
22 | 22 | 22 | $78

East 60s | 1011 Third Ave. (bet. 60th & 61st Sts.) | 212-537-0060 | www.texasdebrazil.com
"You can eat forever" at this UES link of the Brazilian churrascaria chain, where the "fun experience" features a "never-ending" set-price parade of grilled meats served "flamboyantly" by gaucho waiters, accompanied by a "phenomenal" salad bar; it's particularly "great for groups" given its "colossal" dimensions.

	FOOD	DECOR	SERVICE	COST

Thai Market *Thai*
23 | 17 | 19 | $26

West 100s | 960 Amsterdam Ave. (bet. 107th & 108th Sts.) | 212-280-4575 | www.thaimarketny.net

"Authentic" dishes that go way "beyond pad Thai" mean this "no-frills" UWS Siamese "fills up quick" at prime times; the "funky" decor evokes "street carts in Bangkok", as do the "reasonable" prices – no surprise, it's a hit with the "college crowd."

Thalassa *Greek/Seafood*
23 | 23 | 22 | $66

TriBeCa | 179 Franklin St. (bet. Greenwich & Hudson Sts.) | 212-941-7661 | www.thalassanyc.com

"Elegant" Greek seafood is the specialty of this "high-end" TriBeCa "special-occasion" option; of course, such "fine" fish comes at a price ("you help pay its airfare"), but "first-rate" service and an "expansive", "Santorini"-esque setting soften the sticker shock.

Thalia *American*
21 | 20 | 21 | $49

West 40s | 828 Eighth Ave. (50th St.) | 212-399-4444 | www.restaurantthalia.com

A "pre-show standby", this "reliable" Theater District vet plies "solid", "well-priced" Americana ferried by "pleasant" staffers who ensure that you'll "make your show" on time; its "lively crowd" can kick up some "noise", but that comes with the "friendly atmosphere."

Thelewala *Indian*
▽ 23 | 10 | 14 | $14

Greenwich Village | 112 MacDougal St. (bet. Bleecker & 3rd Sts.) | 212-614-9100 | www.thelewalany.com

Night owls and NYU students looking for a "quick", "cheap" Indian fix swoop into this Village "hole-in-the-wall" where the "delicious" fare has just the "right amount of spice"; it "gets crowded" fast though, so insiders consider takeout and "order ahead."

Tía Pol *Spanish*
23 | 16 | 21 | $49

Chelsea | 205 10th Ave. (bet. 22nd & 23rd Sts.) | 212-675-8805 | www.tiapol.com

More than a decade on, this West Chelsea Spaniard is ever "amazing" – and still "perpetually packed" – thanks to "delectable" tapas and "well-chosen" Iberian wines served in a beyond-"cozy" space; most take the "cramped" quarters in stride because it stays "crowded for good reason."

Tiella *Italian*
25 | 16 | 24 | $57

East 60s | 1109 First Ave. (bet. 60th & 61st Sts.) | 212-588-0100 | www.tiellanyc.com

"Tiny and special", this "hidden gem" near the Queensboro Bridge fields "superb" takes on Neapolitan fare, notably its "delicious" namesake mini-pizzas and "excellent" pastas; though the "railway car–like" setting can feel "cramped" at the dinner hour, insiders say it's "more relaxed at lunch."

NEW Tijuana Picnic *Mexican*
▽ 21 | 19 | 18 | $43

Lower East Side | 151 Essex St. (Stanton St.) | 212-219-2000 | www.tijuana-picnic.com

Modern Mexican fare gets an Asian spin at this "flavorful" Lower East-sider via Acme alums, offering tapas, skewers and family-style plates alongside "inventive" cocktails; fans like its late-night hours, "cool", vaguely retro look and hopping downstairs tequila bar, Tico's.

	FOOD	DECOR	SERVICE	COST

Tiny's *American* | 21 | 21 | 19 | $50 |

TriBeCa | 135 W. Broadway (bet. Duane & Thomas Sts.) | 212-374-1135 | www.tinysnyc.com

This "cool" TriBeCan from nightlife czar Matt Abramcyk is indeed "tiny", but its "rustic, bohemian" interior tilts more "cute" than "cramped"; its equally compact American menu stars a "to-die-for kale salad", while upstairs the "energetic, dark bar" dispenses "fun" cocktails and nibbles.

Tipsy Parson *Southern* | 19 | 17 | 18 | $45 |

Chelsea | 156 Ninth Ave. (bet. 19th & 20th Sts.) | 212-620-4545 | www.tipsyparson.com

"Like being in Savannah", this midpriced Chelsea "standout" near the High Line dishes up "decadent" Southern standards "with a slightly modern twist", backed by "delish cocktails"; "easy-with-a-smile" service helps keep the mood "happy."

Toby's Estate Coffee *Coffee* | 24 | 23 | 22 | $8 |

Flatiron | 160 Fifth Ave. (bet. 20th & 21st Sts.) | 646-559-0161
NEW **West Village** | 44 Charles St. (7th Ave.) | 646-590-1924
Williamsburg | 125 N. Sixth St. (bet. Bedford Ave. & Berry St.) | Brooklyn | 347-457-6160
www.tobysestate.com

"Top-notch" single-origin, house-roasted beans make for "excellent" coffee (including the "best flat whites") at these Aussie imports that also vend "fresh pastries" and light savories; expect "relaxed" vibrations and "people sitting on their laptops for hours on end."

Tocqueville *American/French* | 26 | 26 | 26 | $95 |

Flatiron | 1 E. 15th St. (bet. 5th Ave. & Union Sq.) | 212-647-1515 | www.tocquevillerestaurant.com

A bona fide "revelation" in the Flatiron, this "foodie's delight" showcases Marco Moreira's "refined" French–New American fare and "stellar" wine list in a "calm", "grown-up" room presided over by a "superb" staff; of course, it's even more "divine" when "someone else is picking up the check", though the $29 prix fixe lunch is a "real buy."

Toloache *Mexican* | 23 | 18 | 21 | $52 |

East 80s | 166 E. 82nd St. (bet. Lexington & 3rd Aves.) | 212-861-4505
Greenwich Village | 205 Thompson St. (bet. Bleecker & W. 3rd Sts.) | 212-420-0600
West 50s | 251 W. 50th St. (bet. B'way & 8th Ave.) | 212-581-1818
Toloache Taqueria *Mexican*
Financial District | 83 Maiden Ln. (bet. Gold & William Sts.) | 212-809-9800
www.toloachenyc.com

"Deservedly popular", these "haute cantinas" ply "palate-pleasing" Mexican fare served by an "aim-to-please" staff; sure, it can be "jammed and noisy", but a "dazzling array" of margaritas provides some distraction; P.S. a FiDi counter-serve taqueria caters to the lunch crowd.

Tommaso *Italian* | 24 | 19 | 22 | $54 |

Bath Beach | 1464 86th St. (bet. Bay 8th St. & 15th Ave.) | Brooklyn | 718-236-9883 | www.tommasoinbrooklyn.com

Although touted for "old-world" red-sauce favorites the "way you remember them", the real draw at this longtime Italian on the border of Bath Beach and Dyker Heights is the "opera floor show" on certain nights; beyond the "festive" vibe and "friendly" service, it also boasts an "amazing" wine cellar.

Tomoe Sushi *Japanese*   26 | 10 | 17 | $44

Greenwich Village | 172 Thompson St. (bet. Bleecker & Houston Sts.) | 212-777-9346 | www.tomoesushi.com

There's "often a line" to get into this longtime Village Japanese touted for its "massive slabs" of "mouthwatering" sushi; the "tiny", "nothing-fancy" digs look like "a step back into the '70s", with yesteryear "value" pricing to match.

Tom's *Diner*   21 | 17 | 23 | $18

Prospect Heights | 782 Washington Ave. (Sterling Pl.) | Brooklyn | 718-636-9738

Tom's Coney Island *Diner*

Coney Island | 1229 Boardwalk W. (Stillwell Ave.) | Brooklyn | 718-942-4200
www.tomsbrooklyn.com

Lines wrap "around the block" on weekend mornings at this circa-1936 Prospect Heights diner beloved as much for its "sweet" service and "kitschy" decor as for its "good prices" and "many pancake options"; it slings breakfast and lunch only, but the Coney Island spin-off stays open later.

Tony's Di Napoli *Italian*   21 | 18 | 22 | $44

East 60s | 1081 Third Ave. (bet. 63rd & 64th Sts.) | 212-888-6333
West 40s | Casablanca Hotel | 147 W. 43rd St. (bet. 6th & 7th Aves.) | 212-221-0100
www.tonysnyc.com

Made for "large groups", these "welcoming" Italians take a page from the "Carmine's" playbook, purveying "heaping" portions of "reliable" red-sauce standards at "affordable" prices; "tons of people" turn up to kick up a "din" and leave "completely satiated."

Topaz *Thai*   21 | 13 | 17 | $32

West 50s | 127 W. 56th St. (bet. 6th & 7th Aves.) | 212-957-8020 | www.newtopaznyc.com

Near Carnegie Hall and City Center, this "simple" Thai slings "flavorful" classics priced way "low" for the zip code; "drab" digs with "no elbow room" and variable service offset the "bargain" tabs, but still it's "always packed."

Torishin *Japanese*   ▽ 25 | — | 22 | $87

West 50s | 362 W. 53rd St. (9th Ave.) | 212-757-0108 | www.torishinny.com

It's "chicken heaven" at this "super-authentic" yakitori specialist recently relocated to Hell's Kitchen, offering "exceptional" skewers showcasing poultry in its every permutation; "sit at the bar and watch the chefs" for the full experience – it's expensive, but cheaper than the "plane ride" to Tokyo.

Toro *Spanish*   24 | 23 | 22 | $67

Chelsea | 85 10th Ave. (bet. 15th & 16th Sts.) | 212-691-2360 | www.toro-nyc.com

"Crazy-creative" small plates and other "awesome" Spanish dishes meet "killer cocktails" at this "sceney" Chelsea "tapas heaven" where "well-informed" staffers preside over a "huge", industrial-cool space; what's "vibrant" to some is "deafening" to others, but overall it's a pretty "amazing experience."

Tortilleria Nixtamal *Mexican*

24	12	19	$21

Corona | 104-05 47th Ave. (bet. 104th & 108th Sts.) | Queens | 718-699-2434 | www.tortillerianixtamal.com

It's "all about the masa" ground in-house at this Corona Mexican renowned for the freshest tortillas "this side of the Rio Grande", as well as "authentic" tacos and "melt-in-your-mouth" tamales; sure, it's a "hole-in-the-wall", but compensations include "friendly" service and "Queens prices."

Tosca *Italian*

23	23	22	$37

Throggs Neck | 4038 E. Tremont Ave. (Miles Ave.) | Bronx | 718-239-3300 | www.toscacafemenu.com

"Eat and be seen" at this "nightclub"-like Throggs Neck venue, whose array of "quite good", "straightforward" Italian eats also features sushi ("quite the combination"); the "large", "loungey" setup includes a "cool roof deck" and "happening" bar, and hosts what may be the Bronx's "best brunch."

Totonno's Pizzeria Napolitano *Pizza*

27	11	16	$22

Coney Island | 1524 Neptune Ave. (bet. 15th & 16th Sts.) | Brooklyn | 718-372-8606 | www.totonnosconeyisland.com

An "old-fashioned place unchanged by time", this 1924-vintage Coney Island pizzeria is renowned for its "terrific" coal-oven pies "lovingly made with the freshest ingredients"; despite "utilitarian" service, "not much atmosphere" and a cash-only rule, fans insist it's a "must-visit" experience.

Totto Ramen *Japanese/Noodle Shop*

24	12	16	$22

 East 50s | 248 E. 52nd St. (2nd Ave.) | 212-421-0052
West 50s | 464 W. 51st St. (bet. 9th & 10th Aves.) | 646-596-9056
West 50s | 366 W. 52nd St. (bet. 8th & 9th Aves.) | 212-582-0052
www.tottoramen.com

Even "more locations" haven't eased the "super-long" waits for a seat at this much-"hyped" ramen mini-chain beloved for its "outstanding" renditions of "heaven in a bowl"; "no reservations", "no-frills" decor and "rushed" service come with the territory, but the payoff is "authentic Tokyo" dining.

Tournesol *French*

23	17	21	$42

Long Island City | 50-12 Vernon Blvd. (bet. 50th & 51st Aves.) | Queens | 718-472-4355 | www.tournesolnyc.com

For a taste of "Paris in Queens", check out this "convivial" LIC bistro offering "*magnifique*" French fare at "easy-on-the-pocketbook" rates; yes, the "cramped space" means "you really have to like your neighbor", but the "warm welcome" from a "most pleasant" staff compensates.

Tra Di Noi *Italian*

23	12	20	$46

Arthur Avenue/Belmont | 622 E. 187th St. (bet. Belmont & Hughes Sts.) | Bronx | 718-295-1784 | www.tradinoi.com

"Like a meal at grandma's house", this family-run "jewel" off Arthur Avenue might offer "not much decor" but is warmed by "welcoming" service; still, it's the "fresh", "cooked-just-right" Italian classics that make it "worth the trip."

	FOOD	DECOR	SERVICE	COST

Traif *Eclectic*   24 | 19 | 22 | $48

Williamsburg | 229 S. Fourth St. (bet. Havemeyer & Roebling Sts.) |
Brooklyn | 347-844-9578 | www.traifny.com

Given its name (which roughly translates as 'non-kosher'), it's no surprise that there's "lots of pork and shellfish" on the "innovative" Eclectic menu of this Williamsburg "pleasure", featuring a small plates–centric format geared toward "sharing"; expect moderate price tags and an "intimate", verging on "tight", setting.

Trattoria Dell'Arte *Italian*   22 | 20 | 22 | $63

West 50s | 900 Seventh Ave. (bet. 56th & 57th Sts.) | 212-245-9800 |
www.trattoriadellarte.com

A "perennial favorite" opposite Carnegie Hall, this "bustling" Tuscan is ever a "safe bet" with its "terrific" pizza, "requisite" antipasti bar and "amusing" body-parts decor; it's "convenient" for a work lunch or "pre-theater", so "bring your appetite – and your credit card."

Trattoria L'incontro *Italian*   26 | 20 | 25 | $60

Astoria | 21-76 31st St. (Ditmars Blvd.) | Queens | 718-721-3532 |
www.trattorialincontro.com

A "worthy destination", this "family-oriented" Astoria Italian boasts a "dizzying" number of "outstanding" specials recited from memory by "entertaining" staffers, along with an "endless" printed menu; a "welcoming" greeting from chef Rocco Sacramone adds to the "happy", "never-boring" vibe.

Trattoria Romana *Italian*   26 | 18 | 23 | $53

Dongan Hills | 1476 Hylan Blvd. (Benton Ave.) | Staten Island |
718-980-3113 | www.trattoriaromanasi.com

A good "reason to visit Staten Island", this Dongan Hills Italian "favorite" offers "high-quality" cooking prepared by a chef who "makes you feel at home"; granted, it can be "noisy" and "tightly packed" since it's "always filled with customers", but overall it's a "great dining experience."

Trattoria Trecolori *Italian*   22 | 18 | 22 | $47

West 40s | 254 W. 47th St. (B'way) | 212-997-4540 |
www.trattoriatrecolori.com

The staff "makes everyone feel at home" at this "inviting" Theater District Italian, a "red-sauce" mainstay that earns ovations for its "value" pricing and "lively" atmosphere; it gets "packed" pre- and post-curtain, making reservations "a must."

Tres Carnes *Tex-Mex*   22 | 13 | 17 | $16

NEW **East 40s** | 817 Second Ave. (44th St.) | 212-201-0715
East 50s | 954 Third Ave. (bet. 57th & 58th Sts.) | 212-355-8226
Flatiron | 688 Sixth Ave. (22nd St.) | 212-989-8737
www.trescarnes.com

"Tasty", "smoky" meats are the lure at these Tex-Mex quick stops, but the tacos, burritos and bowls are also available with a "plethora of veggie choices"; counter-serve setups have many saying "best to take out" – either way it'll only run "a few pesos."

	FOOD	DECOR	SERVICE	COST

Trestle on Tenth *American*

23 | 20 | 21 | $55

Chelsea | 242 10th Ave. (24th St.) | 212-645-5659 |
www.trestleontenth.com

"Rustic" New American cuisine with Swiss inflections and an "intelligent" wine list appeal to gallery-goers and High Line hoofers alike at this brick-lined Chelsea "oasis"; a "lovely" garden out back and "accommodating" staffers take the edge off of the slightly "pricey" tabs.

Tribeca Grill *American*

23 | 22 | 23 | $67

TriBeCa | 375 Greenwich St. (Franklin St.) | 212-941-3900 |
www.myriadrestaurantgroup.com

"Still a winner", Drew Nieporent and Robert De Niro's "iconic", longtime TriBeCan maintains its "high standards" with "delicious" New American fare and a "masterfully chosen", 2,000 label–strong wine list; the "focused" service and "airy", "upbeat" milieu help keep it "popular", while the $29 prix fixe lunch dodges otherwise "pricey tabs."

Triomphe *French*

23 | 22 | 24 | $72

West 40s | Iroquois Hotel | 49 W. 44th St. (6th Ave.) | 212-453-4233 |
www.triomphe-newyork.com

A "real find" in the Theater District, this all-day French "jewel box" in the Iroquois Hotel turns out "excellent" cuisine in "pleasing-to-the-eye" presentations; its "tiny", "quiet" quarters and "superb service" help take the sting out of "expensive" prices.

Tulsi *Indian*

23 | 22 | 21 | $59

East 40s | 211 E. 46th St. (bet. 2nd & 3rd Aves.) | 212-888-0820 |
www.tulsinyc.com

"Refined" contemporary Indian cooking including some "unusual" specialties is yours at this "classy" standout near Grand Central; true, it's "not cheap", but compensations include "accommodating" service and a "peaceful" setting with "quaint netting between tables."

NEW Tuome *American*

26 | 20 | 22 | $63

East Village | 536 E. Fifth St. (Ave. B) | 646-833-7811 |
www.tuomenyc.com

"Big" flavors arrive in "small" digs at this "inspired" East Village New American fielding a "progressive", Asian-accented menu highlighted by its signature 'Pig Out', a "killer" pork belly dish; "pleasant" staffers and a "spare" but "cozy" setting enhance its "satisfying" feel.

Turkish Cuisine *Turkish*

20 | 14 | 19 | $41

West 40s | 631 Ninth Ave. (bet. 44th & 45th Sts.) | 212-397-9650 |
www.turkishcuisinenyc.com

"Consistent", "tasty" Turkish fare at "reasonable" rates make this Theater District veteran a "delightful" choice "pre-curtain"; fans focus on the "pleasant" service rather than the "down-to-earth" decor, or head for the back garden.

Turkish Kitchen *Turkish*

22 | 18 | 20 | $42

Murray Hill | 386 Third Ave. (bet. 27th & 28th Sts.) | 212-679-6633 |
www.turkishkitchen.com

"As real as it gets", this "tried-and-true" Murray Hill Turk earns "undying loyalty" with "high-quality" traditional eats at "modest" prices; "courteous" staffers oversee the "comfortable" setting, and the "lavish" Sunday brunch "defeats all efforts at self-control."

Turkuaz *Turkish*

20 | 18 | 21 | $40

West 90s | 2637 Broadway (100th St.) | 212-665-9541 | www.turkuazrestaurant.com

"Tasty", well-priced Turkish food served by "costumed" waiters in a room channeling a "sultan's private tent" draw "armchair travelers" and "belly-dancing" buffs to this "amenable" Upper Westsider; the "plentiful" Sunday buffet is an additional lure.

Tuscany Grill *Italian*

23 | 18 | 21 | $50

Bay Ridge | 8620 Third Ave. (bet. 86th & 87th Sts.) | Brooklyn | 718-921-5633 | www.tuscanygrillbrooklyn.com

Beloved in Bay Ridge for its "excellent" contemporary Tuscan food at midrange prices, this "quiet", "cozy little neighborhood" Italian caters to a "mature, upscale" crowd; valet parking and "welcoming" service are further reasons it's "been around for years."

12th Street Bar & Grill *American*

22 | 20 | 22 | $41

Park Slope | 1123 Eighth Ave. (12th St.) | Brooklyn | 718-965-9526 | www.12thstreetbarandgrill.com

A locals' "go-to", this South Sloper is an "old reliable" for "well-prepared" yet "affordable" New Americana delivered by an "accommodating" crew; the "pretty" main dining room is fit for a casual "date", while the round-the-corner pub offers the same menu with "sports on the telly."

12 Chairs *American/Mideastern*

24 | 19 | 21 | $26

SoHo | 56 MacDougal St. (bet. Houston & Prince Sts.) | 212-254-8640

12 Chairs Cafe *American/Mideastern*

NEW Williamsburg | 342 Wythe Ave. (2nd St.) | Brooklyn | 347-227-7077 www.12chairscafe.com

"Locals know" about these "low-key" cafes, a "comforting" "default" for "simple and delicious" American-Mideastern eats served with "no pretensions" at "reasonable prices"; while "nothing fancy", they're "pretty enjoyable" for a "meet-up" and "definitely get busy."

21 Club *American*

23 | 25 | 25 | $81

West 50s | 21 W. 52nd St. (bet. 5th & 6th Aves.) | 212-582-7200 | www.21club.com

"Old NY" is "preserved at its finest" at this circa-1929 former speakeasy, a "one-of-a-kind" Midtown "icon" where "well-prepared" American "classics" come via "accommodating" staffers in "throwback" surrounds with "interesting" old toys hanging from the ceiling and private rooms upstairs; you'll need to "bring your credit card" and "be sure to dress" (jackets required, no jeans), but it's one for the "bucket list."

26 Seats *French*

22 | 18 | 21 | $49

East Village | 168 Ave. B (bet. 10th & 11th Sts.) | 212-677-4787 | www.26seatsbistro.com

A "date night" to remember kicks into gear at this "romantic" Alphabet City option, a "cozy" French bistro featuring "delightful" classics, "lovely" service and endearingly "mismatched decor"; yes, it's as "minuscule" as the name implies, but skimpy square footage aside, "great value" abounds.

| | FOOD | DECOR | SERVICE | COST |

Two Boots *Pizza*   19 | 13 | 15 | $15

East 40s | Grand Central | 89 E. 42nd St., Lower Dining Concourse
(Vanderbilt Ave.) | 212-557-7992
East 80s | 1617 Second Ave. (84th St.) | 212-734-0317
East Village | 42 Ave. A (bet. 3rd & 4th Sts.) | 212-254-1919
West 40s | 625 Ninth Ave. (bet. 44th & 45th Sts.) | 212-956-2668
West 90s | 2547 Broadway (bet. 95th & 96th Sts.) | 212-280-2668
West Village | 201 W. 11th St. (7th Ave. S.) | 212-633-9096
NEW **Park Slope** | 284 Fifth Ave. (1st St.) | Brooklyn | 718-499-0008
Williamsburg | 558 Driggs Ave. (7th St.) | Brooklyn | 718-387-2668
"Nontraditional" is the word for these "Cajun-inspired" pizzerias where
a "crunchy" cornmeal crust, "yummy" toppings and "provocative"
names add some "N'Awlins" flavor; the settings and service are "casual"
and tailor-made for "kids."

2 Duck Goose *Chinese*   19 | 16 | 17 | $41

Gowanus | 400 Fourth Ave. (6th St.) | Brooklyn | 347-987-4808 |
www.2duckgoose.com
Looking to Hong Kong, this "tiny" Gowanus spot plies an "enjoyable"
lineup of "classic" Cantonese dishes goosed up with "creative" contemporary touches in "bare-bones" digs; though a few feel it's "uninspired",
more deem it a "nice addition to the neighborhood."

Two Hands *Australian*   ∇ 23 | 23 | 20 | $19

Little Italy | 164 Mott St. (Broome St.) | no phone | www.twohandsnyc.com
This "trendy", daytime-only Aussie cafe in Little Italy "excites taste buds"
with its "tasty", "Instagram"-ready breakfast and lunch offerings; "cheery
baristas" pull flat-whites in the "small", "charming" space, leaving "long
weekend waits" as the sole drawback.

NEW **212 Steakhouse** *Steak*   22 | 20 | 20 | $69

East 50s | 316 E. 53rd St. (bet. 1st & 2nd Aves.) | 212-858-0646 |
www.212steakhouse.com
"*The* place for Kobe" beef (as well as "tender" Wagyu), this "unpretentious" Midtown meatery offers "quality" renderings of the premium Japanese cuts in a "comfy" modern setting; service can be "swell" or "erratic",
but "good value" makes it an "inviting" "alternative" for carnivores.

Txikito *Spanish*   24 | 16 | 21 | $57

Chelsea | 240 Ninth Ave. (bet. 24th & 25th Sts.) | 212-242-4730 |
www.txikitonyc.com
Those "dreaming of San Sebastián" make for this "lively" Chelsea
Spaniard where "smart" staffers serve an "absolutely delicious", ever-
evolving array of "real-deal" Basque tapas; with "so many wonderful
choices", it "can get expensive in a hurry", but at least the "terrific" wine
selection is "moderately priced."

Umami Burger *Burgers*   21 | 14 | 17 | $25

Battery Park City | Hudson Eats | 230 Vesey St. (West St.) |
917-728-4400
Greenwich Village | 432 Sixth Ave. (bet. 9th & 10th Sts.) | 212-677-8626
NEW **Williamsburg** | 158 N. 4th St. (Bedford Ave.) | Brooklyn |
718-907-5680
www.umamiburger.com
Whether "overhyped" or "living up to the hype", this popular LA-based

patty purveyor offers "unusual", "upscale" burgers packing "strong", umami-rich flavors like Parmesan ("dreamy") and truffle ("a must"); the Village and Williamsburg outlets feature table service and a full bar, while the Hudson Eats branch is just a counter.

NEW Uma Temakeria *Japanese* ▽ 20 | 20 | 22 | $20

Chelsea | 64 Seventh Ave. (14th St.) | 646-360-3260 | www.umatemakeria.com

"Great-tasting" temaki (cone-shaped sushi hand rolls) is the focus of this "fast-casual" Chelsea Japanese overseen by a "cheerful" crew; the "interesting concept" is probably best for takeout, given "limited seating" and "spartan" surroundings.

Umbertos Clam House *Italian* 21 | 14 | 18 | $46

Little Italy | 132 Mulberry St. (bet. Grand & Hester Sts.) | 212-431-7545 | www.umbertosclamhouse.com

Linguine-lovers "dig the clams" and pastas "like mamma used to make" at this "casual" Italian seafooder on Mulberry Street; purists "miss the original location" and knock its "tourist" tendencies, but all appreciate the "fair" pricing.

Uncle Boons *Thai* 25 | 21 | 22 | $52

NoLita | 7 Spring St. (bet. Bowery & Elizabeth St.) | 646-370-6650 | www.uncleboons.com

Something "different from the norm", this "cutting-edge" NoLita Thai offers a "new-school" take on Siamese cuisine via "vibrant flavors" and very "serious spicing"; an "attentive" team presides over the "knickknack"-filled basement space, where "must-try" beer slushies can be ordered from the "cozy" bar.

Uncle Jack's Steakhouse *Steak* 23 | 20 | 22 | $79

West 30s | 440 Ninth Ave. (bet. 34th & 35th Sts.) | 212-244-0005
West 50s | 44 W. 56th St. (bet. 5th & 6th Aves.) | 212-245-1550
Bayside | 39-40 Bell Blvd. (40th Ave.) | Queens | 718-229-1100
www.unclejacks.com

"Perfectly cooked" beef plated in "tremendous" portions is the stock-in-trade of these "pleasing" steakhouses with "old-school" looks and "high" but "worth-every-penny" tabs; bonus points go to an "excellent" staff that treats everyone like "Uncle Jack's favorite niece or nephew."

Uncle Nick's *Greek* 21 | 13 | 19 | $38

Chelsea | 382 Eighth Ave. (29th St.) | 212-609-0500
West 50s | 747 Ninth Ave. (bet. 50th & 51st Sts.) | 212-245-7992
www.unclenicksgreekrestaurant.com

Fans say there's "no need to venture to Astoria" given the "tasty", "stick-to-your-ribs" chow and "affordable" tabs at these "casual" Greek tavernas known for their "wonderful flaming cheese" dish; sure, the settings are on the "shabby" side, but they stay "busy" all the same.

Union Square Cafe *American* 27 | 23 | 26 | $78

Union Square | 21 E. 16th St. (bet. 5th Ave. & Union Sq.) | 212-243-4020 | www.unionsquarecafe.com

A "perennial favorite with good reason", Danny Meyer's "stellar" Union Square "cornerstone" still fires "on all cylinders" with "exceptional" New American food served with "signature warmth" by "informed" staffers in an "inviting", "civilized" milieu; it "can still be a tough reservation", but "go now" as it's closing at the end of 2015 and relocating to Park Avenue South.

Untamed Sandwiches *Sandwiches* | 25 | 20 | 24 | $17 |

West 30s | 43 W. 39th St. (bet. 5th & 6th Aves.) | 646-669-9397 | www.untamedsandwiches.com

"Bringing sandwiches to a new level", this "hip" fast-casual spot near Bryant Park features "creative combos" of "killer" braised meats and veggies, plus beer and wine; "friendly" service and "affordable" tabs add to its "understated" appeal.

Untitled *American* | – | – | – | E |

Meatpacking District | Whitney Museum | 99 Gansevoort St. (bet. 10th Ave. & Washington St.) | 212-570-3670 | www.untitledatthewhitney.com

In tandem with the Whitney Museum's move to the Meatpacking District comes the relocation of this Danny Meyer New American, where chef Michael Anthony (Gramercy Tavern) offers a seasonal, vegetable-centric menu in airy, industrial-chic digs with glass walls and soaring ceilings; outdoor dining adds some additional seating, but be prepared for big crowds – it's parked at the foot of a High Line exit.

NEW Upholstery Store *American* | ∇ 25 | 26 | 25 | $47 |

West Village | 713 Washington St. (bet. 11th & Perry Sts.) | 212-929-6384 | www.kg-ny.com

They "take pride in the details" at Kurt Gutenbrunner's West Village wine bar, back on the scene following a revamp and now offering "simple" yet "exceptional" American small plates; a rustic-chic setting and "solid" vino list burnish its "sophisticated" ambiance.

NEW Upland *Californian* | 25 | 26 | 24 | $73 |

Murray Hill | 345 Park Ave. S. (26th St.) | 212-686-1006 | www.uplandnyc.com

There's a "hip scene" in progress at this "much-hyped" Californian off Park Avenue South where chef Justin Smillie offers a "novel", Italian-accented menu led by "outstanding pastas"; "difficult reservations" are offset by "patient" service, a "lively", "beautiful" crowd and that swoon-worthy, golden-hued setting.

Upstate *Seafood* | 27 | 19 | 23 | $45 |

East Village | 95 First Ave. (bet. 5th & 6th Sts.) | 917-408-3395 | www.upstatenyc.com

Bivalve "connoisseurs" dig this "lively" East Village oyster bar for its "first-rate" seafood and "revolving" craft beer list; a no-rezzie rule and "ridiculously small" dimensions can make for "long waits", but payoffs include "on-point" service and "reasonable" tabs.

Uskudar *Turkish* | 23 | 13 | 21 | $39 |

East 70s | 1405 Second Ave. (bet. 73rd & 74th Sts.) | 212-988-4046 | www.uskudarnyc.com

Although "narrow" with just a "handful of tables", this "welcoming" UES "hole-in-the-wall" does a brisk business thanks to its "delicious", "straightforward" Turkish cuisine and "personal" service; "easy-on-the-wallet" prices seal the deal.

	FOOD	DECOR	SERVICE	COST

Utsav *Indian*
21 | 18 | 19 | $41

West 40s | 1185 Sixth Ave. (bet. 46th & 47th Sts.) | 212-575-2525 | www.utsavny.com

Although somewhat "difficult to find", this Theater District Indian delivers "above-average" classics in "civilized" modern digs manned by a "gracious" crew; if prices seem a "little high", the daily lunch buffet and $35 pre-theater prix fixe are a relative "bargain."

Uva *Italian*
22 | 21 | 21 | $46

East 70s | 1486 Second Ave. (bet. 77th & 78th Sts.) | 212-472-4552 | www.uvawinebar.com

"Beautiful food" and "beautiful people" collide at this "bustling", "noisy" UES "date destination" trading in "delicious" Italian dishes and "wonderful wines"; an "enchanting" back garden, "decent" prices and "attentive" service secure its standing as a "neighborhood favorite."

Valbella *Italian*
24 | 24 | 24 | $92

East 50s | 11 E. 53rd St. (bet. 5th & Madison Aves.) | 212-888-8955
Meatpacking District | 421 W. 13th St. (bet. 9th Ave. & Washington St.) | 212-645-7777
www.valbellarestaurants.com

Thanks to "excellent" Italian cuisine, "terrific" wines, "lavish" settings and "solicitous" service, these "classy" destinations draw a "mix of ages" in the mood to "celebrate"; just "bring an appetite" and your "expense account" – and keep their "unbelievable private rooms" in mind for "special occasions."

The Vanderbilt *American*
22 | 21 | 21 | $39

Prospect Heights | 570 Vanderbilt Ave (Bergen St.) | Brooklyn | 718-623-0570 | www.thevanderbiltnyc.com

Now a bona fide "standby" on Prospect Heights' happening Vanderbilt Avenue strip, Saul Bolton's "stylish", midpriced American gastropub trades in "delightful", "strictly-in-season" small plates washed down with "delicious cocktails"; locals dub it a "friendly", "no-hassles" experience.

Vanessa's Dumpling House *Chinese*
22 | 8 | 13 | $10

East Village | 220 E. 14th St. (bet. 2nd & 3rd Aves.) | 212-529-1329
Lower East Side | 118 Eldridge St. (bet. Broome & Grand Sts.) | 212-625-8008
Williamsburg | 310 Bedford Ave. (bet. 1st & 2nd Sts.) | Brooklyn | 718-218-8809
www.vanessas.com

Just a few dollars fund a "pig out" at these "always-busy" dumpling dispensers whose "amazing" namesake specialty is fried or steamed "while you wait"; the setups with minimal seating are "utilitarian" and service is "insouciant" at best, but for a "fast, filling" nosh, you "can't beat" 'em.

Vatan *Indian/Vegetarian*
24 | 25 | 24 | $41

Murray Hill | 409 Third Ave. (29th St.) | 212-689-5666 | www.vatanny.com

An "incredible variety of flavors" from "delicate" to "spicy" emerges from the kitchen of this Murray Hill vegetarian Indian where the "authentic Gujarati" specialties come in an all-you-can-eat Thali format for $32; "accommodating" service and a transporting "village" setting complete the "totally unique experience."

	FOOD	DECOR	SERVICE	COST

Veselka *Ukrainian*

21 | 14 | 17 | $25

East Village | 144 Second Ave. (9th St.) | 212-228-9682 | www.veselka.com
The "all-encompassing menu" of "hearty", "fair-priced" Ukrainian
staples (think "handmade pierogi", "terrific borscht") at this 24/7 East
Village "institution" draws everyone from "families" to the "post-party
crowd"; maybe there's "no decor" to speak of, but it's got "old-time
atmosphere" to spare.

Vesta *Italian*

26 | 20 | 24 | $39

Astoria | 21-02 30th Ave. (21st St.) | Queens | 718-545-5550 |
www.vestavino.com
"Neighborhood" spots don't get much more "cozy" than this "off-the-
beaten-path" Astoria Italian fielding "spot-on", "farm-to-table" fare
dispatched by an "attentive" team; though the menu is rather "limited",
it "changes often", while the "warm, intimate" vibe is a constant.

Vesuvio *Italian*

22 | 17 | 21 | $29

Bay Ridge | 7305 Third Ave. (bet. 73rd & 74th Sts.) | Brooklyn |
718-745-0222 | www.vesuviobayridge.com
It may "not have the name recognition" of other Brooklyn pizza stalwarts,
but this "comfortable" neighborhood Italian in Bay Ridge has been slinging
"delicious" pies since 1953, along with an "abundance" of pastas; "friendly" staffers, "fair" tabs and "never a long wait" keep regulars regular.

Vezzo *Pizza*

24 | 15 | 17 | $28

Murray Hill | 178 Lexington Ave. (31st St.) | 212-839-8300 |
www.vezzothincrust.com
"Paper-thin", "crispy"-crusted pies with "toppings to suit any taste" are
the specialty of this "busy", "bargain-priced" Murray Hill pizzeria; the
digs are "tight" and service can be "slooow", but all's forgiven after a bite
of that "outstanding" Shroomtown pie.

NEW Via Carota *Italian*

24 | 21 | 23 | $64

West Village | 51 Grove St. (bet. Bleecker St. & 7th Ave. S.) | no phone |
www.viacarota.com
The "love child of Buvette and I Sodi", this "charming" West Village Italian via chefs Jody Williams and Rita Sodi offers a "delicious", somewhat
"pricey" menu (with particularly "spot-on" vegetable dishes) in a "spacious", rustic-chic room; "no reservations" means "plan accordingly", or
join the "vibrant scene" at the bar.

Via Emilia *Italian*

22 | 16 | 21 | $48

Flatiron | 47 E. 21st St. (bet. B'way & Park Ave. S.) | 212-505-3072 |
www.viaemilianyc.net
Known for its "delectable" Emilia-Romagnan food paired with "excellent wines from the region" (including "the best Lambruscos"), this
"friendly" Flatiron Italian is also appreciated for its "reasonable prices";
the "bright" setting may be on the "stark" side, but at least there's
"elbow room" between tables.

Via Quadronno *Italian*

22 | 17 | 17 | $44

East 50s | 767 Fifth Ave. (59th St.) | 212-421-5300
East 70s | 25 E. 73rd St. (bet. 5th & Madison Aves.) | 212-650-9880

continued

NEW **East 80s** | 1228 Madison Ave. (bet. 88th & 89th Sts.) | 212-369-9000
www.viaquadronno.com

"Rub elbows" with all the "chic Euro moms" over panini and espresso at these "seriously clubby" UES renditions of a Milanese bar (with a counter-service spin-off in the GM building); granted, tabs are "pricey" and the "cozy" digs can be "tight", but it's perfect "before shopping or the museums."

ViceVersa *Italian* 24 | 22 | 24 | $61

West 50s | 325 W. 51st St. (bet. 8th & 9th Aves.) | 212-399-9291 | www.viceversanyc.com

At this "vibrant" Theater District staple, the "top-notch" Italian cooking garners as much praise as the "attentive" staffers who will "get you out in time" for your curtain; factor in a "sleek" interior augmented with a "delightful" back patio, and it's an all-around "pleasant" dining experience.

NEW Vic's *Italian/Mediterranean* 22 | 21 | 22 | $55

NoHo | 31 Great Jones St. (bet. Bowery & Lafayette St.) | 212-253-5700 | www.vicsnewyork.com

A thorough reinvention of the former Five Points, this "laid-back" NoHo Italian-Med from the Cookshop team features an "interesting" menu highlighted by "wonderful" housemade pasta and "creative pizza" from its wood-burning oven; an "open floor plan" with "well-spaced tables" adds to the "welcoming" vibe, though critics say it "doesn't seem like it's firing on all cylinders" yet.

Victor's Cafe *Cuban* 23 | 21 | 22 | $58

West 50s | 236 W. 52nd St. (bet. B'way & 8th Ave.) | 212-586-7714 | www.victorscafe.com

In business since 1963, this Theater District Cuban "doesn't rest on its laurels", supplying "solid" food and "fantastic" mojitos in "energetic" environs exuding classic "Havana style" – "ceiling fans and all"; "old-world" service and live music enhance this "welcome respite", but be prepared for "noise" and "tourists."

Vietnaam *Vietnamese* 22 | 14 | 20 | $27

East 80s | 1700 Second Ave. (88th St.) | 212-722-0558 | www.vietnaam88.com

"Excellent renditions" of Vietnamese standards make this "under-the-radar" Upper Eastsider a "delightful" find for classic satays and noodle dishes; "satisfying" service and "good-value" prices seal the deal – locals are "so glad to have it" in the neighborhood.

The View *American* 18 | 23 | 18 | $109

West 40s | Marriott Marquis Hotel | 1535 Broadway (bet. 45th & 46th Sts.) | 212-704-8900 | www.theviewny.com

"As the name implies", it's all about the "second-to-none" 360-degree views of Manhattan at this "revolving" Times Square hotel eatery; just "be prepared to spend" to dine on "so-so" prix fixe-only American fare with "lots of tourists", though even jaded natives admit it can be a "fun experience."

	FOOD	DECOR	SERVICE	COST

Villa Berulia *Italian* — 25 | 20 | 27 | $54

Murray Hill | 107 E. 34th St. (bet. Lexington & Park Aves.) | 212-689-1970 | www.villaberulia.com

"Exceptional" hospitality is the strong suit of this Murray Hill "family affair" that follows through with "excellent" Italian fare and "even better specials"; the "throwback" mood pleases its "older crowd", and "fair prices" seal the deal.

Villa Mosconi *Italian* — 22 | 16 | 22 | $55

Greenwich Village | 69 MacDougal St. (bet. Bleecker & Houston Sts.) | 212-674-0320 | www.villamosconi.com

Red-sauce fanciers endorse this "old-school" Village Italian "throwback" (since 1976) for its "generous portions" of "smack-your-lips-good" classics delivered by "delightful" staffers; maybe the "old-world" digs could "use updating", but "decent prices" please its "longtime" regulars.

Vincent's *Italian* — 22 | 16 | 21 | $49

Little Italy | 119 Mott St. (Hester St.) | 212-226-8133 | www.02de1be.netsolhost.com

A Little Italy fixture since "before you were born", this 1904-vintage Italian is renowned for its "incredible" hot marinara sauce that "makes the dishes sing"; "quick" service, comfy "old-school" digs and "price-is-right" tabs cement its "standby" status.

NEW **The Vine** *Italian* — — | — | — | M

Chelsea | Eventi Hotel | 851 Sixth Ave. (30th St.) | 212-201-4065 | www.eventihotel.com

Set in Chelsea's Eventi Hotel, this airy cocktail lounge offers classic tipples, craft beers and a Euro-centric wine list in sleek digs that open onto a leafy patio; chef Laurent Tourondel provides the accompanying Italian menu, featuring dishes like crostini and wood-fired pizzas.

Vinegar Hill House *American* — 23 | 22 | 21 | $52

Vinegar Hill | 72 Hudson Ave. (bet. Front & Water Sts.) | Brooklyn | 718-522-1018 | www.vinegarhillhouse.com

"Brooklyn to its core", this "hipster magnet" in "middle-of-nowhere" Vinegar Hill is "worth seeking out" for "appealing" New American "market cooking" served in "funky", "cozy" digs complete with the "most romantic garden"; the only rubs are "cramped" conditions and "long waits" (reservations are recommended).

Virgil's Real Barbecue *BBQ* — 21 | 15 | 18 | $38

West 40s | 152 W. 44th St. (bet. B'way & 6th Ave.) | 212-921-9494 | www.virgilsbbq.com

"Solid" BBQ turns up in Times Square at this longtime "crowd-pleaser" that rolls out "huge portions" of "greasy" grub in "massive" digs; OK, it's "not Texas" and the setup's "nothing memorable", but you'd never know it from the hordes of "tourists" crowding in.

NEW **Virginia's** *American* — ∇ 23 | 17 | 22 | $45

East Village | 647 E. 11th St. (Ave. C) | 212-658-0182 | www.virginiasnyc.com

Per Se and Locanda Verde alums are behind this "small" East Village bistro offering a "limited menu" of "original", market-driven American dishes; framed vintage menus from world-famous restaurants line its whitewashed walls, while vaulted ceilings and leather banquettes lend a "comfortable" feel.

Vitae *American*

24 | 20 | 21 | $65

East 40s | 4 E. 46th St. (bet. 5th & Madison Aves.) | 212-682-3562 | www.vitaenyc.com

A "beautiful", "modern" bi-level space and "even better" seasonal American cooking have fans calling this upscale Midtowner a Grand Central–area "gem"; a roomy front bar offering lots of by-the-glass wines, a "quieter", "romantic" upstairs with a "view of the scene below" and "personable" service help justify the "expensive" bill.

Vivolo *Italian*

20 | 20 | 21 | $53

East 70s | 140 E. 74th St. (Lexington Ave.) | 212-737-3533

Cucina Vivolo *Italian*

East 70s | 138 E. 74th St. (Lexington Ave.) | 212-717-4700 www.cucinavivolo.com

An "old-school" enclave set in a "fireplace"-equipped townhouse, this circa-1977 UES Italian seduces its mature fan base with "simple", "satisfying" repasts, "clubby" looks and "welcoming" service; its next-door cafe is more casual and less expensive.

V-Note *Vegan*

24 | 21 | 22 | $41

East 70s | 1522 First Ave. (bet. 79th & 80th Sts.) | 212-249-5009 | www.v-notenyc.com

"Who could imagine that vegan food could become addictive?" marvel those "hooked" on this Upper Eastsider's "artfully prepared", comfort-oriented dishes; a "refined", often-"quiet" setting, organic wines and "reasonable" tabs complete the "pleasant surprise."

Wa Jeal *Chinese*

23 | 15 | 18 | $36

East 80s | 1588 Second Ave. (bet. 82nd & 83rd Sts.) | 212-396-3339 | www.wajeal.com

For a "10-alarm fire" of the taste buds, diners turn to this "exotic" UES Chinese praised for its "incendiary" but "nuanced" Sichuan cooking (there are also milder dishes for blander palates); factor in "quick service" and "comfortable prices", and no one minds that the decor's just "so-so."

Walker's *Pub Food*

19 | 15 | 20 | $36

TriBeCa | 16 N. Moore St. (Varick St.) | 212-941-0142 | www.walkersnyc.com

"As local as it gets in TriBeCa", this "quintessential" neighborhood pub is populated by everyone from area "families" and "bankers" to "film people shooting nearby"; "welcoming" vibes, "funky" digs and "quality" bar food at "value" rates keep the place humming.

Wallflower *French*

24 | 23 | 24 | $60

West Village | 235 W. 12th St. (Greenwich Ave.) | 646-682-9842 | www.wallflowernyc.com

Locals are "charmed" by this "unpretentious" West Village French boîte where a "limited menu" of "delicious, thoughtfully crafted" Gallic bites is served alongside "unique" cocktails; "small, intimate" confines and "super-attentive" service make it a "perfect date spot."

	FOOD	DECOR	SERVICE	COST

Wallsé *Austrian* 25 | 22 | 23 | $86

West Village | 344 W. 11th St. (Washington St.) | 212-352-2300 |
www.kg-ny.com

The "only thing missing is an Alpine view" at this "vunderful" West Village Austrian via chef Kurt Gutenbrunner, whose "haute" menu "always surprises"; "European-style service" and a "serene", "arty" setting hung with paintings by Julian Schnabel help justify the "special-occasion" tabs.

Walter Foods *American* 23 | 23 | 21 | $41

Williamsburg | 253 Grand St. (Roebling St.) | Brooklyn | 718-387-8783
Walter's *American*
Fort Greene | 166 DeKalb Ave. (Cumberland St.) | Brooklyn |
718-488-7800
www.walterfoods.com

Embodying Brooklyn's "Socratic ideal of a neighborhood place", these "pub-ish" spots supply "solid", spiffed-up American comfort fare and "killer" cocktails; "reasonable" prices and "comfortable" interiors seal the deal – they "care about the details and it shows."

Water Club *American* 23 | 25 | 24 | $76

Murray Hill | East River & 30th St. (enter on 23rd St.) | 212-683-3333 |
www.thewaterclub.com

"Inspiring water views" from a barge docked on the East River off Murray Hill lend a "romantic" air to this "charming" destination, where a "pro" staff serves "dependably good" American fare (including a "terrific" Sunday brunch); sure, it's "geared toward tourists" and best enjoyed "when your rich uncle is in town", but it's hard to top for "special-occasion" dining.

Water's Edge *American/Seafood* 22 | 25 | 21 | $69

Long Island City | East River & 44th Dr. (Vernon Blvd.) | Queens |
718-482-0033 | www.watersedgenyc.com

"Romantic" is the word for this LIC "special-occasion" favorite where the "magnificent" Manhattan skyline views induce swoons; the "well-prepared" American seafood may be "expensive for what you get", but not when you factor in the "exceptional ambiance."

Water Table *New England* — | — | — | VE

Greenpoint | India St. Pier (at FDR Dr. & 23rd St.) | Brooklyn |
917-499-5727 | www.thewatertablenyc.com

This dinner boat sailing from the India Street pier in Greenpoint serves locavore-oriented New England fare in a $75 three-course prix fixe, plus cocktails and East Coast beers and wines; the WWII-era vessel, outfitted with wooden tables and benches, exudes rollicking, rock 'n' roll vibrations.

Watty & Meg *American* 19 | 20 | 20 | $39

Cobble Hill | 248 Court St. (Kane St.) | Brooklyn | 718-643-0007 |
www.wattyandmeg.com

"Flavor abounds" in the "interesting" "market-to-table" New American dishes at this "welcoming" Cobble Hill "neighborhood place"; the "comfortable", "spacious" interior and "quaint" sidewalk seating are all "kid-friendly", yet the noise level usually "isn't too bad", so "proper conversation is possible."

	FOOD	DECOR	SERVICE	COST

Waverly Inn *American*

22 **23** **21** **$74**

West Village | 16 Bank St. (Waverly Pl.) | 917-828-1154 |
www.waverlynyc.com

Maybe the "celebrity buzz has slowed", but Graydon Carter's "clubby" West Villager still offers "high-end" spins on American "home-cooking" favorites in "cozy" confines (festooned with droll Edward Sorel murals); in winter, regulars say a "cozy booth by the fireplace" is "where it's at."

West Bank Cafe *American*

20 **17** **21** **$46**

West 40s | 407 W. 42nd St. (bet. 9th & 10th Aves.) | 212-695-6909 |
www.westbankcafe.com

Convenient to 42nd Street's Theater Row, this pre-curtain "standby" keeps its audience coming back with "satisfying" American chow served in "congenial" environs; the menu "may not be the most exciting", but the prices are "fair" and they get you "out on time" for your show.

Westville *American*

23 **15** **19** **$28**

Chelsea | 246 W. 18th St. (8th Ave.) | 212-924-2223
East Village | 173 Ave. A (11th St.) | 212-677-2033
Hudson Square | 333 Hudson St. (bet. Charlton & Vandam Sts.) |
212-776-1404
West Village | 210 W. 10th St. (Bleecker St.) | 212-741-7971
www.westvillenyc.com

These "homey" standbys maintain a loyal fan base with "wonderful", market-oriented American fare that includes many "interesting vegetable dishes" at "super-value" tabs; overseen by a "courteous" crew, they're predictably "busy", but the waits are "well worth it."

White Bear *Chinese*

25 **3** **11** **$9**

Flushing | 135-02 Roosevelt Ave. (Prince St.) | Queens | 718-961-2322

"Delish" and "addictive", the spicy chili oil wontons are the "signature dish" at this "must-stop" Flushing Chinese also known for its "awesome noodles" and "price-is-right" tabs; "broken-English" service and a "tiny", "hole-in-the-wall" setting make most "take it to go."

White Street *American*

22 **24** **21** **$86**

TriBeCa | 221 W. Broadway (bet. Franklin & White Sts.) | 212-944-8378 |
www.whitestreetnyc.com

With its "breathtaking" chandeliers and "comfy" banquettes, this "romantic" TriBeCa dining room makes a "grand" backdrop for "innovative" New American cooking that gets "a little kick" via global spices; optimists see "potential" once it "works out the kinks."

'Wichcraft *Sandwiches*

18 **13** **16** **$17**

Chelsea | 601 W. 26th St. (bet. 11th & 12th Aves.) | 212-780-0577
Chelsea | 269 11th Ave. (bet. 27th & 28th Sts.) | 212-780-0577
East 40s | 555 Fifth Ave. (46th St.) | 212-780-0577
East 40s | 245 Park Ave. (47th St.) | 212-780-0577
Flatiron | 11 E. 20th St. (B'way) | 212-780-0577
Greenwich Village | 60 E. Eighth St. (Mercer St.) | 212-780-0577
TriBeCa | 397 Greenwich St. (Beach St.) | 212-780-0577
West 40s | Rockefeller Ctr. | 1 Rockefeller Plaza (bet. 5th & 6th Aves.) |
212-780-0577

	FOOD	DECOR	SERVICE	COST

continued

West 60s | 61 W. 62nd St. (Columbus Ave.) | 212-780-0577
www.wichcraft.com

"Original" sandwiches and "on-the-go" snacks made from "quality" in-gredients justify the "premium" price tags at this "quick-bite" chain from *Top Chef*'s Tom Colicchio; "no-frills" setups and "inconsistent" service don't deter the lunchtime "masses."

NEW Wildair *American* 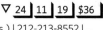 – | – | – | M

Lower East Side | 142 Orchard St. (Rivington St.) | 646-964-5624 |
www.wildair.nyc

From the owners of the tasting menu–only Contra, this nearby LES American is a bit more casual, offering à la carte dinner items (the bread course is a must) served in a pared-down room sporting an open kitchen and communal high-top tables; natural wines are a focus of the vino list, which leans toward contemporary French bottles.

Wild Edibles *Seafood* ▽ 24 | 11 | 19 | $36

Murray Hill | 535 Third Ave. (bet. 35th & 36th Sts.) | 212-213-8552 |
www.wildedibles.com

"Fresh-off-the-boat" catch – from fish 'n' chips to "all the oyster varieties you could ever want" – lures diners to this moderately priced Murray Hill seafooder; despite the "cramped quarters" and sometimes "slow" service, fans applaud the "feeling of integrity about the place."

Wild Ginger *Asian/Vegan* 23 | 20 | 22 | $28

Little Italy | 380 Broome St. (bet. Mott & Mulberry Sts.) | 212-966-1883
Cobble Hill | 112 Smith St. (bet. Dean & Pacific Sts.) | Brooklyn |
718-858-3880
NEW Williamsburg | 182 N. 10th St. (bet. Bedford & Driggs Aves.) |
Brooklyn | 718-218-8828
www.wildgingerny.com

For a "healthy change of pace", find "vegan paradise" at these separately owned standbys where the "creative", "flavorful" Pan-Asian dishes showcase "mock meats" that "even carnivores can enjoy"; "cheap" prices complete the "wholesome" picture.

NEW Willow *American* ▽ 20 | 20 | 20 | M

Bedford-Stuyvesant | 506 Franklin Ave. (Fulton St.) | Brooklyn |
718-399-2384 | www.willowbk.com

The concise menu matches the compact setting of this "good-vibes" Bed-Stuy New American offering "delicious" hyper-seasonal fare crafted from local ingredients; brought to you by the folks behind Gowanus' The Pines, it's done up in standard Brooklyn style – think exposed brick, rows of wine bottles – though high ceilings keep the claustrophobia factor low.

Wilma Jean *Southern* 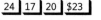 24 | 17 | 20 | $23

Carroll Gardens | 345 Smith St. (Carroll St.) | Brooklyn | 718-422-0444 |
www.wilmajean345.com

"Seriously delectable" fried chicken and "sides your mama wishes she could make" comprise the "perfectly edited menu" at this "casual" Carroll Gardens Southerner that's more than "worth the calories"; "excellent" beer and "good-value" tabs make this one a "neighborhood" keeper.

	FOOD	DECOR	SERVICE	COST

Wo Hop *Chinese*

22 | **6** | **15** | **$20**

Chinatown | 17 Mott St. (bet. Mosco & Worth Sts.) | 212-962-8617 |
www.wohopnyc.com

"Old-school" is an understatement when it comes to this 1938-vintage Chinatown double-decker known for "tried-and-true" Cantonese cooking at "rock-bottom", cash-only rates; despite "abrupt" service and "dingy" digs decorated with a "zillion photos", "long lines" are the norm – especially "late-night."

Wolfgang's Steakhouse *Steak*

26 | **21** | **23** | **$88**

NEW **East 40s** | 16 E. 46th St. (bet. 5th & Madison Aves.) |
212-490-8300

East 50s | 200 E. 54th St. (3rd Ave.) | 212-588-9653
Murray Hill | 4 Park Ave. (33rd St.) | 212-889-3369
TriBeCa | 409 Greenwich St. (bet. Beach & Hubert Sts.) | 212-925-0350
West 40s | NY Times Bldg. | 250 W. 41st St. (bet. 7th & 8th Aves.) |
212-921-3720
www.wolfgangssteakhouse.net

"Masterfully done" steaks "with all the trimmings" lure "mostly men" to these "high-energy" chop shops also touted for their "outstanding" wine lists, "old-school" service and "awesome ceilings" in the Park Avenue outlet; "holler"-worthy noise and "sticker-shock" tabs notwithstanding, it's a "top contender" in its genre.

Wollensky's Grill *Steak*

24 | **19** | **23** | **$68**

East 40s | 201 E. 49th St. (3rd Ave.) | 212-753-0444 |
www.smithandwollenskynyc.com

"Less highfalutin" and somewhat "cheaper" than its next-door big brother, Smith & Wollensky, this "casual" East Midtowner serves "dynamite" steaks and burgers in "high-energy" environs; it's especially beloved for its "late-dining" hours – open nightly till 2 AM.

Wondee Siam *Thai*

19 | **10** | **17** | **$26**

West 50s | 792 Ninth Ave. (bet. 52nd & 53rd Sts.) | 212-459-9057
West 50s | 813 Ninth Ave. (bet. 53rd & 54th Sts.) | 917-286-1726
West 100s | 969 Amsterdam Ave. (bet. 107th & 108th Sts.) |
212-531-1788
www.wondeesiam2.com

"Consistently delicious" Thai fare brings back "memories of Bangkok" at these "hole-in-the-wall" Westsiders; OK, they're "not fancy" and "seating is limited", but service is "fast" and regulars say the "rock-bottom prices" are the key to their enduring "popularity."

Writing Room *American*

20 | **21** | **19** | **$55**

East 80s | 1703 Second Ave. (bet. 88th & 89th Sts.) | 212-335-0075 |
www.thewritingroomnyc.com

"Paying homage to its predecessor, Elaine's", this UES American is lined with photos of "famous patrons" from back in the day, while their literary works enjoy pride of place in the "inviting" rear study; expect "solid" food, "friendly" service and a bar "packed" with a "fiftysomething crowd."

Wu Liang Ye *Chinese*

24 | **11** | **15** | **$39**

West 40s | 36 W. 48th St. (bet. 5th & 6th Aves.) | 212-398-2308 |
www.wuliangyenyc.com

Just off Rock Center and "one of the best Chinese restaurants north of C-town" is this source for "lip-tingling", "real-deal" Sichuan cooking ("bring tissues to deal with your runny nose"); "bargain prices" outweigh the "glum" decor and "indifferent" service.

Xi'an Famous Foods *Chinese/Noodle Shop* | 23 | 8 | 14 | $15 |

Chinatown | 67 Bayard St. (bet. Bowery & Mott St.) | 718-885-7788
NEW East 70s | 328 E. 78th St. (bet. 1st & 2nd Aves.) | 212-786-2068
East Village | 81 St. Marks Pl. (1st Ave.) | 212-786-2068
NEW Murray Hill | 14 E. 34th St. (bet. 5th & Madison Aves.) | 212-786-2068
West 40s | 24 W. 45th St. (bet. 5th & 6th Aves.) | 212-786-2068
West 100s | 2675 Broadway (bet. 101st & 102nd Sts.) | 212-786-2068
NEW Greenpoint | 648 Manhattan Ave. (bet. Nassau & Norman Aves.) | Brooklyn | 212-786-2068
Flushing | Golden Shopping Mall | 41-28 Main St. (41st Rd.) | Queens | 718-888-7713
www.xianfoods.com

Fans of "banging" hand-pulled noodles discover "fiery" "nirvana" at this "burgeoning" Western Chinese chain also famed for cumin-lamb burgers so "insanely good" that they have their own "cult following"; "zero decor" and "cramped" seating are offset by ultra-"cheap" tabs.

Xixa *Mexican* ▽ | 25 | 22 | 25 | $52 |

Williamsburg | 241 S. Fourth St. (Havemeyer St.) | Brooklyn | 718-388-8860 | www.xixany.com

A Williamsburg "scene – in a good way" – this "innovative" Mexican from the Traif team rolls out a "unique", small plates-centric menu paired with "sinful" cocktails; "affordable" tabs and "attentive without being annoying" service make for "lovely" dining at this "highly recommended" spot.

Yakitori Taisho *Japanese* | 24 | 14 | 15 | $31 |

East Village | 5 St. Marks Pl. (bet. 2nd & 3rd Aves.) | 212-228-5086

The "secret is out" – this "fun", "loud" East Village Japanese rolls out an "extensive" variety of "really good" yakitori; sure, the "dingy" digs "need a big-time renovation", but ultra-"cheap" tabs and late-"late hours" keep it "always packed with students."

Yakitori Totto *Japanese* | 24 | 16 | 18 | $52 |

West 50s | 251 W. 55th St. (bet. B'way & 8th Ave.) | 212-245-4555 | www.tottonyc.com

"If it can be put on a skewer, they'll do it" at this "small", "popular" Midtown yakitori den where "heavenly" meats, veggies and "chicken parts you never knew existed" are grilled on sticks; it's a real "excursion to Tokyo" complete with "cramped", "noisy" digs, "long waits" and tabs that can "add up quickly."

Yama *Japanese* | 24 | 13 | 17 | $44 |

East 40s | 308 E. 49th St. (bet. 1st & 2nd Aves.) | 212-355-3370
Gramercy Park | 122 E. 17th St. (Irving Pl.) | 212-475-0969
www.yamasushinyc.com

"Bigger is better" declare sushiphiles of these East Side Japanese "go-tos" for "monster-size" slabs of the "freshest fish", offered at a "decent price"; the price of popularity: "drab", "crowded" settings with "long waits" at prime times.

	FOOD	DECOR	SERVICE	COST

Yefsi Estiatorio *Greek* — 24 | 17 | 21 | $57

East 70s | 1481 York Ave. (bet. 78th & 79th Sts.) | 212-535-0293 |
www.yefsiestiatorio.com

Be "transported to Greece" at this "upscale", "real-deal" Yorkville "favorite" where "wonderful" mezes are the focus, and the service is "warm and friendly"; the "rustic", "like-in-Athens" setting can get "noisy", but in summer there's always the "charming garden."

Yerba Buena *Pan-Latin* — 22 | 18 | 20 | $52

East Village | 23 Ave. A (bet. 1st & 2nd Sts.) | 212-529-2919
West Village | 1 Perry St. (Greenwich Ave.) | 212-620-0808
www.ybnyc.com

Chef Julian Medina delivers "inventive" Pan-Latin fare matched with "creative drinks" at these "stylish" crosstown siblings manned by a "helpful" crew; just be aware that the settings are "tight" and the "noise level rises a few decibels" as the night wears on.

Yuca Bar *Pan-Latin* — 23 | 18 | 20 | $27

East Village | 111 Ave. A (7th St.) | 212-982-9533 | www.yucabarnyc.com
"Upbeat" and "crowded" with "good-looking" types, this "colorful" East Villager mixes "better-than-average", well-priced Pan-Latin fare with "killer" drinks; it gets "loud" and service can lag, but for "people-watching" by the open doors and windows, it's hard to beat.

Yuka *Japanese* — 23 | 12 | 19 | $31

East 80s | 1557 Second Ave. (81st St.) | 212-772-9675 |
www.yukasushi.com

"Talk about a bargain", this "busy" Yorkville Japanese veteran offers "super-fresh", all-you-can-eat sushi for just $21 per person; the space and service are pretty basic, so most diners focus on the "amazing deal."

Yura on Madison *Sandwiches* — 21 | 12 | 13 | $22

East 90s | 1292 Madison Ave. (92nd St.) | 212-860-1707 |
www.yuraonmadison.com

A "perfect pre-museum stop", this "pricey" Carnegie Hill cafe vending "consistently delicious" sandwiches, salads and baked goods is also a "hangout" for local "prep-school girls" and their "Madison Avenue moms"; it "needs more seating", so many go the "take-out" route.

Zabb Elee *Thai* — 24 | 13 | 18 | $28

East Village | 75 Second Ave. (bet. 4th & 5th Sts.) | 212-505-9533
Elmhurst | 71-28 Roosevelt Ave. (72nd St.) | Queens | 718-426-7992
www.zabbelee.com

"Complex flavors" – some of them "blistering hot" – distinguish these "affordable" Thais that serve up "delicious", "unusual" Northeastern Isan dishes; "friendly" staffers add warmth to the otherwise "sterile" environs.

Zaitzeff *Burgers* — 22 | 10 | 14 | $17

Financial District | 72 Nassau St. (John St.) | 212-571-7272 |
www.zaitzeffnyc.com

"Tasty" patties of all persuasions – Kobe beef, sirloin, turkey, vegetable – made with "quality" ingredients and served on "terrific Portuguese rolls" are the draw at this FiDi burger-and-beer purveyor; "small" dimensions make it more enjoyable either before or after the "lunch crush."

	FOOD	DECOR	SERVICE	COST

Zaytoons *Mideastern*

21 | 15 | 19 | $21

Carroll Gardens | 283 Smith St. (Sackett St.) | Brooklyn | 718-875-1880
Clinton Hill | 472 Myrtle Ave. (bet. Hall St. & Washington Ave.) |
Brooklyn | 718-623-5522
Prospect Heights | 594 Vanderbilt Ave. (St Marks Ave.) | Brooklyn |
718-230-3200
www.zaytoons.com

For "tasty", "reliable" Middle Eastern fare, stay tooned to these nothing-fancy Brooklyn standbys where "tables are close" but the prices are "terrific"; Carroll Gardens and Clinton Hill are BYO, while Prospect Heights boasts a "pleasant garden."

Zengo *Pan-Latin*

20 | 23 | 19 | $57

East 40s | 622 Third Ave. (40th St.) | 212-808-8110 |
www.richardsandoval.com

A "beautiful" tri-level space designed by AvroKO sets the stage for a "special" experience at this Grand Central–area Pan-Latin presenting Richard Sandoval's "imaginative" Asian-accented cuisine; "pricey" tabs and "tiny portions" can vex, but "welcoming" service and a "cool" downstairs tequila lounge tip the balance.

Zenkichi *Japanese*

26 | 26 | 26 | $78

Williamsburg | 77 N. Sixth St. (Wythe Ave.) | Brooklyn | 718-388-8985 |
www.zenkichi.com

"Zen is the appropriate word" for this "special" Williamsburg Japanese featuring "peaceful" private cubicles where "mindful" staffers can be summoned with the "press of a button"; adding to the "romantic" mood is an "excellent" izakaya-style small-plates menu paired with "top-notch" sakes.

Zen Palate *Asian/Vegetarian*

21 | 16 | 18 | $30

Murray Hill | 516 Third Ave. (34th St.) | 212-685-6888 |
www.zenpalate.com

It's "amazing what they do with tofu" at this Asian-influenced vegetarian standby in Murray Hill featuring a variety of "fake-meat" dishes that "even a carnivore can love"; foes yawn"stereotypical", but at least the "fair pricing" outweighs the "harried" service and "dingy" decor.

Zero Otto Nove *Italian/Pizza*

23 | 21 | 22 | $46

Flatiron | 15 W. 21st St. (bet. 5th & 6th Aves.) | 212-242-0899
Arthur Avenue/Belmont | 2357 Arthur Ave. (186th St.) | Bronx |
718-220-1027
www.089bx.roberto089.com

"Fabulous pizzas and pastas" top the list of "hearty" Southern Italian specialties offered at these "reliable" "favorites"; the Arthur Avenue original (done up like an "old-fashioned" courtyard) doesn't take reservations, so "be prepared to wait" – or check out the "large" Flatiron offshoot.

Zito's Sandwich Shoppe *Sandwiches*

22 | 18 | 20 | $18

Bay Ridge | 7604 Third Ave. (76th St.) | Brooklyn | 718-836-7777 |
www.zitossandwichshoppe.com

The "old-time Brooklyn" submarine sandwich shop gets an update via this Bay Ridge counter-service joint slinging "tasty" classic Italian heros prepared with "quality ingredients", accompanied by craft brews; expect decor as "simple" as the pricing.

	FOOD	DECOR	SERVICE	COST

Zizi Limona *Mediterranean/Mideastern*

▽ 25 | 23 | 20 | $32

Williamsburg | 129 Havemeyer St. (1st St.) | Brooklyn | 347-763-1463 |
www.zizilimona.com

A "delicious" variety of Med–Middle Eastern classics draws "hipsters" to this Williamsburg spot where "friendly servers" preside over a "homey", brick-walled room; "fair prices", "surprisingly good" wines and a small grocery in the rear add additional "neighborhood" appeal.

Zona Rosa *Mexican*

▽ 21 | 23 | 19 | $28

Williamsburg | 571 Lorimer St. (Metropolitan Ave.) | Brooklyn | 917-324-7423 | www.zonarosabrooklyn.com

"Fabulous, quirky design" – complete with a "sublime rooftop deck" and kitchen "built inside an Airstream trailer" – and a "greatest-party-in-Brooklyn" vibe collide at this Williamsburg taqueria; fueling the fiesta are "delicious" Mexican dishes and "incredible margaritas."

NEW Zuma *Japanese*

22 | 24 | 19 | $98

Murray Hill | 261 Madison Ave. (bet. 38th & 39th Sts.) | 212-544-9862 | www.zumarestaurant.com

The first NYC outpost of the "swank" global chain, this "high-energy" Murray Hill Japanese delivers "inventive" izakaya-style bites along with sushi and robata-grilled dishes in a "dramatic" duplex space; "sky-high" tabs and "service kinks" aren't keeping its "good-looking" crowd away from its "cool-as-can-be" upstairs lounge.

Zum Schneider *German*

21 | 18 | 19 | $34

East Village | 107 Ave. C (7th St.) | 212-598-1098 | www.nyc.zumschneider.com

It's all about the "humongous" Bavarian steins of beer and German brats at this affordable East Village "slice of Munich" that's a "boisterous" "haus away from home" where "every day's a party"; hit the ATM first since it's "cash only", and prepare to wait during Oktoberfest.

Zum Stammtisch *German*

24 | 20 | 23 | $42

Glendale | 69-46 Myrtle Ave. (bet. 69th Pl. & 70th St.) | Queens | 718-386-3014 | www.zumstammtisch.com

"Go with an appetite" to this 1972-vintage Glendale German, where the "hearty" classics come in "you-won't-leave-hungry" portions for "moderate" sums; "pleasant frauleins in Alpine costume" toting steins of "frosty beer" bolster the kitschy "hofbrauhaus-in-Bavaria" vibe.

Zutto *Japanese/Noodle Shop*

20 | 15 | 18 | $47

TriBeCa | 77 Hudson St. (Harrison St.) | 212-233-3287 | www.zuttonyc.com

"They do ramen – and everything else – right" at this TriBeCa Japanese whose menu also includes "high-quality" sushi, buns and more; with a "laid-back ambiance", service that "makes you feel at home" and "easy-going" prices, "no wonder it's been here forever."

ZZ's Clam Bar *Seafood*

▽ 23 | 20 | 20 | $129

Greenwich Village | 169 Thompson St. (bet. Bleecker & Houston Sts.) | 212-254-3000 | www.zzsclambar.com

The Torrisi guys are behind this beyond-"tiny" Village boîte with a "speak-easy" vibe, where the "elevated raw-bar" fare and fancy libations are served by a "friendly" staff; the "outrageous" pricing has some going just "for cocktails and apps" – but with only 12 seats, "good luck getting in."

INDEXES

Special Features

Listings cover the best in each category and include names, locations and Food ratings. Multi-location restaurants' features may vary by branch.

BAR/SINGLES SCENES

All'onda | **G Vill**	23
Arlington Club | **E 70s**	21
Atlantic Grill | **E 70s**	23
Bagatelle | **Meatpacking**	18
Beauty & Essex | **LES**	23
Berg'n | **Crown Hts**	23
Blue Ribbon | **multi.**	25
Blue Water | **Union Sq**	24
Bodega Negra | **Chelsea**	22
NEW Bowery Meat Co. | **E Vill**	25
Breslin | **NoMad**	22
Bryant Pk Grill/Cafe | **W 40s**	18
Buddakan | **Chelsea**	25
Cabana | **multi.**	22
Catch | **Meatpacking**	23
NEW Chevalier | **W 50s**	22
NEW Clocktower | **Flatiron**	24
Crave Fishbar | **E 50s**	24
DBGB | **E Vill**	22
Del Frisco's | **multi.**	25
Dirty French | **LES**	24
Dos Caminos | **multi.**	19
Dutch | **SoHo**	22
East Pole | **E 60s**	23
El Toro Blanco | **W Vill**	21
Freemans | **LES**	22
Gato | **NoHo**	26
Harlow | **E 50s**	20
Hillstone | **multi.**	22
Hudson Clearwater | **W Vill**	25
NEW Hunt & Fish | **W 40s**	19
NEW Javelina | **Gramercy**	26
Joya | **Cobble Hill**	22
La Esquina | **SoHo**	23
Lafayette | **NoHo**	22
Lavo | **E 50s**	20
Lure Fishbar | **SoHo**	25
Macao Trading | **TriBeCa**	22
Margaux | **G Vill**	18
Maysville | **NoMad**	22
Miss Lily's | **G Vill**	23
Otto | **G Vill**	22
Penrose | **E 80s**	22
Perla | **G Vill**	23
NEW Pier A Harbor Hse. | **BPC**	18
NEW Porchlight | **Chelsea**	21
Rist. Morini | **E 80s**	24

Rosemary's | **W Vill**	22
NEW Rosie's | **E Vill**	24
Salvation Taco | **Murray Hill**	20
Saxon & Parole | **NoHo**	24
Smith | **multi.**	19
Spice Market | **Meatpacking**	24
Standard Grill | **Meatpacking**	21
Stanton Social | **LES**	23
STK | **Meatpacking**	23
Tao | **multi.**	24
NEW Tijuana Picnic | **LES**	21
Toro | **Chelsea**	24
NEW Upland | **Murray Hill**	25
NEW Zuma | **Murray Hill**	22

BEER STANDOUTS

B. Café | **W 80s**	20
Berg'n | **Crown Hts**	23
Birreria | **Flatiron**	21
Black Forest Bklyn | **Ft Greene**	20
Blue Smoke | **multi.**	22
Breslin | **NoMad**	22
BXL | **multi.**	20
Café d'Alsace | **E 80s**	21
Cannibal | **W 40s**	22
Colicchio/Sons | **Chelsea**	26
DBGB | **E Vill**	22
Dinosaur BBQ | **multi.**	22
Eleven Madison | **Flatiron**	28
Fette Sau | **W'burg**	26
NEW Finch | **Clinton Hill**	22
5 Napkin Burger | **multi.**	21
Flex Mussels | **multi.**	23
Fraunces Tav. | **Financial**	18
Gander | **Flatiron**	20
Gramercy Tavern | **Flatiron**	28
Heidelberg | **E 80s**	19
Jacob's Pickles | **W 80s**	22
Jake's Steakhse. | **Fieldston**	24
Jimmy's No. 43 | **E Vill**	20
John Brown Smokehse. | **LIC**	22
Luksus | **Greenpt**	25
Markt | **Flatiron**	20
Petite Abeille | **multi.**	19
Press 195 | **Bayside**	25
Queens Kickshaw | **Astoria**	23
Resto | **Murray Hill**	21
Spotted Pig | **W Vill**	24
Upstate | **E Vill**	27

More on zagat.com

Zum Schneider | **E Vill**   21

BREAKFAST

Balthazar | **SoHo**   24
Barney Greengrass | **W 80s**   25
Baz Bagel | **L Italy**   21
Brasserie | **E 50s**   22
Breslin | **NoMad**   22
Bubby's | **multi.**   21
Butter | **W 40s**   23
Buvette | **W Vill**   25
Cafe Cluny | **W Vill**   23
Cafe Luxembourg | **W 70s**   21
Cafe Gitane | **multi.**   22
Cafe Mogador | **E Vill**   24
Café Sabarsky/Fledermaus | **E 80s** 22
Carnegie Deli | **W 50s**   23
Casa Lever | **E 50s**   22
City Bakery | **Flatiron**   23
Clinton St. Baking | **LES**   25
Community | **Morningside Hts**   23
Cookshop | **Chelsea**   23
Coppelia | **Chelsea**   23
E.A.T. | **E 80s**   19
Egg | **W'burg**   24
Five Leaves | **Greenpt**   25
Forty Four | **W 40s**   22
Friedman's | **multi.**   22
Hudson Clearwater | **W Vill**   25
Hudson Eats | **BPC**   19
Jean-Georges | **W 60s**   28
Jean-Georges' Noug. | **W 60s**   27
Jeffrey's Grocery | **W Vill**   23
Joseph Leonard | **W Vill**   24
Katz's Deli | **LES**   25
Kitchenette | **Morningside Hts**   20
Krupa | **Windsor Terr.**   25
Ladurée | **SoHo**   22
Lafayette | **NoHo**   22
Lambs Club | **W 40s**   21
Landmarc | **W 50s**   19
Le Pain Q. | **multi.**   18
NEW Little Park | **TriBeCa**   26
Locanda Verde | **TriBeCa**   25
Machiavelli | **W 80s**   21
Maialino | **Gramercy**   25
Maison Kayser | **multi.**   21
Margaux | **G Vill**   18
Marlow/Sons | **W'burg**   23
Michael's | **W 50s**   23
Morandi | **W Vill**   23
Nice Matin | **W 70s**   19

NoHo Star | **NoHo**   20
Norma's | **W 50s**   25
Odeon | **TriBeCa**   21
Okonomi | **W'burg**   25
Palm Court | **W 50s**   23
Penelope | **Murray Hill**   22
Regency B&G | **E 60s**   24
Reynard | **W'burg**   23
Rosemary's | **W Vill**   22
Sant Ambroeus | **multi.**   22
Sarabeth's | **multi.**   20
Standard Grill | **Meatpacking**   21
Tartine | **W Vill**   22
Tom's | **Prospect Hts**   21
Two Hands | **L Italy**   23
Veselka | **E Vill**   21

BRUNCH

ABC Kitchen | **Flatiron**   26
Aita | **multi.**   24
Allswell | **W'burg**   23
Almond | **multi.**   20
Amy Ruth's | **Harlem**   23
Applewood | **Park Slope**   24
Aquagrill | **SoHo**   27
Artisanal | **Murray Hill**   21
Atlantic Grill | **E 70s**   23
A Voce | **W 50s**   23
Back Forty West | **SoHo**   21
Bagatelle | **Meatpacking**   18
Balaboosta | **NoLita**   25
Balthazar | **SoHo**   24
Bar Americain | **W 50s**   23
Barbounia | **Flatiron**   21
Barney Greengrass | **W 80s**   25
Bar Tabac | **Cobble Hill**   20
Baz Bagel | **L Italy**   21
Black Whale | **City Is**   21
Blue Ribbon | **W Vill**   25
Blue Water | **Union Sq**   24
Brasserie 8½ | **W 50s**   22
Bubby's | **multi.**   21
Buttermilk | **Carroll Gdns**   26
Cafe Cluny | **W Vill**   23
Café d'Alsace | **E 80s**   21
Cafe Loup | **W Vill**   20
Cafe Luluc | **Cobble Hill**   21
Cafe Luxembourg | **W 70s**   21
Cafe Mogador | **E Vill**   24
Carlyle | **E 70s**   24
Cebu | **Bay Ridge**   22
Cecil | **Harlem**   23
Celeste | **W 80s**   23

Chalk Point | **SoHo**	24
Clam | **W Vill**	25
Clinton St. Baking | **LES**	25
Colicchio/Sons | **Chelsea**	26
Colonia Verde | **Ft Greene**	21
Colonie | **Bklyn Hts**	25
Community | **Morningside Hts**	23
Cookshop | **Chelsea**	23
Cornelia St. | **W Vill**	18
Craftbar | **Flatiron**	22
db Bistro Moderne | **W 40s**	24
DBGB | **E Vill**	22
NEW Delaware & Hudson | **W'burg**	26
Dell'anima | **W Vill**	24
Diner | **W'burg**	25
Dutch | **SoHo**	22
East Pole | **E 60s**	23
Edi & The Wolf | **E Vill**	22
Egg | **W'burg**	24
Élan | **Flatiron**	23
El Quinto Pino | **Chelsea**	23
Emily | **Clinton Hill**	26
Empellón Taqueria | **W Vill**	22
Empire Diner | **Chelsea**	19
Estela | **NoLita**	27
Extra Virgin | **W Vill**	22
Fat Radish | **LES**	22
Five Leaves | **Greenpt**	25
Flatbush Farm | **Park Slope**	21
44 & X/44½ | **W 40s**	23
Fourth | **G Vill**	20
French Louie | **Boerum Hill**	25
Friend/Farmer | **Gramercy**	19
Gander | **Flatiron**	20
Good | **W Vill**	21
Great Jones Cafe | **NoHo**	21
Hearth | **E Vill**	25
Hope & Anchor | **Red Hook**	20
Hundred Acres | **SoHo**	21
Il Gattopardo | **W 50s**	24
Ilili | **NoMad**	24
Isabella's | **W 70s**	20
Jack the Horse | **Bklyn Hts**	24
Jack's Wife Freda | **multi.**	23
Jacob's Pickles | **W 80s**	22
James | **Prospect Hts**	24
Jane | **G Vill**	22
JoJo | **E 60s**	24
Joseph Leonard | **W Vill**	24
Kin Shop | **W Vill**	25
Kitchenette | **Morningside Hts**	20
Ladurée | **SoHo**	22

Lafayette | **NoHo**	22
Lambs Club | **W 40s**	21
L'Apicio | **E Vill**	23
Lavo | **E 50s**	20
Le Gigot | **W Vill**	25
Leopard/des Artistes | **W 60s**	21
Le Philosophe | **NoHo**	22
LIC Market | **LIC**	26
Lido | **Harlem**	23
Lion | **G Vill**	18
Little Prince | **SoHo**	22
Locanda Verde | **TriBeCa**	25
Maialino | **Gramercy**	25
Má Pêche | **W 50s**	23
Mark | **E 70s**	23
Marshal | **W 40s**	24
Meadowsweet | **W'burg**	25
Mile End | **Boerum Hill**	22
Minetta Tavern | **G Vill**	25
Miriam | **Park Slope**	22
Miss Lily's | **G Vill**	23
Miss Mamie's | **W 100s**	22
Mon Petit Cafe | **E 60s**	21
Montmartre | **Chelsea**	19
Murray's Cheese Bar | **W Vill**	24
Narcissa | **E Vill**	25
Nice Matin | **W 70s**	19
Norma's | **W 50s**	25
Northern Spy | **E Vill**	21
Ocean Grill | **W 70s**	23
Odeon | **TriBeCa**	21
Ofrenda | **W Vill**	24
Olea | **Ft Greene**	27
Palm Court | **W 50s**	23
Penelope | **Murray Hill**	22
Penrose | **E 80s**	22
Perilla | **W Vill**	24
Petrossian | **W 50s**	24
NEW Pizza Beach | **E 80s**	19
Prune | **E Vill**	24
Public | **NoLita**	24
Queens Comfort | **Astoria**	24
NEW Rainbow Rm. | **W 50s**	23
Red Rooster | **Harlem**	22
Resto | **Murray Hill**	21
Rist. Morini | **E 80s**	24
River Café | **Dumbo**	26
Riverpark | **Murray Hill**	26
River Styx | **Greenpt**	23
Roberta's | **Bushwick**	26
Rocking Horse | **Chelsea**	22
Root & Bone | **E Vill**	24
Rosemary's | **W Vill**	22

Rose Water | **Park Slope**	26
Runner & Stone | **Gowanus**	22
Russ/Daughters Cafe | **LES**	26
Salvation Taco | **Murray Hill**	20
Sanford's | **Astoria**	23
Sarabeth's | **multi.**	20
Saxon & Parole | **NoHo**	24
Scottadito | **Park Slope**	23
Seva Indian | **Astoria**	24
Shalom Japan | **W'burg**	24
Smith | **multi.**	19
Spotted Pig | **W Vill**	24
Stanton Social | **LES**	23
Stella 34 | **W 30s**	22
Stone Park | **Park Slope**	25
Sylvia's | **Harlem**	20
Tartine | **W Vill**	22
Tavern/Green | **Central Pk**	15
Telepan | **W 60s**	26
Tertulia | **W Vill**	24
Tipsy Parson | **Chelsea**	19
Tom's | **Prospect Hts**	21
Tribeca Grill | **TriBeCa**	23
Turkish Kitchen | **Murray Hill**	22
Union Sq. Cafe | **Union Sq**	27
NEW Upland | **Murray Hill**	25
Vanderbilt | **Prospect Hts**	22
NEW Vic's | **NoHo**	22
Water Club | **Murray Hill**	23
Waverly Inn | **W Vill**	22
Writing Room | **E 80s**	20

BUFFET

(Check availability)

Benares | **multi.**	21
Bukhara Grill | **E 40s**	24
Chola | **E 50s**	23
Churrascaria | **W 40s**	24
Darbar | **multi.**	21
Dhaba | **Murray Hill**	23
Fogo de Chão | **W 50s**	25
Indus Valley | **W 90s**	22
Jackson Diner | **multi.**	23
Sapphire Indian | **W 60s**	21
Seva Indian | **Astoria**	24
Texas de Brazil | **E 60s**	22
Turkuaz | **W 90s**	20
Utsav | **W 40s**	21
View | **W 40s**	18

BYO

Afghan Kebab | **multi.**	21
Buddha Bodai | **Chinatown**	22

Di Fara | **Midwood**	26
Gazala's | **W 40s**	22
Kuma Inn | **LES**	23
Little Poland | **E Vill**	21
Lucali | **Carroll Gdns**	26
Oaxaca | **multi.**	23
Peking Duck | **Chinatown**	23
Pho Bang | **L Italy**	23
Phoenix Gdn. | **E 40s**	23
Poke | **E 80s**	23
Qi | **W'burg**	22
Queens Comfort | **Astoria**	24
Sauce | **LES**	22
Taci's Beyti | **Sheepshead**	26
Tanoshi | **E 70s**	25
Tartine | **W Vill**	22
Tea & Sympathy | **W Vill**	22
Wondee Siam | **W 50s**	19
Zaytoons | **multi.**	21

CELEBRITY CHEFS

Einat Admony

Balaboosta | **NoLita**	25
Bar Bolonat | **W Vill**	25
Taïm | **multi.**	26

Dominique Ansel

Dominique Ansel Bakery | **SoHo**	25
NEW Dominique Ansel Kit. | **W Vill**	—

Michael Anthony

Gramercy Tavern | **Flatiron**	28
Untitled | **Meatpacking**	—

Dan Barber

Blue Hill | **G Vill**	28

Lidia Bastianich

Becco | **W 40s**	23
Felidia | **E 50s**	25

Mario Batali

Babbo | **G Vill**	26
Casa Mono | **Gramercy**	25
Del Posto | **Chelsea**	27
Eataly | **Flatiron**	24
Esca | **W 40s**	25
Lupa | **G Vill**	25
Manzo | **Flatiron**	25
Otto | **G Vill**	22

Jonathan Benno

Lincoln | **W 60s**	25

April Bloomfield
- Breslin | **NoMad** — 22
- John Dory Oyster | **NoMad** — 21
- Salvation Taco | **Murray Hill** — 20
- Spotted Pig | **W Vill** — 24

Saul Bolton
- Red Gravy | **Bklyn Hts** — 20
- Saul | **Prospect Hts** — 24
- Vanderbilt | **Prospect Hts** — 22

David Bouley
- Bouley | **TriBeCa** — 29
- Brushstroke/Ichimura | **TriBeCa** — 26

Daniel Boulud
- Bar Boulud | **W 60s** — 24
- Boulud Sud | **W 60s** — 25
- Café Boulud | **E 70s** — 27
- Daniel | **E 60s** — 29
- db Bistro Moderne | **W 40s** — 24
- DBGB | **E Vill** — 22

Danny Bowien
- Mission Cantina | **LES** — 21
- Mission Chinese | **LES** — 22

Terrance Brennan
- Artisanal | **Murray Hill** — 21
- Picholine | **W 60s** — 26

David Burke
- David Burke Fab. | **W 30s** — 24
- David Burke Fishtail | **E 60s** — 24
- David Burke Kitchen | **SoHo** — 25

Marco Canora
- **NEW** Fifty Paces | **E Vill** — 22
- Hearth | **E Vill** — 25

Mario Carbone/Rich Torrisi
- Carbone | **G Vill** — 24
- Dirty French | **LES** — 24
- Parm | **multi.** — 21
- Santina | **Meatpacking** — 23
- ZZ's Clam Bar | **G Vill** — 23

Andrew Carmellini
- Bar Primi | **E Vill** — 24
- Dutch | **SoHo** — 22
- Lafayette | **NoHo** — 22
- Library/Public | **G Vill** — 19
- **NEW** Little Park | **TriBeCa** — 26
- Locanda Verde | **TriBeCa** — 25

David Chang
- **NEW** Fuku | **E Vill** — —
- Má Pêche | **W 50s** — 23
- Momofuku Ko | **E Vill** — 26
- Momofuku Noodle | **E Vill** — 25
- Momofuku Ssäm Bar | **E Vill** — 26

Rebecca Charles
- Pearl Oyster | **W Vill** — 27

Amanda Cohen
- Dirt Candy | **LES** — 25

Tom Colicchio
- Colicchio/Sons | **Chelsea** — 26
- Craft | **Flatiron** — 25
- Craftbar | **Flatiron** — 22
- Riverpark | **Murray Hill** — 26
- 'Wichcraft | **multi.** — 18

John DeLucie
- Bill's Food/Drink | **E 50s** — 18
- Lion | **G Vill** — 18

Alain Ducasse
- Benoit | **W 50s** — 23

Todd English
- Ça Va | **W 40s** — 21
- Plaza Food Hall | **W 50s** — 21

Bobby Flay
- Bar Americain | **W 50s** — 23
- Gato | **NoHo** — 26

Marc Forgione
- American Cut | **TriBeCa** — 24
- Khe-Yo | **TriBeCa** — 24
- Marc Forgione | **TriBeCa** — 26

John Fraser
- Dovetail | **W 70s** — 25
- Narcissa | **E Vill** — 25

Alex Guarnaschelli
- Butter | **W 40s** — 23

Kurt Gutenbrunner
- Blaue Gans | **TriBeCa** — 22
- Café Sabarsky/Fledermaus | **E 80s** — 22
- **NEW** Upholstery Store | **W Vill** — 25
- Wallsé | **W Vill** — 25

Ilan Hall
- Gorbals | **W'burg** — 25

Gabrielle Hamilton
- Prune | **E Vill** — 24

Peter Hoffman
- Back Forty West | **SoHo** — 21

Daniel Humm
- Eleven Madison | **Flatiron** — 28
- NoMad | **NoMad** — 26
- NoMad Bar | **NoMad** — 25

Eiji Ichimura
- Brushstroke/Ichimura | **TriBeCa** — 26

Sara Jenkins
- Porchetta | **E Vill** — 22
- Porsena | **E Vill** — 24

Thomas Keller
  Bouchon Bakery | **multi.** — 22
  Per Se | **W 50s** — 28
Mark Ladner
  Del Posto | **Chelsea** — 27
Anita Lo
  Annisa | **W Vill** — 27
Michael Lomonaco
  Porter House | **W 50s** — 26
Nobu Matsuhisa
  Nobu | **multi.** — 27
Jehangir Mehta
  Graffiti | **E Vill** — 28
  Mehtaphor | **TriBeCa** — 28
Carlo Mirarchi
  Blanca | **Bushwick** — 26
  Roberta's | **Bushwick** — 26
Marco Moreira
  15 East | **Union Sq** — 27
  Tocqueville | **Flatiron** — 26
Masaharu Morimoto
  Morimoto | **Chelsea** — 26
Seamus Mullen
  El Colmado | **multi.** — 19
  Tertulia | **W Vill** — 24
Marc Murphy
  Landmarc | **multi.** — 19
Daisuke Nakazawa
  Sushi Nakazawa | **W Vill** — 27
Enrique Olvera
  NEW Cosme | **Flatiron** — 25
Ivan Orkin
  Ivan Ramen | **multi.** — 22
Charlie Palmer
  Aureole | **W 40s** — 25
  Charlie Palmer | **E 50s** — 24
  NEW Charlie Palmer at
  The Knick | **W 40s** — 27
  NEW Crimson & Rye | **E 50s** — 20
David Pasternack
  Esca | **W 40s** — 25
Alfred Portale
  Gotham B&G | **G Vill** — 28
Michael Psilakis
  FishTag | **W 70s** — 22
  Kefi | **W 80s** — 22
  MP Taverna | **multi.** — 24
Cesar Ramirez
  Chef's/Brooklyn Fare |
  Downtown Bklyn — 26
Mary Redding
  Mary's Fish | **W Vill** — 24

Andy Ricker
  Pok Pok Ny | **Columbia St.** — 26
  Pok Pok Phat | **Columbia St.** — 25
Eric Ripert
  Le Bernardin | **W 50s** — 29
Marcus Samuelsson
  Red Rooster | **Harlem** — 22
  NEW Streetbird | **Harlem** — 18
Richard Sandoval
  Maya | **E 60s** — 22
  Pampano | **E 40s** — 24
  Zengo | **E 40s** — 20
Alex Stupak
  NEW Empellón al Pastor |
  E Vill — 19
  Empellón Cocina | **E Vill** — 23
  Empellón Taqueria | **W Vill** — 22
Gari Sugio
  Gari | **multi.** — 26
Masayoshi Takayama
  NEW Kappo Masa | **E 70s** — 25
  Masa/Bar Masa | **W 50s** — 26
Dale Talde
  Pork Slope | **Park Slope** — 20
  Talde | **Park Slope** — 24
Bill Telepan
  Telepan | **W 60s** — 26
Jean-Georges Vongerichten
  ABC Cocina | **Flatiron** — 25
  ABC Kitchen | **Flatiron** — 26
  Jean-Georges | **W 60s** — 28
  JoJo | **E 60s** — 24
  Mark | **E 70s** — 23
  Mercer Kitchen | **SoHo** — 23
  Perry St. | **W Vill** — 26
  Spice Market | **Meatpacking** — 24
David Waltuck
  Élan | **Flatiron** — 23
Jonathan Waxman
  Barbuto | **W Vill** — 24
  NEW Jams | **W 50s** — —
Michael White
  Ai Fiori | **W 30s** — 26
  Butterfly | **TriBeCa** — 19
  Costata | **SoHo** — 23
  Marea | **W 50s** — 27
  Nicoletta | **E Vill** — 22
  Osteria Morini | **SoHo** — 26
  Rist. Morini | **E 80s** — 24
Jody Williams
  Buvette | **W Vill** — 25
  NEW Via Carota | **W Vill** — 24

Geoffrey Zakarian
   Lambs Club | **W 40s** — 21
   National | **E 50s** — 20
   Palm Court | **W 50s** — 23
Galen Zamarra
   NEW Almanac | **W Vill** — 26
   Mas | **W Vill** — 26

CELEBRITY SIGHTINGS

Antica Pesa | **W'burg** — 24
Balthazar | **SoHo** — 24
Bar Pitti | **G Vill** — 23
Beautique | **W 50s** — 20
Bond St | **NoHo** — 25
Cafe Cluny | **W Vill** — 23
Cafe Luxembourg | **W 70s** — 21
Carbone | **G Vill** — 24
Catch | **Meatpacking** — 23
Da Silvano | **G Vill** — 21
Elio's | **E 80s** — 25
NEW Hunt & Fish | **W 40s** — 19
Joe Allen | **W 40s** — 18
Le Bilboquet | **E 60s** — 22
Leopard/des Artistes | **W 60s** — 21
Marea | **W 50s** — 27
Michael's | **W 50s** — 23
Minetta Tavern | **G Vill** — 25
NoMad | **NoMad** — 26
Orso | **W 40s** — 23
Philippe | **E 60s** — 22
NEW Polo Bar | **E 50s** — 20
Primola | **E 60s** — 22
Rao's | **E Harlem** — 23
Spotted Pig | **W Vill** — 24
Waverly Inn | **W Vill** — 22

CHILD-FRIENDLY

(* children's menu available)
Alice's Tea* | **multi.** — 20
Allswell | **W'burg** — 23
Amorina* | **Prospect Hts** — 22
Ample Hills | **multi.** — 27
Amy Ruth's | **Harlem** — 23
Arirang Hibachi* | **multi.** — 23
Artie's* | **City Is** — 21
Atlantic Grill* | **multi.** — 23
Bamonte's | **W'burg** — 23
Bareburger* | **multi.** — 21
Bark | **multi.** — 20
Barney Greengrass | **W 80s** — 25
Baz Bagel | **L Italy** — 21
Blue Ribbon* | **multi.** — 25
Blue Smoke* | **multi.** — 22

Blue Water* | **Union Sq** — 24
Boathouse* | **Central Pk** — 18
Brasserie Cognac* | **multi.** — 18
Brennan | **Sheepshead** — 22
Brooklyn Crab | **Red Hook** — 20
Brooklyn Farmacy | **Carroll Gdns** — 24
Bubby's* | **multi.** — 21
Buttermilk* | **Carroll Gdns** — 26
Café Habana/Outpost | **Ft Greene** — 23
Calexico | **multi.** — 21
Carmine's* | **W 40s** — 22
ChipShop* | **multi.** — 20
Cowgirl* | **W Vill** — 17
Crema | **Chelsea** — 23
DBGB* | **E Vill** — 22
Dinosaur BBQ* | **multi.** — 22
Eddie's Sweet Shop | **Forest Hills** — 25
El Vez | **Battery Pk** — 20
Emily | **Clinton Hill** — 26
Farm/Adderley* | **Ditmas Pk** — 23
5 Napkin Burger* | **multi.** — 21
Flatbush Farm | **Park Slope** — 21
Fogo de Chão | **W 50s** — 25
Franny's | **Park Slope** — 23
Friend/Farmer* | **Gramercy** — 19
Ganso | **Downtown Bklyn** — 21
Gargiulo's | **Coney Is** — 23
Gigino* | **multi.** — 21
Good Enough* | **W 80s** — 19
Grey Dog* | **multi.** — 22
Han Dynasty* | **multi.** — 23
Hill Country | **Flatiron** — 22
Hill Country Chicken | **multi.** — 21
Hometown | **Red Hook** — 25
Isabella's* | **W 70s** — 20
Jackson Hole* | **multi.** — 20
Jack the Horse | **Bklyn Hts** — 24
Joe & Pat's | **Castelton Cnrs** — 24
Junior's* | **multi.** — 19
L&B Spumoni* | **Gravesend** — 24
Landmarc* | **W 50s** — 19
La Villa Pizzeria | **multi.** — 24
Le Pain Q.* | **multi.** — 18
London Lennie's* | **Middle Vill** — 24
Mable's Smokehse. | **W'burg** — 23
Melt Shop | **multi.** — 22
Mermaid* | **multi.** — 23
Miss Mamie's | **W 100s** — 22
Nick's | **multi.** — 24
Ninja | **TriBeCa** — 16

Noodle Pudding | **Bklyn Hts**	25
Otto | **G Vill**	22
Palm* | **W 50s**	23
Peanut Butter Co. | **G Vill**	22
Pera* | **E 40s**	21
Rock Center Café* | **W 40s**	18
Rosa Mexicano* | **multi.**	22
Ruby Foo's* | **W 50s**	18
Sammy's Fishbox* | **City Is**	23
Sammy's Shrimp* | **City Is**	23
Sarabeth's | **multi.**	20
Schiller's | **LES**	20
Sea Grill* | **W 40s**	24
2nd Ave Deli | **multi.**	23
Serendipity 3 | **E 60s**	19
Shabu-Shabu 70 | **E 70s**	21
Shake Shack | **multi.**	22
S'MAC | **multi.**	22
Smorgas Chef* | **Murray Hill**	20
Sylvia's* | **Harlem**	20
Texas de Brazil | **E 60s**	22
Tony's Di Napoli | **W 40s**	21
Two Boots* | **multi.**	19
Veselka | **E Vill**	21
View* | **W 40s**	18
Virgil's* | **W 40s**	21
Zero Otto | **Arthur Ave./Belmont**	23
Zum Stammtisch | **Glendale**	24

COCKTAIL STARS

Atera | **TriBeCa**	24
Bacchanal | **L Italy**	22
Bar Chuko | **Prospect Hts**	26
Bar Primi | **E Vill**	24
Beatrice Inn | **W Vill**	21
Beautique | **W 50s**	20
Beauty & Essex | **LES**	23
Bergen Hill | **Carroll Gdns**	27
Betony | **W 50s**	25
Black Ant | **E Vill**	24
NEW Cosme | **Flatiron**	25
Crif Dogs | **E Vill**	22
NEW Crimson & Rye | **E 50s**	20
Dead Rabbit | **Financial**	22
Decoy | **W Vill**	26
Distilled | **TriBeCa**	20
Dutch | **SoHo**	22
Eleven Madison | **Flatiron**	28
Empellón Taqueria | **W Vill**	22
Estela | **NoLita**	27
Fort Defiance | **Red Hook**	23
Franny's | **Park Slope**	23

French Louie | **Boerum Hill**	25
Fung Tu | **LES**	25
NEW Grand Army | **Downtown Bklyn**	22
Hudson Clearwater | **W Vill**	25
Macao Trading | **TriBeCa**	22
Mayahuel | **E Vill**	23
Maysville | **NoMad**	22
Minetta Tavern | **G Vill**	25
Momofuku Ssäm Bar | **E Vill**	26
Monkey Bar | **E 50s**	20
M. Wells Steakhse. | **LIC**	24
Navy | **SoHo**	21
NoMad Bar | **NoMad**	25
NEW Oleanders | **W'burg**	–
Pachanga Patterson | **Astoria**	24
Perla | **G Vill**	23
Piora | **W Vill**	25
P.J. Clarke's | **multi.**	18
NEW Porchlight | **Chelsea**	21
Prime Meats | **Carroll Gdns**	24
Red Rooster | **Harlem**	22
River Styx | **Greenpt**	23
Root & Bone | **E Vill**	24
Rye | **W'burg**	25
Salvation Taco | **Murray Hill**	20
NEW Santina | **Meatpacking**	23
Saxon & Parole | **NoHo**	24
NEW Tijuana Picnic | **LES**	21
Tiny's | **TriBeCa**	21
Toro | **Chelsea**	24
Yerba Buena | **multi.**	22
ZZ's Clam Bar | **G Vill**	23

COLLEGE-CENTRIC

Columbia
Community | **Morningside Hts**	23
Kitchenette | **Morningside Hts**	20
Max SoHa/Caffe | **Morningside Hts**	21
Miss Mamie's | **W 100s**	22
Pisticci | **Morningside Hts**	24
Thai Market | **W 100s**	23

NYU
Angelica Kit. | **E Vill**	23
Artichoke Basille | **multi.**	22
BaoHaus | **E Vill**	23
Café Habana/Outpost | **NoLita**	23
Caracas | **E Vill**	26
Crif Dogs | **E Vill**	22
Dos Toros | **G Vill**	22
Gyu-Kaku | **multi.**	21

Ippudo | **multi.**	25
John's/12th St. | **E Vill**	22
NEW Kiin Thai | **G Vill**	22
La Esquina | **SoHo**	23
Mamoun's | **multi.**	23
99 Miles/Philly | **G Vill**	21
Num Pang | **G Vill**	23
100 Montaditos | **G Vill**	19
Otto | **G Vill**	22
Quantum Leap | **G Vill**	22
Republic | **Union Sq**	19
NEW Saki | **G Vill**	—
S'MAC | **multi.**	22
Smith | **multi.**	19
Spice | **G Vill**	20
Vanessa's Dumpling | **E Vill**	22
Veselka | **E Vill**	21

COMMUTER OASIS

Grand Central

Ammos | **E 40s**	22
Aretsky's Patroon | **E 40s**	23
Benjamin Steak | **E 40s**	27
Bobby Van's | **E 40s**	23
Cafe Centro | **E 40s**	22
Capital Grille | **E 40s**	25
Cipriani | **E 40s**	23
Docks Oyster | **E 40s**	21
Hatsuhana | **E 40s**	25
Junior's | **multi.**	19
La Fonda/Sol | **E 40s**	22
Luke's Lobster | **E 40s**	24
Michael Jordan | **E 40s**	21
Morton's | **E 40s**	23
Nanni | **E 40s**	23
Naples 45 | **E 40s**	19
Naya | **E 40s**	22
Num Pang | **E 40s**	23
Osteria Laguna | **E 40s**	22
Oyster Bar | **E 40s**	22
Palm | **E 40s**	25
Pera | **E 40s**	21
Pietro's | **E 40s**	23
Sakagura | **E 40s**	25
Shake Shack | **E 40s**	22
Sinigual | **E 40s**	21
Soba Totto | **E 40s**	23
Sparks | **E 40s**	25
Sushi Yasuda | **E 40s**	27
Tulsi | **E 40s**	23
Two Boots | **E 40s**	19
Zengo | **E 40s**	20

Penn Station

Arno | **W 30s**	22
Casa Nonna | **W 30s**	22
David Burke Fab. | **W 30s**	24
Delmonico's | **W 30s**	24
Frankie & Johnnie's | **W 30s**	21
Gaonnuri | **W 30s**	19
Keens | **W 30s**	26
Larb Ubol | **W 30s**	22
Nick & Stef's | **W 30s**	22
NEW State Grill | **W 30s**	25
Uncle Jack's | **W 30s**	23
Uncle Nick's | **Chelsea**	21

Port Authority

Ça Va | **W 40s**	21
Chez Josephine | **W 40s**	22
Chimichurri Grill | **W 40s**	24
NEW City Kitchen | **W 40s**	25
Dafni | **W 40s**	21
Esca | **W 40s**	25
Etc. Etc. | **W 40s**	23
5 Napkin Burger | **W 40s**	21
Hakkasan | **W 40s**	24
Inakaya | **W 40s**	24
John's Pizzeria | **W 40s**	23
Marseille | **W 40s**	21
Mercato | **W 30s**	23
Qi | **W 40s**	22
Schnipper's | **W 40s**	19
Shake Shack | **W 40s**	22
Shorty's | **W 40s**	21
West Bank | **W 40s**	20
Wolfgang's | **W 40s**	26

FIREPLACES

Alberto | **Forest Hills**	24
Alta | **G Vill**	25
Antica Pesa | **W'burg**	24
Applewood | **Park Slope**	24
Battery Gdns. | **Financial**	19
Beatrice Inn | **W Vill**	21
Benjamin Steak | **E 40s**	27
Boathouse | **Central Pk**	18
Bouley | **TriBeCa**	29
Blossom | **W Vill**	25
Ça Va | **W 40s**	21
Cebu | **Bay Ridge**	22
Christos | **Astoria**	24
Club A Steak | **E 50s**	26
Cornelia St. | **W Vill**	18
Donovan's | **Bayside**	21
Dutch | **SoHo**	22
F & J Pine | **Van Nest**	23

Forty Four | **W 40s**	22
Friend/Farmer | **Gramercy**	19
Glass House | **W 40s**	20
House | **Gramercy**	24
I Trulli | **Murray Hill**	23
JoJo | **E 60s**	24
Keens | **W 30s**	26
Lady Mendl's | **Gramercy**	21
La Lanterna | **G Vill**	20
Lambs Club | **W 40s**	21
Manetta's | **LIC**	25
Marco Polo | **Carroll Gdns**	22
Molly's | **Gramercy**	21
NoMad | **NoMad**	26
NoMad Bar | **NoMad**	25
Northeast Kingdom | **Bushwick**	25
One if by Land | **W Vill**	23
Peacock | **Murray Hill**	22
Per Se | **W 50s**	28
Place | **W Vill**	24
Public | **NoLita**	24
Quality Meats | **W 50s**	26
Salinas | **Chelsea**	24
Scottadito | **Park Slope**	23
Sea Fire Grill | **E 40s**	27
Telly's Taverna | **Astoria**	25
Tiny's | **TriBeCa**	21
Triomphe | **W 40s**	23
21 Club | **W 50s**	23
Vinegar Hill Hse. | **Vinegar Hill**	23
Vivolo | **E 70s**	20
Water Club | **Murray Hill**	23
Waverly Inn | **W Vill**	22
Writing Room | **E 80s**	20

FOOD HALLS

Berg'n | **Crown Hts**	23
NEW City Kitchen | **W 40s**	25
Eataly | **Flatiron**	24
NEW Gansevoort Mkt. | **Meatpacking**	–
Gotham West | **W 40s**	20
Hudson Eats | **BPC**	19
NEW Le District | **BPC**	–
New World Mall | **Flushing**	22
Plaza Food Hall | **W 50s**	21
Smorgasburg | **multi.**	26

GLUTEN-FREE OPTIONS

(Call to discuss specific needs)

Alta | **G Vill**	25
Amali | **E 60s**	25
Angelica Kit. | **E Vill**	23
Bareburger | **multi.**	21

Betony | **W 50s**	25
Bistango | **multi.**	21
Blue Smoke | **multi.**	22
Candle 79 | **E 70s**	26
Caracas | **E Vill**	26
China Grill | **W 50s**	22
Del Posto | **Chelsea**	27
Don Antonio | **W 50s**	23
Etc. Etc. | **W 40s**	23
5 Napkin Burger | **multi.**	21
Friedman's | **multi.**	22
Galli | **multi.**	24
Hill Country | **Flatiron**	22
Hu Kitchen | **G Vill**	24
Hummus Pl. | **multi.**	22
Keste Pizza | **W Vill**	23
NEW Little Beet | **Murray Hill**	22
Nice Matin | **W 70s**	19
Nizza | **W 40s**	20
Nom Wah Tea | **Chinatown**	21
Palm Court | **W 50s**	23
Pappardella | **W 70s**	21
Peacefood Café | **multi.**	24
Risotteria | **multi.**	23
Risotteria Melotti | **E Vill**	25
Rosa Mexicano | **multi.**	22
Rubirosa | **NoLita**	26
Ruby Foo's | **W 50s**	18
S'MAC | **multi.**	22
Smith | **multi.**	19
Tao | **multi.**	24
V-Note | **E 70s**	24
Zengo | **E 40s**	20

GREEN/LOCAL/ORGANIC

Brucie | **Cobble Hill**	21
ABC Cocina | **Flatiron**	25
ABC Kitchen | **Flatiron**	26
Aita | **multi.**	24
Aldea | **Flatiron**	24
All'onda | **G Vill**	23
Amali | **E 60s**	25
Ample Hills | **multi.**	27
Angelica Kit. | **E Vill**	23
Applewood | **Park Slope**	24
Aroma Kitchen | **NoHo**	22
Aureole | **W 40s**	25
Aurora | **multi.**	24
Babbo | **G Vill**	26
Back Forty West | **SoHo**	21
Bar Boulud | **W 60s**	24
Barbuto | **W Vill**	24

Bareburger | **multi.**	21
Bark | **multi.**	20
Battersby | **Boerum Hill**	26
Bell Book/Candle | **W Vill**	22
Betony | **W 50s**	25
Blossom | **multi.**	25
Blue Hill | **G Vill**	28
Brooklyn Farmacy | **Carroll Gdns**	24
Buttermilk | **Carroll Gdns**	26
NEW Cafe Clover | **W Vill**	24
Café Habana/Outpost | **multi.**	23
Candle Cafe | **multi.**	24
Candle 79 | **E 70s**	26
Caravan/Dreams | **E Vill**	23
City Bakery | **Flatiron**	23
Clinton St. Baking | **LES**	25
Colicchio/Sons | **Chelsea**	26
Colonie | **Bklyn Hts**	25
Community | **Morningside Hts**	23
Contra | **LES**	25
Cookshop | **Chelsea**	23
Craft | **Flatiron**	25
NEW Delaware & Hudson | **W'burg**	26
Dell'anima | **W Vill**	24
Del Posto | **Chelsea**	27
Diner | **W'burg**	25
Dover | **Carroll Gdns**	26
East Pole | **E 60s**	23
Eddy | **E Vill**	26
Egg | **W'burg**	24
Eleven Madison | **Flatiron**	28
Emily | **Clinton Hill**	26
Esca | **W 40s**	25
Farm/Adderley | **Ditmas Pk**	23
Fat Radish | **LES**	22
Fette Sau | **W'burg**	26
Flatbush Farm | **Park Slope**	21
Fletcher's | **multi.**	22
Frankies | **multi.**	25
Franny's | **Park Slope**	23
French Louie | **Boerum Hill**	25
Glasserie | **Greenpt**	25
Good Fork | **Red Hook**	25
Gotham B&G | **G Vill**	28
Gramercy Tavern | **Flatiron**	28
Hearth | **E Vill**	25
NEW Houseman | **Hudson Sq**	—
Hundred Acres | **SoHo**	21
Il Buco | **NoHo**	25
Kin Shop | **W Vill**	25
L'Artusi | **W Vill**	27
La Vara | **Cobble Hill**	27

Le Pain Q. | **multi.**	18
Lincoln | **W 60s**	25
NEW Little Beet | **Murray Hill**	22
NEW Little Park | **TriBeCa**	26
Locanda Verde | **TriBeCa**	25
Lupa | **G Vill**	25
Marc Forgione | **TriBeCa**	26
Market Table | **W Vill**	23
Marlow/Sons | **W'burg**	23
Marshal | **W 40s**	24
Mas | **W Vill**	26
Meadowsweet | **W'burg**	25
Meat Hook | **W'burg**	23
Mimi Cheng's | **E Vill**	24
Momofuku Ko | **E Vill**	26
Momofuku Noodle | **E Vill**	25
Momofuku Ssäm Bar | **E Vill**	26
Narcissa | **E Vill**	25
Navy | **SoHo**	21
Nightingale 9 | **Carroll Gdns**	21
NoMad | **NoMad**	26
Northern Spy | **E Vill**	21
Paulie Gee's | **Greenpt**	27
Peaches | **Bed-Stuy**	24
Pearl Oyster | **W Vill**	27
Per Se | **W 50s**	28
Prime Meats | **Carroll Gdns**	24
Print | **W 40s**	24
Prune | **E Vill**	24
Redhead | **E Vill**	23
Riverpark | **Murray Hill**	26
Roberta's | **Bushwick**	26
Roman's | **Ft Greene**	25
Root & Bone | **E Vill**	24
Rosemary's | **W Vill**	22
Rose Water | **Park Slope**	26
Rucola | **Boerum Hill**	25
Saul | **Prospect Hts**	24
NEW Semilla | **W'burg**	26
Sfoglia | **E 90s**	23
Smoke Joint | **Ft Greene**	20
Smorgas Chef | **multi.**	20
Snack | **multi.**	23
Stone Park | **Park Slope**	25
Telepan | **W 60s**	26
Tía Pol | **Chelsea**	23
Tocqueville | **Flatiron**	26
Tortilleria Nixtamal | **Corona**	24
Trestle on 10th | **Chelsea**	23
Txikito | **Chelsea**	24
Union Sq. Cafe | **Union Sq**	27
Upstate | **E Vill**	27
Vanderbilt | **Prospect Hts**	22

More on zagat.com

Veselka | **E Vill**	21
Vesta | **Astoria**	26
NEW Virginia's | **E Vill**	23
Wilma Jean | **Carroll Gdns**	24

GROUP DINING

Almayass | **Flatiron**	24
Almond | **multi.**	20
Alta | **G Vill**	25
Arirang Hibachi | **multi.**	23
Artisanal | **Murray Hill**	21
Atlantic Grill | **E 70s**	23
Back Forty West | **SoHo**	21
Balthazar | **SoHo**	24
Bar Americain | **W 50s**	23
Beauty & Essex | **LES**	23
Blaue Gans | **TriBeCa**	22
BLT Prime | **Gramercy**	26
BLT Steak | **E 50s**	25
Blue Fin | **W 40s**	22
Blue Smoke | **multi.**	22
Blue Water | **Union Sq**	24
Boathouse | **Central Pk**	18
Bond 45 | **W 40s**	19
Buddakan | **Chelsea**	25
Cabana | **multi.**	22
Calle Ocho | **W 80s**	21
Carmine's | **multi.**	22
Casa Nonna | **W 30s**	22
China Grill | **W 50s**	22
Churrascaria | **W 40s**	24
Colicchio/Sons | **Chelsea**	26
Congee | **LES**	21
Crispo | **W Vill**	25
DBGB | **E Vill**	22
Decoy | **W Vill**	26
Del Frisco's | **multi.**	25
Dinosaur BBQ | **multi.**	22
Dominick's | **Arthur Ave./Belmont**	22
Don Peppe | **S Ozone Pk**	26
Dos Caminos | **multi.**	19
El Vez | **Battery Pk**	20
F & J Pine | **Van Nest**	23
Fette Sau | **W'burg**	26
Fig & Olive | **multi.**	21
Fogo de Chão | **W 50s**	25
Golden Unicorn | **Chinatown**	21
Gyu-Kaku | **multi.**	21
Havana Central | **W 40s**	22
Hill Country | **Flatiron**	22
Ilili | **NoMad**	24
Jing Fong | **Chinatown**	21

NEW Kang Ho Dong | **Murray Hill**	23
Kuma Inn | **LES**	23
Kum Gang San | **multi.**	21
Landmarc | **W 50s**	19
Má Pêche | **W 50s**	23
Mission Chinese | **LES**	22
Momofuku Ssäm Bar | **E Vill**	26
Morimoto | **Chelsea**	26
Ninja | **TriBeCa**	16
NoMad Bar | **NoMad**	25
Otto | **G Vill**	22
Oyster Bar | **E 40s**	22
Pacificana | **Sunset Pk**	24
Park Avenue | **Flatiron**	25
Peking Duck | **Chinatown**	23
Peter Luger | **W'burg**	28
NEW Pier A Harbor Hse. | **BPC**	18
Public | **NoLita**	24
Quality Meats | **W 50s**	26
Redeye Grill | **W 50s**	21
Red Rooster | **Harlem**	22
Rosa Mexicano | **multi.**	22
NEW Rosie's | **E Vill**	24
Ruby Foo's | **W 50s**	18
Sahara | **Sheepshead**	22
Sammy's Roumanian | **LES**	19
Sik Gaek | **multi.**	23
Spice Market | **Meatpacking**	24
Standard Grill | **Meatpacking**	21
Stanton Social | **LES**	23
Stella 34 | **W 30s**	22
Tamarind | **TriBeCa**	26
Tanoreen | **Bay Ridge**	26
Tao | **multi.**	24
Tavern/Green | **Central Pk**	15
Texas de Brazil | **E 60s**	22
NEW Tijuana Picnic | **LES**	21
Tony's Di Napoli | **W 40s**	21
Toro | **Chelsea**	24
Tribeca Grill | **TriBeCa**	23
2 Duck Goose | **Gowanus**	19
Victor's Cafe | **W 50s**	23
Yerba Buena | **multi.**	22
Zengo | **E 40s**	20
NEW Zuma | **Murray Hill**	22

HAPPY HOURS

Allswell | **W'burg**	23
Atrium Dumbo | **Dumbo**	23
A Voce | **W 50s**	23
Back Forty West | **SoHo**	21
Bell Book/Candle | **W Vill**	22

Brooklyn Star	**W'burg**	25
Clam	**W Vill**	25
Costata	**SoHo**	23
Crave Fishbar	**E 50s**	24
Cull & Pistol	**Chelsea**	24
Distilled	**TriBeCa**	20
Docks Oyster	**E 40s**	21
Ed's Chowder	**W 60s**	20
El Colmado	**multi.**	19
Emporio	**NoLita**	23
FishTag	**W 70s**	22
Flex Mussels	**multi.**	23
Fonda	**multi.**	23
Gyu-Kaku	**multi.**	21
Haru	**multi.**	21
John Dory Oyster	**NoMad**	21
Littleneck	**multi.**	23
Lobster Joint	**multi.**	24
Maialino	**Gramercy**	25
Marco Polo	**Carroll Gdns**	22
Mermaid	**multi.**	23
Móle	**multi.**	21
MP Taverna	**multi.**	24
Ofrenda	**W Vill**	24
Oyster Bar	**E 40s**	22
NEW Porchlight	**Chelsea**	21
Red Rooster	**Harlem**	22
Rist. Morini	**E 80s**	24
Rosa Mexicano	**multi.**	22
Rye	**W'burg**	25
Sala One Nine	**Flatiron**	21
Sea Fire Grill	**E 40s**	27
Sotto 13	**W Vill**	23
Thalia	**W 40s**	21
Penrose	**E 80s**	22
Upstate	**E Vill**	27

HISTORIC PLACES

(Year opened; * building)

1763	Fraunces Tav.*	**Financial**	18
1787	One if by Land*	**W Vill**	23
1863	City Hall*	**TriBeCa**	22
1868	Landmark Tav.*	**W 40s**	19
1870	Kings' Carriage*	**E 80s**	23
1873	Paris Cafe	**Seaport**	18
1884	P.J. Clarke's	**multi.**	18
1885	Keens	**W 30s**	26
NEW 1886	Pier A Harbor Hse.*	**BPC**	18
1887	Peter Luger	**W'burg**	28
1888	Katz's Deli	**LES**	25
1892	Ferrara	**L Italy**	24

1896	Rao's	**E Harlem**	23
1900	Bamonte's	**W'burg**	23
1902	Angelo's/Mulberry	**L Italy**	23
1904	Vincent's	**L Italy**	22
1905	Morgan*	**Murray Hill**	23
1906	Barbetta	**W 40s**	22
1907	Gargiulo's	**Coney Is**	23
1908	Barney Greengrass	**W 80s**	25
1908	John's/12th St.	**E Vill**	22
1910	Wolfgang's*	**multi.**	26
1913	Oyster Bar	**E 40s**	22
1917	Leopard/des Artistes*	**W 60s**	21
1919	Mario's	**Arthur Ave./Belmont**	21
1920	Leo's Latticini/Corona	**Corona**	24
1920	Nom Wah Tea	**Chinatown**	21
1920	Waverly Inn	**W Vill**	22
1921	Sardi's	**W 40s**	18
1922	Sanford's	**Astoria**	23
1924	Totonno Pizza	**Coney Is**	27
1926	Frankie & Johnnie's	**W 40s**	21
1927	Ann & Tony's	**Arthur Ave./Belmont**	22
1927	Russian Tea	**W 50s**	20
1929	Eisenberg's	**Flatiron**	20
1929	Empire Diner	**Chelsea**	19
1929	John's Pizzeria	**W 40s**	23
1929	21 Club	**W 50s**	23
1930	Carlyle	**E 70s**	24
1930	El Quijote	**Chelsea**	22
1932	Papaya King	**E 80s**	22
1932	Pietro's	**E 40s**	23
1933	Patsy's	**W 50s**	21
1934	Tavern/Green	**Central Pk**	15
1936	Heidelberg	**E 80s**	19
1936	Monkey Bar*	**E 50s**	20
1936	Tom's	**Prospect Hts**	21
1937	Carnegie Deli	**W 50s**	23
1937	Denino's	**Elm Pk**	26
1937	Le Veau d'Or	**E 60s**	19
1937	Minetta Tavern*	**G Vill**	25
1938	Wo Hop	**Chinatown**	22
1941	Sevilla	**W Vill**	24
1942	B & H Dairy	**E Vill**	23
1944	Patsy's	**W 50s**	21

1945 | Ben's Best | **Rego Pk**	23
1950 | Junior's | **W 40s**	19
1953 | Liebman's | **Riverdale**	24
1953 | Vesuvio | **Bay Ridge**	22
1954 | Serendipity 3 | **E 60s**	19
1954 | Veselka | **E Vill**	21
1957 | Arturo's | **G Vill**	23
1958 | Queen | **Bklyn Hts**	24
1959 | Brasserie | **E 50s**	22
1959 | El Parador | **Murray Hill**	22
1959 | Four Seasons | **E 50s**	26
1959 | London Lennie's | **Middle Vill**	24
1960 | Bull & Bear | **E 40s**	21
1960 | Chez Napoléon | **W 50s**	22
1960 | Joe & Pat's | **Castelton Cnrs**	24
1961 | Corner Bistro | **W Vill**	23
1962 | La Grenouille | **E 50s**	27
1962 | Sylvia's | **Harlem**	20
1963 | Victor's Cafe | **W 50s**	23
1964 | Di Fara | **Midwood**	26
1964 | Le Perigord | **E 50s**	25
1965 | Joe Allen | **W 40s**	18
1966 | Sparks | **E 40s**	25

HOTEL DINING

Ace Hotel	
Breslin | **NoMad**	22
John Dory Oyster | **NoMad**	21
No. 7 | **NoMad**	21
Stumptown | **NoMad**	23
Affinia Shelburne Hotel	
Rare B&G | **Murray Hill**	20
Amsterdam Court Hotel	
Natsumi | **W 50s**	22
Archer Hotel	
David Burke Fab. | **W 30s**	24
Baccarat Hotel	
NEW Chevalier | **W 50s**	22
Benjamin Hotel	
National | **E 50s**	20
Blakely Hotel	
Abboccato | **W 50s**	21
Bowery Hotel	
Gemma | **E Vill**	21
Bryant Park Hotel	
Koi | **W 40s**	24
Carlyle Hotel	
Carlyle | **E 70s**	24
Casablanca Hotel	
Tony's Di Napoli | **W 40s**	21

Cassa Hotel	
Butter | **W 40s**	23
Chambers Hotel	
Má Pêche | **W 50s**	23
Chandler Hotel	
Juni | **Murray Hill**	27
Chatwal Hotel	
Lambs Club | **W 40s**	21
City Club Hotel	
db Bistro Moderne | **W 40s**	24
Dream Hotel	
Serafina | **W 50s**	19
Dream Downtown Hotel	
Bodega Negra | **Chelsea**	22
Cherry | **Chelsea**	22
Duane Street Hotel	
Mehtaphor | **TriBeCa**	28
Dylan Hotel	
Benjamin Steak | **E 40s**	27
Edition Hotel	
NEW Clocktower | **Flatiron**	24
Elysée Hotel	
Monkey Bar | **E 50s**	20
Empire Hotel	
Ed's Chowder | **W 60s**	20
Eventi Hotel	
NEW Vine | **Chelsea**	—
Excelsior Hotel	
Calle Ocho | **W 80s**	21
Gramercy Park Hotel	
Maialino | **Gramercy**	25
Greenwich Hotel	
Locanda Verde | **TriBeCa**	25
Hilton NY Fashion District Hotel	
Rare B&G | **Murray Hill**	20
Hyatt Union Sq. Hotel	
Fourth | **G Vill**	20
Ink48 Hotel	
Print | **W 40s**	24
Inn at Irving Pl.	
Lady Mendl's | **Gramercy**	21
InterContinental Hotel Times Sq.	
Ça Va | **W 40s**	21
Iroquois Hotel	
Triomphe | **W 40s**	23
James Hotel	
David Burke Kitchen | **SoHo**	25
Jane Hotel	
Cafe Gitane | **W Vill**	22
Knickerbocker Hotel	
NEW Charlie Palmer at The Knick | **W 40s**	27

Langham Place Fifth Ave. Hotel
Ai Fiori | **W 30s** 26

Le Parker Meridien
Burger Joint | **W 50s** 25
Norma's | **W 50s** 25

Lombardy Hotel
Harlow | **E 50s** 20

London NYC Hotel
Maze | **W 50s** 22

Ludlow Hotel
Dirty French | **LES** 24

Mandarin Oriental Hotel
Asiate | **W 50s** 24

Maritime Hotel
Tao | **Chelsea** 24

Mark Hotel
Mark | **E 70s** 23

Marlton Hotel
Margaux | **G Vill** 18

Marriott Marquis Hotel
View | **W 40s** 18

Martha Washington Hotel
Marta | **NoMad** 24

McCarren Hotel
NEW Oleanders | **W'burg** —

Mela Hotel
Saju Bistro | **W 40s** 22

Mercer Hotel
Mercer Kitchen | **SoHo** 23

NoMad Hotel
NoMad | **NoMad** 26

NYLO Hotel
Serafina | **W 70s** 19

1 Hotel Central Park
NEW Jams | **W 50s** —

Park Hyatt Hotel
Back Rm at One57 | **W 50s** 24

Park South Hotel
NEW O Ya | **Murray Hill** —

Pierre Hotel
Sirio | **E 60s** 21

Plaza Hotel
Palm Court | **W 50s** 23
Plaza Food Hall | **W 50s** 21

Pod 39 Hotel
Salvation Taco | **Murray Hill** 20

Regency Hotel
Regency B&G | **E 60s** 24

Royalton Hotel
Forty Four | **W 40s** 22

Sherry-Netherland Hotel
Harry Cipriani | **E 50s** 24

6 Columbus Hotel
Blue Ribbon Sushi | **SoHo** 25

Sixty Hotel
NEW Sessanta | **SoHo** —

Sixty LES Hotel
Blue Ribbon Sushi | **LES** 25

Smyth Hotel
NEW Little Park | **TriBeCa** 26

Sohotel
Bacchanal | **L Italy** 22

Standard Hotel
Standard Grill | **Meatpacking** 21

Standard East Village Hotel
Narcissa | **E Vill** 25

Surrey Hotel
Café Boulud | **E 70s** 27

Time Hotel
Serafina | **W 50s** 19

Trump Int'l Hotel
Jean-Georges | **W 60s** 28
Jean-Georges' Noug. | **W 60s** 27

Trump SoHo Hotel
Koi | **Hudson Sq** 24

W Hotel Times Sq.
Blue Fin | **W 40s** 22

Waldorf-Astoria Hotel
Bull & Bear | **E 40s** 21

Wales Hotel
Paola's | **E 90s** 24

Washington Sq. Hotel
North Sq. | **G Vill** 24

Wellington Hotel
Molyvos | **W 50s** 23

William Hotel
Peacock | **Murray Hill** 22

Wythe Hotel
Reynard | **W'burg** 23

HOT SPOTS

ABC Cocina | **Flatiron** 25
Bagatelle | **Meatpacking** 18
Bar Bolonat | **W Vill** 25
Bar Primi | **E Vill** 24
Bâtard | **TriBeCa** 27
Beautique | **W 50s** 20
Beauty & Essex | **LES** 23
Berg'n | **Crown Hts** 23
Bodega Negra | **Chelsea** 22
NEW Cafe Clover | **W Vill** 24
Carbone | **G Vill** 24
Cecil | **Harlem** 23
Charlie Bird | **SoHo** 23
Cherry | **W'burg** 22

Clam | **W Vill**	25
Claudette | **G Vill**	21
NEW Clocktower | **Flatiron**	24
Contra | **LES**	25
NEW Cosme | **Flatiron**	25
Decoy | **W Vill**	26
Dirt Candy | **LES**	25
Dirty French | **LES**	24
Dover | **Carroll Gdns**	26
East Pole | **E 60s**	23
Emily | **Clinton Hill**	26
Estela | **NoLita**	27
French Louie | **Boerum Hill**	25
Gato | **NoHo**	26
Glady's | **Crown Hts**	24
Glasserie | **Greenpt**	25
Ivan Ramen | **multi.**	22
NEW Javelina | **Gramercy**	26
Lavo | **E 50s**	20
Meadowsweet | **W'burg**	25
Minetta Tavern | **G Vill**	25
Mission Chinese | **LES**	22
Miss Lily's | **G Vill**	23
M. Wells Steakhse. | **LIC**	24
Narcissa | **E Vill**	25
Navy | **SoHo**	21
NoMad | **NoMad**	26
NoMad Bar | **NoMad**	25
Okonomi | **W'burg**	25
Perla | **G Vill**	23
NEW Pizza Beach | **E 80s**	19
Pok Pok Ny | **Columbia St.**	26
NEW Polo Bar | **E 50s**	20
Red Rooster | **Harlem**	22
Reynard | **W'burg**	23
Rist. Morini | **E 80s**	24
River Styx | **Greenpt**	23
Root & Bone | **E Vill**	24
Rosemary's | **W Vill**	22
NEW Rosie's | **E Vill**	24
NEW Santina | **Meatpacking**	23
Spotted Pig | **W Vill**	24
Sushi Nakazawa | **W Vill**	27
Toro | **Chelsea**	24
NEW Upland | **Murray Hill**	25

JACKET REQUIRED

Carlyle | **E 70s**	24
Daniel | **E 60s**	29
Four Seasons | **E 50s**	26
Jean-Georges | **W 60s**	28
La Grenouille | **E 50s**	27
Le Bernardin | **W 50s**	29

Le Cirque | **E 50s**	24
Per Se | **W 50s**	28
River Café | **Dumbo**	26
21 Club | **W 50s**	23

MEET FOR A DRINK

ABC Cocina | **Flatiron**	25
Acme | **NoHo**	20
Aldo Sohm | **W 50s**	21
All'onda | **G Vill**	23
American Cut | **TriBeCa**	24
Aretsky's Patroon | **E 40s**	23
Artisanal | **Murray Hill**	21
NEW Asia de Cuba | **G Vill**	23
Astor Room | **Astoria**	21
Atlantic Grill | **E 70s**	23
Atrium Dumbo | **Dumbo**	23
Aurora | **multi.**	24
Back Forty West | **SoHo**	21
Bar Boulud | **W 60s**	24
Barbounia | **Flatiron**	21
Betony | **W 50s**	25
Bill's Food/Drink | **E 50s**	18
Blue Fin | **W 40s**	22
Blue Water | **Union Sq**	24
Bodega Negra | **Chelsea**	22
Bond St | **NoHo**	25
Boqueria | **multi.**	23
NEW Bowery Meat Co. | **E Vill**	25
Bryant Pk Grill/Cafe | **W 40s**	18
Buddakan | **Chelsea**	25
Butterfly | **TriBeCa**	19
Cafe El Pres. | **Flatiron**	20
Cafe Luxembourg | **W 70s**	21
Cafe Tallulah | **W 70s**	20
Casa Lever | **E 50s**	22
Catch | **Meatpacking**	23
Chalk Point | **SoHo**	24
City Hall | **TriBeCa**	22
NEW Clocktower | **Flatiron**	24
Colicchio/Sons | **Chelsea**	26
NEW Crimson & Rye | **E 50s**	20
Daniel | **E 60s**	29
DBGB | **E Vill**	22
Dead Rabbit | **Financial**	22
Del Frisco's | **multi.**	25
Dos Caminos | **multi.**	19
Dutch | **SoHo**	22
Eddy | **E Vill**	26
Élan | **Flatiron**	23
El Toro Blanco | **W Vill**	21
El Vez | **Battery Pk**	20
NEW Eugene & Co. | **Bed-Stuy**	—

Flatbush Farm | **Park Slope**	21
Four Seasons | **E 50s**	26
Freemans | **LES**	22
French Louie | **Boerum Hill**	25
NEW Gabriel Kreuther | **W 40s**	—
NEW Gardenia | **W Vill**	—
Gato | **NoHo**	26
Glass House | **W 40s**	20
Gotham B&G | **G Vill**	28
Gramercy Tavern | **Flatiron**	28
NEW Grand Army | **Downtown Bklyn**	22
Gran Electrica | **Dumbo**	25
Hakkasan | **W 40s**	24
Harlow | **E 50s**	20
Harry's Cafe | **Financial**	23
Hillstone | **multi.**	22
Huertas | **E Vill**	25
Jack the Horse | **Bklyn Hts**	24
Jean-Georges | **W 60s**	28
J.G. Melon | **multi.**	22
Keens | **W 30s**	26
Kellari Taverna | **W 40s**	22
Koi | **W 40s**	24
Lafayette | **NoHo**	22
La Fonda/Sol | **E 40s**	22
Lambs Club | **W 40s**	21
Landmarc | **W 50s**	19
Lavo | **E 50s**	20
Le Bernardin | **W 50s**	29
Le Cirque | **E 50s**	24
Le Colonial | **E 50s**	22
Library/Public | **G Vill**	19
Lincoln | **W 60s**	25
Macao Trading | **TriBeCa**	22
Maialino | **Gramercy**	25
Mari Vanna | **Flatiron**	20
Mark | **E 70s**	23
Masa/Bar Masa | **W 50s**	26
Mayahuel | **E Vill**	23
Maysville | **NoMad**	22
Michael Jordan | **E 40s**	21
NEW Milling Rm. | **W 80s**	24
Minetta Tavern | **G Vill**	25
Modern | **W 50s**	26
Monkey Bar | **E 50s**	20
National | **E 50s**	20
Natsumi | **W 50s**	22
Nobu | **multi.**	27
NoMad | **NoMad**	26
Northeast Kingdom | **Bushwick**	25
North End Grill | **Battery Pk**	25
Odeon | **TriBeCa**	21
NEW Oleanders | **W'burg**	—
Orsay | **E 70s**	20
Park | **Chelsea**	19
Park Avenue | **Flatiron**	25
Penrose | **E 80s**	22
NEW Pier A Harbor Hse. | **BPC**	18
Pies-N-Thighs | **W'burg**	24
P.J. Clarke's | **multi.**	18
NEW Porchlight | **Chelsea**	21
NEW Prova | **Chelsea**	24
Quality Italian | **W 50s**	24
Raoul's | **SoHo**	23
NEW Rebelle | **NoLita**	18
Red Rooster | **Harlem**	22
Reynard | **W'burg**	23
NEW Ribbon | **W 70s**	—
Roberta's | **Bushwick**	26
Roebling Tea Room | **W'burg**	24
Roman's | **Ft Greene**	25
Salvation Taco | **Murray Hill**	20
Saxon & Parole | **NoHo**	24
Spice Market | **Meatpacking**	24
Standard Grill | **Meatpacking**	21
Stanton Social | **LES**	23
STK | **Meatpacking**	23
Stone Park | **Park Slope**	25
Talde | **Park Slope**	24
Tao | **multi.**	24
Tavern/Green | **Central Pk**	15
Tessa | **W 70s**	23
Toro | **Chelsea**	24
21 Club | **W 50s**	23
Untitled | **Meatpacking**	—
NEW Upland | **Murray Hill**	25
NEW Vic's | **NoHo**	22
Wollensky's | **E 40s**	24
Zengo | **E 40s**	20

MUSIC/LIVE ENTERTAINMENT

(Call for types and times of performances)

Blue Smoke | **multi.**	22
Blue Water | **Union Sq**	24
Cávo | **Astoria**	20
Chez Josephine | **W 40s**	22
Cornelia St. | **W Vill**	18
Knickerbocker | **G Vill**	21
La Lanterna | **G Vill**	20
River Café | **Dumbo**	26
Sylvia's | **Harlem**	20
Tommaso | **Bath Bch**	24

More on zagat.com

NEWCOMERS

Almanac | **W Vill**	26
Asia de Cuba | **G Vill**	23
Baba's Pierogies | **Gowanus**	—
Babu Ji | **E Vill**	—
Bara | **E Vill**	—
Bar Bolinas | **Clinton Hill**	—
Beaubourg | **BPC**	20
Birds & Bubbles | **LES**	21
BKB | **E 70s**	23
Black Tap | **SoHo**	20
Bowery Meat Co. | **E Vill**	25
Bricolage | **Park Slope**	—
Burger & Lobster | **Flatiron**	24
Cafe Clover | **W Vill**	24
Charlie Palmer at The Knick | **W 40s**	27
Chefs Club | **NoLita**	24
Chevalier | **W 50s**	22
Chomp Chomp | **W Vill**	—
City Kitchen | **W 40s**	25
Clocktower | **Flatiron**	24
Cosme | **Flatiron**	25
Crimson & Rye | **E 50s**	20
Delaware & Hudson | **W'burg**	26
Dominique Ansel Kit. | **W Vill**	—
Eli's Table | **E 80s**	22
El Rey | **LES**	25
Empellón al Pastor | **E Vill**	19
Esme | **Greenpt**	23
Eugene & Co. | **Bed-Stuy**	—
Faro | **Bushwick**	—
Finch | **Clinton Hill**	22
Florian | **Gramercy**	22
Fuku | **E Vill**	—
Gabriel Kreuther | **W 40s**	—
Gansevoort Mkt. | **Meatpacking**	—
Ganso Yaki | **Downtown Bklyn**	—
Gardenia | **W Vill**	—
Gelso & Grand | **L Italy**	18
Goemon Curry | **NoLita**	—
Grand Army | **Downtown Bklyn**	22
Haldi | **Murray Hill**	19
Houseman | **Hudson Sq**	—
Hudson Garden | **Bronx Park**	—
Hugo & Sons | **Park Slope**	23
Hunt & Fish | **W 40s**	19
Il Falco | **LIC**	24
Industry Kitchen | **Financial**	—
Jams | **W 50s**	—
Javelina | **Gramercy**	26
June Wine | **Cobble Hill**	20
Kang Ho Dong | **Murray Hill**	23

Kao Soy | **Red Hook**	21
Kappo Masa | **E 70s**	25
Kiin Thai | **G Vill**	22
King Bee | **E Vill**	21
Korilla | **E Vill**	23
Kottu House | **LES**	—
La Gamelle | **LES**	—
L'Antagoniste | **Bed-Stuy**	23
Le District | **BPC**	—
Limani | **W 50s**	23
Lincoln Sq. Steak | **W 70s**	20
Little Beet Table | **Murray Hill**	22
Little Park | **TriBeCa**	26
Loi Estiatorio | **W 50s**	25
Lupulo | **Chelsea**	—
Maman | **L Italy**	20
Mamo | **SoHo**	—
Mastro's Steak | **W 50s**	25
Milling Rm. | **W 80s**	24
Milton | **E 90s**	23
Monte Carlo | **E 70s**	23
Mu Ramen | **LIC**	24
Noreetuh | **E Vill**	—
Oiji | **E Vill**	—
Oleanders | **W'burg**	—
One Dine | **Financial**	—
O Ya | **Murray Hill**	—
Pardon My French | **E Vill**	27
Pier A Harbor Hse. | **BPC**	18
Pizza Beach | **E 80s**	19
Polo Bar | **E 50s**	20
Porchlight | **Chelsea**	21
Prova | **Chelsea**	24
Rainbow Rm. | **W 50s**	23
Ramen Lab | **NoLita**	26
Rebelle | **NoLita**	18
Red Stixs | **E 40s**	20
Ribbon | **W 70s**	—
River Dock | **St. George**	—
Rocky Slims | **Murray Hill**	21
Rose's | **Prospect Hts**	—
Rosie's | **E Vill**	24
Saki | **G Vill**	—
Santina | **Meatpacking**	23
Seamore's | **L Italy**	—
Semilla | **W'burg**	26
Sessanta | **SoHo**	—
Shuko | **G Vill**	26
Spaghetti Incident | **LES**	—
State Grill | **W 30S**	25
Streetbird | **Harlem**	18
Superiority Burger | **E Vill**	—
Tacuba | **Astoria**	20

Tasca Chino | **Gramercy**	19
Tijuana Picnic | **LES**	21
Tuome | **E Vill**	26
212 Steakhse. | **E 50s**	22
Uma Temakeria | **Chelsea**	20
Upholstery Store | **W Vill**	25
Upland | **Murray Hill**	25
Via Carota | **W Vill**	24
Vic's | **NoHo**	22
Vine | **Chelsea**	—
Virginia's | **E Vill**	23
Wildair | **LES**	—
Willow | **Bed-Stuy**	20
Zuma | **Murray Hill**	22

NOTEWORTHY CLOSINGS

Alder
Barchetta
BLT B&G
BLT Fish
Char No. 4
Chin Chin
Cleveland
Commerce
Crown
Edison Cafe
Elm
Five Points
Grocery
Harrison
Josie's
L'Absinthe
Louro
Marco's
Marrow
Megu
Monarch Rm.
Olives
Ouest
Rayuela
Seäsonal
The Palm (837 2nd Ave.)
Willow Road
Ze Café

OUTDOOR DINING

Agnanti | **Astoria**	25
Alma | **Columbia St.**	20
Altesi | **E 60s**	22
A.O.C. | **W Vill**	20
Aquagrill | **SoHo**	27
Aurora | **W'burg**	24
Avra | **E 40s**	26

Bacchus | **Downtown Bklyn**	21
Barbetta | **W 40s**	22
Bar Corvo | **Prospect Hts**	25
Battery Gdns. | **Financial**	19
NEW Beaubourg | **BPC**	20
Berg'n | **Crown Hts**	23
Blue Water | **Union Sq**	24
Boathouse | **Central Pk**	18
Bobo | **W Vill**	23
Bogota | **Park Slope**	24
Bottega | **E 70s**	20
NEW Bowery Meat Co. | **E Vill**	25
Brass. Ruhlmann | **W 50s**	18
Bryant Pk Grill/Cafe | **W 40s**	18
Cacio e Pepe | **E Vill**	22
Cafe Asean | **W Vill**	23
Cafe Centro | **E 40s**	22
Cafe Mogador | **E Vill**	24
Cávo | **Astoria**	20
Conviv. Osteria | **Park Slope**	26
Da Nico | **L Italy**	21
Dinosaur BBQ | **multi.**	22
Dominique Ansel Bakery | **SoHo**	25
NEW Dominique Ansel Kit. | **W Vill**	—
Edi & The Wolf | **E Vill**	22
Empire Diner | **Chelsea**	19
Esca | **W 40s**	25
Farm/Adderley | **Ditmas Pk**	23
Flatbush Farm | **Park Slope**	21
44 & X/44½ | **W 40s**	23
Frankies | **multi.**	25
French Louie | **Boerum Hill**	25
Gigino | **BPC**	21
Gnocco | **E Vill**	22
Good Fork | **Red Hook**	25
Gran Electrica | **Dumbo**	25
Hudson Eats | **BPC**	19
NEW Industry Kitchen | **Financial**	—
Isabella's | **W 70s**	20
I Trulli | **Murray Hill**	23
Ivan Ramen | **multi.**	22
Ladurée | **SoHo**	22
La Esquina | **SoHo**	23
La Lanterna | **G Vill**	20
La Mangeoire | **E 50s**	22
L&B Spumoni | **Gravesend**	24
Montmartre | **Chelsea**	19
M. Wells Dinette | **LIC**	22
M. Wells Steakhse. | **LIC**	24
New Leaf | **Inwood**	—
Pachanga Patterson | **Astoria**	24

Palma	**W Vill**	24	Lion	**G Vill**	18
Pera	**SoHo**	21	Marea	**W 50s**	27
NEW Pier A Harbor Hse.	**BPC**	18	Margaux	**G Vill**	18
Pines	**Gowanus**	25	Michael's	**W 50s**	23
Pine Tree Cafe	**Bronx Pk**	24	Minetta Tavern	**G Vill**	25
Pizzetteria Brunetti	**W Vill**	26	Nello	**E 60s**	18
NEW River Dock	**St. George**	–	Nicola's	**E 80s**	22
Riverpark	**Murray Hill**	26	NoMad	**NoMad**	26
Roberta's	**Bushwick**	26	Orso	**W 40s**	23
Roebling Tea Room	**W'burg**	24	Philippe	**E 60s**	22
NEW Rosie's	**E Vill**	24	NEW Polo Bar	**E 50s**	20
Salinas	**Chelsea**	24	Rao's	**E Harlem**	23
San Pietro	**E 50s**	24	Red Rooster	**Harlem**	22
NEW Santina	**Meatpacking**	23	Reynard	**W'burg**	23
Sripraphai	**Woodside**	26	Roberta's	**Bushwick**	26
Tartine	**W Vill**	22	Rosemary's	**W Vill**	22
Tavern/Green	**Central Pk**	15	Sant Ambroeus	**multi.**	22
Traif	**W'burg**	24	NEW Santina	**Meatpacking**	23
Trestle on 10th	**Chelsea**	23	Sette Mezzo	**E 70s**	23
ViceVersa	**W 50s**	24	Sparks	**E 40s**	25
Vinegar Hill Hse.	**Vinegar Hill**	23	Spice Market	**Meatpacking**	24
Water Club	**Murray Hill**	23	Spotted Pig	**W Vill**	24
Water's Edge	**LIC**	22	Standard Grill	**Meatpacking**	21
Untitled	**Meatpacking**	–	Swifty's	**E 70s**	17
NEW Vine	**Chelsea**	–	21 Club	**W 50s**	23
Zona Rosa	**W'burg**	21	Via Quadronno	**E 70s**	22

PEOPLE-WATCHING

Acme	**NoHo**	20
Amaranth	**E 60s**	21
Antica Pesa	**W'burg**	24
Bagatelle	**Meatpacking**	18
Balthazar	**SoHo**	24
Beatrice Inn	**W Vill**	21
Beautique	**W 50s**	20
Breslin	**NoMad**	22
Café Boulud	**E 70s**	27
Cafe Gitane	**multi.**	22
Casa Lever	**E 50s**	22
Cherche Midi	**NoLita**	22
Cipriani	**SoHo**	23
Da Silvano	**G Vill**	21
Elio's	**E 80s**	25
Four Seasons	**E 50s**	26
Fred's at Barneys	**E 60s**	20
Harlow	**E 50s**	20
Indochine	**G Vill**	23
Joe Allen	**W 40s**	18
Katz's Deli	**LES**	25
Lavo	**E 50s**	20
Le Bilboquet	**E 60s**	22
Le Cirque	**E 50s**	24
Leopard/des Artistes	**W 60s**	21

POWER SCENES

ABC Kitchen	**Flatiron**	26
Ai Fiori	**W 30s**	26
Balthazar	**SoHo**	24
Betony	**W 50s**	25
BLT Prime	**Gramercy**	26
BLT Steak	**E 50s**	25
Bobby Van's	**multi.**	23
Bull & Bear	**E 40s**	21
Carlyle	**E 70s**	24
Casa Lever	**E 50s**	22
NEW Chevalier	**W 50s**	22
China Grill	**W 50s**	22
Cipriani	**Financial**	23
City Hall	**TriBeCa**	22
Daniel	**E 60s**	29
Del Frisco's	**multi.**	25
Del Posto	**Chelsea**	27
Elio's	**E 80s**	25
Four Seasons	**E 50s**	26
Fresco	**E 50s**	22
NEW Gabriel Kreuther	**W 40s**	–
Gotham B&G	**G Vill**	28
Harry's Cafe	**Financial**	23
Jean-Georges	**W 60s**	28
NEW Kappo Masa	**E 70s**	25

Keens | **W 30s**	26
La Grenouille | **E 50s**	27
Lambs Club | **W 40s**	21
Le Bernardin | **W 50s**	29
Le Bilboquet | **E 60s**	22
Le Cirque | **E 50s**	24
Marea | **W 50s**	27
Michael's | **W 50s**	23
Modern | **W 50s**	26
Morton's | **E 40s**	23
Nobu | **multi.**	27
NoMad | **NoMad**	26
Norma's | **W 50s**	25
North End Grill | **Battery Pk**	25
Peter Luger | **W'burg**	28
Rao's | **E Harlem**	23
Regency B&G | **E 60s**	24
Russian Tea | **W 50s**	20
San Pietro | **E 50s**	24
Sant Ambroeus | **multi.**	22
Sirio | **E 60s**	21
Smith/Wollensky | **E 40s**	24
Sparks | **E 40s**	25
21 Club | **W 50s**	23

PRIVATE ROOMS/ PARTIES

Acme | **NoHo**	20
Ai Fiori | **W 30s**	26
Aldea | **Flatiron**	24
Alta | **G Vill**	25
Ample Hills | **multi.**	27
Aquavit | **E 50s**	26
Aretsky's Patroon | **E 40s**	23
Aroma Kitchen | **NoHo**	22
Astor Room | **Astoria**	21
Aureole | **W 40s**	25
A Voce | **W 50s**	23
Bacaro | **LES**	21
Bar Americain | **W 50s**	23
Barbetta | **W 40s**	22
Bar Boulud | **W 60s**	24
Battery Gdns. | **Financial**	19
Beauty & Essex | **LES**	23
Benoit | **W 50s**	23
Betony | **W 50s**	25
BLT Prime | **Gramercy**	26
BLT Steak | **E 50s**	25
Blue Hill | **G Vill**	28
Blue Smoke | **multi.**	22
Blue Water | **Union Sq**	24
Bodega Negra | **Chelsea**	22
Bond St | **NoHo**	25

Bouley | **TriBeCa**	29
Breslin | **NoMad**	22
Buddakan | **Chelsea**	25
Café Boulud | **E 70s**	27
Capital Grille | **E 40s**	25
Casa Lever | **E 50s**	22
Casa Nonna | **W 30s**	22
Catch | **Meatpacking**	23
Ça Va | **W 40s**	21
Cellini | **E 50s**	22
City Hall | **TriBeCa**	22
Colicchio/Sons | **Chelsea**	26
Conviv. Osteria | **Park Slope**	26
Craft | **Flatiron**	25
Daniel | **E 60s**	29
David Burke Kitchen | **SoHo**	25
db Bistro Moderne | **W 40s**	24
Del Frisco's | **multi.**	25
Delmonico's | **W 30s**	24
Del Posto | **Chelsea**	27
Dinosaur BBQ | **multi.**	22
Docks Oyster | **E 40s**	21
Eleven Madison | **Flatiron**	28
EN Japanese | **W Vill**	25
Felidia | **E 50s**	25
Fig & Olive | **multi.**	21
Four Seasons | **E 50s**	26
Fourth | **G Vill**	20
Frankies | **multi.**	25
Fraunces Tav. | **Financial**	18
Freemans | **LES**	22
Fresco | **E 50s**	22
NEW Gabriel Kreuther | **W 40s**	—
Gabriel's | **W 60s**	21
Gander | **Flatiron**	20
Gramercy Tavern | **Flatiron**	28
Hakkasan | **W 40s**	24
Harry's Cafe | **Financial**	23
Hecho en Dumbo | **NoHo**	22
Hudson Clearwater | **W Vill**	25
Il Buco | **NoHo**	25
Il Buco Alimentari | **NoHo**	24
Il Cortile | **L Italy**	23
Ilili | **NoMad**	24
Jean-Georges | **W 60s**	28
Jungsik | **TriBeCa**	26
Keens | **W 30s**	26
Lafayette | **NoHo**	22
La Grenouille | **E 50s**	27
Le Bernardin | **W 50s**	29
Le Cirque | **E 50s**	24
Le Perigord | **E 50s**	25
Le Zie | **Chelsea**	21

Lincoln	**W 60s**	25
Locanda Verde	**TriBeCa**	25
Lupa	**G Vill**	25
Lure Fishbar	**SoHo**	25
Macelleria	**Meatpacking**	22
Maialino	**Gramercy**	25
Maloney & Porcelli	**E 50s**	25
Marcony	**Murray Hill**	24
Marea	**W 50s**	27
Mas	**W Vill**	26
Michael's	**W 50s**	23
Milos	**W 50s**	27
Modern	**W 50s**	26
Mr. Chow	**E 50s**	23
Mr. K's	**E 50s**	23
National	**E 50s**	20
Nerai	**E 50s**	24
Nobu	**multi.**	27
NoMad	**NoMad**	26
Oceana	**W 40s**	25
Palma	**W Vill**	24
Park	**Chelsea**	19
Parlor Steakhse.	**E 80s**	21
Pera	**SoHo**	21
Periyali	**Flatiron**	24
Perry St.	**W Vill**	26
Per Se	**W 50s**	28
Picholine	**W 60s**	26
Print	**W 40s**	24
Public	**NoLita**	24
Quality Meats	**W 50s**	26
Raoul's	**SoHo**	23
Redeye Grill	**W 50s**	21
Remi	**W 50s**	22
River Café	**Dumbo**	26
Rock Center Café	**W 40s**	18
Rotisserie Georgette	**E 60s**	22
Russian Tea	**W 50s**	20
Salinas	**Chelsea**	24
Saxon & Parole	**NoHo**	24
Scarpetta	**Chelsea**	25
Scottadito	**Park Slope**	23
Sea Fire Grill	**E 40s**	27
Sea Grill	**W 40s**	24
Shun Lee Palace	**E 50s**	23
Sparks	**E 40s**	25
Spice Market	**Meatpacking**	24
Stanton Social	**LES**	23
STK	**Meatpacking**	23
Stone Park	**Park Slope**	25
Tamarind	**TriBeCa**	26
Tao	**multi.**	24
Tavern/Green	**Central Pk**	15

Thalassa	**TriBeCa**	23
Tocqueville	**Flatiron**	26
Toro	**Chelsea**	24
Tratt. L'incontro	**Astoria**	26
Tribeca Grill	**TriBeCa**	23
21 Club	**W 50s**	23
Uncle Jack's	**W 50s**	23
Uva	**E 70s**	22
Valbella	**Meatpacking**	24
Victor's Cafe	**W 50s**	23
Vitae	**E 40s**	24
Water Club	**Murray Hill**	23
Yerba Buena	**multi.**	22
Zengo	**E 40s**	20
Zizi Limona	**W'burg**	25

QUICK BITES

Arepas	**Astoria**	23
A Salt & Battery	**W Vill**	22
Azuri Cafe	**W 50s**	23
BaoHaus	**E Vill**	23
Bark	**multi.**	20
Baz Bagel	**L Italy**	21
Berg'n	**Crown Hts**	23
Blossom du Jour	**multi.**	25
Bouchon Bakery	**multi.**	22
Bread	**multi.**	21
Cafe El Pres.	**Flatiron**	20
Calexico	**multi.**	21
Caracas	**multi.**	26
NEW Chomp Chomp	**W Vill**	–
City Bakery	**Flatiron**	23
NEW City Kitchen	**W 40s**	25
Counter	**W 40s**	20
Crif Dogs	**multi.**	22
Daisy May's	**W 40s**	22
Dos Toros	**multi.**	22
Eataly	**Flatiron**	24
NEW Fuku	**E Vill**	–
NEW Gansevoort Mkt.	**Meatpacking**	–
Gotham West	**W 40s**	20
Gray's Papaya	**W 70s**	21
Halal Guys	**multi.**	22
Harlem Shake	**Harlem**	20
Hudson Eats	**BPC**	19
Hu Kitchen	**G Vill**	24
Hummus Pl.	**multi.**	22
Island Burgers	**multi.**	21
Joe's Pizza	**multi.**	24
Kati Roll	**multi.**	23
La Bonne Soupe	**W 50s**	19
La Esquina	**SoHo**	23

NEW Le District | **BPC**	—
Los Tacos | **Chelsea**	27
Luke's Lobster | **multi.**	24
NEW Maman | **L Italy**	20
Mamoun's | **multi.**	23
Meatball Shop | **multi.**	21
Melt Shop | **multi.**	22
Mimi Cheng's | **E Vill**	24
Miss Lily's | **multi.**	23
Naya Express | **multi.**	22
New World Mall | **Flushing**	22
Nice Green Bo | **Chinatown**	21
99 Miles/Philly | **multi.**	21
Oaxaca | **multi.**	23
100 Montaditos | **G Vill**	19
Papaya King | **multi.**	22
Plaza Food Hall | **W 50s**	21
Porchetta | **E Vill**	22
Prosperity Dumpling | **LES**	24
Schnipper's | **multi.**	19
Shake Shack | **multi.**	22
Smile to Go | **SoHo**	20
Smorgasburg | **multi.**	26
NEW Superiority Burger | **E Vill**	—
Taboonette | **G Vill**	23
Taïm | **multi.**	26
Tres Carnes | **multi.**	22
Two Boots | **multi.**	19
NEW Untamed Sandwiches | **W 30s**	25
Vanessa's Dumpling | **multi.**	22
Via Quadronno | **multi.**	22

QUIET CONVERSATION

Ammos | **E 40s**	22
Annisa | **W Vill**	27
Aroma Kitchen | **NoHo**	22
Asiate | **W 50s**	24
Aureole | **W 40s**	25
Basso56 | **W 50s**	22
Blue Hill | **G Vill**	28
Bosie Tea Parlor | **W Vill**	21
Brasserie 8½ | **W 50s**	22
Cellini | **E 50s**	22
NEW Charlie Palmer at the Knick | **W 40s**	27
Chef's/Brooklyn Fare | **Downtown Bklyn**	26
NEW Chevalier | **W 50s**	22
Clement Rest. | **W 50s**	25
Da Umberto | **Chelsea**	25
Dawat | **E 50s**	24
EN Japanese | **W Vill**	25

NEW Gabriel Kreuther | **W 40s**	—
Giovanni | **E 80s**	25
Il Tinello | **W 50s**	24
Jean-Georges | **W 60s**	28
Jungsik | **TriBeCa**	26
NEW Kappo Masa | **E 70s**	25
Kings' Carriage | **E 80s**	23
La Grenouille | **E 50s**	27
Le Bernardin | **W 50s**	29
Left Bank | **W Vill**	25
Madison Bistro | **Murray Hill**	21
Marea | **W 50s**	27
Mas | **W Vill**	26
Masa/Bar Masa | **W 50s**	26
Montebello | **E 50s**	22
Mr. K's | **E 50s**	23
Nerai | **E 50s**	24
North Sq. | **G Vill**	24
Palm Court | **W 50s**	23
Periyali | **Flatiron**	24
Perry St. | **W Vill**	26
Per Se | **W 50s**	28
Petrossian | **W 50s**	24
Picholine | **W 60s**	26
Pietro's | **E 40s**	23
Radiance Tea | **multi.**	21
Remi | **W 50s**	22
Rosanjin | **TriBeCa**	25
Sapphire Indian | **W 60s**	21
Scaletta | **W 70s**	21
Sfoglia | **E 90s**	23
Sirio | **E 60s**	21
Solera | **E 50s**	22
Tocqueville | **Flatiron**	26
Triomphe | **W 40s**	23
Villa Berulia | **Murray Hill**	25
Zenkichi | **W'burg**	26

RAW BARS

Ammos | **E 40s**	22
Anassa Taverna | **E 60s**	21
Aquagrill | **SoHo**	27
Atlantic Grill | **E 70s**	23
Balthazar | **SoHo**	24
Bar Americain | **W 50s**	23
Beaubourg | **BPC**	20
Blue Fin | **W 40s**	22
Blue Ribbon | **multi.**	25
Blue Water | **Union Sq**	24
Brooklyn Crab | **Red Hook**	20
Catch | **Meatpacking**	23
City Hall | **TriBeCa**	22
City Lobster/Steak | **W 50s**	20

Clam | **W Vill**	25
Crave Fishbar | **E 50s**	24
Cull & Pistol | **Chelsea**	24
David Burke Fishtail | **E 60s**	24
Docks Oyster | **E 40s**	21
Dutch | **SoHo**	22
Ed's Chowder | **W 60s**	20
Ed's Lobster Bar | **multi.**	25
Esca | **W 40s**	25
Fish | **W Vill**	23
Flex Mussels | **multi.**	23
Jack the Horse | **Bklyn Hts**	24
Jeffrey's Grocery | **W Vill**	23
John Dory Oyster | **NoMad**	21
Jordans Lobster | **Sheepshead**	22
Kanoyama | **E Vill**	24
NEW King Bee | **E Vill**	21
L & W Oyster | **NoMad**	20
Littleneck | **multi.**	23
London Lennie's | **Middle Vill**	24
Lure Fishbar | **SoHo**	25
Maison Premiere | **W'burg**	26
Mark | **E 70s**	23
Marlow/Sons | **W'burg**	23
Mercer Kitchen | **SoHo**	23
Mermaid | **multi.**	23
M. Wells Steakhse. | **LIC**	24
Navy | **SoHo**	21
Oceana | **W 40s**	25
Ocean Grill | **W 70s**	23
Oyster Bar | **multi.**	22
Parlor Steakhse. | **E 80s**	21
Pearl Oyster | **W Vill**	27
Pearl Room | **Bay Ridge**	20
P.J. Clarke's | **multi.**	18
Plaza Food Hall | **W 50s**	21
Randazzo's | **Sheepshead**	22
NEW Ribbon | **W 70s**	—
Standard Grill | **Meatpacking**	21
Thalia | **W 40s**	21
21 Club | **W 50s**	23
Uncle Jack's | **multi.**	23
Upstate | **E Vill**	27
Walter | **multi.**	23
ZZ's Clam Bar | **G Vill**	23

ROMANTIC PLACES

Alberto | **Forest Hills**	24
Al Di La | **Park Slope**	26
Alta | **G Vill**	25
Annisa | **W Vill**	27
Antica Pesa | **W'burg**	24
Asiate | **W 50s**	24
Aurora | **multi.**	24
Bacaro | **LES**	21
Barbetta | **W 40s**	22
Blue Hill | **G Vill**	28
Boathouse | **Central Pk**	18
Bobo | **W Vill**	23
Bottino | **Chelsea**	20
Bouley | **TriBeCa**	29
Caviar Russe | **E 50s**	24
Cherry | **Chelsea**	22
Cómodo | **SoHo**	25
Conviv. Osteria | **Park Slope**	26
Daniel | **E 60s**	29
Del Posto | **Chelsea**	27
Eleven Madison | **Flatiron**	28
El Quinto Pino | **Chelsea**	23
Erminia | **E 80s**	24
Esme | **Greenpt**	23
Firenze | **E 80s**	21
Four Seasons | **E 50s**	26
Gemma | **E Vill**	21
Good Fork | **Red Hook**	25
Gramercy Tavern | **Flatiron**	28
House | **Gramercy**	24
Il Buco | **NoHo**	25
I Sodi | **W Vill**	25
I Trulli | **Murray Hill**	23
JoJo | **E 60s**	24
Kings' Carriage | **E 80s**	23
La Grenouille | **E 50s**	27
La Lanterna | **G Vill**	20
La Mangeoire | **E 50s**	22
Lambs Club | **W 40s**	21
L'Artusi | **W Vill**	27
La Vara | **Cobble Hill**	27
Le Gigot | **W Vill**	25
Little Owl | **W Vill**	26
Machiavelli | **W 80s**	21
Mas | **W Vill**	26
Morimoto | **Chelsea**	26
Mr. K's | **E 50s**	23
NoMad | **NoMad**	26
Olea | **Ft Greene**	27
One if by Land | **W Vill**	23
Ovelia | **Astoria**	23
Palma | **W Vill**	24
Paola's | **E 90s**	24
Peasant | **NoLita**	24
Piora | **W Vill**	25
Place | **W Vill**	24
NEW Rainbow Rm. | **W 50s**	23
Raoul's | **SoHo**	23
River Café | **Dumbo**	26

Rouge et Blanc | **SoHo**	25
Rye | **W'burg**	25
Salinas | **Chelsea**	24
Scalini Fedeli | **TriBeCa**	26
Scarpetta | **Chelsea**	25
Sfoglia | **E 90s**	23
Sistina | **E 80s**	25
Spiga | **W 80s**	23
Tocqueville | **Flatiron**	26
Uva | **E 70s**	22
View | **W 40s**	18
Vinegar Hill Hse. | **Vinegar Hill**	23
Wallsé | **W Vill**	25
Water Club | **Murray Hill**	23
Water's Edge | **LIC**	22
Zenkichi | **W'burg**	26

SENIOR APPEAL

Artie's | **City Is**	21
Aureole | **W 40s**	25
Bamonte's | **W'burg**	23
Barbetta | **W 40s**	22
Barney Greengrass | **W 80s**	25
Benoit | **W 50s**	23
Bistro Vendôme | **E 50s**	22
Caravaggio | **E 70s**	25
NEW Chevalier | **W 50s**	22
Chez Napoléon | **W 50s**	22
Club A Steak | **E 50s**	26
Dawat | **E 50s**	24
DeGrezia | **E 50s**	24
Delmonico's | **W 30s**	24
Del Posto | **Chelsea**	27
Due | **E 70s**	22
Felidia | **E 50s**	25
Gabriel's | **W 60s**	21
Giovanni | **E 80s**	25
Grifone | **E 40s**	24
Il Gattopardo | **W 50s**	24
Il Tinello | **W 50s**	24
Ithaka | **E 80s**	20
Jubilee | **E 50s**	21
Kings' Carriage | **E 80s**	23
La Bonne Soupe | **W 50s**	19
La Grenouille | **E 50s**	27
La Mangeoire | **E 50s**	22
Lattanzi | **W 40s**	22
Le Cirque | **E 50s**	24
Leopard/des Artistes | **W 60s**	21
Le Perigord | **E 50s**	25
Lusardi's | **E 70s**	24
Mark | **E 70s**	23
Mr. K's | **E 50s**	23

Nerai | **E 50s**	24
Nicola's | **E 80s**	22
Nippon | **W 50s**	23
Piccolo Angolo | **W Vill**	26
Pietro's | **E 40s**	23
Ponticello | **Astoria**	23
Primola | **E 60s**	22
Quatorze Bis | **E 70s**	22
NEW Rainbow Rm. | **W 50s**	23
Remi | **W 50s**	22
Rist. Morini | **E 80s**	24
River Café | **Dumbo**	26
Rossini's | **Murray Hill**	22
Rotisserie Georgette | **E 60s**	22
Russian Tea | **W 50s**	20
San Pietro | **E 50s**	24
Sardi's | **W 40s**	18
Scaletta | **W 70s**	21
Shun Lee West | **W 60s**	22
Sirio | **E 60s**	21
Sistina | **E 80s**	25
Triomphe | **W 40s**	23
Tuscany Grill | **Bay Ridge**	23
Villa Berulia | **Murray Hill**	25
Vivolo | **E 70s**	20

TOUGH TICKETS

ABC Kitchen | **Flatiron**	26
Babbo | **G Vill**	26
Blanca | **Bushwick**	26
Carbone | **G Vill**	24
Chef's/Brooklyn Fare | **Downtown Bklyn**	26
NEW Cosme | **Flatiron**	25
Dirt Candy | **LES**	25
Dirty French | **LES**	24
Gato | **NoHo**	26
Luksus | **Greenpt**	25
Minetta Tavern | **G Vill**	25
Momofuku Ko | **E Vill**	26
NEW Polo Bar | **E 50s**	20
Rao's | **E Harlem**	23
NEW Shuko | **G Vill**	26
Sushi Nakazawa | **W Vill**	27
Take Root | **Carroll Gdns**	23
ZZ's Clam Bar | **G Vill**	23

TRANSPORTING EXPERIENCES

Asiate | **W 50s**	24
Balthazar | **SoHo**	24
Beauty & Essex | **LES**	23
Boathouse | **Central Pk**	18
Buddakan | **Chelsea**	25

Cafe China | **Murray Hill**	24
Il Buco | **NoHo**	25
Ilili | **NoMad**	24
Keens | **W 30s**	26
La Grenouille | **E 50s**	27
Lambs Club | **W 40s**	21
Le Colonial | **E 50s**	22
Library/Public | **G Vill**	19
NEW Limani | **W 50s**	23
Masa/Bar Masa | **W 50s**	26
Monkey Bar | **E 50s**	20
Ninja | **TriBeCa**	16
Per Se | **W 50s**	28
Qi | **W'burg**	22
NEW Rainbow Rm. | **W 50s**	23
Rao's | **E Harlem**	23
Spice Market | **Meatpacking**	24
Tao | **multi.**	24
Tavern/Green | **Central Pk**	15
Water's Edge | **LIC**	22
Water Table | **Greenpt**	—
Waverly Inn | **W Vill**	22

24-HOUR DINING

BCD Tofu | **W 30s**	23
Bubby's | **multi.**	21
Cafeteria | **Chelsea**	20
Coppelia | **Chelsea**	23
Gray's Papaya | **W 70s**	21
Kang Suh | **W 30s**	18
Kum Gang San | **multi.**	21
Kunjip | **W 30s**	21
New WonJo | **W 30s**	24
Sanford's | **Astoria**	23
Sarge's Deli | **Murray Hill**	23
Veselka | **E Vill**	21

VIEWS

Alma | **Columbia St.**	20
Angelina's | **Tottenville**	24
Asiate | **W 50s**	24
A Voce | **W 50s**	23
Battery Gdns. | **Financial**	19
Birreria | **Flatiron**	21
Boathouse | **Central Pk**	18
Brooklyn Crab | **Red Hook**	20
Bryant Pk Grill/Cafe | **W 40s**	18
City Is. Lobster | **City Is**	22
Gaonnuri | **W 30s**	19
Gigino | **BPC**	21
Hudson Eats | **BPC**	19
Industry Kitchen | **Financial**	—
Jake's Steakhse. | **Fieldston**	24
Lincoln | **W 60s**	25

Michael Jordan | **E 40s**	21
Modern | **W 50s**	26
Morso | **E 50s**	25
NEW One Dine | **Financial**	—
Per Se | **W 50s**	28
NEW Pier A Harbor Hse. | **BPC**	18
Pine Tree Cafe | **Bronx Pk**	24
P.J. Clarke's | **multi.**	18
Porter House | **W 50s**	26
NEW Rainbow Rm. | **W 50s**	23
Randazzo's | **Sheepshead**	22
Rare B&G | **Murray Hill**	20
River Café | **Dumbo**	26
NEW River Dock | **St. George**	—
Riverpark | **Murray Hill**	26
Robert | **W 50s**	21
Rock Center Café | **W 40s**	18
Sea Grill | **W 40s**	24
Shi | **LIC**	23
Stella 34 | **W 30s**	22
View | **W 40s**	18
Water Club | **Murray Hill**	23
Water's Edge | **LIC**	22

VISITORS ON EXPENSE ACCOUNT

Ai Fiori | **W 30s**	26
American Cut | **TriBeCa**	24
Aureole | **W 40s**	25
Babbo | **G Vill**	26
Bâtard | **TriBeCa**	27
Bouley | **TriBeCa**	29
Café Boulud | **E 70s**	27
Carbone | **G Vill**	24
NEW Chevalier | **W 50s**	22
Craft | **Flatiron**	25
Daniel | **E 60s**	29
Del Frisco's | **multi.**	25
Del Posto | **Chelsea**	27
Dovetail | **W 70s**	25
Eleven Madison | **Flatiron**	28
Four Seasons | **E 50s**	26
Gramercy Tavern | **Flatiron**	28
Hakkasan | **W 40s**	24
Il Mulino | **G Vill**	25
Jean-Georges | **W 60s**	28
NEW Kappo Masa | **E 70s**	25
Keens | **W 30s**	26
Kurumazushi | **E 40s**	24
La Grenouille | **E 50s**	27
Le Bernardin | **W 50s**	29
Le Cirque | **E 50s**	24
Marea | **W 50s**	27

Masa/Bar Masa | **W 50s**	26
Milos | **W 50s**	27
Modern | **W 50s**	26
Nobu | **multi.**	27
NEW O Ya | **Murray Hill**	–
Palm | **E 40s**	25
Per Se | **W 50s**	28
Peter Luger | **W'burg**	28
Picholine | **W 60s**	26
Rist. Morini | **E 80s**	24
River Café | **Dumbo**	26
NEW Shuko | **G Vill**	26
Sushi Nakazawa | **W Vill**	27
Sushi Yasuda | **E 40s**	27
Union Sq. Cafe | **Union Sq**	27

WINE BARS

Aldo Sohm | **W 50s**	21
Alta | **G Vill**	25
Aroma Kitchen | **NoHo**	22
Bacaro | **LES**	21
Bacchus | **Downtown Bklyn**	21
Balkanika | **W 40s**	20
Bar Boulud | **W 60s**	24
Bar Jamón | **Gramercy**	24
Casellula | **W 50s**	25
Corkbuzz | **multi.**	20
Danny Brown | **Forest Hills**	26
El Quinto Pino | **Chelsea**	23
Felice | **E 60s**	21
NEW Fifty Paces | **E Vill**	–
Il Buco Alimentari | **NoHo**	24
I Trulli | **Murray Hill**	23
NEW June Wine | **Cobble Hill**	20
Le Bernardin | **W 50s**	29
Murray's Cheese Bar | **W Vill**	24
Otto | **G Vill**	22
Palma | **W Vill**	24
Peasant | **NoLita**	24
Racines | **TriBeCa**	22
NEW Upholstery Store | **W Vill**	25
Uva | **E 70s**	22
Vesta | **Astoria**	26

WINNING WINE LISTS

ABC Cocina | **Flatiron**	25
ABC Kitchen | **Flatiron**	26
Aldea | **Flatiron**	24
All'onda | **G Vill**	23
Alta | **G Vill**	25
Amali | **E 60s**	25
Annisa | **W Vill**	27
Asiate | **W 50s**	24
Aureole | **W 40s**	25

A Voce | **W 50s**	23
Babbo | **G Vill**	26
Bacchanal | **L Italy**	22
Balthazar | **SoHo**	24
Barbetta | **W 40s**	22
Bar Boulud | **W 60s**	24
Bâtard | **TriBeCa**	27
Becco | **W 40s**	23
Betony | **W 50s**	25
NEW Birds & Bubbles | **LES**	21
BLT Prime | **Gramercy**	26
BLT Steak | **E 50s**	25
Blue Fin | **W 40s**	22
Blue Hill | **G Vill**	28
Bobby Van's | **multi.**	23
Bouley | **TriBeCa**	29
Brushstroke/Ichimura | **TriBeCa**	26
Café Boulud | **E 70s**	27
Cafe Katja | **LES**	25
Caffe e Vino | **Ft Greene**	22
Capital Grille | **E 40s**	25
Carbone | **G Vill**	24
Casa Mono | **Gramercy**	25
'Cesca | **W 70s**	22
Charlie Bird | **SoHo**	23
Chef's/Brooklyn Fare | **Downtown Bklyn**	26
City Hall | **TriBeCa**	22
Claudette | **G Vill**	21
Cocotte | **SoHo**	23
Costata | **SoHo**	23
Craft | **Flatiron**	25
Daniel | **E 60s**	29
db Bistro Moderne | **W 40s**	24
Del Frisco's | **multi.**	25
Dell'anima | **W Vill**	24
Del Posto | **Chelsea**	27
Diner | **W'burg**	25
Dovetail | **W 70s**	25
Élan | **Flatiron**	23
Eleven Madison | **Flatiron**	28
Esca | **W 40s**	25
Estela | **NoLita**	27
Felidia | **E 50s**	25
Frankies | **multi.**	25
Franny's | **Park Slope**	23
NEW Gabriel Kreuther | **W 40s**	–
Gander | **Flatiron**	20
Gato | **NoHo**	26
Gotham B&G | **G Vill**	28
Gramercy Tavern | **Flatiron**	28
Harry's Cafe | **Financial**	23
Hearth | **E Vill**	25

Il Buco | **NoHo**	25
I Trulli | **Murray Hill**	23
Jean-Georges | **W 60s**	28
Junoon | **Flatiron**	24
Lafayette | **NoHo**	22
Lambs Club | **W 40s**	21
Landmarc | **W 50s**	19
La Pizza Fresca | **Flatiron**	24
La Vara | **Cobble Hill**	27
Le Bernardin | **W 50s**	29
Le Cirque | **E 50s**	24
Lupa | **G Vill**	25
Maialino | **Gramercy**	25
Má Pêche | **W 50s**	23
Marc Forgione | **TriBeCa**	26
Marea | **W 50s**	27
Marta | **NoMad**	24
Mas | **W Vill**	26
Michael's | **W 50s**	23
Milos | **W 50s**	27
Minetta Tavern | **G Vill**	25
Modern | **W 50s**	26
Molyvos | **W 50s**	23
Momofuku Ko | **E Vill**	26
Musket Room | **NoLita**	26
M. Wells Steakhse. | **LIC**	24
Narcissa | **E Vill**	25
Nice Matin | **W 70s**	19
NoMad | **NoMad**	26
Oceana | **W 40s**	25
Osteria Morini | **SoHo**	26
Otto | **G Vill**	22
NEW O Ya | **Murray Hill**	—
Pearl & Ash | **NoLita**	24
Per Se | **W 50s**	28
Picholine | **W 60s**	26
Porter House | **W 50s**	26
Racines | **TriBeCa**	22
Raoul's | **SoHo**	23
NEW Rebelle | **NoLita**	18
Reynard | **W'burg**	23
Rist. Morini | **E 80s**	24
River Café | **Dumbo**	26
Roman's | **Ft Greene**	25
Rotisserie Georgette | **E 60s**	22
Rouge et Blanc | **SoHo**	25
San Pietro | **E 50s**	24
Scalini Fedeli | **TriBeCa**	26
Scarpetta | **Chelsea**	25
Simone | **E 80s**	25
Sirio | **E 60s**	21
Sistina | **E 80s**	25
Smith/Wollensky | **E 40s**	24

Solera | **E 50s**	22
Sparks | **E 40s**	25
Thalassa | **TriBeCa**	23
Tía Pol | **Chelsea**	23
Tocqueville | **Flatiron**	26
Tommaso | **Bath Bch**	24
Trestle on 10th | **Chelsea**	23
Tribeca Grill | **TriBeCa**	23
21 Club | **W 50s**	23
Txikito | **Chelsea**	24
Union Sq. Cafe | **Union Sq**	27
NEW Upland | **Murray Hill**	25
Valbella | **Meatpacking**	24
Via Emilia | **Flatiron**	22
Vinegar Hill Hse. | **Vinegar Hill**	23
Wallsé | **W Vill**	25
Water's Edge | **LIC**	22
NEW Wildair | **LES**	—

Cuisines

Includes names, locations and Food ratings.

AFGHAN

Afghan Kebab | **multi.**	21

AFRICAN

Ponty Bistro | **multi.**	22

AMERICAN

ABC Kitchen | **Flatiron**	26
Acme | **NoHo**	20
Alice's Tea | **multi.**	20
NEW Almanac | **W Vill**	26
Alobar | **LIC**	20
Annisa | **W Vill**	27
Applewood | **Park Slope**	24
Aretsky's Patroon | **E 40s**	23
Asiate | **W 50s**	24
Astor Room | **Astoria**	21
Atera | **TriBeCa**	24
Atrium Dumbo | **Dumbo**	23
August | **E 60s**	21
Aureole | **W 40s**	25
Bacchanal | **L Italy**	22
Back Forty West | **SoHo**	21
Back Rm at One57 | **W 50s**	24
Bar Americain | **W 50s**	23
BarBacon | **W 50s**	20
NEW Bar Bolinas | **Clinton Hill**	—
Bâtard | **TriBeCa**	27
Battersby | **Boerum Hill**	26
Battery Gdns. | **Financial**	19
Beatrice Inn | **W Vill**	21
Beautique | **W 50s**	20
Beauty & Essex | **LES**	23
Beecher's Cellar | **Flatiron**	23
Bell Book/Candle | **W Vill**	22
Benchmark | **Park Slope**	23
Betony | **W 50s**	25
Bill's Food/Drink | **E 50s**	18
Black Whale | **City Is**	21
Blanca | **Bushwick**	26
Blenheim | **W Vill**	20
Blue Hill | **G Vill**	28
Blue Ribbon | **multi.**	25
Blue Ribbon Fried | **E Vill**	21
Boathouse | **Central Pk**	18
Boulton & Watt | **E Vill**	21

Brindle Room | **E Vill**	24
Bryant Pk Grill/Cafe | **W 40s**	18
Bubby's | **multi.**	21
NEW Burger & Lobster | **Flatiron**	24
Butter | **W 40s**	23
Butterfly | **TriBeCa**	19
Buttermilk | **Carroll Gdns**	26
NEW Cafe Clover | **W Vill**	24
Cafe Cluny | **W Vill**	23
Cafe Orlin | **E Vill**	22
Cafeteria | **Chelsea**	20
Casellula | **W 50s**	25
Caviar Russe | **E 50s**	24
Cecil | **Harlem**	23
Chadwick's | **Bay Ridge**	24
Chalk Point | **SoHo**	24
Charlie Bird | **SoHo**	23
NEW Charlie Palmer at The Knick | **W 40s**	27
NEW Chefs Club | **NoLita**	24
Cibo | **E 40s**	20
Clement Rest. | **W 50s**	25
Clinton St. Baking | **LES**	25
NEW Clocktower | **Flatiron**	24
Clyde Frazier's | **W 30S**	21
Coffee Shop | **Union Sq**	17
Colicchio/Sons | **Chelsea**	26
Colonie | **Bklyn Hts**	25
Community | **Morningside Hts**	23
Contra | **LES**	25
Cookshop | **Chelsea**	23
Cornelia St. | **W Vill**	18
Craft | **Flatiron**	25
Craftbar | **Flatiron**	22
NEW Crimson & Rye | **E 50s**	20
David Burke Fab. | **W 30s**	24
David Burke Kitchen | **SoHo**	25
Degustation | **E Vill**	25
NEW Delaware & Hudson | **W'burg**	26
Delicatessen | **NoLita**	23
Dimes | **LES**	23
Diner | **W'burg**	25
Distilled | **TriBeCa**	20

Donovan's | **multi.**	21
Dover | **Carroll Gdns**	26
Dovetail | **W 70s**	25
Dutch | **SoHo**	22
East End Kitchen | **E 80s**	20
East Pole | **E 60s**	23
E.A.T. | **E 80s**	19
Eatery | **W 50s**	19
Eddy | **E Vill**	26
Egg Shop | **NoLita**	24
Élan | **Flatiron**	23
Eleven Madison | **Flatiron**	28
NEW Eli's Table | **E 80s**	22
NEW El Rey | **LES**	25
NEW Esme | **Greenpt**	23
Estela | **NoLita**	27
NEW Eugene & Co. | **Bed-Stuy**	—
Farm/Adderley | **Ditmas Pk**	23
Fat Radish | **LES**	22
Fedora | **W Vill**	22
NEW Fifty Paces | **E Vill**	22
NEW Finch | **Clinton Hill**	22
5 & Diamond | **Harlem**	21
Five Leaves | **Greenpt**	25
Flatbush Farm | **Park Slope**	21
Foragers City Table | **Chelsea**	22
Fort Defiance | **Red Hook**	23
Forty Four | **W 40s**	22
44 & X/44½ | **W 40s**	23
Four Seasons | **E 50s**	26
Fourth | **G Vill**	20
Fred's at Barneys | **E 60s**	20
Freemans | **LES**	22
French Louie | **Boerum Hill**	25
Friedman's | **multi.**	22
Friend/Farmer | **Gramercy**	19
Gander | **Flatiron**	20
Giorgio's | **Flatiron**	22
GG's | **E Vill**	22
Glass House | **W 40s**	20
Good | **W Vill**	21
Good Enough/Eat | **W 80s**	19
Good Fork | **Red Hook**	25
Gotham B&G | **G Vill**	28
Gramercy Tavern | **Flatiron**	28
Grand Tier | **W 60s**	21
Grey Dog | **multi.**	22
Hearth | **E Vill**	25

Henry's End | **Bklyn Hts**	25
Hillstone | **multi.**	22
Home Rest. | **W Vill**	21
House | **Gramercy**	24
NEW Houseman | **Hudson Sq**	—
Hudson Clearwater | **W Vill**	25
NEW Hudson Garden | **Bronx Park**	—
Hundred Acres | **SoHo**	21
NEW Industry Kitchen | **Financial**	—
Isabella's | **W 70s**	20
Jack's Wife Freda | **multi.**	23
Jack the Horse | **Bklyn Hts**	24
Jacob's Pickles | **W 80s**	22
James | **Prospect Hts**	24
NEW Jams | **W 50s**	—
Jane | **G Vill**	22
Jeffrey's Grocery | **W Vill**	23
Joe Allen | **W 40s**	18
Joseph Leonard | **W Vill**	24
NEW June Wine | **Cobble Hill**	20
Juni | **Murray Hill**	27
Kings' Carriage | **E 80s**	23
Knickerbocker | **G Vill**	21
Krupa | **Windsor Terr.**	25
Lambs Club | **W 40s**	21
Left Bank | **W Vill**	25
Library/Public | **G Vill**	19
LIC Market | **LIC**	26
Lion | **G Vill**	18
Little Beet | **multi.**	22
Little Owl | **W Vill**	26
NEW Little Park | **TriBeCa**	26
Luksus | **Greenpt**	25
NEW Maman | **L Italy**	20
Má Pêche | **W 50s**	23
Marc Forgione | **TriBeCa**	26
Mark | **E 70s**	23
Market Table | **W Vill**	23
Marlow/Sons | **W'burg**	23
Marshal | **W 40s**	24
Martha | **Ft Greene**	21
Mas | **W Vill**	26
Mayfield | **Crown Hts**	25
Maysville | **NoMad**	22
Meadowsweet | **W'burg**	25
Melba's | **Harlem**	25

Mercer Kitchen | **SoHo**	23
Mike's Bistro | **E 50s**	26
NEW Milling Rm. | **W 80s**	24
Modern | **W 50s**	26
Momofuku Ko | **E Vill**	26
Momofuku Noodle | **E Vill**	25
Momofuku Ssäm Bar | **E Vill**	26
Monkey Bar | **E 50s**	20
Monument Lane | **W Vill**	24
Morgan Dining Rm. | **Murray Hill**	23
Murray's Cheese Bar | **W Vill**	24
Narcissa | **E Vill**	25
National | **E 50s**	20
New Leaf | **Inwood**	—
NoHo Star | **NoHo**	20
NoMad | **NoMad**	26
NoMad Bar | **NoMad**	25
Norma's | **W 50s**	25
Northeast Kingdom | **Bushwick**	25
North End Grill | **Battery Pk**	25
Northern Spy | **E Vill**	21
North Sq. | **G Vill**	24
No. 7 | **multi.**	21
Oceana | **W 40s**	25
Odeon | **TriBeCa**	21
NEW Oleanders | **W'burg**	—
NEW One Dine | **Financial**	—
One if by Land | **W Vill**	23
Palm Court | **W 50s**	23
Park Avenue | **Flatiron**	25
Pearl & Ash | **NoLita**	24
Penelope | **Murray Hill**	22
Penrose | **E 80s**	22
Perilla | **W Vill**	24
Perry St. | **W Vill**	26
Per Se | **W 50s**	28
NEW Pier A Harbor Hse. | **BPC**	18
Pines | **Gowanus**	25
Pine Tree Cafe | **Bronx Pk**	24
Piora | **W Vill**	25
Place | **W Vill**	24
NEW Polo Bar | **E 50s**	20
NEW Porchlight | **Chelsea**	21
Prime Meats | **Carroll Gdns**	24
Print | **W 40s**	24
Prune | **E Vill**	24
Quality Meats | **W 50s**	26
NEW Rainbow Rm. | **W 50s**	23
Recette | **W Vill**	23
Red Cat | **Chelsea**	23
Redeye Grill | **W 50s**	21
Red Rooster | **Harlem**	22
Regency B&G | **E 60s**	24
Reynard | **W'burg**	23
NEW Ribbon | **W 70s**	—
River Café | **Dumbo**	26
Riverpark | **Murray Hill**	26
River Styx | **Greenpt**	23
Robert | **W 50s**	21
Rock Center Café | **W 40s**	18
Roebling Tea Room | **W'burg**	24
NEW Rose's | **Prospect Hts**	—
Rose Water | **Park Slope**	26
Runner & Stone | **Gowanus**	22
Rye | **W'burg**	25
Salt & Fat | **Sunnyside**	24
Sarabeth's | **multi.**	20
Saul | **Prospect Hts**	24
Saxon & Parole | **NoHo**	24
Schnipper's | **multi.**	19
NEW Semilla | **W'burg**	26
Serendipity 3 | **E 60s**	19
S'MAC | **multi.**	22
Smith | **multi.**	19
Sojourn | **E 70s**	23
Standard Grill | **Meatpacking**	21
St. Anselm | **W'burg**	27
NEW State Grill | **W 30S**	25
Stone Park | **Park Slope**	25
Swifty's | **E 70s**	17
Table d'Hôte | **E 90s**	22
Take Root | **Carroll Gdns**	23
Tavern/Green | **Central Pk**	15
Telepan | **W 60s**	26
Thalia | **W 40s**	21
Tiny's | **TriBeCa**	21
Tocqueville | **Flatiron**	26
Trestle on 10th | **Chelsea**	23
Tribeca Grill | **TriBeCa**	23
NEW Tuome | **E Vill**	26
12th St. B&G | **Park Slope**	22
12 Chairs | **multi.**	24
21 Club | **W 50s**	23
Union Sq. Cafe | **Union Sq**	27
Untitled | **Meatpacking**	—

NEW Upholstery Store | **W Vill**	25
Vanderbilt | **Prospect Hts**	22
View | **W 40s**	18
Vinegar Hill Hse. | **Vinegar Hill**	23
NEW Virginia's | **E Vill**	23
Vitae | **E 40s**	24
Walter | **multi.**	23
Water Club | **Murray Hill**	23
Water's Edge | **LIC**	22
Watty & Meg | **Cobble Hill**	19
Waverly Inn | **W Vill**	22
West Bank | **W 40s**	20
Westville | **multi.**	23
White Street | **TriBeCa**	22
NEW Wildair | **LES**	—
NEW Willow | **Bed-Stuy**	20

ARGENTINEAN

Buenos Aires | **E Vill**	23
Chimichurri Grill | **W 40s**	24

ARMENIAN

Almayass | **Flatiron**	24

ASIAN

NEW Asia de Cuba | **G Vill**	23
Asiate | **W 50s**	24
Buddakan | **Chelsea**	25
Cafe Asean | **W Vill**	23
China Grill | **W 50s**	22
Fatty Fish | **E 60s**	20
Jimmy's No. 43 | **E Vill**	20
Mooncake Foods | **multi.**	21
Obao | **multi.**	20
Pig and Khao | **LES**	26
Purple Yam | **Ditmas Pk**	21
Qi | **multi.**	22
Red Bamboo | **G Vill**	24
Ruby Foo's | **W 50s**	18
Salt & Fat | **Sunnyside**	24
Shi | **LIC**	23
Spice Market | **Meatpacking**	24
Talde | **Park Slope**	24
Tao | **multi.**	24
Wild Ginger | **multi.**	23
Zengo | **E 40s**	20
Zen Palate | **Murray Hill**	21

AUSTRALIAN

Burke & Wills | **W 70s**	23
Flinders Lane | **E Vill**	25

Two Hands | **L Italy**	23

AUSTRIAN

Blaue Gans | **TriBeCa**	22
Cafe Katja | **LES**	25
Café Sabarsky/Fledermaus | **E 80s**	22
Edi & The Wolf | **E Vill**	22
Mont Blanc | **W 40s**	23
Wallsé | **W Vill**	25

BAKERIES

Bakeri | **multi.**	26
Balthazar | **SoHo**	24
Baz Bagel | **L Italy**	21
Bouchon Bakery | **multi.**	22
ChikaLicious | **multi.**	25
City Bakery | **Flatiron**	23
Clinton St. Baking | **LES**	25
Dominique Ansel Bakery | **SoHo**	25
NEW Dominique Ansel Kit. | **W Vill**	—
Ferrara | **L Italy**	24
Four & Twenty | **multi.**	25
La Bergamote | **multi.**	24
Ladurée | **SoHo**	22
Lafayette | **NoHo**	22
Le Pain Q. | **multi.**	18
Maison Kayser | **multi.**	21
Runner & Stone | **Gowanus**	22

BARBECUE

Blue Smoke | **multi.**	22
BrisketTown | **W'burg**	24
Butcher Bar | **Astoria**	24
Daisy May's | **W 40s**	22
Dinosaur BBQ | **multi.**	22
Fette Sau | **W'burg**	26
Fletcher's | **multi.**	22
Hill Country | **multi.**	22
Hometown | **Red Hook**	25
John Brown Smokehse. | **LIC**	22
Mable's Smokehse. | **W'burg**	23
Mighty Quinn's | **multi.**	25
Morgans BBQ | **Prospect Hts**	23
Pork Slope | **Park Slope**	20
Smoke Joint | **Ft Greene**	20
Strand Smokehse. | **Astoria**	20
Virgil's | **W 40s**	21

CUISINES

BELGIAN

B. Café	multi.	20
BXL Cafe	multi.	20
Cannibal	multi.	22
Le Pain Q.	multi.	18
Markt	Flatiron	20
Petite Abeille	multi.	19
Resto	Murray Hill	21

BRAZILIAN

Churrascaria	W 40s	24
Coffee Shop	Union Sq	17
Fogo de Chão	W 50s	25
Ipanema	W 40s	20
SushiSamba	W Vill	24
Texas de Brazil	E 60s	22

BRITISH

A Salt & Battery	W Vill	22
Breslin	NoMad	22
ChipShop	multi.	20
East Pole	E 60s	23
Jones Wood Foundry	E 70s	20
NEW Milton	E 90s	23
Peacock	Murray Hill	22
Tea & Sympathy	W Vill	22

BURGERS

Amsterdam Burger Co.	W 90s	24
Back Forty West	SoHo	21
Bareburger	multi.	21
Black Iron Burger	E Vill	23
NEW Black Tap	SoHo	20
Bonnie's Grill	Park Slope	21
Burger & Barrel	SoHo	22
NEW Burger & Lobster	Flatiron	24
Burger Bistro	multi.	22
Burger Joint	multi.	25
Corner Bistro	multi.	23
Counter	W 40s	20
db Bistro Moderne	W 40s	24
Donovan's	multi.	21
DuMont Burger	W'burg	23
Emily	Clinton Hill	26
5 Napkin Burger	multi.	21
Harlem Shake	Harlem	20
Island Burgers	multi.	21
Jackson Hole	multi.	20
J.G. Melon	multi.	22
Keens	W 30s	26
Little Prince	SoHo	22
Minetta Tavern	G Vill	25
Peter Luger	W'burg	28
P.J. Clarke's	multi.	18
Pork Slope	Park Slope	20
Rare B&G	multi.	20
Schnipper's	multi.	19
Shake Shack	multi.	22
67 Burger	multi.	21
Spotted Pig	W Vill	24
NEW Superiority Burger	E Vill	—
21 Club	W 50s	23
Umami Burger	multi.	21

CAJUN/CREOLE

Bayou	Rosebank	24
Catfish	Crown Hts	22
Great Jones Cafe	NoHo	21
NEW King Bee	E Vill	21
Sugar Freak	Astoria	21

CALIFORNIAN

Michael's	W 50s	23
NEW Jams	W 50s	—
NEW Upland	Murray Hill	25

CAMBODIAN

Num Pang	multi.	23

CARIBBEAN

Ali's Roti	multi.	23
Glady's	Crown Hts	24
Lolo's	multi.	25
Negril	G Vill	23

CAVIAR

Caviar Russe	E 50s	24
Petrossian	W 50s	24
Russ/Daughters Cafe	LES	26
Russian Tea	W 50s	20

CHEESE SPECIALISTS

Artisanal	Murray Hill	21
Beecher's Cellar	Flatiron	23
Casellula	W 50s	25
Murray's Cheese Bar	W Vill	24
Picholine	W 60s	26

CHEESESTEAKS

99 Miles/Philly	multi.	21
Shorty's	multi.	21

CHICKEN

BarKogi | **E 50s**	22
NEW Birds & Bubbles | **LES**	21
Blue Ribbon Fried | **E Vill**	21
BonChon | **multi.**	23
Coco Roco | **multi.**	21
Flor/Mayo | **W 100s**	23
NEW Fuku | **E Vill**	—
Hill Country Chicken | **multi.**	21
Kyochon | **multi.**	21
Malecon | **multi.**	23
Pies-N-Thighs | **multi.**	24
Pio Pio | **multi.**	23
NEW Streetbird | **Harlem**	18
Torishin | **E 60s**	25
Yakitori Totto | **W 50s**	24

CHINESE
(* dim sum specialist)

Amazing 66 | **Chinatown**	22
Bao | **E Vill**	23
BaoHaus | **E Vill**	23
Biang! | **Flushing**	25
Big Wong | **Chinatown**	22
Bo-Ky | **multi.**	22
Buddha Bodai* | **Chinatown**	22
Cafe China | **Murray Hill**	24
Cafe Evergreen* | **E 70s**	20
Chef Ho's | **E 80s**	22
Congee | **LES**	21
Decoy | **W Vill**	26
Dim Sum Go Go* | **Chinatown**	21
Dumpling Galaxy | **Flushing**	22
Dumpling Man | **E Vill**	24
Excellent Dumpling* | **Chinatown**	22
Flor/Mayo | **multi.**	23
456 Shanghai | **Chinatown**	23
Fung Tu | **LES**	25
Golden Shopping Mall | **Flushing**	22
Golden Unicorn* | **Chinatown**	21
Grand Sichuan | **multi.**	21
Great NY Noodle | **Chinatown**	24
Hakkasan | **W 40s**	24
Han Dynasty | **multi.**	23
Hop Kee | **Chinatown**	22
Jing Fong* | **Chinatown**	21
Joe's Ginger | **Chinatown**	20

Joe's Shanghai | **multi.**	22
Lychee House* | **E 50s**	21
Macao Trading | **TriBeCa**	22
Mission Chinese | **LES**	22
Mr. Chow | **multi.**	23
Mr. K's | **E 50s**	23
Nice Green Bo | **Chinatown**	21
NoHo Star | **NoHo**	20
Nom Wah Tea* | **Chinatown**	21
Oriental Gdn.* | **Chinatown**	23
Pacificana* | **Sunset Pk**	24
Peking Duck | **multi.**	23
Philippe | **E 60s**	22
Phoenix Gdn. | **E 40s**	23
Pig Heaven | **E 80s**	20
Ping's* | **multi.**	22
Prosperity Dumpling | **LES**	24
Red Egg | **L Italy**	20
RedFarm* | **multi.**	24
NEW Red Stixs | **E 40s**	20
Shanghai Cafe | **L Italy**	24
Shun Lee Palace | **E 50s**	23
Shun Lee West | **W 60s**	22
Spicy & Tasty | **Flushing**	24
Szechuan Gourmet | **multi.**	22
Tang Pavilion | **W 50s**	22
NEW Tasca Chino* | **Gramercy**	19
Tasty Hand-Pulled | **Chinatown**	23
2 Duck Goose | **Gowanus**	19
Vanessa's Dumpling | **multi.**	22
Wa Jeal | **E 80s**	23
White Bear | **Flushing**	25
Wo Hop | **Chinatown**	22
Wu Liang Ye | **W 40s**	24
Xi'an | **multi.**	23

COFFEE

Abraço Espresso | **E Vill**	24
Bakeri | **multi.**	26
Birch Coffee | **multi.**	25
Blue Bottle | **multi.**	24
Cafe Lalo | **W 80s**	18
Café Sabarsky/Fledermaus | **E 80s**	22
East End Kitchen | **E 80s**	20
NEW El Rey | **LES**	25
Five Leaves | **Greenpt**	25
Grey Dog | **multi.**	22
Joe | **multi.**	21

La Colombe	**multi.**	25
Le Pain Q.	**multi.**	18
Margaux	**G Vill**	18
Ninth St Espresso	**multi.**	23
Omonia	**multi.**	19
Oslo Coffee	**multi.**	22
Queens Kickshaw	**Astoria**	23
Rucola	**Boerum Hill**	25
San Matteo	**E 80s**	26
Sant Ambroeus	**multi.**	22
Saraghina	**Bed-Stuy**	23
Smile	**multi.**	20
Stumptown	**multi.**	23
Sweetleaf	**multi.**	23
Toby's Estate	**multi.**	24
Via Quadronno	**multi.**	22

CONTINENTAL

Battery Gdns.	**Financial**	19
Cebu	**Bay Ridge**	22
Petrossian	**W 50s**	24
Russian Samovar	**W 50s**	19
Russian Tea	**W 50s**	20
Russian Vodka	**W 50s**	18
Sardi's	**W 40s**	18

CUBAN

Amor Cubano	**E Harlem**	21
NEW Asia de Cuba	**G Vill**	23
Café Habana/Outpost	**multi.**	23
Cuba	**G Vill**	24
Cubana Café	**Park Slope**	21
Guantanamera	**W 50s**	23
Havana Alma	**W Vill**	23
Havana Central	**W 40s**	22
Victor's Cafe	**W 50s**	23

DELIS

B & H Dairy	**E Vill**	23
Barney Greengrass	**W 80s**	25
Ben's Best	**Rego Pk**	23
Ben's Kosher	**multi.**	19
Carnegie Deli	**W 50s**	23
David's Brisket	**multi.**	25
Katz's Deli	**LES**	25
Leo's Latticini/Corona	**multi.**	24
Liebman's	**Riverdale**	24
Mile End	**multi.**	22
Mill Basin Deli	**Flatlands**	25
Pastrami Queen	**E 70s**	23

Sarge's Deli	**Murray Hill**	23
2nd Ave Deli	**multi.**	23

DESSERT

Bouchon Bakery	**multi.**	22
Brooklyn Farmacy	**Carroll Gdns**	24
Cafe Lalo	**W 80s**	18
Café Sabarsky/Fledermaus	**E 80s**	22
ChikaLicious	**multi.**	25
Chocolate Room	**multi.**	25
City Bakery	**Flatiron**	23
Dominique Ansel Bakery	**SoHo**	25
NEW Dominique Ansel Kit.	**W Vill**	—
Ferrara	**L Italy**	24
Junior's	**multi.**	19
Lady Mendl's	**Gramercy**	21
L&B Spumoni	**Gravesend**	24
Omonia	**multi.**	19
Sant Ambroeus	**multi.**	22
Serendipity 3	**E 60s**	19
Spot	**multi.**	24

DINER

Bonnie's Grill	**Park Slope**	21
Brooklyn Farmacy	**Carroll Gdns**	24
Coppelia	**Chelsea**	23
Diner	**W'burg**	25
Empire Diner	**Chelsea**	19
Hope & Anchor	**Red Hook**	20
Junior's	**multi.**	19
Little Poland	**E Vill**	21
Sanford's	**Astoria**	23
Schnipper's	**multi.**	19
Teresa's	**Bklyn Hts**	20
Tom's	**multi.**	21

DOMINICAN

Malecon	**multi.**	23
Mamajuana	**multi.**	22

EASTERN EUROPEAN

NEW Baba's Pierogies	**Gowanus**	—
Kafana	**E Vill**	24
Sammy's Roumanian	**LES**	19

ECLECTIC

Abigael's	**W 30s**	21
Baoburg	**W'burg**	25
Berg'n	**Crown Hts**	23

Carol's Cafe	**Todt Hill**	24
Cecil	**Harlem**	23
Corkbuzz	**multi.**	20
Do or Dine	**Bed-Stuy**	25
Ducks Eatery	**E Vill**	25
Gorbals	**W'burg**	25
Graffiti	**E Vill**	28
Mehtaphor	**TriBeCa**	28
Public	**NoLita**	24
Schiller's	**LES**	20
Stanton Social	**LES**	23
Traif	**W'burg**	24

ETHIOPIAN

Awash	**multi.**	21
Bunna Cafe	**Bushwick**	25
Injera	**W Vill**	23
Queen of Sheba	**W 40s**	23

EUROPEAN

Bakeri	**multi.**	26
Danny Brown	**Forest Hills**	26
Fushimi	**multi.**	24
NoMad	**NoMad**	26
Spotted Pig	**W Vill**	24

FILIPINO

Jeepney	**E Vill**	23
Jimmy's No. 43	**E Vill**	20
Kuma Inn	**LES**	23
Maharlika	**E Vill**	22

FONDUE

Artisanal	**Murray Hill**	21
Chocolate Room	**multi.**	25
Kashkaval	**W 50s**	24
Mont Blanc	**W 40s**	23
Murray's Cheese Bar	**W Vill**	24

FRENCH

Aldo Sohm	**W 50s**	21
Au Za'atar	**E Vill**	20
Bagatelle	**Meatpacking**	18
NEW Bara	**E Vill**	–
Barbès	**Murray Hill**	21
Bobo	**W Vill**	23
Bouchon Bakery	**multi.**	22
Bouley	**TriBeCa**	29
Bourgeois Pig	**G Vill**	23
Buvette	**W Vill**	25
Café Boulud	**E 70s**	27

Cafe Centro	**E 40s**	22
Cafe Gitane	**multi.**	22
Café Henri	**LIC**	23
Carlyle	**E 70s**	24
Chef's/Brooklyn Fare	**Downtown Bklyn**	26
Daniel	**E 60s**	29
DBGB	**E Vill**	22
Degustation	**E Vill**	25
Dirty French	**LES**	24
Dominique Ansel Bakery	**SoHo**	25
NEW Dominique Ansel Kit.	**W Vill**	–
Fedora	**W Vill**	22
French Louie	**Boerum Hill**	25
NEW Gabriel Kreuther	**W 40s**	–
Indochine	**G Vill**	23
Jean-Georges	**W 60s**	28
Jean-Georges' Noug.	**W 60s**	27
NEW King Bee	**E Vill**	21
La Baraka	**Douglaston**	23
La Bergamote	**multi.**	24
La Boîte en Bois	**W 60s**	20
Ladurée	**SoHo**	22
Lafayette	**NoHo**	22
La Grenouille	**E 50s**	27
La Mangeoire	**E 50s**	22
NEW L'Antagoniste	**Bed-Stuy**	23
La Tarte Flambee	**multi.**	20
Le Bernardin	**W 50s**	29
Le Cirque	**E 50s**	24
Le Colonial	**E 50s**	22
Le Gigot	**W Vill**	25
Le Marais	**W 40s**	23
Le Perigord	**E 50s**	25
Le Rivage	**W 40s**	21
Maison Kayser	**multi.**	21
NEW Maman	**L Italy**	20
Margaux	**G Vill**	18
Marseille	**W 40s**	21
Maze	**W 50s**	22
Mercer Kitchen	**SoHo**	23
Minetta Tavern	**G Vill**	25
Modern	**W 50s**	26
NEW Monte Carlo	**E 70s**	23
Nizza	**W 40s**	20
Odeon	**TriBeCa**	21
Pascalou	**E 90s**	22

CUISINES

Per Se	**W 50s**	28
Petrossian	**W 50s**	24
Picholine	**W 60s**	26
Ponty Bistro	**multi.**	22
Racines	**TriBeCa**	22
NEW Rebelle	**NoLita**	18
Rotisserie Georgette	**E 60s**	22
Rouge et Blanc	**SoHo**	25
Simone	**E 80s**	25
Tartinery	**multi.**	20
Tocqueville	**Flatiron**	26
Triomphe	**W 40s**	23
Wallflower	**W Vill**	24

FRENCH (BISTRO)

Almond	**multi.**	20
A.O.C.	**W Vill**	20
Bacchus	**Downtown Bklyn**	21
Bar Boulud	**W 60s**	24
Bar Tabac	**Cobble Hill**	20
NEW Beaubourg	**BPC**	20
Benoit	**W 50s**	23
Bistro Cassis	**W 70s**	20
Bistro Chat Noir	**E 60s**	21
Bistro Vendôme	**E 50s**	22
Cafe Cluny	**W Vill**	23
Cafe Loup	**W Vill**	20
Cafe Luluc	**Cobble Hill**	21
Cafe Luxembourg	**W 70s**	21
Cherche Midi	**NoLita**	22
Chez Jacqueline	**G Vill**	20
Chez Josephine	**W 40s**	22
Chez Lucienne	**Harlem**	22
Chez Napoléon	**W 50s**	22
Claudette	**G Vill**	21
Cocotte	**SoHo**	23
Cornelia St.	**W Vill**	18
db Bistro Moderne	**W 40s**	24
Deux Amis	**E 50s**	20
JoJo	**E 60s**	24
Jubilee	**E 50s**	21
La Bonne Soupe	**W 50s**	19
La Lunchonette	**Chelsea**	23
Landmarc	**multi.**	19
La Sirène	**Hudson Sq**	24
Le Bilboquet	**E 60s**	22
Le Parisien	**Murray Hill**	22
Le Philosophe	**NoHo**	22
Le Veau d'Or	**E 60s**	19

Little Prince	**SoHo**	22
Lucien	**E Vill**	24
Madison Bistro	**Murray Hill**	21
Maison Harlem	**Manhattanville**	22
Mon Petit Cafe	**E 60s**	21
Montmartre	**Chelsea**	19
Nice Matin	**W 70s**	19
NEW Pardon My French	**E Vill**	27
Quatorze Bis	**E 70s**	22
Raoul's	**SoHo**	23
Saju Bistro	**W 40s**	22
Table d'Hôte	**E 90s**	22
Tartine	**W Vill**	22
Tournesol	**LIC**	23
26 Seats	**E Vill**	22

FRENCH (BRASSERIE)

Artisanal	**Murray Hill**	21
Balthazar	**SoHo**	24
Brasserie	**E 50s**	22
Brasserie Cognac	**multi.**	18
Brasserie 8½	**W 50s**	22
Brass. Ruhlmann	**W 50s**	18
Café d'Alsace	**E 80s**	21
Cafe Tallulah	**W 70s**	20
Ça Va	**W 40s**	21
NEW Chevalier	**W 50s**	22
Jacques	**multi.**	20
NEW La Gamelle	**LES**	—
NEW Le District	**BPC**	—
Le Relais	**E 50s**	20
Les Halles	**multi.**	20
Marseille	**W 40s**	21
Orsay	**E 70s**	20
Rue 57	**W 50s**	20

GASTROPUB

BarBacon	Amer.	**W 50s**	20
Boulton & Watt	Amer.	**E Vill**	21
Cannibal	Belgian	**multi.**	22
DBGB	French	**E Vill**	22
Penrose	Amer.	**E 80s**	22
Resto	Belgian	**Murray Hill**	21
Spotted Pig	Euro.	**W Vill**	24
Vanderbilt	Amer.	**Prospect Hts**	22

GEORGIAN

Old Tbilisi Gdn.	**G Vill**	22

GERMAN

Berlyn	**Ft Greene**	21
Black Forest Bklyn	**Ft Greene**	20
Blaue Gans	**TriBeCa**	22
Heidelberg	**E 80s**	19
Nurnberger Bierhaus	**Randall Manor**	21
Rolf's	**Gramercy**	15
Zum Schneider	**E Vill**	21
Zum Stammtisch	**Glendale**	24

GREEK

Agnanti	**Astoria**	25
Agora Tav.	**Forest Hills**	20
Ammos	**E 40s**	22
Anassa Taverna	**E 60s**	21
Avra	**E 40s**	26
Bahari Estiatorio	**Astoria**	24
Cávo	**Astoria**	20
Dafni	**W 40s**	21
Eliá	**Bay Ridge**	26
Elias Corner	**Astoria**	25
Ethos	**multi.**	22
FishTag	**W 70s**	22
Greek Kitchen	**W 50s**	21
Ithaka	**E 80s**	20
Kefi	**W 80s**	22
Kellari Taverna	**W 40s**	22
NEW Loi Estiatorio	**W 50s**	25
Loukoumi	**Astoria**	23
Milos	**W 50s**	27
Molyvos	**W 50s**	23
MP Taverna	**multi.**	24
Nerai	**E 50s**	24
Okeanos	**Park Slope**	21
Omonia	**multi.**	19
Ovelia	**Astoria**	23
Periyali	**Flatiron**	24
Pylos	**E Vill**	26
Snack	**multi.**	23
Stamatis	**Astoria**	23
Taverna Kyclades	**multi.**	26
Telly's Taverna	**Astoria**	25
Thalassa	**TriBeCa**	23
Uncle Nick's	**multi.**	21
Yefsi Estiatorio	**E 70s**	24

HAWAIIAN

NEW Noreetuh	**E Vill**	—

HEALTH FOOD

(See also Vegetarian)

Community	**Morningside Hts**	23
Hu Kitchen	**G Vill**	24
Quantum Leap	**G Vill**	22
Roast Kit.	**multi.**	21
Spring/Natural	**multi.**	20

HOT DOGS

Bark	**multi.**	20
Cannibal	**multi.**	22
Crif Dogs	**multi.**	22
Gray's Papaya	**W 70s**	21
Katz's Deli	**LES**	25
Mile End	**multi.**	22
Papaya King	**multi.**	22
Shake Shack	**multi.**	22
Smoke Joint	**Ft Greene**	20
Westville	**multi.**	23

ICE CREAM

Amorino	**multi.**	25
Ample Hills	**multi.**	27
Big Gay Ice Cream	**multi.**	25
Brooklyn Farmacy	**Carroll Gdns**	24
Eddie's Sweet Shop	**Forest Hills**	25
Grom	**multi.**	25
Il Laboratorio	**LES**	25
Jacques Torres	**multi.**	26
Khe-Yo	**TriBeCa**	24
L&B Spumoni	**Gravesend**	24
Lemon Ice King	**Corona**	26
Manducatis Rustica	**LIC**	24
Morgenstern's	**LES**	26
Ralph's Famous	**multi.**	25
Serendipity 3	**E 60s**	19
Stella 34	**W 30s**	22

INDIAN

Amma	**E 50s**	25
Awadh	**W 90s**	24
NEW Babu Ji	**E Vill**	—
Baluchi's	**multi.**	21
Benares	**multi.**	21
Brick Ln. Curry	**multi.**	21
Bukhara Grill	**E 40s**	24
Chola	**E 50s**	23
Darbar	**multi.**	21
Dawat	**E 50s**	24
Dhaba	**Murray Hill**	23

CUISINES

NEW Haldi | **Murray Hill**	19
Hampton Chutney | **multi.**	22
Haveli | **E Vill**	23
Indus Valley | **W 90s**	22
Jackson Diner | **multi.**	23
Junoon | **Flatiron**	24
Kati Roll | **multi.**	23
Moti Mahal | **E 60s**	24
Nirvana | **Murray Hill**	22
Pippali | **Murray Hill**	24
Sapphire Indian | **W 60s**	21
Saravanaa Bhavan | **multi.**	23
Seva Indian | **Astoria**	24
Tamarind | **TriBeCa**	26
Thelewala | **G Vill**	23
Tulsi | **E 40s**	23
Utsav | **W 40s**	21
Vatan | **Murray Hill**	24

ISRAELI

Azuri Cafe | **W 50s**	23
Bar Bolonat | **W Vill**	25
Hummus Pl. | **multi.**	22
Miriam | **Park Slope**	22
Taïm | **multi.**	26

ITALIAN
(N=Northern; S=Southern)

Abboccato | **W 50s**	21
Acappella | N | **TriBeCa**	23
Acqua at Peck Slip | **Seaport**	21
Ai Fiori | **W 30s**	26
Aita | **multi.**	24
Alberto | N | **Forest Hills**	24
Al Di La | N | **Park Slope**	26
Alfredo 100 | S | **E 50s**	21
Alidoro | **multi.**	27
All'onda | N | **G Vill**	23
Altesi Rist. | **E 60s**	22
Amarone | **W 40s**	22
Amorina | **Prospect Hts**	22
Angelina's | **Tottenville**	24
Angelo's/Mulberry | S | **L Italy**	23
Angelo's Pizzeria | **multi.**	21
Annabel | **W 50s**	21
Ann & Tony's | **Arthur Ave./Belmont**	22
Antica Pesa | **W'burg**	24
Antonucci | **E 80s**	23
Ápizz | **LES**	24

Areo | **Bay Ridge**	24
Armani Rist. | N | **E 50s**	23
Arno | N | **W 30s**	22
Aroma Kitchen | **NoHo**	22
Arturo's | **G Vill**	23
Aurora | **multi.**	24
A Voce | **multi.**	23
Babbo | **G Vill**	26
Bacaro | N | **LES**	21
Baci & Abbracci | **W'burg**	23
Baker & Co. | **W Vill**	24
Bamonte's | **W'burg**	23
Barbetta | N | **W 40s**	22
Barbuto | **W Vill**	24
Bar Corvo | N | **Prospect Hts**	25
Bar Eolo | S | **Chelsea**	23
Bar Italia | **E 60s**	21
Barosa | **Rego Pk**	23
Bar Pitti | **G Vill**	23
Bar Primi | **E Vill**	24
Basso56 | S | **W 50s**	22
Basta Pasta | **Flatiron**	23
Becco | **W 40s**	23
Beccofino | **Riverdale**	24
Bella Blu | N | **E 70s**	22
Bella Via | **LIC**	23
Best Pizza | **W'burg**	22
Bianca | N | **NoHo**	25
Birreria | **Flatiron**	21
Bistango | **multi.**	21
Bocca | S | **Flatiron**	22
Bocelli | **Old Town**	25
Bond 45 | **W 40s**	19
Bottega | **E 70s**	20
Bottino | N | **Chelsea**	20
Bread | **multi.**	21
Bricco | **W 50s**	20
Brick Cafe | **Astoria**	21
Brioso | **New Dorp**	24
Brucie | **Cobble Hill**	21
Cacio e Pepe | S | **E Vill**	22
Cafe Fiorello | **W 60s**	20
Caffe e Vino | **Ft Greene**	22
Caffe Storico | N | **W 70s**	21
Campagnola | **E 70s**	24
Cara Mia | **W 40s**	21
Caravaggio | **E 70s**	25
Carbone | **G Vill**	24

Carmine's | S | **multi.**	22
Casa Lever | N | **E 50s**	22
Casa Nonna | **W 30s**	22
Celeste | S | **W 80s**	23
Cellini | **E 50s**	22
'Cesca | S | **W 70s**	22
Cibo | N | **E 40s**	20
Cipriani | **multi.**	23
Circo | N | **W 50s**	22
Coppola's | **multi.**	20
Costata | **SoHo**	23
Cotta | **W 80s**	20
Covo | **Hamilton Hts**	23
Crispo | N | **W Vill**	25
Da Andrea | **G Vill**	23
Da Nico | **multi.**	21
Da Noi | N | **multi.**	22
Da Silvano | N | **G Vill**	21
Da Umberto | N | **Chelsea**	25
Defonte's | **multi.**	24
DeGrezia | **E 50s**	24
Dell'anima | **W Vill**	24
Del Posto | **Chelsea**	27
Dominick's | **Arthur Ave./Belmont**	22
Don Antonio | S | **W 50s**	23
Don Peppe | **S Ozone Pk**	26
Due | N | **E 70s**	22
Eataly | **Flatiron**	24
Ecco | **TriBeCa**	22
83.5 | **E 80s**	22
Elio's | **E 80s**	25
Emilia's | **Arthur Ave./Belmont**	24
Emilio's Ballato | **NoLita**	26
Emporio | **NoLita**	23
Enoteca Maria | **St. George**	26
Enzo's | **multi.**	25
Erminia | S | **E 80s**	24
Esca | S | **W 40s**	25
Etc. Etc. | **W 40s**	23
F & J Pine | **Van Nest**	23
NEW Faro | **Bushwick**	–
Felice | **multi.**	21
Felidia | **E 50s**	25
NEW Fifty Paces | **E Vill**	22
57 Napoli | **E 50s**	24
Fiorentino's | S | **Gravesend**	20
Firenze | N | **E 80s**	21
NEW Florian | **Gramercy**	22
Forcella | S | **multi.**	23
Fornino | **multi.**	24
Fragole | **Carroll Gdns**	24
Frank | **E Vill**	23
Frankies | N | **multi.**	25
Franny's | **Park Slope**	23
Fred's at Barneys | N | **E 60s**	20
Fresco | N | **E 50s**	22
Gabriel's | N | **W 60s**	21
Galli | **multi.**	24
Gargiulo's | S | **Coney Is**	23
NEW Gelso & Grand | **L Italy**	18
Gemma | N | **E Vill**	21
Gennaro | **W 90s**	24
Gigino | N | **multi.**	21
Gino's | **Bay Ridge**	24
Giorgio's | **Flatiron**	22
Giovanni | N | **E 80s**	25
Giovanni Rana | **Chelsea**	23
Gnocco | **E Vill**	22
Gradisca | **W Vill**	24
Grazie | **E 80s**	20
Grifone | N | **E 40s**	24
Harry Cipriani | N | **E 50s**	24
Harry's Italian | N | **multi.**	20
Hearth | N | **E Vill**	25
NEW Hugo & Sons | **Park Slope**	23
Il Bambino | **Astoria**	26
Il Buco | **NoHo**	25
Il Buco Alimentari | **NoHo**	24
Il Cantinori | N | **G Vill**	24
Il Cortile | **L Italy**	23
NEW Il Falco | **LIC**	24
Il Gattopardo | S | **W 50s**	24
Il Mulino | S | **multi.**	25
Il Mulino Prime | **SoHo**	25
Il Postino | **E 40s**	24
Il Riccio | **E 70s**	21
Il Tinello | N | **W 50s**	24
Il Vagabondo | **E 60s**	19
Isle/Capri | **E 60s**	20
I Sodi | N | **W Vill**	25
I Trulli | S | **Murray Hill**	23
Joe & Pat's | **Castelton Cnrs**	24
John's/12th St. | **E Vill**	22
La Follia | **Gramercy**	23
La Lanterna | **G Vill**	20

CUISINES

La Masseria | **multi.**	24
La Mela | S | **L Italy**	20
L&B Spumoni | **Gravesend**	24
L'Apicio | **E Vill**	23
La Pizza Fresca | **Flatiron**	24
La Rivista | **W 40s**	20
L'Artusi | **W Vill**	27
Lattanzi | S | **W 40s**	22
Lavagna | N | **E Vill**	24
La Vigna | **Forest Hills**	25
La Villa Pizzeria | **multi.**	24
Lavo | **E 50s**	20
Leopard/des Artistes | S | **W 60s**	21
Leo's Latticini/Corona | **multi.**	24
Le Zie | N | **Chelsea**	21
Lido | N | **Harlem**	23
Lil' Frankie | **E Vill**	23
Lincoln | **W 60s**	25
Locanda Verde | **TriBeCa**	25
Locanda Vini | N | **Clinton Hill**	26
Lorenzo's | **Bloomfield**	22
Lupa | **G Vill**	25
Lusardi's | N | **E 70s**	24
Luzzo's | S | **multi.**	24
Macelleria | N | **Meatpacking**	22
Machiavelli | N | **W 80s**	21
Madison's | **Riverdale**	20
Maialino | **Gramercy**	25
Malatesta | N | **W Vill**	24
NEW Mamo | **SoHo**	—
Manducatis | S | **LIC**	24
Manetta's | **LIC**	25
Manzo | **Flatiron**	25
Marcony | **Murray Hill**	24
Marco Polo | **Carroll Gdns**	22
Marea | **W 50s**	27
Maria Pia | **W 50s**	21
Mario's | S | **Arthur Ave./Belmont**	21
Marta | S | **NoMad**	24
Maruzzella | **E 70s**	20
Max SoHa/Caffe | **multi.**	21
Mercato | **W 30s**	23
Montebello | N | **E 50s**	22
Morandi | **W Vill**	23
Morso | **E 50s**	25
Nanni | N | **E 40s**	23

Naples 45 | S | **E 40s**	19
Nello | N | **E 60s**	18
Nicola's | N | **E 80s**	22
Nicoletta | **E Vill**	22
Nino's | **multi.**	21
Nizza | **W 40s**	20
Nocello | N | **W 50s**	23
Noodle Pudding | **Bklyn Hts**	25
Novitá | N | **Gramercy**	25
Nucci's | **multi.**	22
Numero 28 | **multi.**	22
Obicà Mozzarella | **multi.**	23
Original Crab | **City Is**	25
Orso | N | **W 40s**	23
Osteria al Doge | N | **W 40s**	21
Osteria Laguna | N | **E 40s**	22
Osteria Morini | N | **SoHo**	26
Otto | **G Vill**	22
Pagani | **W Vill**	20
Palma | S | **W Vill**	24
Paola's | **E 90s**	24
Pappardella | **W 70s**	21
Park Side | **Corona**	25
Parm | S | **multi.**	21
Parma | **E 70s**	21
Pasquale Rigoletto | **Arthur Ave./Belmont**	22
Patricia's | **Morris Pk**	23
Patsy's | S | **W 50s**	21
Patsy's Pizzeria | **multi.**	21
Paul & Jimmy's | **Gramercy**	20
Peasant | **NoLita**	24
Pellegrino's | **L Italy**	24
Pepe Giallo/Rosso | **multi.**	23
Pepolino | N | **TriBeCa**	24
Perla | **G Vill**	23
Pescatore | **E 50s**	21
Piccola Venezia | **Astoria**	26
Piccolo Angolo | **W Vill**	26
Piccolo Cafe | **multi.**	22
Pietro's | **E 40s**	23
Pisticci | S | **Morningside Hts**	24
PizzArte | S | **W 50s**	23
Pó | **W Vill**	25
Pomodoro Rosso | **W 70s**	20
Ponticello | N | **Astoria**	23
Porchetta | **E Vill**	22
Porsena | **E Vill**	24

Primola | **E 60s**	22
Quality Italian | **W 50s**	24
Queen | **Bklyn Hts**	24
Rafele | **W Vill**	25
Rao's | S | **E Harlem**	23
Red Gravy | **Bklyn Hts**	20
Remi | N | **W 50s**	22
Ribalta | S | **G Vill**	25
Risotteria | **multi.**	23
Risotteria Melotti | **E Vill**	25
Rist. Morini | **E 80s**	24
Roberta's | **Bushwick**	26
Roberto | **Arthur Ave./Belmont**	25
Roc | **TriBeCa**	22
NEW Rocky Slims | **Murray Hill**	21
Roman's | **Ft Greene**	25
Rosemary's | **W Vill**	22
Rossini's | N | **Murray Hill**	22
Rubirosa | **NoLita**	26
Rucola | N | **Boerum Hill**	25
Sandro's | **E 80s**	23
San Matteo | **E 80s**	26
San Pietro | S | **E 50s**	24
Sant Ambroeus | **multi.**	22
NEW Santina | **Meatpacking**	23
Sauce | S | **LES**	22
Scaletta | N | **W 70s**	21
Scalinatella | **E 60s**	24
Scalini Fedeli | N | **TriBeCa**	26
Scalino | **multi.**	23
Scarlatto | **W 40s**	20
Scarpetta | **Chelsea**	25
Scottadito | N | **Park Slope**	23
Serafina | **multi.**	19
NEW Sessanta | **SoHo**	—
Sette Mezzo | **E 70s**	23
Sfoglia | N | **E 90s**	23
Sirio | N | **E 60s**	21
Sistina | N | **E 80s**	25
Sotto 13 | **W Vill**	23
NEW Spaghetti Incident | **LES**	—
Speedy Romeo | **Clinton Hill**	25
Spiga | **W 80s**	23
Spigolo | **E 70s**	22
Stella 34 | **W 30s**	22
Supper | N | **E Vill**	26
Teodora | N | **E 50s**	21
Testaccio | S | **LIC**	22

Tiella | S | **E 60s**	25
Tommaso | **Bath Bch**	24
Tony's Di Napoli | S | **multi.**	21
Tosca | **Throggs Neck**	23
Tra Di Noi | **Arthur Ave./Belmont**	23
Trattoria Dell'Arte | N | **W 50s**	22
Tratt. L'incontro | **Astoria**	26
Tratt. Romana | **Dongan Hills**	26
Trattoria Trecolori | **W 40s**	22
Tuscany Grill | N | **Bay Ridge**	23
Umbertos Clam Hse. | **L Italy**	21
Uva | **E 70s**	22
Valbella | N | **multi.**	24
Vesta | **Astoria**	26
Vesuvio | **Bay Ridge**	22
Vezzo | **Murray Hill**	24
NEW Via Carota | **W Vill**	24
Via Emilia | N | **Flatiron**	22
Via Quadronno | N | **multi.**	22
ViceVersa | **W 50s**	24
NEW Vic's | **NoHo**	22
Villa Berulia | N | **Murray Hill**	25
Villa Mosconi | **G Vill**	22
Vincent's | **L Italy**	22
NEW Vine | **Chelsea**	—
Vivolo | **E 70s**	20
Zero Otto | S | **multi.**	23

JAMAICAN

Miss Lily's | **multi.**	23
Negril | **G Vill**	23

JAPANESE
(* sushi specialist)

Aburiya Kinnosuke | **E 40s**	24
Aji Sushi* | **Murray Hill**	21
Arirang Hibachi | **multi.**	23
NEW Bara | **E Vill**	—
Bar Chuko | **Prospect Hts**	26
Bassanova | **Chinatown**	21
Blue Fin* | **W 40s**	22
Blue Ginger* | **Chelsea**	22
Blue Ribbon Sushi* | **multi.**	25
Bohemian | **NoHo**	27
Bond St* | **NoHo**	25
Brushstroke/Ichimura | **TriBeCa**	26
Cha An | **E Vill**	22
Cherry* | **multi.**	22
Chuko | **Prospect Hts**	26

Cocoron	multi.	23
EN Japanese	W Vill	25
15 East*	Union Sq	27
Fushimi*	multi.	24
Ganso	Downtown Bklyn	21
NEW Ganso Yaki	Downtown Bklyn	—
Gari*	multi.	26
NEW Goemon Curry	NoLita	—
Gyu-Kaku	multi.	21
Hakata Tonton	W Vill	22
Haru*	multi.	21
Hatsuhana*	E 40s	25
Hibino*	multi.	26
Hide-Chan	E 50s	23
Inakaya	W 40s	24
Ippudo	multi.	25
Ivan Ramen	multi.	22
Japonica*	G Vill	23
Jewel Bako*	E Vill	24
Jin Ramen	multi.	23
Kajitsu	Murray Hill	24
Kanoyama*	E Vill	24
NEW Kappo Masa*	E 70s	25
Katsu-Hama	multi.	22
Ki Sushi*	Cobble Hill	24
Koi*	multi.	24
Ko Sushi*	multi.	20
Kouzan*	W 90s	21
Kurumazushi*	E 40s	24
Kyo Ya	E Vill	26
Masa/Bar Masa*	W 50s	26
Meijin	E 80s	22
Minca	E Vill	24
Momo Sushi Shack*	Bushwick	25
Momoya*	multi.	23
Morimoto	Chelsea	26
NEW Mu Ramen	LIC	24
Naruto	multi.	20
Natsumi*	W 50s	22
Neta*	G Vill	26
New York Sushi Ko*	LES	—
Ninja*	TriBeCa	16
Nippon*	E 50s	24
Nobu	multi.	27
Okonomi	W'burg	25
1 or 8*	W'burg	24
Ootoya	multi.	25

NEW O Ya*	Murray Hill	—
Poke*	E 80s	23
Prime KO*	W 80s	22
NEW Ramen Lab	NoLita	26
Rosanjin	TriBeCa	25
Sakagura*	E 40s	25
Sake Bar Hagi	W 40s	23
NEW Saki*	G Vill	—
Samurai Mama/Papa	W'burg	23
Sasabune*	E 70s	26
Shabu-Shabu 70*	E 70s	21
Shalom Japan	W'burg	24
NEW Shuko*	G Vill	26
Soba Nippon*	W 50s	23
Soba Totto	E 40s	23
Soba-ya	E Vill	23
Soto*	W Vill	25
Sushi Damo*	W 50s	21
Sushiden*	E 40s	24
Sushi Dojo*	multi.	25
Sushi Nakazawa*	W Vill	27
SushiSamba	W Vill	24
Sushi Seki*	multi.	26
Sushi Sen-nin*	Murray Hill	25
Sushi Yasuda*	E 40s	27
Sushi Zen*	W 40s	25
Takahachi*	multi.	24
Takashi	W Vill	26
Tanoshi	E 70s	25
Tenzan*	multi.	21
Tomoe Sushi*	G Vill	26
Torishin	E 60s	25
Totto Ramen	multi.	24
NEW Uma Temakeria*	Chelsea	20
Yakitori Taisho	E Vill	24
Yakitori Totto	W 50s	24
Yama*	multi.	24
Yuka*	E 80s	23
Zenkichi	W'burg	26
NEW Zuma*	Murray Hill	22
Zutto*	TriBeCa	20

JEWISH

B & H Dairy	E Vill	23
Barney Greengrass	W 80s	25
Baz Bagel	L Italy	21
Ben's Best	Rego Pk	23
Ben's Kosher	multi.	19

Carnegie Deli	**W 50s**	23
Katz's Deli	**LES**	25
Lattanzi	**W 40s**	22
Liebman's	**Riverdale**	24
Mile End	**multi.**	22
Mill Basin Deli	**Flatlands**	25
Russ/Daughters Cafe	**LES**	26
Sammy's Roumanian	**LES**	19
Shalom Japan	**W'burg**	24

KOREAN
(* barbecue specialist)

Bann	**W 50s**	22
BarKogi	**E 50s**	22
Barn Joo	**Flatiron**	22
BCD Tofu	**W 30s**	23
BonChon	**multi.**	23
Cho Dang Gol	**W 30s**	23
Danji	**W 50s**	25
Do Hwa*	**W Vill**	23
Franchia	**Murray Hill**	24
Gaonnuri*	**W 30s**	19
Hangawi	**Murray Hill**	24
Hanjan	**Flatiron**	24
Jungsik	**TriBeCa**	26
NEW Kang Ho Dong*	**Murray Hill**	23
Kang Suh	**W 30S**	18
NEW Korilla	**E Vill**	23
Kristalbelli*	**W 30s**	25
Kum Gang San*	**multi.**	21
Kunjip*	**W 30s**	21
Kyochon	**multi.**	21
Madangsui*	**W 30s**	22
Mandoo Bar	**W 30s**	22
Mapo Korean	**Flushing**	24
Miss Korea*	**W 30s**	21
Moim	**Park Slope**	23
Mŏkbar	**Chelsea**	26
New WonJo*	**W 30s**	24
NEW Oiji	**E Vill**	—
Sik Gaek	**multi.**	23

KOSHER/KOSHER-STYLE

Abigael's	**W 30s**	21
Azuri Cafe	**W 50s**	23
Ben's Best	**Rego Pk**	23
Ben's Kosher	**multi.**	19
Buddha Bodai	**Chinatown**	22
Caravan/Dreams	**E Vill**	23

Hummus Pl.	**multi.**	22
Le Marais	**W 40s**	23
Liebman's	**Riverdale**	24
Mike's Bistro	**E 50s**	26
Mill Basin Deli	**Flatlands**	25
Pastrami Queen	**E 70s**	23
Peacefood Café	**multi.**	24
Prime Grill	**E 50s**	23
Prime KO	**W 80s**	22
Reserve Cut	**Financial**	24
Sacred Chow	**G Vill**	23
2nd Ave Deli	**multi.**	23

LAOTIAN

| Khe-Yo | **TriBeCa** | 24 |

LATIN AMERICAN

| Colonia Verde | **Ft Greene** | 21 |

LEBANESE

Al Bustan	**E 50s**	21
Almayass	**Flatiron**	24
Balade	**E Vill**	24
Ilili	**NoMad**	24
Naya	**multi.**	22

MALAYSIAN

Fatty Crab	**Meatpacking**	21
Laut	**Union Sq**	22
Nyonya	**multi.**	23

MEDITERRANEAN

Aldea	**Flatiron**	24
Alta	**G Vill**	25
Amali	**E 60s**	25
Amaranth	**E 60s**	21
Antique Garage	**SoHo**	19
Balaboosta	**NoLita**	25
Balkanika	**W 40s**	20
Barbounia	**Flatiron**	21
Bodrum	**W 80s**	21
Boulud Sud	**W 60s**	25
Bustan	**W 80s**	23
Cafe Centro	**E 40s**	22
Cafe Tallulah	**W 70s**	20
Conviv. Osteria	**Park Slope**	26
Dee's	**Forest Hills**	23
Estela	**NoLita**	27
Extra Virgin	**W Vill**	22
Fig & Olive	**multi.**	21
NEW Gardenia	**W Vill**	—

Gato	**NoHo**	26
Glasserie	**Greenpt**	25
Il Buco	**NoHo**	25
Il Buco Alimentari	**NoHo**	24
Isabella's	**W 70s**	20
Kashkaval	**W 50s**	24
NEW Limani	**W 50s**	23
Little Owl	**W Vill**	26
Margaux	**G Vill**	18
Marseille	**W 40s**	21
Meadowsweet	**W'burg**	25
Mémé	**W Vill**	23
Miriam	**Park Slope**	22
Nice Matin	**W 70s**	19
Nick & Toni	**W 60s**	21
Olea	**Ft Greene**	27
Park	**Chelsea**	19
Pera	**multi.**	21
Picholine	**W 60s**	26
Place	**W Vill**	24
Red Cat	**Chelsea**	23
Smile	**multi.**	20
Taboon	**multi.**	23
Tanoreen	**Bay Ridge**	26
Tessa	**W 70s**	23
NEW Vic's	**NoHo**	22
Zizi Limona	**W'burg**	25

MEXICAN

Alma	**Columbia St.**	20
Añejo	**multi.**	22
Baby Bo's	**Murray Hill**	21
Barrio Chino	**LES**	24
Black Ant	**E Vill**	24
Bodega Negra	**Chelsea**	22
Cafe El Pres.	**Flatiron**	20
Café Frida	**W 70s**	20
Café Habana/Outpost	**multi.**	23
Calexico	**multi.**	21
Casa Enrique	**LIC**	26
Cascabel Taqueria	**multi.**	19
Chavela's	**Crown Hts**	24
NEW Cosme	**Flatiron**	25
Crema	**Chelsea**	23
Dos Caminos	**multi.**	19
Dos Toros	**multi.**	22
El Centro	**W 50s**	23
El Parador	**Murray Hill**	22
El Paso	**multi.**	22

El Vez	**Battery Pk**	20
NEW Empellón al Pastor	**E Vill**	19
Empellón Cocina	**E Vill**	23
Empellón Taqueria	**W Vill**	22
Fonda	**multi.**	23
Gran Electrica	**Dumbo**	25
Hecho en Dumbo	**NoHo**	22
Hell's Kitchen	**W 50s**	23
NEW Korilla	**E Vill**	23
La Esquina	**multi.**	23
La Palapa	**E Vill**	22
La Superior	**W'burg**	25
Los Tacos	**Chelsea**	27
Maya	**E 60s**	22
Mayahuel	**E Vill**	23
Maz Mezcal	**E 80s**	21
Mesa Coyoacan	**W'burg**	24
Mexico Lindo	**Murray Hill**	22
Mexicue	**multi.**	21
Mezzaluna	**E 70s**	20
Mission Cantina	**LES**	21
Mojave	**Astoria**	23
Móle	**multi.**	21
Oaxaca	**multi.**	23
Ofrenda	**W Vill**	24
Pachanga Patterson	**Astoria**	24
Pampano	**E 40s**	24
Rocking Horse	**Chelsea**	22
Rosa Mexicano	**multi.**	22
NEW Rosie's	**E Vill**	24
Salvation Taco	**Murray Hill**	20
Sinigual	**E 40s**	21
Tacombi	**multi.**	24
NEW Tacuba	**Astoria**	20
NEW Tijuana Picnic	**LES**	21
Toloache	**multi.**	23
Tortilleria Nixtamal	**Corona**	24
Xixa	**W'burg**	25
Zona Rosa	**W'burg**	21

MIDDLE EASTERN

Au Za'atar	**E Vill**	20
Balaboosta	**NoLita**	25
Bar Bolonat	**W Vill**	25
Gazala's	**multi.**	22
Halal Guys	**multi.**	22
Mamoun's	**multi.**	23
Maoz	**multi.**	22
Mimi's Hummus	**Ditmas Pk**	24

Moustache	**multi.**	22
Taboon	**multi.**	23
Tanoreen	**Bay Ridge**	26
12 Chairs	**multi.**	24
Zaytoons	**multi.**	21
Zizi Limona	**W'burg**	25

MOROCCAN

Barbès	**Murray Hill**	21
Cafe Gitane	**multi.**	22
Cafe Mogador	**multi.**	24
Mémé	**W Vill**	23

NEW ENGLAND

Littleneck	**multi.**	23
Lobster Joint	**multi.**	24
Luke's Lobster	**multi.**	24
Mary's Fish	**W Vill**	24
Mermaid	**multi.**	23
Pearl Oyster	**W Vill**	27
Water Table	**Greenpt**	—

NEW ZEALAND

Musket Room	**NoLita**	26

NOODLE SHOPS

Bassanova	**Chinatown**	21
Biang!	**Flushing**	25
Bo-Ky	**multi.**	22
Chuko	**Prospect Hts**	26
Ganso	**Downtown Bklyn**	21
Great NY Noodle	**Chinatown**	24
Hide-Chan	**E 50s**	23
Ippudo	**multi.**	25
Ivan Ramen	**multi.**	22
Jin Ramen	**multi.**	23
Kung Fu Ramen	**W 40s**	23
Meijin	**E 80s**	22
Minca	**E Vill**	24
Mökbar	**Chelsea**	26
Momofuku Noodle	**E Vill**	25
NEW Mu Ramen	**LIC**	24
Naruto	**multi.**	20
Nightingale 9	**Carroll Gdns**	21
Ootoya	**multi.**	25
Pho Bang	**multi.**	23
NEW Ramen Lab	**NoLita**	26
Republic	**Union Sq**	19
Soba Nippon	**W 50s**	23
Soba Totto	**E 40s**	23
Soba-ya	**E Vill**	23

Tasty Hand-Pulled	**Chinatown**	23
Totto Ramen	**multi.**	24
Xi'an	**multi.**	23
Zutto	**TriBeCa**	20

NUEVO LATINO

Cabana	**multi.**	22
Calle Ocho	**W 80s**	21
Coppelia	**Chelsea**	23
Mamajuana	**multi.**	22

PAN-LATIN

ABC Cocina	**Flatiron**	25
Bogota	**Park Slope**	24
Coppelia	**Chelsea**	23
Macondo	**multi.**	19
Yerba Buena	**multi.**	22
Yuca Bar	**E Vill**	23
Zengo	**E 40s**	20

PERSIAN

Persepolis	**E 70s**	23
Ravagh	**multi.**	24

PERUVIAN

Coco Roco	**multi.**	21
Flor/Mayo	**multi.**	23
Pio Pio	**multi.**	23
Raymi	**Flatiron**	24

PIZZA

Adrienne's	**Financial**	24
Al Forno	**E 70s**	20
Amorina	**Prospect Hts**	22
Angelo's Pizzeria	**multi.**	21
Annabel	**W 50s**	21
Ápizz	**LES**	24
Artichoke Basille	**multi.**	22
Arturo's	**G Vill**	23
Bella Blu	**E 70s**	22
Bella Via	**LIC**	23
Best Pizza	**W'burg**	22
Bricco	**W 50s**	20
Co.	**Chelsea**	23
Covo	**Hamilton Hts**	23
Dee's	**Forest Hills**	23
Denino's	**Elm Pk**	26
Di Fara	**Midwood**	26
Don Antonio	**W 50s**	23
Emily	**Clinton Hill**	26
57 Napoli	**E 50s**	24

CUISINES

Forcella | **multi.**	23
Fornino | **multi.**	24
Franny's | **Park Slope**	23
GG's | **E Vill**	22
Gigino | **multi.**	21
Grimaldi's | **multi.**	22
Harry's Italian | **multi.**	20
Houdini Kit. | **Ridgewood**	25
Joe & Pat's | **Castelton Cnrs**	24
Joe's Pizza | **multi.**	24
John's/12th St. | **E Vill**	22
John's Pizzeria | **multi.**	23
Juliana's | **Dumbo**	26
Keste Pizza | **W Vill**	23
L&B Spumoni | **Gravesend**	24
La Pizza Fresca | **Flatiron**	24
La Villa Pizzeria | **multi.**	24
Lil' Frankie | **E Vill**	23
Lombardi's | **NoLita**	24
Lucali | **Carroll Gdns**	26
Luzzo's | **multi.**	24
Manducatis Rustica | **LIC**	24
Marta | **NoMad**	24
Motorino | **multi.**	25
Naples 45 | **E 40s**	19
Nick's | **multi.**	24
Nicoletta | **E Vill**	22
Nino's | **multi.**	21
Numero 28 | **multi.**	22
Otto | **G Vill**	22
Ovest | **Chelsea**	23
Patsy's | **W 50s**	21
Paulie Gee's | **Greenpt**	27
NEW Pizza Beach | **E 80s**	19
PizzArte | **W 50s**	23
Pizzetteria Brunetti | **W Vill**	26
Posto | **Gramercy**	23
NEW Prova | **Chelsea**	24
Rizzo's | **multi.**	21
Roberta's | **Bushwick**	26
NEW Rocky Slims | **Murray Hill**	21
Rubirosa | **NoLita**	26
San Matteo | **E 80s**	26
Saraghina | **Bed-Stuy**	23
Speedy Romeo | **Clinton Hill**	25
Spunto | **W Vill**	22
Totonno Pizza | **Coney Is**	27
Two Boots | **multi.**	19

Vesta | **Astoria**	26
Vesuvio | **Bay Ridge**	22
Vezzo | **Murray Hill**	24
Zero Otto | **multi.**	23

POLISH

Little Poland | **E Vill**	21
Teresa's | **Bklyn Hts**	20

PORTUGUESE

Ipanema | **W 40s**	20
NEW Lupulo | **Chelsea**	–
Macao Trading | **TriBeCa**	22

PUB FOOD

Burger & Barrel | **SoHo**	22
Dead Rabbit | **Financial**	22
Donovan's | **multi.**	21
Fraunces Tav. | **Financial**	18
Henry Public | **Cobble Hill**	23
J.G. Melon | **multi.**	22
Landmark Tav. | **W 40s**	19
Molly's | **Gramercy**	21
Neary's | **E 50s**	19
Paris Cafe | **Seaport**	18
Piper's Kilt | **Inwood**	20
P.J. Clarke's | **multi.**	18
Walker's | **TriBeCa**	19

PUERTO RICAN

Don Coqui | **City Is**	22
Sazon | **TriBeCa**	23

QUÉBÉCOIS

M. Wells Dinette | **LIC**	22

RUSSIAN

Mari Vanna | **Flatiron**	20
Russian Samovar | **W 50s**	19
Russian Tea | **W 50s**	20
Russian Vodka | **W 50s**	18

SANDWICHES
(See also Delis)

Alidoro | **multi.**	27
Banh Mi Saigon | **L Italy**	24
Beecher's Cellar | **Flatiron**	23
Best Pizza | **W'burg**	22
Bonnie's Grill | **Park Slope**	21
Bread | **multi.**	21
Brennan | **Sheepshead**	22
Defonte's | **multi.**	24

E.A.T. | **E 80s**	19
Eisenberg's | **Flatiron**	20
Friedman's | **multi.**	22
NEW Fuku | **E Vill**	–
Hanco's | **multi.**	20
Il Bambino | **Astoria**	26
Leo's Latticini/Corona | **multi.**	24
Meatball Shop | **multi.**	21
Meat Hook | **W'burg**	23
Melt Shop | **multi.**	22
Mile End | **multi.**	22
99 Miles/Philly | **multi.**	21
No. 7 | **multi.**	21
Num Pang | **multi.**	23
100 Montaditos | **G Vill**	19
Parm | **multi.**	21
Peanut Butter Co. | **G Vill**	22
Porchetta | **E Vill**	22
Press 195 | **Bayside**	25
Queens Kickshaw | **Astoria**	23
Roll-n-Roaster | **Sheepshead**	22
San Matteo | **E 80s**	26
Sarge's Deli | **Murray Hill**	23
Shorty's | **multi.**	21
Smile | **multi.**	20
Taboon | **multi.**	23
Tartinery | **multi.**	20
Untamed Sandwiches | **W 30S**	25
Via Quadronno | **multi.**	22
'Wichcraft | **multi.**	18
Yura on Madison | **E 90s**	21
Zito's | **Bay Ridge**	–

SCANDINAVIAN

Aquavit | **E 50s**	26
Smorgas Chef | **multi.**	20

SEAFOOD

Ammos | **E 40s**	22
Aquagrill | **SoHo**	27
Artie's | **City Is**	21
Atlantic Grill | **multi.**	23
Avra | **E 40s**	26
Bergen Hill | **Carroll Gdns**	27
NEW BKB | **E 70s**	23
Blue Fin | **W 40s**	22
Blue Water | **Union Sq**	24
Bocelli | **Old Town**	25
Boil | **LES**	23

Brooklyn Crab | **Red Hook**	20
Catch | **Meatpacking**	23
City Hall | **TriBeCa**	22
City Is. Lobster | **City Is**	22
City Lobster/Steak | **W 50s**	20
Clam | **W Vill**	25
Cowgirl | **multi.**	17
Crave Fishbar | **E 50s**	24
Cull & Pistol | **Chelsea**	24
David Burke Fishtail | **E 60s**	24
Docks Oyster | **E 40s**	21
Ed's Chowder | **W 60s**	20
Ed's Lobster Bar | **multi.**	25
Elias Corner | **Astoria**	25
El Toro Blanco | **W Vill**	21
Esca | **W 40s**	25
Ethos | **multi.**	22
Extra Fancy | **W'burg**	23
Fish | **W Vill**	23
FishTag | **W 70s**	22
Flex Mussels | **multi.**	23
Francisco's | **Chelsea**	22
NEW Grand Army | **Downtown Bklyn**	22
Harlow | **E 50s**	20
Ithaka | **E 80s**	20
John Dory Oyster | **NoMad**	21
Jordans Lobster | **Sheepshead**	22
Jubilee | **E 50s**	21
Kellari Taverna | **W 40s**	22
L & W Oyster | **NoMad**	20
Le Bernardin | **W 50s**	29
Littleneck | **multi.**	23
Lobster Joint | **multi.**	24
Lolo's | **multi.**	25
London Lennie's | **Middle Vill**	24
Luke's Lobster | **multi.**	24
Lure Fishbar | **SoHo**	25
Maison Premiere | **W'burg**	26
Marea | **W 50s**	27
Mary's Fish | **W Vill**	24
Mermaid | **multi.**	23
Milos | **W 50s**	27
Navy | **SoHo**	21
North End Grill | **Battery Pk**	25
Oceana | **W 40s**	25
Ocean Grill | **W 70s**	23
Okeanos | **Park Slope**	21

Oriental Gdn.	**Chinatown**	23
Original Crab	**City Is**	25
Oyster Bar	**multi.**	22
Pampano	**E 40s**	24
Pearl Oyster	**W Vill**	27
Pearl Room	**Bay Ridge**	20
Periyali	**Flatiron**	24
Ping's	**multi.**	22
Randazzo's	**Sheepshead**	22
Redeye Grill	**W 50s**	21
Red Hook Lobster	**multi.**	24
NEW River Dock	**St. George**	—
River Styx	**Greenpt**	23
Sammy's Fishbox	**City Is**	23
Sammy's Shrimp	**City Is**	23
Sea Fire Grill	**E 40s**	27
Sea Grill	**W 40s**	24
NEW Seamore's	**L Italy**	—
Sea Shore	**City Is**	23
Sik Gaek	**multi.**	23
Strip House	**multi.**	25
Taverna Kyclades	**multi.**	26
Telly's Taverna	**Astoria**	25
Thalassa	**TriBeCa**	23
Upstate	**E Vill**	27
Water's Edge	**LIC**	22
Wild Edibles	**Murray Hill**	24
ZZ's Clam Bar	**G Vill**	23

SINGAPOREAN

NEW Chomp Chomp	**W Vill**	—

SMALL PLATES
(See also Spanish tapas specialist)

Almayass	Armenian/ Lebanese	**Flatiron**	24
Alta	Med.	**G Vill**	25
Añejo	Mex.	**multi.**	22
Bar Chuko	Japanese	 **Prospect Hts**	26
Bar Primi	Italian	**E Vill**	24
Beauty & Essex	Amer.	**LES**	23
Bergen Hill	Seafood	 **Carroll Gdns**	27
Beyoglu	Turkish	**E 80s**	21
Buvette	French	**W Vill**	25
Caffe Storico	Italian	**W 70s**	21
Cannibal	Belgian	**multi.**	22
Cocotte	French	**SoHo**	23
Danji	Korean	**W 50s**	25

David Burke Fab.	Amer.	 **W 30s**	24
Degustation	French/Spanish	 **E Vill**	25
NEW El Rey	Amer.	**LES**	25
Empellón Cocina	Mex.	**E Vill**	23
Empellón Taqueria	Mex.	 **W Vill**	22
EN Japanese	Japanese	**W Vill**	25
Estela	Amer./Med.	**NoLita**	27
Felice	Italian	**multi.**	21
Forty Four	Amer.	**W 40s**	22
Graffiti	Eclectic	**E Vill**	28
Hanjan	Korean	**Flatiron**	24
NEW June Wine	Amer.	 **Cobble Hill**	20
Kashkaval	Med.	**W 50s**	24
Macondo	Pan-Latin	**multi.**	19
Má Pêche	Amer.	**W 50s**	23
Mayahuel	Mex.	**E Vill**	23
Maze	French	**W 50s**	22
Mehtaphor	Eclectic	**TriBeCa**	28
NEW Oiji	Korean	**E Vill**	—
Recette	Amer.	**W Vill**	23
Sakagura	Japanese	**E 40s**	25
Salt & Fat	Amer./Asian	 **Sunnyside**	24
Sojourn	Amer.	**E 70s**	23
Traif	Eclectic	**W'burg**	24
Uva	Italian	**E 70s**	22
Vanderbilt	Amer.	 **Prospect Hts**	22
NEW Willow	Amer.	**Bed-Stuy**	20
Zenkichi	Japanese	**W'burg**	26

SOUL FOOD

Amy Ruth's	**Harlem**	23
Miss Mamie's	**W 100s**	22
Sylvia's	**Harlem**	20

SOUTH AFRICAN

Madiba	**multi.**	22

SOUTH AMERICAN

Arepa Lady	**Elmhurst**	25

SOUTHERN

Amy Ruth's	**Harlem**	23
NEW Birds & Bubbles	**LES**	21
Brooklyn Star	**W'burg**	25
Commodore	**W'burg**	23

Egg | **W'burg**	24
Hill Country Chicken | **multi.**	21
Jacob's Pickles | **W 80s**	22
Kitchenette | **Morningside Hts**	20
Melba's | **Harlem**	25
Minton's | **Harlem**	21
Miss Mamie's | **W 100s**	22
Peaches | **Bed-Stuy**	24
Pies-N-Thighs | **multi.**	24
Queens Comfort | **Astoria**	24
Redhead | **E Vill**	23
Root & Bone | **E Vill**	24
Sweet Chick | **multi.**	24
Sylvia's | **Harlem**	20
Tipsy Parson | **Chelsea**	19
Wilma Jean | **Carroll Gdns**	24

SOUTHWESTERN

Agave | **W Vill**	19
Cilantro | **multi.**	21
Cowgirl | **multi.**	17

SPANISH
(* tapas specialist)

Alcala Rest.* | **E 40s**	24
Andanada 141* | **W 60s**	22
Bar Jamôn* | **Gramercy**	24
Beso | **St. George**	24
Boqueria* | **multi.**	23
Cafe Espanol | **multi.**	21
Casa Mono* | **Gramercy**	25
Cata | **LES**	22
Degustation | **E Vill**	25
El Charro Espanol* | **W Vill**	24
El Colmado* | **multi.**	19
El Porrón* | **E 60s**	22
El Pote | **Murray Hill**	22
El Quijote | **Chelsea**	22
El Quinto Pino* | **Chelsea**	23
Francisco's | **Chelsea**	22
Huertas* | **E Vill**	25
La Fonda/Sol | **E 40s**	22
La Vara* | **Cobble Hill**	27
Real Madrid | **Mariners Harbor**	21
Sala One Nine* | **Flatiron**	21
Salinas* | **Chelsea**	24
Sevilla | **W Vill**	24
Socarrat* | **multi.**	23
Solera* | **E 50s**	22
NEW Tasca Chino* | **Gramercy**	19

Tertulia* | **W Vill**	24
Tía Pol* | **Chelsea**	23
Toro* | **Chelsea**	24
Txikito* | **Chelsea**	24

SRI LANKAN

NEW Kottu House | **LES**	—

STEAKHOUSES

American Cut | **TriBeCa**	24
Angus Club | **E 50s**	25
Arirang Hibachi | **multi.**	23
Arlington Club | **E 70s**	21
Artie's | **City Is**	21
Ben & Jack's | **NoMad**	24
Benchmark | **Park Slope**	23
Benjamin Steak | **E 40s**	27
Bill's Food/Drink | **E 50s**	18
BLT Prime | **Gramercy**	26
BLT Steak | **E 50s**	25
Bobby Van's | **multi.**	23
Bond 45 | **W 40s**	19
NEW Bowery Meat Co. | **E Vill**	25
Buenos Aires | **E Vill**	23
Bull & Bear | **E 40s**	21
Capital Grille | **multi.**	25
Charlie Palmer | **E 50s**	24
Chimichurri Grill | **W 40s**	24
Christos | **Astoria**	24
Churrascaria | **W 40s**	24
City Hall | **TriBeCa**	22
City Lobster/Steak | **W 50s**	20
Club A Steak | **E 50s**	26
Costata | **SoHo**	23
Del Frisco's | **multi.**	25
Delmonico's | **multi.**	24
E&E Grill Hse. | **W 40s**	21
Empire Steak | **W 50s**	22
Frankie & Johnnie's | **multi.**	21
Gallaghers | **W 50s**	23
Harry's Cafe | **Financial**	23
NEW Hunt & Fish | **W 40s**	19
Il Mulino Prime | **SoHo**	25
Jake's Steakhse. | **Fieldston**	24
Keens | **W 30s**	26
Le Marais | **W 40s**	23
Le Relais | **E 50s**	20
Les Halles | **multi.**	20
NEW Lincoln Sq. Steak | **W 70s**	20

CUISINES

Macelleria | **Meatpacking**	22
Maloney & Porcelli | **E 50s**	25
Manzo | **Flatiron**	25
MarkJoseph | **Seaport**	24
NEW Mastro's Steak | **W 50s**	25
Michael Jordan | **E 40s**	21
Morton's | **multi.**	23
M. Wells Steakhse. | **LIC**	24
Nick & Stef's | **W 30s**	22
Nino's | **multi.**	21
NYY Steak | **multi.**	24
Old Homestead | **Chelsea**	25
Palm | **multi.**	25
Parlor Steakhse. | **E 80s**	21
Peter Luger | **W'burg**	28
Pietro's | **E 40s**	23
Porter House | **W 50s**	26
Prime Grill | **E 50s**	23
Prime KO | **W 80s**	22
Prime Meats | **Carroll Gdns**	24
Quality Italian | **W 50s**	24
Quality Meats | **W 50s**	26
Reserve Cut | **Financial**	24
Ricardo | **E Harlem**	25
Ruth's Chris | **W 50s**	25
Smith/Wollensky | **E 40s**	24
Sparks | **E 40s**	25
S Prime | **Astoria**	23
St. Anselm | **W'burg**	27
STK | **multi.**	23
Strip House | **multi.**	25
T-Bar Steak | **E 70s**	21
Texas de Brazil | **E 60s**	22
Uncle Jack's | **multi.**	23
Wolfgang's | **multi.**	26
Wollensky's | **E 40s**	24

SWISS

Mont Blanc | **W 40s**	23
Trestle on 10th | **Chelsea**	23

TAIWANESE

BaoHaus | **E Vill**	23
Mimi Cheng's | **E Vill**	24

TEAHOUSE

Alice's Tea | **multi.**	20
Bosie Tea Parlor | **W Vill**	21
Cha An | **E Vill**	22
Lady Mendl's | **Gramercy**	21

Radiance Tea | **multi.**	21
Tea & Sympathy | **W Vill**	22

TEX-MEX

NEW Javelina | **Gramercy**	26
Tres Carnes | **multi.**	22

THAI

Ayada | **Elmhurst**	26
Erawan | **Bayside**	24
Jaiya | **multi.**	23
Joya | **Cobble Hill**	22
NEW Kao Soy | **Red Hook**	21
NEW Kiin Thai | **G Vill**	22
Kin Shop | **W Vill**	25
Kuma Inn | **LES**	23
Land Thai | **W 80s**	22
Lan Larb | **multi.**	21
Larb Ubol | **W 30S**	22
Laut | **Union Sq**	22
Ngam | **E Vill**	24
Pam Real Thai | **W 40s**	23
Pok Pok Ny | **Columbia St.**	26
Pok Pok Phat | **Columbia St.**	25
Pure Thai | **W 50s**	26
Qi | **multi.**	22
Room Service | **W 40s**	22
Sea | **W'burg**	23
Somtum Der | **E Vill**	24
Song | **Park Slope**	22
Spice | **multi.**	20
Sripraphai | **Woodside**	26
Thai Market | **W 100s**	23
Topaz | **W 50s**	21
Uncle Boons | **NoLita**	25
Wondee Siam | **multi.**	19
Zabb Elee | **multi.**	24

TURKISH

Akdeniz | **W 40s**	23
A La Turka | **E 70s**	20
Ali Baba | **multi.**	21
Beyoglu | **E 80s**	21
Bodrum | **W 80s**	21
Pasha | **W 70s**	22
Pera | **multi.**	21
Sahara | **Sheepshead**	22
Sip Sak | **E 40s**	23
Taci's Beyti | **Sheepshead**	26
Turkish Cuisine | **W 40s**	20

Turkish Kitchen	**Murray Hill**	22
Turkuaz	**W 90s**	20
Uskudar	**E 70s**	23

UKRAINIAN

Veselka	**E Vill**	21

VEGETARIAN
(* vegan)

Angelica Kit.*	**E Vill**	23
B & H Dairy	**E Vill**	23
Blossom*	**multi.**	25
Bunna Cafe*	**Bushwick**	25
Butcher's Daughter*	**NoLita**	21
Candle Cafe*	**multi.**	24
Candle 79*	**E 70s**	26
Dirt Candy	**LES**	25
Hangawi	**Murray Hill**	24
Hummus Pl.	**multi.**	22
Kajitsu	**Murray Hill**	24
Maoz	**multi.**	22
Peacefood Café*	**multi.**	24
Quantum Leap	**G Vill**	22
Queens Kickshaw	**Astoria**	23
Red Bamboo*	**G Vill**	24
Sacred Chow	**G Vill**	23
Saravanaa Bhavan	**multi.**	23
Taïm	**multi.**	26
Vatan	**Murray Hill**	24
V-Note*	**E 70s**	24
Wild Ginger*	**multi.**	23
Zen Palate*	**Murray Hill**	21

VENEZUELAN

Arepas	**Astoria**	23
Caracas	**multi.**	26

VIETNAMESE

Banh Mi Saigon	**L Italy**	24
Bo-Ky	**multi.**	22
🆕 Bricolage	**Park Slope**	—
Bunker Viet.	**Ridgewood**	26
Hanco's	**multi.**	20
Indochine	**G Vill**	23
Le Colonial	**E 50s**	22
Nha Trang	**Chinatown**	22
Nightingale 9	**Carroll Gdns**	21
Omai	**Chelsea**	23
Pho Bang	**multi.**	23
Rouge et Blanc	**SoHo**	25
Vietnaam	**E 80s**	22

Locations

Includes names, cuisines and Food ratings.

Manhattan

BATTERY PARK CITY

(Chambers St. to Battery Pl., west of West St.)

NEW Beaubourg	*French*	20
Blue Ribbon Sushi	*Japanese*	25
Blue Smoke	*BBQ*	22
Dos Toros	*Mex.*	22
El Vez	*Mex.*	20
Gigino	*Italian*	21
Harry's Italian	*Italian*	20
Hudson Eats	*Food Hall*	19
NEW Le District	*Food Hall/Fr.*	—
Mighty Quinn's	*BBQ*	25
North End Grill	*Amer./Seafood*	25
Num Pang	*Cam./Sandwiches*	23
Parm	*Italian/Sandwiches*	21
NEW Pier A Harbor Hse.	*Amer.*	18
P.J. Clarke's	*Pub*	18
Shake Shack	*Burgers*	22
Tartinery	*French/Sandwiches*	20
Umami Burger	*Burgers*	21

CENTRAL PARK

Boathouse	*Amer.*	18
Maoz	*Mideast./Veg.*	22
Tavern/Green	*Amer.*	15

CHELSEA

(30th to 34th Sts., west of 9th Ave.; 14th to 30th Sts., west of 7th Ave.)

Amorino	*Ice Cream*	25
Artichoke Basille	*Pizza*	22
Bareburger	*Burgers*	21
Bar Eolo	*Italian*	23
Blossom	*Vegan/Veg.*	25
Blue Bottle	*Coffee*	24
Blue Ginger	*Japanese*	22
Bodega Negra	*Mex.*	22
Bottino	*Italian*	20
Buddakan	*Asian*	25
Cafeteria	*Amer.*	20
Cherry	*Japanese*	22
Co.	*Pizza*	23
Colicchio/Sons	*Amer.*	26
Cookshop	*Amer.*	23
Coppelia	*Diner/Pan-Latin*	23

Corkbuzz	*Eclectic*	20
Crema	*Mex.*	23
Cull & Pistol	*Seafood*	24
Da Umberto	*Italian*	25
Del Posto	*Italian*	27
El Quijote	*Spanish*	22
El Quinto Pino	*Spanish*	23
Empire Diner	*Diner*	19
Fonda	*Mex.*	23
Foragers City Table	*Amer.*	22
Francisco's	*Seafood/Spanish*	22
Friedman's	*Amer.*	22
Giovanni Rana	*Italian*	23
Grand Sichuan	*Chinese*	21
Grey Dog	*Amer.*	22
Joe	*Coffee*	21
La Bergamote	*Bakery/French*	24
La Lunchonette	*French*	23
Le Pain Q.	*Bakery/Belgian*	18
Le Zie	*Italian*	21
Los Tacos	*Mex.*	27
NEW Lupulo	*Portug.*	—
Meatball Shop	*Sandwiches*	21
Mexicue	*Mex.*	21
Mökbar	*Korean/Noodle Shop*	26
Momoya	*Japanese*	23
Montmartre	*French*	19
Morimoto	*Japanese*	26
Ninth St Espresso	*Coffee*	23
Num Pang	*Cam./Sandwiches*	23
Old Homestead	*Steak*	25
Omai	*Viet.*	23
Ovest	*Pizza*	23
Park	*Med.*	19
Patsy's Pizzeria	*Pizza*	20
Pepe Giallo/Rosso	*Italian*	23
NEW Porchlight	*Amer.*	21
NEW Prova	*Pizza*	24
Rare B&G	*Burgers*	20
Red Cat	*Amer./Med.*	23
Rocking Horse	*Mex.*	22
Salinas	*Spanish*	24
Sarabeth's	*Amer.*	20
Scarpetta	*Italian*	25
Socarrat	*Spanish*	23
Spice	*Thai*	20

Sushi Seki | *Japanese*	26
Tao | *Asian*	24
Tía Pol | *Spanish*	23
Tipsy Parson | *Southern*	19
Toro | *Spanish*	24
Trestle on 10th | *Amer.*	23
Txikito | *Spanish*	24
NEW Uma Temakeria | *Japanese*	20
Uncle Nick's | *Greek*	21
NEW Vine | *Italian*	—
Westville | *Amer.*	23
'Wichcraft | *Sandwiches*	18

CHINATOWN

(Canal to Pearl Sts., east of B'way)

Amazing 66 | *Chinese*	22
Bassanova | *Japanese/Noodle*	21
Big Wong | *Chinese*	22
Bo-Ky | *Noodle Shop*	22
Buddha Bodai | *Chinese/Kosher*	22
Dim Sum Go Go | *Chinese*	21
Excellent Dumpling | *Chinese*	22
456 Shanghai | *Chinese*	23
Golden Unicorn | *Chinese*	21
Great NY Noodle | *Noodle Shop*	24
Hop Kee | *Chinese*	22
Jing Fong | *Chinese*	21
Joe's Ginger | *Chinese*	20
Joe's Shanghai | *Chinese*	22
Nha Trang | *Viet.*	22
Nice Green Bo | *Chinese*	21
Nom Wah Tea | *Chinese*	21
Oriental Gdn. | *Chinese/Seafood*	23
Peking Duck | *Chinese*	23
Ping's | *Chinese/Seafood*	22
Tasty Hand-Pulled | *Noodle Shop*	23
Wo Hop | *Chinese*	22
Xi'an | *Chinese/Noodle Shop*	23

EAST HARLEM

(100th to 135th Sts., east of 5th Ave.)

Amor Cubano | *Cuban*	21
El Paso | *Mex.*	22
Moustache | *Mideast.*	22
Patsy's Pizzeria | *Pizza*	20
Rao's | *Italian*	23
Ricardo | *Steak*	25

EAST 40s

Aburiya Kinnosuke | *Japanese*	24
Alcala Rest. | *Spanish*	24

Ali Baba | *Turkish*	21
Ammos | *Greek/Seafood*	22
Aretsky's Patroon | *Amer.*	23
Avra | *Greek/Seafood*	26
Benjamin Steak | *Steak*	27
Bobby Van's | *Steak*	23
Bukhara Grill | *Indian*	24
Bull & Bear | *Steak*	21
Cafe Centro | *French/Med.*	22
Capital Grille | *Steak*	25
Cibo | *Amer./Italian*	20
Cipriani | *Italian*	23
Da Noi | *Italian*	22
Darbar | *Indian*	21
Docks Oyster | *Seafood*	21
Dos Toros | *Mex.*	22
Grifone | *Italian*	24
Gyu-Kaku | *Japanese*	21
Hatsuhana | *Japanese*	25
Il Postino | *Italian*	24
Jacques Torres | *Ice Cream*	26
Joe | *Coffee*	21
Junior's | *Diner*	19
Katsu-Hama | *Japanese*	22
Kurumazushi | *Japanese*	24
La Fonda/Sol | *Spanish*	22
Luke's Lobster | *Seafood*	24
Michael Jordan | *Steak*	21
Morton's | *Steak*	23
Nanni | *Italian*	23
Naples 45 | *Italian/Pizza*	19
Naya | *Lebanese*	22
99 Miles/Philly | *Cheestks.*	21
Num Pang | *Cam./Sandwiches*	23
Osteria Laguna | *Italian*	22
Oyster Bar | *Seafood*	22
Palm | *Steak*	25
Pampano | *Mex./Seafood*	24
Patsy's Pizzeria | *Pizza*	20
Pera | *Med.*	21
Phoenix Gdn. | *Chinese*	23
Pietro's | *Italian/Steak*	23
NEW Red Stixs | *Chinese*	20
Roast Kit. | *Health*	21
Sakagura | *Japanese*	25
Sea Fire Grill | *Seafood*	27
Shake Shack | *Burgers*	22
Sinigual | *Mex.*	21
Sip Sak | *Turkish*	23
Smith/Wollensky | *Steak*	24

Soba Totto	Japanese/Noodle	23
Sparks	Steak	25
Sushiden	Japanese	24
Sushi Yasuda	Japanese	27
Tres Carnes	Tex-Mex	22
Tulsi	Indian	23
Two Boots	Pizza	19
Vitae	Amer.	24
'Wichcraft	Sandwiches	18
Wolfgang's	Steak	26
Wollensky's	Steak	24
Yama	Japanese	24
Zengo	Pan-Latin	20

EAST 50s

Al Bustan	Lebanese	21
Alfredo 100	Italian	21
Amma	Indian	25
Angelo's Pizzeria	Pizza	21
Angus Club	Steak	25
Aquavit	Scan.	26
Armani Rist.	Italian	23
BarKogi	Chicken/Korean	22
Bill's Food/Drink	Amer./Steak	18
Bistango	multi.	21
Bistro Vendôme	French	22
BLT Steak	Steak	25
Bobby Van's	Steak	23
Brasserie	French	22
Brick Ln. Curry	Indian	21
BXL Cafe	Belgian	20
Casa Lever	Italian	22
Caviar Russe	Amer.	24
Cellini	Italian	22
Charlie Palmer	Steak	24
Chola	Indian	23
Club A Steak	Steak	26
Crave Fishbar	Seafood	24
NEW Crimson & Rye	Amer.	20
Darbar	Indian	21
Dawat	Indian	24
DeGrezia	Italian	24
Deux Amis	French	20
Dos Caminos	Mex.	19
Ethos	Greek/Seafood	22
Felidia	Italian	25
57 Napoli	Pizza	24
Fig & Olive	Med.	21
Four Seasons	Amer.	26
Fresco	Italian	22

Grand Sichuan	Chinese	21
Harlow	Seafood	20
Harry Cipriani	Italian	24
Hide-Chan	Japanese/Noodle	23
Hillstone	Amer.	22
Jubilee	French	21
Kati Roll	Indian	23
La Grenouille	French	27
La Mangeoire	French	22
Lavo	Italian	20
Le Cirque	French	24
Le Colonial	French/Viet.	22
Le Perigord	French	25
Le Relais	French/Steak	20
Lychee House	Chinese	21
Maloney & Porcelli	Steak	25
Mike's Bistro	Amer./Kosher	26
Monkey Bar	Amer.	20
Montebello	Italian	22
Morso	Italian	25
Mr. Chow	Chinese	23
Mr. K's	Chinese	23
National	Amer.	20
Naya	Lebanese	22
Neary's	Pub	19
Nerai	Greek	24
Ninth St Espresso	Coffee	23
Nippon	Japanese	24
Obao	Asian	20
Obicà Mozzarella	Italian	23
Peking Duck	Chinese	23
Pescatore	Italian	21
P.J. Clarke's	Pub	18
NEW Polo Bar	Amer.	20
Prime Grill	Kosher/Steak	23
Radiance Tea	Teahse.	21
Roast Kit.	Health	21
Rosa Mexicano	Mex.	22
San Pietro	Italian	24
Schnipper's	Amer.	19
Serafina	Italian	19
Shun Lee Palace	Chinese	23
Smith	Amer.	19
Socarrat	Spanish	23
Solera	Spanish	22
Tao	Asian	24
Tenzan	Japanese	21
Teodora	Italian	21
Totto Ramen	Japanese/Noodle	24
Tres Carnes	Tex-Mex	22

NEW 212 Steakhse. | *Steak*	22
Valbella | *Italian*	24
Via Quadronno | *Italian*	22
Wolfgang's | *Steak*	26

EAST 60s

Alice's Tea | *Teahse.*	20
Altesi Rist. | *Italian*	22
Amali | *Med.*	25
Amaranth | *Med.*	21
Anassa Taverna | *Greek*	21
August | *Amer.*	21
Bar Italia | *Italian*	21
Birch Coffee | *Coffee*	25
Bistro Chat Noir | *French*	21
Cabana | *Nuevo Latino*	22
Daniel | *French*	29
David Burke Fishtail | *Seafood*	24
East Pole | *Amer./British*	23
El Porrón | *Spanish*	22
Fatty Fish | *Asian*	20
Felice | *Italian*	21
Fig & Olive | *Med.*	21
Fred's at Barneys | *Amer./Italian*	20
Il Mulino | *Italian*	25
Il Vagabondo | *Italian*	19
Isle/Capri | *Italian*	20
Jackson Hole | *Burgers*	20
JoJo | *French*	24
Le Bilboquet | *French*	22
Le Pain Q. | *Bakery/Belgian*	18
Le Veau d'Or | *French*	19
Maya | *Mex.*	22
Mon Petit Cafe | *French*	21
Moti Mahal | *Indian*	24
Nello | *Italian*	18
Patsy's Pizzeria | *Pizza*	20
Philippe | *Chinese*	22
Primola | *Italian*	22
Ravagh | *Persian*	24
Regency B&G | *Amer.*	24
Rotisserie Georgette | *French*	22
Sant Ambroeus | *Italian*	22
Scalinatella | *Italian*	24
Serafina | *Italian*	19
Serendipity 3 | *Dessert*	19
Sirio | *Italian*	21
Sushi Seki | *Japanese*	26
Texas de Brazil | *Brazilian/Steak*	22
Tiella | *Italian*	25
Tony's Di Napoli | *Italian*	21

EAST 70s

Afghan Kebab | *Afghan*	21
A La Turka | *Turkish*	20
Al Forno | *Pizza*	20
Arlington Club | *Steak*	21
Atlantic Grill | *Seafood*	23
Bareburger | *Burgers*	21
B. Café | *Belgian*	20
Bella Blu | *Italian*	22
NEW BKB | *Seafood*	23
Boqueria | *Spanish*	23
Bottega | *Italian*	20
Brasserie Cognac | *French*	18
Café Boulud | *French*	27
Cafe Evergreen | *Chinese*	20
Campagnola | *Italian*	24
Candle Cafe | *Vegan/Veg.*	24
Candle 79 | *Vegan/Veg.*	26
Caravaggio | *Italian*	25
Carlyle | *French*	24
Cilantro | *SW*	21
Dos Toros | *Mex.*	22
Due | *Italian*	22
Gari | *Japanese*	26
Haru | *Japanese*	21
Il Riccio | *Italian*	21
J.G. Melon | *Pub*	22
Joe | *Coffee*	21
Jones Wood Foundry | *British*	20
NEW Kappo Masa | *Japanese*	25
Ko Sushi | *Japanese*	20
Le Pain Q. | *Bakery/Belgian*	18
Lusardi's | *Italian*	24
Maison Kayser | *Bakery/French*	21
Mark | *Amer.*	23
Maruzzella | *Italian*	20
Meatball Shop | *Sandwiches*	21
Mezzaluna | *Italian*	20
NEW Monte Carlo | *French*	23
Nino's | *Italian*	21
Numero 28 | *Pizza*	22
Orsay | *French*	20
Oslo Coffee | *Coffee*	22
Parma | *Italian*	21
Pastrami Queen | *Deli/Kosher*	23
Persepolis | *Persian*	23
Quatorze Bis | *French*	22
Sant Ambroeus | *Italian*	22
Sasabune | *Japanese*	26
2nd Ave Deli | *Deli/Kosher*	23

Serafina | *Italian*	19
Sette Mezzo | *Italian*	23
Shabu-Shabu 70 | *Japanese*	21
Sojourn | *Amer.*	23
Spice | *Thai*	20
Spigolo | *Italian*	22
Swifty's | *Amer.*	17
Szechuan Gourmet | *Chinese*	22
Tanoshi | *Japanese*	25
T-Bar Steak | *Steak*	21
Uskudar | *Turkish*	23
Uva | *Italian*	22
Via Quadronno | *Italian*	22
Vivolo | *Italian*	20
V-Note | *Vegan*	24
Xi'an | *Chinese/Noodle Shop*	23
Yefsi Estiatorio | *Greek*	24

EAST 80s

Alice's Tea | *Teahse.*	20
Antonucci | *Italian*	23
Baluchi's | *Indian*	21
Bareburger | *Burgers*	21
Beyoglu | *Turkish*	21
Burger Bistro | *Burgers*	22
Café d'Alsace | *French*	21
Café Sabarsky/ Fledermaus | *Austrian*	22
Cascabel Taqueria | *Mex.*	19
Chef Ho's | *Chinese*	22
East End Kitchen | *Amer.*	20
E.A.T. | *Amer.*	19
83.5 | *Italian*	22
Elio's | *Italian*	25
NEW Eli's Table | *Amer.*	22
Erminia | *Italian*	24
Felice | *Italian*	21
Firenze | *Italian*	21
Flex Mussels | *Seafood*	23
Giovanni | *Italian*	25
Grazie | *Italian*	20
Heidelberg | *German*	19
Ithaka | *Greek/Seafood*	20
Jacques | *French*	20
Jaiya | *Thai*	23
Kings' Carriage | *Amer.*	23
Ko Sushi | *Japanese*	20
Le Pain Q. | *Bakery/Belgian*	18
Luke's Lobster | *Seafood*	24
Maison Kayser | *Bakery/French*	21
Maz Mezcal | *Mex.*	21

Meijin | *Japanese/Noodle*	22
Móle | *Mex.*	21
Naruto | *Japanese/Noodle Shop*	20
Nicola's | *Italian*	22
Papaya King | *Hot Dogs*	22
Parlor Steakhse. | *Steak*	21
Penrose | *Amer.*	22
Pig Heaven | *Chinese*	20
NEW Pizza Beach | *Pizza*	19
Poke | *Japanese*	23
Rist. Morini | *Italian*	24
Sandro's | *Italian*	23
San Matteo | *Italian/Pizza*	26
Shake Shack | *Burgers*	22
Shorty's | *Cheesestks.*	21
Simone | *French*	25
Sistina | *Italian*	25
Tenzan | *Japanese*	21
Toloache | *Mex.*	23
Two Boots | *Pizza*	19
Via Quadronno | *Italian*	22
Vietnaam | *Viet.*	22
Wa Jeal | *Chinese*	23
Writing Room | *Amer.*	20
Yuka | *Japanese*	23

EAST 90s

Brick Ln. Curry | *Indian*	21
El Paso | *Mex.*	22
La Tarte Flambee | *French*	20
NEW Milton | *British*	23
Nick's | *Pizza*	24
Paola's | *Italian*	24
Pascalou | *French*	22
Pio Pio | *Peruvian*	23
Rizzo's | *Pizza*	21
Sarabeth's | *Amer.*	20
Sfoglia | *Italian*	23
Table d'Hôte | *Amer./French*	22
Yura on Madison | *Sandwiches*	21

EAST VILLAGE

(14th to Houston Sts., east of 3rd Ave.)

Abraço Espresso | *Coffee*	24
Angelica Kit. | *Vegan/Veg.*	23
Artichoke Basille | *Pizza*	22
Au Za'atar | *French/Mideast.*	20
Awash | *Ethiopian*	21
NEW Babu Ji | *Indian*	—
Balade | *Lebanese*	24

B & H Dairy | *Deli/Veg.*	23
Bao | *Chinese*	23
BaoHaus | *Taiwanese*	23
NEW Bara | *French/Japanese*	—
Bareburger | *Burgers*	21
Bar Primi | *Italian*	24
Big Gay Ice Cream | *Ice Cream*	25
Black Ant | *Mex.*	24
Black Iron Burger | *Burgers*	23
Blue Ribbon Fried | *Chicken*	21
Boulton & Watt | *Amer.*	21
NEW Bowery Meat Co. | *Steak*	25
Brick Ln. Curry | *Indian*	21
Brindle Room | *Amer.*	24
Buenos Aires | *Argent./Steak*	23
Cacio e Pepe | *Italian*	22
Cafe Mogador | *Moroccan*	24
Cafe Orlin | *Amer.*	22
Caracas | *Venez.*	26
Caravan/Dreams | *Kosher/Veg.*	23
Cha An | *Japanese/Teahse.*	22
ChikaLicious | *Dessert*	25
Crif Dogs | *Hot Dogs*	22
DBGB | *French*	22
Degustation | *Amer.*	25
Ducks Eatery | *Eclectic*	25
Dumpling Man | *Chinese*	24
Eddy | *Amer.*	26
Edi & The Wolf | *Austrian*	22
NEW Empellón al Pastor | *Mex.*	19
Empellón Cocina | *Mex.*	23
NEW Fifty Paces | *Amer.*	22
Flinders Lane | *Australian*	25
Fonda | *Mex.*	23
Frank | *Italian*	23
NEW Fuku | *Chicken/ Sandwiches*	—
Gemma | *Italian*	21
GG's | *Amer./Pizza*	22
Gnocco | *Italian*	22
Graffiti | *Eclectic*	28
Grand Sichuan | *Chinese*	21
Haveli | *Indian*	23
Hearth | *Amer./Italian*	25
Huertas | *Spanish*	25
Jeepney | *Filipino*	23
Jewel Bako | *Japanese*	24
Jimmy's No. 43 | *SE Asian*	20
John's/12th St. | *Italian*	22
Kafana | *E Euro.*	24
Kanoyama | *Japanese*	24
NEW King Bee | *Cajun/French*	21
NEW Korilla | *Korean/Mex.*	23
Kyo Ya | *Japanese*	26
La Palapa | *Mex.*	22
L'Apicio | *Italian*	23
Lavagna | *Italian*	24
Lil' Frankie | *Italian/Pizza*	23
Little Poland | *Diner/Polish*	21
Lucien | *French*	24
Luke's Lobster | *Seafood*	24
Luzzo's | *Pizza*	24
Maharlika | *Filipino*	22
Mamoun's | *Mideast.*	23
Mayahuel | *Mex.*	23
Mermaid | *Seafood*	23
Mighty Quinn's | *BBQ*	25
Mimi Cheng's | *Taiwanese*	24
Minca | *Japanese/Noodle Shop*	24
Miss Lily's | *Jamaican*	23
Momofuku Ko | *Amer.*	26
Momofuku Noodle | *Amer.*	25
Momofuku Ssäm Bar | *Amer.*	26
Motorino | *Pizza*	25
Moustache | *Mideast.*	22
Narcissa | *Amer.*	25
Ngam | *Thai*	24
Nicoletta | *Italian/Pizza*	22
Ninth St Espresso | *Coffee*	23
NEW Noreetuh | *Hawaiian*	—
Northern Spy | *Amer.*	21
Numero 28 | *Pizza*	22
NEW Oiji | *Korean*	—
Papaya King | *Hot Dogs*	22
NEW Pardon My French | *French*	27
Porchetta | *Italian/Sandwiches*	22
Porsena | *Italian*	24
Prune | *Amer.*	24
Pylos | *Greek*	26
Ravagh | *Persian*	24
Redhead | *Southern*	23
Red Hook Lobster | *Seafood*	24
Risotteria Melotti | *Italian*	25
Root & Bone | *Southern*	24
NEW Rosie's | *Mex.*	24
S'MAC | *Amer.*	22
Smith | *Amer.*	19
Soba-ya | *Japanese/Noodle Shop*	23
Somtum Der | *Thai*	24
Spot | *Dessert*	24

LOCATIONS

NEW Superiority Burger | Burgers —

Supper | *Italian* 26

Sushi Dojo | *Japanese* 25

Takahachi | *Japanese* 24

Taverna Kyclades | *Greek/Seafood* 26

NEW Tuome | *Amer.* 26

26 Seats | *French* 22

Two Boots | *Pizza* 19

Upstate | *Seafood* 27

Vanessa's Dumpling | *Seafood* 22

Veselka | *Ukrainian* 21

NEW Virginia's | *Amer.* 23

Westville | *Amer.* 23

Xi'an | *Chinese/Noodle Shop* 23

Yakitori Taisho | *Japanese* 24

Yerba Buena | *Pan-Latin* 22

Yuca Bar | *Pan-Latin* 23

Zabb Elee | *Thai* 24

Zum Schneider | *German* 21

FINANCIAL DISTRICT

(South of Civic Center, excluding South St. Seaport)

Adrienne's | *Pizza* 24

Bareburger | *Burgers* 21

Battery Gdns. | *Amer./Cont.* 19

Bobby Van's | *Steak* 23

BonChon | *Chicken* 23

Capital Grille | *Steak* 25

Cipriani | *Italian* 23

Dead Rabbit | *Pub* 22

Delmonico's | *Steak* 24

Felice | *Italian* 21

Fraunces Tav. | *Pub* 18

Harry's Cafe | *Steak* 23

Harry's Italian | *Italian* 20

Haru | *Japanese* 21

NEW Industry Kitchen | *Amer.* —

Les Halles | *French/Steak* 20

Luke's Lobster | *Seafood* 24

Melt Shop | *Sandwiches* 22

Mooncake Foods | *Pan-Asian* 21

Morton's | *Steak* 23

Obao | *Asian* 20

NEW One Dine | *Amer.* —

Reserve Cut | *Kosher/Steak* 24

Schnipper's | *Amer.* 19

Shorty's | *Cheestks.* 21

Smashburger | *Burgers* 20

Smorgas Chef | *Scan.* 20

Toloache | *Mex.* 23

Zaitzeff | *Burgers* 22

FLATIRON

(14th to 30th Sts., 7th Ave. to Park Ave. So., excluding Union Sq.)

ABC Cocina | *Pan-Latin* 25

ABC Kitchen | *Amer.* 26

Aldea | *Med.* 24

Almayass | *Armenian/Lebanese* 24

Almond | *French* 20

A Voce | *Italian* 23

Barbounia | *Med.* 21

Barn Joo | *Korean* 22

Basta Pasta | *Italian* 23

Beecher's Cellar | *Amer.* 23

Birreria | *Italian* 21

Bocca | *Italian* 22

Boqueria | *Spanish* 23

NEW Burger & Lobster | *Amer.* 24

BXL Cafe | *Belgian* 20

Cafe El Pres. | *Mex.* 20

City Bakery | *Bakery* 23

NEW Clocktower | *Amer.* 24

NEW Cosme | *Mex.* 25

Craft | *Amer.* 25

Craftbar | *Amer.* 22

Eataly | *Food Hall/Italian* 24

Eisenberg's | *Sandwiches* 20

Élan | *Amer.* 23

Eleven Madison | *Amer.* 28

Gander | *Amer.* 20

Giorgio's | *Amer./Italian* 22

Gramercy Tavern | *Amer.* 28

Grimaldi's | *Pizza* 22

Hanjan | *Korean* 24

Hill Country | *BBQ* 22

Hill Country Chicken | *Chicken/Southern* 21

Il Mulino | *Italian* 25

Junoon | *Indian* 24

La Pizza Fresca | *Italian/Pizza* 24

Le Pain Q. | *Bakery/Belgian* 18

Maison Kayser | *Bakery/French* 21

Manzo | *Italian/Steak* 25

Mari Vanna | *Russian* 20

Markt | *Belgian* 20

Num Pang | *Cam./Sandwiches* 23

Obicà Mozzarella | *Italian* 23

Ootoya | *Japanese/Noodle Shop* 25

Park Avenue | *Amer.*	25
Periyali | *Greek*	24
Petite Abeille | *Belgian*	19
Qi | *Asian/Thai*	22
Raymi | *Peruvian*	24
Rosa Mexicano | *Mex.*	22
Sala One Nine | *Spanish*	21
Schnipper's | *Amer.*	19
Shake Shack | *Burgers*	22
Tacombi | *Mex.*	24
Toby's Estate | *Coffee*	24
Tocqueville | *Amer./French*	26
Tres Carnes | *Tex-Mex*	22
Via Emilia | *Italian*	22
'Wichcraft | *Sandwiches*	18
Zero Otto | *Italian/Pizza*	23

GRAMERCY PARK

(14th to 23rd Sts., 1st Ave. to Park Ave. So., excluding Union Sq.)

Bar Jamón | *Spanish*	24
BLT Prime | *Steak*	26
Casa Mono | *Spanish*	25
Dos Toros | *Mex.*	22
NEW Florian | *Italian*	22
Friend/Farmer | *Amer.*	19
Halal Guys | *Mideast.*	22
House | *Amer.*	24
NEW Javelina | *Tex-Mex*	26
Lady Mendl's | *Teahse.*	21
La Follia | *Italian*	23
Maialino | *Italian*	25
Molly's | *Pub*	21
NEW Morton's | *Steak*	23
Novitá | *Italian*	25
Paul & Jimmy's | *Italian*	20
Piccolo Cafe | *Coffee/Italian*	22
Ponty Bistro | *African/French*	22
Posto | *Pizza*	23
Rolf's | *German*	15
NEW Tasca Chino | *Chinese/ Spanish*	19
Yama | *Japanese*	24

GREENWICH VILLAGE

(Houston to 14th Sts., 3rd to 6th Aves., excluding NoHo)

All'onda | *Italian*	23
Alta | *Med.*	25
Amorino | *Ice Cream*	25
Artichoke Basille | *Pizza*	22
Arturo's | *Pizza*	23

NEW Asia de Cuba | *Asian/ Cuban*	23
Babbo | *Italian*	26
Bareburger | *Burgers*	21
Bark | *Hot Dogs*	20
Bar Pitti | *Italian*	23
Blue Hill | *Amer.*	28
Bourgeois Pig | *French*	23
Burger Joint | *Burgers*	25
Cafe Espanol | *Spanish*	21
Carbone | *Italian*	24
Chez Jacqueline | *French*	20
Claudette | *French*	21
Corkbuzz | *Eclectic*	20
Cuba | *Cuban*	24
Da Andrea | *Italian*	23
Da Silvano | *Italian*	21
Dos Toros | *Mex.*	22
5 Napkin Burger | *Burgers*	21
Fourth | *Amer.*	20
Gotham B&G | *Amer.*	28
Grey Dog | *Amer.*	22
Gyu-Kaku | *Japanese*	21
Han Dynasty | *Chinese*	23
Hu Kitchen | *Health*	24
Il Cantinori | *Italian*	24
Il Mulino | *Italian*	25
Indochine | *French/Viet.*	23
Ippudo | *Japanese/Noodle Shop*	25
Jane | *Amer.*	22
Japonica | *Japanese*	23
J.G. Melon | *Pub*	22
Joe | *Coffee*	21
Joe's Pizza | *Pizza*	24
Kati Roll | *Indian*	23
NEW Kiin Thai | *Thai*	22
Knickerbocker | *Amer.*	21
La Colombe | *Coffee*	25
La Lanterna | *Italian*	20
Le Pain Q. | *Bakery/Belgian*	18
Library/Public | *Amer.*	19
Lion | *Amer.*	18
Lupa | *Italian*	25
Mamoun's | *Mideast.*	23
Maoz | *Mideast./Veg.*	22
Margaux | *French/Med.*	18
Mermaid | *Seafood*	23
Minetta Tavern | *French*	25
Miss Lily's | *Jamaican*	23
Negril | *Carib./Jamaican*	23

Neta	*Japanese*	26
99 Miles/Philly	*Cheestks.*	21
North Sq.	*Amer.*	24
Num Pang	*Cam./Sandwiches*	23
Old Tbilisi Gdn.	*Georgian*	22
100 Montaditos	*Sandwiches*	19
Ootoya	*Japanese/Noodle Shop*	25
Otto	*Italian/Pizza*	22
Patsy's Pizzeria	*Pizza*	20
Peacefood Café	*Kosher/ Vegan/Veg.*	24
Peanut Butter Co.	*Sandwiches*	22
Perla	*Italian*	23
Quantum Leap	*Health/Veg.*	22
Red Bamboo	*Asian/Vegan*	24
Ribalta	*Italian*	25
Roast Kit.	*Health*	21
Sacred Chow	*Kosher/Vegan/ Veg.*	23
NEW Saki	*Japanese*	—
NEW Shuko	*Japanese*	26
Spice	*Thai*	20
Strip House	*Steak*	25
Stumptown	*Coffee*	23
Taboon	*Sandwiches*	23
Thelewala	*Indian*	23
Toloache	*Mex.*	23
Tomoe Sushi	*Japanese*	26
Umami Burger	*Burgers*	21
Villa Mosconi	*Italian*	22
'Wichcraft	*Sandwiches*	18
ZZ's Clam Bar	*Seafood*	23

HAMILTON HEIGHTS

Covo	*Italian*	23

HARLEM

(110th to 155th Sts., 5th to St. Nicholas Aves.)

Amy Ruth's	*Soul Food*	23
Cecil	*Amer./Eclectic*	23
Chez Lucienne	*French*	22
5 & Diamond	*Amer.*	21
Harlem Shake	*Burgers*	20
Lido	*Italian*	23
Lolo's	*Caribb./Seafood*	25
Madiba	*S African*	22
Melba's	*Amer./Southern*	25
Minton's	*Southern*	21
Ponty Bistro	*African/French*	22
Red Rooster	*Amer.*	22

NEW Streetbird	*Chicken*	18
Sylvia's	*Soul Food/Southern*	20

HUDSON SQUARE

(Canal to Houston Sts., west of 6th Ave.)

NEW Houseman	*Amer.*	—
Koi	*Japanese*	24
La Colombe	*Coffee*	25
La Sirène	*French*	24
Westville	*Amer.*	23

INWOOD

Mamajuana	*Dominican/ Nuevo Latino*	22
New Leaf	*Amer.*	—
Piper's Kilt	*Pub*	20

LITTLE ITALY

(Broome to Canal Sts., Bowery to Centre St.)

Angelo's/Mulberry	*Italian*	23
Bacchanal	*Amer.*	22
Banh Mi Saigon	*Sandwiches/ Viet.*	24
Baz Bagel	*Bakery/Jewish*	21
Bo-Ky	*Noodle Shop*	22
Da Nico	*Italian*	21
Ferrara	*Bakery*	24
NEW Gelso & Grand	*Italian*	18
Il Cortile	*Italian*	23
La Mela	*Italian*	20
Lan Larb	*Thai*	21
NEW Maman	*Amer./French*	20
Nyonya	*Malaysian*	23
Pellegrino's	*Italian*	24
Pepe Giallo/Rosso	*Italian*	23
Pho Bang	*Noodle Shop/Viet.*	23
Red Egg	*Chinese*	20
NEW Seamore's	*Seafood*	—
Shanghai Cafe	*Chinese*	24
Two Hands	*Australian*	23
Umbertos Clam Hse.	*Italian*	21
Vincent's	*Italian*	22
Wild Ginger	*Asian/Vegan*	23

LOWER EAST SIDE

(South of Houston St., east of Bowery & Pike St.)

Ápizz	*Italian*	24
Bacaro	*Italian*	21
Barrio Chino	*Mex.*	24
Beauty & Essex	*Amer.*	23

🆕 Birds & Bubbles | *Southern*	21
Blue Ribbon Sushi | *Japanese*	25
Boil | *Seafood*	23
Cafe Katja | *Austrian*	25
Calexico | *Mex.*	21
Cata | *Spanish*	22
Clinton St. Baking | *Amer.*	25
Cocoron | *Japanese*	23
Congee | *Chinese*	21
Contra | *Amer.*	25
Dimes | *Amer.*	23
Dirt Candy | *Veg.*	25
Dirty French | *French*	24
🆕 El Rey | *Amer.*	25
Fat Radish | *Amer.*	22
Freemans | *Amer.*	22
Fung Tu | *Amer./Chinese*	25
Galli | *Italian*	24
Il Laboratorio | *Ice Cream*	25
Ivan Ramen | *Japanese/Noodle*	22
Katz's Deli | *Deli*	25
🆕 Kottu House | *Sri Lankan*	—
Kuma Inn | *Filipino/Thai*	23
🆕 La Gamelle | *French*	—
Macondo | *Pan-Latin*	19
Meatball Shop | *Sandwiches*	21
Mission Cantina | *Mex.*	21
Mission Chinese | *Chinese*	22
Morgenstern's | *Ice Cream*	26
New York Sushi Ko | *Japanese*	—
Pies-N-Thighs | *Southern*	24
Pig and Khao | *SE Asian*	26
Prosperity Dumpling | *Chinese*	24
Rizzo's | *Pizza*	21
Russ/Daughters Cafe | *Jewish*	26
Sammy's Roumanian | *Jewish*	19
Sauce | *Italian*	22
Schiller's | *Cont.*	20
🆕 Spaghetti Incident | *Italian*	—
Stanton Social | *Eclectic*	23
Sweet Chick | *Southern*	24
🆕 Tijuana Picnic | *Mex.*	21
Vanessa's Dumpling | *Seafood*	22
🆕 Wildair | *Amer.*	—

MANHATTANVILLE

Maison Harlem | *French*	22

MEATPACKING

(14th to Horatio Sts., west of Hudson St.)

Bagatelle | *French*	18

Bubby's | *Amer.*	21
Catch | *Seafood*	23
Dos Caminos | *Mex.*	19
Ed's Lobster Bar | *Seafood*	25
El Colmado | *Spanish*	19
Fatty Crab | *Malaysian*	21
Fig & Olive | *Med.*	21
🆕 Gansevoort Mkt. | *Food Hall*	—
Macelleria | *Italian/Steak*	22
🆕 Santina | *Italian*	23
Serafina | *Italian*	19
Spice Market | *SE Asian*	24
Standard Grill | *Amer.*	21
STK | *Steak*	23
Sushi Dojo | *Japanese*	25
Tacombi | *Mex.*	24
Untitled | *Amer.*	—
Valbella | *Italian*	24

MORNINGSIDE HEIGHTS

Community | *Amer.*	23
Dinosaur BBQ | *BBQ*	22
Friedman's | *Amer.*	22
Jin Ramen | *Japanese/Noodle*	23
Joe | *Coffee*	21
Kitchenette | *Southern*	20
Max SoHa/Caffe | *Italian*	21
Pisticci | *Italian*	24
Serafina | *Italian*	19

MURRAY HILL

(34th to 42nd Sts., east of Park Ave.)

Aji Sushi | *Japanese*	21
Ali Baba | *Turkish*	21
Alidoro | *Italian/Sandwiches*	27
Artisanal | *French*	21
Baby Bo's | *Mex.*	21
Baluchi's | *Indian*	21
Barbès | *French/Moroccan*	21
Bareburger | *Burgers*	21
Birch Coffee | *Coffee*	25
Bistango | *multi.*	21
Blue Smoke | *BBQ*	22
BonChon | *Chicken*	23
Cafe China | *Chinese*	24
Cannibal | *Belgian*	22
Coppola's | *Italian*	20
Dhaba | *Indian*	23
Dos Caminos | *Mex.*	19
El Parador | *Mex.*	22

El Pote	*Spanish*	22
Ethos	*Greek/Seafood*	22
Forcella	*Pizza*	23
Franchia	*Korean*	24
NEW Haldi	*Indian*	19
Hangawi	*Korean/Veg.*	24
I Trulli	*Italian*	23
Jackson Hole	*Burgers*	20
Jaiya	*Thai*	23
Juni	*Amer.*	27
Kajitsu	*Japanese/Veg.*	24
NEW Kang Ho Dong	*Korean*	23
Kyochon	*Chicken*	21
Lan Larb	*Thai*	21
La Tarte Flambee	*French*	20
Le Parisien	*French*	22
Les Halles	*French/Steak*	20
Little Beet	*Amer.*	22
Madison Bistro	*French*	21
Marcony	*Italian*	24
Mexico Lindo	*Mex.*	22
Morgan Dining Rm.	*Amer.*	23
Nick's	*Pizza*	24
Nirvana	*Indian*	22
Oaxaca	*Mex.*	23
NEW O Ya	*Japanese*	—
Peacock	*British*	22
Penelope	*Amer.*	22
Piccolo Cafe	*Coffee/Italian*	22
Pio Pio	*Chicken/Peruvian*	23
Pippali	*Indian*	24
Ralph's Famous	*Ice Cream*	25
Rare B&G	*Burgers*	20
Ravagh	*Persian*	24
Resto	*Belgian*	21
Riverpark	*Amer.*	26
NEW Rocky Slims	*Italian/Pizza*	21
Rossini's	*Italian*	22
Sachi	*Asian*	23
Salvation Taco	*Mex.*	20
Sarabeth's	*Amer.*	20
Saravanaa Bhavan	*Indian/Veg.*	23
Sarge's Deli	*Deli/Sandwiches*	23
2nd Ave Deli	*Deli/Kosher*	23
Shake Shack	*Burgers*	22
S'MAC	*Amer.*	22
Smorgas Chef	*Scan.*	20
Sushi Sen-nin	*Japanese*	25
Turkish Kitchen	*Turkish*	22
NEW Upland	*Cal.*	25

Vatan	*Indian/Veg.*	24
Vezzo	*Pizza*	24
Villa Berulia	*Italian*	25
Water Club	*Amer.*	23
Wild Edibles	*Seafood*	24
Wolfgang's	*Steak*	26
Xi'an	*Chinese/Noodle Shop*	23
Zen Palate	*Asian/Veg.*	21
NEW Zuma	*Japanese*	22

NOHO

(Houston to 4th Sts., Bowery to B'way)

Acme	*Amer.*	20
Aroma Kitchen	*Italian*	22
Bianca	*Italian*	25
Bohemian	*Japanese*	27
Bond St	*Japanese*	25
Gato	*Med.*	26
Great Jones Cafe	*Cajun*	21
Hecho en Dumbo	*Mex.*	22
Il Buco	*Italian/Med.*	25
Il Buco Alimentari	*Italian/Med.*	24
Lafayette	*French*	22
Le Pain Q.| *Bakery/Belgian*	18
Le Philosophe	*French*	22
Mile End	*Deli/Sandwiches*	22
NoHo Star	*Amer./Asian*	20
Saxon & Parole	*Amer.*	24
Smile	*Med.*	20
NEW Vic's	*Italian/Med.*	22

NOLITA

(Houston to Kenmare Sts., Bowery to Lafayette St.)

Balaboosta	*Med./Mideast.*	25
Bread	*Italian/Sandwiches*	21
Butcher's Daughter	*Vegan*	21
Cafe Gitane	*French/Moroccan*	22
Café Habana/Outpost	*Cuban/Mex.*	23
NEW Chefs Club	*Amer.*	24
Cherche Midi	*French*	22
Cocoron	*Japanese*	23
Delicatessen	*Amer.*	23
Egg Shop	*Amer.*	24
Emilio's Ballato	*Italian*	26
Emporio	*Italian*	23
Estela	*Amer./Med.*	27
NEW Goemon Curry	*Japanese*	—
Grey Dog	*Amer.*	22
Jacques	*French*	20

Lombardi's | *Pizza*	24
Musket Room | *New Zealand*	26
Parm | *Italian/Sandwiches*	21
Pearl & Ash | *Amer.*	24
Peasant | *Italian*	24
Public | *Eclectic*	24
NEW Ramen Lab | *Japanese/ Noodle Shop*	26
NEW Rebelle | *French*	18
Rubirosa | *Italian/Pizza*	26
Sant Ambroeus | *Italian*	22
Socarrat | *Spanish*	23
Tacombi | *Mex.*	24
Taïm | *Israeli/Veg.*	26
Tartinery | *French/Sandwiches*	20
Uncle Boons | *Thai*	25

NOMAD

Ben & Jack's | *Steak*	24
Birch Coffee | *Coffee*	25
Breslin | *British*	22
Hillstone | *Amer.*	22
Ilili | *Lebanese*	24
John Dory Oyster | *Seafood*	21
L & W Oyster | *Seafood*	20
Marta | *Italian/Pizza*	24
Maysville | *Amer.*	22
Melt Shop | *Sandwiches*	22
Mexicue | *Mex.*	21
NoMad | *Amer./Euro.*	26
NoMad Bar | *Amer.*	25
Shorty's | *Cheestks.*	21
Stumptown | *Coffee*	23

SOHO

(Canal to Houston Sts., 6th Ave. to Lafayette St.)

Alidoro | *Italian/Sandwiches*	27
Antique Garage | *Med.*	19
Aquagrill | *Seafood*	27
Aurora | *Italian*	24
Back Forty West | *Amer.*	21
Balthazar | *French*	24
Bistro Les Amis | *French*	22
NEW Black Tap | *Burgers*	20
Blue Ribbon | *Amer.*	25
Blue Ribbon Sushi | *Japanese*	25
Boqueria | *Spanish*	23
Burger & Barrel | *Burgers/Pub*	22
Chalk Point | *Amer.*	24
Charlie Bird | *Amer.*	23
Cipriani | *Italian*	23

Cocotte | *French*	23
Cómodo | *Latin Amer.*	25
Costata | *Italian/Steak*	23
David Burke Kitchen | *Amer.*	25
Dominique Ansel Bakery | *Bakery/French*	25
Dos Caminos | *Mex.*	19
Dutch | *Amer.*	22
Ed's Lobster Bar | *Seafood*	25
Galli | *Italian*	24
Hampton Chutney | *Indian*	22
Hundred Acres | *Amer.*	21
Il Mulino Prime | *Italian/Steak*	25
Jack's Wife Freda | *Amer.*	23
La Colombe | *Coffee*	25
Ladurée | *Bakery/French*	22
La Esquina | *Mex.*	23
Le Pain Q. | *Bakery/Belgian*	18
Little Prince | *French*	22
Lure Fishbar | *Seafood*	25
NEW Mamo | *Italian*	—
Mercer Kitchen | *Amer./French*	23
Mooncake Foods | *Pan-Asian*	21
Navy | *Seafood*	21
Osteria Morini | *Italian*	26
Pepe Giallo/Rosso | *Italian*	23
Pera | *Med.*	21
Raoul's | *French*	23
Rouge et Blanc | *French/Viet.*	25
NEW Sessanta | *Italian*	—
Smile | *Med.*	20
Snack | *Greek*	23
Spice | *Thai*	20
Spring/Natural | *Health*	20
12 Chairs | *Amer./Mideast.*	24

SOUTH STREET SEAPORT

Acqua at Peck Slip | *Italian*	21
Cowgirl | *SW*	17
MarkJoseph | *Steak*	24
Paris Cafe | *Pub*	18
Roast Kit. | *Health*	21
Smorgasburg | *Food Hall*	26

STUYVESANT TOWN/ PETER COOPER VILLAGE

Petite Abeille | *Belgian*	19

TRIBECA

(Barclay to Canal Sts., west of B'way)

Acappella | *Italian*	23

LOCATIONS

Almond	French	20
American Cut	Steak	24
Añejo	Mex.	22
Atera	Amer.	24
Bâtard	Amer.	27
Benares	Indian	21
Blaue Gans	Austrian/German	22
Bouley	French	29
Brushstroke/Ichimura	Japanese	26
Bubby's	Amer.	21
Butterfly	Amer.	19
City Hall	Seafood/Steak	22
Distilled	Amer.	20
Ecco	Italian	22
Gari	Japanese	26
Gigino	Italian	21
Jungsik	Korean	26
Khe-Yo	Laotian	24
La Colombe	Coffee	25
Landmarc	French	19
🆕 Little Park	Amer.	26
Locanda Verde	Italian	25
Macao Trading	Chinese/Portug.	22
Maison Kayser	Bakery/French	21
Marc Forgione	Amer.	26
Mehtaphor	Eclectic	28
Mr. Chow	Chinese	23
Ninja	Japanese	16
Nobu	Japanese	27
Odeon	Amer./French	21
Palm	Steak	25
Pepolino	Italian	24
Racines	French	22
Roc	Italian	22
Rosanjin	Japanese	25
Sarabeth's	Amer.	20
Sazon	Puerto Rican	23
Scalini Fedeli	Italian	26
Takahachi	Japanese	24
Tamarind	Indian	26
Thalassa	Greek/Seafood	23
Tiny's	Amer.	21
Tribeca Grill	Amer.	23
Walker's	Pub	19
White Street	Amer.	22
'Wichcraft	Sandwiches	18
Wolfgang's	Steak	26
Zutto	Japanese/Noodle Shop	20

UNION SQUARE

(14th to 18th Sts., 5th Ave. to Irving Pl.)

Blue Water	Seafood	24
Coffee Shop	S Amer.	17
15 East	Japanese	27
Haru	Japanese	21
Laut	Malaysian/Thai	22
Maoz	Mideast./Veg.	22
Republic	Asian	19
Union Sq. Cafe	Amer.	27

WASHINGTON HEIGHTS

| Malecon | Dominican | 23 |

WEST 30s

Abigael's	Eclectic/Kosher	21
Ai Fiori	Italian	26
Arno	Italian	22
BCD Tofu	Korean	23
Ben's Kosher	Deli/Kosher	19
BonChon	Chicken	23
Casa Nonna	Italian	22
Cho Dang Gol	Korean	23
Clyde Frazier's	Amer.	21
David Burke Fab.	Amer.	24
Delmonico's	Steak	24
Frankie & Johnnie's	Steak	21
Friedman's	Amer.	22
Gaonnuri	Korean	19
Kang Suh	Korean	18
Kati Roll	Indian	23
Keens	Steak	26
Kristalbelli	Korean	25
Kunjip	Korean	21
Larb Ubol	Thai	22
Madangsui	Korean	22
Mandoo Bar	Korean	22
Maoz	Mideast./Veg.	22
Mercato	Italian	23
Miss Korea	Korean	21
Mooncake Foods	Pan-Asian	21
New WonJo	Korean	24
Nick & Stef's	Steak	22
Sarabeth's	Amer.	20
Smashburger	Burgers	20
Snack	Greek	23
Spot	Dessert	24
🆕 State Grill	Amer.	25
Stella 34	Italian	22
Szechuan Gourmet	Chinese	22

Uncle Jack's | *Steak*	23	Grand Sichuan | *Chinese*	21
Untamed Sandwiches | *Sandwiches*	25	Gyu-Kaku | *Japanese*	21
		Hakkasan | *Chinese*	24

WEST 40s

Akdeniz | *Turkish*	23	Haru | *Japanese*	21
Amarone | *Italian*	22	Havana Central | *Cuban*	22
Ample Hills | *Ice Cream*	27	**NEW** Hunt & Fish | *Steak*	19
Añejo | *Mex.*	22	Inakaya | *Japanese*	24
Aureole | *Amer.*	25	Ipanema | *Brazilian/Portuguese*	20
Balkanika | *Med.*	20	Ivan Ramen | *Japanese/Noodle*	22
Barbetta | *Italian*	22	Joe Allen | *Amer.*	18
Bareburger | *Burgers*	21	John's Pizzeria | *Pizza*	23
Becco | *Italian*	23	Junior's | *Diner*	19
Blossom | *Vegan/Veg.*	25	Kellari Taverna | *Greek/Seafood*	22
Blue Bottle | *Coffee*	24	Koi | *Japanese*	24
Blue Fin | *Seafood*	22	Kung Fu Ramen | *Noodle Shop*	23
Bobby Van's | *Steak*	23	La Masseria | *Italian*	24
Bond 45 | *Italian/Steak*	19	Lambs Club | *Amer.*	21
Bouchon Bakery | *Amer./French*	22	Landmark Tav. | *Pub*	19
Bryant Pk Grill/Cafe | *Amer.*	18	La Rivista | *Italian*	20
Butter | *Amer.*	23	Lattanzi | *Italian*	22
BXL Cafe | *Belgian*	20	Le Marais | *French/Kosher/Steak*	23
Cannibal | *Belgian*	22	Le Pain Q. | *Bakery/Belgian*	18
Cara Mia | *Italian*	21	Le Rivage | *French*	21
Carmine's | *Italian*	22	Luke's Lobster | *Seafood*	24
Ça Va | *French*	21	Maison Kayser | *Bakery/French*	21
NEW Charlie Palmer at The Knick | *Amer.*	27	Maoz | *Mideast./Veg.*	22
		Marseille | *French/Med.*	21
Chez Josephine | *French*	22	Marshal | *Amer.*	24
Chimichurri Grill | *Argent./Steak*	24	Mexicue | *Mex.*	21
Churrascaria | *Brazilian/Steak*	24	Mont Blanc | *Austrian/Swiss*	23
NEW City Kitchen | *Food Hall*	25	Nizza | *Italian*	20
Counter | *Burgers*	20	Num Pang | *Cam./Sandwiches*	23
Dafni | *Greek*	21	Oaxaca | *Mex.*	23
Daisy May's | *BBQ*	22	Obao | *Asian*	20
db Bistro Moderne | *French*	24	Oceana | *Amer./Seafood*	25
Del Frisco's | *Steak*	25	Ootoya | *Japanese/Noodle Shop*	25
E&E Grill Hse. | *Steak*	21	Orso | *Italian*	23
El Colmado | *Spanish*	19	Osteria al Doge | *Italian*	21
Esca | *Italian/Seafood*	25	Pam Real Thai | *Thai*	23
Etc. Etc. | *Italian*	23	Piccolo Cafe | *Coffee/Italian*	22
5 Napkin Burger | *Burgers*	21	Pio Pio | *Chicken/Peruvian*	23
Forty Four | *Amer.*	22	Print | *Amer.*	24
44 & X/44½ | *Amer.*	23	Qi | *Asian/Thai*	22
Frankie & Johnnie's | *Steak*	21	Queen of Sheba | *Ethiopian*	23
NEW Gabriel Kreuther | *French*	—	Roast Kit. | *Health*	21
Gari | *Japanese*	26	Rock Center Café | *Amer.*	18
Gazala's | *Mideast.*	22	Room Service | *Thai*	22
Glass House | *Amer.*	20	Saju Bistro | *French*	22
Gotham West | *Food Hall*	20	Sake Bar Hagi | *Japanese*	23
		Sardi's | *Cont.*	18

L O C A T I O N S

Scarlatto | *Italian*	20
Schnipper's | *Amer.*	19
Sea Grill | *Seafood*	24
Serafina | *Italian*	19
Shake Shack | *Burgers*	22
Shorty's | *Cheestks.*	21
STK | *Steak*	23
Strip House | *Steak*	25
Sushiden | *Japanese*	24
Sushi Zen | *Japanese*	25
Thalia | *Amer.*	21
Tony's Di Napoli | *Italian*	21
Trattoria Trecolori | *Italian*	22
Triomphe | *French*	23
Turkish Cuisine | *Turkish*	20
Two Boots | *Pizza*	19
Utsav | *Indian*	21
View | *Amer.*	18
Virgil's | *BBQ*	21
West Bank | *Amer.*	20
'Wichcraft | *Sandwiches*	18
Wolfgang's | *Steak*	26
Wu Liang Ye | *Chinese*	24
Xi'an | *Chinese/Noodle Shop*	23

WEST 50s

Abboccato | *Italian*	21
Afghan Kebab | *Afghan*	21
Aldo Sohm | *French*	21
Angelo's Pizzeria | *Pizza*	21
Annabel | *Italian/Pizza*	21
Asiate | *Amer./Asian*	24
A Voce | *Italian*	23
Azuri Cafe | *Israeli/Kosher*	23
Back Rm at One57 | *Amer.*	24
Bann | *Korean*	22
Bar Americain | *Amer.*	23
BarBacon | *Amer.*	20
Bareburger | *Burgers*	21
Basso56 | *Italian*	22
Beautique | *Amer./French*	20
Benares | *Indian*	21
Benoit | *French*	23
Betony | *Amer.*	25
Blue Ribbon Sushi | *Japanese*	25
Bobby Van's | *Steak*	23
Bouchon Bakery | *Amer./French*	22
Brasserie Cognac | *French*	18
Brasserie 8½ | *French*	22
Brass. Ruhlmann | *French*	18
Bricco | *Italian*	20

Burger Joint | *Burgers*	25
Capital Grille | *Steak*	25
Carnegie Deli | *Deli*	23
Casellula | *Amer.*	25
NEW Chevalier | *French*	22
Chez Napoléon | *French*	22
China Grill | *Asian*	22
Circo | *Italian*	22
City Lobster/Steak | *Seafood/ Steak*	20
Clement Rest. | *Amer.*	25
Danji | *Korean*	25
Del Frisco's | *Steak*	25
Don Antonio | *Pizza*	23
Eatery | *Amer.*	19
El Centro | *Mex.*	23
Empire Steak | *Steak*	22
Fogo de Chão | *Brazilian*	25
Gallaghers | *Steak*	23
Greek Kitchen | *Greek*	21
Grom | *Ice Cream*	25
Guantanamera | *Cuban*	23
Harry's Italian | *Italian*	20
Hell's Kitchen | *Mex.*	23
Il Gattopardo | *Italian*	24
Il Tinello | *Italian*	24
Ippudo | *Japanese/Noodle Shop*	25
Island Burgers | *Burgers*	21
NEW Jams | *Cal.*	—
Joe's Shanghai | *Chinese*	22
Kashkaval | *Med.*	24
Katsu-Hama | *Japanese*	22
La Bergamote | *Bakery/French*	24
La Bonne Soupe | *French*	19
La Masseria | *Italian*	24
Landmarc | *French*	19
Le Bernardin | *French/Seafood*	29
Le Pain Q. | *Bakery/Belgian*	18
NEW Limani | *Med.*	23
Little Beet | *Amer.*	22
NEW Loi Estiatorio | *Greek*	25
Luke's Lobster | *Seafood*	24
Maison Kayser | *Bakery/French*	21
Má Pêche | *Amer.*	23
Marea | *Italian/Seafood*	27
Maria Pia | *Italian*	21
Masa/Bar Masa | *Japanese*	26
NEW Mastro's Steak | *Steak*	25
Maze | *French*	22
Melt Shop | *Sandwiches*	22

Michael's | *Cal.*	23
Milos | *Greek/Seafood*	27
Modern | *Amer./French*	26
Molyvos | *Greek*	23
Mooncake Foods | *Pan-Asian*	21
Natsumi | *Japanese*	22
Naya | *Lebanese*	22
Nino's | *Italian/Steak*	21
Nobu | *Japanese*	27
Nocello | *Italian*	23
Norma's | *Amer.*	25
No. 7 | *Sandwiches*	21
NYY Steak | *Steak*	24
Palm | *Steak*	25
Palm Court | *Amer.*	23
Patsy's | *Italian*	21
Per Se | *Amer./French*	28
Petrossian | *Cont./French*	24
PizzArte | *Pizza*	23
Plaza Food Hall | *Food Hall*	21
Porter House | *Steak*	26
Pure Thai | *Thai*	26
Quality Italian | *Italian/Steak*	24
Quality Meats | *Amer./Steak*	26
Radiance Tea | *Teahse.*	21
NEW Rainbow Rm. | *Amer.*	23
Redeye Grill | *Amer./Seafood*	21
Remi | *Italian*	22
Robert | *Amer.*	21
Ruby Foo's | *Asian*	18
Rue 57 | *French*	20
Russian Samovar | *Cont./Russian*	19
Russian Tea | *Cont./Russian*	20
Russian Vodka | *Cont./Russian*	18
Ruth's Chris | *Steak*	25
Sarabeth's | *Amer.*	20
Serafina | *Italian*	19
Soba Nippon | *Japanese/Noodle*	23
Sushi Damo | *Japanese*	21
Szechuan Gourmet | *Chinese*	22
Taboon | *Med./Mideast.*	23
Tang Pavilion | *Chinese*	22
Tartinery | *French/Sandwiches*	20
Toloache | *Mex.*	23
Topaz | *Thai*	21
Torishin | *Japanese*	25
Totto Ramen | *Japanese/Noodle*	24
Trattoria Dell'Arte | *Italian*	22
21 Club | *Amer.*	23

Uncle Nick's | *Greek*	21
ViceVersa | *Italian*	24
Victor's Cafe | *Cuban*	23
Wondee Siam | *Thai*	19
Yakitori Totto | *Japanese*	24

WEST 60s

Andanada 141 | *Spanish*	22
Atlantic Grill | *Seafood*	23
Bar Boulud | *French*	24
Blossom | *Vegan/Veg.*	25
Boulud Sud | *Med.*	25
Cafe Fiorello | *Italian*	20
Ed's Chowder | *Seafood*	20
Gabriel's | *Italian*	21
Grand Tier | *Amer.*	21
Jean-Georges | *French*	28
Jean-Georges' Noug. | *French*	27
Joe | *Coffee*	21
La Boîte en Bois | *French*	20
Leopard/des Artistes | *Italian*	21
Le Pain Q. | *Bakery/Belgian*	18
Lincoln | *Italian*	25
Nick & Toni | *Med.*	21
Picholine | *French/Med.*	26
P.J. Clarke's | *Pub*	18
Rosa Mexicano | *Mex.*	22
Sapphire Indian | *Indian*	21
Shun Lee West | *Chinese*	22
Smith | *Amer.*	19
Telepan | *Amer.*	26
'Wichcraft | *Sandwiches*	18

WEST 70s

Alice's Tea | *Teahse.*	20
Bistro Cassis | *French*	20
Burke & Wills | *Australian*	23
Café Frida | *Mex.*	20
Cafe Luxembourg | *French*	21
Cafe Tallulah | *French/Med.*	20
Caffe Storico | *Italian*	21
'Cesca | *Italian*	22
Coppola's | *Italian*	20
Dovetail | *Amer.*	25
FishTag | *Greek/Seafood*	22
Gari | *Japanese*	26
Grand Sichuan | *Chinese*	21
Gray's Papaya | *Hot Dogs*	21
Hummus Pl. | *Israeli/Kosher/Veg.*	22
Isabella's | *Amer./Med.*	20

LOCATIONS

Le Pain Q. | *Bakery/Belgian* 18
NEW Lincoln Sq. Steak | *Steak* 20
Maoz | *Mideast./Veg.* 22
Nice Matin | *French/Med.* 19
Ocean Grill | *Seafood* 23
Pappardella | *Italian* 21
Parm | *Italian/Sandwiches* 21
Pasha | *Turkish* 22
Patsy's Pizzeria | *Pizza* 20
Piccolo Cafe | *Coffee/Italian* 22
Pomodoro Rosso | *Italian* 20
RedFarm | *Chinese* 24
NEW Ribbon | *Amer.* —
Risotteria | *Italian* 23
Saravanaa Bhavan | *Indian/Veg.* 23
Scaletta | *Italian* 21
Serafina | *Italian* 19
Shake Shack | *Burgers* 22
Tenzan | *Japanese* 21
Tessa | *Med.* 23

WEST 80s

Barney Greengrass | *Deli* 25
B. Café | *Belgian* 20
Blossom | *Vegan/Veg.* 25
Bodrum | *Med./Turkish* 21
Bustan | *Med.* 23
Cafe Lalo | *Coffee/Dessert* 18
Calle Ocho | *Nuevo Latino* 21
Candle Cafe | *Vegan/Veg.* 24
Celeste | *Italian* 23
Cilantro | *SW* 21
Cotta | *Italian* 20
5 Napkin Burger | *Burgers* 21
Good Enough/Eat | *Amer.* 19
Hampton Chutney | *Indian* 22
Han Dynasty | *Chinese* 23
Haru | *Japanese* 21
Island Burgers | *Burgers* 21
Jackson Hole | *Burgers* 20
Jacob's Pickles | *Southern* 22
Jin Ramen | *Japanese/Noodle* 23
Joe | *Coffee* 21
Kefi | *Greek* 22
Land Thai | *Thai* 22
Luke's Lobster | *Seafood* 24
Machiavelli | *Italian* 21
Meatball Shop | *Sandwiches* 21
Mermaid | *Seafood* 23
NEW Milling Rm. | *Amer.* 24
Momoya | *Japanese* 23

Oaxaca | *Mex.* 23
Peacefood Café | *Kosher/ Vegan/Veg.* 24
Prime KO | *Japanese/Kosher/ Steak* 22
Sarabeth's | *Amer.* 20
Spice | *Thai* 20
Spiga | *Italian* 23
Spring/Natural | *Health* 20

WEST 90s

Amsterdam Burger Co. | *Burgers* 24
Awadh | *Indian* 24
Bareburger | *Burgers* 21
Birch Coffee | *Coffee* 25
Carmine's | *Italian* 22
Gennaro | *Italian* 24
Halal Guys | *Mideast.* 22
Indus Valley | *Indian* 22
Kouzan | *Japanese* 21
Le Pain Q. | *Bakery/Belgian* 18
Malecon | *Dominican* 23
Numero 28 | *Pizza* 22
Pio Pio | *Chicken/Peruvian* 23
Turkuaz | *Turkish* 20
Two Boots | *Pizza* 19

WEST 100s

(See also Harlem/East Harlem)
Awash | *Ethiopian* 21
Cascabel Taqueria | *Mex.* 19
Flor/Mayo | *Chinese/Peruvian* 23
Miss Mamie's | *Soul Food/ Southern* 22
Spice | *Thai* 20
Szechuan Gourmet | *Chinese* 22
Thai Market | *Thai* 23
Wondee Siam | *Thai* 19
Xi'an | *Chinese/Noodle Shop* 23

WEST VILLAGE

(14th to Houston Sts., west of 6th Ave., excluding Meatpacking)
Agave | *SW* 19
NEW Almanac | *Amer.* 26
Annisa | *Amer.* 27
A.O.C. | *French* 20
A Salt & Battery | *British* 22
Baker & Co. | *Italian* 24
Bar Bolonat | *Israeli/Mideast.* 25
Barbuto | *Italian* 24
Beatrice Inn | *Amer.* 21
Bell Book/Candle | *Amer.* 22

Big Gay Ice Cream	*Ice Cream*	25	Jack's Wife Freda	*Amer.*	23
Birch Coffee	*Coffee*	25	Jeffrey's Grocery	*Amer.*	23
Blenheim	*Amer.*	20	Joe	*Coffee*	21
Blossom	*Vegan/Veg.*	25	Joe's Pizza	*Pizza*	24
Blue Ribbon	*Amer.*	25	John's Pizzeria	*Pizza*	23
Bobo	*French*	23	Joseph Leonard	*Amer.*	24
Bosie Tea Parlor	*Teahse.*	21	Keste Pizza	*Pizza*	23
Bread	*Italian/Sandwiches*	21	Kin Shop	*Thai*	25
Buvette	*French*	25	L'Artusi	*Italian*	27
Cafe Asean	*SE Asian*	23	Left Bank	*Amer.*	25
NEW Cafe Clover	*Amer.*	24	Le Gigot	*French*	25
Cafe Cluny	*Amer./French*	23	Little Owl	*Amer./Med.*	26
Cafe Gitane	*French/Moroccan*	22	Macondo	*Pan-Latin*	19
Cafe Loup	*French*	20	Malatesta	*Italian*	24
ChikaLicious	*Dessert*	25	Market Table	*Amer.*	23
NEW Chomp Chomp	*Singapor.*	—	Mary's Fish	*Seafood*	24
Clam	*Seafood*	25	Mas	*Amer.*	26
Cornelia St.	*Amer.*	18	Meatball Shop	*Sandwiches*	21
Corner Bistro	*Burgers*	23	Mémé	*Med./Moroccan*	23
Cowgirl	*SW*	17	Mighty Quinn's	*BBQ*	25
Crispo	*Italian*	25	Móle	*Mex.*	21
Decoy	*Chinese*	26	Monument Lane	*Amer.*	24
Dell'anima	*Italian*	24	Morandi	*Italian*	23
Do Hwa	*Korean*	23	Moustache	*Mideast.*	22
NEW Dominique Ansel Kit.	*Bakery/French*	—	Murray's Cheese Bar	*Amer.*	24
Dos Toros	*Mex.*	22	Numero 28	*Pizza*	22
El Charro Espanol	*Spanish*	24	Oaxaca	*Mex.*	23
El Toro Blanco	*Mex.*	21	Ofrenda	*Mex.*	24
Empellón Taqueria	*Mex.*	22	One if by Land	*Amer.*	23
EN Japanese	*Japanese*	25	Pagani	*Italian*	20
Extra Virgin	*Med.*	22	Palma	*Italian*	24
Fedora	*Amer./French*	22	Pearl Oyster	*New Eng./Seafood*	27
Fish	*Seafood*	23	Perilla	*Amer.*	24
Flex Mussels	*Seafood*	23	Perry St.	*Amer.*	26
Frankies	*Italian*	25	Piccolo Angolo	*Italian*	26
NEW Gardenia	*Med.*	—	Piora	*Amer.*	25
Good	*Amer.*	21	Pizzetteria Brunetti	*Pizza*	26
Gradisca	*Italian*	24	Place	*Amer./Med.*	24
Grand Sichuan	*Chinese*	21	Pó	*Italian*	25
Grey Dog	*Amer.*	22	Rafele	*Italian*	25
Grom	*Ice Cream*	25	Recette	*Amer.*	23
Hakata Tonton	*Japanese*	22	RedFarm	*Chinese*	24
Havana Alma	*Cuban*	23	Risotteria	*Italian*	23
Home Rest.	*Amer.*	21	Rosemary's	*Italian*	22
Hudson Clearwater	*Amer.*	25	Sant Ambroeus	*Italian*	22
Hummus Pl.	*Israeli/Kosher/Veg.*	22	Sevilla	*Spanish*	24
			Snack	*Greek*	23
Injera	*Ethiopian*	23	Soto	*Japanese*	25
I Sodi	*Italian*	25	Sotto 13	*Italian*	23
			Spotted Pig	*Euro.*	24

LOCATIONS

Spunto | *Pizza*	22
Sushi Nakazawa | *Japanese*	27
SushiSamba | *Brazilian/Japanese*	24
Taïm | *Israeli/Veg.*	26
Takashi | *Japanese*	26
Tartine | *French*	22
Tea & Sympathy | *Teahse.*	22
Tertulia | *Spanish*	24
Toby's Estate | *Coffee*	24
Two Boots | *Pizza*	19
NEW Upholstery Store | *Amer.*	25
NEW Via Carota | *Italian*	24
Wallflower | *French*	24
Wallsé | *Austrian*	25
Waverly Inn | *Amer.*	22
Westville | *Amer.*	23
Yerba Buena | *Pan-Latin*	22

Bronx

ARTHUR AVENUE/ BELMONT

Ann & Tony's | *Italian*	22
Dominick's | *Italian*	22
Emilia's | *Italian*	24
Enzo's | *Italian*	25
John's Pizzeria | *Pizza*	23
Mario's | *Italian*	21
Pasquale Rigoletto | *Italian*	22
Roberto | *Italian*	25
Tra Di Noi | *Italian*	23
Zero Otto | *Italian/Pizza*	23

BRONX PARK

NEW Hudson Garden | *Amer.*	—
Pine Tree Cafe | *Amer.*	24

CITY ISLAND

Artie's | *Seafood/Steak*	21
Black Whale | *Amer.*	21
City Is. Lobster | *Seafood*	22
Don Coqui | *S Amer.*	22
Original Crab | *Italian/Seafood*	25
Sammy's Fishbox | *Seafood*	23
Sammy's Shrimp | *Seafood*	23
Sea Shore | *Seafood*	23

CONCOURSE/DOWNTOWN

NYY Steak | *Steak*	24

FIELDSTON

Jake's Steakhse. | *Steak*	24

KINGSBRIDGE

Malecon | *Dominican*	23
Smashburger | *Burgers*	20

MORRIS PARK

Enzo's | *Italian*	25
Patricia's | *Italian*	23

MOTT HAVEN

Pio Pio | *Chicken/Peruvian*	23

RIVERDALE

Beccofino | *Italian*	24
Liebman's | *Deli/Kosher*	24
Madison's | *Italian*	20

THROGGS NECK

Tosca | *Italian*	23

VAN NEST

F & J Pine | *Italian*	23

WAKEFIELD

Ali's Roti | *Carib.*	23

Brooklyn

BATH BEACH

Nyonya | *Malaysian*	23
Tommaso | *Italian*	24

BAY RIDGE

Areo | *Italian*	24
Arirang Hibachi | *Japanese*	23
Burger Bistro | *Burgers*	22
Cebu | *Cont.*	22
Chadwick's | *Amer.*	24
David's Brisket | *Deli*	25
Eliá | *Greek*	26
Fushimi | *Japanese*	24
Gino's | *Italian*	24
Omonia | *Coffee/Greek*	19
Pearl Room | *Seafood*	20
Tanoreen | *Med./Mideast.*	26
Tuscany Grill | *Italian*	23
Vesuvio | *Italian*	22
Zito's | *Sandwiches*	—

BEDFORD-STUYVESANT

Ali's Roti | *Carib.*	23
David's Brisket | *Deli*	25
Do or Dine | *Eclectic*	25
NEW Eugene & Co. | *Amer.*	—
NEW L'Antagoniste | *French*	23
Oaxaca | *Mex.*	23

Peaches	*Southern*	24
Saraghina	*Pizza*	23
NEW Willow	*Amer.*	20

BENSONHURST

Tenzan	*Japanese*	21

BOERUM HILL

Battersby	*Amer.*	26
Blue Bottle	*Coffee*	24
French Louie	*Amer./French*	25
Mile End	*Deli/Sandwiches*	22
Rucola	*Italian*	25
Spice	*Thai*	20

BROOKLYN HEIGHTS

Ample Hills	*Ice Cream*	27
ChipShop	*British*	20
Colonie	*Amer.*	25
Fornino	*Pizza*	24
Hanco's	*Viet.*	20
Henry's End	*Amer.*	25
Jack the Horse	*Amer.*	24
Le Pain Q.	*Bakery/Belgian*	18
Luzzo's	*Pizza*	24
Noodle Pudding	*Italian*	25
Queen	*Italian*	24
Red Gravy	*Italian*	20
Teresa's	*Diner/Polish*	20

BUSHWICK

Blanca	*Amer.*	26
Bunna Cafe	*Ethiopian/Vegan*	25
NEW Faro	*Italian*	—
Momo Sushi Shack	*Japanese*	25
Northeast Kingdom	*Amer.*	25
Roberta's	*Italian/Pizza*	26

CARROLL GARDENS

Bergen Hill	*Seafood*	27
Brooklyn Farmacy	*Ice Cream*	24
Buttermilk	*Amer.*	26
Dover	*Amer.*	26
Fragole	*Italian*	24
Frankies	*Italian*	25
Lucali	*Pizza*	26
Marco Polo	*Italian*	22
Nightingale 9	*Viet.*	21
Prime Meats	*Amer./Steak*	24
Take Root	*Amer.*	23
Wilma Jean	*Southern*	24
Zaytoons	*Mideast.*	21

CLINTON HILL

Aita	*Italian*	24
NEW Bar Bolinas	*Amer.*	—
Emily	*Pizza*	26
NEW Finch	*Amer.*	22
Locanda Vini	*Italian*	26
Speedy Romeo	*Italian/Pizza*	25
Zaytoons	*Mideast.*	21

COBBLE HILL

Awash	*Ethiopian*	21
Bareburger	*Burgers*	21
Bar Tabac	*French*	20
Brucie	*Italian*	21
Cafe Luluc	*French*	21
Chocolate Room	*Dessert*	25
Hanco's	*Viet.*	20
Henry Public	*Pub*	23
Hibino	*Japanese*	26
Joya	*Thai*	22
NEW June Wine	*Amer.*	20
Ki Sushi	*Japanese*	24
La Vara	*Spanish*	27
Watty & Meg	*Amer.*	19
Wild Ginger	*Asian/Vegan*	23

COLUMBIA STREET WATERFRONT DISTRICT

Alma	*Mex.*	20
Calexico	*Mex.*	21
Pok Pok NY	*Thai*	26
Pok Pok Phat	*Thai*	25

CONEY ISLAND

Gargiulo's	*Italian*	23
Grimaldi's	*Pizza*	22
Smorgasburg	*Food Hall*	26
Tom's	*Diner*	21
Totonno Pizza	*Pizza*	27

CROWN HEIGHTS

Aita	*Italian*	24
Ali's Roti	*Carib.*	23
Berg'n	*Food Hall*	23
Catfish	*Cajun*	22
Chavela's	*Mex.*	24
Glady's	*Carib.*	24
Mayfield	*Amer.*	25
Mighty Quinn's	*BBQ*	25

DITMAS PARK

Farm/Adderley	*Amer.*	23
Mimi's Hummus	*Mideast.*	24

LOCATIONS

Purple Yam | *Asian* 21

DOWNTOWN BROOKLYN

Bacchus | *French* 21
Chef's/Brooklyn Fare | *French* 26
Ganso | *Japanese/Noodle Shop* 21
NEW Ganso Yaki | *Japanese* —
NEW Grand Army | *Seafood* 22
Hill Country | *BBQ* 22
Hill Country Chicken | *Chicken/ Southern* 21
Junior's | *Diner* 19
Oaxaca | *Mex.* 23
Shake Shack | *Burgers* 22

DUMBO

Atrium Dumbo | *French* 23
Gran Electrica | *Mex.* 25
Grimaldi's | *Pizza* 22
Jacques Torres | *Ice Cream* 26
Juliana's | *Pizza* 26
Luke's Lobster | *Seafood* 24
No. 7 | *Sandwiches* 21
River Café | *Amer.* 26
Shake Shack | *Burgers* 22

EAST NEW YORK

Smashburger | *Burgers* 20

FLATLANDS

Mill Basin Deli | *Deli/Kosher* 25

FORT GREENE

Berlyn | *German* 21
Black Forest Bklyn | *German* 20
Café Habana/Outpost | *Cuban/Mex.* 23
Caffe e Vino | *Italian* 22
Colonia Verde | *Latin Amer.* 21
Madiba | *S African* 22
Martha | *Amer.* 21
No. 7 | *Amer.* 21
Oaxaca | *Mex.* 23
Olea | *Med.* 27
Roman's | *Italian* 25
67 Burger | *Burgers* 21
Smashburger | *Burgers* 20
Smoke Joint | *BBQ* 20
Walter | *Amer.* 23

GOWANUS

Ample Hills | *Ice Cream* 27
NEW Baba's Pierogies | *E Euro.* —
Dinosaur BBQ | *BBQ* 22

Fletcher's | *BBQ* 22
Four & Twenty | *Bakery* 25
Littleneck | *Seafood* 23
Ninth St Espresso | *Coffee* 23
Oaxaca | *Mex.* 23
Pines | *Amer.* 25
Runner & Stone | *Amer./Bakery* 22
2 Duck Goose | *Chinese* 19

GRAVESEND

Fiorentino's | *Italian* 20
L&B Spumoni | *Ice Cream/Pizza* 24

GREENPOINT

Bakeri | *Bakery/Euro.* 26
Calexico | *Mex.* 21
NEW Esme | *Amer.* 23
Five Leaves | *Amer.* 25
Fornino | *Pizza* 24
Glasserie | *Med.* 25
Littleneck | *Seafood* 23
Lobster Joint | *New Eng./ Seafood* 24
Luksus | *Amer.* 25
No. 7 | *Sandwiches* 21
Paulie Gee's | *Pizza* 27
River Styx | *Amer.* 23
Scalino | *Italian* 23
Water Table | *New Eng.* —
Xi'an | *Chinese/Noodle Shop* 23

MIDWOOD

Di Fara | *Pizza* 26

MILL BASIN

La Villa Pizzeria | *Pizza* 24

PARK SLOPE

Al Di La | *Italian* 26
Applewood | *Amer.* 24
Artichoke Basille | *Pizza* 22
Bareburger | *Burgers* 21
Bark | *Hot Dogs* 20
Benchmark | *Amer./Steak* 23
Blue Ribbon | *Amer.* 25
Bogota | *Pan-Latin* 24
Bonnie's Grill | *Burgers* 21
NEW Bricolage | *Viet.* —
Burger Bistro | *Burgers* 22
Calexico | *Mex.* 21
Chocolate Room | *Dessert* 25
Coco Roco | *Chicken/Peruvian* 21
Conviv. Osteria | *Med.* 26

Cubana Café | *Cuban*	21
Flatbush Farm | *Amer.*	21
Fonda | *Mex.*	23
Franny's | *Italian/Pizza*	23
Hanco's | *Viet.*	20
NEW Hugo & Sons | *Italian*	23
La Villa Pizzeria | *Pizza*	24
Luke's Lobster | *Seafood*	24
Miriam | *Israeli/Med.*	22
Moim | *Korean*	23
Naruto | *Japanese/Noodle Shop*	20
Numero 28 | *Pizza*	22
Okeanos | *Greek*	21
Oyster Bar | *Seafood*	22
Patsy's Pizzeria | *Pizza*	20
Pork Slope | *Pub*	20
Rose Water | *Amer.*	26
Scalino | *Italian*	23
Scottadito | *Italian*	23
Shake Shack | *Burgers*	22
67 Burger | *Burgers*	21
Song | *Thai*	22
Spice | *Thai*	20
Stone Park | *Amer.*	25
Talde | *Asian*	24
12th St. B&G | *Amer.*	22
Two Boots | *Pizza*	19

PROSPECT PARK

Smorgasburg | *Food Hall*	26

PROSPECT HEIGHTS

Amorina | *Italian/Pizza*	22
Ample Hills | *Ice Cream*	27
Bar Chuko | *Japanese*	26
Bar Corvo | *Italian*	25
Chuko | *Japanese/Noodle Shop*	26
Four & Twenty | *Bakery*	25
James | *Amer.*	24
Morgans BBQ | *BBQ*	23
NEW Rose's B&G | *Amer.*	—
Saul | *Amer.*	24
Tom's | *Diner*	21
Vanderbilt | *Amer.*	22
Zaytoons | *Mideast.*	21

PROSPECT LEFFERTS GARDENS

Ali's Roti | *Carib.*	23

RED HOOK

Brooklyn Crab | *Seafood*	20

Defonte's | *Sandwiches*	24
Fort Defiance | *Amer.*	23
Good Fork | *Amer.*	25
Hometown | *BBQ*	25
Hope & Anchor | *Diner*	20
NEW Kao Soy | *Thai*	21
Red Hook Lobster | *Seafood*	24

SHEEPSHEAD BAY

Brennan | *Sandwiches*	22
Jordans Lobster | *Seafood*	22
Randazzo's | *Seafood*	22
Roll-n-Roaster | *Sandwiches*	22
Sahara | *Turkish*	22
Taci's Beyti | *Turkish*	26

SUNSET PARK

Nyonya | *Malaysian*	23
Pacificana | *Chinese*	24

VINEGAR HILL

Vinegar Hill Hse. | *Amer.*	23

WILLIAMSBURG

Allswell | *Amer.*	23
Antica Pesa | *Italian*	24
Aurora | *Italian*	24
Baci & Abbracci | *Italian*	23
Bakeri | *Bakery/Euro.*	26
Bamonte's | *Italian*	23
Baoburg | *Eclectic*	25
Best Pizza | *Pizza*	22
Blue Bottle | *Coffee*	24
Blue Ribbon | *Amer.*	25
BrisketTown | *BBQ*	24
Brooklyn Star | *Southern*	25
Cafe Mogador | *Moroccan*	24
Caracas | *Venez.*	26
Cherry | *Japanese*	22
Commodore | *Southern*	23
Crif Dogs | *Hot Dogs*	22
NEW Delaware & Hudson | *Amer.*	26
Diner | *Amer.*	25
Dos Toros | *Mex.*	22
DuMont Burger | *Burgers*	23
Egg | *Southern*	24
Extra Fancy | *New Eng.*	23
Fette Sau | *BBQ*	26
Forcella | *Pizza*	23
Fornino | *Pizza*	24
Fushimi | *Japanese*	24

Gorbals	*Eclectic*	25
Joe's Pizza	*Pizza*	24
La Esquina	*Mex.*	23
La Superior	*Mex.*	25
Mable's Smokehse.	*BBQ*	23
Maison Premiere	*Seafood*	26
Marlow/Sons	*Amer.*	23
Meadowsweet	*Amer./Med.*	25
Meatball Shop	*Sandwiches*	21
Meat Hook	*Sandwiches*	23
Mesa Coyoacan	*Mex.*	24
Móle	*Mex.*	21
Motorino	*Pizza*	25
MP Taverna	*Greek*	24
Oaxaca	*Mex.*	23
Okonomi	*Japanese*	25
𝗡𝗘𝗪 Oleanders	*Amer.*	–
1 or 8	*Japanese*	24
Oslo Coffee	*Coffee*	22
Peter Luger	*Steak*	28
Pies-N-Thighs	*Southern*	24
Qi	*Asian/Thai*	22
Reynard	*Amer.*	23
Roebling Tea Room	*Amer.*	24
Rye	*Amer.*	25
Samurai Mama/Papa	*Japanese*	23
Sea	*Thai*	23
𝗡𝗘𝗪 Semilla	*Amer.*	26
Shalom Japan	*Japanese/Jewish*	24
Smorgasburg	*Food Hall*	26
St. Anselm	*Amer./Steak*	27
Sweet Chick	*Southern*	24
Sweetleaf	*Coffee*	23
Toby's Estate	*Coffee*	24
Traif	*Eclectic*	24
12 Chairs	*Amer./Mideast.*	24
Two Boots	*Pizza*	19
Umami Burger	*Burgers*	21
Vanessa's Dumpling	*Seafood*	22
Walter	*Amer.*	23
Wild Ginger	*Asian/Vegan*	23
Xixa	*Mex.*	25
Zenkichi	*Japanese*	26
Zizi Limona	*Med./Mideast.*	25
Zona Rosa	*Mex.*	21

WINDSOR TERRACE

Krupa	*Amer.*	25

Queens

ASTORIA

Agnanti	*Greek*	25
Arepas	*Venez.*	23
Artichoke Basille	*Pizza*	22
Astor Room	*Amer.*	21
Bahari Estiatorio	*Greek*	24
Bareburger	*Burgers*	21
BonChon	*Chicken*	23
Brick Cafe	*Italian*	21
Butcher Bar	*BBQ*	24
Cávo	*Greek*	20
Christos	*Steak*	24
Elias Corner	*Greek/Seafood*	25
Il Bambino	*Italian/Sandwiches*	26
Loukoumi	*Greek*	23
Mojave	*Mex.*	23
MP Taverna	*Greek*	24
Omonia	*Coffee/Greek*	19
Ovelia	*Greek*	23
Pachanga Patterson	*Mex.*	24
Piccola Venezia	*Italian*	26
Ponticello	*Italian*	23
Queens Comfort	*Southern*	24
Queens Kickshaw	*Coffee/ Sandwiches*	23
Rizzo's	*Pizza*	21
Sanford's	*Diner*	23
Seva Indian	*Indian*	24
S Prime	*Steak*	23
Stamatis	*Greek*	23
Strand Smokehse.	*BBQ*	20
Sugar Freak	*Cajun/Creole*	21
𝗡𝗘𝗪 Tacuba	*Mex.*	20
Taverna Kyclades	*Greek/ Seafood*	26
Telly's Taverna	*Greek/Seafood*	25
Tratt. L'incontro	*Italian*	26
Vesta	*Italian*	26

BAYSIDE

Ben's Kosher	*Deli/Kosher*	19
BonChon	*Chicken*	23
Donovan's	*Amer.*	21
Erawan	*Thai*	24
Jackson Hole	*Burgers*	20
Press 195	*Sandwiches*	25
Ralph's Famous	*Ice Cream*	25
Uncle Jack's	*Steak*	23

BELLEROSE

Jackson Diner | *Indian*   23

CORONA

Lemon Ice King | *Ice Cream*   26
Leo's Latticini/Corona | *Italian/*   24
   Sandwiches
Park Side | *Italian*   25
Tortilleria Nixtamal | *Mex.*   24

DOUGLASTON

Grimaldi's | *Pizza*   22
La Baraka | *French*   23

EAST ELMHURST

Jackson Hole | *Burgers*   20

ELMHURST

Arepa Lady | *S Amer.*   25
Ayada | *Thai*   26
Pho Bang | *Noodle Shop/Viet.*   23
Ping's | *Chinese/Seafood*   22
Zabb Elee | *Thai*   24

FLUSHING

Biang! | *Chinese/Noodle Shop*   25
Dumpling Galaxy | *Chinese*   22
Golden Shopping Mall | *Chinese*   22
Joe's Shanghai | *Chinese*   22
Kum Gang San | *Korean*   21
Kyochon | *Chicken*   21
Mapo Korean | *Korean*   24
New World Mall | *Food Hall*   22
Pho Bang | *Noodle Shop/Viet.*   23
Sik Gaek | *Korean*   23
Spicy & Tasty | *Chinese*   24
Szechuan Gourmet | *Chinese*   22
White Bear | *Chinese*   25
Xi'an | *Chinese/Noodle Shop*   23

FOREST HILLS

Agora Tav. | *Greek*   20
Alberto | *Italian*   24
Cabana | *Nuevo Latino*   22
Danny Brown | *Euro.*   26
Dee's | *Pizza*   23
Eddie's Sweet Shop | *Ice Cream*   25
La Vigna | *Italian*   25
Nick's | *Pizza*   24

GLEN OAKS

Ralph's Famous | *Ice Cream*   25

GLENDALE

Zum Stammtisch | *German*   24

HOWARD BEACH

La Villa Pizzeria | *Pizza*   24

JACKSON HEIGHTS

Jackson Diner | *Indian*   23
Pio Pio | *Chicken/Peruvian*   23

LONG ISLAND CITY

Alobar | *Amer.*   20
Bareburger | *Burgers*   21
Bella Via | *Italian*   23
Birch Coffee | *Coffee*   25
Café Henri | *French*   23
Casa Enrique | *Mex.*   26
Corner Bistro | *Burgers*   23
Hibino | *Japanese*   26
NEW Il Falco | *Italian*   24
John Brown Smokehse. | *BBQ*   22
LIC Market | *Amer.*   26
Manducatis | *Italian*   24
Manducatis Rustica | *Italian*   24
Manetta's | *Italian*   25
NEW Mu Ramen | *Japanese/*   24
   Noodle Shop
M. Wells Dinette | *Québécois*   22
M. Wells Steakhse. | *Steak*   24
Shi | *Asian*   23
Smorgasburg | *Food Hall*   26
Spice | *Thai*   20
Sweetleaf | *Coffee*   23
Testaccio | *Italian*   22
Tournesol | *French*   23
Water's Edge | *Amer./Seafood*   22

MIDDLE VILLAGE

London Lennie's | *Seafood*   24
Pio Pio | *Chicken/Peruvian*   23

REGO PARK

Barosa | *Italian*   23
Ben's Best | *Deli/Kosher*   23

RIDGEWOOD

Bunker Viet. | *Viet.*   26
Houdini Kit. | *Pizza*   25

ROCKAWAY BEACH

Caracas | *Venez.*   26

ROXBURY

Fletcher's | *BBQ*   22

SOUTH OZONE PARK
Don Peppe | *Italian* — 26

SUNNYSIDE
Salt & Fat | *Amer./Asian* — 24
Sik Gaek | *Korean* — 23

WHITESTONE
Ralph's Famous | *Ice Cream* — 25

WILLETS POINT
Leo's Latticini/Corona | *Italian/Sandwiches* — 24
Shake Shack | *Burgers* — 22

WOODSIDE
Donovan's | *Amer.* — 21
Mamajuana | *Dominican/Nuevo Latino* — 22
Sripraphai | *Thai* — 26

Staten Island

ARDEN HEIGHTS
Ralph's Famous | *Ice Cream* — 25

BLOOMFIELD
Lorenzo's | *Italian* — 22

CASTLETON CORNERS
Joe & Pat's | *Italian/Pizza* — 24

DONGAN HILLS
Tratt. Romana | *Italian* — 26

ELM PARK
Denino's | *Pizza* — 26
Ralph's Famous | *Ice Cream* — 25

ELTINGVILLE
Ralph's Famous | *Ice Cream* — 25

GRANT CITY
Fushimi | *Japanese* — 24

GREAT KILLS
Arirang Hibachi | *Japanese* — 23

MARINERS HARBOR
Real Madrid | *Spanish* — 21

NEW DORP
Brioso | *Italian* — 24
Ralph's Famous | *Ice Cream* — 25

OLD TOWN
Bocelli | *Italian/Seafood* — 25

PRINCE'S BAY
Ralph's Famous | *Ice Cream* — 25

RANDALL MANOR
Nurnberger Bierhaus | *German* — 21

ROSEBANK
Bayou | *Cajun* — 24

SHORE ACRES
Da Noi | *Italian* — 22

ST. GEORGE
Beso | *Spanish* — 24
Enoteca Maria | *Italian* — 26
NEW River Dock | *Seafood* — —

STAPLETON
Defonte's | *Sandwiches* — 24

TODT HILL
Carol's Cafe | *Eclectic* — 24

TOTTENVILLE
Angelina's | *Italian* — 24
Da Nico | *Italian* — 21
Nucci's | *Italian* — 22

TRAVIS-CHELSEA
Da Noi | *Italian* — 22

WEST BRIGHTON
Nucci's | *Italian* — 22

More on zagat.com